Sources of Gain in
Counseling and Psychotherapy

READINGS AND COMMENTARY

Sources of Gain in Counseling and Psychotherapy

READINGS AND COMMENTARY

WITHDRAWN

EDITED BY

BERNARD G. BERENSON

University of Arkansas, Fayetteville

ROBERT R. CARKHUFF

State University of New York, Buffalo

New York   Chicago   San Francisco   Toronto

ISBN: 0-03-059195-3
Printed in the United States of America
56789 090 1514131211

Preface

We are first and foremost therapists. As a vital part of this identity, we ask questions about the efficacy of our work. Because of, or perhaps in spite of, our rigorous training in scientific psychology, we press our skills to translate them into human benefits.

In one way, however, the term "therapist" does not fit us. We do not separate "therapy" from life: we no longer see "patients"—only human beings. This simple and almost naïve breakthrough has had far-reaching implications for the people we try to help, as well as for our awareness of our own humanity in all its strengths and weaknesses.

In order to be effective practitioners, we attempt to learn what the major orientations to counseling and therapy can teach. We have discovered that certain conditions which cut across all of the major therapeutic systems appear to constitute a core of effective therapeutic ingredients. In addition, there appear to be a number of dimensions which, under certain specifiable conditions, may constitute additional sources of effectiveness. Although there are many dimensions that simply remain unknown to us, we probe the unknown so that we may not be fearful of it, just as we strive to understand the contributions of the major systems so that we can be free of any one of them.

It is our hope that with the readings and commentaries that follow, counselors, psychotherapists, guidance and personnel workers, and their students will reexamine their positions to include all potential sources of gain in counseling and psychotherapy, independent of their theoretical orientation. In collecting these works, we reject fully the stance that the experiential and the experimental approaches are antithetical. At the same time, we raise questions in an attempt to point up the logical implications of each of these positions.

This book is meant to serve as an introduction to a meaningful and potent eclectic stance in counseling and psychotherapy. We hope that it will be of value in both graduate and undergraduate programs in education, psychology, social work, and medicine. In addition, as a commentary on a society with a great need to seek out effective means of providing

v

the individual with the freedom and courage to emerge as a full human, this book should be of interest to all of those nonprofessionals who are concerned with constructive human relationships.

We feel that we have collected the most significant efforts made by a number of authors to cut across the various cults of psychotherapy. We hope that these readings and commentaries create a synthesis of the emerging facilitative conditions and truly therapeutic processes which, we believe, will constitute the building blocks for future developments in the helping professions. We also hope that these new developments in psychotherapy will illuminate the workings and meanings of *all* significant interpersonal relationships.

Books on counseling and psychotherapy often end by stressing essentially the same point: *the individual practitioner must come to know himself fully and develop his own personalized approach in order to effect the greatest degree of constructive change in his clients.* It is unfortunate that these texts postscript this point, for the "self-understanding" which may follow implicitly takes place within the very narrow and delimited context of the particular orientation to the "helping" that has preceded. We would begin where others end.

In developing a response to the long repressed challenges to counseling and psychotherapy and identifying sources of gain and emerging directions, we have taken the liberty of changing the original titles of some of the readings to better reflect our stance. Each reading is preceded and followed by editorial comments which are meant to be the connective tissues of the book.

We are grateful to our colleagues who provided a stimulating context within which to do our work and writing, and particularly grateful to Dr. David Aspy, John Douds (M.S.W.), Dr. Myron Manley, Dr. Theodore Sarbin, and Drs. Alexander and Lena Astin. In addition, the responses of our students have provided the testing ground for our presentation: in particular, we would like to mention Mae Alexik, Theodore Friel, Todd Holder, Daniel Kratochvil, and Richard Pierce. We also gratefully acknowledge the administrative and secretarial assistance of Bernice Carkhuff and Marcia Mason. Finally, we wish to thank our wives who have been most long-suffering in their tolerance of our commitment to our work.

B. G. B.
R. R. C.

Amherst, Massachusetts
September 1966

Contents

Preface   v

INTRODUCTION: A Personalized Approach to Counseling
  and Psychotherapy   1

ROBERT R. CARKHUFF   *Requiem or Reveille?*   8

PART ONE: The Challenge to the Helping Professions   21

HANS J. EYSENCK   *The Inefficacy of Therapeutic Processes with
  Adults*   22
  An Aroused Audience   31

EUGENE E. LEVITT   *The Undemonstrated Effectiveness of
  Therapeutic Processes with Children*   33
  The Burden of Proof Is a Burden Indeed   45

ALLEN E. BERGIN   *Negative Results Revisited*   47
  For Better or for Worse   55

PART TWO: Cross-Cult Dimensions of Counseling and
  Psychotherapy   57

  The Clinical Approaches   57

FRIEDA FROMM-REICHMANN   *The Prerequisites of Therapy from an
  Analytic Viewpoint*   58
  The Client's Future and the Therapist's Past   62

LAURANCE F. SHAFFER and EDWARD J. SHOBEN, JR.   *Common Aspects
  of Psychotherapy*   63
  Communication between Closed Doors   70

CARL R. ROGERS *The Conditions of Change from a Client-Centered Viewpoint* 71
  Both Model and Agent 85

ROBERT A. HARPER *Some Common Effects of Diverse Approaches* 86
  The Bland Leading the Blind 98

JEROME D. FRANK *Modifications in the Assumptive World* 99
  Some Assumptive Extensions 113

NICHOLAS HOBBS *A New Cosmology* 114
  Insight: Hindsight and Foresight 125

FORREST L. VANCE and THEODORE C. VOLSKY *Psychological Discordance Reduction* 126
  Beyond Our Pathological Noses 136

WILLIAM SCHOFIELD *Some General Factors in Counseling and Therapy* 137
  Reflections of Friendship 146

FRANZ ALEXANDER *Psychoanalysis and Learning Theory* 147
  In Process 161

  The Experimental Approaches 162

EDWARD J. SHOBEN, JR. *Psychotherapy as a Problem in Learning Theory* 163
  Relationship Conditions for Effective Counterconditioning 192

LEONARD KRASNER *The Reinforcement Machine* 193
  The Final Plunge 240

S. RACHMAN *Behavior Therapy* 241
  A Bagful of Techniques 259

PART THREE: Out of the Darkness 260

  Research Developments and Directions 260

ALBERT BANDURA *Psychotherapy as Social Learning* 261
  People Can Learn from People 283

G. GAIL GARDNER *The Facilitative Relationship* 284
    To Care or Not to Care 300

JOHN M. GROSSBERG *Behavior Therapy: More or Less* 301
    Compatible Partners 322

LOUIS BREGER and JAMES L. MCGAUGH *Another View of Behavior Therapy* 323
    Errors in Programs: Stops and Checks 357

CHARLES B. TRUAX and ROBERT R. CARKHUFF *New Directions in Clinical Research* 358
    Hope and Confidence 390

Integrations and Implications for Facilitative Processes and Constructive Outcomes 392

EDWARD J. MURRAY *The Sociotropic Stance* 393
    A Rehabilitation Learning Theory 400

ALLEN E. BERGIN *Some Implications of Psychotherapy Research for Therapeutic Practice* 401
    In Reverse Order 421

ROBERT R. CARKHUFF *An Integration of Practice and Training* 423
    All Anger Is Not Destructive 436

SUMMARY: Emerging Directions: A Synthesis 439

Sources of Gain in
Counseling and Psychotherapy

READINGS AND COMMENTARY

INTRODUCTION

*"It is the fundamental paradox
of Nature as we now see it
that its universal plasticity
seems suddenly to have hardened."*

PIERRE TEILHARD DE CHARDIN

A Personalized Approach
to Counseling and Psychotherapy

In the face of the burgeoning gap between social needs and social services it is ironical that an otherwise pragmatic and empirical America has for so long looked with disdain upon eclecticism in therapeutic treatment. Instead of being shaped by what is effective for those we serve, we retreat into highly cognitive theories and flee from an examination of the fundamental assumptions and outcomes of our cosmologies.

For the patient (and perhaps even for the therapist) the therapeutic encounter can be "for better or for worse." This sobering point has profound implications for our current modes of training and practice. The traditional "schools" and theories cannot alone identify those ingredients which, when present in therapy, culminate in positive change and which, when absent, result in deteriorative consequences.

The need is acute to go beyond the usual definitions of roles, images, theories of dynamics, screening, selection, and techniques. No one school or technique of therapy has demonstrated its efficacy with all or even a significant number of patient populations. Furthermore, much of the literature gives good reason for doubting the usefulness of therapy in any specific instance. If the cults of therapy have anything constructive to offer, they must share certain common dimensions. For example, effective therapists from a variety of backgrounds of training are alike in

1

several critical characteristics: they believe in the possibility of constructive personality change; they do not know fully before termination the shape of the emerging, changing personality of the patient (although they implicitly hope that the client will live more effectively); they care deeply for others; and they are confident. There are many more characteristics that they share. It is our contention that, given a reasonable length of time, such therapists could become effective with a wide range of patient populations. Their clinical practices and lives have been dedicated to searching out what works within the framework of self-awareness, thus creating a deep and secure level of congruence. *They are shaped by what is effective for the client, given a particular interaction of therapist, client, and contextual variables.* This attitude denies the possibility of a strict adherence to a school.

These effective therapists do not suffer from the usual professional schizophrenia. To them, *therapy is a significantly personal way of relating and is integrated with life—and not necessarily to the exclusion of some particularly useful techniques of demonstrated efficacy.* The less effective among us ask our patients to join our world or doubt the possibility of constructive personality change. We all know the therapist who, when asked if he feels that people can really change, shrugs his shoulders. We know the counselor who assigns an IQ test to force the client to face the "reality" that he (the client) is not able to do most things well. We may even mention the therapist who complains that he has "never seen a healthy person" in his office. One is tempted to ask: Has he ever seen a healthy person in his home or in the mirror?

THE THERAPIST AND HIS ASSUMPTIONS
ABOUT EFFECTIVE THERAPY

If we are ever to address ourselves to the facilitative aspects of all interpersonal relationships, we need to take a questioning view of the histories of the traditional approaches as well as of many new approaches to therapy and translate what we find into more constructive training programs. Most approaches are replete with increasingly higher levels of abstractions in the theories themselves and as they relate to behavior and practice. The abstractions leave less room for the individual therapist and for the unique aspects of what might develop into a truly therapeutic relationship between the particular therapist and patient.

If during therapy the therapist is preoccupied with his membership in a school he may well be divorcing the therapy process from its outcome as well as from the broader and more basic aspects of life. There is good reason to feel today that unless the therapist is keenly, confidently, and comfortably aware of *who he is* and *is becoming,* he is not providing the patients or clients with the most effective experience.

In addition, the more traditional highly abstract intellectualizations (and here we mean not only the psychoanalytic and vocational counseling movements but also the nondirective and even the behavioristic) carry with them far-reaching implications that may well be in need of re-examination in the light of recent findings. Several of these assumptions that have for too long influenced the nature of our training programs and our relationships to our clients and patients can be stated concretely as follows:

1. Effective counseling and therapy can be accomplished only by those who have graduated from approved medical or graduate or post-graduate programs.
2. Effective counseling and therapy can be accomplished only by those who know and adhere to a recognized school of therapy.
3. Effective counseling and therapy can be accomplished only by those who have passed the screening procedures of a particular school of therapy.
4. Effective counseling and therapy can be accomplished only by the intellectually superior.
5. Effective counseling and therapy can be accomplished only by those who fully understand personality dynamics.
6. Effective counseling and therapy can be accomplished only by those who can remain objective and who do not become involved in the lives of their patients.
7. Effective counseling and therapy can be accomplished only by those who have first learned to distrust their own experiences, impulses, and feelings.
8. Effective counseling and therapy can be accomplished only by those persons who are more "therapist" than "human."
9. Effective counseling and therapy can be accomplished only by those who make their major commitment to the broader aspects and values of the social and institutional establishment.
10. Effective counseling and psychotherapy involving the personal problems of clients can only be accomplished by an impersonal approach.

There are more, many more. In the light of recent theoretical and research developments, it may be meaningful to reword these assumptions as follows:

1A. Effective counseling and therapy can be accomplished by non-professional persons trained to offer high levels of psychological conditions that correlate with constructive change.
2A. Effective counseling and therapy can be accomplished by persons

providing high levels of facilitative interpersonal conditions independent of schools of therapy.

3A. Effective counseling and therapy can be accomplished by many persons who have not passed the screening procedures of a particular school of therapy.

4A. Effective counseling and therapy can be accomplished by persons representing a wide range of levels of intellectual functioning.

5A. Effective counseling and therapy can be accomplished by persons who may or may not understand fully the complexities of personality dynamics.

6A. Effective counseling and therapy can be accomplished only by those who become involved at some deep level in the lives of their patients.

7A. Effective counseling and therapy can be accomplished only by those who have first learned to trust their own experiences, impulses, and feelings.

8A. Effective counseling and therapy can be accomplished only by those persons who are more "human" than "therapist."

9A. Effective counseling and therapy can be accomplished only by those who make a basic commitment to their clients, who challenge the establishment with new learnings and are continuously re-examining old learnings.

10A. Effective counseling and psychotherapy involving the personal problems of clients can only be accomplished by the most personal of approaches.

A meaningful synthesis of these and many more points is necessary if future therapy training and practice is to effectively meet the needs of individuals and society.

THE THERAPIST AND HIS SCHOOL

For the most part, descriptions of therapeutic processes and theories present each school or approach (its history, assumptions, and techniques) in such a way that the reader or student is left with the task of choosing which, for him, is the most workable system. Inherent in such presentations is the implication that some choice and commitment of allegiance must be made if one is to be a good therapist. In other presentations there is the implication that eclecticism somehow robs the student or therapist of a basic aspect of identification. Even among therapists, the need to belong may be stronger than the perspective necessary to evaluate the present stage of the literature in theory and practice. Membership in a group or school of therapy allows the therapist to demonstrate where he stands, and it allows others to identify his position and assume certain things about the kind of therapy he does. However, these assumptions may be so far removed from the real encounter and context that in fact they tell us little of what goes on in the therapeutic session. Furthermore, they tell us little about the efficacy of his therapy, his kind of commitments, and his feelings. More important, they may fail to communicate enough about who the therapist is as a person.

There is good reason to believe that belonging and adherence to a specific school provides the therapist with a much needed level of confidence. However, it may not only be necessary, but also critically important to examine other sources of confidence both in the life history of the therapist and in the training process. It is interesting to note that after having successfully completed a traditionally oriented training program, so many therapists rely on the dictates and principles of a school of therapy, ignoring and perhaps denying their own life experiences. The confidence that such a therapist has in his school far exceeds that which he has in himself.

When we consider the possibility that the level of confidence the therapist has in himself may correlate with experience, it becomes critical that we allow a significant level of therapist confidence to emerge early in practice and training, so that we not only save patients anguish and failure experiences, but in addition, provide the therapist with successes earlier in his professional life. Training and exposure to *those* aspects of psychotherapy that appear to cut across major schools of psychotherapy, may provide some of the necessary and important conditions for training programs. Goals for our patients may be quite fitting as goals for practicum students.

THE BEGINNINGS OF POTENT PRACTICES

The necessary beginning point of any effective helping process is the counselor or therapist himself. How he thinks and feels about himself will be reflected in how he thinks and feels about others or, conversely, how he thinks and feels about others will reflect how he thinks and feels about himself. In order to have a truly therapeutic effect upon another individual, the counselor must have a profound depth of understanding of his own fully experienced personal needs and conflicts so that they do not intrude in a deleterious manner. Above all, he must trust his own motives. *The counselor must trust his own experience, for in the end all that he has to offer the client is 100 percent of his own experience.*

Such a view is not antiintellectual in the sense that it disallows consideration of a variety of potentially effective theories, techniques, and other methodologies. Rather, the self-knowing counselor or therapist is constantly seeking better handles on his own experience—this implies more cognitive constructs—and more effective methods of functioning.

Not unlike the beginning tennis player, the modes of functioning of the counselor that are initially less natural or lower on a given response hierarchy are often ultimately incorporated in his most effective way of operating in a given situation. Indeed, the constructs that the effective practitioner in any situation can articulate are closely congruent with his experience in that situation.

Trusting his own motives and experience will enable the counselor to be open to the feedback that he gets from his client. Trusting the feedback that he gets from his client will enable him to be shaped by what is effective for the client. Implicit in this viewpoint is a basic equation of valuing the client to the degree one values oneself. In other words, in order to improve the client's level of functioning, *the effective counselor will do anything for the client that, given the same circumstances, he would do for himself.* It is precisely this *active attempt* to change and improve the level of functioning of those with whom we are concerned that differentiates the potent and personalized eclectic practitioner from his tradition-bound colleagues.

In employing the term "eclecticism," we are not describing a particular approach or absence of approach. Rather we are underscoring the recognition that no one theoretical orientation or series of techniques is adequate to deal with the complexities of multiple persons in potentially constructive interactions. For us, eclecticism connotes the counselor's bringing himself to bear fully within the therapeutic encounter, employing all of his own experience as well as appropriate and relevant knowledge and techniques in a dedicated attempt to translate his efforts to client benefits.

It is the implementation of a prescribed role that renders the counselor impotent in settings and with persons very different from those that gave birth to the model for therapy in the first place. Considering the extensive number of variables impinging upon the therapeutic encounter and the differences in these variables, adherence to one orientation means that nearly all therapeutic encounters will be limited in their effectiveness by the dominance of one traditional model, whether it is psychoanalytic or trait and factor counseling, Rogersian, existential or behavioristic.

The beginnings of potent practice, therefore, involve a self-experiencing and self-knowing counselor who is shaped by what is facilitative for his client. *By facilitative we simply mean that which frees the individual to attain higher and more personally rewarding levels of intrapersonal and interpersonal functioning.* While facilitative may also connote the behavioral change resultant from the symptom and/or anxiety reduction due to techniques such as systematic counterconditioning, we employ the construct primarily to denote those counselor dimensions of attitude and sensitivity that create a therapeutic atmosphere enabling the client to relate constructively to the counselor and to himself within the therapeutic encounter. Dimensions such as the counselor's accurate empathic understanding of the client, his respect for the client, his genuineness within the encounter, and the concreteness or specificity with which counselor and client deal with feelings and problem-expressions, enable the client to explore himself constructively in his areas of concern. The increased self-understanding and self-experiencing leads to increased experimentation with alternative ways of functioning. In conjunction with an improved repertoire of methods, more relevant and meaningful information, the elimination of serious and handicapping symptomatology, and the neutralization of disabling anxiety and situational obstacles, the client evidences constructive behavioral change in improved ways of relating to others and in his own personal self-fulfillment.

Furthermore, counselors who are functioning at high levels of facilitative conditions have clients who improve in their own functioning because the counselors are personally more potent reinforcers and because they elicit a high degree of reciprocating affect in the client. The client's level of positive self-reinforcement and the level of positive affect is communicated to others and, in turn, received by the clients from others. Improvement on a variety of indices of functioning follows. Conversely, the clients of counselors communicating low levels of facilitative conditions are involved in a process eliciting negative affect, negative self-regard, negative regard from others, and consequent behavioral deterioration.

In regard to questionable clinical practices in general, it is noteworthy that exactly 14 years after Eysenck questioned the effectiveness of professional practitioners, the following review of the literature in the training area suggests that *there are no professional training programs which have demonstrated their efficacy in terms of a translation to constructive behavioral gains in clients.* Not unlike the effective practitioner, our efforts in the following pages will be dedicated to searching out what conditions make the therapeutic process work most effectively.

REQUIEM OR REVEILLE? *

Robert R. Carkhuff

It is clear that traditional counseling and clinical training programs of all kinds have simply not established their efficacy in terms of client benefits. Indeed, the dominant programs are universally resistant to the notion of assessing the outcomes of their programs. They settle too early for process variables (such as grades) which research in counseling and psychotherapy has long since laid to rest. The few carefully controlled studies present a distressing composite picture. The trained clinician's ability to judge the personality characteristics of others bears an inverse relationship to the actual measured characteristics (Taft, 1954). With increasing training and expressions of confidence in clinical judgment, we find decreasing validities (Kelly and Fiske, 1950) and reliabilities (Arnhoff, 1954) in these judgments. Further, persons with the same amount of graduate training (physical scientists), irrelevant to the understanding and judgment of behavior, judge personality characteristics with a high degree of accuracy (Taft, 1954) and are better predictors of behavior with increasing information and personal encounters (Weiss, 1963). To be sure, we might even question the relationship to client benefits of these inquiries into the effects of training. However, one study stands out in this regard as the most enlightened and systematic effort to relate training process variables to client outcome variables. Bergin and Soloman (1963) found the level of empathic understanding of final year, postinternship graduate students (a level which was remarkably low compared to the base-rate findings of Berenson, Carkhuff, and Myrus, 1965; Martin, Carkhuff, and Berenson, 1965; and Pierce, 1965, suggesting, perhaps, the deteriorative consequences of traditional graduate training) in a long-standing program of some repute to be positively correlated with therapeutic competence. Their study is another in a long and growing list of studies relating the dimensions such as empathy to a variety of outcome criteria. However, Bergin and Soloman found their ratings of *empathy to be slightly negatively correlated with both the students' grade point averages—and most important—the students' practicum grade averages,* with the judgments of the clinical faculty once again being brought into doubt.

Rather than an ultimate concern with client outcome variables, an

* Training in counseling and psychotherapy: Requiem or reveille? *Journal of Counseling Psychology*, 1966, *13*, 360-367. Reprinted by permission.

analysis of the training literature, in general, in all of the helping professions suggest an interesting analogue of personality and process. Medical educators (Lester *et al.*, 1962; Roman, 1961, Schwartz and Abel, 1955; Ward, 1962; Wolberg, 1954) in the great majority focus primarily upon the more pedagogic dimension of "shaping" behavior in training and treatment to develop "rational understanding." Social workers (Austin, 1963; Bloom and Chére, 1958; Boehm, 1961; Towles, 1961; Wessel, 1961) by and large emphasize the therapeutic dimensions involved in a nurturant supervisor-supervisee relationship calculated to cultivate the experiential base leading to the kind of self-understanding which might free the student to become his most facilitative self. Clinical and counseling psychology and education, especially in its counseling emphasis, run the gamut from the direct control in training beginning with Korner and Brown (1952) and presently implied by Krasner (1962) to the views of Rogers (1957) which emphasize the experiential base. Fluctuating in between these extremes are the views promulgated by Arbuckle (1963), Patterson (1964), and others. One cannot help but conjecture that the attitudes and orientations found in the literature reflect the dominant and assertive disposition of the medical profession, the passive and submissive disposition of social work, and the intensified role conflicts of applied psychology. Even further, the possible dominance of the emphasized dimensions by the attitudinal dispositions of the professions involved brings into clear focus the question of the critical and artificially exclusionary nature of any one of these dimensions. Indeed, both the didactic and the experiential dimensions as well as other dimensions such as the oft-neglected role model provided by those designated as "more knowing" may constitute significant sources of learning in all effective interpersonal learning processes.

Consistent with the emphasis upon the direct shaping of behavior, a number of impersonal programmed training approaches have been implemented with the main finding being that trainees change their response patterns in the direction of their recorded supervisors (Fosmire and Palmer, 1964; Palmer *et al.*, 1963) but that they do not demonstrate gains in conditions related to therapeutic outcome (Baldwin and Lee, 1964). These findings question the possibility of programming conditions such as empathy, warmth, and congruence in the contextual absence of such conditions (Berlin and Wyckoff, 1964; Ward, 1962). In this regard, Magoon's (1964) suggestion for the use of audio-visual films in brief and vicarious occupational counseling may be extended to supervisory films which make supervisory sessions unnecessary; supervisory films may be matched to trainee types who provide counseling films matched to counselee types. *No one has to see anyone!*

While a number of programs have advocated the direct experiential involvement of the trainees in supervision and client treatment (Adams, 1958; Arbuckle, 1963; Fleming and Hamburg, 1958; Flint and Rioch, 1963; Lott, 1957; Patterson, 1964; University of Minnesota counselor education staff, 1960; Werkman, 1961), none have researched the process or outcome of their programs. More specifically integrative programs (Adams *et al.*, 1964; Fleming, 1953; Fleming and Benedek, 1964; Truax, Carkhuff, and Douds, 1964) have focused upon essentially three principal sources of learning which operate consistently and concurrently in training or for that matter counseling or psychotherapy: 1) the didactic or direct shaping of behavior; 2) the experiential base of learning; and 3) the role model for effective counseling which the trainer establishes. Research evidence related to both therapy process and outcome variables for integrated programs, systematically implemented and researched is promising (Berenson, Carkhuff, and Myrus, 1965; Carkhuff and Truax, 1965, 1965a); trainee products offer high levels of empathy, positive regard, genuineness, and concreteness and elicit client process involvement and movement demonstrating constructive gain or change. A number of less systematically implemented and researched NDEA guidance institutes (Demos, 1964; Demos and Zuwaylif, 1963; Hansen and Barker, 1964; Jones, 1963; Munger and Johnson, 1960; Webb and Harris, 1963) have established essentially the same findings, an increased tendency for trainees to make more understanding and less evaluative responses, with the problem of possible short-term effects (Enelow, Adler, and Manning, 1964; Munger, Myers, and Brown, 1963) and the lack of demonstration of substantial changes in actual counselor behavior (Meadow and Tillem, 1963) perhaps reflecting the short-term nature of training.

It is interesting to note that one area where researchers have vigorously and rigorously sought to assess the translation of their training efforts in terms of client benefits is the area of lay counselor training, many of the programs of which have been built in large part around a central core of facilitative conditions of empathy, positive regard, and congruence (Carkhuff and Truax, 1964b; Truax and Carkhuff, 1964) and all of which have striven primarily to enable the trainees to become their most facilitative selves. Here the evidence is extensive that the lay trainees demonstrate counseling outcomes at least as constructive as their training supervisors or professional practitioners in general (Appleby, 1963; Carkhuff and Truax, 1965, 1965a; Harvey, 1964; Mendel and Rapport, 1963; Rioch *et al.*, 1963; Tudor, 1952).

A RESEARCH OVERVIEW

The conjectured dimensions and process findings (where one process measure correlates with another but neither has an established relationship with the client's improvement in functioning) are, to be sure, interesting. However, we must conclude the following: *There are no well-designed, controlled, and implemented studies assessing the efficacy of training programs.* There are few systematic attempts to provide appropriate training control groups and pre- and post-training measures. With few notable exceptions, there are no systematic specifications of the antecedent training conditions of the behavioral change which we have implicitly asked for from our trainees in therapeutic training. With the exception of the highly positive body of literature on lay therapist training, there have been no systematic assessments of the translation of training to client or patient improvement or deterioration in functioning. An example may be warranted here. In assessing, for example, a program providing training in a dimension such as empathy we might attempt to accomplish the following: 1) to make some kind of naturalistic assessment of the level of empathy currently offered and the outcome currently achieved in therapeutic processes in a particular setting; 2) to assess in some way the level of empathy offered by both the trainees and their controls both prior to and subsequent to the training; 3) to introduce control groups including those which meet together for a similar amount of time with an instructor for obtuse purposes other than therapeutic training per se; 4) to specify the more didactic methods by which empathy will be taught; 5) to assess in some way the level of empathy provided the trainees in the context of the training; and lastly, and perhaps most important, 6) to assess the patient encounters and conduct follow-up studies in order to determine whether or not the training program has indeed led to better results than those established in the initial naturalistic studies. To be sure, process and outcome measures continue to provide great difficulty, but strides of progress have been made in the last decade (Truax and Carkhuff, 1964). With the possible exception of the lay training programs no consistent and extensive body of training literature has established its ultimate efficacy in terms of client and patient benefits.

Thus, there is substantial support for a solid core of the helping processes, a body of primary facilitative interpersonal dimensions that account for much of the variability in a variety of the outcome criteria which we may employ to assess our "helping." While, for example, the weights of these dimensions may vary with therapist, client, and contextual variables, preliminary evidence suggests that in the general case we may be able to account for between one third to one half of the variability in our change indices at this point in time (Truax, 1961; Truax and Carkhuff, 1964).

Some qualifications are in order. If we are talking of dimensions common to all effective interpersonal processes we may not be talking so much about the "techniques" of making empathic responses like the reflective technique, etc., which in the past may have bogged us down in our thinking and doing, as we are about "a way of life," a way of living effectively in facilitating others and ourselves. In addition, secondary dimensions may, for some therapists, clients, and situations, singularly or in their various interactions, operate to facilitate or even retard the effects of the primary conditions. Figure 1 demonstrates several notable possibilities concerning possible "preferred" modes of treatment. Given particular interaction patterns of therapist, client, and contextual variables, brief educational or vocational counseling, nondirective therapy, behavioristic conditioning, psychoanalytic therapy, or any one of the many other available approaches may, with all their full implications

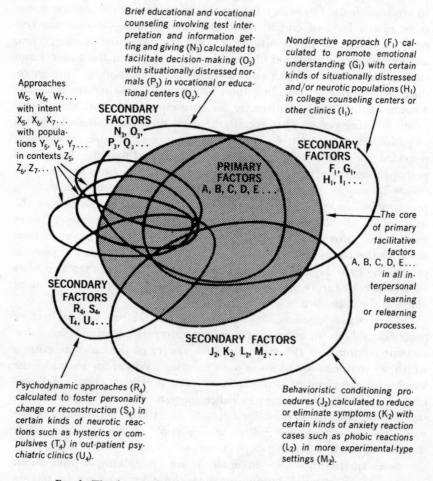

Brief educational and vocational counseling involving test interpretation and information getting and giving (N_3) calculated to facilitate decision-making (O_3) with situationally distressed normals (P_3) in vocational or educational centers (Q_3).

Nondirective approach (F_1) calculated to promote emotional understanding (G_1) with certain kinds of situationally distressed and/or neurotic populations (H_1) in college counseling centers or other clinics (I_1).

Approaches W_5, W_6, W_7... with intent X_5, X_6, X_7... with populations Y_5, Y_6, Y_7... in contexts Z_5, Z_6, Z_7...

SECONDARY FACTORS N_3, O_3, P_3, Q_3...

PRIMARY FACTORS A, B, C, D, E...

SECONDARY FACTORS F_1, G_1, H_1, I_1...

The core of primary facilitative factors A, B, C, D, E... in all interpersonal learning or relearning processes.

SECONDARY FACTORS R_4, S_4, T_4, U_4...

SECONDARY FACTORS J_2, K_2, L_2, M_2...

Psychodynamic approaches (R_4) calculated to foster personality change or reconstruction (S_4) in certain kinds of neurotic reactions such as hysterics or compulsives (T_4) in out-patient psychiatric clinics (U_4).

Behavioristic conditioning procedures (J_2) calculated to reduce or eliminate symptoms (K_2) with certain kinds of anxiety reaction cases such as phobic reactions (L_2) in more experimental-type settings (M_2).

FIG. 1. The interpersonal core of primary facilitative factors and some possible examples of secondary factors.

concerning goals, techniques, etc., constitute preferred modes of treatment. Further elucidation may be warranted here. For example, a knowledge of psychodynamic developmental phenomena may increase the accountable variability 10 percent for a psychoanalytically-oriented therapist working with a case involving an adjustment reaction to adolescence or, on the other hand, contribute nothing or actually depress the predictability for a hospitalized psychotic patient.

Clinical psychology and psychiatric and social work training centers throughout the country, in their focus upon psychodynamic thinking, have built their programs around what may be a negligible, albeit at times an important, contribution to the treatment process, when compared to the contribution of the central core of facilitative conditions. Some counseling psychology programs have mistakenly followed suit. Others have variously concentrated upon personality, interest, and aptitude testing, and interpretation, "theories" of vocational choice, and educational and vocational information getting and giving, all of which are, perhaps, significant in and of themselves but for each of which there is no support for the likelihood of accounting for a major part of the variation in the change indices. Most programs have neglected or disregarded any systematic attention to the core of facilitative interpersonal conditions.

The intent is not to negate the potential significance of the various training orientations, but rather to put them in proper perspective in building around a common interpersonal core. Due attention must be given those other aspects of the helping processes according to their efficacy in a given interaction of therapist, client, and contextual variables. A dramatic and current case in point deserves some comprehensive attention, that is, the therapist employing the conditioning principle of reciprocal inhibition with a phobic patient (Wolpe, Salter, and Reyna, 1964) where the statistics cited for symptomatic improvement or recovery are truly strong, although not unqualified. "Behavior" therapy may well be the preferred mode of treatment here with these particular goals— *in the context of high levels of facilitative conditions.* In this regard, Murray (1963) has challenged the need of many behavior therapists to conduct an impersonal therapy and has found support for his challenge in the warm, personal, and empathic relationships of the therapists in the conditioning therapy and theory of many leading behaviorists. In addition, the behavior therapists, if pushed to their logical extensions, must hold some hope for the symptom reduction in patients to lead to improvement in other areas of functioning, including especially the potential ability to engage in constructive love relationships (with appropriate discrimination learning, of course). It might be facilitative to offer the patient such an experience in any therapy.

It is clear, however, that the success rate, at least as assessed by the goals established, which Wolpe and others have achieved in counter-conditioning certain kinds of anxiety reactions cannot be accounted for by interpersonal factors alone. Wolpe (1958), himself, while attributing nearly all "fundamental psychotherapeutic effects" of all treatment approaches to the reciprocal inhibition of neurotic anxiety responses, that is, the complete or partial suppression of the anxiety responses as a consequence of the simultaneous evocation by nonspecific "relationship" factors of other responses physiologically antagonistic to anxiety, concedes the following: "If the favorable results of the present series are, to the extent of 60 percent, regarded as due to the nonspecific reciprocal inhibition that would occur in any kind of interview situation, the additional 30 percent of good results appear to be attributable to the special measures for obtaining reciprocal inhibition. . . ." In particular cases, the conditioning process may account for more variability than the facilitative conditions, but together these two aspects of learning may constitute independent sources of effect and account for a significantly greater success rate. We are continually reminded that learning theory in no way dictates that the therapist be an impersonal programmed reinforcement machine, but rather, if carried to its logical conclusion, must indeed indicate a very personal process. We are continually reminded that the magnitude of certain response patterns and reinforcement effects may well be contingent upon certain personal relationship factors.

To be sure, it becomes incumbent upon all training programs to incorporate more than a passing educational exposure to approaches constituting possible preferred modes of treatment. Further, we have good reason to believe that the very evolution of different treatment cults is born of continuing experiences involving particular interaction patterns of therapist, client, and situational variables.

Nevertheless, the overwhelming preponderance of systematic evidence available today indicates that the primary conditions of effective treatment are conditions which minimally trained nonprofessional persons can provide. The conditions are not the monopoly of doctoral training, and there is strong reason to believe that they are often not achieved in doctoral training. In some cases graduate training may even retard or contribute to the deterioration of the trainee's ability to offer these conditions. At the very minimum, the extensive psychoanalytic training program of Rioch et al (1963), which can be severely questioned on many counts, has established that one does not need a doctorate degree of any kind to operate at the level of experienced doctoral-trained clinicians when seen from the viewpoint of continuing traditional, albeit questionable, modes of practice.

It would then appear that helping persons can be trained in less than the four or usually more years it takes for doctoral training. The growing social urgency can be met most effectively and efficiently in shorter term programs for practitioners, perhaps a one- or two-year "mental health counselor" program designed to produce "therapeutic agents." It is clear that these minimally trained persons can provide the levels of conditions commensurate to those of their trainers. It also appears, however, that training and supervision are essential (with some issues involved here concerning who provides the training). The primary role of the doctoral person as we see it would be to attempt to explicate the effective dimensions in the therapeutic or facilitative processes, to implement these constructs in training, and to assess the efficacy of the training, especially in its client and patient outcome. To do so, with all due consideration to our early developmental levels reflected in our limitations in both research as well as practice, necessitates the possession of some research skills and tools, and not simply reading or consumption skills.

CONCLUSIONS

Resistance is to be anticipated. The effect of recommendations is always in large part contingent upon the readiness of the profession. However, if we were to do properly controlled research on the practice of law and found that, all other things being equal, defendants who were defended by minimally trained, nonprofessional "friends" were as likely or even more likely to obtain acquittal than those who had professional counsel, we would be horrified and would call for extensive reform in professional legal practice. The studies reviewed here demand that we in the applied psychological sciences do likewise. How many such studies must we mount before we will take action?

We appeal for the same change in many of the practicing members of our profession which we must ask for in our trainees or for that matter, our clients: a chance to become their most open and flexible, facilitative selves. We appeal to the unbiased among our colleagues to find in themselves the dimensions of those relationships which have been most rewarding and fulfilling for both parties and in which they have been most efficacious. Or, if they cannot find these experiences in themselves, perhaps they can open up and attempt to understand the encounters of their colleagues whose clients improve in functioning as a consequence of "real" helping relationships. Perhaps we can further operationalize these dimensions and implement investigations of them. Perhaps we can build our programs around those dimensions for which we find extensive support. Bordin's (1962) editorial suggests the critical need for the study of that form of intervention which can best enhance the psychological growth of the individual client. We might add a concern for that form of intervention which might best enhance the growth of the trainee, for if change cannot occur for the individual trainee in the direction of effective and facilitative functioning in four or five years and several thousand hours of graduate study, then how can we expect to effect change in from one to 50 or even 100 sessions of counseling or psychotherapy with clients? To put the question another way: If we believe constructive change or gain can occur in 10 or 20 sessions, then how much more can we achieve in years of graduate study? We might also add a concern for that form of intervention which might enhance the growth of practitioners whose clients and own personal experiences are not left improved for the counseling or therapeutic encounter, and, in some frighteningly large number of cases, as indicated by extensive research now available to us, are retarded in their development.

Our plea is not for a more delimited and dichotomous sphere of operation in practice and research as the Clark report (Clark *et al.,* 1964) recommends, but rather for an expanded role. The intent is neither to downgrade the doctorate nor to attempt to attain a perhaps unattainable Frommian society. Rather, the intent is to upgrade the position to one involving effective training and practices. We would attempt to establish shorter-term programs which facilitate the development of the interpersonal skills which allow those individuals who are not likely to make profound contributions at other levels to make the optimum contribution to a client's welfare. The preponderance of evidence of the foregoing review suggests that the outcomes of "low level" lay therapist training programs, and possibly some NDEA institute programs, constructed primarily around a core of "cross-cult" dimensions of effective interpersonal functioning, have been most impressive, whereas more traditional, highly cognitive programs are of highly questionable and certainly unestablished efficacy.

If lay persons can accomplish in the therapeutic encounter results comparable to those of professionals, then what is it that those of us with doctorates have to offer if not some skill in explicating, operationalizing, and implementing in training, practice, research, and consultation the dimensions of effective interpersonal learning and relearning processes? For example, I envisualize the doctoral person in a service setting, continually assessing ongoing forms of training and treatment based upon extensive documentation. I see him serving to train, as well as to consult on preferred modes of treatment with perhaps ten mental health counselors who can then pass the benefits on to one hundred patients instead of carrying his present ten-patient caseload (which may be a high estimate from what is known about doctoral persons in most service settings). In addition, I see the doctoral practitioner overseeing continuous and comprehensive community care. In brief, I see the

doctoral person knowing *all* that is knowable concerning truly therapeutic processes—and continually striving for more understanding and
effectiveness.

Surely "the rights and interests of society are paramount" (Clark
et al., 1964). We must strive to broaden our training efforts so that new
understanding can be translated into benefits for clients and patients
by trained therapeutic agents such as mental health counselors of more
limited educational backgrounds. The need for doctoral-status, "pure"
practitioners would appear to be *superfluous,* except insofar as the doctoral training equips the practitioners to make enlightened and systematic inquiry into that which they are attempting to accomplish and
to provide the appropriate training and consultation in the hope of improving the efficacy of the therapeutic or facilitative processes involving
those for whom we serve.

REFERENCES

Adams, W. R. The psychiatrist in an ambulatory clerkship for comprehensive
medical care in a new curriculum. *J. med. Educ.,* 1958, *33,* 211-220.

Adams, W. R., Ham, T. H., Mawardi, Betty H., Scali, H. A., and Weisman,
R. A. A naturalistic study of teaching in a clinical clerkship. *J. med. Educ.,*
1964, *39,* 164-174.

Appleby, L. Evaluation of treatment methods for chronic schizophrenia. *Arch.
gen. Psychiat.,* 1963, *8,* 8-21.

Arbuckle, D. S. The learning of counseling: Process not product. *J. counsel.
Psychol.,* 1963, *10,* 163-168.

Arnhoff, F. N. Some factors influencing the unreliability of clinical judgments.
J. clin. Psychol., 1954, *10,* 272-275.

Austin, Lucille N. The changing role of the supervisor. In *Ego-oriented casework: Problems and perspectives,* H. Parad and R. Miller (Eds.). New York:
Family Service Assoc. of America, 1963, pp. 273-291.

Baldwin, T., and Lee, Joan. Evaluation of programmed instruction in human
relations. *Amer. Psychologist,* 1965, *20,* 489 (Abstract).

Berenson, B. G., Carkhuff, R. R., and Myrus, Pamela. An investigation of the
level of interpersonal functioning of college students. *J. counsel. Psychol.,*
in press, 1966.

Bergin, A., and Soloman, Sandra. Personality and performance correlates of empathic understanding in psychotherapy. Paper read at Amer. Psychol. Assoc.,
Philadelphia, Sept., 1963.

Berlin, J. I., and Wyckoff, L. B. Human relations training through dyadic programmed instruction. Paper presented, Amer. Personnel Guid. Assoc., 1964.

Bloom, L., and Chére, H. A problem of relationship in supervision. *Soc. casework,* 1958, *37,* 402-406.

Boehm, W. Social work: Science and art. *Soc. Serv. Rev.,* 1961, *35,* 144-151.

Bordin, E. S. Editorial: Narrowness or breadth? *J. counsel. Psychol.*, 1962, *10*, 2.

Carkhuff, R. R., and Truax, C. B. Training in counseling and psychotherapy: An evaluation of an integrated didactic and experiential approach. *J. consult. Psychol.*, 1965, *29*, 333-336.

Carkhuff, R. R., and Truax, C. B. Lay mental health counseling: The effects of lay group counseling. *J. consult. Psychol.*, in press, 1965. (a)

Carkhuff, R. R., and Truax, C. B. Toward explication of facilitation and retardation in interpersonal learning processes. *Personnel guid. J.*, in press, 1965 (b).

Clark, K. E. *et al.* Committee on the scientific and professional aims of psychology. Report to Board of Directors and Council of Representatives of APA, *Amer. Psychologist*, 1964, *20*, 95-100.

Demos, G. D. The application of certain principles of client-centered therapy to short-term vocational counseling. *J. counsel. Psychol.*, 1964, *11*, 280-284.

Demos, G. D., and Zuwaylif, F. H. Counselor movement as a result of an intensive six-week training program in counseling. *Personnel guid. J.*, 1963, *42*, 125-128.

Enelow, A. J., Adler, L. M., and Manning, P. R. A supervised psychotherapy course for practicing physicians. *J. med. Educ.*, 1964, *39*, 140-146.

Fleming, Joan. The role of supervision in psychiatric training. *Bull. Menning. Clin.*, 1953, *17*, 157-169.

Fleming, Joan, and Benedek, Therese. Supervision: A method of teaching psychoanalysis. *Psychoanal. Quart.*, 1964, *33*, 71-86.

Fleming, Joan, and Hamburg, D. A. An analysis of methods for teaching psychotherapy with a description of a new approach. *AMA Arch. Neurol. Psychiat.*, 1958, *79*, 179-200.

Flint, A. A., and Rioch, Margaret J. An experiment in teaching family dynamics. *Amer. J. Psychiat.*, 1963, *118*, 940-944.

Fosmire, F. R., and Palmer, B. E. A comparison of a method of programmed instruction and of personal supervision in psychotherapy. Paper presented, National Society for Programmed Instruction, Trinity Univer., San Antonio, Texas, April, 1964.

Hansen, J. C., and Barker, E. N. Experiencing and the supervisory relationship. *J. counsel. Psychol.*, 1964, *11*, 107-111.

Harvey, L. V. The use of nonprofessional auxiliary counselors in staffing a counseling service. *J. counsel. Psychol.*, 1964, *11*, 348-357.

Jones, V. Attitude changes in an NDEA Institute. *Personnel guid. J.*, 1963, *42*, 387-389.

Kelly, E. L., and Fiske, D. W. The prediction of success in the VA training program in clinical psychology. *Amer. Psychologist*, 1950, *5*, 395-406.

Korner, I. N., and Brown, W. H. The mechanical third ear. *J. consult. Psychol.*, 1952, *16*, 81-84.

Krasner, L. The therapist as a social reinforcement machine. In H. H. Strupp and L. Luborsky (Eds.), *Research in psychotherapy*, Vol. 2. Washington, D.C., Amer. Psychol. Assoc., 1962.

Lester, B. K., Gussen, J., Yamamoto, J., and West, L. J. Teaching psychotherapy in a longitudinal curriculum. *J. med. Educ.*, 1962, *37*, 28-32.

Lott, G. M. Multiple psychotherapy: The efficient use of psychiatric treatment and training time. *Psychiat. Quart.*, 1957, *2*, 1-19.

Magoon, T. Innovations in counseling. *J. counsel. Psychol.*, 1964, *11*, 342-347.

Martin, J. C., Carkhuff, R. R., and Berenson, B. G. Process variables in counseling and psychotherapy: A study of counseling and friendship. *J. counsel. Psychol.*, 1966, *13*, 356-359.

Meadow, L., and Tillem, K. Evaluating the effectiveness of a workshop rehabilitation program. *Personnel guid. J.*, 1963, *42*, 541-545.

Mendel, W. M., and Rapport, S. Out-patient treatment for chronic schizophrenic patients: Therapeutic consequences of an existential view. *Arch. gen. Psychiat.*, 1963, *8*, 190-196.

Munger, P. F., and Johnson, C. A. Changes in attitudes associated with an NDEA counseling and guidance institute. *Personnel guid. J.*, 1960, *38*, 751-753.

Munger, P. F., Myers, R. A., and Brown, D. F. Guidance institutes and the persistence of attitudes. *Personnel guid. J.*, 1963, *41*, 415-419.

Murray, E. J. Learning theory and psychotherapy: Biotropic versus sociotropic approaches. *J. counsel. Psychol.*, 1963, *10*, 250-255.

Palmer, B., Fosmire, F. R. Breger, L., Straughan, J. H., and Patterson, G. R. First report of a program of research in psychotherapy training. Mimeographed manuscript, Univer. of Oregon Psychological Clinic, 1963.

Patterson, C. H. Supervising students in the counseling practicum. *J. counsel. Psychol.*, 1964, *11*, 47-53.

Pierce, R. An investigation of the relationship between grade point average and the level of interpersonal functioning. Unpublished dissertation, Univer. of Massachusetts, 1965.

Rioch, Margaret J., Elkes, C., Flint, A. A., Udansky, B. S., Newman, R. G., and Silber, E. NIMH pilot study in training mental health counselors. *Amer. J. Orthopsychiat.*, 1963, *33*, 678-689.

Rogers, C. R. Training individuals to engage in the therapeutic process. In C. R. Strother (Ed.), *Psychology and Mental Health*. Washington, D.C.: Amer. Psychol. Assoc., 1957.

Romano, J. Teaching of psychiatry to medical students. *Lancet,* July, 1961, 93-95.

Taft, R. The ability to judge people. *Psychol. Bull.*, 1955, *52*, 1-23.

Towles, Charlotte. Role of the supervisor in the union of cause and function in social work. *Soc. Serv. Rev.*, 1961, *35*, 144-151.

Truax, C. B. The process of group psychotherapy. *Psychol. Monogr.*, 1961, *75*, No. 14 (Whole No. 511).

Truax, C. B., and Carkhuff, R. R. Significant developments in psychotherapy research. In *Progress in clinical Psychology*, Vol. VI, L. E. Abt and B. F. Reiss (Eds.). New York: Grune & Stratton, 1964 (a).

Truax, C. B., Carkhuff, R. R., and Douds, J. Toward an integration of the didactic and experiential approaches to training in counseling and psychotherapy. *J. counsel. Psychol.*, 1964, *11*, 240-247.

Tudor, Gwenn. A socio-psychiatric nursing approach to intervention in problem of mutual withdrawal on a mental hospital ward. *Psychiat.*, 1952, *15*, 193-217.

Univer. of Minnesota counselor education staff. Supervised field practice in student personnel work. *Personnel guid. J.*, 1960, *39*, 308-309.

Ward, C. H. Electronic preceptoring in teaching beginning psychotherapy. *J. med. Educ.*, 1962, *37*, 1128-1129.

Webb, A. P., and Harris, J. T. A semantic differential study of counselors in an NDEA institute. *Personnel guid. J.*, 1963, *42*, 260-263.

Weiss, J. H. The effect of professional training and amount and accuracy of information on behavioral prediction. *J. consult. Psychol.*, 1963, *27*, 257-262.

Werkman, S. L. Teaching the interpretive process to medical students. *Amer. J. Psychiat.*, 1961, *117*, 897-902.

Wessel, Rosa. Social work education and practice. *Soc. Serv. Rev.*, 1961, *35*, 151-160.

Wolberg, L. R. *The technique of psychotherapy*. New York: Grune & Stratton, 1954.

Wolpe, J. *Psychotherapy by reciprocal inhibition*. London: Oxford Univer. Press, 1958.

Wolpe, J., Salter, A., and Reyna, L. J. *The conditioning therapies: The challenge in psychotherapy*. New York: Holt, Rinehart and Winston, 1964.

PART ONE

*"We can never
fully understand
but we can increase
our penetration."*

ALFRED C. WHITEHEAD

The Challenge to the Helping Professions

We who have devoted our lives to various phases of the "helping" profession are not eagerly disposed toward questioning the efficacy of our
efforts. We know in our viscera the experience of freeing another to
become a productive, fulfilled member of society, or at the very least,
of enabling a previously institutionalized person to make a marginal,
however tenuous, adjustment on "the outside." We know from staff
meetings and clinical conferences that our equally dedicated colleagues
have had similar positive experiences with clients and patients. We are
reinforced periodically at local and national conventions by the program
titles and talks, all of which take some basic client benefits for granted.
All that we know and experience makes us believe that our efforts are
not in vain.

Because we continually desire to make more potent social service
contributions, we intermittently attempt to search or research the
processes and outcomes of our work. We wish to explicate effective
processes so that we can pass on to others in training the means to
elicit positive gains in clients and patients. In this vein, Knight, a psychoanalyst, in 1941 established criteria to assess the basic efficacy of treatment
efforts. He suggested, among others: symptomatic improvement, increased
productivity, improved adjustment and pleasure in sex, improved interpersonal relationships, and the ability to handle ordinary psychological
conflicts and reasonable stress. These seem to be immediately and intui-

21

tively satisfactory criteria; yet, after more than a quarter of a century of continuing and expanding forms of traditional counseling and psychotherapy, *we have not met the challenge of these indices.*

After a careful review of well-controlled research exploring the outcome of various psychotherapeutic, counseling, and guidance activities, Eysenck in 1952 drew and substantiated the conclusion that the helping professions were *not* effective in producing patient improvement in adult neurotics. Eysenck's research and review, interpreted liberally, established that at the minimum there were *no average differences in the outcome indices of persons who were treated and persons who were not treated.* At the maximum, there is cause for even greater alarm: *There may be justification for leaving some patients alone and relying upon the phenomenon of spontaneous remission rather than treating them in the most traditional psychoanalytic mode of practice.* At the minimum, *therapeutic practices have failed to establish their efficacy.* At the maximum, *they may be very questionable modes of intervention with highly dubious outcomes.*

Eysenck presented a challenge to therapeutic practitioners. We accept the challenge. We accept the proposition that the burden of proof is with those who lay claim to the efficacy of therapeutic intervention. Psychotherapy should not be "an unidentified technique applied to unspecified problems with unpredictable outcomes (for which we recommend rigorous training)" [Raimy, 1950].

In this light, Eysenck's (1952) now classic article will prove a most meaningful starting point.

THE INEFFICACY OF THERAPEUTIC PROCESSES WITH ADULTS*

Hans J. Eysenck

The recommendation of the Committee on Training in Clinical Psychology of the American Psychological Association regarding the training of clinical psychologists in the field of psychotherapy has been criticized by the writer in a series of papers (10, 11, 12). Of the arguments

* The effects of psychotherapy: An evaluation. *Journal of Consulting Psychology,* 1952, *16,* 319-324. Reprinted by permission of author and publisher. A subsequent review of the literature by Eysenck, "The Effects of Psychotherapy," appeared in *The handbook of abnormal psychology,* New York: Basic Books, 1960.

presented in favor of the policy advocated by the Committee, the most cogent one is perhaps that which refers to the social need for the skills possessed by the psychotherapist. In view of the importance of the issues involved, it seemed worthwhile to examine the evidence relating to the actual effects of psychotherapy, in an attempt to seek clarification on a point of fact.

BASE LINE AND UNIT OF MEASUREMENT

In the only previous attempt to carry out such an evaluation, Landis has pointed out that "before any sort of measurement can be made, it is necessary to establish a base line and a common unit of measure. The only unit of measure available is the report made by the physician stating that the patient has recovered, is much improved, is improved, or unimproved. This unit is probably as satisfactory as any type of human subjective judgment, partaking of both the good and bad points of such judgments" (26, p. 156). For a unit Landis suggests "that of expressing therapeutic results in terms of the number of patients recovered or improved per 100 cases admitted to the hospital." As an alternative, he suggests "the statement of therapeutic outcome for some given group of patients during some stated interval of time."

Landis realized quite clearly that in order to evaluate the effectiveness of any form of therapy, data from a control group of nontreated patients would be required in order to compare the effects of therapy with the spontaneous remission rate. In the absence of anything better, he used the amelioration rate in state mental hospitals for patients diagnosed under the heading of "neuroses." As he points out:

> There are several objections to the use of the consolidated amelioration rate . . . of the . . . state hospitals . . . as a base rate for spontaneous recovery. The fact that psychoneurotic cases are not usually committed to state hospitals unless in a very bad condition; the relatively small number of voluntary patients in the group; the fact that such patients do get some degree of psychotherapy especially in the reception hospitals; and the probably quite different economic, educational, and social status of the State Hospital group compared to the patients reported from each of the other hospitals—all argue against the acceptance of [this] figure . . . as a truly satisfactory base line, but in the absence of any other better figure this must serve (26, p. 168).

Actually the various figures quoted by Landis agree very well. The percentage of neurotic patients discharged annually as recovered or improved from New York state hospitals is 70 (for the years 1925-1934); for the United States as a whole it is 68 (for the years 1926 to 1933). The percentage of neurotics discharged as recovered or improved within one year of admission is 66 for the United States (1933) and 68 for New York (1914). The consolidated amelioration rate of New York state hospitals, 1917-1934, is 72 percent. As this is the figure chosen by Landis, we may accept it in preference to the other very similar ones quoted. By and large, we may thus say that of severe neurotics receiving in the main custodial care, and very little if any psychotherapy, over two-thirds recovered or improved to a considerable extent. "Although this is not, strictly speaking, a basic figure for 'spontaneous' recovery, still any therapeutic method must show an appreciably greater size than this to be seriously considered" (26, p. 160).

Another estimate of the required "base line" is provided by Denker:

Five hundred consecutive disability claims due to psychoneurosis, treated by general practitioners throughout the country, and not by accredited specialists or sanatoria, were reviewed. All types of neurosis were included, and no attempt made to differentiate the neurasthenic, anxiety, compulsive, hysteric, or other states, but the greatest care was taken to eliminate the true psychotic or organic lesions which in the early stages of illness so often simulate neurosis. These cases were taken consecutively from the files of the Equitable Life Assurance Society of the United States, were from all parts of the country, and all had been ill of a neurosis for at least three months before claims were submitted. They, therefore, could be fairly called "severe," since they had been totally disabled for at least a three months' period, and rendered unable to carry on with any "occupation for remuneration or profit" for at least that time (9, p. 2164).

These patients were regularly seen and treated by their own physicians with sedatives, tonics, suggestion, and reassurance, but in no case was any attempt made at anything but this most superficial type of "psychotherapy" which has always been the stock-in-trade of the general practitioner. Repeated statements, every three months or so by their physicians, as well as independent investigations by the insurance company, confirmed the fact that these people actually were not engaged in productive work during the period of their illness. During their disablement, these cases received disability benefits. As Denker points out, "It is appreciated that this fact of disability income may have actually prolonged the total period of disability and acted as a barrier to incentive for recovery. One would, therefore, not expect the therapeutic results in such a group of cases to be as favorable as in other groups where the economic factor might act as an important spur in helping the sick patient adjust to his neurotic conflict and illness" (9, p. 2165).

The cases were all followed up for at least a five-year period, and often as long as ten years after the period of disability had begun. The criteria of "recovery" used by Denker were as follows: (a) return to work, and ability to carry on well in economic adjustments for at least a five-year period; (b) complaint of no further or very slight difficulties; (c) making of successful social adjustments. Using these criteria, which are very similar to those usually used by psychiatrists, Denker found that 45 percent of the patients recovered after one year, another 27 percent after two years, making 72 percent in all. Another 10 percent, 5 percent, and 4 percent recovered during the third, fourth, and fifth years, respectively, making a total of 91 percent recoveries after five years.

This sample contrasts in many ways with that used by Landis. The cases on which Denker reports were probably not quite as severe as those summarized by Landis; they were all voluntary, nonhospitalized patients, and came from a much higher socioeconomic stratum. The majority of Denker's patients were clerical workers, executives, teachers, and professional men. In spite of these differences, the recovery figures for the two samples are almost identical. The most suitable figure to choose from those given by Denker is probably that for the two-year recovery rate, as follow-up studies seldom go beyond two years and the higher figures for three-, four-, and five-year follow-up would overestimate the efficiency of this "base line" procedure. Using, therefore, the two-year recovery figure of 72 percent, we find that Denker's figure agrees exactly with that given by Landis. We may, therefore, conclude with some confidence that our estimate of some two-thirds of severe neurotics showing recovery or considerable improvement without the benefit of systematic psychotherapy is not likely to be very far out.

EFFECTS OF PSYCHOTHERAPY

We may now turn to the effects of psychotherapeutic treatment. The results of nineteen studies reported in the literature, covering over 7000 cases, and dealing with both psychoanalytic and eclectic types of treatment, are quoted in detail in Table 1. An attempt has been made to report results under the four headings: (a) Cured, or much improved; (b) Improved; (c) Slightly improved; (d) Not improved, died, discontinued treatment, etc. It was usually easy to reduce additional categories given by some writers to these basic four; some writers give only two or three categories, and in those cases it was, of course, impossible to subdivide further, and the figures for combined categories are given.[1] A slight degree of subjectivity inevitably enters into this procedure, but it is doubtful if it has caused much distortion. A somewhat greater degree of subjectivity is probably implied in the writer's judgment as to which

---

[1] In one or two cases where patients who improved or improved slightly were combined by the original author, the total figure has been divided equally between the two categories.

TABLE 1

Summary of Reports of the Results of Psychotherapy

	N	Cured; much im- proved	Im- proved	Slightly im- proved	Not im- proved; died; left treat- ment	% Cured; much im- proved; im- proved
(A) *Psychoanalytic*						
1. Fenichel (13, pp. 28–40)	484	104	84	99	197	39
2. Kessel and Hyman (24)	34	16	5	4	9	62
3. Jones (22, pp. 12–14)	59	20	8	28	3	47
4. Alexander (1, pp. 30–43)	141	28	42	23	48	50
5. Knight (25)	42	8	20	7	7	67
All cases	760	335			425	44%
(B) *Eclectic*						
1. Huddleson (20)	200	19	74	80	27	46
2. Matz (30)	775	10	310	310	145	41
3. Maudsley Hospital Report (1931)	1721	288	900		533	69
4. Maudsley Hospital Report (1935)	1711	371	765		575	64
5. Neustatter (32)	46	9	14	8	15	50
6. Luff and Garrod (27)	500	140	135	26	199	55
7. Luff and Garrod (27)	210	38	84	54	34	68
8. Ross (34)	1089	547	306		236	77
9. Yaskin (40)	100	29	29		42	58
10. Curran (7)	83		51		32	61
11. Masserman and Carmichael (29)	50	7	20	5	18	54
12. Carmichael and Masserman (4)	77	16	25	14	22	53
13. Schilder (35)	35	11	11	6	7	63
14. Hamilton and Wall (16)	100	32	34	17	17	66
15. Hamilton *et al.* (15)	100	48	5	17	32	51
16. Landis (26)	119	40	47		32	73
17. Institute Med. Psychol. (quoted Neustatter)	270	58	132	55	25	70
18. Wilder (39)	54	3	24	16	11	50
19. Miles *et al.* (31)	53	13	18	13	9	58
All cases	7293	4661			2632	64%

disorders and diagnoses should be considered to fall under the heading of "neurosis." Schizophrenic, manic-depressive, and paranoid states have been excluded; organ neuroses, psychopathic states, and character disturbances have been included. The number of cases where there was genuine doubt is probably too small to make much change in the final figures, regardless of how they are allocated.

A number of studies have been excluded because of such factors as excessive inadequacy of follow-up, partial duplication of cases with others included in our table, failure to indicate type of treatment used, and other reasons which made the results useless from our point of view. Papers thus rejected are those by Thorley and Craske (37), Bennett and Semrad (2), H. I. Harris (19), Hardcastle (17), A. Harris (18), Jacobson and Wright (21), Friess and Nelson (14), Comroe (5), Wenger (38), Orbison (33), Coon and Raymond (6), Denker (8), and Bond and Braceland (3). Their inclusion would not have altered our conclusions to any considerable degree, although, as Miles *et al.* point out: "When the various studies are compared in terms of thoroughness, careful planning, strictness of criteria and objectivity, there is often an inverse correlation between these factors and the percentage of successful results reported" (31, p. 88).

Certain difficulties have arisen from the inability of some writers to make their column figures agree with their totals, or to calculate percentages accurately. Again, the writer has exercised his judgment as to which figures to accept. In certain cases, writers have given figures of cases where there was a recurrence of the disorder after apparent cure or improvement, without indicating how many patients were affected in these two groups respectively. All recurrences of this kind have been subtracted from the "cured" and "improved" totals, taking half from each. The total number of cases involved in all these adjustments is quite small. Another investigator making all decisions exactly in the opposite direction to the present writer's would hardly alter the final percentage figures by more than 1 or 2 percent.

We may now turn to the figures as presented. Patients treated by means of psychoanalysis improve to the extent of 44 percent; patients treated eclectically improve to the extent of 64 percent; patients treated only custodially or by general practitioners improve to the extent of 72 percent. There thus appears to be an inverse correlation between recovery and psychotherapy; the more psychotherapy, the smaller the recovery rate. This conclusion requires certain qualifications.

In our tabulation of psychoanalytic results, we have classed those who stopped treatment together with those not improved. This appears to be reasonable; a patient who fails to finish his treatment, and is not improved, is surely a therapeutic failure. The same rule has been followed with the data summarized under "eclectic" treatment, except when the patient who did not finish treatment was definitely classified as "improved" by the therapist. However, in view of the peculiarities of Freudian procedures it may appear to some readers to be more just to class those cases separately, and deal only with the percentage of completed treatments which are successful. Approximately one-third of the psychoanalytic patients listed broke off treatment, so that the percentage of successful treatments of patients who finished their course must be put at approximately 66 percent. It would appear, then, that when we discount the risk the patient runs of stopping treatment altogether, his chances of improvement under psychoanalysis are approximately equal to his chances of improvement under eclectic treatment, and slightly worse than his chances under a general practitioner or custodial treatment.

Two further points require clarification: (a) Are patients in our "control" groups (Landis and Denker) as seriously ill as those in our "experimental" groups? (b) Are standards of recovery perhaps less stringent in our "control" than in our "experimental" groups? It is difficult to answer these questions definitely, in view of the great divergence of opinion between psychiatrists. From a close scrutiny of the literature it appears that the "control" patients were probably at least as seriously ill as the "experimental" patients, and possibly more so. As regards standards of recovery, those in Denker's study are as stringent as most of those used by psychoanalysts and eclectic psychiatrists, but those used by the State Hospitals whose figures Landis quotes are very probably more lenient. In the absence of agreed standards of severity of illness, or of extent of recovery, it is not possible to go further.

In general, certain conclusions are possible from these data. They fail to prove that psychotherapy, Freudian or otherwise, facilitates the recovery of neurotic patients. They show that roughly two-thirds of a group of neurotic patients will recover or improve to a marked extent within about two years of the onset of their illness, whether they are treated by means of psychotherapy or not. This figure appears to be remarkably stable from one investigation to another, regardless of type of patient treated, standard of recovery employed, or method of therapy used. From the point of view of the neurotic, these figures are encouraging; from the point of view of the psychotherapist, they can hardly be called very favorable to his claims.

The figures quoted do not necessarily disprove the possibility of therapeutic effectiveness. There are obvious shortcomings in any actuarial comparison and these shortcomings are particularly serious when there is so little agreement among psychiatrists relating even to the most fundamental concepts and definitions. Definite proof would require a special investigation, carefully planned and methodologically more adequate than these *ad hoc* comparisons. But even the much more modest conclusions that the figures fail to show any favorable effects of psychotherapy should give pause to those who would wish to give an important part in the training of clinical psychologists to a skill the existence and effectiveness of which is still unsupported by any scientifically acceptable evidence.

These results and conclusions will no doubt contradict the strong feeling of usefulness and therapeutic success which many psychiatrists and clinical psychologists hold. While it is true that subjective feelings of this type have no place in science, they are likely to prevent an easy acceptance of the general argument presented here. This contradiction between objective fact and subjective certainty has been remarked on in other connections by Kelly and Fiske, who found that "One aspect of our findings is most disconcerting to us: the inverse relationship between the confidence of staff members at the time of making a prediction and the measured validity of that prediction. Why is it, for example, that our staff members tended to make their best predictions at a time when they subjectively felt relatively unacquainted with the candidate, when they had constructed no systematic picture of his personality structure? Or conversely, why is it that with increasing confidence in clinical judgment . . . we find decreasing validities of predictions?" (23, p. 406).

In the absence of agreement between fact and belief, there is urgent need for a decrease in the strength of belief, and for an increase in the number of facts available. Until such facts as may be discovered in a process of rigorous analysis support the prevalent belief in therapeutic effectiveness of psychological treatment, it seems premature to insist on the inclusion of training in such treatment in the curriculum of the clinical psychologist.

SUMMARY

A survey was made of reports on the improvement of neurotic patients after psychotherapy, and the results compared with the best available estimates of recovery without benefit of such therapy. The figures fail to support the hypothesis that psychotherapy facilitates recovery from neurotic disorder. In view of the many difficulties attending such actuarial comparisons, no further conclusions could be derived from the data whose shortcomings highlight the necessity of properly planned and executed experimental studies into this important field.

REFERENCES

1. Alexander, F. *Five-year report of the Chicago Institute for Psychoanalysis, 1932-1937.*

2. Bennett, A. E., and Semrad, E. V. Common errors in diagnosis and treat-

ment of the psychoneurotic patient—a study of 100 case histories. *Nebr. med. J.*, 1936, *21*, 90-92.

3. Bond, E. D., and Braceland, F. J. Prognosis in mental disease. *Amer. J. Psychiat.*, 1937, *94*, 263-274.

4. Carmichael, H. T., and Masserman, T. H. Results of treatment in a psychiatric outpatients' department. *J. Amer. med. Assoc.*, 1939, *113*, 2292-2298.

5. Comroe, B. I. Follow-up study of 100 patients diagnosed as "neurosis." *J. nerv. ment. Dis.*, 1936, *83*, 679-684.

6. Coon, G. P., and Raymond, A. A review of the psychoneuroses at Stockbridge. Stockbridge, Mass.: Austen Riggs Foundation, Inc., 1940.

7. Curran, D. The problem of assessing psychiatric treatment. *Lancet*, 1937, II, 1005-1009.

8. Denker, P. G. Prognosis and life expectancy in the psychoneuroses. *Proc. Assoc. Life Insur. med. Dir. Amer.*, 1937, *24*, 179.

9. Denker, R. Results of treatment of psychoneuroses by the general practitioner. A follow-up study of 500 cases. *N. Y. State J. Med.*, 1946, *46*, 2164-2166.

10. Eysenck, H. J. Training in clinical psychology: An English point of view. *Amer. Psychologist*, 1949, *4*, 173-176.

11. Eysenck, H. J. The relation between medicine and psychology in England. In W. Dennis (Ed.), *Current trends in the relation of psychology and medicine*. Pittsburgh: Univer. of Pittsburgh Press, 1950.

12. Eysenck, H. J. Function and training of the clinical psychologist. *J. ment. Sci.*, 1950, *96*, 1-16.

13. Fenichel, O. *Ten years of the Berlin Psychoanalysis Institute, 1920-1930.*

14. Friess, C., and Nelson, M. J. Psychoneurotics five years later. *Amer. J. ment. Sci.*, 1942, *203*, 539-558.

15. Hamilton, D. M., Vanney, I. H., and Wall, T. H. Hospital treatment of patients with psychoneurotic disorder. *Amer. J. Psychiat.*, 1942, *99*, 243-247.

16. Hamilton, D. M., and Wall, T. H. Hospital treatment of patients with psychoneurotic disorder. *Amer. J. Psychiat.*, 1941, *98*, 551-557.

17. Hardcastle, D. H. A follow-up study of 100 cases made for the Department of Psychological Medicine, Guy's Hospital. *J. ment. Sci.*, 1934, *90*, 536-549.

18. Harris, A. The prognosis of anxiety states. *Brit. med. J.*, 1938, 2, 649-654.

19. Harris, H. I. Efficient psychotherapy for the large out-patient clinic. *New England J. Med.*, 1939, *221*, 1-5.

20. Huddleson, J. H. Psychotherapy in 200 cases of psychoneurosis. *Mil. Surgeon*, 1927, *60*, 161-170.

21. Jacobson, J. R., and Wright, K. W. Review of a year of group psychotherapy. *Psychiat. Quart.*, 1942, *16*, 744-764.

22. Jones, E. *Decennial report of the London Clinic of Psychoanalysis, 1926-1936.*

23. Kelly, E. L., and Fiske, D. W. The prediction of success in the VA training program in clinical psychology. *Amer. Psychologist*, 1950, *5*, 395-406.

24. Kessel, L., and Hyman, H. T. The value of psychoanalysis as a therapeutic procedure. *J. Amer. med. Assoc.*, 1933, *101*, 1612-1615.

25. Knight, R. O. Evaluation of the results of psychoanalytic therapy. *Amer. J. Psychiat.*, 1941, *98*, 434-446.

26. Landis, C. Statistical evaluation of psychotherapeutic methods. In S. E. Hinsie (Ed.), *Concepts and problems of psychotherapy*. London: Heinemann, 1938. Pp. 155-165.

27. Luff, M. C., and Garrod, M. The after-results of psychotherapy in 500 adult cases. *Brit. med. J.*, 1935, *2*, 54-59.

28. Mapother, E. Discussion. *Brit. J. med. Psychol.*, 1927, *7*, 57.

29. Masserman, T. H., and Carmichael, H. T. Diagnosis and prognosis in psychiatry, *J. ment. Sci.*, 1938, *84*, 893-946.

30. Matz, P. B. Outcome of hospital treatment of ex-service patients with nervous and mental disease in the U. S. Veteran's Bureau, *U. S. Vet. Bur. med. Bull.*, 1929, *5*, 829-842.

31. Miles, H. H. W., Barrabee, E. L., and Finesinger, J. E. Evaluation of psychotherapy. *Psychosom. Med.*, 1951, *13*, 83-105.

32. Neustatter, W. L. The results of 50 cases treated by psychotherapy. *Lancet*, 1935, I, 796-799.

33. Orbison, T. J. The psychoneuroses: Psychasthenia, neurasthenia, and hysteria, with special reference to a certain method of treatment. *Calif. west. Med.*, 1925, *23*, 1132-1136.

34. Ross, T. A. *An enquiry into prognosis in the neuroses*. London: Cambridge Univer. Press, 1936.

35. Schilder, P. Results and problems of group psychotherapy in severe neuroses. *Ment. Hyg., N. Y.*, 1939, *23*, 87-98.

36. Skottowe, I., and Lockwood, M. R. The fate of 150 psychiatric outpatients. *J. ment. Sci.*, 1935, *81*, 502-508.

37. Thorley, A. S., and Craske, N. Comparison and estimate of group and individual method of treatment. *Brit. med. J.*, 1950, *1*, 97-100.

38. Wenger, P. Uber weitere Ergebnisse der Psychotherapie in Rahmen einer Medizinischen Poliklinik. *Wien. med. Wschr.*, 1934, *84*, 320-325.

39. Wilder, J. Facts and figures on psychotherapy, *J. clin. Psychopath.*, 1945, *7*, 311-347.

40. Yaskin, J. C. The psychoneuroses and neuroses. A review of 100 cases with special reference to treatment and results. *Amer. J. Psychiat.*, 1936, *93*, 107-125.

An Aroused Audience

"There appears to be an inverse correlation between recovery and psychotherapy. . . ." This is Eysenck's challenge, and it stimulated a violent reaction. Sanford (1953) immediately concluded: ". . . the only sensible course with respect to such a challenge is to ignore it." For many practitioners, the whole notion of questioning the efficiency of the therapeutic processes "seemed slightly blasphemous, as if we were attempting a statistical test of the efficacy of prayer. . . ." (Teuber and Powers, 1953). Others were more critically systematic in their emotion-laden observations, calling attention to the many uncontrolled variables in Eysenck's actuarial study and concluding in effect that there were no data on the basis of which to evaluate the therapeutic effects of psychotherapy (De Charms, Levy, and Wertheimer, 1954; Luborsky, 1954; Rosenzweig, 1954).

The attacks were appropriate, often fought on Eysenck's own grounds. An insight such as Rosenzweig's that the higher standard of recovery for more intensive therapy necessarily yields a smaller degree of success speaks for itself. Yet we are left with a lingering doubt about the fact that the psychotherapeutic processes have not demonstrated their efficacy. We are left with the feeling that the major pleas are almost apologies: the therapist's motives are good, even if we cannot prove that he does any good. At the very minimum, Eysenck would seem to have pushed the issue of efficacy squarely before us.

Eysenck's initial challenge found some reluctant support from prominent persons involved in training counselors and therapists. Meehl (1955) suggested: "The history of the healing arts furnishes ample grounds for skepticism as to our nonsystematic clinical observations." He was stimulated by Eysenck, and advised that "critics such as Eysenck deserve experimental, statistical answers." Shoben (1956) reviewed the responses of Eysenck's critics and concluded: ". . . their argument that his data were inadequate in many ways says nothing that Eysenck himself did not say, and the conclusive evidence of therapeutic effectiveness must come not from argument but from relevant and rigorous research."

Despite Shoben, by 1956 the controversy had apparently died. The resistance of the helping profession seemed to have successfully overcome the probing of the critic. However, in 1957 Levitt published the distressing findings of his search into the efficacy of treatment process with children. He was not in the Eysenck tradition, and yet he rediscovered the same figures that Eysenck had reported in his earlier study with adults: *There are no average differences in the outcome indices of treatment and control groups.*

THE UNDEMONSTRATED EFFECTIVENESS
OF THERAPEUTIC PROCESSES
WITH CHILDREN *

Eugene E. Levitt

A compendium of results of psychotherapy with adults was published a few years ago by Eysenck (16). It included reports from 24 sources on more than 8000 cases treated by an assortment of psychotherapeutic techniques. The average percentage of cases reported as improved (that is, cured, improved, much improved, adjusted, well, etc.) is about 65.[1] Eysenck's control or base line data estimating the remission rate in the absence of formal psychotherapy come from two sources. Those of Landis (32) for hospitalized neurotics, and those of Denker (14) for neurotics treated at home by general practitioners, show similar remission rates of about 70 percent for a two-year period. Comparing these figures with the average for the treated cases, Eysenck concluded, ". . . roughly two-thirds of a group of neurotic patients will recover or improve to a marked extent within about two years of the onset of their illness, whether they are treated by means of psychotherapy or not" (16, p. 322). He concludes further that "the figures fail to support the hypothesis that psychotherapy facilitates recovery from neurotic disorder" (16, p. 323).

The difficulties attending an evaluation of psychotherapy have been detailed many times, most recently by Rosenzweig (47) in a critique of Eysenck's findings. Other thoughtful and well-organized delineations of evaluation problems include those of Thorne (50), Zubin (56, 57), and Greenhill (22), among others. It is not within the province of the present paper to repeat these accounts.

* The results of psychotherapy with children. *Journal of Consulting Psychology*, 1957, *21*, 189-196. Reprinted by permission of author and publisher. A subsequent review of the literature by Dr. Levitt, "Psychotherapy with children: A further evaluation," appeared in *Behavior Research and Theory*, 1963, *1*, 45-51.

[1] The data, however, are not quite as "remarkably stable from one investigation to another" as Eysenck appears to believe. The 19 reports of the results of eclectic therapy differ significantly among themselves when frequencies of improvement and nonimprovement are compared. A chi square is 38.11 with a p beyond the .01 level for 18 degrees of freedom. Eysenck's point is nonetheless basically reasonable; the range of percent improvement of from 41 to 77 represents considerable stability when one considers the differences in population, chronology, treatment, classification, and terminology among the studies.

The purpose of this paper is to summarize available reports of the results of psychotherapy with children using Eysenck's article (16) as a model.[2] Certain departures will be necessitated by the nature of the data, but in the main, the form will follow that of Eysenck.

BASE LINE AND UNIT OF MEASUREMENT

As in Eysenck's study, the "unit of measurement" used here will be evaluations of the degree of improvement of the patient by concerned clinicians. Individuals listed as "much improved, improved, partially improved, successful, partially successful, adjusted, partially adjusted, satisfactory," etc., will be grouped under the general heading of Improved. The Unimproved cases were found in groupings like "slightly improved, unimproved, unadjusted, failure, worse," etc.

The use of the discharge rate of children's wards in state hospitals as a base line for evaluating the effects of psychotherapy is not recommended. It is most likely that hospitalized children are initially more disturbed than those brought to the child guidance clinics and family service agencies from which the data on treatment are drawn. Few guidance clinics or family service agencies accept psychotic children for treatment, tending instead to refer them to the state hospital. Furthermore, as Rosenzweig (47) points out, the criteria for discharge from a state hospital are probably less stringent than those leading to an appraisal of Improved by other agencies. For these reasons, available statistics of state hospital populations such as those of Witmer (52), McFie (38), and Robins and O'Neal (46) are not used as base line data.

Follow-up evaluations of changes in behavior problems in normal children also do not furnish satisfactory control data. Studies such as those of McFie (38) and Cummings (12) report markedly conflicting results, probably as a function of differences in ages of the subjects, and of varying follow-up intervals. More importantly, behavior like nail biting and nose picking can hardly be regarded as comparable to the problems for which children are referred to guidance clinics.

The use of a follow-up control group of cases closed as unsuccessful, as in the study of Shirley, Baum, and Polsky (49), suffers from obvious weaknesses. Such a group is not comparable to an untreated sample; it appears to represent the segment of the treatment population for which a poor prognosis has been already established.

A common phenomenon of the child guidance clinic is the patient

---

[2] Compendia similar to, and overlapping Eysenck's have been published by Zubin (57) and by Miles, Barrabee, and Finesinger (39). These tend to be more detailed and descriptive. Eysenck's work is most concise; in it, descriptions and discussions of individual studies have been subordinated to the presentation of over-all results. The present writer feels that this is the most provocative, and hence most fruitful, way of evaluating a collection of psychotherapeutic results.

who is accepted for treatment, but who voluntarily breaks off the clinic relationship without ever being treated. In institutions where the service load is heavy and the waiting period between acceptance and onset of treatment may range up to 6 months, this group of patients is often quite large. Theoretically, they have the characteristics of an adequate control group. So far as is known, they are similar to treated groups in every respect except for the factor of treatment itself.

Nevertheless, the use of this type of group as a control is not common in follow-up evaluations of the efficacy of treatment. Three studies report follow-up data on such groups. Of these, the data of Morris and Soroker (40) are not suitable for the purposes of this paper. Of their 72 cases, at least 11 had treatment elsewhere between the last formal contact with the clinic and the point of evaluation, while an indeterminate number had problems too minor to warrant clinic treatment.

The samples in the remaining two studies appear satisfactory as sources of base line data. Witmer and Keller (55) appraised their group 8 to 13 years after clinic treatment, and reported that 78 percent were Improved. In the Lehrman study (34), a one-year follow-up interval found 70 percent Improved. The over-all rate of improvement for 160 cases in both reports is 72.5 percent. This figure will be used as the base line for evaluating the results of treatment of children.

THE RESULTS OF PSYCHOTHERAPY

Studies showing outcome at close of treatment are not distinguished from follow-up studies in Eysenck's aggregation. The distinction seems logical, and is also meaningful in the predictive sense, as the analyses of this paper will indicate. Of the reports providing data for the present evaluation, thirteen present data at close, twelve give follow-up results, and five furnish both types, making a total of eighteen evaluations at close and seventeen at follow-up. The data of two reports (29, 30) are based on a combined close-follow-up rating. Results for the three kinds of evaluations will be presented separately.

The age range covered by all studies is from preschool to 21 years at the time of original clinic contact, the customary juncture for the determination of age for the descriptive data. However, very few patients were over 18 years at that time, and not many were over 17. The median age, roughly estimated from the ranges, would be about 10 years.

The usual psychiatric classification of mental illnesses is not always appropriate for childhood disorders. The writer has attempted to include only cases which would crudely be termed neuroses, by eliminating the data on delinquents, mental defectives, and psychotics whenever possible. The latter two groups constituted a very small proportion of the clinic cases. The proportion of delinquent cases is also small at some clinics but fairly large at others. Since the data as presented were not always amenable to these excisions, an unknown number of delinquent cases are included. However, the outcomes for the separated delinquents are much the same as those for the entire included group.

As in Eysenck's study, a number of reports were excluded here for various reasons. The investigations of Healy and Bronner (24), Feiker (18), Ellis (15), Mann (37), and Giddings (20) were eliminated because of overlap, partial overlap, or suspected overlap of the sample with samples of included reports. Those of Bennett and Rogers (3), Rich (45), Hunt, Blenkner, and Kogan (27), Schiffmann and Olson (48), and Heckman and Stone (25) were not useable either because of peculiar or inadequate presentation of data, or because results for children and adults were inseparable.

The number of categories in which patients were classified varied from study to study. Most used either a three-, four-, or five-point scale. A few used only two categories, while one had twelve. Classification systems with more than five points were compressed into smaller scales. The data are presented tabularly in their original form, but the totals are pooled into three categories, Much Improved, Partially Improved, and Unimproved. A summation of the former two categories gives the frequency of Improved Cases.

A summary of results at close is shown in Table 1. Results of follow-up evaluations are summarized in Table 2, while the results from two studies using a combined close-follow-up evaluation are presented in Table 3. In the latter two tables, the follow-up interval is given as a range of years, the usual form of presentation in the studies. An attempt has been made to compute an average interval per case, using the midpoint of the range as a median when necessary. These averages are tenuous since it cannot be safely assumed that the midpoint actually is the median value. For example, in the Healy-Bronner investigation (23), the range of intervals is 1 to 20 years, but the median is given as $2\frac{1}{2}$ years. Since the proportion of cases which can be located is likely to vary inversely with the number of years of last clinic contact, the averages of 4.8 years for the follow-up studies and 2.3 years for the close-follow-up studies are probably overestimates.

Table 1 shows that the average percentage of improvement, that is, the combined percentages in the Much Improved and Partially Improved categories is 67.05 at close. It is not quite accurate to say that the data are consistent from study to study. A chi-square analysis of improvement and unimprovement yields a value of 230.37, which is significant beyond the .001 level for 17 df. However, as in the case of Eysenck's data, there is a considerable amount of consistency considering the interstudy differences in methodology, definition, etc.

TABLE 1

Summary of Results of Psychotherapy with Children at Close

Study	N	Much improved	Partially improved		Unimproved		Percent improved
(11)	57	16	18	12	8	3	80.7
(26)	100	13	18	42	26	1	73.0
(28)	70	12	29	19	10		85.7
(44)	250	54	82	46	68		72.8
(34)	196	76	52		68		65.3
(31)	50	15	18		17		66.0
(10)	126	25	54		47		62.7
(53)	290	75	154		61		79.0
(2)	814	207	398		209		74.3
(43)	72	26	31		15		79.2
(33)	196	93	61		42		78.6
(6)	27	5	11		11		59.3
(9)	31	13	8		10		67.7
(8)	23	2	9		12		47.8
(7)	75	35	22		18		76.0
(1)	80	31	21		28		65.0
(35)	522	225			297		43.1
(13)	420	251			169		59.8
All cases	3399	1174	1105		1120		67.05
Percent	100.00	34.54	32.51		32.95		

The average percentage of improvement in the follow-up studies is given in Table 2 as 78.22. The percentage for the combined close-follow-up evaluations is 73.98, roughly between the other two. The percentage of improvement in the control studies was 72.5, slightly higher than the improvement at close and slightly lower than at follow-up. It would appear that treated children are no better off at close than untreated children, but that they continue to improve over the years and eventually surpass the untreated group.

This conclusion is probably specious, perhaps unfortunately. One of the two control studies was an evaluation one year after the last clinic contact, the other 8 to 13 years after. The former study reports only 70 percent improvement while the longer interval provided 78 percent improvement. The figure for the one-year interval is similar to the results at close, while the percentage of improvement for the control with the 8- to 13-year interval is almost identical with that for the follow-up studies.

The point of the analysis is more easily seen if the results at close and at follow-up are pooled. This combination gives the same sort of estimate as that furnished by the two control groups pooled since one

TABLE 2

Summary of Results of Psychotherapy with Children at Follow-up

Study	Interval in years	N	Much improved		Partially improved		Unimproved		Percent improved
(33)	1–5	197	49		55	39	38	16	72.6
(5)	2	33	8		11	7	6	1	78.8
(11)	2–3	57	25		17	6	6	3	84.2
(52)[a]	1–10	366		81	78	106	101		72.4
(28)	2–3	70	21		30	13	6		91.4
(51)	5–8	17	7			3	4	3	58.8
(34)	1	196	99		46		51		74.0
(41)	16–27	34	22		11		1		97.1
(2)	1–20	705	358		225		122		82.7
(4)	5–18	650	355		181		114		82.5
(36)	3–15	484	111		264		109		77.5
(19)	1–4	732	179		398		155		78.8
(13)	5	359	228		80		51		85.8
(21)	1–2	25	6		12		7		72.0
(42)	1–2	25	10		6		9		64.0
(35)	$\frac{1}{2}$–$1\frac{1}{2}$	191	82				109		42.9
(23)	1–20	78	71				7		91.0
All cases	4.8[b]	4219	1712		1588		919		78.22
Percent		100.00	40.58		37.64		21.78		

[a] Data based on 13 studies originally reported in (54); results of 8 of these are included here.

[b] Estimated average follow-up interval per case.

of them is a long-interval follow-up while the other was examined only a short time after clinic contact. The pooled percentage of improvement based on 7987 cases in both close and follow-up studies is 73.27, which is practically the same as the percentage of 72.5 for the controls.

It now appears that Eysenck's conclusion concerning the data for adult psychotherapy is applicable to children as well; the results do not support the hypothesis that recovery from neurotic disorder is facilitated by psychotherapy.

The discrepancy between results at close and at follow-up suggests that time is a factor in improvement. Denker's report (14) also indicated the operation of a time factor. He found that 45 percent of the patients had recovered by the end of one year, 72 percent had recovered by the end of two years, 82 percent by three years, 87 percent by four years, and 91 percent by five years. The rate of improvement as a function of time in Denker's data is clearly negatively accelerating.

A Spearman rank-order correlation between estimated median fol-

TABLE 3

Summary of Results of Psychotherapy with Children Based on
Combined Close-Follow-up Evaluation

Study	Interval in years	N	Much improved	Partially improved		Unimproved		Percent improved
(29)	1–10	339	94	81	76	42	46	74.04
(30)	1–10	30	9	13		8		73.33
All cases	5.5[a]	369	103	170		96		73.98
Percent		100.00	27.91	46.07		26.02		

[a] Estimated average follow-up interval per case.

low-up interval and percentage of improvement in the 17 studies in Table 2 is .48, $p = .05$. This estimate of relationship should be viewed with caution because of the aforementioned difficulty in determining median intervals. However, it is uncorrected for tied ranks, which tends to make it a conservative null test. It is also, of course, insensitive to the curve of the bivariate distribution.

The percentage of improvement as a function of time interval is shown by the data of Table 4. The studies have been grouped at five

TABLE 4

Improvement as a Function of the Interval Between Last
Clinic Contact and Follow-up

Estimated median interval in years	Number of reports	Total N	N improved	Percent improved
1–1$\frac{1}{2}$	4	437	261	59.73
2–2$\frac{1}{2}$	6	1167	929	79.61
5–6$\frac{1}{2}$	3	742	583	78.57
10	2	1189	958	80.57
12	2	684	569	83.19
All cases	17	4219	3300	78.22

time-interval points in the table. There are four studies with estimated median intervals of 1-1$\frac{1}{2}$ years, six with intervals of 2-2$\frac{1}{2}$ years, three with 5-6$\frac{1}{2}$ years, two with 10 years, and two with 12 years.

The data of Table 4 indicate that most of the correlation between improvement and time-interval is accounted for by the studies with the shortest intervals, and those with the largest. The curve is more or less the same as that of Denker's data, negatively accelerating with most of the improvement accomplished by $2\frac{1}{4}$ years. It is peculiar that the improvement after $1\frac{1}{2}$ years is about 60 percent, less than the 67 percent improvement at close. However, the difference is not too great to attribute to variations in methodology and sampling among the concerned studies. Another potential explanation will be offered shortly.

This analysis suggests that improvement is in part a function of time, though the mechanisms involved remain purely speculative. Future comparisons of the results of psychotherapy should properly take this factor into consideration.

Inspection of the data in Table 1 discloses another potential factor in the improvement rate. The studies in which only two rating categories, improved and unimproved, have been used, appear to furnish lower percentages of improvement than the average. In the two reports of this kind in Table 1, the average improvement is only 50.5 percent compared with the overall 67 percent. A complete analysis of percentage of improvement as a function of number of categories is shown in Table 5.

TABLE 5

Improvement as a Function of the Number of Points on the Rating Scale in Evaluation at Close

Number of points	Number of reports	Total N	N improved	Percent improved
2	2	942	476	50.53
3	12	1980	1442	72.83
4	2	320	242	75.63
5	2	157	119	75.80
All cases	18	3399	2279	67.05

Examination of Table 5 indicates that three-, four-, and five-point rating scales produce about the same percentage of improvement. The use of a two-point scale, however, results in over 20 percent less improvement than the others.[3] This kind of analysis cannot be applied to the data in Table 2 since it will be confounded by the time factor.

Evidently, a certain proportion of the unimproved cases in the studies

---

[3] The marked difference between the two-point scale studies and those using finer scales is reflected in the consistency analysis. The chi square for 17 df was 230.37, but when the two-category studies are eliminated, it falls to 52.66 for 15 df. The value is significant beyond the .01 level, but the original chi square has been decreased by more than 75 percent with a loss of only two df.

using two categories would have fallen in partially improved categories if they had been utilized. A number of cases in which a fair amount of improvement was manifested are forced into the unimproved category when central points are not available. A two-point scale thus seems to be overly coarse. It is desirable that finer scales be used in future evaluation studies.

The study of Maas et al. (35), which furnishes three-quarters of the cases in the 1-1½ year interval group in Table 4, used a two-point scale. The percentage of improvement is only 43, which may account for the fact that this time-interval group has a lower percentage of improvement than in the studies at close.

There are a number of different kinds of therapies which have been used in the studies reported here. The therapists have been psychiatrists, social workers, and teams of clinicians operating at different points in the patient's milieu. Therapeutic approaches included counseling, guidance, placement, and recommendations to schools and parents, as well as deeper level therapies. In some instances the patient alone was the focus of attention. In others, parents and siblings were also treated. The studies apparently encompassed a variety of theoretical viewpoints, although these are not usually specified. Viewed as a body, the studies providing the data for Tables 1, 2, and 3 are therapeutically eclectic, a plurality, perhaps, reflecting psychoanalytic approaches.

Thus we may say that the therapeutic eclecticism, the number of subjects, the results, and the conclusions of this paper are markedly similar to those of Eysenck's study. Two-thirds of the patients examined at close and about three-quarters seen in follow-up have improved. Approximately the same percentages of improvement are found for comparable groups of untreated children.

As Eysenck pointed out (17) in a sequel to his evaluation, such appraisal does not *prove* that psychotherapy is futile. The present evaluation of child psychotherapy, like its adult counterpart, fails to support the hypothesis that treatment is effective, but it *does not* force the acceptance of a contrary hypothesis. The distinction is an important one, especially in view of the differences among the concerned studies, and their generally poor caliber of methodology and analysis. Until additional evidence from well-planned investigations becomes available, a cautious, tongue-in-cheek attitude toward child psychotherapy is recommended.

SUMMARY

A survey of eighteen reports of evaluations at close, and seventeen at follow-up, was compared with similar evaluations of untreated children. Two-thirds of the evaluations at close, and three-quarters at follow-up, showed improvement. Roughly the same percentages were found for the respective control groups. A crude analysis indicates that time is a factor in improvement in the follow-up studies: the rate of improvement with time is negatively accelerating. Further analysis contraindicates the use of only two categories in evaluation. The scale tends to give much lower rates of improvement than three-, four-, and five-point scales.

It is concluded that the results of the present study fail to support the view that psychotherapy with "neurotic" children is effective.

References

1. Albright, Sue, and Gambrell, Helen. Personality traits as criteria for the psychiatric treatment of adolescents. *Smith Coll. Stud. soc. Wk,* 1938, *9,* 1-26.

2. Barbour, R. F. Selected surveys prepared for the inter-clinic conference. In J. F. Davidson (Chmn.), Follow-up on child guidance cases. Ninth Child Guidance Inter-Clinic Conference, London, 1951. Pp. 49-59.

3. Bennett, C. C., and Rogers, C. R. Predicting the outcomes of treatment. *Amer. J. Orthopsychiat.,* 1941, *11,* 210-221.

4. Bronner, Augusta F. Treatment and what happened afterward. *Amer. J. Orthopsychiat.,* 1944, *14,* 28-35.

5. Brown, Jane L. The follow-up procedure of an intermittent child guidance clinic. Unpublished master's thesis, Smith Coll., 1931.

6. Brown, Marjorie. Adolescents treatable by a family agency. *Smith Coll. Stud. soc. Wk,* 1947, *18,* 37-67.

7. Burlingham, Susan. A quantitative analysis of psychiatric social treatment carried out in seventy-five cases at the Institute for Juvenile Research. Unpublished master's thesis, Smith Coll., 1931.

8. Canaday, Louise J. A way of predicting the probable outcome of treatment of young children who run away. Unpublished master's thesis, Smith Coll., 1940.

9. Carpenter, Jean A. Some factors relating to the method and outcome of casework treatment with the adolescent girl when the girl herself is the focus of treatment. Unpublished master's thesis, Smith Coll., 1939.

10. Christianson, Eva, Gates, Mary, and Coleman, Fay. A survey of the intake of a mental hygiene clinic with special reference to the outcome of treatment. *Smith Coll. Stud. soc. Wk,* 1934, *5,* 211-212.

11. Cohen, Marion, and Davis, Ellen. Factors related to the outcome of treatment in a child guidance clinic. *Smith Coll. Stud. soc. Wk,* 1934, *5,* 212-214.

12. Cummings, Jean D. A follow-up study of emotional symptoms in school children. *Brit. J. educ. Psychol.,* 1946, *16,* 163-177.

13. Cunningham, J. M., Westerman, Hester H., and Fischhoff, J. A follow-up study of children seen in a psychiatric clinic for children. Paper read at Amer. Orthopsychiat. Assoc., Chicago, March, 1955.

14. Denker, P. G. Results of treatment of psychoneuroses by the general practitioner, *N. Y. State med. J.,* 1946, *46,* 2164-2166.

15. Ellis, Florine J. A study of one hundred children treated by the Northern New Jersey Mental Hygiene clinics. *Smith Coll. Stud. soc. Wk,* 1936, *6,* 277-278.

16. Eysenck, H. J. The effects of psychotherapy: An evaluation. *J. consult. Psychol.,* 1952, *16,* 319-324.

17. Eysenck, H. J. The effects of psychotherapy: A reply. *J. abnorm. soc. Psychol.,* 1955, *50,* 147-148.

18. Feiker, Hazel A. A comparative study of the methods of case work of adolescent boys in the years 1928-1930 and 1938-1940 at a child guidance clinic. Unpublished master's thesis, Smith Coll., 1941.

19. Fenton, N., and Wallace, Ramona. Child guidance in California communities, Part 6. Follow-up study of Bureau cases. *J. juv. Res.,* 1938, *22,* 43-60.

20. Giddings, Elizabeth R. Some factors affecting the outcome of treatment of Negro cases in a child guidance clinic. Unpublished master's thesis, Smith Coll., 1940.

21. Gollander, Barbara. A study of overinhibited and unsocialized aggressive children. III. Later adjustment. Unpublished master's thesis, Smith Coll., 1944.

22. Greenhill, M. H. *et al.* Evaluation in mental health. *Publ. Hlth Serv. Publ. No. 413,* Washington: U. S. Gov't Printing Off., 1955.

23. Healy, W., Bronner, Augusta F., Baylor, Edith M., and Murphy, J. P. *Reconstructing behavior in youth: a study of problem children in foster families.* New York: Knopf, 1929.

24. Healy, W., and Bronner, Augusta F. *Treatment and what happened afterward.* Boston: Judge Baker Guidance Clinic, 1939.

25. Heckman, A. A., and Stone, A. Testing casework results: Forging new tools. *Surv. Midmonthly,* 1947, *83,* 267-270.

26. Hubbard, Ruth M., and Adams, Christine F. Factors affecting the success of child guidance treatment. *Amer. J. Orthopsychiat.,* 1936, *6,* 81-102.

27. Hunt, J. McV., Blenkner, Margaret, and Kogan, L. S. A field-test of the Movement Scale. *Soc. Casewk,* 1950, *31,* 267-277.

28. Irgens, Effie M. Must parents' attitudes become modified in order to bring about adjustment in problem children? *Smith. Coll. Stud. soc. Wk,* 1936, *7,* 17-45.

29. Jacobsen, Virginia. Influential factors in the outcome of treatment of school phobia. *Smith Coll. Stud. soc. Wk,* 1948, *18,* 181-202.

30. Johnson, Lillian J., and Reid, J. H. An evaluation of ten years' work with emotionally disturbed children. *Ryther Child Cent. Monogr.* IV, 1947.

31. La More, Mary T. An evaluation of a state hospital child guidance clinic. *Smith Coll. Stud. soc. Wk,* 1941, *12,* 137-164.

32. Landis, C. A statistical evaluation of psychotherapeutic methods. In L. E. Hinsie (Ed.), *Concepts and problems of psychotherapy.* New York: Columbia Univer. Press, 1937.

33. Lee, P. R., and Kenworthy, M. E. *Mental hygiene and social work.* New York: Commonwealth Fund, 1929.

34. Lehrman, L. J., Sirluck, Hilda, Black, B. J., and Glick, Selma J. Success and failure of treatment of children in the child guidance clinics of the Jewish Board of Guardians, New York City. *Jewish Bd. Guard. Res. Monogr.,* 1949, No. 1.

35. Maas, H. S. *et al.* Socio-cultural factors in psychiatric clinic services for children: A collaborative study in the New York and San Francisco metropolitan areas. *Smith Coll. Stud. soc. Wk,* 1955, *25,* 1-90.

36. Maberly, A., and Sturge, Brenda. After-results of child guidance. *Brit. med. J.,* 1939, *1,* 1130-1134.

37. Mann, Ida L. Results with child guidance patients diagnosed as psychoneurotic. *Smith Coll. Stud. soc. Wk,* 1942, *13,* 160-161.

38. McFie, Bernice S. Behavior and personality difficulties in school children. *Brit. J. educ. Psychol.,* 1934, *4,* 30-46.

39. Miles, H. H. W., Barrabee, Edna L., and Finesinger, J. E. Evaluation of psychotherapy. *Psychosom. Med.,* 1951, *8,* 83-105.

40. Morris, D. P., and Soroker, Eleanor. A follow-up study of a guidance-clinic waiting list. *Ment. Hyg., N. Y.,* 1953, *37,* 84-88.

41. Morris, D. P., Soroker, Eleanor, and Burress, Genette. Follow-up studies of shy, withdrawn children—I. Evaluation of later adjustment. *Amer. J. Orthopsychiat.,* 1954, *24,* 743-754.

42. Moses, Jane. A study of overinhibited and unsocialized aggressive children. Part IV: The later adjustment of unsocialized aggressive children. Unpublished master's thesis, Smith Coll., 1944.

43. Newell, N. W. The methods of child guidance adapted to a public school system. *Ment. Hyg., N. Y.,* 1934, *18,* 362-373.

44. Reid, J. H., and Hagan, Helen R. *Residential treatment of emotionally disturbed children.* New York: Child Welfare League of America, 1952.

45. Rich, G. J. Preschool clinical service and follow-up in a city health department. *Amer. J. Orthopsychiat.,* 1948, *18,* 134-139.

46. Robins, E., and O'Neal, Patricia. Clinical features of hysteria in children, with a note on prognosis. A two- to seventeen-year follow-up study of 41 patients. *Nerv. Child,* 1953, *10,* 246-271.

47. Rosenzweig, S. A transvaluation of psychotherapy—A reply to Hans Eysenck. *J. abnorm. soc. Psychol.,* 1954, *49,* 298-304.

48. Schiffmann, Frances, and Olson, Elma. *A study in family case work: An attempt to evaluate service.* Evanston, Ill.: Family Welfare Assoc., 1939.

49. Shirley, Mary, Baum, Betty, and Polsky, Sylvia. Outgrowing childhood's problems: A follow-up study of child guidance patients. *Smith Coll. Stud. soc. Wk,* 1940, *11,* 31-60.

50. Thorne, F. C. Rules of evidence in the evaluation of the effects of psychotherapy. *J. clin. Psychol.*, 1952, *8*, 38-41.

51. Walcott, Esther. A study of the present adjustment made by solitary children who had withdrawn into an imaginary world. Unpublished master's thesis, Smith Coll., 1931.

52. Witmer, Helen L. A comparison of treatment results in various types of child guidance clinics. *Amer. J. Orthopsychiat.*, 1935, *5*, 351-360.

53. Witmer, Helen L. *et al.* The outcome of treatment in a child guidance clinic: A comparison and an evaluation. *Smith Coll. Stud. soc. Wk,* 1933, *3*, 339-399.

54. Witmer, Helen L. *et al.* The later adjustment of problem children. *Smith Coll. Stud. soc. Wk,* 1935, *6*, 1-98.

55. Witmer, Helen L., and Keller, Jane. Outgrowing childhood problems: A study in the value of child guidance treatment. *Smith Coll. Stud. soc. Wk,* 1942, *13*, 74-90.

56. Zubin, J. Design for the evaluation of therapy. *Res. Publ. Assoc. Res. nerv. ment. Dis.,* 1953, *31*, 10-15.

57. Zubin, J. Evaluation of therapeutic outcome in mental disorders. *J. nerv. ment. Dis.,* 1953, *117*, 95-111.

The Burden of Proof Is a Burden Indeed

After the furor had died and doubt had been cast upon Eysenck's statistical compilation of outcome indices for adult therapy cases, Levitt arrived at "markedly similar" figures for child psychotherapy: approximately two-thirds at the close of the study and three-quarters at follow-up of both the treatment and control patients improved. He concluded, that "the results of the present study fail to support the view that psychotherapy with 'neurotic' children is effective." Levitt's illuminating insight indicates that only the temporal factor is a relevant and significantly positive correlate of positive patient outcome.

The implications are profound. Two independent sources of data were reviewed by two rigorous researchers who were also clinically astute —and both found a lack of demonstrable results for child and adult treatment. Yet Levitt's support for Eysenck's stance was not met with the excited upheaval that greeted the earlier work. It was met with neither applause nor resistance.

The most significant effect of Levitt's replication with child therapy is that: Levitt *did* replicate Eysenck. A criteria of rigor alone might lead us to focus upon the multitude of uncontrolled variables. *A criteria of meaning* might suggest that in spite of the multitude of uncontrolled variables, *the phenomenon explored is so significant that without controls it will replicate again and again.*

Reinforced by Levitt's findings, Eysenck (1960) became delightfully disparaging:

> To judge by their writings, some advocates of psychotherapy appear to take an attitude similar to that adapted by Galen, the father of modern medicine, in his advocacy of the wondrous powers of Samian clay: "All who drink this remedy recover in a short time, except those whom it does not help, who all die and have no relief from any other medicine. Therefore it is obvious that it fails only in incurable cases."

Eysenck went on to take aim at the promulgators of major cults of therapy, suggesting that the "quantitative indices . . . are better than professions of faith bolstered by the therapist's prestige and the skillful use of the illustrative case." His all-too-evident conclusion is that "the burden of proof is on anyone who claims specific results for a given form of therapy."

Despite Eysenck's implications, the full hypothesis has not been proven. Nevertheless, although the results of Eysenck and Levitt do not prove that psychotherapy is "futile" (Eysenck, 1955), they should cause clinical practitioners to také long, hard looks at their therapeutic activities and their outcomes. The failure of both Eysenck and Levitt to find an unambiguous base line figure for untreated groups provides a "most eloquent testimony" to the inability of most clinical practitioners to take seriously their responsibility for studying therapy process and outcome.

Bergin (1963) is one of the few clinical psychologists who is responsive to the challenges of Eysenck and Levitt. In addition, he flies fully in the face of the critics of outcome research: "There are no such phenomena as culture-free or values-free people; consequently it seems inevitable that specific attention and action is required on the part of both practitioners and researchers with regard to these facts. This involves becoming explicit about the values to which we are committed, doing all we can to specify their meaning in precise psychological terms, and finally, devoting ourselves to developing ways of achieving these ends."

NEGATIVE RESULTS REVISITED*

Allen E. Bergin

The questions raised by Eysenck (1952) ten years ago regarding the effectiveness of psychotherapy when compared with the effects of no-treatment can be rephrased today in much more sophisticated and scientific terminology, but they are still questions. For Eysenck, and perhaps others, there is in fact no longer a question; psychotherapy is *not* effective in ameliorating psychopathology. Indeed, in his most recent and depressing review we find Eysenck (1960, p. 697) expressing his pessimism by quoting Galen thusly:

> All who drink this remedy recover in a short time, except those whom it does not help, who all die and have no relief from any other medicine. Therefore it is obvious that it fails only in incurable cases.

For the rest of us who require more persuasive evidence before believing that a null hypothesis has been thoroughly confirmed, there remain questions regarding the validity of this challenging, but seemingly unrefuted, assertion.

Let it be recognized that this conclusion, and the question which stimulated its derivation is highly simplified and ignores essential underlying complexities in outcome research; nevertheless, let us consider first of all the current validity of the challenge embodied in the general proposition that psychotherapy has no unique effect upon personality change.

CONTROLLED STUDIES OF THERAPEUTIC EFFECTS

On the basis of an extensive review we are forced to conclude that the requirements for an adequate test of this proposition have rarely been fully met. It is unusual to find independent pre-, post-, and follow-up measures as well as the use of equivalent treatment and non-treatment control groups all in the same study. I wish to discuss with you six of these more adequately designed studies representing the major findings to date with regard to the main point at issue.

* The effects of psychotherapy: Negative results revisited. *Journal of Counseling Psychology*, 1963, *10*, 244-255. Reprinted by permission of author and publisher. This paper was originally read at a symposium held at the annual meeting of the American Psychological Association, St. Louis, Missouri, August 30-September 6, 1962, Edward J. Shoben, Jr., Chairman.

The Chicago study of client-centered therapy edited by Rogers and Dymond (1954) was once considered the epitome of good research design in studying the effects of psychotherapy; however, its presumed demonstration of positive change for psychotherapy subjects and not for control subjects is subject to important limitations. First of all, the study utilizes a normal rather than a neurotic control group. The neurotics in therapy *do* change significantly but the study provides little evidence on "spontaneous" changes in control neurotics over time which was the point Eysenck originally raised. Would an equivalent group of neurotics tested over an eight-month period, as was the case with the experimentals, show as much change as the experimentals? The two-month pre-therapy testing of the experimentals offers evidence on the basis of own-control data that neurotics do not change spontaneously over time while waiting for psychotherapy; nevertheless, we do not know whether or not they would have changed if the testing had been done at an eight-month interval rather than at a two-month interval. The data are conclusive with respect to normals and are indeed suggestive with regard to neurotics; but they do not conclusively demonstrate that psychotherapy has an effect upon neurotically disturbed persons which does not occur with equal potency outside of psychotherapy.

Another major project, the Cambridge-Somerville Youth Study of delinquency prevention (Powers and Witmer, 1951) was an impressive, well-designed study of 650 boys, 325 experimentals and 325 controls, over approximately a ten-year period. The results were utterly negative; in fact, if anything, the controls may have been slightly better off than the experimentals at the conclusion of the experiment. However, there are serious problems with this study also, one upon which Eysenck leans heavily in support of his current, more pessimistic position regarding the effects of psychotherapy. First, the treatment cannot be truly said to have been what most of us would term psychotherapy. It consisted of a variation of social casework which involved primarily the counselor's being a warm, interested friend of the boy—in fact, the intent of the study was to determine whether boys would model themselves after a positive figure who was simply warmly and humanly interested in them. Second, we have no assurance in this nor any other instance where a control group of disturbed persons is used, that the controls are genuine controls.

Perhaps, here, as in other cases, neurotic persons seek counsel and advice from a variety of sources including friends, relatives, clergymen, and physicians or in other ways informally seek out resources for promoting change. In this case, parents or other environmental figures may have been agents promoting such contacts. It is known, for instance, that at least 10 percent of the control boys had contacts with other treatment centers. We cannot be assured, either, that the effects of such extratherapeutic contacts are randomized across experimental and control groups for it is unlikely that persons already in a psychotherapy or counseling relationship will be strongly motivated to seek additional help from other sources. Thus, we cannot say that the only difference between the experimental and control groups is the administration of the treatment.

Two other studies utilizing control groups provide interesting data in the present context. The Barron and Leary study (1955) utilizes an out-patient waiting list control group and the Cartwright and Vogel study (1960) utilizes an own-control design. Both studies meet the requirement of equal time periods between testings for experimental and control groups. Both studies provide evidence of change in the experimental group which is matched by a similar amount of change in the control group; thus the data are negative in both instances with regard to the proposition at issue. It has been noted, however, that the experimentals in both of these instances manifested significantly greater variability in criterion scores at the conclusion of psychotherapy than did the controls. The Cartwright and Vogel study provides interesting additional data that appear to explain this result. It was found that when therapists were divided into experienced and inexperienced groups that the experienced therapists produced positive change whereas the clients seen by inexperienced therapists actually got worse. This is striking and requires further analysis. We shall return to it in a moment.

Shlien, Mosak, and Dreikurs (1962) report a fascinating research comparing time-limited client-centered and Adlerian psychotherapy on the basis of pre-, post-, and follow-up self-ideal Q sorts. The data indicate very similar and statistically significant changes in both experimental groups after 20 sessions of therapy and no change in two equivalent control groups, one a group of normals, the other a group of neurotics. Of the six studies we are reporting, this is the only one that provides unequivocally positive results.

The final study is as yet unpublished, but the quality of design and the results, which have been privately circulated, require inclusion in our own survey because of their importance. This large program of intensive research with schizophrenics underway at Wisconsin (Gendlin, 1962; Rogers, 1959, 1961; Truax, 1962) has begun to yield its results, some of which pertain directly to the question at issue. The study involves unusually thorough matching of experimental and control groups and an extensive program of outcome evaluation. It is, at least in design, a paradigm for all research addressed to the basic, simple question of whether psychotherapy has any effect at all. Since the treatment studied was applied to schizophrenic subjects, many of them severely regressed, we hesitate to include these data in our analysis; nevertheless certain aspects of the results provide an interesting comparison with the work already cited by Cartwright and Vogel.

In the present instance, preliminary data show no significant differences between experimental and control subjects; however, when experimental subjects are divided according to qualities of the therapist it was found that patients of therapists who provided high therapeutic conditions (high empathy, positive regard, and congruence) improved significantly whereas patients of therapists who provided low therapeutic conditions (low empathy, positive regard, and congruence) became significantly worse. The effectiveness of the one group of therapists is cancelled out by the negative effects of the other group when the two are combined into a single experimental group and compared with the controls. This clearly shown result is an exciting breakthrough. It confirms what was suggested in the Cartwright and Vogel and perhaps the Barron and Leary study, that change does indeed occur in psychotherapy, but in two opposite directions, the direction depending upon therapist qualities. This may indeed be the answer to the series of negative findings on the generalized effectiveness of psychotherapy. The positive results in the Shlien study and the partially positive findings in the Rogers and Dymond study may be explainable in this context on the basis of good therapist selection.

IMPLICATIONS OF THE DATA
FOR NEW RESEARCH FRONTIERS

There are no simple generalizations which derive readily from the foregoing studies or the class of studies which they represent. They provide many stimuli for further theorizing and for further research exploration and in this sense are eminently fruitful. Let us pursue for a moment three interesting directions from among those which these data lead us to consider.

Control Groups Not Control Groups

One of the most provocative implications of the series of negative findings cited here and the additional ones cited in the two Eysenck papers is that neurotics change positively with time without the benefits of psychotherapy. Many of the studies using adequate control groups and reporting negative results show significant changes in the tested subjects. The fact that the changes are of similar degree among both experimental and control subjects should not prevent us from noting the significant fact that change *does* occur! This finding has now reached the stage of being a repeatedly replicated fact. What is going on in these control groups? Why do these people change? The fact is that we have little knowledge whatsoever as to what goes on in these control groups. It is tacitly assumed that since they do not receive formal psychotherapy that they are controls equal in every other way with the experimentals. But are they? I know of no controlled study which has provided sampling of the subject's daily life experiences which might affect his adjustment or personality disturbance. It should be recalled here that we have no reason to assume that outside experience effects should be randomized across therapy and no-therapy groups.

I would like to propose the following solution to this puzzle. The control groups in these studies are not control groups; they are therapy groups! We have substantial evidence from two independent and thoroughly done studies that anxious or disturbed people seek help but not from psychotherapists. Jerome Frank (1961) reports that during a $4\frac{1}{2}$ year follow-up period of the cases which had been seen for six months in an experimental therapy design, *one-half* of them had contacts with a medical or nonmedical "help-giving person that was more than casual and lasted some time." He states that "In light of the help-seeking activities of the patients in this study, their progressive improvement in social effectiveness probably represents the average effect of nonspecific help" (p. 212). One of the many projects stimulated by the Joint Commission on Mental Illness and Health involved a survey of how *Americans View Their Mental Health* (Gurin, Veroff, and Feld, 1960). One of the striking findings in the study was the report that when people became seriously upset they sought help but with significantly greater frequency from clergymen, physicians, friends, teachers, etc. than from mental health professionals. Perhaps, then, the changes occurring in control groups can be attributed to this type of help-seeking. If this is so it suggests that what may actually be the effective ingredient in the psychotherapeutic process is not specific to psychotherapy.

Therapeutic Conditions among Professionals and Nonprofessionals

This brings us to the second deduction which can be made from our brief analysis of outcome research. It was noted in several instances that a negative outcome, that is no difference in amount of change between experimentals and controls, could be accounted for by the mutually cancelling effects of two different kinds of therapists having provided treatment—one kind apparently promotes positive change and the other kind promotes negative change. The evidence regarding exactly *who* produces which kind of change is not altogether clear. This ability appears to have some relationship to amount of experience, but the more impressive data concern attitudinal qualities of the therapist. Truax (1962) reports from the Wisconsin project that among these qualities are empathic understanding, congruence, and unconditional positive regard.

Additional information is provided in the studies by Whitehorn and Betz (Betz, 1962) in which therapists who were successful in treating schizophrenics were clearly distinguishable from those therapists who were unsuccessful. The more effective therapists were measurably more democratic, nonauthoritarian, noninterpretive, and personal in their approach and were especially perceptive of the "individualistic inner experiences of the patient." (However, McNair, Callahan, and Lorr demonstrate that the picture may be more complex than this, 1962.)

It is interesting to consider the thought that these qualities could very likely characterize the experienced client-centered and Adlerian therapists in the Shlien study which is the only report demonstrating an unequivocally positive outcome. The deduction to be drawn from this reasoning is obvious. The therapists who produce positive results are those who have certain personal qualities and ways of responding to others rather than a well-trained armamentarium of techniques; therefore it is no vain stretch of the imagination to hypothesize that our so-called control subjects who change in spite of being controls are seeking help from and being influenced by people who have the same personal qualities as those therapists who produce positive personality change. The proposition tendered for consideration here suggests that not only have our control groups not been control groups, but that what we have called psychotherapy is not in fact the psychotherapeutic agent. Future research, then, calls for greater precision in specifying controls, the dimensionalizing of therapist qualities in order to better specify our antecedent variable, and, finally, experimentation with new forms of psychotherapy based upon newly hypothesized change agents.

Stimuli toward the Assessment of Valued Outcomes

This stage of our argument leads to the third and final observation which derives from the survey of outcome studies. It does not pertain directly to research results, but rather to broader conclusions about the direction and meaning of therapy outcome research. The studies reviewed here and the larger number which they represent exemplify the fact that subjective value judgments underlie the selection of all outcome criteria. This fact has presented an enduring problem in specifying the effects of psychotherapy. Disagreement regarding the acceptability of criteria on both theoretical and practical levels is pervasively commonplace and is undoubtedly traceable to issues of personal values. The present studies are suggestive of how such a state of affairs produces great diversity in indices of psychotherapy's effect. The outcome measures in these reports include self-ideal discrepancy, a TAT index of adjustment, social effectiveness, personal comfort-discomfort, MMPI indices, number of arrests or court appearances, behavior rating scales, and therapist judgments.

It is no longer original to conclude from such evidence that outcome can mean many things, that different and important outcome criteria tend to be uncorrelated, and that discrepant research results are to be expected under such conditions. All this is well demonstrated and simply punctuates the need for as much specificity with regard to measured consequences as is needed with regard to antecedent conditions of therapeutic promise. In fact, it should be noted that neither the term "psychotherapy" nor the term "outcome" are denotative and that they refer neither to a specified antecedent variable nor a specified consequent. There are dozens of now precisely specified variables, which could serve as referents for these terms, but there is little agreement as to which ones are the most relevant and useful. In an attempt to remedy such an unseemly condition, the problem of outcome has been minimized in favor of process analyses and experimental analogues of psychotherapy (Astin, 1961). Let us discover, it was heralded, what leads to what! That is true science! Once we know what conditions lead to what results, then we or someone else can worry about whether the results are desirable or not. The psychotherapy situation became, then, a laboratory for the study of interpersonal processes and the problem of outcome was often set aside, not because outcome analysis was a scientifically unfertile field, but because the valuational issues presented were something that modern psychology was ill-equipped to deal with.

It is clear that this solution has side-stepped, rather than resolved the problem of determining the quality of therapeutic results. As an alternative, I would like to propose that psychotherapy research will become most fruitful when it is not only scientifically correct but is socially sensitive, when research and practice are geared toward the discovery and application of means toward accomplishing specifically valued goals. We never have and, I believe, never will strictly agree upon the goals or outcomes to be strived for, but to me it is folly to suppose that the research enterprise in psychotherapy will become optimally fruitful until it includes an enlarged devotion toward valued ends. The folly lies, in part, in the implicit and inhibiting notion that we ought to have culture-free criteria. There are no such phenomena as culture-free or values-free people; consequently it seems inevitable that specific attention and action is required on the part of both practitioners and researchers with regard to these facts. This involves becoming explicit about the values to which we are committed, doing all we can to specify their meaning in precise psychological terms, and finally, devoting ourselves to developing ways of achieving those ends. Our research frustrations in this area can be alleviated only by studying how specifically valued goals can best be achieved as consequences of therapeutic regimes organized to accomplish such purposes. It seems axiomatic to me that we cannot escape this requirement and that to do so would necessarily undermine the potential contribution of the psychotherapy research enterprise.

SUMMARY

To sum up, we find that the question of the effects of psychotherapy has led to a series of researches which has raised a number of alternative questions or problems. These vexations of the scientific spirit appear on the verge of stimulating important breakthroughs in the analysis of psychotherapeutic effects even though the majority of findings are negative with regard to the global question of the effects of psychotherapy. First, the studies reviewed appear to have demonstrated that control groups may actually represent a test of the effectiveness of nonprofessional therapeutic conditions, that these conditions may very well exist in professional psychotherapy as well, but that they are found primarily among a selected group of therapists and that the remainder of therapists have a negative effect which accounts for the unimpressive results among experimental groups. We have noted also the need for additional precision in specifying both antecedents and consequents in psychotherapy, and have suggested that in particular the problem of specifying therapeutic consequences can only be addressed in terms of values, that this should then be the basis for positive action with regard to promoting what we value rather than dilly-dallying in midstream because we are afraid to assert openly what we believe and act upon privately.

Finally, perhaps we can all feel at one with Jerome Frank (1961, p. 207) when he cited Alice in Wonderland as having a true kinship with the psychotherapy researcher:

> . . . the croquet balls were live hedgehogs, and the mallets live flamingoes, and the soldiers had to double themselves up and stand on their hands and feet to make the arches—Alice soon came to the conclusion that it was a difficult game indeed.

REFERENCES

Astin, A. W. The functional autonomy of psychotherapy. *Amer. Psychologist,* 1961, *16,* 75-78.

Barron, F., and Leary, T. Changes in psychoneurotic patients with and without psychotherapy. *J. consult. Psychol.,* 1955, *19,* 239-245.

Betz, Barbara J. Experiences in research in psychotherapy with schizophrenic patients. In H. H. Strupp and L. Luborsky (Eds.), *Research in psychotherapy.* Vol. 2. Washington, D. C.: Amer. Psychol. Assoc., 1962, pp. 41-60.

Cartwright, Rosalind Dymond, and Vogel, J. L. A comparison of changes in psychoneurotic patients during matched periods of therapy and no-therapy. *J. consult. Psychol.*, 1960, *24*, 121-127.

Eysenck, H. J. The effects of psychotherapy: An evaluation. *J. consult. Psychol.*, 1952, *16*, 319-324.

Eysenck, H. J. The effects of psychotherapy. In H. J. Eysenck (Ed.), *Handbook of abnormal psychology*. New York: Basic Books, 1960, pp. 697-725.

Frank, J. D. *Persuasion and healing*. Baltimore: Johns Hopkins Press, 1961.

Gendlin, E. T. Client-centered developments and work with schizophrenics. *J. counsel. Psychol.*, 1962, *9*, 205-211.

Gurin, G., Veroff, J., and Feld, Sheila. *Americans view their mental health*. New York: Basic Books, 1960.

McNair, D. M., Callahan, D. M., and Lorr, M. Therapist "type" and patient response to psychotherapy. *J. consult. Psychol.*, 1962, *26*, 425-429.

Powers, E., and Witmer, Helen. *An experiment in the prevention of delinquency*. New York: Columbia Univer. Press, 1951.

Rogers, C. R., and Dymond, Rosalind F. *Psychotherapy and personality change*. Chicago: Univer. of Chicago Press, 1954.

Rogers, C. R. The process of personality change in schizophrenics and normals during psychotherapy: A research investigation. Unpublished manuscript, Univer. of Wisconsin, 1959.

Rogers, C. R. Introduction to the Symposium. Paper read at a symposium: Therapeutic and research progress in a program of psychotherapy with hospitalized schizophrenics. Amer. Psychol. Assoc. Convention, New York, 1961.

Shlien, J. M., Mosak, H. H., and Dreikurs, R. Effect of time limits: A comparison of two psychotherapies. *J. counsel. Psychol.*, 1962, *9*, 31-34.

Truax, C. B. Effective ingredients in psychotherapy: An approach to unraveling the patient-therapist interaction. *J. counsel. Psychol.*, 1963, *10*, 256-263.

For Better or For Worse

Bergin reminds us of the significance of what we in our distressful concern often overlook. Both in the control and the treatment groups *changes do occur*.

We have an effect, he shows, although his "we" enlarges to incorporate the "clergymen, physicians, friends, teachers" sought out by the members of the control group in their urgency. All helpers, however, are not equally effective. The significantly increased variability in the change indices of the treatment group suggests that the efforts of professional helpers tend to have more far-reaching implications for clients than those of nonprofessionals. Formal counseling and psychotherapeutic processes appear to incorporate the extremes of facilitation and retardation of client development—extremes which in the past have cancelled each other out. Perhaps the members of the mental health profession possess the same sensitivities and communicative skills on the average as nonprofessional helpers, only more so—or less so.

The task before us is to explicate the facilitative and retarding learning or relearning experiences. Although we might study the processes in both the professional helping encounters and the nonprofessional helping encounters, it makes most sense to concentrate on the heightened processes producing the extremes of outcome—professional counseling and psychotherapy. *The hope for the profession lies in understanding the work of those counselors and therapists whose clients get well.*

PART TWO

*"If the artist himself
is not converted by the Word
what hope can there be
for the masses who read him."*

HENRY MILLER

Cross-Cult Dimensions of Counseling and Psychotherapy

THE CLINICAL APPROACHES

In our attempts to explicate the facilitative or retarding effects of our therapeutic efforts, we must look primarily at those therapists whose clients tend to improve on a variety of outcome indices. In order to study relevant process variables, we begin with attempts by a number of prominent therapists and theorists to postulate effective dimensions that cut across the multitude of approaches to counseling and psychotherapy.

The attempts reviewed here run a full loop from a selection from Frieda Fromm-Reichmann's relatively traditional and monumental psychoanalytic work to Franz Alexander's now-classic attempt to integrate psychoanalytic practice with learning theory. It is a loop rather than a circle because Alexander attempts to bridge a gap between two hitherto mutually exclusive stances. In between, we consider a number of cross-cult attempts from a variety of different vantage points. In the second part of this section, we review several of the more experimental approaches to counseling and psychotherapy.

While the following selection by Fromm-Reichmann (1950) is not specifically dedicated to discerning dimensions that cut across the cults of therapy, she is succinct and lucid in her attempt to illuminate the efficacy of psychoanalytic processes.

THE PREREQUISITES OF THERAPY
FROM AN ANALYTIC VIEWPOINT *

Frieda Fromm-Reichmann

This [discussion] presents formulations of principles of intensive psychotherapy with psychoneurotics and psychotics. These psychotherapeutic principles are offered on the basis of a general dynamic and psychiatric orientation; more specifically, they are suggested to the reader on the basis of my training in and my experience with the application of Sigmund Freud's concepts of psychoanalytic psychotherapy with neurotics, the development of these teachings during the last fifty years, and especially of H. S. Sullivan's operational interpersonal conceptions. These doctrines form the background for my scientific orientation concerning the nature of and the procedure in intensive psychotherapy.

In view of the multitude of existing schools of psychotherapeutic thinking, . . . I will briefly define the guiding concepts of this discussion of intensive psychotherapy. The therapeutic procedure presented is intended to effect mitigation of a person's emotional difficulties in living and to bring about recovery from his mental symptoms. The psychotherapeutic process is designed to bring about understanding for and insight into the historical and dynamic factors which, unknown to the patient, are among the causes of the mental disturbance for which he seeks psychiatric help.

The technique used in this process, . . . very briefly outlined here, comprises: the clarification of a patient's difficulties with his fellow-men through observation and investigation of the vicissitudes of the mutual interrelationship between doctor and patient; the encouragement of recall of forgotten memories; the investigation and scrutiny of the anxiety connected with such recall, including the patient's resistance against this recall and his security operations with the psychiatrist who tries to effect it. It is in the light of these memories and of the patient's and doctor's

* Introduction. Reprinted from *The principles of intensive psychotherapy* by Frieda Fromm-Reichmann by permission of The University of Chicago Press. Copyright 1950 by The University of Chicago Press.

interpersonal experiences with each other that the patient's communications are interpreted with regard to their unconscious genetic and dynamic implications.

The goal of intensive psychotherapy therefore, as I see it . . . is understood to be: alleviation of patients' emotional difficulties in living and elimination of the symptomatology, this goal to be reached by gaining insight into and understanding of the unconscious roots of patients' problems, the genetics and dynamics, on the part of both patient and psychiatrist, whereby such understanding and insight may frequently promote changes in the dynamic structure of the patient's personality.[1]

This therapeutic goal of intensive psychotherapy is in contradistinction to the aim of other important psychotherapeutic methods and techniques, such as brief psychotherapy, suggestive psychotherapy, hypnotherapy, etc. Their goal is to cure symptoms and effect social recoveries. They operate without promoting personality changes and without producing insight into the genetics and dynamics of a patient's problems, or they center upon only a limited focal amount of insight. . . . [I believe] that it is *not only the wording per se* (that is, the interpretive give-and-take) which relieves the patient but also the discharge of affect plus insight gained by the patient. The nonverbal interplay experienced between patient and doctor which accompanies verbalized interchange also plays an integral part in all intensive psychotherapy. . . .[2]

It is my belief that the problems and emotional difficulties of mental patients, neurotics or psychotics, are, in principle, rather similar to one another and also to the emotional difficulties in living from which we all suffer at times. Should these difficulties become so great that a person is unable to resolve them without help, thereby feeling the need for assistance, he may become a mental patient in need of psychotherapy. . . .

[It is] my firm belief that the first prerequisite for successful psychotherapy is the respect that the psychiatrist must extend to the mental patient. Such respect can be valid only if the psychiatrist realizes that his patient's difficulties in living are not too different from his own. This statement is not just a humanitarian or charitable hypothesis but a scientific conviction. There are various well-known psychiatric facts that point in this direction.[3]

The first of these is the two-sidedness of motivation that the modes

---

[1] From this formulation of "intensive psychotherapy" my psychiatric philosophy becomes evident: that there is no valid *intensive* psychotherapy other than that which is psychoanalytic or psychoanalytically oriented.

[2] *Editor's note.* Fromm-Reichmann describes some "indispensable affective concomitants to the psychotherapeutic process" in her sections on "The Psychiatrist," "Transference and Parataxic Distortions," "Security Operations, Resistance," and "Acting Out."

[3] Although I have elaborated upon them in a previous publication, I will repeat them here because of their bearing upon the attitude of respect between the psychiatrist and the mental patient.

of expression of the so-called "healthy" have in common with many modes of expression of the mentally disturbed, as they present themselves in their symptoms. Many emotional reactions of both mentally disturbed and mentally stable people are an expression of a continuous or transitory disturbance of their emotional stability in terms of difficulties in their interpersonal relationships as well as an expression of their motivation toward alleviating or overcoming these difficulties. For instance, consider an obsessional person suffering from compulsive handwashing. He has to wash his hands from fifteen to thirty times daily, each time he touches certain things or persons from which he fears contamination. This compulsion is a mental symptom which seriously interferes with the maintenance of the person's interpersonal contacts. However, were he not to give in to the compulsion, his fear of contamination, which he fights with his compulsive handwashing, would interfere even more seriously with his contacts with other people.

Another example would be a withdrawn, aloof, seclusive schizophrenic. His aloofness constitutes a serious interpersonal difficulty. At the same time, it is motivated by a tendency to forego even more serious interpersonal difficulties. As one patient put it, it may be meant to forego "another rebuke," in the long row of thwarting rebuffs which the schizophrenic has experienced in his early childhood and which have conditioned him to expect repetition (4). Or it may serve the purpose of avoiding the outbursts of hostility against other people by which so many schizophrenics feel threatened within themselves.

Now, consider any average so-called "healthy" person who suffers from anxiety, that is, from a very unpleasant interference with his interpersonal contacts. Since he lives in a society and in a culture where the display of fear or anxiety are coexistent with an alleged or real decrease of prestige or self-respect, he may tend to convert his anxiety into anger, preferably against the person who is the cause of his anxiety. While this anger is an expression of a transitory interpersonal difficulty, it is, therefore, also the expression of a tendency toward alleviating this difficulty if and when it is masked as anxiety (2).

Again, consider a healthy person who is given to boasting and bragging to cover up his sense of inferiority. Pseudo-megalomanic outbursts certainly constitute a nuisance in our interpersonal world. However, the feelings of inferiority for whose overcompensation these outbursts are staged, constitute a much more serious interpersonal interference, that is, transitory difficulty in living. The realization and display of lack of self-respect will always be accompanied by a reduction of one's respect for others and therefore by the expectation of a decrease of the respect which one may expect from others. "One can respect others only to the extent that one respects oneself," as H.S. Sullivan put it (3, 6, 7).

So much for the two-sidedness of motivation which prevails equally in many emotional reactions of mentally disturbed and mentally healthy people. The other type of psychological expression which is evidenced by mentally healthy, as well as by mentally disturbed, people are the means of expression used by the mentally healthy while asleep, in their dreams, and by the mentally disturbed while awake, in their psychotic productions. Dreams and psychotic productions are actually analogous. To mention only a few of the operations common to them, both the dreamer and the psychotic express themselves in allusions, symbols, and pictures and by means of distortions and condensations. Both experience illusions and hallucinations. In both states, thinking does not follow the rules of logic, and the sense of time and space are not congruent with the chronological and topographical concepts of time and space which are valid with the healthy while awake (1, 5, 7). In brief, the psychotic operates along the lines of thinking and uses the means of expression with which the psychiatrist, who is familiar with the principles of psychoanalytic dream interpretation, is well acquainted. . . . Considered from the aspect of teleological thinking, one may even say that dreams follow the same pattern of two-sidedness in motivation as do other emotional experiences mentioned above. The dream constitutes, as it were, a transitory psychotic state through which we all pass once within a period of twenty-four hours. Some psychiatrists feel that it may be assumed that, in doing so, we safeguard against the danger of developing continuous psychotic states while awake. So much to corroborate the statement about the similarity in operation of the emotional difficulties of mental patients and those of healthy people.

What, then, is the nature of these difficulties? Emotional difficulties in living are difficulties in interpersonal relationships; and a person is not emotionally hampered, that is, he is mentally healthy to the extent to which he is able to be aware of, and therefore to handle, his interpersonal relationships (7). In stating this and, by implication, defining psychiatry and psychotherapy as the science and art of interpersonal relationships, I not only wish to say that a person is mentally healthy to the extent to which he is able to be aware of and to handle his overt relationships with other people. But I also wish to refer to a much more far-reaching fact. We can understand human personality only in terms of interpersonal relationships. There is no way to know about human personality other than by means of what one person conveys to another, that is, in terms of his relationship with him. Moreover, the private mental and emotional experiences, his *covert inner* thought and reverie processes are *also* in terms of interpersonal experiences.

From this interpersonal concept of psychiatry it ensues that intensive psychotherapy comprises the investigation and understanding of a person's overt and covert mental operations as interpersonal processes. Neither of these processes can be scrutinized or understood other than in terms of a person's interpersonal exchange with another person, be it in reality, as in overt relationships, or in fantasy, as in one's thought—and reverie—processes. When the experience is a psychotherapeutic one, it is the interpersonal exchange between the patient and the psychiatrist as a participant observer which carries the possibility of therapeutically valid interpersonal investigation and formulation.

We assume that it is true that emotional problems in general and the symptomatology of a mental patient in particular are due to difficulties in interpersonal relationships, for which there is reduced awareness. Subsequently, then, the principal problem of the psychotherapeutic interview is to facilitate the accession to awareness of information about interpersonal problems and difficulties which will help to clarify for the patient the troublesome aspects of his life and ultimately to resolve his symptomatology (7). This information must be sought with the patient and given by him as communication to another person, the psychiatrist. Hence it follows that the psychotherapeutic process is of a strictly interpersonal nature as to procedure and as to contents.

As we set out to investigate and clarify the principles of intensive psychotherapy, we must study, therefore, not only the psychotherapeutic process as such, or the patient's personality in terms of his interpersonal processes, but also the personality of the participant observer, the psychiatrist, in terms of his interpersonal relationships.

REFERENCES

1. Freud, S. *The interpretation of dreams.* New York: Macmillan, 1931. Also in *The basic writings of Sigmund Freud.* New York: Modern Library, Random House, 1938.

2. Freud, S. *The problem of anxiety.* New York: Norton, 1936.

3. Freud, S. Selfishness and self-love. *Psychiatry*, 1939, *2*, 507-523.

4. Fromm-Reichmann, Frieda. A preliminary note on the emotional significance of stereotypes in schizophrenics. *Bull. Forest Sanitarium*, 1942, *1*, 17-21.

5. Jung, C. G. The psychology of dementia praecox. *Nerv. ment. dis. monographs*, 1936, *3*, pp. 10-11, 22, 82-83.

6. Menninger, K. *Love against hate.* New York: Harcourt, Brace and World, 1942.

7. Sullivan, H. S. Conceptions of modern psychiatry. *Psychiatry*, 1940, *3*, 1-117.

The Client's Future and the Therapist's Past

Fromm-Reichmann focuses upon psychotherapy as an interpersonal process between therapist and patient. She underscores the necessity of understanding the interpersonal functioning of the therapist as well as that of the client. Most important, she prescribes two critical variables of truly therapeutic processes: (1) ". . . the first prerequisite for successful psychotherapy is the respect that the psychiatrist must extend to the mental patient"; (2) ". . . the principal problem of the psychotherapeutic interview is to facilitate the accession to awareness of information about interpersonal problems and difficulties which will help to clarify for the patient the troublesome aspects of his life and ultimately to resolve his symptomatology."

In order to involve the client in a deep process of self-exploration and understanding within the therapeutic encounter, as well as in a lifelong process leading to constructive personality change, the therapist must realize "that his patient's difficulties in living are not too different from his own." The therapist must provide conditions conducive to the client's feeling of freedom and security so that the client can come to experience himself and experiment with himself. In the end, the client's self-understanding and respect are in large part contingent upon the therapist's self-understanding and respect for himself. Because the implicit goals of therapy involve the client's becoming in many significant ways like the therapist, the therapist *must* represent a way of living effectively and facilitatively for himself and others.

This selection sets the stage for the remainder of the readings. Constant threads involving facilitative conditions, some of which appear in this introductory reading, will be found interwoven through all of the readings. Some of the concepts that Fromm-Reichmann emphasizes will be found under new constructs in the following integrative effort of Shaffer and Shoben (1956).

COMMON ASPECTS OF PSYCHOTHERAPY *

Laurance F. Shaffer
and
Edward J. Shoben, Jr.

Brief extracts from psychotherapeutic interviews cannot, of course, demonstrate the changes that take place during a full therapeutic experience, which often runs into dozens or scores of hours. But even

* Common aspects of psychotherapy. From *Psychotherapy: Learning new adjustments,* chapter in *The psychology of adjustment.* Boston: Houghton Mifflin Company, 1956, pp. 522-529. Reprinted by permission of authors and publisher.

brief quotations serve several useful purposes. They convey some of the flavor of a counseling process. They indicate that counseling is primarily a conversation between client and therapist, intended to explore the former's feelings, increase his self-understanding, and eventually help him discover new and more effective ways of living. Although the excerpts are drawn from presumably different "schools" of psychotherapy—psychoanalytic, client-centered, and general or eclectic—they suggest that the similarities of these approaches are somewhat greater than their differences. Where differences occur, they are more of degree than of kind. All types of psychotherapy share, in varying degrees, certain common dimensions of the therapeutic process.

INTERPRETATION AND RESPONSIBILITY

One dimension of the counseling process is the degree to which the clinician *interprets* what the client tells him (1). The therapist's responses may range from merely restating what the client has said, to drawing inferences about his unconscious impulses. A few examples may clarify the continuum of interpretative responses.

The least interpretative reaction, which merely repeats the content of a patient's statement, is illustrated by this interchange:

> *Cl.* I've been awfully nervous and high-strung lately. It's hard for me to get to work and concentrate on what I have to do. I think it's perfectly natural though. I had a pretty big operation not long ago, and I haven't really got my strength back yet.
>
> *Th.* You feel your nervousness and inability to work are just a natural aftermath of your operation.

The therapist has said nothing that the client has not already put into words. Interpretation is at a minimum. Nevertheless, the clinician's response helps to achieve two goals. First, it indicates that the counselor is listening in an attentive, genuinely interested, accepting way, and that the client is quite free to think with him further about his disturbing nervousness. Second, it objectifies the reason that the client gives to explain his uneasiness. It is probable that his recent operation is more a rationalization than an adequate reason for the anxiety that the client feels. But it is more likely that he can consider his own defensive behavior constructively when he hears it expressed by another person than when he hears himself say it, or when someone argues with him.

At the other end of the scale of interpretation are attempts to uncover profoundly unconscious concerns in the client. Usually, the more interpretative the therapist's response, the more it involves the integration of previous statements by the client with his current ones.

The clinician is responding not only to what the client says but also to what he has previously said. A suicidal patient in a hospital, for example, has told his therapist about a number of phobias, including fears of crossing streets and bridges. The therapist also knows that the patient attempted to take his own life by drowning, that he was in a panic of anxiety when he did it, and that he suffers from very low self-esteem. The patient says:

> Pt. It's got so bad I can't even drive over a bridge any more without feeling so scared it's all I can do not to leave the car and run away.

The therapist responds as follows:

> Th. It seems to me that these phobias are all associated with your destructive impulses toward yourself. You think of yourself as a very worthless person and hate yourself for being so inadequate in your own eyes. Streets and bridges symbolize the river in which you could drown this person whom you despise so, and every time you cross them, they arouse this urge to do yourself harm. No wonder you get anxious to the point of panic.

Here the clinician is trying to clarify the patient's behavior by relating his attempted suicide to his lack of self-regard, and by uncovering the unconscious meanings that streets and bridges have for him. Whether such interpretations are helpful may be debatable. The only point with which we are concerned here is the illustration of a highly interpretative response by the psychotherapist.

. . . The client-centered therapist tends to use statements that fall closer to the low end of the interpretative scale; the psychoanalyst tends to work much more interpretatively; the eclectic clinician lies somewhere between.[1] All three, however, vary somewhat in their degree of interpretativeness, depending on the issue the client is discussing and on the extent to which they feel he is ready to consider new interpretations of his behavior. One experimental study, which compared the techniques of analytic and client-centered therapists, showed that the psychoanalysts asked more exploratory questions (2). The client-centered therapists tended to reflect and clarify the clients' expressions of feeling. The analysts also gave more interpretations, but only 10 percent of their responses were interpretative.

Another dimension of psychotherapy is the degree of responsibility assumed by the clinician for maintaining and developing the therapeutic

---

[1] *Editor's Note:* On pp. 516 to 522 of their book, Shaffer and Shoben provided illustrative case material, from which they offer their own cogent interpretations.

relationship. If the therapist asks many questions, determines the topics discussed, advises the client about the decisions he should make in his everyday life, or tells the client to get in touch with him whenever he feels anxious or upset, then he would be rated high on this dimension because he assumes virtually all responsibility for the therapeutic development. On the other hand, the therapist who is primarily an understanding listener, permits the client to choose the topics discussed, encourages the client to think with him about any problems that arise, but offers neither advice nor direction, and essentially limits the client's contacts with him to the consulting room would be rated low because he places most of the responsibility on the client.

It is probable that varying degrees of responsibility are desirable at different points in the therapeutic process. For example, it may be important for the clinician to assume greater responsibility in the earlier stages of counseling than later. Nevertheless, our three excerpts again suggest differences in degree of responsibility assumed by the three therapists. The client-centered counselor listens attentively and reflects feelings sensitively, but he does little to steer the course of the interview. The psychoanalyst, on the other hand, takes full responsibility for instructing his client to associate freely to the elements of his dream. The analyst opens the discussion of the client's possible resentment against his mother. The eclectic therapist is again intermediate, listening carefully and permitting the client to follow her own lines of thought, but often determining the topic to a considerable degree. But the three counselors vary from moment to moment in the amount of responsibility they accept. They seem to overlap in their assumption of responsibility. Their differences are of emphasis, and do not mark them off from one another as representatives of completely independent doctrines.

THE COUNSELING RELATIONSHIP

Psychotherapy is a *relationship* between two people. In this respect, psychotherapeutic service differs markedly from the service rendered by other professional persons such as general medical practitioners or lawyers. In such instances, one divulges his difficulties and problems in matters of health, or involving some legal issue, and expects that the doctor or attorney will prescribe a course of action which will lead to a solution. While it helps if the physician or lawyer has a pleasant manner and a reassuring way of dealing with people, he is called on primarily for his technical skill and expertness.

In counseling, however, the situation is quite different. Psychological difficulties arise primarily from handicapping interpersonal relations. Their cure understandably lies in an opportunity for new social learning.

The personal aspect of the relationship is therefore an integral part of the client's therapeutic experience.

Fiedler has shown that the relationship in psychotherapy is more a function of the experience and expertness of clinicians than of their "schools" or theoretical affiliations (3). He secured recorded interviews from ten therapists representing psychoanalytic, Adlerian, and client-centered approaches. These recordings were then evaluated by other therapists in terms of how well they approximated an ideal counseling relationship. The findings were that the more expert and experienced clinicians created relationships closer to the ideal than did the non-experts, and that the relationships created by experts of one school more closely resembled those created by experts of *other* schools than those created by nonexperts of the *same* school. Similarly, expert therapists of different schools agreed better among themselves as to what constituted an ideal counseling relationship than they did with nonexpert members of the same schools.

The psychotherapeutic relationship is characterized by three fundamental attitudes on the part of the therapist (4). The first of these attitudes may be called *warm concern*. The clinician is genuinely interested in his client as a person and is fully committed to the task of being as helpful as possible. There is no necessary implication of "liking" a client; many psychotherapeutic subjects are not very likeable people, and their unhappy and troubled awareness of this fact is one of the motivations for their entering therapy. All that is meant is that the therapist devotes all his attention during the time he is with his client to understanding the client's feelings as sensitively and as fully as he can. He respects and values the client as a human being and not merely as a "case."

Second, the relationship is characterized by a *nonretaliatory permissiveness*. The clinician gives the client extensive freedom to discuss any topic he chooses, including his reactions to the therapist himself and to the therapeutic situation. Regardless of the topic chosen, the therapist remains calm and unshocked. Even when the client attacks him verbally, he is more interested in understanding the attack than in retaliation or revenge. Consequently, the relationship is a safe one for the client because he is never rejected or subjected to punishment for the behavior he reports or for the attitudes and feelings he verbalizes. On the other hand, the clinician does not express his approval of what the client does or reports. He merely accepts it as an expression of the client's personality and attempts to work with it constructively.

The third hallmark of an effective counseling relationship is *honesty of communication*. The therapist constantly tries to clarify the interaction between himself and his client, and to enlarge his conception of the client's behavior. What is the client really trying to say? How can the client be encouraged to think more clearly about himself? How can the therapist communicate back to the client a clarified understanding of what has been expressed, both intellectually and in terms of feelings? The therapist has to think and feel with the client. At times, the efforts to communicate honestly involve calling painful issues to the client's attention, such as his tendency to feel sorry for himself, his resentment bordering on hatred for his mother, or his competitive tendencies that are destructive of good relations with others. But much of a therapist's skill lies in his ability to combine this kind of honesty and directness with a sensitive understanding of the client's feelings. The therapist may point out personality problems, but he does not condemn them.

Unlike other relationships of comparable intimacy and intensity, the psychotherapeutic one is sharply limited by its utilitarian purpose (5). The goal of counseling is the improvement of the client's adjustment to a point where the therapist is no longer needed. Consequently, although he accepts the client as a person in difficulty, and is warmly and genuinely interested in him, the clinician gives of himself only insofar as it will help, not please, the client. He limits the relationship to the clinic or consulting room, and generally refrains from any intervention in the client's extraclinical life. The therapist certainly does not become involved with him in informal, extraprofessional ways. The relationship is designed so that it has a termination point, even though the termination point may be indefinite. The relationship is to last only so long as the client needs the therapist's help. Finally, the therapist establishes the relationship in an essentially one-sided fashion. The clinician does not share his own troubles or pleasures with his clients, nor does he usually permit his own personal values or affairs to intrude into the interviews.

The result of these limitations is a considerable amount of anonymity on the part of the therapist. The client knows the clinician primarily in his professional role only, and that role is maintained with a high degree of consistency and integrity. Thus, while the therapeutic relationship develops into one of trust, confidence, and warmth, the distinctive personality of the clinician is decidedly minimized.

THE CONTENT OF THERAPEUTIC INTERVIEWS

The content of psychotherapeutic interviews tends to cut across the lines of the "schools," as do the qualities of interpretation and relationship. Counseling is mainly a series of conversations. Whether the therapy is psychoanalytic, client-centered, or eclectic in orientation, the conversational content is typically concerned with the client's values, motives, and emotions, and with the situations to which he feels they are relevant. These situations may be either current or recollected from his history.

One situation of considerable importance is the counseling process and the counseling relationship. Indeed, there is much more focus in psychotherapy on the changing qualities of the client-clinician relationship than in any interpersonal situation outside the clinic walls.

The topics of psychotherapy are often not easy to discuss but the most difficult conversational items are often the most helpful. In one study, for example, forty-three clients judged the therapeutic value of fifteen topics which had been considered in the course of counseling (6). The clients agreed well among themselves as to the relative value of the topics, and their ratings showed a high correlation between a topic's "helpfulness" and its "disturbing" qualities. Thus, the topic called "shame and guilt" was judged as extremely upsetting, but the discussion of it in the course of counseling was regarded as highly helpful. When a group of psychologists rated the topics for their "intimacy," their personal significance for clients, the ratings showed a high positive relationship with clients' judgments of helpfulness.

It is not surprising, then, that therapeutic conversations are centered on the client's anxiety, guilt feelings, and feelings of inferiority or inadequacy, and on the occurrences that engender them. Obviously, such topics are precisely the ones that are most difficult for the patient to talk about. One of the hindrances to successful counseling is that it depends on discussing the very things that the client is least inclined to discuss and which are most susceptible to repression. For this reason, psychotherapy is a time-consuming process and often holds many painful moments for the client.

Psychotherapy thus appears to be an interpersonal relationship of great warmth and genuine interest within which the concerns most disturbing to the client are discussed. How does this therapeutic process function: How does the client learn new ways of adjusting to his needs and to his world?

REFERENCES

1. Collier, R. M. A basis for integration rather than fragmentation in psychotherapy. *J. consult. Psychol.*, 1950, *14*, 199-205.

2. Strupp, H. H. An objective comparison of Rogerian and psychoanalytic techniques. *J. consult. Psychol.*, 1955, *19*, 1-7.

3. Fiedler, F. E. A comparison of therapeutic relationships in psychoanalytic, nondirective, and Adlerian therapy. *J. consult. Psychol.*, 1950, *14*, 436-445. Also see Fiedler, F. E. The concept of an ideal therapeutic relationship. *J. consult. Psychol.*, 1950, *14*, 239-245.

4. Shoben, E. J., Jr. A theoretical approach to psychotherapy as personality modification. *Harvard educ. Rev.*, 1953, *23*, 128-142.

5. Weinberg, S. K. *Society and personality disorders.* Englewood Cliffs, N. J.: Prentice-Hall, 1952.

6. Talland, G. A., and Clark, D. H. Evaluation of topics in therapy group discussion. *J. clin. Psychol.*, 1954, *10*, 131-137.

7. Shoben, E. J., Jr. Psychotherapy as a problem in learning theory. *Psychol. Bull.*, 1949, *46*, 366-392.

Communication between Closed Doors

Shaffer and Shoben were among the earliest to point up the commonalities of the various counseling and therapeutic approaches. Their starting point is clear: "Psychological difficulties arise primarily from handicapping interpersonal relations." The personal aspect of the relationship which is for Shaffer and Shoben "an integral part of the client's therapeutic experience" is *calculated* to enable the client to explore his feelings, "increase his understanding and eventually help him discover new and more effective ways of living." We use "calculated" advisedly, for while Shaffer and Shoben are helpful in distinguishing many of the common aspects of psychotherapy, their elaborations of these dimensions disturb us.

For example, they write of "honesty of communication," yet illustrate a one-sided relationship in which the therapist remains "calm" under all circumstances, as if his profound understanding of the client enables him to control his feelings or reactions to the client—as if the client were not another person in this encounter, or as if the therapist himself were not a responsive person. The warm concern and nonretaliatory permissiveness they discuss appear to be implemented from an acknowledged repertoire of responses and seem to leave no room for responding directly to the client. There is no recognition that unconditionality must be a technique in any phase beyond the initial instances of all significant human encounters, in which sensitive people suspend their judgments, their values, and their feelings, in order to comprehend more fully the impact of their potential self-disclosure. The therapist who is unconditional after 20 hours of therapy must be very conditional indeed.

In sum, the therapist's offerings appear independent of the client, and there is no place for a human encounter. The therapist keeps saying: "Whatever you do, I will not allow my feelings to show." Contrast this with the therapist, teacher, or any person who is shaped in large part by what is effective for those with whom he is interacting as well as for himself, and who remains genuine in a relationship that acknowledges some varying degree of reciprocity without denying the power implicit in his role.

We are constantly struck by the emphasis upon one source of learning in counseling, such as the experiential or didactic, to the exclusion of others, as the model for effective and facilitative living which the therapist must implicitly become for the client. We read that the therapist cannot disclose himself or "permit his own personal values or affairs to intrude into the interviews." Yet *he cannot avoid these things; he has no alternatives.* He and his activities are living examples of culturally determined values, the first exercise of which is the decision to see the client because the therapist feels that he can help the client to live more effectively. Implicitly by the very act of counseling, the therapist becomes for the client a representative of a way of living facilitatively. It follows that the degree to which the therapist is genuinely facilitative, and not simply exercising and implementing a role model and its techniques within the encounter, will determine in large part the degree to which the client can achieve a similar level of effective living.

In the next reading, Rogers (1957) draws upon his years of clinical experience in dealing with similar-appearing constructs in his heroic effort to discern "the necessary and sufficient conditions of therapeutic personality change."

THE CONDITIONS OF CHANGE FROM A CLIENT-CENTERED VIEWPOINT *

Carl R. Rogers

For many years I have been engaged in psychotherapy with individuals in distress. In recent years I have found myself increasingly concerned with the process of abstracting from that experience the general principles which appear to be involved in it. I have endeavored to discover any orderliness, any unity which seems to inhere in the subtle, complex tissue of interpersonal relationship in which I have so constantly been immersed in therapeutic work. One of the products of this concern is an attempt to state, in formal terms, a theory of psychotherapy, of personality, and of interpersonal relationships which will encompass and

* The necessary and sufficient conditions of therapeutic personality change. *Journal of Consulting Psychology*, 1957, *21*, 95-103. Reprinted by permission of author and publisher.

contain the phenomena of my experience.[1] What I wish to do in this paper is to take one very small segment of that theory, spell it out more completely, and explore its meaning and usefulness.

THE PROBLEM

The question to which I wish to address myself is this: Is it possible to state, in terms which are clearly definable and measurable, the psychological conditions which are both necessary and sufficient to bring about constructive personality change? Do we, in other words, know with any precision those elements which are essential if psychotherapeutic change is to ensue?

Before proceeding to the major task let me dispose very briefly of the second portion of the question. What is meant by such phrases as "psychotherapeutic change," "constructive personality change"? This problem also deserves deep and serious consideration, but for the moment let me suggest a common-sense type of meaning upon which we can perhaps agree for purposes of this paper. By these phrases is meant: change in the personality structure of the individual, at both surface and deeper levels, in a direction which clinicians would agree means greater integration, less internal conflict, more energy utilizable for effective living; change in behavior away from behaviors generally regarded as immature and toward behaviors regarded as mature. This brief description may suffice to indicate the kind of change for which we are considering the preconditions. It may also suggest the ways in which this criterion of change may be determined.[2]

THE CONDITIONS

As I have considered my own clinical experience and that of my colleagues, together with the pertinent research which is available, I have drawn out several conditions which seem to me to be *necessary* to initiate constructive personality change, and which, taken together, appear to be *sufficient* to inaugurate that process. As I have worked on this problem I have found myself surprised at the simplictiy of what has emerged. The statement which follows is not offered with any assurance as to its correctness, but with the expectation that it will have the value of any theory, namely that it states or implies a series of hypotheses which are open to proof or disproof, thereby clarifying and extending our knowledge of the field.

---

[1] This formal statement is entitled A theory of therapy, personality, and interpersonal relationships, as developed in the client-centered framework. In S. Koch (Ed.), *Psychology: A study of a science,* Vol. III. New York: McGraw-Hill, 1959, pp. 184-256.

[2] That this is a measurable and determinable criterion has been shown in research already completed. See (7), especially Chapters 8, 13, and 17.

Since I am not, in this paper, trying to achieve suspense, I will state at once, in severely rigorous and summarized terms, the six conditions which I have come to feel are basic to the process of personality change. The meaning of a number of the terms is not immediately evident, but will be clarified in the explanatory sections which follow. It is hoped that this brief statement will have much more significance to the reader when he has completed the paper. Without further introduction let me state the basic theoretical position.

For constructive personality change to occur, it is necessary that these conditions exist and continue over a period of time:

1. Two persons are in psychological contact.
2. The first, whom we shall term the client, is in a state of incongruence, being vulnerable or anxious.
3. The second person, whom we shall term the therapist, is congruent or integrated in the relationship.
4. The therapist experiences unconditional positive regard for the client.
5. The therapist experiences an empathic understanding of the client's internal frame of reference and endeavors to communicate this experience to the client.
6. The communication to the client of the therapist's empathic understanding and unconditional positive regard is to a minimal degree achieved.

No other conditions are necessary. If these six conditions exist, and continue over a period of time, this is sufficient. The process of constructive personality change will follow.

A Relationship

The first condition specifies that a minimal relationship, a psychological contact, must exist. I am hypothesizing that significant positive personality change does not occur except in a relationship. This is of course an hypothesis, and it may be disproved.

Conditions 2 through 6 define the characteristics of the relationship which are regarded as essential by defining the necessary characteristics of each person in the relationship. All that is intended by this first condition is to specify that the two people are to some degree in contact, that each makes some perceived difference in the experiential field of the other. Probably it is sufficient if each makes some "subceived" difference, even though the individual may not be consciously aware of this impact. Thus it might be difficult to know whether a catatonic patient perceives a therapist's presence as making a difference to him—a difference of any kind—but it is almost certain that at some organic level he does sense this difference.

Except in such a difficult borderline situation as that just mentioned, it would be relatively easy to define this condition in operational terms and thus determine, from a hard-boiled research point of view, whether the condition does, or does not, exist. The simplest method of determination involves simply the awareness of both client and therapist. If each is aware of being in personal or psychological contact with the other, then this condition is met.

This first condition of therapeutic change is such a simple one that perhaps it should be labeled an assumption or a precondition in order to set it apart from those that follow. Without it, however, the remaining items would have no meaning, and that is the reason for including it.

The State of the Client

It was specified that it is necessary that the client be "in a state of incongruence, being vulnerable or anxious." What is the meaning of these terms?

Incongruence is a basic construct in the theory we have been developing. It refers to a discrepancy between the actual experience of the organism and the self picture of the individual insofar as it represents that experience. Thus a student may experience, at a total or organismic level, a fear of the university and of examinations which are given on the third floor of a certain building, since these may demonstrate a fundamental inadequacy in him. Since such a fear of his inadequacy is decidedly at odds with his concept of himself, this experience is represented (distortedly) in his awareness as an unreasonable fear of climbing stairs in this building, or any building, and soon an unreasonable fear of crossing the open campus. Thus there is a fundamental discrepancy between the experienced meaning of the situation as it registers in his organism and the symbolic representation of that experience in awareness in such a way that it does not conflict with the picture he has of himself. In this case to admit a fear of inadequacy would contradict the picture he holds of himself; to admit incomprehensible fears does not contradict his self-contempt.

Another instance would be the mother who develops vague illnesses whenever her only son makes plans to leave home. The actual desire is to hold on to her only source of satisfaction. To perceive this in awareness would be inconsistent with the picture she holds of herself as a good mother. Illness, however, is consistent with her self concept, and the experience is symbolized in this distorted fashion. Thus again there is a basic incongruence between the self as perceived (in this case as an ill mother needing attention) and the actual experience (in this case the desire to hold on to her son).

When the individual has no awareness of such incongruence in himself, then he is merely vulnerable to the possibility of anxiety and disorganization. Some experience might occur so suddenly or so obviously that the incongruence could not be denied. Therefore, the person is vulnerable to such a possibility.

If the individual dimly perceives such an incongruence in himself, then a tension state occurs which is known as anxiety. The incongruence need not be sharply perceived. It is enough that it is subceived—that is, discriminated as threatening to the self without any awareness of the content of that threat. Such anxiety is often seen in therapy as the individual approaches awareness of some element of his experience which is in sharp contradiction to his self concept.

It is not easy to give precise operational definition to this second of the six conditions, yet to some degree this has been achieved. Several research workers have defined the self concept by means of a Q sort by the individual of a list of self-referent items. This gives us an operational picture of the self. The total experiencing of the individual is more difficult to capture. Chodorkoff (2) has defined it as a Q sort made by a clinician who sorts the same self-referent items independently, basing his sorting on the picture he has obtained of the individual from projective tests. His sort thus includes unconscious as well as conscious elements of the individual's experience, thus representing (in an admittedly imperfect way) the totality of the client's experience. The correlation between these two sortings gives a crude operational measure of incongruence between self and experience, low or negative correlation representing of course a high degree of incongruence.

The Therapist's Genuineness in the Relationship

The third condition is that the therapist should be, within the confines of this relationship, a congruent, genuine, integrated person. It means that within the relationship he is freely and deeply himself, with his actual experience accurately represented by his awareness of himself. It is the opposite of presenting a façade, either knowingly or unknowingly.

It is not necessary (nor is it possible) that the therapist be a paragon who exhibits this degree of integration, of wholeness, in every aspect of his life. It is sufficient that he is accurately himself in this hour of this relationship, that in this basic sense he is what he actually is, in this moment of time.

It should be clear that this includes being himself even in ways which are not regarded as ideal for psychotherapy. His experience may be "I am afraid of this client" or "My attention is so focused on my own problems that I can scarcely listen to him." If the therapist is not denying these feelings to awareness, but is able freely to be them (as well as being his other feelings), then the condition we have stated is met.

It would take us too far afield to consider the puzzling matter as to the degree to which the therapist overtly communicates this reality in himself to the client. Certainly the aim is not for the therapist to express or talk out his own feelings, but primarily that he should not be deceiving the client as to himself. At times he may need to talk out some of his own feelings (either to the client, or to a colleague or supervisor) if they are standing in the way of the two following conditions.

It is not too difficult to suggest an operational definition for this third condition. We resort again to Q technique. If the therapist sorts a series of items relevant to the relationship (using a list similar to the ones developed by Fiedler [3, 4] and Bown [1]), this will give his perception of his experience in the relationship. If several judges who have observed the interview or listened to a recording of it (or observed a sound movie of it) now sort the same items to represent *their* perception of the relationship, this second sorting should catch those elements of the therapist's behavior and inferred attitudes of which he is unaware, as well as those of which he is aware. Thus a high correlation between the therapist's sort and the observer's sort would represent in crude form an operational definition of the therapist's congruence or integration in the relationship; and a low correlation, the opposite.

Unconditional Positive Regard

To the extent that the therapist finds himself experiencing a warm acceptance of each aspect of the client's experience as being a part of that client, he is experiencing unconditional positive regard. This concept has been developed by Standal (8). It means that there are no *conditions* of acceptance, no feeling of "I like you only *if* you are thus and so." It means a "prizing" of the person, as Dewey has used that term. It is at the opposite pole from a selective evaluating attitude—"You are bad in these ways, good in those." It involves as much feeling of acceptance for the client's expression of negative, "bad," painful, fearful, defensive, abnormal feelings as for his expression of "good," positive, mature, confident, social feelings, as much acceptance of ways in which he is inconsistent as of ways in which he is consistent. It means a caring for the client, but not in a possessive way or in such a way as simply to satisfy the therapist's own needs. It means a caring for the client as a *separate* person, with permission to have his own feelings, his own experiences. One client describes the therapist as "fostering my possession of my own experience . . . that [this] is *my* experience and that I am actually having it: thinking what I think, feeling what I feel, wanting what I want, fearing what I fear: no 'ifs,' 'buts,' or 'not reallys.' " This is the type of acceptance which is hypothesized as being necessary if personality change is to occur.

Like the two previous conditions, this fourth condition is a matter of degree,[3] as immediately becomes apparent if we attempt to define it in terms of specific research operations. One such method of giving it definition would be to consider the Q sort for the relationship as described under Condition 3. To the extent that items expressive of unconditional positive regard are sorted as characteristic of the relationship by both the therapist and the observers, unconditional positive regard might be said to exist. Such items might include statements of this order: "I feel no revulsion at anything the client says"; "I feel neither approval nor disapproval of the client and his statements—simply acceptance"; "I feel warmly toward the client—toward his weaknesses and problems as well as his potentialities"; "I am not inclined to pass judgment on what the client tells me"; "I like the client." To the extent that both therapist and observers perceive these items as characteristic, or their opposites as uncharacteristic, Condition 4 might be said to be met.

Empathy

The fifth condition is that the therapist is experiencing an accurate, empathic understanding of the client's awareness of his own experience. To sense the client's private world as if it were your own, but without ever losing the "as if" quality—this is empathy, and this seems essential to therapy. To sense the client's anger, fear, or confusion as if it were your own, yet without your own anger, fear, or confusion getting bound up in it, is the condition we are endeavoring to describe. When the client's world is this clear to the therapist, and he moves about in it freely, then he can both communicate his understanding of what is clearly known to the client and can also voice meanings in the client's experience of which the client is scarcely aware. As one client described this second aspect: "Every now and again, with me in a tangle of thought and feeling, screwed up in a web of mutually divergent lines of movement, with impulses from different parts of me, and me feeling the feeling of its

---

[3] The phrase "unconditional positive regard" may be an unfortunate one, since it sounds like an absolute, an all or nothing dispositional concept. It is probably evident from the description that completely unconditional positive regard would never exist except in theory. From a clinical and experiential point of view I believe the most accurate statement is that the effective therapist experiences unconditional positive regard for the client during many moments of his contact with him, yet from time to time he experiences only a conditional positive regard—and perhaps at times a negative regard, though this is not likely in effective therapy. It is in this sense that unconditional positive regard exists as a matter of degree in any relationship.

being all too much and suchlike—then whomp, just like a sunbeam thrusting its way through cloudbanks and tangles of foliage to spread a circle of light on a tangle of forest paths, came some comment from you. [It was] clarity, even disentanglement, an additional twist to the picture, a putting in place. Then the consequence—the sense of moving on, the relaxation. These were sunbeams." That such penetrating empathy is important for therapy is indicated by Fiedler's research (3) in which items such as the following placed high in the description of relationships created by experienced therapists:

> The therapist is well able to understand the patient's feelings.
> The therapist is never in any doubt about what the patient means.
> The therapist's remarks fit in just right with the patient's mood and content.
> The therapist's tone of voice conveys the complete ability to share the patient's feelings.

An operational definition of the therapist's empathy could be provided in different ways. Use might be made of the Q sort described under Condition 3. To the degree that items descriptive of accurate empathy were sorted as characteristic by both the therapist and the observers, this condition would be regarded as existing.

Another way of defining this condition would be for both client and therapist to sort a list of items descriptive of client feelings. Each would sort independently, the task being to represent the feelings which the client had experienced during a just completed interview. If the correlation between client and therapist sortings were high, accurate empathy would be said to exist, a low correlation indicating the opposite conclusion.

Still another way of measuring empathy would be for trained judges to rate the depth and accuracy of the therapist's empathy on the basis of listening to recorded interviews.

The Client's Perception of the Therapist

The final condition as stated is that the client perceives, to a minimal degree, the acceptance and empathy which the therapist experiences for him. Unless some communication of these attitudes has been achieved, then such attitudes do not exist in the relationship as far as the client is concerned, and the therapeutic process could not, by our hypothesis, be initiated.

Since attitudes cannot be directly perceived, it might be somewhat more accurate to state that therapist behaviors and words are perceived by the client as meaning that to some degree the therapist accepts and understands him.

An operational definition of this condition would not be difficult. The client might, after an interview, sort a Q-sort list of items referring to qualities representing the relationship between himself and the therapist. (The same list could be used as for Condition 3.) If several items descriptive of acceptance and empathy are sorted by the client as characteristic of the relationship, then this condition could be regarded as met. In the present state of our knowledge the meaning of "to a minimal degree" would have to be arbitrary.

Some Comments

Up to this point the effort has been made to present, briefly and factually, the conditions which I have come to regard as essential for psychotherapeutic change. I have not tried to give the theoretical context of these conditions nor to explain what seem to me to be the dynamics of their effectiveness. Such explanatory material is available, to the reader who is interested, in the document already mentioned (see footnote 1).

I have, however, given at least one means of defining, in operational terms, each of the conditions mentioned. I have done this in order to stress the fact that I am not speaking of vague qualities which ideally should be present if some other vague result is to occur. I am presenting conditions which are crudely measurable even in the present state of our technology, and have suggested specific operations in each instance even though I am sure that more adequate methods of measurement could be devised by a serious investigator.

My purpose has been to stress the notion that in my opinion we are dealing with an if-then phenomenon in which knowledge of the dynamics is not essential to testing the hypotheses. Thus, to illustrate from another field: if one substance, shown by a series of operations to be the substance known as hydrochloric acid, is mixed with another substance, shown by another series of operations to be sodium hydroxide, then salt and water will be products of this mixture. This is true whether one regards the results as due to magic, or whether one explains it in the most adequate terms of modern chemical theory. In the same way it is being postulated here that certain definable conditions precede certain definable changes and that this fact exists independently of our efforts to account for it.

THE RESULTING HYPOTHESES

The major value of stating any theory in unequivocal terms is that specific hypotheses may be drawn from it which are capable of proof or disproof. Thus, even if the conditions which have been postulated as necessary and sufficient conditions are more incorrect than correct (which

I hope they are not), they could still advance science in this field by providing a base of operations from which fact could be winnowed out from error.

The hypotheses which would follow from the theory given would be of this order:

If these six conditions (as operationally defined) exist, then constructive personality change (as defined) will occur in the client.

If one or more of these conditions is not present, constructive personality change will not occur.

These hypotheses hold in any situation whether it is or is not labeled "psychotherapy."

Only Condition 1 is dichotomous (it either is present or is not), and the remaining five occur in varying degree, each on its continuum. Since this is true, another hypothesis follows, and it is likely that this would be the simplest to test:

If all six conditions are present, then the greater the degree to which Conditions 2 to 6 exist, the more marked will be the constructive personality change in the client.

At the present time the above hypothesis can only be stated in this general form—which implies that all of the conditions have equal weight. Empirical studies will no doubt make possible much more refinement of this hypothesis. It may be, for example, that if anxiety is high in the client, then the other conditions are less important. Or if unconditional positive regard is high (as in a mother's love for her child), then perhaps a modest degree of empathy is sufficient. But at the moment we can only speculate on such possibilities.

SOME IMPLICATIONS

Significant Omissions

If there is any startling feature in the formulation which has been given as to the necessary conditions for therapy, it probably lies in the elements that are omitted. In present-day clinical practice, therapists operate as though there were many other conditions in addition to those described, which are essential for psychotherapy. To point this up it may be well to mention a few of the conditions which, after thoughtful consideration of our research and our experience, are not included.

For example, it is *not* stated that these conditions apply to one type of client, and that other conditions are necessary to bring about psychotherapeutic change with other types of client. Probably no idea is so prevalent in clinical work today as that one works with neurotics in one way, with psychotics in another; that certain therapeutic conditions must be provided for compulsives, others for homosexuals, etc. Because of this heavy weight of clinical opinion to the contrary, it is with some "fear and trembling" that I advance the concept that the essential conditions of psychotherapy exist in a single configuration, even though the client or patient may use them very differently.[4]

It is *not* stated that these six conditions are the essential conditions for client-centered therapy, and that other conditions are essential for other types of psychotherapy. I certainly am heavily influenced by my own experience, and that experience has led me to a viewpoint which is termed "client-centered." Nevertheless my aim in stating this theory is to state the conditions which apply to *any* situation in which constructive personality change occurs, whether we are thinking of classical psychoanalysis, or any of its modern offshoots, or Adlerian psychotherapy, or any other. It will be obvious then that in my judgment much of what is considered to be essential would not be found, empirically, to be essential. Testing of some of the stated hypotheses would throw light on this perplexing issue. We may of course find that various therapies produce various types of personality change, and that for each psychotherapy a separate set of conditions is necessary. Until and unless this is demonstrated, I am hypothesizing that effective psychotherapy of any sort produces similar changes in personality and behavior, and that a single set of preconditions is necessary.

It is *not* stated that psychotherapy is a special kind of relationship, different in kind from all others which occur in everyday life. It will be evident instead that for brief moments, at least, many good friendships fulfill the six conditions. Usually this is only momentarily, however, and then empathy falters, the positive regard becomes conditional, or the congruence of the "therapist" friend becomes overlaid by some degree of façade or defensiveness. Thus the therapeutic relationship is seen as a heightening of the constructive qualities which often exist in part in other relationships, and an extension through time of qualities which in other relationships tend at best to be momentary.

It is *not* stated that special intellectual professional knowledge— psychological, psychiatric, medical, or religious—is required of the ther-

---

[4] I cling to this statement of my hypothesis even though it is challenged by a study by Kirtner (5). Kirtner has found, in a group of 26 cases from the Counseling Center at the University of Chicago, that there are sharp differences in the client's mode of approach to the resolution of life difficulties, and that these differences are related to success in psychotherapy. Briefly, the client who sees his problem as involving his relationships, and who feels that he contributes to this problem and wants to change it, is likely to be successful. The client who externalizes his problem, feeling little self-responsibility, is much more likely to be a failure. Thus the implication is that some other conditions need to be provided for psychotherapy with this group. For the present, however, I will stand by my hypothesis as given, until Kirtner's study is confirmed, and until we know an alternative hypothesis to take its place.

apist. Conditions 3, 4, and 5, which apply especially to the therapist, are qualities of experience, not intellectual information. If they are to be acquired, they must, in my opinion, be acquired through an experiential training—which may be, but usually is not, a part of professional training. It troubles me to hold such a radical point of view, but I can draw no other conclusion from my experience. Intellectual training and the acquiring of information has, I believe, many valuable results—but becoming a therapist is not one of those results.

It is *not* stated that it is necessary for psychotherapy that the therapist have an accurate psychological diagnosis of the client. Here too it troubles me to hold a viewpoint so at variance with my clinical colleagues. When one thinks of the vast proportion of time spent in any psychological, psychiatric, or mental hygiene center on the exhaustive psychological evaluation of the client or patient, it seems as though this *must* serve a useful purpose insofar as psychotherapy is concerned. Yet the more I have observed therapists, and the more closely I have studied research such as that done by Fiedler and others (4), the more I am forced to the conclusion that such diagnostic knowledge is not essential to psychotherapy.[5] It may even be that its defense as a necessary prelude to psychotherapy is simply a protective alternative to the admission that it is, for the most part, a colossal waste of time. There is only one useful purpose I have been able to observe which relates to psychotherapy. Some therapists cannot feel secure in the relationship with the client unless they possess such diagnostic knowledge. Without it they feel fearful of him, unable to be empathic, unable to experience unconditional regard, finding it necessary to put up a pretense in the relationship. If they know in *advance* of suicidal impulses they can somehow be more acceptant of them. Thus, for some therapists, the security they perceive in diagnostic information may be a basis for permitting themselves to be integrated in the relationship, and to experience empathy and full acceptance. In these instances a psychological diagnosis would certainly be justified as adding to the comfort and hence the effectiveness of the therapist. But even here it does not appear to be a basic precondition for psychotherapy.[6]

Perhaps I have given enough illustrations to indicate that the conditions I have hypothesized as necessary and sufficient for psychotherapy are striking and unusual primarily by virtue of what they omit. If we

---

[5] There is no intent here to maintain that diagnostic evaluation is useless. We have ourselves made heavy use of such methods in our research studies of change in personality. It is its usefulness as a precondition to psychotherapy which is questioned.

[6] In a facetious moment I have suggested that such therapists might be made equally comfortable by being given the diagnosis of some other individual, not of this patient or client. The fact that the diagnosis proved inaccurate as psychotherapy continued would not be particularly disturbing, because one always expects to find inaccuracies in the diagnosis as one works with the individual.

were to determine, by a survey of the behaviors of therapists, those hypotheses which they appear to regard as necessary to psychotherapy, the list would be a great deal longer and more complex.

Is This Theoretical Formulation Useful?

Aside from the personal satisfaction it gives as a venture in abstraction and generalization, what is the value of a theoretical statement such as has been offered in this paper? I should like to spell out more fully the usefulness which I believe it may have.

In the field of research it may give both direction and impetus to investigation. Since it sees the conditions of constructive personality change as general, it greatly broadens the opportunities for study. Psychotherapy is not the only situation aimed at constructive personality change. Programs of training for leadership in industry and programs of training for military leadership often aim at such change. Educational institutions or programs frequently aim at development of character and personality as well as at intellectual skills. Community agencies aim at personality and behavioral change in delinquents and criminals. Such programs would provide an opportunity for the broad testing of the hypotheses offered. If it is found that constructive personality change occurs in such programs when the hypothesized conditions are not fulfilled, then the theory would have to be revised. If however the hypotheses are upheld, then the results, both for the planning of such programs and for our knowledge of human dynamics, would be significant. In the field of psychotherapy itself, the application of consistent hypotheses to the work of various schools of therapists may prove highly profitable. Again the disproof of the hypotheses offered would be as important as their confirmation, either result adding significantly to our knowledge.

For the practice of psychotherapy the theory also offers significant problems for consideration. One of its implications is that the techniques of the various therapies are relatively unimportant except to the extent that they serve as channels for fulfilling one of the conditions. In client-centered therapy, for example, the technique of "reflecting feelings" has been described and commented on (6, pp. 26-36). In terms of the theory here being presented, this technique is by no means an essential condition of therapy. To the extent, however, that it provides a channel by which the therapist communicates a sensitive empathy and an unconditional positive regard, then it may serve as a technical channel by which the essential conditions of therapy are fulfilled. In the same way, the theory I have presented would see no essential value to therapy of such techniques as interpretation of personality dynamics, free association, analysis of dreams, analysis of the transference, hypnosis, interpretation of life style, suggestion, and the like. Each of these techniques may, however, become a channel for communicating the essential conditions which have been formulated. An interpretation may be given in a way which communicates the unconditional positive regard of the therapist. A stream of free association may be listened to in a way which communicates an empathy which the therapist is experiencing. In the handling of the transference an effective therapist often communicates his own wholeness and congruence in the relationship. Similarly for the other techniques. But just as these techniques *may* communicate the elements which are essential for therapy, so any one of them may communicate attitudes and experiences sharply contradictory to the hypothesized conditions of therapy. Feeling may be "reflected" in a way which communicates the therapist's lack of empathy. Interpretations may be rendered in a way which indicates the highly conditional regard of the therapist. Any of the techniques may communicate the fact that the therapist is expressing one attitude at a surface level, and another contradictory attitude which is denied to his own awareness. Thus one value of such a theoretical formulation as we have offered is that it may assist therapists to think more critically about those elements of their experience, attitudes, and behaviors which are essential to psychotherapy, and those which are nonessential or even deleterious to psychotherapy.

Finally, in those programs—educational, correctional, military, or industrial—which aim toward constructive changes in the personality structure and behavior of the individual, this formulation may serve as a very tentative criterion against which to measure the program. Until it is much further tested by research, it cannot be thought of as a valid criterion, but, as in the field of psychotherapy, it may help to stimulate critical analysis and the formulation of alternative conditions and alternative hypotheses.

SUMMARY

Drawing from a larger theoretical context, six conditions are postulated as necessary and sufficient conditions for the initiation of a process of constructive personality change. A brief explanation is given of each condition, and suggestions are made as to how each may be operationally defined for research purposes. The implications of this theory for research, for psychotherapy, and for educational and training programs aimed at constructive personality change, are indicated. It is pointed out that many of the conditions which are commonly regarded as necessary to psychotherapy are, in terms of this theory, nonessential.

REFERENCES

1. Bown, O. H. An investigation of therapeutic relationship in client-centered therapy. Unpublished doctor's dissertation, Univer. of Chicago, 1954.

2. Chodorkoff, B. Self-perception, perceptual defense, and adjustment. *J. abnorm. soc. Psychol.*, 1954, *49*, 508-512.

3. Fiedler, F. E. A comparison of therapeutic relationships in psychoanalytic, nondirective, and Adlerian therapy. *J. consult. Psychol.*, 1950, *14*, 436-445.

4. Fiedler, F. E. Quantitative studies on the role of therapists' feelings toward their patients. In O. H. Mowrer (Ed.), *Psychotherapy: Theory and research.* New York: Ronald, 1953.

5. Kirtner, W. L. Success and failure in client-centered therapy as a function of personality variables. Unpublished master's thesis, Univer. of Chicago, 1955.

6. Rogers, C. R. *Client-centered therapy*. Boston: Houghton Mifflin, 1951.

7. Rogers, C. R., and Dymond, Rosalind F. (Eds.). *Psychotherapy and personality change.* Chicago: Univer. of Chicago Press, 1954.

8. Standal, S. The need for positive regard: A contribution to client-centered theory. Unpublished doctor's dissertation, Univer. of Chicago, 1954.

Both Model and Agent

Rogers is boldly challenging in his statement of conditions and in his points on outcome, training, diagnosis, and technique. His is a most distinctive contribution, which, however, suffers from generalization. It is unlikely, for example, at our present developmental level that any one series of conditions is "necessary" and "sufficient." Furthermore, if the conditions are viewed as primary or general factors, it is likely that the weights of these factors will vary with therapist, client, and environmental variables, alone and in their various interactions. In addition, secondary factors in a given interaction of relevant variables may operate to facilitate or retard the effects of the principal conditions, as well as to contribute to effective processes (Carkhuff, 1963).

Rogers' model indicates a congruent therapist who involves the client in a process of therapeutic self-exploration and immediacy of experiencing, so that the client may become more congruent. We feel that a logical extension of this model is a similar therapeutic movement for the therapist; that is, in the past as well as in the present, he has been able to explore and come to some deep and comprehensive understanding of himself. There is a cycle of "agentry." Someone provided the conditions that facilitated the therapist's growth to congruence and the therapist, in turn, provides the conditions for the client's growth to congruence. In a very real sense, *the therapist is both model and agent for facilitation.*

Let us examine this more closely. The therapist makes a decision to see the client. Why does he make this decision? Because he believes that he can help the client to move, as Rogers writes, "away from behaviors generally regarded as immature and toward behaviors regarded as mature." Why does he believe he can help? Because he believes that he himself lives more effectively—more maturely. Among many other things, he lives with understanding and respect for himself and others. He is genuine with himself and others and honest in his communications. Implicitly, *these are the conditions of facilitative living, as well as the goals of counseling.* They are structural goals and not necessarily content-bound. The therapist teaches a structural approach to an effective way of living. When the client has developed a sufficient or minimal amount of these dimensions, he is terminated.

The reader can perceive that we have drawn the therapist out of counseling and put him back in "real life." That is, the effective counselor is not simply genuine "within the confines of the therapeutic relationship," but he is genuine in his living; if not, he has nothing to sell. Hopefully his empathy will not "falter," his positive regard become "conditional," and his congruence become "overlaid by some degree of façade of genuineness."

Rogers believes that friends are unable to provide sustaining levels of the necessary and sufficient conditions of personality change. However, a vast number of persons function in life without ever seeing a therapist; vast numbers of patients get well without treatment. With full awareness that the reciprocal relationships of friends are not predicated upon the change of either of the parties, we still ask: Can different forms or levels of friendship effect change at crisis points?

In the following article, Harper (1959) is extremely helpful in pulling together some of the common effects in clients of good counseling and therapy. In addition, he is candid in his comments on the sufficiency of the conditions prescribed by Rogers.

SOME COMMON EFFECTS
OF DIVERSE APPROACHES *

Robert A. Harper

. . . Our difficult task is to try to ascertain, in as clear and objective a manner as possible, what the various systems of psychotherapy each have to offer.

* Critique and overview. In *Psychoanalysis and psychotherapy*, by Robert A. Harper. © 1959. Reprinted by permission of Prentice-Hall, Inc., Englewood Cliffs, N. J.

Let us make a broad division of the various schools into two main categories: A. the emotionally oriented, or affective, therapies and B. the intellectually oriented, or cognitive, therapies. Group A constitutes the great bulk of psychotherapeutic systems: all types of psychoanalysis, with the exception of Adler's individual psychology (which is discussed as a form of psychoanalysis more for historical than content purposes), client-centered therapy, Gestalt therapy, hypnotherapy, experiential therapy, conditioned reflex therapy, therapy by reciprocal inhibition and all of the group psychotherapies except didactic group therapy. At times the dynamic culturalists (especially Sullivan and Fromm) veer in the cognitive direction, but most of their therapeutic efforts, like those of the rest of Group A, are directed toward what may be called emotional reconditioning.

Group B may be considered therapeutic nonconformists. The psychobiologic therapists belong primarily in this group, even though they pay some token respect to certain psychoanalytic techniques and theories. Adlerians, who have frankly developed what they refer to as an educational type of therapy, may be considered cognitive therapists. The entire group in Chapter 8[1] are mainly oriented toward intellectual reconditioning. And that, with the addition of the already mentioned didactic group therapists, is the whole of Group B. None of the therapists in this group have an extensive following.

It would seem, therefore, that Group B is swimming against the therapeutic current, and so it is in some ways. Yet actually the affective vs. cognitive issue is not so simple as it at first appears. Not only have the dynamic culturalists brought increasing emphasis on ego instead of id in deviant psychoanalytic circles, but even the classical analytic group has in practice spent more and more of its time and attention in analysis of the ego defenses, rather than prolonged unwinding of the id impulses. This is a trend in the direction of greater attention to the cognitive, the executive, the less deeply unconscious (if not actually conscious) aspects of the personality.

The client-centered therapists are deep within the affective division of therapy. They speak almost exclusively of feelings, emotional experience, acceptance, emotional safety, love, positive regard, empathy, and similar topics of affect. The Rogersians are actually relying, in final analysis, on the ability of the patient to emerge from the warm, accepting atmosphere of therapy with more rational, logical, efficient, realistic ego structure. They feel that the cognitive aspects of the personality can function adequately once the emotional blocks are dissolved by the accepting therapeutic environment. Although the Rogersians conduct much rationally oriented research, the weight of the influence of their thera-

---

[1] *Editors' note.* Practitioners of "directive psychotherapy, general semantics, learning theory therapy, assertion-structured therapy, and rational therapy."

peutic system strikes this writer as being in the reactionary tradition of mysticism and art rather than in the direction of advancing rationality and science.

The experiential therapy of Whitaker and Malone, though startlingly "radical" in some of its techniques (such as the occasional use of aggression and therapeutic sleeping), is even more reactionary in its impact, for it advocates a return to the early psychoanalytic emphasis on the deep unconscious forces (the id impulses). These therapists direct their whole effort toward removing the rational, cognitive ego functions from the treatment situation and concentrating on primary processes of communication: fantasy relationships between therapist's id and patient's id. Such activities by their very nature tend to rule out the application of the rational tools of science. We must, however, acknowledge a further factor. It is quite apparent that much of the work undertaken by Whitaker and Malone is with very sick persons, for the most part psychotics. A rational, realistic approach is considerably less effective with a person who has renounced rationality and has escaped from reality than with a neurotic who is simply exhibiting various self-defeating patterns of reality. Understood in this sense, experiential therapy may be a necessary therapeutic departure from rationality for the purpose of meeting and helping the psychotic in his own world of unreality.

The Rogersians, on the other hand, are dealing primarily with mildly disturbed patients, and their rejection of a cognitive approach to their patients' needs to be understood in another frame of reference.

Client-centered therapy, it seems to me, is most clearly and objectively perceived as a historical correction. Rogers developed his emphasis on permissiveness as a reaction to a kind of totalitarianism which had developed in the field of psychotherapy in the late thirties. The Freudians in the twenties and early thirties were the unrecognized minority in the psychiatric fraternity. By the late thirties they had not only won their battle for legitimate recognition among psychiatrists and the general public, but were experiencing a wave of high prestige. Psychoanalysis was being much sought after as a kind of general cure-all for social, as well as personal, problems. As is true of many minorities who newly acquire power, arrogant and dictatorial attitudes were not uncommon among psychoanalytically trained psychiatrists. These attitudes are still to be encountered, but there is a growing realistic humility today regarding the limitations of both the techniques and theories of psychoanalysis among many analysts.

This atmosphere of totalitarianism in psychotherapy in the thirties was further strengthened by the attitudes of psychiatric social workers who came to function in ancillary roles to psychiatrists in clinics, hospitals, and private and public agencies. The service concept was so effectively drilled into most social workers of at least that generation that most of them functioned in devoted, unquestioning servitude (a servitude which was further enhanced by the fact that most psychiatrists were men and most social workers were women). The psychoanalyst's utterance was the not-to-be-disputed word of authority.

It required an intelligent, emotionally independent, male psychologist, free of any feeling of need to be beholden to the psychiatric group or the psychoanalytic sub-group, to lead a successful rebellion against the father figure of the psychoanalyst. The need for such a psychologist was filled by Carl Rogers, and the way he rebelled was naturally structured by his personal and professional predispositions. His method can be fairly compared to the route taken by Ghandi and his followers in achieving Indian independence of the British. Like Ghandi, Rogers brought about no head-on clash of bristling authority with bristling counter-authority. He quietly emulated Ghandi by nonviolently resisting the dictates of authority. He demonstrated in theory, in practice, and in research that people can be just as effectively helped without the complicated psychoanalytic superstructure of technique and mythology of theory. His nonviolent rebellion gathered momentum by being joined not only by many other psychologists, but by dissatisfied elements in other professions: ministers, educators, sociologists, social workers, and even a few psychiatrists. Part of the strength of the client-centered approach was drawn from its appeal to factors deep within the American culture.[2]

The psychotherapeutic revolutionary war would seem to have been won by the rebels. Psychologists and others than psychiatrists and psychoanalysts are increasingly practicing psychotherapy of their own individual choosing.

But some of the post-independence problems of psychotherapy seem resistive to solution by the methods of the revolution. Just as the Indians have found that passive nonresistance does not solve difficulties that they have had to face since the departure of the British, the realistic psychotherapist must admit that not all the therapeutic problems respond to emotional permissiveness in the clinical setting.

What Rogers has recently suggested as the necessary and sufficient conditions for psychotherapeutic personality change[3] may be what he has labeled them for some *slightly* disturbed patients. Such conditions may even be necessary and sufficient for some moderately to severely disturbed patients whose main problem has been a feeling of being unloved and unaccepted. But this writer shares the point of view of

---

[2] *Editors' note.* This subject is discussed early in Chapter 6 of Harper's book.

[3] *Editors' note.* This subject is discussed in the latter part of Chapter 6 of Harper's book.

other non-Rogersian clinicians that there are many quite disturbed patients for whom unconditional positive regard and empathic understanding, however well communicated, are insufficient to effect psychotherapeutic personality change. While awaiting the research for which Rogers calls to test these and other therapeutic hypotheses, many clinicians join Thorne[4] in emphasizing the need of many patients for therapeutic direction, diagnosis, and recovery plans based increasingly on the tools of rationality.

In a sense, the client-centered therapeutic atmosphere is the best possible recapture of the uterine environment for the patient. Although Rogers admits his partial dependence on Otto Rank, it is doubtful if he would approve our harking back to the heart of Rankian theory: emotional disturbance mainly traceable to the birth trauma. But the patient who experiences an approximation of unconditional positive regard for and empathic understanding of all his characteristics is getting the closest he will ever get in adult life to the completely satisfying, undemanding environment of prenatal life. To a considerable degree (but perhaps not always to what sounds like an overly seductive, Rogersian degree), acceptance and reassurance may be considered helpful *pre*-conditions to the serious, often cognitive, sometimes directive business which then needs to follow, as many non-Rogersian therapists would see it. This "further business" of therapy is the help needed by an individual who has seriously failed to adapt himself to life as an adult. A brief sojourn in the womblike atmosphere of Rogersian therapy may give such a person the recuperative strength he needs to face the job of learning how to handle the problems of the very unwomblike, nontherapeutic world of adult reality. But many such persons need direct guidance, specific education, in how to utilize their energies in effective, rational, realistic adaptation to interpersonal actualities. Thus it seems, at least, to a non-Rogersian.

What are the most valuable forms of direct guidance and specific education? Much would seem to depend upon specific diagnosis in each instance. But it must be admitted that the best of current psychological and psychiatric diagnostic methods, from Sullivanian analysis of early interpersonal acculturation through psychometric tests to Freudian dream interpretation via free association, are crude, largely unvalidated, and often unreliable tools. This brings us back to the undeniable realization that much more research is needed. But we cannot wait for the results of research in order to proceed to meet the psychotherapeutic needs of many members of our society. Meantime, a number of rational, though not yet scientifically established, guides can be explored by therapists who are willing to experiment with some unfamiliar approaches (a

---

[4] *Editors' note.* See Chapter 8 of Harper's book.

notable example of which is the rational reconditioning process suggested by Albert Ellis).

Such experimentation calls for less rigid adherence to any particular system of psychotherapy, and one wonders if the time has not arrived for greater emphasis on eclecticism, synthesis, flexibility in the use of differing therapeutic techniques. The dogmatic schools of psychotherapy were perhaps historically necessary for various desirable changes of public and professional climate (of which the Rogersian revolution was simply the most recent). It seems likely now, however, that further progress is more blocked than enhanced by clinging to psychotherapeutic "religions." There are two characteristics of rigid systemists: (1) their closed minds about points of view and outright facts which fail to fit their system and (2) their manifestation of what the psychoanalysts call "reaction formations." Let us illustrate these two assertions.

First, we have the current ruling class in psychotherapy: the Freudians. Although . . . humility is beginning to become a part of their personalities, there is still a persisting tendency among many in this group to believe they have the *only* valid answers to the nature of the human psyche and the treatment of psychic disorders. The more rigid and fanatic of the Freudians react roughly in the fashion of religious fundamentalists. Tell a fundamentalist that you think many Biblical stories are to be viewed as allegories and myths, and he has had enough of you. Tell a fundamentalist Freudian that you question the efficiency of free association, the universality of the Oedipus complex or the three stages of infantile sexuality, and his reaction is much the same. He does not care what brand of the devil you have assumed—dynamic culturalist, client-centered therapist, Adlerian, Jungian, or psychobiologist—he knows that your understanding of human behavior is *superficial* (the Freudian equivalent of Satanic) and that your resistance to Freudian doctrine is a manifestation of your own ego defenses against psychosexual truth. Such defensiveness, such repression of the point of view of the "enemy," would indicate in the Freudians, by their own analytical theories, feelings of insecurity. For the patient to admit hate, as well as love, for a parent, is an intolerable ego threat. For an orthodox Freudian to admit doubt in, as well as faith and acceptance of, classical psychoanalytic theory, may be a similarly intolerable ego threat. Such unswerving Freudian faith is suspiciously symptomatic of a reaction formation.

Closed minds and reaction formations are equally evident in fanatics of other persuasions. The psychoanalysis-hating Salter, the Freud-biting Horney, the Freud-repressing Sullivan, the Freud-rejecting Adler and Jung (and those who orthodoxly follow these and other therapeutic messiahs) show an unwillingness to listen objectively and to consider the possible merit of opposing positions. Because of their permissive exterior, such dogmatism is, though present, less evident, in the Rogersians. They are quite fearful of and incapable of dealing adequately with strong, opposing points of view and with authoritarian figures because of their anxiety about their own repressed tendencies toward dictatorial behavior. A Salter who violently overthrows *all* Freudian procedures and theories as utter nonsense must be, by the hypothesis of reaction formation, fighting down some pro-analytic tendencies inside himself that frighten him. The client-centered therapist who pushes down *all* therapist direction, *all* diagnosis, *all* functions of the therapist other than exudence of positive regard and empathy for the omnipotent client, must, by this same hypothesis, be repressing strong authoritarian impulses in himself that he fears and doubts that he can handle. In fairness, it should be pointed out that those therapists who emphatically reject everything the Rogersians have to offer are undoubtedly afraid of soft, accepting, love-giving tendencies in *their* repressed psyches.

While we await research findings (and for definitively helpful results, it is bound to be a long wait), it would appear that many therapists and their patients are likely to profit from a flexible repertoire of therapeutic techniques, rather than from a rigid adherence to a single system of psychotherapy. It is encouraging to observe a growing trend of eclecticism among therapists of many persuasions. (This trend is being fought, however, by some classical analysts, some Rogersians, and others.)

Phillips and Ellis are two cognitively oriented therapists whose writings to date in support of assertion-structured therapy and rational psychotherapy, respectively, give the appearance of anti-eclecticism. It is possible, however, that at least part of their denunciation of other systems is designed to attract greater attention to their own genuine contributions. Both have made significant eclectic contributions prior to the development of their own therapeutic systems, and there is every reason to believe they will do so in the future. Meantime, their systems of psychotherapy serve as an effective challenge to psychoanalysts, client-centered therapists, and others that concentrate largely on emotional reconditioning.

Wolpe brings, in some ways, an even stronger challenge to the theoretical superstructures and the elaborate techniques of many of the therapies in both groups A and B. While it seems likely at this point that his system is based on an oversimplification of human behavior, emotional disturbance, and the therapeutic process, new experimental testing of therapy will be stimulated by his theories and techniques.

The coolest eclectics and rationalists to date in this warm, emotional springtime of psychotherapy would seem to be the learning theory therapists, the psychobiologists, and Thorne. The latter two are eclectics in the full sense of the term, and their major influence in the whole field has been that of pointing out neglected techniques and theories of aid in treating all types of disturbed persons. The learning theory therapists have made their main emphasis that of clearing away mysticism from many varieties of approaches and offering ways of testing by future research many of the hypotheses about human personality, its pathological developments, and methods of treating these pathologies (to this point, however, their actual research production falls considerably below that of Rogers and associates). Thorne and the psychobiologists have likewise underlined reliance on the products of science in the training and functioning of therapists.

The general semanticists have made a contribution which has begun to be absorbed into the general therapeutic stream: namely, the focus of much more careful attention on the whole communicative process, both inside and outside the treatment setting. Much more needs to be learned here, but even now the therapist can function more effectively (whatever other techniques he uses or theories he holds) by devoting a considerable portion of his perceptive skills to his and the patient's transmission of meaning.

The experiments or exercises offered by the Gestaltists need to be explored much more carefully by therapists of many differing points of view. Without necessarily holding to all of the theories of Perls and his associates, the eclectic therapist may find here a technique for rendering more effective the attitude change of some patients.

Hypnosis is being re-explored in a number of therapeutic settings. Caution is needed here, as Wolberg has pointed out, because of the magical aura associated with the technique in the minds of many people. As a tool to be selectively employed, however, hypnosis is part of the legitimate equipment of the skilled therapist.

While Whitaker and Malone may in a sense lead us further away from a rational, scientific approach to psychotherapy by their emphasis on id communication, their techniques have certainly had a healthful effect in challenging *any* rigid, dogmatic assumptions about what will or will not work in psychotherapy. Other imaginative and instructive techniques (including the use of multiple therapists) . . . continue to emerge from the Atlanta psychiatric center. Future therapeutic developments must certainly take into account the experimental proceedings of Whitaker, Malone, and associates.

The simple technique outlined by Ellis of getting patients to understand the self-verbalized perpetuations of their negative emotions and to learn to substitute more rational and realistic thought which will (allegedly) produce neutral or positive emotional conditions needs much further investigation and therapeutic experimentation. Research which will pit the accepting, affective approach of Rogers, for example, against the directive, cognitive techniques of Ellis should prove valuable. It is encouraging to report that both Rogers and Ellis have independently indicated strong interest in such research.

The group psychotherapies not only offer new ways for helping patients to facilitate the development of greater insights into personality characteristics that they have tended to repress, dissociate, or disown, but also present a practice situation in which the patient can develop his skills in interpersonal relations. To this point, enthusiasm for systems and particular techniques have followed to some extent the route of individual psychotherapy. However, the group experience itself is destructive of dogmatism and rigidity in the therapist, and so a great deal of imaginative trial-and-accidental-success learning has tended to ensue. This has made some contribution to the flexibility of individual therapeutic practices. It is hoped that at least some of the future experimentation in group psychotherapy can develop along systematic research lines which encourage scientific reduplication.

What, then, of psychoanalysis? It seems indisputable that at this point in the development of psychotherapy many of the Freudian theories (especially with certain of the more moderate "corrections" of the dynamic culturalists) are still the best available for an over-all working hypothesis regarding the functioning of the human personality. The more thinking of Freud's critics draw heavily (as many of them admit) upon his insights even in the course of their criticisms. In the writer's opinion, the most sagacious eclectic therapists of at least this generation are likely to be theoretically, and to some extent technically, psychoanalytically oriented. Meantime, many of the psychoanalytic hypotheses can be reformulated (as some already have) in operational terms and tested, along with other hypotheses in large, co-ordinated research projects (still largely in a fantasy stage).

What is the common ground of all these therapies we have considered? How can people be helped by such divergent procedures as those of the classical analyst or the client-centered therapist, on the one hand, and those of the rational therapist or the assertion-structured therapist, on the other?

The following observations about common aspects of psychotherapy are in terms of *effects.* . . .[5] They are presented in the form of assertions, but are to be considered tentative hypotheses to be tested by future research. Not all of these observations apply to all patients at all times with all forms of psychotherapy, nor are these common effects the totality of results of any particular system of therapy. They are simply current conceptions of frequently occurring results of the work of many therapists with many of the patients with whom they seem to have success.

---

[5] *Editors' note.* Aspects of techniques were discussed in Chapter 1 of Harper's book.

First of all, weak egos (those of the patients) at least temporarily gain support from strong egos (those of the therapists). Stated differently, persons with initially low self-esteem gain in this area through intimate association with persons of generally high self-esteem. "*He* (the self-respecting therapist) likes and accepts and gives attention to and cares for and is concerned about *me*. I, therefore, must be better, more worthwhile, less hopeless, etc., than I had thought."

The first effect can be achieved in numerous ways. It can be done by a very nondirective method of largely listening, noncritically feeding back what the patient has said, showing infinite patience and acceptance. Or it can be done relatively impersonally behind the couch on which the patient rests, but with occasional interpretations which demonstrate that the analyst has been listening carefully and that the patient has a fascinating and complicated unconscious (otherwise, the patient feels, why would the analyst consider it worthwhile to spend three or four hours per week listening and interpreting?). Or it can be done by rational instruction, emotional reconditioning (including Wolpe's point of reciprocal inhibition), confirmation and disconfirmation, sharing of fantasy experiences, and consideration of alleged symbols of an alleged collective unconscious. Any of these methods and many others give the patient attention at the very minimum and often understanding, acceptance, and love. As with the child (and in any therapeutic system this is the role the patient at least temporarily takes), even punitive attention from the parent (therapist) brings the feeling that "I am at least worthy of this strong person's time and energy, and I am, hence, of some importance."

The second common effect of psychotherapy is that less rational and less reality-oriented persons (patients) at least temporarily learn more realistic ways of handling life problems from more rational and reality-oriented persons (therapists). They can be specifically told how better to deal with reality, or they can gradually come to imitate the examples set by the therapists over a period of time. But directly or indirectly they are taught (yes, *taught*—though this is a rejected word in many a therapist's vocabulary, the process goes on) by therapists how to behave less disturbedly in confronting their life activities.

Third, patients also learn (again, the methods may be very direct or very devious) that a lot of the things that they have fretted, stewed, or panicked over are not as important as they thought. (The observation that psychotherapy is the process whereby the unbland learn to be led by the bland into becoming bland has some truth in it.) In one way or another, successful therapy reduces anxiety by communicating to the patient that his concerns about what his neighbors think, his guilt feelings about not having been nice to his mother before she died, his worries about not being acceptable to the members of a social club, etc., are at best unnecessary and at worst idiotic. He is directly taught such things, or he indirectly comes to "catch on" to them by associating with a person who is quite bland about such matters.

Fourth, patients learn patience. One of the most frequent difficulties of persons with emotional immaturity and certain forms of emotional disturbance is a low tension capacity. The very process of going through the long and tedious process of therapy week after week, discussing the frequently recurring problems and hearing or otherwise sensing the same suggested ways of handling these difficulties, develops the person's tension capacity, his ability to be patient. Stated differently, patients gradually learn to be less childish, more adult. They learn to insist less on immediately satisfying goal-responses and to put up with tensions necessary to achieve long-term goals. They learn sometimes by instruction, sometimes by example—usually by both.

Fifth, patients learn new sets of myths (a "new faith"), which at least seem to be more scientific, more closely related to contemporary social reality, than their old sets of myths. The myths the patients adopt are their perceptions of the therapists' beliefs. Whether or not the therapists and the patients are aware of the myth-adopting process seems to have little effect on its efficiency. Therapists of a few of the systems (Ellis, Phillips, Salter, and the Adlerians, for several examples) would seem to be frank propagandists: they admit they are attempting to instill their systems of value in their patients. But others, including the most nondirective of the Rogersians and the most classically impersonal of the Freudians, have their patients as evidence that they, too, transmit their values. Patients even come to dream the kinds of dreams, in some instances, that they feel are most appreciated by their therapist.

Since it is very likely that even the most unrealistic myth system of a fairly healthy therapist will function more effectively (at least for a time) than the probably quite confused myth system the patient brought with him to therapy, improvement is likely to ensue from the change in values for the patient.

Sixth, patients gain perspective about their emotions and their interactional difficulties from talking about them and hearing the therapist talk about them. Such talk in itself tends to objectify fears, anxieties, feelings of inadequacy, and so on. The patient finds it gradually more difficult to react with intense fear to, say, open spaces, after all the angles of the nature and possible causes of his phobic fear have been discussed at length by the therapist and himself. Another patient who has always been late to appointments, who postpones other responsibilities, and lies late abed each morning begins to lose his neurotic satisfaction from such tactics of avoidance after he and the therapist have conversationally dealt with these and related factors at great length. The personal privacy, the hidden subjectivity, of various aspects of neurosis can be removed by talk alone (even if the talk is devoid of insight into causation and does nothing other than expose the problems to objective discussion), and sometimes the emotional disturbance loses its power with its privacy.

Seventh, by focusing so much attention on present anxieties while in therapy, patients are likely to find future anxieties less threatening. Not only have the old problems lost a lot of their ego-damaging punch (for such reasons as those discussed in the foregoing points), but new problems often seem weak, pale, and manageable in contrast to the former anxiety investments in the problems subjected to the tedious inspection of psychotherapy. "Nothing can throw me after I live through this" is a sometimes valid reaction of the patient in the process of therapy.

Patients often emerge from therapy with the feeling that the therapist is a part of them and, hence, life will never again be so lonely or so difficult. This intense emotional experience derives from the personal, intimate, problem-inspecting process with even a relatively cold and impersonal therapist. "He's there; he understands; he thinks I am worthwhile. I am not alone; I have some of his strength; I can handle whatever lies ahead."

The points we have just brought out are, we think, observable in psychotherapy as a whole. It should be understood, however, that some systems may more consistently and efficiently achieve these and other important effects. And some therapists, regardless of system affiliation or lack of same, achieve much better results than their colleagues. With any therapist and any system, such results as those we have discussed are by no means inevitable—failures seem at least as plentiful as successes.

Psychotherapy is, if we may now generalize from our list of common effects, a contemporary means for individuals with poorly functioning value systems to find the support of an apparently strong and successful person in learning a new value system and how to live more effectively thereby. None of these value systems learned in therapy may be considered totally satisfactory for meeting the problems of present-day social turbulence. They are varyingly successful stopgap measures for persons who no longer get sufficient ego strength and relationship support from such long-standing institutions (value systems) as the church, the school, marriage, and the family.

We use the term "stopgap measure" advisedly, for it seems quite evident that as the ever-brighter light of science increasingly penetrates psychotherapy, all the systems of this make-shift institution will reveal more fiction than fact, more myth than science. The day may not be too distant—with the advances of biochemistry, physiology, and biophysics, as well as psychology itself—that what we now call psychotherapy will relate to the scientific treatment and prevention of behavioral disorders as astrology now relates to astronomy.

While we look to that day, however, much work must be done with the present primitive tools of psychotherapy. Blunt instruments are surely rendered no sharper by rigidity, dogmatism, and fanatic adherence to a particular system. Young therapists in training should be encouraged to expose themselves to the full range of therapeutic theories and to experiment with the complete repertory of therapeutic techniques. Such therapists, in this period which is hopefully a prelude to more scientific procedures, are more likely, we firmly believe, to be helpful to a great number of patients than therapists conditioned in one theoretical orientation and its limited techniques.

But this is the outlook of an eclectic, and an eclectic is often less acceptable to fanatics than even fanatics of opposing persuasions. . . . We are saying, in effect: look around, reserve judgment for a while and then make it tentative, and experiment with many theories and techniques. Until science brings us definitive answers—if science does—let us try to avoid commitment to a rigid religion of psychotherapy. Let us learn from and constructively employ the arts of many therapies.

The Bland Leading the Blind

Harper emphasizes the need for "eclecticism, synthesis, and flexibility in the use of differing therapeutic techniques" in order to enable "individuals with poorly functioning value systems" to learn new value systems and how to live more effectively thereby. He points out, quite appropriately, that empathy and similar dimensions by themselves may be insufficient to effect psychotherapeutic personality change. Specific treatment techniques are critical sources of effective treatment processes. These specific modes of treatment must be tied to specific diagnoses.

Harper states that therapeutic diagnostic categories and instruments are "crude." However, even if the traditional diagnostic categories and instruments were sharpened up, they would be *most meaningless* for *present* treatment programs. Our own attitude towards diagnosis has evolved from a negative beginning. When we started practicing, we found diagnosis intellectually repugnant in our quest for more effective treatment processes. As we continue, however, we find that the effectiveness of preferred modes of treatment in the context of a primary core of critical therapeutic ingredients necessitates another view, which can be elaborated as follows: The central core of dimensions shared by all processes involves the structure of the dimensions of the relationship, such as genuineness, understanding, respect, and concreteness. The secondary factors that operate in the context of this core might involve a variety of techniques calculated to achieve most effectively the goals inherent in a therapeutic process involving a particular interaction of therapist, client, and contextual variables. More meaningful client dimensions must be discerned: *only those dimensions which can be related to differential treatment are meaningful.*

Harper favors "advancing rationality and science." We would like to point out that this viewpoint need not exclude the more emotional, attitudinal conditions of experience. (In this regard, we underscore Harper's advice to novitiates: "Be as open and flexible as you would have your clients become.") His study of the common effects of the psychotherapeutic process upon the behavior of the client in relationship to that of the therapist makes inroads upon the mysticism of therapy. He shows that the clients become stronger, more realistic, and reasonable. They find future anxieties less threatening as they gain perspective from learning "a new set of myths," or as Frank (1961) puts it in the next article, from making modifications in their "assumptive worlds" so that fewer critical errors occur.

MODIFICATIONS IN THE ASSUMPTIVE WORLD*

Jerome Frank

The attempt to describe features common to all forms of psychotherapy requires consideration of a wide variety of patterned personal and social interactions. To keep our bearings in this exploration, a general conceptual framework is needed. Such a scheme should be able to relate a person's inner life to his interactions with other persons and to his group allegiances. It should suggest how certain kinds of distress might arise from and contribute to disturbed relationships with others, and how particular types of interpersonal experience might help to ameliorate both. This is obviously a very big order, and to handle it adequately would require a complete theory of personality development and structure as related to social and cultural influences, which is beyond

* A conceptual framework of psychotherapy. In *Persuasion and healing.* Baltimore: Johns Hopkins Press, 1961, pp. 18-34. Reprinted by permission of author and publisher.

---

[1] A manful attempt to construct such a scheme has been made by Kardiner *et al.* (1945). A brilliant, if less inclusive, scheme for relating personality to culture is offered by Spiro (1961). See also Kluckhohn *et al.* (1953).

the scope of this book.[1] The following presentation attempts only to sketch a few useful concepts in sufficient detail for orientation purposes. It makes no pretense at completeness. Although the exposition is primarily in terms of psychiatric patients and psychotherapy as they exist in America, with slight modifications it also applies to the other forms of influence and healing to be considered.

PSYCHOTHERAPY AND ADAPTATION TO STRESS

Although the conditions for which psychotherapy may be used are protean, they can all be viewed as temporary or persistent unsuccessful adaptations to stress. Everyone repeatedly must deal with experiences that temporarily disturb his equanimity and bring him into conflict with others. The healthy person is able to handle most of them promptly and effectively, without excessive expenditure of energy. Thus he can push ever forward and may often seek stress to enjoy the triumph of mastering it, like Sir Edmund Hillary, who was impelled to climb Mt. Everest simply because it was there.

The psychiatric patient, the ill savage, the person on the verge of religious conversion, and the prisoner of the Communists all are in distress because of their inability to master certain stresses, which arise in large part from their interactions with other persons or groups, present or past. Failures of adaptation are determined by an imbalance between the stress and the person's susceptibility to it. Sometimes the stress is so great that it exceeds the adaptive capacity of almost everyone. Examples are the prisoner who finally yields to the prolonged tortures and deprivations of thought reform, the soldier who collapses after overwhelming battle stress,[2] or the housewife with no income, six young children, and an alcoholic husband who mistreats her. That persons show emotional strain under such circumstances is hardly surprising, but their treatment obviously must focus on alleviating the environmental stress.

Failures of adaptation caused by personal inadequacies arising from personally meaningful life experiences are our primary concern. For completeness, however, brief mention may be made of impersonal or organic handicaps limiting adaptive capacity. One of these is aging, which is characterized by generalized reduction of ability to adjust to stress. There may also be constitutional differences in adaptive capacity. Some persons seem unduly inflexible, others perhaps too flexible so that they are at the mercy of every new experience.

The ability to cope with stress may be limited by inborn bodily defects or by damage occurring any time after conception. Many disabilities formerly thought to be genetic in origin apparently may be pro-

[2] Glass (1957) reports that both the intensity and the duration of combat are related to the rate of neuropsychiatric breakdown.

duced by prenatal mishaps.[3] After birth, a host of illnesses may limit adjustive capacity through nonprogressive handicaps such as a residual paralysis from poliomyelitis or, more seriously, through progressive chronic disease. Psychotherapy may have something to offer such patients by enabling them to modify their concepts of the implications of these handicaps for future happiness and ability to function. Since they account for only a small portion of the distress for which people come to psychotherapists, however, and their relevance to psychotherapy is largely indirect, they may be passed over with this brief mention.

Let us now turn to the task of characterizing defects in adaptive mechanisms that arise from interpersonal experiences and result in more or less persistent maladaptations, reflected in both a person's relationships with others and his inner life.

THE ASSUMPTIVE WORLD

In order to be able to function at all, everyone must impose an order and regularity on the welter of experiences impinging upon him. To do this, he develops out of his personal experiences a set of more or less implicit assumptions about the nature of the world in which he lives, which enables him to predict the behavior of others and the outcome of his own actions. The totality of each person's assumptions may be conveniently termed his "assumptive world." [4]

This is a short-hand expression for a highly structured, complex, interacting set of values, expectations, and images of oneself and others, which guide and in turn are guided by a person's perceptions and behavior and which are closely related to his emotional states and his feelings of well-being. Assumptions range widely in scope. An example of one extreme would be assumptions connected with the importance of brushing one's teeth; of the other, those concerning the nature of God. They also vary in their time reference, some being primarily concerned with the past, some with the present, and some with the future.

Assumptive systems may be enduring or transient. Assumptions about the attractiveness of a hat can usually be changed as easily as the hat itself; not so assumptions about the nature of God. Some assumptions are held only tentatively, others with firm conviction. The degree of sub-

---

[3] Pasamanick and Lilienfeld (1955), for example, report a statistically significant association between mental retardation and damaging prenatal experiences.

[4] This term has been borrowed from Cantril, but it is given a much wider meaning here. He confines it to the sphere of perceptions only, but his discussion of the "assumptive form world" seems to justify the broader use. For example, he says: "The net result of our purposive actions is that we create for ourselves a set of assumptions which serve as guides and bases for future actions." (Cantril, 1950, p. 87.)

Kelley (1955, p. 561) has developed an elaborate theory of psychological functioning and a psychotherapeutic method based on the "fundamental postulate" that a "person's processes are psychologically channelized by the ways in which he anticipates events."

jective conviction accompanying them need not parallel their persistence —a lady may be absolutely convinced that a hat becomes her one day and that it is hideous the next—but conviction and tenacity do tend to vary together.

Different parts of the assumptive world exist at different levels of consciousness. Only a minute part of it is in awareness at any one time, and the relative accessibility to awareness of different aspects of it may differ greatly. A person may be clearly aware of his assumptions about the nuclear arms race, let us say, but be oblivious of his assumption that he must be perfect in order to gain his mother's love. Yet the latter conviction may have considerably more effect on his behavior than the former. Unconscious assumptive systems are especially pertinent to psychotherapy, not only because they are of profound importance to personal functioning but because, for reasons to be considered shortly, they resist change.

Assumptive systems may vary in their degree of mutual harmony or conflict. Internal conflicts are major sources of distress and disability, and much of psychotherapy can be viewed as an effort to help the patient resolve them.

A person's assumptive systems powerfully affect and are affected by his emotional states. Those systems that lead to a sense of uncertainty or confusion or to the prediction of an unfavorable outcome of a course of action tend to generate unpleasant emotions such as anxiety, panic, and despair. Those that give the person a sense of security and promise a better future are related to feelings of hope, faith, and the like. As will be seen, these emotional states not only have direct bearing on a person's ability to modify his perceptions and behavior, but also largely determine his state of well-being.

Anything that casts doubt on an established assumptive system seems to arouse an emotional reaction. An experience that does not meet expectations arouses a feeling of surprise. This may be tinged with fear or other unpleasant feelings if the person doubts his ability to make the necessary adjustment, or exhilaration if he is confident he can cope with the situation. That is, the emotional impact of an experience seems related to the extent to which it implies the necessity of a change in the assumptive world. It seems as if the more extensive, and possibly the more abrupt, the change required, the greater is the concomitant emotional upheaval. Contrast the emotions accompanying the discovery that what one took to be a robin is really a bluebird with those accompanying a religious conversion involving far-reaching changes in the convert's values.

Although it seems likely that no change in a person's assumptive world takes place without a concomitant emotional reaction, an emotional upheaval in itself is not sufficient to produce major change. Even when a person is much upset by being compelled to reorganize an error in his assumptive world, no correction occurs automatically. He may, however, be strongly motivated by the experience to re-examine his assumptions and seek more reliable guides to expectation.

In order to function successfully and enjoy life, a person must possess an integrated set of assumptions that correspond to conditions as they actually are. For it is only to the extent that a person can successfully predict the results of his acts that he can behave in such a way as to maximize chances for success and minimize those for failure. Thus everyone is strongly motivated constantly to check the validity of his assumptions, and every act is both a consequence of a more or less explicit expectation and a test of its validity. If the consequences of the act fail to confirm the prediction, the person is in trouble. He must either modify his expectations and the corresponding behavior or resort to maneuvers to conceal their incorrectness and evade their unfortunate consequences. This process for the most part goes on automatically and outside of awareness.

The validity of some aspects of the assumptive world can be checked against experiences unmediated by other persons. For example, the test of the assumption that a glowing poker is hot is to touch it. But since man is a social creature, his most significant experiences are with other persons, and those aspects of his assumptive world most essential to his functioning—his attitudes and values—can only be validated through his interactions with others, individually or in groups. An example of an interaction chain between two persons, which is guided by, and helps to form, the attitudes of each, is the following:

A man comes home late for supper after a hard day at the office and greets his wife with a warm kiss. She responds in kind and makes a sympathetic remark about his work load as they go in to supper. This encourages him to tell her about the events of the day. She shows interest, so he continues until he has gotten everything off his chest. Then he is prepared to listen to his wife's account of her doings, which he encourages with appropriate signs of interest, and so they have a pleasant chatty meal. Such an interactional chain is based on mutual expectations of affection and understanding and, in turn, strengthens these expectations, increasing the likelihood of similar mutually gratifying behavior on subsequent occasions. Thus the favorable behavior and assumptive systems of each member of the couple with respect to their relationship continually reinforce each other.

Starting the same way, the interaction might run quite a different course. The wife does not return her husband's kiss, but says coldly that he is late for supper again. As they go in to dinner he makes an angry rejoinder to which she responds in kind. He picks up the paper and buries himself in it while he eats. She does the same with a book. Here the husband's initial favorable expectations, which he expressed by a warm kiss, are disappointed by his wife's coolness. This leads him to alter his assumption about his wife's attitude and to change his behavior correspondingly. The subsequent interactions lead to a progressive breakdown of communication, confirming the unfavorable mutual expectancies of each spouse and increasing the likelihood that future interactional chains will run the same unsatisfactory course. This example illustrates how interactions between two persons form a mutually regulative system in which the behavior of each influences the other and simultaneously helps each to form his own psychic life.

Interactions with the members of a person's family, especially during his early years, are important formative influences of his assumptive world. If the family group provides a rich variety of experiences enabling the person to develop a wide repertory of adaptive skills, and if his parents make him feel loved and wanted and treat him as if he is capable and good, then he comes to see himself as a well-equipped, competent, lovable person in a friendly, secure universe. The world is his oyster. He welcomes new experiences, tackles them with confidence, and easily modifies his behavior and assumptive world according to the outcome. Thus he readily learns and develops.

The family environment may fall short of this ideal in many ways. It may be lacking in opportunities for certain experience. For example, there may be no adequate father figure or inadequate opportunity to play with other children. Thus the child may grow up lacking certain important assumptive systems simply for want of a chance to develop them. More serious difficulties occur if the child is unfortunate enough to have unloving or inconsistent parents. If they are profoundly inconsistent, he may become so confused that he loses all confidence in his ability to interpret experience. This may be a major source of schizophrenia.[5] Parental rejection may lead him to see himself as unlovable, in a hostile world: "I a stranger and afraid. In a world I never made."[6] If he has been constantly belittled, he may grow up feeling inadequate to deal with many situations. Assumptive systems like these obviously tend to cause a person to avoid new experiences since he fears the worst from them.

Persons often try to resolve stresses initially created by their families by means that bring temporary relief but lay the ground for future trouble. The following example of a miniature neurosis illustrates how a person resorted to such a solution in childhood and was able to correct

---

[5] This is the "double-bind" hypothesis of the etiology of schizophrenia (Bateson et al., 1956).

[6] A. E. Housman, *Last Poems*. London: Richards Press Ltd., 1922.

it years later through a lucky combination of circumstances. A scientist walking with some professional colleagues on the boardwalk at Atlantic City suddenly launched into an angry diatribe against the worthlessness of the merchandise in the curio shops. Although his remarks had some justification, the intensity of his feelings was so disproportionate as to arouse quizzical looks. Noting this, he became uncomfortable and began to wonder about it himself. He then suddenly remembered a long-forgotten childhood experience. At the age of seven he spent a few days at Atlantic City with his mother and grandmother. To give his grandmother a birthday present he emptied his piggy bank and bought her a cuckoo clock. Instead of being pleased, the grandmother angrily criticized his mother for letting him be so extravagant. As he told of this, he laughed and seemed relieved.

Let us describe this little episode in theoretical terms. In giving a birthday present to his grandmother the boy was acting on the assumption that she would be pleased. The unexpected failure of his prediction must have been most unpleasant for him. He probably felt resentment and anger at his grandmother as well as guilt for upsetting her and especially for the pain that he had inadvertently caused his mother. He might even have been angry at his mother for letting him get into such a fix.

A young child obviously cannot resolve such feelings by "having it out" with the adults who caused them, but must resort to more oblique solutions. Our patient, if he may be so termed for the moment, resorted to two common neurotic "mechanisms of defense" [7]—repression and displacement. He blotted the unpleasant episode from awareness, and displaced the object of his angry feelings from his grandmother to the curio shops. This solution had two advantages. It afforded a less dangerous object for his anger than his grandmother, and it allowed him to relieve his guilt by blaming the shops instead of himself. Like all neurotic solutions, however, it also had drawbacks. It left him with an error in his assumptive world and prevented him from correcting it through subsequent experience, because its source was unconscious. It also left him with a definite, if trivial, psychic scar, in that curio shops aroused an unduly unpleasant feeling in him. When circumstances again brought him in contact with these shops, he experienced this unpleasant feeling. By sharing it with his peers, he was implicitly validating it, and they failed to confirm it. Their quizzical looks communicated that they did not share this aspect of his assumptive world. This led him to examine himself for the source of his inappropriate feeling, and he discovered a

---

[7] This psychoanalytic term refers to more-or-less automatic and unconscious ways of protecting the self against unpleasant emotions, especially anxiety. See Fenichel (1945), Chapter IX, pp. 141-167.

past situation for which the feeling had been appropriate. By the same act he realized that this situation no longer existed. That is, he gained insight and with it was able to bring his assumptive systems into line with those of his colleagues.

Emotions were involved when his grandmother initially failed to confirm his assumptive world, leading him to modify it, and again when he modified it years later on the basis of his insight based on a different interaction, as shown by his discomfiture and his laugh. It is worth noting that the supportive, relaxed attitude of his colleagues made it relatively easy for him first to express his feelings, then to search himself for their source, and finally to offer a bit of self-revelation that explained and resolved them.

The family is only one source of experiences from which a person develops his assumptive world. He also interacts with many other groups, who transmit not only their own cultures, but also aspects of the larger culture of which they are a part. The relative power of the cultural assumptions depends on how well knit the culture is and on the extent to which its world view permeates the lives of its members. The assumptive worlds of, let us say, the members of an isolated tribe on a small Pacific atoll probably have more in common than those of twentieth-century Americans.

How the assumptive world of a culture affects the perceptions of its members can be demonstrated by a stereopticon. This device permits the presentation of two different pictures simultaneously, one to each eye. It has been found that if a picture of a baseball player is shown to one eye and a bullfighter to the other, Americans tend to see the baseball player, Mexicans the bullfighter. Thus members of each culture select from the stimuli reaching them those that best accord with their assumptive worlds.[8]

Societies often contain built-in conflicts, or sources of stress, which create disharmonies in the assumptive worlds of their members. Often a society also contains institutionalized ways of resolving the stresses it creates. As we shall see, societies that believe in witchcraft, for example, also have ways of counteracting witches' spells. However, too often there is no readily available institutionalized way of handling a conflict engendered by discrepancies in the assumptive world of a society. Americans, for example, often have considerable difficulty in reconciling within themselves the disapproval of violence conveyed by the "official" American Christian ideology and its glorification in the media of mass communication. This conflict at a social level may be reflected in confused individual attitudes towards violence, often accompanied by feelings of anxiety or guilt.

---

[8] The example is from Cantril (1957).

How the assumptive world of a group can pose virtually insoluble conflicts for its members, and how these conflicts can predispose to solutions that aggravate them, is illustrated by an "experiment of nature"—an outbreak of a fluke infestation know as schistosomiasis among American troops in the Philippines in World War II.[9] Many patients hospitalized with this disease seemed to stay sick after obvious signs of infestation had disappeared, suggesting that emotional reactions might be contributing importantly to their persistent invalidism. Accordingly, fifty patients who had been hospitalized for two to four months were selected at random and interviewed about their attitudes. Only two seemed completely well. Of the remaining forty-eight, only seven had objective signs of schistosomiasis and most of these were questionable, so forty-one, or four-fifths, of these patients had complaints with nothing physical to show for them. The complaints were mainly weakness, shakiness, headaches, and upper abdominal cramps. Review of the attitudes of all fifty patients showed that all but seven were anxious, resentful, or confused, or showed some combination of these feelings.

The assumptive world of the little society in which these men lived confronted them with a vague menace against which there was no clearly indicated course of action. It should be emphasized that this threat arose solely from the meaning of the situation to them. They were well fed and housed, did not feel very ill, and most had never been very uncomfortable at any time. Nor, as their subsequent recovery showed, were they in any actual danger from the disease. Yet they were badly demoralized. At least three aspects of their assumptive world contributed to this. First they believed the disease to be a threat to their survival since prognosis was considered uncertain and the efficacy of treatment questionable. Only two of the fifty were convinced that they had been cured, while thirty-two expected either to die of the disease or to become invalids. Second, the situation was highly ambiguous. Doctors could not avoid conveying their own uncertainties to the patients. They might say different things at different times, or different doctors might contradict each other. As one man put it, "(The doctors) tell you one thing one day and kind of contradict themselves. Like they say the sickness is all in your head and then they want to give you more shots." Moreover, at the same moment that the doctors were trying to be reassuring, the radio on the wards carried alarmist reports of the disastrous nature of the disease to discourage bathing in infected streams. The soldiers did not know whom to believe: "Either the radio or the doctors are screwed up about something. I suppose the doctors are right, but then I suppose the doctors write the radio programs."

Finally, the soldiers felt that nobody really cared about them. This

[9] The example is from Frank (1946a).

feeling seemed to have been created by fluctuations in disposition policies, reflecting the lack of knowledge about the disease, so that the decisions to return some soldiers to duty, hold others in the hospital, and promptly send others home appeared to the men to be purely capricious. The feeling of abandonment was accentuated by the attitudes of the harassed doctors, who, burdened with huge caseloads and not knowing what to make of the patients' endless complaints, inevitably tended to become somewhat aloof: "I tell them something and they pass it off as though it didn't exist. I feel I might as well be talking to myself."

The healthy way of coping with an ambiguous, threatening assumptive world is to clear up the uncertainty by getting more information, and the soldiers went at this with a vengeance. They read every scrap of literature on schistosomiasis they could find, wrote friends to look up the disease in medical texts, pestered the treatment staff for information, and compared notes with each other. Of course, this only made matters worse. The lack of authoritative information, the inability to comprehend the information that was available, and the general level of anxiety conspired to create a mass of rumors that enhanced the general confusion and intensified the morbid atmosphere.

Concomitantly with unsuccessful efforts to deal with the threat in appropriate fashion, the patients inevitably fell back on patterns of behavior that they had developed in early life to cope with similar predicaments. They "regressed" in that, like children, their complaints became a way of trying to elicit signs of interest and caring from the doctors, who were, in a sense, parent surrogates. Their symptoms, furthermore, afforded an indirect and acceptable way of expressing their resentment towards the treatment staff. A patient can legitimately complain that his headache has not been relieved, but it is considerably more difficult to complain of the doctor's incompetence.

This regressive way of dealing with the stressful assumptive world tended to confirm and heighten its threatening quality. By constantly dwelling on their symptoms, patients heightened their fears and forebodings. The variety and vagueness of their complaints added to the doctors' confusion and increased their uneasiness. They reacted by becoming impatient, intensifying the patients' anxiety and resentment.

It must be emphasized, however, that despite the self-aggravating nature of the threat and its apparent insolubility, individual reactions to it varied greatly. At one extreme, as already mentioned, two soldiers in the sample interviewed were apparently completely unscathed, while at the other, two were so disturbed emotionally as to require hospitalization on this basis alone. Even when an assumptive world is widely shared, people show widely differing abilities to cope with it successfully.

THE ASSUMPTIVE WORLD OF THE PSYCHIATRIC
PATIENT IN RELATION TO PSYCHOTHERAPY

According to the formulation offered here, the aim of psychotherapy is to help a person to feel and function better by enabling him to make appropriate modifications in his assumptive world. What helps or hinders such changes? In general, assumptive systems, once established, tend to resist change. Facts and experiences contradictory to assumptions do not universally, immediately, and automatically lead to their revision, but are more apt to be ignored or rationalized away. There are several reasons for the stability of assumptive systems. A major one is that they are anchored to internalized reference points.

The examples illustrate how the assumptive systems of persons or groups present at the moment can influence the assumptive systems of individuals exposed to them. Most groups against which a person tests his assumptions, however, are not actually present at the time, but exist as the residues of past experiences that he has internalized. These "reference groups" range from single concrete individuals such as "my father" to groups that exist only as concepts—such as "the scientific community" or "patriotic Americans." These internalized standards of reference are necessary for a stable personality organization, and they help a person withstand the temporary pressures of the groups he may be in at different times. At the same time, they may impair his ability to profit from new experiences that might lead to beneficial change.

Another reason why assumptive systems tend to perpetuate and reinforce themselves lies in the reciprocal nature of many interactions. Each participant tends to elicit from another responses in kind. Friendliness tends to beget friendly responses, and anger, angry ones, thus strengthening the assumptions on which the initial act was based. Furthermore, a person's own behavior, guided by his expectations, influences his interpretation of the other person's response. Thus in the example cited earlier, the husband would interpret the same response of the wife quite differently, depending on how he perceived his own initial greeting. If he saw it as friendly, this would predispose him to interpret her response as such; if he meant it to be cool, he would be inclined to interpret her response as being similar. In either case, he would guide his next action accordingly, predisposing the wife to respond in accord with his expectations. Thus a continuing relationship tends to lead each participant to develop an enduring, structured set of expectations about himself and the other person, with corresponding behaviors, which become ever harder to modify by new experience.

Unhealthy assumptive worlds of mental patients present certain special obstacles to change. It would lead too far afield to consider in detail how various neurotic resolutions of stress tend to impede new learning. Repression, as used by the man who hated curio shops, may serve as an illustration. Blotting an experience from awareness prevents the erroneous conclusion that has been drawn from it from being modified by subsequent experiences, in part because the patient cannot link them to the original one. Moreover, repressed emotions or thoughts reduce both a person's adaptive capacity and his sense of security. He must expend some effort to keep them out of awareness, thus decreasing energy available for meeting current stresses. Since repression is seldom perfect, repressed emotions or thoughts are apt to erupt into consciousness attached to obviously inappropriate objects or at inappropriate times, so that they are mysterious to the patient. In the example, the scientist was startled at the inappropriate intensity of his dislike of the shops. The sense of not being able to account for one's feelings or thoughts may be partly responsible for the common fear of psychiatric patients that they are going crazy.

In addition to presenting specific blocks to new learning, such as repression, the faulty assumptive systems of mental patients impede their ability to benefit from new experiences in more general ways. To the extent that the assumptive world of a person is erroneous, his predictions as to the behavior of others will be wrong, leading him to suffer repeated shocks, failures, and frustrations. Chronic frustration arouses anger and other unacceptable feelings, which increase his feelings of unworthiness. He may be further demoralized by the knowledge that he is not living up to his capacities. Finally, the contempt or impatience of those about him, reflecting cultural attitudes towards mental illness, contributes to his loss of self-esteem, and he may view his need for psychotherapy as conclusive evidence of his inferiority.

Emotions like anxiety, depression, and feelings of inadequacy tend to reduce a person's willingness and capacity to experiment. Since nothing is more anxiety-producing than uncertainty, a chronically anxious patient clings fearfully to his old solutions, however inadequate, because they are familiar, whereas experimentation would require venturing into unknown territory. The depressed patient cannot muster the necessary energy or interest to attempt a change. Although moderate anxiety and depression cause some persons to seek help and so facilitate psychotherapy, they tend to cause others to withdraw. Isolation from others, besides being distressing in itself, reduces opportunities to correct errors in one's assumptive world by checking them against the assumptions of others.

But probably the greatest block to new learning in psychiatric patients is that they are saddled with ways of dealing with stress that aggravate rather than alleviate it. The major problem here arises from the reciprocal nature of human transactions, mentioned earlier. A person's behavior tends to "train" others to respond in such a way as to confirm his expectations. This training is especially effective if the patient's behavior is already restricted to a narrow range so that he does the same thing repeatedly.[10] A paranoid patient, who is convinced that everyone hates him, may by his surly, suspicious manner antagonize a person who initially bore him no ill will. The reaction he receives confirms the patient's belief that everyone dislikes him, intensifying his dislike-creating behavior. In the schistosomiasis example, patients came to expect the doctors to confuse them and show a lack of interest in them. By their vague but constant complaining they tended to elicit from the doctors precisely such behavior. This, in turn, aggravated their complaints. Thus patients tend to get caught in "self-fulfilling prophecies,"[11] and their behavior is both self-perpetuating and self-defeating. Breaking these vicious circles is the main goal of psychotherapy.

In view of the resistance of assumptive systems, especially unhealthy ones, to change, the psychotherapist's task would appear to be well-nigh hopeless, and the extent of the personality changes he can help patients to achieve is indeed limited. However, these changes need not be negligible, for the psychotherapist may be able to mobilize powerful influencing forces.

To oversimplify vastly, the two major sources of interpersonal influence are individuals on whom a person feels dependent and those whom he perceives to be like himself. The former, first represented by his parents, later by teachers, bosses, and so on, gain their power through their direct control of his well-being. The sources of influence of the latter—his friends and colleagues—are not so apparent, but probably spring in part from the fact that their attitudes of acceptance or rejection determine his sense of group belonging.[12]

A person's feelings of dependency on others may spring from his perception of them as possessing information that would be useful to him, or as being able to harm or help him in a variety of ways. Perceived power to harm readily induces outward conformity to escape reprisal, but at the same time generates feelings such as resentment, which may impede genuine acceptance of the powerful figure's goals or ideas. Per-

---

[10] See discussion by Leary (1957), pp. 91-131, of the interpersonal reflex for a good account of this process.

[11] The concept of the self-fulfilling prophecy is developed by Merton (1957), pp. 421-436.

[12] Another important source of the influence of one's peers may lie in a postulated drive to evaluate one's opinions and abilities by comparison with others. This tendency is stronger, the greater the perceived similarity between the opinions and abilities of others and one's own (Festinger, 1954).

ceived power to help seems to be a particularly potent source of influence. Through engendering hope, it directly improves the perceiver's sense of well-being, and heightens his self-confidence, increasing his willingness to modify his attitudes and behavior. At the same time it strengthens his sense of dependence without directly stirring up conflicting emotions.

The psychotherapist gains his potential power to influence the patient's assumptive world from all these sources. Patients who have similar educational and social backgrounds perceive him as like themselves. In many settings he is a representative of the larger culture, so that his acceptance of the patient implies acceptance by the larger group. He may use specific group methods to take full advantage of the patient's hunger for group acceptance. His cultural role and special training predispose the patient to perceive him both as an expert in problems of living and as a healer. These favorable, socially determined perceptions are complicated, especially in long-term therapy, by idiosyncratic ones encompassed by the term "transference." That is, patients tend to transfer to the therapist emotions that are really appropriate to other persons in their lives. Transference reactions may both help and impede the therapist's power depending on whom he represents to the patient.

Consideration of the sources and nature of the psychotherapist's influence is a major object of this book. For the present, it suffices to indicate that although patients may present formidable resistance to change, the psychotherapist often has forces at his disposal that can overcome this, at least to some extent.

SUMMARY

Psychotherapy tries to relieve a person's distress and improve his functioning by helping him to correct errors and resolve conflicts in his assumptions concerning himself and others. These assumptions are organized into systems existing at varying levels of consciousness and in harmonious or conflicting relationships with one another. They affect and are affected by emotional states, and changes in them are regularly accompanied by emotion. Healthy assumptive systems are characterized by internal consistency and close correspondence with actual conditions. They thus lead to reliable, satisfactory interactions with other persons, accompanied by a sense of competence, inner security, and well-being, which enables them to be readily modified when necessary. Unhealthy assumptive systems are internally full of conflict and do not accurately correspond to circumstances, leading to experiences of frustration and failure. Efforts to cope with or evade these feelings tend to intensify distortions and conflicts and to become both self-perpetuating and self-defeating, resulting in cumulative adaptational difficulties.

Despite the stubbornness of maladaptive assumptive systems, the psychotherapist, as a socially sanctioned expert and healer and a representative of the larger society, may be able to mobilize forces sufficiently powerful to produce beneficial changes in them.

REFERENCES

Bateson, G., Jackson, D. D., Haley, J., and Weakland, J. Toward a theory of schizophrenia. *Behav. Sci., 1,* 251-264.

Cantril, H. Perception and interpersonal relations. *Amer. J. Psychiat., 114,* 119-126.

Cantril, H. *The "why" of man's experience.* New York: Macmillan, 1950.

Fenichel, O. *The psychoanalytic theory of neurosis.* New York: Norton, 1945.

Festinger, L. A theory of social comparison processes. *Hum. Relat., 7,* 117-140. Reprinted in Hare, A. P., Borgatta, E. F., and Bales, R. F. (Eds.), *Small groups: Studies in social interaction.* New York: Knopf, 1955. Pp. 163-187.

Frank, J. D. Emotional reactions of American soldiers to an unfamiliar disease. *Amer. J. Psychiat., 102,* 631-640. (1946a)

Glass, A. J. Observations upon the epidemiology of mental illness in troops during warfare. In *Symposium on preventive and social psychiatry.* Washington, D. C.: Walter Reed Army Institute of Research, 1957.

Kardiner, A., Linton, R., DuBois, C., and West, J. *The psychological frontiers of society.* New York: Columbia Univer. Press, 1945.

Kelley, G. A. *The psychology of personal constructs,* Vol. 2, *Clinical diagnosis and psychotherapy.* New York: Norton, 1955.

Kluckhohn, C., Murray, H. A., and Schneider, D. M. *Personality in nature, society, and culture.* New York: Knopf, 1953.

Leary, T. F. *Interpersonal diagnosis of personality.* New York: Ronald, 1957.

Merton, R. K. *Social theory and social structure.* Glencoe, Ill.: Free Press, 1957.

Pasamanick, B., and Lilienfeld, A. M. Association of maternal and fetal factors with development of mental deficiency: 1. abnormalities in the prenatal and parental periods. *J. Amer. Med. Assoc.,* 1955, *159,* 155-160.

Spiro, M. E. Social system, personality, and functional analysis. In Kaplan, B. (Ed.), *Studying personality cross-culturally.* Evanston, Ill.: Row, Petersen, 1961.

Some Assumptive Extensions

For Frank, psychotherapy is an attempt to help patients resolve their internal and interpersonal conflicts by modifying their erroneous assumptive worlds. While he does not cover in this reading all the therapist dimensions that contribute to changes, there are several conditions to which he gives repeated attention: the conditions of love, support, attention, and concern. These conditions make it relatively easy for the client "to express his feelings, then to search himself for their source, and finally to offer a bit of self-revelation that explained and resolved them."

We think that Frank presents the beginnings of a developmental model which can be stated as follows: The child growing up in the unloving and inconsistent home develops errors in some important assumptive systems and fails to develop other important systems. The conditions for imposing order and regularity upon experience are not present. As a consequence, he loses all confidence in his ability to understand his experience, and sometimes develops a severe psychopathological state. The conditions that were absent in the child's home in the first place, that is, love and the genuine and sensitive understanding and respect that it implies, are instituted in the therapy process. Variations in communication of these conditions in counseling may be dictated by this model. For example, direct and explicit communication of the conditions facilitative for self-exploration and ultimate revisions in the assumptive system may be necessary for the extremely pathological person who has never experienced them. However, these facilitative conditions may be taken for granted in working with the situationally distressed normal person who has few errors in his assumptive world, and greater attention may be given to more cognitive concerns.

Hobbs (1962) is relevant in this regard. He challenges the traditional view of insight as an antecedent of change in suggesting that insight may be possible only after extensive personality reorganization has taken place. In addition, he attempts to discern the principal sources of gain in psychotherapy.

A NEW COSMOLOGY *

Nicholas Hobbs

This paper needs a subtitle. Let it be: "Five Hypotheses in Search of a Theory." One of the firmly rooted assumptions in psychotherapeutic practice is that the development of insight on the part of the client is both a major goal of the therapeutic endeavor, intrinsically worth promoting, and a primary means of achieving, step by step in the

* Sources of gain in psychotherapy, *American Psychologist,* 1962, *17,* 18-34. Reprinted by permission of author and publisher. This paper was presented as the Presidential Address to the Division of Clinical Psychology at the 1961 meeting of the American Psychological Association.

therapeutic process, the over-all objective of more effective functioning. If a client can be helped to understand why he behaves as he does or to recognize and understand the origin of the neurotic tactics that continually defeat him, he will gradually abandon the inappropriate behavior and substitute therefore more rational tactics in the management of his life. Increased self-understanding is regarded as inherently good and as a means to the end of good psychological health.

The promotion of insight is thus the tactic most heavily relied upon by most therapists who write about their work. Other strategies—the encouragement of catharsis, of abreaction, of transference—are valued to the extent that they lay the groundwork for the achievement of insight. The interpretation of behavior, perhaps the most widely used tactic of all, is aimed directly at the promotion of self-understanding. Furthermore, the achievement of insight by a client is a welcomed signal to the therapist that his efforts are paying off, and that his client, armed with new understanding, will gain a new measure of control over his life. All of this is a part of the folklore, both amateur and professional, of helping people by talking with them. But I have come seriously to doubt the presumed relationship between the achievement of insight and the achievement of more effective functioning.

My doubts about the efficacy of insight as a change agent were first aroused a number of years ago while working in a clinic with a staff with diverse theoretical persuasions. In staff discussions of therapy cases, the occurrence of a significant insight on the part of a client was greeted with approval and satisfaction and with the expectation that there should follow some change for the better in the client's behavior. When anticipated changes did not occur there was general discomfort. If the client persisted in behaving contrary to theory, as some obstinate clients did, we countered with a very useful, theory-preserving gambit. We said, "Well, it is obvious that the client did not have real insight. He may have had 'intellectual insight'," we said, "but he did not have 'emotional insight'." This was always an after-the-fact adjustment. We were not attracted to the obvious alternate interpretation, namely, that insight need not lead to changes in behavior. We were too much a part of our culture, both general and professional, to question the time-honored relationship between self-understanding and effective functioning.

I began to wonder why we never examined the alternate explanation of the failure of insight to produce changes in behavior. Once jarred from the point of usual perspective on this issue, I began to see a number of arguments for an alternate explanation, namely, that insight may have nothing to do with behavior change at all, or is, at best, an event that may or may not occur as a result of more fundamental personality reorganizations. Here are some of the arguments:

Item 1. In interpretive therapies, great stress is placed on the exquisite timing of interpretations. The thought occurs that an interpretation may be acceptable to a client only after he has achieved sufficient self-reorganization for the interpretation no longer to be relevant. He can accept, but he no longer "needs," the interpretation.

Item 2. In play therapy with young children most therapists do not bother to try to develop insight. Rational formulations are adult fare, a consequence of the adult's addiction to words. Instead, therapists provide children concrete experiences in relationship with a particular kind of adult and get good results.

Item 3. The equipotentiality of diverse interpretations is a bothersome thing. It is quite apparent that therapists of different theoretical persuasions seem to promote different but equally effective insights. An Adlerian interpretation based on assumed relationships between organ inferiority and life style seems just as effective as a Freudian interpretation based on disjunctions among id, ego, and superego requirements. A Jungian interpretation based on the relationship between the individual and the cosmos seems as effective as an existential interpretation of the estrangement of man resulting from the subject-object dichotomy, currently described as an invention of Descartes. Or the therapist can get equally good results by making no interpretations at all, as Rogers has shown. All this suggests that the occurrence of an insight merely means that the client is catching on to the therapist's personal system for interpreting the world of behavior. The therapist does not have to be right; he mainly has to be convincing.

There are other arguments but these will suffice. They do not, of course, disprove the accepted relationship between insight and change in behavior but they do suggest that one should give serious consideration to an alternate hypothesis. It seems to me that the traditional formulation of the relationship between self-understanding and effective behavior may be backwards. I suggest that insight is not a cause of change but a possible result of change. It is not a source of therapeutic gain but one among a number of possible consequences of gain. It may or may not occur in therapy; whether it does or not is inconsequential, since it reflects only the preferred modes of expression of the therapist or the client. It is not a change agent, it is a by-product of change. In a word, insight is an epiphenomenon.

The role of insight in therapeutic progress has probably escaped detailed analysis because we have no good definitions of what is meant by the term. Particularly are we lacking in criteria for differentiating between intellectual insight and emotional insight, if there are, indeed, two such entities, which I doubt.

The best definition that I have been able to come up with is this:

Insight is manifested when a client makes a statement about himself that agrees with the therapist's notions of what is the matter with him. This is not a particularly useful formulation.

The acceptance of insight as the sovereign remedy for all neuroses represents both an unwarranted extrapolation from Freud's position and a failure to take into account the kinds of neuroses generated by Viennese life at the turn of the century and by American or European life today. Freud could not have been more explicit in insisting that his method worked best, if not solely, in cases of massive repression with accompanying conversion symptomatology. Contemporary culture often produces a kind of neurosis different from that described by Freud. Contemporary neuroses are frequently characterized not so much by repression and conversion as by an awful awareness and a merciless raw anxiety. The problem of the contemporary neurotic is not lack of insight but lack of a sense of identity, of purpose, of meaning in life. Because of a dehumanization of existence, as Kierkegaard pointed out, he has a sickness unto death. Indeed, in many of the people I work with there seems to be a substantial component of realism in their neurotic condition. Nothing can make a person more anxious, or more guilty, than an unrelentingly clear appreciation of the absurd and desperate condition of man today.

Let us suppose for the moment that insight plays no significant role in the therapeutic process. How then does change come about? What are the sources of gain in psychotherapy? My effort will be to identify sources of change that are common to all approaches to therapy, with the hope that the analysis will provide a theoretical matrix for more adequate quantitative and comparative studies of the therapeutic process. At present it seems to me that there are five major sources of gain, five kinds of experiences that are the well-springs of personality reorganization. I might add that these experiences often occur in daily life quite apart from psychotherapy and are the sources of healthy integrations and re-integrations that develop throughout the life span. Psychotherapy is a unique life situation deliberately designed to make these five sources of gain available in an intense and usable form in a compressed time span, especially for those people who are unable, because of their neurotic tendencies, to avail themselves of the normal healing and nurturing experiences of life. Psychotherapy may thus be practiced, as indeed it is, by anyone who comes into intimate contact with a client on a professional basis.

The first source of gain is in the therapeutic relationship itself. This is a widely accepted notion, and I only wish to specify, which is seldom done, what it is about the relationship that has therapeutic impact. It is this: The client has a sustained experience of intimacy with another human being without getting hurt. He has an experience of contact, of engagement, of commitment. He learns directly and immediately, by concrete experience, that it is possible to risk being close to another, to be open and honest, to let things happen to his feelings in the presence of another, and indeed, even to go so far as to dare to include the therapist himself as an object of these feelings. The neurotic, on the basis of earlier attempts at intimate relationships with important life persons, primarily his mother and father, has come to the deep-seated conviction that other people cannot be trusted, that it is terribly dangerous to open oneself up to them. This conviction may well have a very realistic basis: When he reached out to his parents he was rebuffed. When he made tentative, affective overtures to other important life persons, he got clobbered. On the basis of these hurtful experiences, he has adopted the tactic of alienation that is so characteristic of the neurotic. He may simply withdraw from significant human contacts. He may live and work in proximity with others, but let it be known that the relationship stops where his self begins. Or he may get engaged with others in intense relationships that should lead to intimacy but always with reservations, always on terms that guarantee that he is not really exposed. These are the counterfeit friendships and marriages of the neurotic. And in all this, of course, he will not even be intimate with himself; he cannot let himself feel how he actually feels about himself and others. Now I argue that human intimacy is necessary for human survival. Intimacy may be an instinctual, a biological requirement. But even if it is not a built-in requirement, the prolonged period of dependency of the human infant with its all but inevitable experience of some sustaining intimacy provides ample time to acquire, to learn a need to be close to others. The risking and handling of intimacy are learned by immediate experiencing; talking about intimacy, acquiring insight about intimacy, do not help much.

Now psychotherapy is a situation carefully designed to make it possible for a client to learn to be close to another person without getting hurt. For example, the therapist does not, or should not, punish the client's tentative and fearful efforts at being open and honest about his feelings. On the contrary, he is alert to and reinforces any reaching-out behavior. The therapist permits the client to use him to learn how to be intimate, but he does not make reciprocal demands of a personal character, such as those inevitably involved in friendship or marriage, for these would be too threatening to the client. The therapist may make formal demands but not personal ones. In this special accepting situation, where the ground rules are clear, the client dares to establish a fully honest relationship with another person, and finds it a tremendously reinforcing experience. He is encouraged on the basis of this concrete learning experience to risk more open relationships outside of therapy.

Of course, he takes the chance of getting hurt again, as in childhood, but more likely than not he finds that others are responsive and that he is after all capable of richer, of more giving and more sustaining relationships with other people. This first source of gain lends itself readily to analysis in learning theory terms.

Now, source number two. Much of the time in psychotherapy is spent, or should be spent, in helping the client divest verbal and other symbols of their anxiety-producing potential. Shaffer is the author of the rich-declarative sentence: "Man is forever signalling to himself." It is man's ability to acquire, store, and manipulate symbols, and signal to himself in symbolic form, that makes him so distinctive, and so interesting. It also makes him uniquely susceptible to neurosis. Each of us has a tremendous store of symbols that are the residuals of experiences with which they were originally associated. In the domain of interpersonal relationships, some people have a collection of symbols that, for the most part, set off in them at the deepest and most pervasive somatic level feelings of well being, of comfort, of safety, of assurance. Other people, the ones we call neurotic, have a collection of symbols that set off in them, for the most part, feelings of anxiety and guilt or of somatic distress of specific or pervasive character. Actually, most of us have a mixed collection of distressing and sustaining symbols, and we call ourselves psychologically healthy if we have a clearly favorable algebraic balance of the positive and the negative. The negative symbols, associated with earlier life experiences of a hurtful nature, tend to stick tenaciously with us. In ordinary life circumstances we do not have an opportunity to learn new and more appropriate responses to them. Here is what seems to happen. A child suffers more than he can tolerate at the hands of his father. The concrete experiences get associated with specific symbols that are a product of this unique relationship and its attending circumstances. As an adult, even after his father has long been dead, experiences with authority figures evoke the symbols which evoke anxiety, guilt, hostility, or perhaps headaches, nausea, or other somatic reactions. Because of the distress that has been aroused, he retreats either literally or psychologically from the situation. His distress diminishes, thus reinforcing the avoidance of the authority relationship, and leaving the symbols as strong as ever. But authority cannot be avoided, and the cycle gets repeated over and over again. The crucial thing to note is that he never has an opportunity to learn new and more appropriate responses to the symbols that are evoking in him what we call neurotic behavior. The conditioned response cannot get extinguished.

The task of the therapist is not to help the client gain insight into the fact that he has trouble with authority figures because of his unfortunate experiences with his own father. This is far too abstract a formulation to be of help. He has got to be helped to identify and use comfortably the specific symbols that are elicited in him by authority figures. The symbols must be divested of their anxiety-producing potential.

At this point my communication problem becomes exceedingly difficult because there is no general way to identify or categorize these symbols. They are all highly personal, highly concrete, highly specific to the particular individual. And they have got to be talked about by the client in highly specific, hot, personal, intimate terms. The terms used must get as close as possible to the client's own idiosyncratic symbol system. A bright girl who had frequent attacks of nausea explained early in therapy that she feared she was homosexual and that she recognized the unsatisfactory character of her relationship with her mother, a fine insightful statement. Much later, after she was sure that it was safe to talk to the therapist using the same symbols that she used when talking to her most private self, she described in specific detail the experiences she felt had warped her relationship with her mother. At the end of the very difficult hour, she said, "This is the blackness that I have been trying to vomit."

The transference relationship is a third source of gain in psychotherapy. It also provides the clearest illustration of the differences between therapies which stress, respectively, the rational, abstract, and verbal, or the nonrational, concrete, and experiential components of the therapeutic process. Freud's discovery of the transference situation was a brilliant achievement. It made available to the therapist a most valuable instrument, comparable to the microscope or telescope in its clarifying powers. The essence of the situation is this: The client does not talk about his neurosis, he acts it out. His neurotic stratagems are no longer filtered through semantic screens; they are tried out in concrete, specific acts of hostility, overdependency, seduction, dissimulation, and so on. The therapist and the client are both immediately involved in the client's desperate and always self-defeating and yet so very human ploys and gambits.

In the Freudian prescription for the handling of transference one finds the great psychoanalytic paradox: The cure for unreason is reason. Freud gave us a twentieth-century discovery that unreasonable (that is, neurotic) behavior is determined by specific life experiences, thousands of them probably, and that neurotic behavior is unconscious and preeminently nonrational in origin. He could have said that neurosis is a summary term describing an extensive matrix of conditioned responses built up in a lifetime of hurtful relationships with important life persons, hardened around an armature of assumed guilt. He might further have observed that no man by taking thought becomes neurotic. But for this twentieth-century diagnosis, Freud had a nineteenth-century prescription:

Be rational. Transference represents the neurosis in microcosm; when transference appears it should be interpreted. As Fenichel so clearly instructs us, the client should be shown that he is behaving in an irrational manner.

Now I think it likely that this tactic will result in the client's learning that certain neurotic stratagems are not approved of, and they may well be abandoned in favor of other protective mechanisms. In the face of repeated interpretations, he may learn to repress particular transference symptoms. But nothing has been done about his need for these symptoms; his underlying distrust of himself and of other people remains untouched by the therapist's efforts to promote insight by interpreting the transference.

Transference develops when the client feels that the relationship with the therapist is becoming too dangerous, that he is losing control of the situation. He does not know how to handle the growing intimacy of the relationship without resorting to well established neurotic defenses. He does not need to be told that his tactics are inappropriate, that they are characteristic of his way of life, but he needs to learn through an immediate experience with another human being that the tactics are not necessary. Transference is best handled by providing the client with the kind of understanding and unqualified acceptance that have been so notably absent in his life. Transference stratagems disappear when the client has an opportunity to learn through concrete experience that it is possible to establish a simple, honest, open relationship with another person.

A fourth source of gain is available in those therapies which place the locus of control of the situation in the client rather than in the therapist. The client has hundreds of opportunities to practice decision-making, to learn to be responsible for himself, to develop a concept of himself as a person capable of managing his own life. Here again, you will note the emphasis not on insight but on specific opportunities for the acquisition of new ways of behaving.

Before proceeding to examine a fifth source of gain which seems to be different in character from the four already mentioned, I should like to discuss briefly two possible explanations for our confident advocacy of insight as a primary change agent in psychotherapy.

Insight and understanding appeal to us as central mechanisms in therapy because of our strong general commitment to rationality in problem solving. As F. S. C. Northrup has pointed out, western culture (in spite of its immense irrationalities) has a deeply ingrained rational component. For us, reason is a faith. From earliest childhood we are taught to apply rational principles to the solution of many kinds of problems. If our automobile breaks down we do not ordinarily kick it, pray over it, or assume that its spirit has departed, as a person from a primitive culture might do. We first try to discover what is wrong and then make appropriate interventions to correct the difficulty. It is perhaps the very strength of our faith that has led to a curious short-circuiting in the domain of psychotherapy. Faced with a breakdown of personal functioning, we seem to assume that the development of understanding itself is a sufficient intervention to correct the difficulty. If a person can be helped to understand the origins and current manifestations of his neurotic behavior, particularly if he feels deeply while he is gaining this insight, the neurotic behavior should disappear. A good rational question is: Why should it disappear unless appropriate learning experiences follow?

Even if we do have a cultural bias regarding the importance of insight and understanding, our convictions would gradually be extinguished in the therapy situation if they were not occasionally reinforced. And they are. Insight sometimes does lead to changes in behavior—but not for the reasons commonly assumed. Insight is usually thought of as a freeing or releasing mechanism. I think it may actually operate through the facilitation of repression and the elimination of a particular symptom. A good example is provided by Dollard and Miller. A girl had a habit of thumbing rides with truck drivers at night and then being surprised when men "took advantage of her." The therapist pointed out to her what she was doing and she stopped doing it, thus seeming to validate the assumption of insight as a releasing influence. But Miller's conflict theory provides a better explanation of her behavior, I think. She could either give up hitchhiking or run the risk, as she would see it, of incurring the disappointment of her valued therapist. She might be expected to repress her hitchhiking symptom. But nothing would have been done about her neurotic need for affection.

The same insight-related mechanism may operate outside of therapy to change behavior through repression. A person who expresses his hostility through malicious gossiping reads in a newspaper column that if he gossips he will inevitably alienate all his friends. If this prospect arouses enough anxiety, he will feel much in conflict and may repress his tendency to gossip. But since he is as hostile as ever, he may now become sarcastic or learn to excel at bridge. Again nothing would have been done about his neurotic need to be hostile. It should be pointed out that the repression of some symptoms may have subsequent therapeutic benefits if the person is thereby brought into more intimate human relationships that are intrinsically healing in accordance with the four sources of gain already described. Some symptoms are better than others. The worst symptoms are those that engender most alienation from significant others for this cuts the person off from the normal sources of therapeutic gain in daily living.

There is a fifth source of gain common to all psychotherapies that is qualitatively quite different from the four sources that have already been described. You may have noted in the preceding arguments not only a disavowal of the efficacy of insight as a change agent but also the strong emphasis on specific and concrete opportunities for learning new ways of responding, new ways of relating to other people, and new ways of perceiving oneself. The stress is on immediate experience and specific behaviors. Throughout the discussion there is an implicit invitation to recast the analysis in terms of learning theory of a general reinforcement type. Now the fifth source of gain involves a different level of abstraction and can best be talked about in terms of cognitive processes. I, of course, imply no disjunction between learning and cognition, but simply accept the fact that, at its current stage of development, psychology tends to use different constructs to describe these two aspects of human behavior.

All approaches to psychotherapy seem to have a more or less elaborated conception of the nature of man, which they, in essence, teach to the client. In doing so, they tie in with an ongoing process which is a unique and most exciting and engaging characteristic of man. Man constantly engages in building and repairing and extending and modifying cognitive structures that help him make personal sense of the world. The individual has got to have a cognitive house to live in to protect himself from the incomprehensibilities of existence as well as to provide some architecture for daily experiencing. He has to build defenses against the absurd in the human condition and at the same time find a scheme that will make possible reasonably accurate predictions of his own behavior and of the behavior of his wife, his boss, his professor, his physician, his neighbor, and of the policeman on the corner. He must adopt or invent a personal cosmology. When he invests this cosmology with passion, we may call it his personal mystique.

There are many available cosmologies for ordering the universe and increasing predictive efficiency in daily life. One of the first of these was provided by Pythagorous, some 3000 years ago. Contemporary religious systems seem useful in reducing uncertainty in at least some realms of experience, and for some people. Religions with established dogmas, elaborated rituals, and extensive use of personification appear to have widest appeal, as one would expect. Those with almost no formal doctrine probably appeal most to people who have at hand alternate systems for construing the world. Psychoanalysis provides a cognitive structure of remarkable cogency. Its range of applicability is not cosmic but mundane, which is one source of its appeal among pragmatic people. Its metaphor is engaging; its extensive use of reification simplifies matters, but not too much; its formulation of behavior dynamics is occasionally useful in predicting one's own behavior and the behavior of others. On the other hand, existential therapies would seem to be most acceptable to people who have come to suspect all institutionalized solutions (such as psychoanalysis) to the problem of meaning. Albert Ellis' rational therapy seems eminently suited to his clientele. I would guess that he works largely with bright, articulate, nonreligious, and reasonably well educated but not too disenchanted people who find the process and the model of rational analysis appealing and convincing. Client-centered therapy probably works best with clients who already have well developed but conflicting cognitive structures; they do not need to be taught a system for bringing order into their lives, but rather need to be helped to discover which system makes sense and feels right to them. George Kelly's fixed role therapy is, of course, the most forthright and charming method for providing a client with a cognitive structure for construing his world.

I think it possible to identify some criteria for assessing the adequacy of a personal cosmology and thus provide a therapist with some guidelines for dealing with the cognitive structures of the individual. Above all a person's cosmology must be convincing to him; when doubt occurs, anxiety mounts. Second, it should overlap reasonably well with the cosmologies of the people with whom he associates. If a person adopts a too divergent cosmology, he runs the risk of being declared psychotic and incarcerated. Then it should be perceived by the individual as internally consistent—or relatively so. When there is too great a discrepancy between self and self-ideal, for example, discontent ensues. It should contain, on the other hand, some dissonances of either internal or external origin. With a bit of dissonance, the individual will work to strengthen his major propositions about himself and his world. In addition, it should bring him into more intimate relationships with other people, for without such sustenance the spirit withers. Finally, it should have built in requirements for revision, for to live is to change, and to remain static is to die.

The individual seeks psychotherapy (or some other source of cognitive control) when his cosmology, his personal system for imposing order on the world, breaks down to an alarming degree. With increasing anxiety, order must be restored.

There are two summary points that I would make about this fifth source of gain in psychotherapy: (a) Man by his nature is going to erect cognitive structures to increase his feeling of control over his destiny, and (b) there is no way of establishing the validity of a particular order-giving structure independently of the individual who is going to use it. The concept of insight can have meaning only as a part of the process of elaborating on some particular system for interpreting events. There are no true insights, only more or less useful ones.

All systems of psychotherapy involve in varying measures the five kinds of experiences that I have described. Their effectiveness will depend on the extent to which they provide an opportunity for the client to experience closeness to another human being without getting hurt, to divest symbols associated with traumatic experiences of their anxiety producing potential, to use the transference situation to learn not to need neurotic distortions, to practice being responsible for himself, and to clarify an old or learn a new cognitive system for ordering his world. I am not prepared at the moment to assign beta weights to these several functions.

Insight: Hindsight and Foresight

Hobbs challenges many of our traditional assumptions concerning psychotherapy. He questions the whole notion of "help by talk" and points up the lack of words in the concrete experience of play therapy with children. His "well-springs" of therapeutic personality reorganization reflect many nonverbal sources of effect. With full recognition that therapy is a communication process, he raises the issue of whether "the adult fare" of "rational formulations" are the necessary modes of communication. Hobbs questions whether rational behavior emanates from insight or whether, instead, it takes place only after extensive personality and behavior reorganization. The whole notion of insight, Hobbs suggests, involves the client's "catching on to the therapist's personal system for interpreting the world of behavior." The therapist does not have to be right but he must be convincing.

It may well be that the main effect of the theoretical orientation that gives birth to insights is the confidence that it gives to the therapists involved. It provides the therapist with a cognitive map of the direction therapy is taking, and the consequent confidence that the therapist communicates to the client is a significant source of effective interpersonal processes. Rather than setting insight as a goal of therapy, however, Hobbs focuses upon the therapeutic relationship as an analogue of life. His five sources of gain in therapy revolve around conditions that provide an intimate, nonthreatening experience that affords the client a specific and concrete opportunity to look into himself and his relationꜱhip with the therapist, and to find "new ways of responding, new ways of relating to other people, and new ways of perceiving oneself." In sum, the client learns a new cosmology which makes possible more effective and facilitative intra- and interpersonal living.

In the following reading, Vance and Volsky (1962) concentrate on still another principal effect of counseling and psychotherapy. They borrow from the then-raging vogue in psychology, cognitive dissonance, and term one of the principal therapeutic goals "psychological discordance reduction."

PSYCHOLOGICAL DISCORDANCE
REDUCTION*

Forrest L. Vance
and
Theodore C. Volsky, Jr.

Many psychologists claim to engage in counseling; others claim to practice psychotherapy; some would say they do both. More often than not, we suspect, the self-description is contingent on the individual's willingness (or unwillingness) to work with clients who have been diagnosed, by self or others, as having "emotional problems." In some cases, the label may be related to whether or not the practitioner tends to place primary focus on emotive facets of behavior, regardless of the client's diagnostic status.

Clinical psychologists seem relatively content with this situation. They are secure in the belief that the term psychotherapy is generally understood. They take comfort in the wide acceptance and high prestige which the art enjoys with the professional community and with the public. This position is further reinforced by the popularization of abnormal psychology, psychiatry, and psychotherapeutic techniques in the mass media.

Counseling psychologists, on the other hand, apparently lack any comforting group conviction about what counseling is. The ambiguity

* Counseling and psychotherapy: Split personality or Siamese twins? *American Psychologist*, 1952, *17*, 565-570. Reprinted by permission of author and publisher.

of the term is a perennial topic of discussion, in dignified journal articles and learned symposia as well as in coffee cup seminars, without notable progress in the direction of agreement.

A bewildering variety of functions have been gathered under the general rubric, "counseling." A listing would include educative, evaluative, consultative, administrative, therapeutic, and advisory practices, with plenty of ground left to cover.

Brayfield (1961) has stated the problem forcefully. He has also conveyed the frustration of the counseling psychologist who, believing that "counseling" refers to something important, is unable to find the terminology adequate to describe or discuss it. We, too, are convinced that the current terminology is not adequate to communicate, with clear meaning, the psychologically complex work of the counseling psychologist. We also believe that strong action will be required to develop adequate, acceptable definitions in a discipline addicted to disagreement about basic terms.

The proposals which follow are made with the recognition that their usefulness depends on acceptance by the professional "body politic" which cannot be coerced by citing evidence or by appealing to theoretical authority. The meaning of a term or phrase is dependent on general acceptance, though much of our past theoretical and research work would lead us to conclude that some absolute meaning will be discovered in our data pools. The merits of these proposals are argued on the basis of the clarification they may provide and their fruitfulness in leading to researchable hypotheses.

DISENTANGLING PROCESS AND PRACTITIONER

The terms "psychotherapist" and "counselor" often are used as if the associated processes, psychotherapy and counseling, were plainly distinguishable and mutually exclusive activities. If this were true, these activities would indeed provide an obvious basis for identifying two independent specialties. In actual practice the specific activities of psychologists practicing these applied arts cannot be predicted accurately from their specialty designation alone. "Counselors" engage in psychotherapy and "psychotherapists" counsel. The only meaningful specialty designations within psychology are those like "clinical psychologist" and "counseling psychologist," as defined for membership purposes by the appropriate divisions of the American Psychological Association. These designations precisely identify the respective specialties, not on the basis of exclusive functions, but on the basis of a broad set of criteria involving type of training, professional setting, research interests, and the like; and are subject to redefinition at the will of the membership. On the other hand, terms such as "psychotherapy" or "counseling," which describe goal-related processes, can best be defined by studying those processes, without reference to the specialist using them.

A DEFINITION OF PSYCHOTHERAPY AS PROCESS

Psychotherapy can have reasonably clear meaning when viewed as a process and not as a profession. This meaning can be made more specific when modifiers such as client centered or psychoanalytic are also used.

In our view, psychotherapy denotes a process, usually implemented by interview techniques, which seeks to alter the client's receptor or response system in such a way that healthy behavior will occur in situations where unhealthy behavior has been typical. It is, in short, a kind of *re*learning, or *re*-education. It should also be emphasized that the old behavior is seen as pathological, and the new behavior is seen as healthy.

Psychotherapeutic processes aim to change the mechanisms of stimulus-response mediation in the direction of greater "healthfulness." In some theories, such as those identified with nondirective or client-centered techniques, attempts are made to achieve healthfulness in behavior as interpreted by the client's self-perception, hoping that changes will also be evident to others. Other techniques, such as the rational-emotive therapy of Ellis (1957, 1959a, 1959b), emphasize change in observable behavior, with the hope that self-perception will also change as a consequence. Regardless of variations in technique, however, psychotherapy deals with the pathological and seeks to cure.

A DEFINITION OF COUNSELING AS PROCESS

The situation in the realm of counseling is more troublesome. The term counseling has no traditional, generalized meaning other than the redundant expression, "the work done by counselors" or "a personalized helping relationship." The concept is not restricted to work done by counseling psychologists, or to work done within the psychologically oriented professions. To give greater specificity of meaning to the term requires more than redefinition. It might be possible to add to a definition such as "the use of datum and theory from the science of psychology as it bears relevance to the personalized helping relationship," such qualifiers as "by a certified or licensed psychologist," "by a qualified person," etc. However, this would not resolve the problem. The terminology would still be inadequate to communicate, even within the field of psychology, what the counseling process is.

In order to describe the psychologically complex work done by the counseling psychologist, we believe it is necessary to replace (rather than redefine) the term counseling, when used in reference to goal-related process, with unambiguous, theoretically useful concepts.

In contrast to clinical psychology, counseling psychology has not had a group of professional ancestors from whom to inherit a ready-made, well-established terminology for classifying a nonpathological clientele and for describing techniques used with this clientele. Counseling psychologists wishing to place the empirical data of their domain in the context of a dynamic psychology have tended to borrow ideas which belong to the study of psychopathology. In recent years, this has led to counseling theory and research more appropriate to the process of psychotherapy, as we have defined it, and to processes historically relevant to the goals of counseling psychologists.

Such terms as repression, projection, and displacement have been used to explain the behavioral phenomena of underachievement, job dissatisfaction, vocational uncertainty, and the like. This approach makes it appear that conflicts, choices, problem-solving behavior, and every form of psychological distress is associated with some form of mental illness. It is as though problem situations would not exist but for pathological response tendencies on the part of the individual. Or if affective expression is involved to any degree, it would seem to follow, when viewed against a criterion of current treatment methodologies, that the behavior is pathological, since emotional involvement of any sort is characteristically dealt with by means developed (and generally validated) for the treatment of emotional illness. If all emotional distress is pathological, then a psychologist must either practice psychotherapy or limit his functions to diagnostic work and providing information or simple advisory assistance.

This point of view is discouraging and, we believe, fallacious. It is our intent to make a case for the legitimate area of professional concern which exists between the definable extremes of psychometrics and psychotherapy. In the following paragraphs, we will attempt to describe a kind of nonpathological emotional distress that is clearly the special province of the counseling psychologist, using terms growing out of the situations with which he works and the techniques he employs.

SOME PSYCHOLOGICAL VARIABLES RELEVANT TO THE COUNSELING SITUATION

The situations that lead one to seek the help of a counseling psychologist are descriptively as well as psychologically complex, but some groups of descriptive concepts can be identified, around which practitioners tend to organize their data. Even at this purely descriptive level, no listing of variables relevant to client behavior could hope to be exhaustive, or to satisfy the preferences of all counseling psychologists. We will list some, for purposes of discussion, and leave the system incomplete to permit the addition of other important factors.

1. Abilities-aptitudes: capacities inferred from performance or from test data validated against performance criteria
2. Interests: measured commonalities with vocational reference groups
3. Performance: quantitative measures of significant productive activity
4. Personality: individual differences in the emotional-affective realm
5. Tangible assets-liabilities: physical, social, or economic factors influencing opportunity
6. External pressures: pervasive environmental influences.
7. Goals: client's preferred outcome of his present situation

Data related to these dimensions of client status are collected and used to select personnel, plan academic programs, suggest vocational objectives, resolve personal problems, plan budgets, resolve family disputes, and to perform any other function that can be gathered under that "cover-all" term, counseling. This list of diverse "counseling" functions suggests that there is no single goal-directed process by which counseling in general can be defined. There are a multitude of goals, each with a system of aims and procedures by which to achieve them. When these specific kinds of counseling are described, the result is a collection of unrelated functions which in no wise defines a unitary basic process.

Many of these separate kinds of counseling are readily describable, and are not at all likely to be confused with psychotherapy. However, when a counseling psychologist talks about "resolving personal problems," one might suspect that this is a method of smuggling psychotherapeutic techniques into his office. Many problems arise from attempts to define "counseling" or "counseling psychology" or "psychological counseling," or most recently, "clinical counseling" in a way that includes or excludes particular processes related to specific goals. Novel meanings for familiar terms do not achieve general acceptance, and the resulting failure of communication adds to the conceptual confusion. It is this kind of maneuver that Brayfield (1961) is criticizing in his reaction to what he calls the "positive mental health kick."

In the remainder of this paper, we will try to describe and give a neutral name to one type of psychological distress that is not pathological. Related counseling goals will also be discussed. This is seen as a first step toward clarification of what, to us, is a truly confused conceptual area of applied psychology.

PSYCHOLOGICAL DISCORDANCE
AS A SOURCE OF DISTRESS

When a client is unhappy because his goals call for abilities he lacks, or because he is required by external pressures to perform a job that is incompatible with his interests, it would be folly to label his distress neurotic. In fact, it would be easier to make a case for abnormality if he were undisturbed by such a situation. This kind of disturbance differs from pathology, in that it is judged to be appropriate to the realities of the client's situation. Still, personal problem-solving skills are impaired by this discordance-produced distress, just as they might be by pathological conditions.

People who seek counseling frequently complain of unhappiness related to incompatibilities among two or more aspects of their current situation. For example, inconsistencies may arise between interests and abilities, or abilities and performance, or goals and external pressures, and so on. Or, perhaps three or more of these factors may form an incompatible, discordant cluster. In such a situation, the counseling psychologist faces the task of helping an individual achieve harmony or some form of acceptable compromise among these discordant influences. While this paper is not concerned with a review of the literature, it is worth noting that the line of thought being developed finds support in research findings. There is a body of literature centered around investigation of the self-concept which contains many studies of psychological inconsistency. In particular, studies of actual self-concept in relation to idealized self-concept indicate that discrepancies between these perceptions, which we would interpret as a form of discordance, are associated with emotional-motivational states (Wylie, 1961). Festinger and his associates have done some highly relevant work. He has developed an extensive theory of social behavior around a concept of cognitive dissonance. This kind of discordance is a discrepancy between belief and behavior, and Festinger has shown that this state of affairs has motivational characteristics (1947, pp. 18, 275-279, 291). The concept of discordance in the present paper can be viewed as an expansion of this conceptualization which includes the consequences of discrepancies among any subset of a very large number of psychological variables, of which we have listed several examples particularly relevant to the counseling situation.

PSYCHOLOGICAL DISCORDANCE REDUCTION

When a counseling psychologist seeks to help a client find techniques of resolving a discordant situation, he is practicing an art that easily can be confused with psychotherapy. We know of no unambiguous, concise term for this process, and have labeled it "psychological discordance reduction" for discussion purposes, and will hereafter abbreviate it by the initials PDR. PDR is a general term for the psychologically sophisticated counseling procedures through which a client learns to improvise discordance-reducing behaviors.

No attempt is made to represent PDR as a term synonymous with counseling but rather as a system of related processes with a common generalized goal which can be culled from the greater pool of work done by the counseling psychologist. This culling also helps make clear that not all types of counseling are relevant to a discussion of the relationship between counseling and psychotherapy. Using psychological information to help a young person choose an appropriate college would not easily be confused with psychotherapy. And, if such a situation does involve evidence of discordance, it is not necessarily of such a magnitude as to be accompanied by a marked degree of emotional distress.

Many of the functions usually classified as counseling deal neither with pathology nor with discordance. PDR stands distinctively apart from both psychotherapy and other types of counseling functions. It does not seek to alter old and well-established response systems. Neither does it seek to displace behaviors which have been judged pathological by the self or an observer-other. PDR refers to educative rather than re-educative processes. The object is to aid the individual by adding new responses or perceptions to his repertoire, which can be used to achieve a less discordant behavior pattern in the future.

Confusion can arise at this point unless it is firmly kept in mind that neither PDR nor psychotherapy is practiced exclusively by any one professional group. All psychologists who offer personal interview services of either type inevitably will become involved in many kinds of processes. It is an unfortunate fact that practitioners often identify themselves with one process, in part by studiously attempting to avoid the others. In cases involving emotional distress, this can only lead to failure in the total job of psychological treatment, unless psychopathology and discordance are mutually exclusive processes. Our own experience leads us to believe they are not. Distressed clients frequently seem to present either a primarily pathological or a primarily discordant situation with a secondary involvement in the alternative area. Or a client may fluctuate between psychotherapeutic needs and PDR or other counseling needs within a series of interviews, or even within a single interview. The following model attempts to clarify this situation.

A TWO-FACTOR THEORY
OF PSYCHOLOGICAL DISTRESS

In Figure 1, psychopathology and psychological discordance have been plotted as two dimensions of a multivariate model. A third dimension labeled "decision making" represents only one more of the possible relevant variables which would exist in an "N" dimensional representation of the work of the counseling psychologist. The light vertical and horizontal lines divide this surface into regions of low, moderate, and high levels of discordance, psychopathology, or complexity of the decision-making process. Within some of these major regions we have indi-

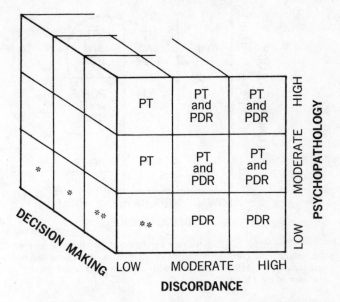

Fig. 1. A multivariate model of psychological treatment methodologies. Two asterisks indicate advisory services with minimal psychological involvement on the part of the client. One asterisk indicates relevant treatment methodologies for aiding the individual to resolve moderate or highly complex decisions. (The assumption in this representation is that this complexity can vary independently of affective involvement on the part of the individual.)

cated either **PDR** or psychotherapy (**PT**), or both, as relevant treatments. On the assumption that the various dimensions of behavior are uncorrelated, there would seem to be a set of situations in which *either* PDR or psychotherapy would be an appropriate treatment. This state of affairs would offer some justification for the existence of service centers devoted exclusively to one or the other of these functions. Such independence might also justify highly specialized, minimally overlapping training programs oriented towards only one of these kinds of psychological treatment.

If, however, the dimensions of discordance and psychopathology are correlated (as illustrated in Figure 2), as we would hypothesize, then the need for psychotherapy and PDR will covary, and combined treatment will generally be desirable. In this situation, it is harder to justify totally divergent training or treatment programs. The real meaning of the distinction between counseling psychology and clinical psychology seems to us to be a matter of emphasis on one or the other of these processes. It also seems clear to us that some extensive cross-fertilization is essential to the welfare of clients seeking help from practitioners of either spe-

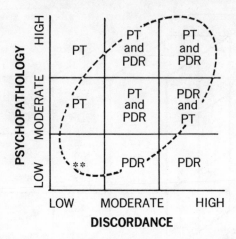

Fig. 2. The expected distribution of clients if psychopathology and discordance are correlated diagnostic categories. Two asterisks indicate advisory services with minimal psychological involvement on the part of the client.

cialty. We are convinced that all psychologists who attempt to offer personalized treatment services, inevitably will become involved in situations requiring both of the treatments we have tried to describe. Unfortunately, practitioners usually seek to identify themselves with one process by assiduously disclaiming the other, and thus increase the likelihood of failure in the total job of psychological treatment.

Clinical psychologists have focused on behavior pathology and its treatment to such an extent that they rarely are able to conceive of personality in nonpathological terms. From this perspective they are prone to indiscriminately label all PDR activities as inadvisable treatment of symptoms. One shudders to think how frequently psychotherapy is attempted as the sole treatment with individuals who complain of being unhappy or disinterested in their work. It is no less frightening to observe the nonpsychotherapeutic treatment such an individual receives from a vocationally naive psychiatrist or clinical psychologist *who does* recognize the nonpathological aspects of the situation. We are not forgetting those counseling psychologists who are unable or unwilling to recognize pathology in their clients. It is not unheard of to mistake delusions of grandeur for unrealistic goals, or to mistake a severe depression as vocational dissatisfaction. However, inept diagnosis on the part of either specialty provides no justification for less than adequate services.

Of course many counseling or clinical psychologists use the opportunities provided by their work to teach themselves skills in the alternate specialty. Some actually undergo a kind of professional metamorphosis, and are transformed completely into the alternate role. This kind of muddle might be avoided by training programs which recognize that many treatment processes are likely to be required in a sound program of psychological assistance for any particular individual seeking help. We have tried to describe and distinguish two of these treatment areas, and are convinced that there are few cases calling for either PDR or psychotherapy alone. Furthermore, our combined experience in observing, and practicing both PDR and psychotherapy, leads us to doubt that any practitioner manages to restrict himself to either of these processes exclusively in working with distressed individuals. Our clients force us to move back and forth from one treatment process to another as variations occur in the relative predominance of pathological versus discordant factors, sometimes even during a single interview.

This is not to claim that every psychologist must become an expert in all types of counseling and in psychotherapy, but rather that an expert in either field needs a sound basic background in the science of psychology and ought to have some competence in alternate diagnostic and treatment methodologies. Referral to a specialist in a complementary field will always be sound practice whenever it becomes apparent that this is in the client's best interest. Also, there are cases of severe discordance and pathology where joint treatment by two specialists is desirable.

Other common treatment processes which we have alluded to but not dealt with in this paper could be abstracted from the applied psychologist's domain by viewing additional situations with which this group is willing to deal, and the means by which they deal with them. For instance, it is desirable and encouraged behavior for high school graduates to seek a counseling psychologist when making a choice of college or career. Neither pathology nor discordance are necessarily involved. An alternate goal-related treatment method would probably best serve his needs. This illustrates the need for definition of other common psychological helping processes beyond those we have described.

Separate research needs and traditions have developed around a variety of specialized treatment processes in applied psychology. This is perhaps both inevitable and desirable, but it must not mislead us into believing that any given individual seeking psychological help can be understood fully from any one of these standpoints alone, or that he can be given adequate assistance without considering many of these aspects of his behavior. We have tried to explicate two such aspects of psychological distress and treatment. In the language of our title, we have come to see psychotherapy and at least one type of counseling, psychological discordance reduction, as Siamese twins. These processes are two distinct but closely related entities that share some vital concerns. Perhaps one

or both of these twins have split personalities, but the distinction between them is not delusional.

REFERENCES

Brayfield, A. H. Counseling psychology: Some dilemmas in the graduate school.
J. counsel. Psychol., 1961, *8*, 17-19.

Ellis, A. Rational psychotherapy and individual psychology. *J. indiv. Psychol.*,
1957, *13*, 38-44.

Ellis, A. Outcome of employing three techniques of psychotherapy. *J. clin.
Psychol.*, 1959, *13*, 344-350. (a)

Ellis, A. Rationalism and its therapeutic applications. *Ann. Psychother.*, 1959, *1*,
55-64. (b)

Festinger, L. *A theory of cognitive dissonance.* Evanston, Ill.: Peterson, 1957.

Wylie, Ruth C. *Self-concept: A critical survey of pertinent research literature.*
Lincoln: Univ. of Nebraska Press, 1961.

Beyond Our Pathological Noses

By our use of the terms "counseling" and "psychotherapy" in an
interchangeable fashion throughout this book, we have implied that
counseling and psychotherapy are additional instances of all interpersonal processes. Vance and Volsky make explicit some of the implications of the terms. We would, as they finally conclude, focus upon the
integrative rather than the differentiating characteristics of the two processes.

From a clarification of old terms, the authors go on to coin and
define a new one, "psychological discordance reduction." This term describes a technique that is helpful in enabling us to see beyond our
pathological noses and make us more effective practitioners. (We cannot
emphasize too often what we have said before: The psychotherapist is
shaped by what is effective for the client or he has no business counseling.) PDR is useful in helping clients because, as Vance and Volsky say,
it does not "seek to alter old and well-established response systems" and
yet does not exclude new and alternate responses.

We do not, however, see the technique as being in the "special
realm" of the counseling psychologist or anyone else. We prefer to
think of a mental health profession instead of the diverse characterizations of psychiatry and social work, guidance, personnel, and clinical and
counseling psychology. With that viewpoint, we hope to see more clearly
the commonalities of human encounters. Rather than focusing upon the
peculiarities of any one helping area (Vance and Volsky characterize

counselors as data collectors who "select . . . plan . . . suggest . . . re-solve . . ."), we would prefer to discover the means by which all of these working relationships begin—now the client is involved in process. In the next article, Schofield (1964) provides an extensive review of the common factors of counseling and psychotherapy.

SOME GENERAL FACTORS
IN COUNSELING AND THERAPY *
William Schofield

The controversial survey of the available statistics on the amount of recovery or significant improvement which is achieved by neurotics under psychotherapy was interpreted by its author [Eysenck] as failing to demonstrate that such therapy is effective. He used as control groups neurotics admitted to state hospitals and psychologically disabled patients treated by general physicians, interpreting the recovery rates of those patients as expressive of the base rate of "spontaneous recovery" in the absence of specific psychotherapy. His use of the hospitalized neurotics and the insured disability cases as controls has been criticized on the grounds both that they were atypical of the patients usually seen for outpatient psychotherapy and that they were actually the recipients of psychotherapeutic influences although these might have been casual and seemingly incidental to other aspects of their treatment. Persons taking this position with respect to the control samples, whose recovery and improvement rates were not reliably less than those of the patients who were treated by skilled psychotherapists, could make the interpretation that the data really show that psychotherapy is effective to a certain degree and that its effectiveness is not a function of specifics of method or of setting.

> "Statistical studies of psychotherapy consistently report that about two-thirds of neurotic patients . . . are improved immediately after treatment, regardless of the type of psychotherapy they have received, and the same improvement rate has been found for patients who have not received any treatment that was *deliberately* psychotherapeutic." (2) (Italics ours.)

---

* This reading is part of a chapter titled "The nature of the process: General factors," in *Psychotherapy: The purchase of friendship.* © 1964. Reprinted by permission of Prentice-Hall, Englewood Cliffs, N. J.

Such interpretations of the limited statistical data are consonant with the frequently offered casual observation, based on the testimonial literature, that all schools of psychotherapy claim a fair number of successes. Together the actuarial interpretation and the clinical overview are consistent with the thesis of *common factors*. This thesis, based upon arm-chair analyses of the irreducible minimum variables in any psychotherapeutic interaction between persons, was stated by psychologists in 1936 (7) and 1952 (1), by an eminent psychiatrist (2), and by still another psychologist (5), in 1961. Briefly stated, this thesis holds that there are certain basic factors (processes, forces, or dimensions) that occur in every form of psychotherapy and that play essentially the same role in every psychotherapeutic model, that it is the factors common to all types of therapy that account for whatever positive results are obtained by any of them. Separate analyses of the common factors have enumerated as few as three or four to as many as five or six. In recent years there have been some ingenious researches designed to tease out the nature and number of uniformities across "schools." [1]

In a psychological analysis of potential common factors in various methods of psychotherapy it is well to start with a clear view of those differences which are explicit. A "school" of psychotherapy is identified by: (a) a theory of personality or of psychopathology, and (b) a set of techniques and rules for the conduct of therapy. Schools vary in the degree to which their prominence or uniqueness is related to the features of their *theory* or to the nature of their *tactics*. Freud wrote extensively on the theory of psychoanalysis but was relatively silent about treatment technique. The early appeal of Roger's "nondirective" therapy was largely in the explicitness and simplicity of the methods he espoused rather than in his theory of personality. To the extent that each system of psychotherapy has an articulated theory it is easy to point out the differences among them at the level of *theory*. But, the theories do not have direct impact on the patient; patients do not "experience" the theories. Therapists of different theoretical persuasion may be of differing effectiveness because of the differences in their respective theories only in measure as those theoretical differences lead to differences in the way in which they conduct therapy—the actual process by which they interact with, learn about, and influence their patients.

Apparently extensive differences in two theories need not be paralleled by notable differences in therapeutic technique, especially as some theories of therapy specify very little about the tactics of treatment. Even where extensive differences are spelled out in the specific procedures of therapy associated with particular systems, it is not certain that these differences will be clearly manifested in the actual conduct of therapeutic

---

[1] *Editors' note*. Pertinent findings are reviewed in Chapter 5 of Schofield's book.

interviews by representatives of the systems. In one survey of orthodox psychoanalysts who were "card-carrying" adherents to the Freudian school, it was found that there was striking lack of consistency with respect to a wide range of specific practices (3).

The differences among systems of psychotherapy either at the level of their personality theory or their prescribed modes of treatment will account for any potentially demonstrated difference in their effectiveness only to the extent that it is demonstrated that the clinicians practicing each system do in fact carry out significantly different processes in their patient contacts. But, as one factor common to all systems there is some theory, some more or less highly explicated theoretical formulation of psychopathology and the therapeutic process. It has been suggested that some sort of "systematic ideology" may be an essential element in successful therapy:

> Whether the therapist talks in terms of psychoanalysis or Christian Science is from this point of view relatively unimportant as compared with the *formal consistency* with which the doctrine employed is adhered to, for by virtue of this consistency the patient receives a schema for achieving some sort and degree of personality organization. (7)

If we examine the broad outlines of psychotherapy as an interpersonal transaction, certain structural properties emerge which are unavoidably common to all forms of psychotherapy; these common factors do not contribute to differences in the conduct of the treatment and they cannot explain any differences in results which might be demonstrated for the "different" approaches. But these common factors may well be of considerable *potency* and may account for most of the positive results which each of the schools claim.

In essence, psychotherapy is conversation with therapeutic intent. As conversation it entails all of the modes of communication (some facilitant and some deterrent) that are active whenever two persons speak to one another. Language carries the major mediational load and is the primary transmitter of communication in conversation. We have long been aware of the distinctions between connotative and denotative language—words have "agreed upon" meanings as specified by the dictionary, but they also have more or less individualistic meanings for each person who uses them. Communication would be easier (simpler and more accurate) if it were humanly possible for persons to restrict their language to purely denotative words; it is not. While members of a culture may share the same official dictionary, they naturally do not share in identical personal experiences whereby words acquire the personal connotations that individuals unconsciously seek to use in their conversations. Some words make for better communication because they have a scientifically precise definition, or in the nature of the things to which they refer there is a limited range of possible connotations; other words tend to contribute a lot of "static" to communication because they do not permit of objective definition but rather represent certain personal meanings of high frequency in a particular group of persons. The following lists will suggest this aspect of the communication problem:

More denotative words	More connotative words
Inch	Good
Minute	Strong
Black	Liberal
Round	Pretty
North	Smart

This is only one of the problem areas receiving intensive investigation in the rapidly evolving technical fields knows as psycholinguistics and communication theory.

Man has long been aware that his oral communications are neither given nor received purely in terms of the words spoken (and their explicit or implicit meanings) but that additional and particular meanings are communicated by the general context of their utterance. The most important part of this contextual communication is undoubtedly the facial expression of the conversants. The particular meaning of a word is frequently signaled by a frown or a smile or a grimace. And responses to questions or assertions may be wordlessly communicated by a nod, by a smile, by "silence freighted with meaning." When communication is emotionally charged, when the topic of conversation is loaded with emotional "meanings" as is frequently the case in psychotherapy, it is imperative that the therapist be skilled in receiving (and sending?) wordless messages or words whose meaning has been silently labeled by the emotional attitude of the sender. In accepting candidates for advanced training in the specialty of psychotherapy, it is generally true that considerable emphasis is given to intellectual ability, with applicants of very superior general intelligence being preferred. There is little in the nature of substantive information or treatment technique to be learned that justifies such emphasis. However, sensitivity to the subtle aspects of the wordless communications in psychotherapy is a most important dimension of therapeutic skill. This skill is not too readily learned but rather reflects native or very early acquired aptitudes that are highly correlated with general intelligence. And a high level of general intelligence is required to meet the scholastic requirements (many of them irrelevant to psychotherapy) that loom large in the formal education of the physician, psychologist, and social worker.[2]

---

[2] *Editors' note.* See Chapter 6 of Schofield's book.

This nonlinguistic aspect of oral communication is a difficult area for research but it is part of the total domain of psycholinguistics. Any general theory of communication must and will encompass the conversations of psychotherapy and, as a general theory, the researches generated by it must inevitably show those particulars of the communication process which are common to all such conversations. Thus, the essentials of the communication process are identical regardless of the school of psychotherapy under whose aegis a particular therapeutic conversation is being conducted. The participants do not have access to special communication media beyond those of any other conversation—they are limited to words and sentences, to assertions and questions, to the silent "labels" of smiles and frowns, tics and tears, and to silences. Within the frame of the communality of the communication process which is shared by all approaches to psychotherapy is a particular common factor—the therapist. Regardless of his theoretical allegiance, the therapist is an expert conversationalist whose specialized equipment include: sensitivity to the emotional nuances of the patient's communication, an ability to listen selectively, facility in encouraging the patient to start and continue conversation, deftness in leading the patient to particular topics, capacity both to tolerate the patient's silences and to use his own silence in communicating. These are basic common skills of all expert psychotherapists, contributing to their capacity to establish and maintain communication. The presence of these skills in high degree is, unfortunately, not necessarily correlated with the achievement of a valid understanding of the patient (a common goal of most schools), nor with achievement of successful treatment (the ultimate goal of all schools).

Although this section is concerned with the factors common to all psychotherapies, it is well to point out those areas in which explicit differences are clearly possible and even likely. The essential elements and processes of communication are shared alike by all schools, but the selection and emphasis of *topics* for conversation may well differ systematically. In accordance with one theory, the therapist may emphasize certain topics for exploration (and explanation) to the exclusion of others, and in a variety of ways restrict the therapeutic conversation to these topics. Another school will emphasize that the topics for discussion should be arrived at spontaneously and determined primarily by the patient. One theory may emphasize the self-concept as the topic of therapeutic conversation while another may focus on specific symptomatology. A theory which was more "correct" about the topics to be conversed about might achieve some potentially demonstrable margin of success beyond that of other approaches by virtue of this "correctness."

Indirect research evidence suggests that there may be less actual consistent variation in the favored topics of different therapists than their theories would suggest. For example, one would expect psychoanalytically oriented therapists to encourage their patients to reveal their sex attitudes and histories. When a group of such therapists was asked for extended, structured descriptions of patients whom they had been treating for at least 25 hours, it was found that they frequently did not have information about such matters as attitudes toward masturbation, extra-marital relations, and other topics (4).

There are additional structural aspects of the therapeutic conversation which set it apart from other classes of person-to-person communication but which are common to all forms of psychotherapy. One of these is the status relationships of therapy. The therapist has a certain status of ascendancy, authority, or power. This status is expressed through certain symbols: he has a title (most frequently that of "doctor"), he has certificates and diplomas which imply that he has received special, technical training, he is a member of (or closely affiliated with members of) an established profession from which he derives his visible identification as a "socially sanctioned healer" (2, p. 2). He may derive additional symbolic identification from his place of business (clinic or hospital), from his professional dress (the white coat), or from his "tools" (for example, Rorschach cards, tape recorder).

Part of the ascendant status of the therapist is reflective of the fact that his client is supplicant. The patient, suffering and wanting to be helped, seeks out the therapist and comes to him. "Almost all psychotherapy is to some degree disturbing to the patient because it is deflating to the ego to be so maladjusted that it becomes necessary to place oneself in the embarrassing position of having to admit failure and seek help from others" (8). This subjectively experienced lowered status of the client has potential for effecting the therapeutic process positively at the beginning of treatment and negatively in later stages. In the beginning he may be more ready to accept the suggestions of the ascendant therapist while later on, when less acutely distressed, his persisting sensitivity to the status differential can motivate obstinacies that are too luxuriously interpreted as "transference" phenomena (1, p. 304).

This status relationship which is common, at least initially, to all psychotherapies generates or supports certain psychological qualities that are universal. In brief, both the therapist and the patient from their respective positions have certain expectancies. The therapist honestly expects to be able to help his client; he knows the dimensions of his status and from these dimensions (training, experience, membership) he expects to be helpful. From this underlying expectation his basic attitude is one of confidence and in a variety of ways his positive expectation and confidence are communicated to the patient.

The patient expects to be helped because in seeking out the therapist he is following the general recommendation of his society as to where he is to expect to be helped. Some patients go reluctantly, even resentfully, to the therapist and without any preformed faith in the process. But even these, since they are never literally forced, cannot be thoroughly convinced that nothing will happen. Increasingly in our society because of the improved education of the public the patient brings to his therapist a readiness to be helped and some faith in the process. Together these initial expectancies of the therapist and the patient provide a positive psychological atmosphere for the powerful healing effects of implicit suggestion. These implicit forces of suggestion are augmented by the social structuring of the on-going therapy as a series of controlled conversations in which, according to some theory that yields "formal consistency," the therapist seeks to persuade the patient (and the patient to be persuaded?) toward new views of himself, and of his problems. These status-derived forces of general suggestion and persuasion are common to all forms of psychotherapy.

Apart from the status roles of the two participants, still another structural factor is common to all approaches. The relationship between the therapist and his patient is not a spontaneous one but rather a controlled, circumscribed, or limited one (1, 2). The frequency of visits, generally regular (and most commonly weekly), their timing and duration, are explicitly determined. What is permissible and desirable for the patient to do during the treatment hour is controlled and what demands he may make of his therapist are very definitely limited. In light of the prolonged nature of the relationship, the intimacy of the material shared, and the qualities of rapport and mutual respect that are engendered, this fact of definite controls on what the patient may do or fail to do, and what he can require of the therapist, constitutes what may be the most distinctive feature of the therapeutic relationship. This feature of controlled relationship is espoused in nearly all methods of psychotherapy.

The quality of the relationship is given specific attention in all formulations of psychotherapy and certain aspects of the relationship are given universal emphasis. There is general agreement that it is the responsibility of the therapist to be accepting of the patient and to communicate his acceptance to the patient. This acceptance of the patient is a complex of therapist attitudes that includes respect for the patient as an individual, positive regard for his personality and his potential, warmth, kindness, and continuing willingness to help no matter what the symptoms or defects of the patient. Most crucially, this attitude of acceptance requires that the therapist relate to his patient in a nonjudgmental, noncritical, nonpunitive way. Of course, failures of conformity, socially inimical attitudes, or even antisocial behavior may not be at the heart of the problem for which the patient seeks help and the therapist may learn of them only incidentally, but he must avoid value assessments which cause him inadvertently to communicate a rejection of the patient. This is a difficult quality of relationship both to describe and to establish effectively. The therapist may share many of his society's values and mores and will not think that it is good for them to be violated or neglected, but it is not his function to condemn or to try to recreate an individual in his own image. This quality of "acceptance" *in our culture at this time* is peculiarly restricted to the psychotherapeutic contract, but it is common to all such contracts. In this sense, psychotherapy provides a very special, perhaps ideal, form of friendship.

It is reasonable to presume that a further reflection of the communality of the quality of acceptance is found in the expectation of the average patient who seeks a therapeutic relationship. The hopeful expectation of "unconditional positive regard" from somebody may well be one of the common factors leading to an increasing demand for psychotherapy and contributing to a positive response when it is available (6).

Whether or not the impact of the mental health movement and its attendant educational programs has created a general expectation of the therapeutically prescribed acceptance, it seems that a majority of patients have an expectation that their revelation of self and others will be treated with complete confidentiality. Again, in the principle that the patient's communications are "privileged" and protected in principle and by law from release in any form or medium which would cause him or others embarrassment or hurt, we have a structural factor shared by all schools of psychotherapy. As a common factor of the therapy contract, it may significantly contribute to the total therapeutic impact of the relationship. It is, by contrast, a notable characteristic of our general culture that we are gossipy and notoriously indifferent to the ethics of personal confidences!

We have reviewed aspects of psychotherapeutic relationship that are basically of a structural nature, that stem from the universal status factors of supplicant and benefactor and from the general provisions of the psychotherapeutic contract. Are there any aspects of the *process* of psychotherapy that permit of the possibility of being general and not restricted to those therapeutic conversations which eventuate under the aegis of a particular theory? Over fifty years ago, when psychotherapy was aborning, Josef Breuer discovered the principle of catharsis. He observed that patients who were able to recall the origins of a symptom and to give uninhibited expression to the emotions attendant upon the situation in which it evolved were subsequently relieved symptomatically and generally improved in their over-all adjustment. This function of emotional purging or catharsis came gradually to be perceived as but one phase of a more general process in which the patient, under the accepting, encouraging, and supportive friendship of the therapist, was enabled to give expression to his conflicts, his anxiety, his guilts, his resentments, to relieve his previously bottled up feelings without fear of rejection or misunderstanding. To this basic process whereby the suffering supplicant is helped to achieve release from the tormenting burden of his previously suppressed (or repressed) emotions, from the personal isolation stemming from his previously unshared feelings, is given the name ventilation. Catharsis and ventilation are the naturally inevitable first steps in any truly intimate personal relationship, requiring nothing more than an *accepting* (and probably understanding) auditor. It is difficult to imagine any formal psychotherapy which could either in theory or *expert* practice deliberately prevent the occurrence of such ventilation.[3] And ventilation and catharsis as general factors may prove to account for a sizable portion of the total therapeutic impact of all psychotherapies.

In the prolonged relationships of intensive psychotherapy, it must be recognized that the patient has opportunity for repeated expression of "punishable" ideas and feelings which do not lead in therapy to punishment or rejection. The anxiety originally accompanying the thoughts is gradually extinguished or reduced through repeated expression without pain. Then it is possible for the patient to see his *bêtes noires* differently, to think differently about them, and to plan imaginatively to react differently to their real life representations. Eventually, with the support and positive suggestion of the therapist, he is able to experiment with new modes of response to those persons and situations which are anxiety symbols and, eventually, to extend the process of learning (and extinction of inappropriate, anxious responses) to the "real" world outside of his therapist's office.

Although there are differences in interpretation as to the elements of the process, differences in emphasis as to whether it is mostly an extinction of old, inappropriate responses or an acquisition of new, more appropiate responses, differences as to whether there are basic generalities or necessary specifics in the content of neurosis, nearly all psychotherapists agree that psychotherapy is a learning process. In this learning, the therapist serves as guide, tutor, model, and primary source of reward. To the extent that all therapists partake of the role of teacher, self-acknowledged or not, we have yet another common dimension.

Considering the range and basic nature of these dimensions and processes which are common to all forms of conversation with therapeutic intent, it is remarkable that so many have found so much to say about such a variety of apparent diversities in theory and practice. But in our

---

[3] It is possible that full ventilation may be prevented or delayed by the inexperienced, insensitive, or inept therapist who is overly active and insufficiently appreciative of the self-curative forces in nature.

culture it is far more acceptable to present oneself as an expert in some moderately occult and complex professionalized technique than to suggest the more modest (grandiose?) claim to being generally perceptive and intelligent about personal problems. Certainly the average counselor can much sooner be confident that he is technically proficient than he can be assured that he is wise.

In view of the extensive variety and possibly sizable therapeutic power of those factors which do appear to be shared by all schools of psychotherapy, it is suggested that we might do well to concentrate our researches on these potential mechanisms of the psychotherapeutic effect, and to emphasize carefully the methods of optimizing their influence when selecting and training psychotherapists, rather than to pursue almost exclusively the search for differences in therapeutic practice that *theoretically* should be there and *theoretically* should make a difference.

REFERENCES

1. Black, J. D. Common factors of the patient-therapist relationships in diverse psychotherapies. *J. clin. Psychol.*, 1952, *8*, 302-306.
2. Frank, J. D. *Persuasion and healing: A comparative study of psychotherapy.* Baltimore: Johns Hopkins Press, 1961.
3. Glover, E. *The technique of psychoanalysis.* New York: International Universities Press, 1955.
4. Glueck, B. C., Meehl, P. E., and Schofield, W. The skilled clinician's assessment of personality. Research project, Univer. of Minnesota, Dept. of Psychiatry, and Institute of Living, Hartford, Connecticut.
5. Hobbs, N. Sources of gain in psychotherapy. *Amer. Psychologist,* 1962, *17*, 741-747.
6. Rogers, C. R. The necessary and sufficient conditions of therapeutic personality change. *J. consult. Psychol.*, 1957, *21*, 95-103.
7. Rosenzweig, S. Some implicit common factors in diverse methods of psychotherapy. *Amer. J. Orthopsychiat.*, 1936, *6*, 412-415.
8. Thorne, F. C. A critique of nondirective methods of psychotherapy. *J. abnorm. soc. Psychol.*, 1944, *39*, 459-470.

Reflections of Friendship

Schofield's comprehensive review of the commonalities of counseling and psychotherapy leads us to one definite conclusion: *The therapist has what the client wants.* That is, the therapist expects to help and the client expects to be helped, the therapist is confident and the client lacks confidence, and so forth. The model concerning what the therapist has and what the client does not have may be extended to its logical conclusion in which the therapist, possessing the inverse of those dimensions of the client's condition, serves as a true model for the client's ultimate level of functioning. Thus, not only does the therapist serve as "guide, tutor, model, and primary source of reward," but the client comes to look in many ways like the effective or the ineffective therapist. Even *not to act* is to accept responsibility for the client's learning not to act.

In this regard, it is important to note that one of the commonalities in therapy, as Schofield points out, is that "the relationship between the therapist and his patient is not a spontaneous one but rather a controlled, circumscribed, and limited one." Again and again the mode of enabling the client to achieve authenticity and spontaneity is a process that lacks authenticity and spontaneity. We place great faith in the client's ultimate strength to break free of this most destructive feature of the therapeutic relationship. Concerning the "very special, perhaps ideal, form of friendship" that Schofield describes as being provided by the "nonjudgmental, noncritical," nonevaluative therapist, we have only one question: Who can benefit from a relationship with someone who does not respond naturally? We cannot imaging any partners more incompatible than those in a friendship *controlled* by a *nonjudgmental* person.

In the next article, Alexander (1963) suggests a rapprochement between clinical and learning theories and practices.

PSYCHOANALYSIS AND LEARNING THEORY *

Franz Alexander

Most of what we know about the basic dynamic principles of psychotherapy is derived from the psychoanalytic process.

One of the striking facts in this field is that the intricate procedure of psychoanalytic treatment underwent so few changes since its guiding principles were formulated by Freud between 1912 and 1915 (7-11). Meanwhile substantial developments took place in theoretical knowledge, particularly in ego psychology. Moreover, in all other fields of medicine, treatments underwent radical changes resulting from a steadily improving

* The dynamics of psychotherapy in the light of learning theory. *American Journal of Psychiatry*, 1963, *201*, 440-448. Reprinted by permission of publisher. This paper was originally read at the 119th annual meeting of The American Psychiatric Association, St. Louis, Missouri, May 1963.

understanding of human physiology and pathology. No medical practitioner could treat patients with the same methods he learned 50 years
ago without being considered antiquated. In contrast, during the same
period the standard psychoanalytic treatment method as it is taught
today in psychoanalytic institutes remained practically unchanged.

It is not easy to account for this conservatism. Is it due to the
perfection of the standard procedure which because of its excellence does
not require reevaluation and improvement, or does it have some other
cultural rather than scientific reasons?

Among several factors one is outstanding: to be a reformer of psychoanalytic treatment was never a popular role. The need for unity
among the pioneer psychoanalysts, who were universally rejected by
outsiders, is one of the deep cultural roots of this stress on conformity.
The majority of those who had critical views became "dissenters" either
voluntarily or by excommunication. Some of these became known as
neo-Freudians. Some of the critics, however, remained in the psychoanalytic fold.

(Some analysts jocularly expressed the view that the stress on conformity was a defense against the analyst's unconscious identification
with Freud, each wanting to become himself a latter day Freud and
founder of a new school. Conformity was a defense against too many
prima donnas.) Another important factor is the bewildering complexity
of the psychodynamic processes occurring during treatment. It appears
that the insecurity which this intricate field necessarily provokes creates
a defensive dogmatism which gives its followers a pseudo-security. Almost
all statements concerning technique could be legitimately only highly
tentative. "Tolerance of uncertainty" is generally low in human beings.
A dogmatic reassertion of some traditionally accepted views—seeking
for a kind of consensus—is a common defense against uncertainty.

In spite of all this, there seems to be little doubt that the essential
psychodynamic principles on which psychoanalytic treatment rests have
solid observational foundations. These constitute the areas of agreement
among psychoanalysts of different theoretical persuasion. Briefly, they
consist in the following observations and evaluations:

1. During treatment unconscious (repressed) material becomes conscious.
   This increases the action radius of the conscious ego: the ego becomes
   cognizant of unconscious impulses and thus is able to coordinate
   (integrate) the latter with the rest of conscious content.
2. The mobilization of unconscious material is achieved mainly by two
   basic therapeutic factors: interpretation of material emerging during
   free association and the patient's emotional interpersonal experiences

in the therapeutic situation (transference). The therapist's relatively objective, nonevaluative, impersonal attitude is the principal factor in mobilizing unconscious material.

3. The patient shows resistance against recognizing unconscious content. Overcoming this resistance is one of the primary technical problems of the treatment.

4. It is only natural that the neurotic patient will sooner or later direct his typical neurotic attitude toward his therapist. He develops a transference which is the repetition of interpersonal attitudes, mostly the feelings of the child to his parents. This process is favored by the therapist encouraging the patient to be himself as much as he can during the interviews. The therapist's objective nonevaluative attitude is the main factor, not only in mobilizing unconscious material during the process of free association, but also in facilitating the manifestation of transference. The original neurosis of the patient, which is based on his childhood experiences, is thus transformed in an artificial "transference neurosis" which is a less intensive repetition of the patient's "infantile neurosis." The resolution of these revived feelings and behavior patterns—the resolution of the transference neurosis—becomes the aim of the treatment.

There is little disagreement concerning these fundamentals of the treatment. Controversies, which occur sporadically, pertain primarily to the technical means by which the transference neurosis can be resolved. The optimal intensity of the transference neurosis is one of the points of contention.

This is not the place to account in detail the various therapeutic suggestions which arose in recent years. Most of these modifications consisted in particular emphases given to certain aspects of the treatment. There are those who stressed interpretation of resistance (Wilheim Reich, Helmuth Kaiser), while others focused on the interpretation of repressed content. Fenichel stated that resistance cannot be analyzed without making the patient understand what he is resisting (6).

It is most difficult to evaluate all these modifications because it is generally suspected that authors' accounts about their theoretical views do not precisely reflect what they are actually doing while treating patients. The reason for this discrepancy lies in the fact that the therapist is a "participant observer" who is called upon constantly to make decisions on the spot. The actual interactional process between therapist and patient is much more complex than the theoretical accounts about it. In general there were two main trends: 1) emphasis on cognitive insight as a means of breaking up the neurotic patterns; 2) emphasis upon the emotional experiences the patient undergoes during treatment. These are not mutually exclusive, yet most controversies centered around emphasis on the one or the other factor: cognitive versus experiential.

While mostly the similarity between the transference attitude and the original pathogenic childhood situation has been stressed, I emphasized the therapeutic significance of the difference between the old family conflicts and the actual doctor-patient relationship. This difference is what allows "corrective emotional experience" to occur, which I consider as the central therapeutic factor both in psychoanalysis proper and also in analytically oriented psychotherapy. The new settlement of an old unresolved conflict in the transference situation becomes possible not only because the intensity of the transference conflict is less than that of the original conflict, but also because the therapist's actual response to the patient's emotional expressions is quite different from the original treatment of the child by the parents. The fact that the therapist's reaction differs from that of the parent, to whose behavior the child adjusted himself as well as he could with his own neurotic reactions, makes it necessary for the patient to abandon and correct these old emotional patterns. After all, this is precisely one of the ego's basic functions—adjustment to the existing external conditions. As soon as the old neurotic patterns are revived and brought into the realm of consciousness, the ego has the opportunity to readjust them to the changed external and internal conditions. This is the essence of the corrective influence of those series of experiences which occur during treatment (2, 3). As will be seen, however, the emotional detachment of the therapist turned out under observational scrutiny to be less complete than this idealized model postulates.

Since the difference between the patient-therapist and the original child-parent relationship appeared to me a cardinal therapeutic agent, I made technical suggestions derived from these considerations. The therapist in order to increase the effectiveness of the corrective emotional experiences should attempt to create an interpersonal climate which is suited to highlight the discrepancy between the patient's transference attitude and the actual situation as it exists between patient and therapist. For example, if the original childhood situation which the patient repeats in the transference was between a strict punitive father and a frightened son, the therapist should behave in a calculatedly permissive manner. If the father had a doting all-forgiving attitude towards his son, the therapist should take a more impersonal and reserved attitude. This suggestion was criticized by some authors, that these consciously and purposefully adopted attitudes are artificial and will be recognized as such by the patient. I maintained however that the therapist's objective, emotionally not participating attitude is itself artificial inasmuch as it does not exist between human beings in actual life. Neither is it as complete as has been assumed. This controversy will have to wait to be decided by further experiences of practitioners.

I made still other controversial technical suggestions aimed at intensifying the emotional experiences of the patient. One of them was changing the number of interviews in appropriate phases of the treatment in order to make the patient more vividly conscious of his dependency needs by frustrating them.

Another of my suggestions pertains to the ever-puzzling question of termination of treatment. The traditional belief is that the longer an analysis lasts the greater is the probability of recovery. Experienced analysts more and more came to doubt the validity of this generalization. If anything, this is the exception; very long treatments lasting over many years do not seem to be the most successful ones. On the other hand, many so-called "transference cures" after very brief contact have been observed to be lasting. A clear correlation between duration of treatment and its results has not been established. There are no reliable criteria for the proper time of termination. Improvements observed during treatment often prove to be conditioned by the fact that the patient is still being treated. The patient's own inclination to terminate or to continue the treatment is not always a reliable indication. The complexity of the whole procedure and our inability to estimate precisely the proper time of termination induced me to employ the method of experimental temporary interruptions, a method which in my experience is the most satisfactory procedure. At the same time it often reduces the total number of interviews. The technique of tentative temporary interruptions is based on trusting the natural recuperative powers of the human personality, which are largely underestimated by many psychoanalysts. There is an almost general trend toward "overtreatment." A universal regressive trend in human beings has been generally recognized by psychoanalysts. Under sufficient stress every one tends to regress to the helpless state of infancy and seek help from others. The psychoanalytic treatment situation caters to this regressive attitude. As Freud stated, treatments often reach a point where the patient's will to be cured is outweighed by his wish to be treated.

In order to counteract this trend a continuous pressure on the patient is needed to make him ready to take over his own management as soon as possible. During temporary interruptions patients often discover that they can live without their analyst. When they return, the still not worked out emotional problems come clearly to the forefront.[1]

---

[1] This type of "fractioned analysis," which was practiced in the early days of the Out-patient Clinic of the Berlin Institute, is an empirical experimental way to find the correct time for termination.

Furthermore, I called attention to Freud's distinction between two forms of regression. He first described regression to a period of ego-development in which the patient was still happy, in which he functioned well. Later he described regressions to traumatic experiences, which he explained as attempts to master subsequently an overwhelming situation of the past. During psychoanalytic treatment both kinds of regression occur. Regressions to pre-traumatic or pre-conflictual periods—although they offer excellent research opportunity for the study of personality development—are therapeutically not valuable. Often we find that the patient regresses in his free associations to preconflictual early infantile material as a maneuver to evade the essential pathogenic conflicts. This material appears as "deep material" and both patient and therapist in mutual self-deception spend a great deal of time and effort to analyze this essentially evasive material. The recent trend to look always for very early emotional conflicts between mother and infant as the most common source of neurotic disturbances is the result of overlooking this frequent regressive evasion of later essential pathogenic conflicts. Serious disturbances of the early symbiotic mother-child relation occur only with exceptionally disturbed mothers. The most common conflicts begin when the child has already a distinct feeling of being a person (ego-awareness) and relates to his human environment, to his parents and siblings as to individual persons. The oedipus complex and sibling rivalry are accordingly the common early sources of neurotic patterns. There are many exceptions, of course, where the personality growth is disturbed in very early infancy.

Another issue which gained attention in the post-Freudian era is the therapist's neglect of the actual present life situation in favor of preoccupation with the patient's past history. This is based on the tenet that the present life circumstances are merely precipitating factors, mobilizing the patient's infantile neurosis. In general, of course, the present is always determined by the past. Freud in a rather early writing proposed the theory of complementary etiology. A person with severe ego defects acquired in the past will react to slight stress situations in his present life with severe reactions; a person with a relatively healthy past history will require more severe blows of life to regress into a neurotic state (12). Some modern authors like French, Rado, myself, and others feel that there is an unwarranted neglect of the actual life circumstances (1, 15). The patient comes to the therapist when he is at the end of his rope, is entangled in emotional problems which have reached a point when he feels he needs help. These authors feel that the therapist never should allow the patient to forget that he came to him to resolve his present problem. The understanding of the past should always be subordinated to the problems of the present. Therapy is not the same as genetic research. Freud's early emphasis upon the reconstruction of past history was the result of his primary interest in research. At first he felt he must know the nature of the disease he proposes to cure. The interest in past history at the expense of the present is the residue of the historical period when research in personality dynamics of necessity was a prerequisite to the development of a rational treatment method.

These controversial issues will have to wait for the verdict of history. Their significance cannot yet be evaluated with finality. One may state, however, that there is a growing inclination to question the universal validity of some habitual practices handed down by tradition over several generations of psychoanalysts. There is a trend toward greater flexibility in technique, attempting to adjust the technical details to the individual nature of the patient and his problems. This principle of flexibility was explicitly stressed by Edith Weigert, Thomas French, myself and still others.

While there is considerable controversy concerning frequency of interviews, interruptions, termination and the mutual relation between intellectual and emotional factors in treatment, there seems to be a universal consensus about the significance of the therapist's individual personality for the results of the treatment. This interest first manifested itself in several contributions dealing with the therapist's own emotional involvement in the patient—"the countertransference phenomenon." Freud first used the expression, countertransference, in 1910. It took, however, about 30 years before the therapist's unconscious, spontaneous reactions toward the patient were explored as to their significance for the course of the treatment. The reasons for this neglect were both theoretical and practical. Originally Freud conceived the analyst's role in the treatment as a blank screen who carefully keeps his incognito and upon whom the patient can project any role, that of the image of his father (father transference), of mother (mother transference), or of any significant person in his past. In this way the patient can reexperience the important interpersonal events of his past undisturbed by the specific personality of the therapist. The phenomenon called "countertransference" however contradicts sharply the "blank screen" theory.

It is now generally recognized that in reality the analyst does not remain a blank screen, an uninvolved intellect, but is perceived by the patient as a concrete person. There is, however, a great deal of difference among present day authors in the evaluation of the significance of the therapist's personality in general and his countertransference reactions in particular.

Some authors consider countertransference as an undesirable impurity just as the patient's emotional involvement with his therapist (transference) originally was considered as an undesirable complication. The ideal model of the treatment was that the patient should freely associate and thus reveal himself without controlling the train of his ideas, and should consider the therapist only as an expert who is trying to help him. Later, as is well known, the patient's emotional involvement turned out to be the dynamic axis of the treatment. So far as the therapist's involvement is concerned, it is considered by most authors as an unwanted impurity. The therapist should have only one reaction to the patient, the wish to understand him and give him an opportunity for readjustment through the insight offered to him by the therapist's interpretations. The latter should function as a pure intellect without being disturbed by any personal and subjective reactions to the patient.

The prevailing view is that the analyst's own emotional reactions should be considered as disturbing factors of the treatment.

Some authors, among them Edith Weigert, Frieda Fromm-Reichmann, Heimann, Benedek and Salzman, however, mention certain assets of the countertransference; they point out that the analyst's understanding of his countertransference atttitudes may give him a particularly valuable tool for understanding the patient's transference reactions (5, 13, 14, 16). As to the therapeutic significance of the countertransference, there is a great deal of disagreement. While Balint and Balint consider this impurity as negligible for the therapeutic process (4), Benedek states in her paper on countertransference that the therapist's personality is the most important agent of the therapeutic process (5). There is, however, general agreement that a too intensive emotional involvement on the therapist's part is a seriously disturbing factor. Glover speaks of the "analyst's toilet" which he learns in his own personal analysis, which should free him from unwarranted emotional participation in the treatment. This is, indeed, the most important objective of the training analysis; it helps him to know how to control and possibly even to change his spontaneous countertransference reactions.

I believe that the countertransference may be helpful or harmful. It is helpful when it differs from that parental attitude toward the child which contributed to the patient's emotional difficulties. The patient's neurotic attitudes developed not in a vacuum but as reactions to parental attitudes. If the therapist's reactions are different from these parental attitudes, the patient's emotional involvement with therapist is not realistic. This challenges the patient to alter his reaction patterns. If, however, the specific countertransference of the therapist happens to be similar to the parental attitudes toward the child, the patient's neurotic reaction patterns will persist and an interminable analysis may result. There is no incentive for the patient to change his feelings. I recommended therefore that the therapist should be keenly aware of his own spontaneous— no matter how slight—feelings to the patient and should try to replace them by an interpersonal climate which is suited to correct the original neurotic patterns.

One of the most systematic revisions of the standard psychoanalytic procedure was undertaken by Sandor Rado, published in several writings, beginning in 1948 (15). His critical evaluation of psychoanalytic treatment and his suggested modifications deserve particular attention because for many years Rado has been known as one of the most thorough students of Freud's writings.

As years went on, Rado became more and more dissatisfied with the prevailing practice of psychoanalysis, and proposed his adaptational technique based on his "adaptational psychodynamics." As it is the case with many innovators, some of Rado's formulations consist in new terminology. Some of his new emphases, however, are highly significant. He is most concerned, as I am, with those features of the standard technique of psychoanalysis which foster regression without supplying a counterforce toward the patient's progression, that is to say, to his successful adaptation to the actual life situation. He raises the crucial question: Is the patient's understanding of his past development sufficient to induce a change in him? "To overcome repressions and thus be able to recall the past is one thing; to learn from it and be able to act on the new knowledge, another" (15).

Rado recommends, as a means to promote the goal of therapy, raising the patient from his earlier child-like adaptations to an appropriate adult level—"to hold the patient as much as possible at the adult level of cooperation with the physician." The patient following his regressive trend "parentifies" the therapist but the therapist should counteract this trend and not allow himself to be pushed by the patient into the parent role. Rado criticizes orthodox psychoanalytic treatment as furthering the regressive urge of the patient by emphasizing the "punitive parentifying" transference (the patient's dependence upon the parentalized image of the therapist) (15). Rado points out that losing self-confidence is the main reason for the patient to build up the therapist into a powerful parent figure. Rado's main principle, therefore, is to "bolster up the patient's self-confidence on realistic grounds." He stresses the importance of dealing with the patient's actual present life conditions in all possible detail. Interpretations must always embrace the conscious as well as unconscious motivations. In concordance with mine and French's similar emphasis (1) Rado succinctly states: "Even when the biographical material on hand reaches far into the past, interpretation must always begin and end with the patient's present life performance, his present adaptive task. The significance of this rule cannot be overstated."

Rado considers his adaptational technique but a further development of the current psychoanalytic technique, not something basically contradictory to it. It should be pointed out that while criticizing the standard psychoanalytic procedure, Rado in reality criticizes a current practice, but not theory. According to accepted theory, the patient's dependent—in Rado's term—"parentifying" transference should be resolved. The patient during treatment learns to understand his own motivations; this enables him to take over his own management. He assimilates the therapist's interpretations and gradually he can dispense with the therapist, from whom he has received all he needs. The therapeutic process thus recapitulates the process of emotional maturation; the child learns from the parents, incorporates their attitude and eventually will no longer need them for guidance. Rado's point becomes relevant when one points out that the current procedure does not always achieve this goal, and I may add, it unnecessarily prolongs the procedure. The reason for this is that the exploration of the past became an aim in itself, indeed the goal of the treatment. The past should be subordinated to a total grasp of the present life situation and serve as the basis for future adaptive accomplishments.

At this point my emphasis is pertinent, that it is imperative for the therapist to correctly estimate the time when his guidance not only becomes unnecessary but detrimental, inasmuch as it unnecessarily fosters the very dependency of the patient on the therapist which the latter tries to combat. I stated that deeds are stronger than words; the treatment should be interrupted at the right time in order to give the patient the experience that he can now function on his own and thus gain that self-confidence which Rado tries to instill into the patient by "positive interpretations." No matter, however, what technical devices they emphasize, the goal of these reformers is the same: to minimize the danger implicit in the psychotherapeutic situation, namely, encouraging undue regression and evasion of the current adaptive tasks. It is quite true that regression is necessary in order to give the patient opportunity to reexperience his early maladaptive patterns and grapple with them anew to find other more appropriate levels of feeling and behavior. The key to successful psychoanalytic therapy is, however, not to allow regression in the transference to become an aim in itself. It is necessary to control it.

In view of these controversies the need for a careful study of the therapeutic process became more and more recognized. Different research centers initiated programs from grants given by the Ford Foundation to study the therapeutic process. At the Mount Sinai Hospital in Los Angeles under my direction, we undertook a study of the therapeutic process, in which a number of psychoanalysts observed the therapeutic interaction between therapist and patient in several treatment cases. All interviews were sound recorded and both the participant observer—that is the therapist—and the nonparticipant observers recorded their evaluation of the process immediately after each interview. Our assumption was that the therapist being an active participant in the interactional process is not capable of recognizing and describing his own involvements with the same objectivity as those who observe him. His attention is necessarily focused on patient's material and being himself involved in this complex interaction cannot fully appreciate his own part in it. This expectation was fully borne out by our study.

As was expected the processing of the voluminous data thus collected proved to be a prolonged affair which will require several years of collaborative work. Yet even at the present stage of processing, several important conclusions emerge. The most important of these is the fact that the traditional descriptions of the therapeutic process do not adequately reflect the immensely complex interaction between therapist and patient. The patient's reactions cannot be described fully as transference reactions. The patient reacts to the therapist as to a concrete person and not only as a representative of parental figures. The therapist's reactions also far exceed what is usually called countertransference. They include in addition to this, interventions based on conscious deliberations and also his spontaneous idiosyncratic attitudes. Moreover, his own values are conveyed to the patient even if he consistently tries to protect his incognito. The patient reacts to the therapist's overt but also to his nonverbal hidden intentions and the therapist reacts to the patient's reaction to him. It is a truly transactional process.

In studying this transactional material I came to the conviction that the therapeutic process can be best understood in the terms of learning theory. Particularly the principle of reward and punishment and also the influence of repetitive experiences can be clearly recognized. Learning is defined as a change resulting from previous experiences. In every learning process, one can distinguish two components. First the motivational factor, namely, the subjective needs which activate the learning process and second, certain performances by which a new behavioral pattern suitable to fill the motivational need is actually acquired. In most general terms unfulfilled needs no matter what their nature may be—hunger for food, hunger for love, curiosity, the urge for mastery—initiate groping trial and error efforts which cease when an adequate behavioral response is found. Adequate responses lead to need satisfaction which is the reward for the effort. Rewarding responses are repeated until they become automatic and their repetition no longer requires effort and further experimentation. This is identical with the feedback mechanisms described in cybernetics. Every change of the total situation requires learning new adequate responses. Old learned patterns which were adequate in a previous situation must be unlearned. They are impediments to acquiring new adequate patterns.

I am not particularly concerned at this point with the controversy between the more mechanistic concepts of the older behaviorist theory and the newer Gestalt theory of learning. The controversy pertains to the nature of the process by which satisfactory behavior patterns are acquired. This controversy can be reduced to two suppositions. The older Thorndike and Pavlov models operate with the principle of contiguity or connectionism. Whenever a behavioral pattern becomes associated with both a specific motivating need and need satisfaction, the organism will automatically repeat the satisfactory performance whenever the same need arises. This view considers the organism as a passive receptor of external and internal stimuli, which become associated by contiguity. The organism's own active organizing function is neglected. The finding of the satisfactory pattern, according to the classical theory, takes place through blind trial and error.

In contrast, the Gestalt theoretical model operates with the supposition that the trials by which the organism finds satisfactory behavioral responses are not blind but are aided by cognitive processes. They are intelligent trials which are guided by certain generalizations arrived at with the aid of the memory of previous experiences. They imply an active organization of previous experiences. This organizational act amounts to a cognitive grasp of the total situation. I am not concerned at this juncture with the seemingly essential difference between the connectionistic and Gestalt theories of learning. Probably both types of learning exist. The infant learns without much help from previous experiences. In this learning blind trials and errors must of necessity prevail. Common basis in all learning, whether it takes place through blind trials and errors or by intelligent trials, is the forging of a connection between three variables: a specific motivating impulse, a specific behavioral response, and a gratifying experience which is the reward.

Accepting Freud's definition of thinking as a substitute for acting, that is to say, as acting in phantasy, the reward principle can be well applied to intellectual solutions of problems. Groping trials and errors in thought—whether blind or guided by cognitive processes—lead eventually to a solution which clicks. Finding a solution which satisfies all the observations without contradictions is accompanied by a feeling of satisfaction. After a solution is found—occasionally it may be found accidentally—the problem-solving urge, as everyone knows who has tried to solve a mathematical equation or a chess puzzle, ceases and a feeling of satisfaction ensues. The tension state which prevails as long as the problem is not solved, yields to a feeling of rest and fulfillment. This is the reward for the effort, whether it consists of blind or intelligent trials. The principle of reward can be applied not only to a rat learning to run a maze, but to the most complex thought processes as well. The therapeutic process can be well described in these terms of learning theory. The specific problem in therapy consists in finding an adequate interpersonal relation between therapist and patient. Initially this is distorted because the patient applies to this specific human interaction feeling-patterns and behavior-patterns which were formed in the patient's past and do not apply either to the actual therapeutic situation or to his actual life situation. During treatment the patient unlearns the old patterns and learns new ones. This complex process of relearning follows the same principles as the more simple relearning process hitherto studied by experimental psychologists. It contains cognitive elements as well as learning from actual interpersonal experiences which occur during the therapeutic interaction. These two components are intricately interwoven. They were described in psychoanalytic literature with the undefined, rather vague term "emotional insight." The word "emotional" refers to the interpersonal experiences, the word "insight" refers to the cognitive element. The expression does not mean more than the recognition of the presence of both components. The psychological process to which the term refers is not yet spelled out in detail. Our present observational study is focused on a better understanding of this complex psychological phenomenon—emotional insight—which appears to us as the central factor in every learning process including psychoanalytic treatment. Every intellectual grasp, even when it concerns entirely nonutilitarian preoccupations, such as playful puzzle-solving efforts, is motivated by some kind of urge for mastery and is accompanied with tension resolution as its reward. In psychotherapy the reward consists in less conflictful, more harmonious interpersonal relations, which the patient achieves first by adequately relating to his therapist, then to his environment, and eventually to his own ego ideal. At first he tries to gain the therapist's approval by living up to the supreme therapeutic principle—to the basic rule of frank self-expression. At the same time he tries to gain acceptance by living up to the therapist's expectations of him, which he senses in spite of the therapist's overt nonevaluating attitude. And finally, he tries to live up to his own genuine values, to his cherished image of himself. Far-reaching discrepancy between the therapist's and the patient's values is a common source of therapeutic impasse.

This gradually evolving dynamic process can be followed and described step by step in studies made by nonparticipant observers. Current studies give encouragement and hope that we shall eventually be able to understand more adequately this intricate interpersonal process and to account for therapeutic successes and failures. As in every field of science, general assumptions gradually yield to more specific ones which are obtained by meticulous, controlled observations. The history of sciences teaches us that new and more adequate technical devices of observation and reasoning are responsible for advancements. In the field of psychotherapy the long overdue observation of the therapeutic process by non-participant observers is turning out to be the required methodological tool. This in itself, however, is not sufficient. The evaluation of the rich and new observational material calls for new theoretical perspectives. Learning theory appears to be at present the most satisfactory framework for the evaluation of observational data and for making valid generalizations. As it continuously happens at certain phases of thought development in all fields of science, different independent approaches merge and become integrated with each other. At present, we are witnessing the beginnings of a most promising integration of psychoanalytic theory with learning theory, which may lead to unpredictable advances in the theory and practice of the psychotherapies.

REFERENCES

1. Alexander, F., and French, T. M. *Psychoanalytic therapy: Principles and application.* New York: Ronald, 1946.

2. Alexander, F. *Psychoanalysis and psychotherapy.* New York: Norton, 1956.

3. Alexander, F. *Behav. Sci.,* Oct. 1958, *3.*

4. Balint, A., and Balint, M. *Int. J. Psychoanal.,* 1939, *20.*

5. Benedek, T. *Bull. Menninger Clin.,* 1953, *17,* 6.

6. Fenichel, O. *The psychoanalytic theory of neurosis.* New York: Norton, 1945.

7. Freud, S. The dynamics of the transference (1912). *Collected papers,* Vol. II. London: Hogarth, 1924.

8. Freud, S. Recommendations for physicians on the psychoanalytic method of treatment (1912). *Collected papers,* Vol. II. London: Hogarth, 1924.

9. Freud, S. Further recommendations in the technique of psychoanalysis on beginning the treatment. The question of the first communications. The dynamics of the cure (1913). *Collected papers,* Vol. II. London: Hogarth, 1924.

10. Freud, S. Further recommendations in the technique of psychoanalysis. Recollection, repetition, and working through (1914). *Collected papers,* Vol. II. London: Hogarth, 1924.

11. Freud, S. Further recommendations in the technique of psychoanalysis. Observations on transference-love (1915). *Collected papers,* Vol. II. London: Hogarth, 1924.

12. Freud, S. *New introductory lectures on psychoanalysis.* New York: Norton, 1933.

13. Fromm-Reichmann, F. *Principles of intensive psychotherapy.* London: Allen & Unwin, 1957.

14. Heimann, P. *Int. J. Psychoanal.,* 1950, *31.*

15. Rado, S. Psychoanalysis of behavior: *Collected papers*, Vol. I (1922-1956); Vol. II (1956-1961). New York: Grune & Stratton, Vol. I, 1956, Vol. II, 1962.
16. Weigert, E. *J. Amer. Psychoanal. Assoc.*, 1954, 2, 4.

In Process

Perhaps Alexander's most significant contribution is the model for openness to change that he himself represents. His classic article, published in his last year of life, is a tribute to a man in process, with hopes for "unpredictable advances in the theory and practice of the psychotherapies."

Alexander is particularly concerned about the inadequacies of psychoanalytic theory in accounting for the complex interactional process between therapist and patient. This point has been solidly underscored by the recent research of Reneker (1965), which indicates that analysts recall less than 15 percent of the material of their sessions and employ less than 5 percent in making their formulations. As recently as 1951, Fromm-Reichmann went to great lengths to explain why an analyst should not fall asleep in the presence of the client and why he should try to understand what the client is communicating. These considerations are at least obliquely related to Eysenck's suggestion that we might lose 23 potential success cases every time we introduce psychoanalytic treatment.

For Alexander, cognitive insights and emotional experiences are not mutually exclusive, and we might add that they appear to be *inherent aspects of all effective learning processes*. Alexander's bias emphasizes the experiential base that provides the patient with an opportunity to unlearn old patterns and learn new patterns of behavior: "The specific problem in therapy consists in finding an adequate interpersonal relation between therapist and patient." He suggests a calculated technique to intensify the patient's emotional experience in order to effect the optimum level of learning and relearning: "The therapist, in order to increase the effectiveness of the corrective emotional experiences, should attempt to create an interpersonal climate which is suited to highlight the discrepancy between the patient's transference attitude and the actual situation as it exists between patient and therapist." Here we might note how often therapists who are shaped by what is effective for their clients evolve in an interactional process to a stance similar to that which might have been calculated in the first place.

Alexander leads us into a whole new area of consideration in generalizing his thinking to all learning experiences: ". . . this complex psychological phenomenon—emotional insight— . . . appears to us as the central factor in every learning process including psychoanalytic treatment." The readings in the following section concentrate on the mechanisms of all learning processes and apply these mechanisms to counseling and psychotherapy.

THE EXPERIMENTAL APPROACHES

This section moves from Shoben's prophetic pronouncements about the value of uniting psychotherapy with the general psychology of learning theory to Krasner's and Rachman's actual utilization within the therapeutic hour of techniques derived from these learning principles.

Shoben not only points to learning theory as the central process in all therapies but employs it as a vehicle to bring therapy into the body of general psychology. He attempts, as he puts it, "to organize some of the phenomena of clinical practice within the framework of systematic behavior theory." To a large degree the rapprochement sought for and prophetically developed by Shoben has been realized. It has, however, lent more respectability to the clinical specialty while clouding some of the central concerns of the clinician. That is, the clinician knows very little more about how the rapprochement helps him to help his patients than he used to know. Perhaps a rapprochement that goes beyond general psychology is needed, so that there is a common meeting ground for all helping professions.

Shoben is not advocating a learning theory psychotherapy but rather pointing out that learning principles may aid us in our efforts to understand and put into perspective successes regardless of approach or orientation. He reminds us of the similarities (neurotic anxiety) of all patient problems and of the reduction of anxiety as a goal common to all therapies. In addition, he notes that all therapists and counselors rely on communication with their patients within the context of a facilitating relationship.

PSYCHOTHERAPY AS A PROBLEM
IN LEARNING THEORY[*1]

Edward Joseph Shoben, Jr.

It has become increasingly apparent that clinical psychologists are more and more drawing psychotherapy into their compass of activities. If this enlargement of scope is to be something more than a trading of one's psychological birthright for a share of psychiatric pottage, it would seem imperative that the therapeutic functions of the psychologist be regarded from the point of view of research as well as from that of practice. As Sanford (47) puts it,

> What should be of great help to us here is our training in scientific method and our tradition of research-mindedness. It would be hard to name an area in which research is more needed than it is in therapy, or an area in which what is being done lags further behind what might be done. . . . And one might say, furthermore, that it is primarily up to the psychologist to perform this needed research.

The difficulties in the way of such inquiry, however, are enormous, as is well attested to by the paucity of investigations of the therapeutic process in terms of the problems, techniques, and concepts common to general psychology. The nature of some of these barriers to psychological research on a matter of such importance probably merits some brief attention.

In the first place, there are situational deterrents to research in psychotherapy. Counseling[2] usually takes place in a "service" setting and is consequently seldom subject to the kinds of exact manipulation required by rigorous experimentation. Often, attempts to control various

* *Psychological Bulletin*, 1949, *46*, 366-392. Reprinted by permission of author and publisher.

[1] This article represents a revision and extension of an earlier attempt (51) to conceptualize psychotherapy in terms of systematic behavior theory. Acknowledgment must be made to a number of people, foremost among whom is Dr. O. H. Mowrer, who, though he may recognize some of his ideas in the ensuing pages, must not be held responsible either for their form or for the uses to which they are put. Others are Dr. Kenneth Spence and Dr. I. E. Farber, of the University of Iowa, who have been invaluable sources of stimulation and instruction but who are absolved from any responsibility for what is here said.

[2] The terms counseling and psychotherapy are here used interchangeably without regard for any of the distinctions they are sometimes employed to convey.

factors in the therapeutic set-up give rise to serious ethical problems concerning the relationship of the therapist and his agency to their clients, and certainly the pressure of the demand for counseling services frequently conflicts with the requirements of a research program. Secondly, the problem of complexity gives one pause. Psychotherapy is a form of social interaction, an active social situation, in which many subtle, difficult-to-isolate aspects of the personalities of *both* patient and counselor must be taken into consideration. The therapist is not merely the wielder of some supposedly meliorative technique but is deeply involved as a personality in the counseling process. Thus, the psychology of the psychologist, as well as the psychology of the patient and the nature of the therapeutic method, enters into the determination of the therapeutic end product. Third, there are personnel problems militating against effective research in psychotherapy. Psychologists most familiar with the therapeutic process are seldom well schooled in the experimental and conceptual skills basic to fruitful investigations in general psychology, whereas those who are best equipped technically and conceptually as research workers are generally rather untutored in therapeutic techniques, are unfamiliar with clinical material, and are frequently repelled by the admittedly gross and somewhat nebulous notions clinicians use in their efforts to conceptualize the complex phenomena with which they work. In sum, the situational lack of amenability of psychotherapy to experimental inquiry, the enormous complexity of the factors entering into the counseling process, and the differences in training and interest between clinical and laboratory workers all tend to impede a *rapprochement* between psychotherapy and the research functions characteristic of general psychology.

In spite of these difficulties, there is one slender lead that might be profitably followed in the attempt to provide a basis for the conceptualization and investigation of psychotherapy as a problem in general psychology. This is the widespread recognition that psychotherapy is essentially a learning process and should be subject to study as such.

This point of view is not only in harmony with the general conception of counseling as a conversation or series of conversations between two persons, therapist and patient, the goal of which is to resolve the conflicts, reduce the anxiety, or somehow modify the behavior of the latter—a conception which clearly implies learning; it has been more or less clearly so verbalized by a number of clinical workers. Cameron (4) sees the desideratum of counseling as the patient's "acquisition of normal biosocial behavior," a statement which definitely implies the learning of new ways of reacting as a function of the therapeutic process. Alexander and French (1) advance as a basic therapeutic principle the reexposure of the client, within the favorable circumstances of psychotherapy, to emotional situations with which he was unable to deal in the past. Presumably, the justification for such a reexposure rests on the hypothesis that its occurrence "under more favorable conditions" in some way permits the patient to learn more adequate ways of coping with such experiences. Rogers (45) describes the therapeutic process as a freeing of the "growth capacities" of the individual which permits him to acquire "more mature" ways of reacting. If "growth" in this context means (as it must) something more than physiological maturation, and if it is not to be lumped with the old and rather mystic homeopathic notion of the *vis medicatrix naturae*, it must refer to the client's acquisition of new modes of response. Such new modes of response are "more mature" because for a given patient they are less fraught with anxiety or conflict. Thus, Rogers is actually talking about psychotherapy as a learning process. White (64) insists that, "Psychotherapy is designed to bring about learning . . ."; and Darley (7) argues that unless the process of learning in counseling is demonstrated, it is not legitimate to infer that the modifications of behavior that may occur during or following therapy are necessarily outcomes of therapy.

In spite of this widespread acknowledgement of psychotherapy as a learning process, there have been few attempts (11, 25, 49, 50) systematically to formulate therapy in terms of learning theory. This paper represents a tentative, apologetically offered effort to construct a learning-theory intrepretation of counseling that will help to narrow the gap between practitioner and researcher, clinician and experimentalist, and to encourage some much needed investigation.

COMMON FACTORS IN SCHOOLS OF PSYCHOTHERAPY

When one surveys the various theories and practices of psychotherapy in an effort to find those common factors which a learning-theory interpretation of the counseling process must cover, it appears possible to make four summarizing general statements:

1. All schools of psychotherapy can with some justice claim cures (46). Notable successes seem to be the common property of virtually all forms of counseling from moral suasion through nondirective therapy to psychoanalysis.
2. Clinical patients,[3] in spite of their enormous differences, tend to present a similar problem in that one of their primary motivations is

---

[3] The "clinical patients" spoken of in this paper include only those classifiable as neurotic or "maladjusted." Nothing said here is meant to apply to psychotics, psychopaths, or behavior problems associated with endocrine disturbances or lesions of the central or autonomic nervous systems.

anxiety and much of their nonintegrative or "symptomatic" behavior is maintained on the basis of anxiety reduction.

3. The goal common to most psychotherapies is the modification of the client's underlying anxiety. This is related to the hypothesis that once his motivation is altered, the overt habit structures of the patient will change.

4. Finally, all types of counseling employ the techniques of the *therapeutic relationship,* the unique social situation that is formed when therapist and patient meet to discuss the problems of the latter, and of *conversational content,* that is, of talking about certain things within the therapeutic setting rather than others.

A word must be said about each of these four factors which seem to be common to the various forms of counseling, regardless of the doctrinal banners flown.

ALL SCHOOLS REPORT CURES. If it is true that the proponents of various theories of psychotherapy all seem able to claim successes, and if it is true—as has often been pointed out—that successes are no proof of therapeutic theory, then it would seem to follow that an understanding of the counseling process would be furthered by giving more attention to the conditions under which the patient's learning of new modes of reaction takes place within the general clinical setting. If this is a fair notion, based as it is on the conception of therapy as a learning situation, it might be instructive to explore the points in common among the different approaches to counseling in terms of (a) the similarity of patients' problems, (b) the agreement among clinicians as to goals, and (c) the techniques common to nearly all therapeutic enterprises. Such an exploration might lead to a formulation of the learning process in counseling in terms of these three sets of information.

SIMILARITIES IN CLINICAL CASES. While from the practical standpoint of dealing therapeutically with patients it is necessary to consider each case in all its uniqueness, from a theoretical point of view it is instructive to look for similarities. This amounts to asking the rather ambitious questions of (a) What constitutes the core of "neurosis" or "maladjustment"? and (b) What are the common problems faced by therapists in their contacts with patients? While no definitive answer can be given here, it is important to consider these issues as bearing on the goals and techniques employed by counselors of different theoretical persuasions and as factors to be accounted for in attempting to formulate a learning-theory interpretation of the therapeutic process.

A point on which there seems to be widespread agreement is, in Horney's (17) phrase, that "one essential factor common to all neuroses . . . is anxieties and the defenses built up against them." The phenomena clinically identified as feelings of insecurity, feelings of inadequacy, and guilt feelings are all variants of anxiety in the sense that they involve debilitating expectations of future punishment. Likewise, it would seem that the "phenomenological self-concept" of Combs (6) and Rogers (45) refers to little more than a patient's level of anxiety, guilt, or inadequacy, together with his verbalizations, accurate or otherwise, of his defenses against them.

To conceptualize anxiety usefully, it is necessary to discriminate between anxiety and fear or, as Freud (12, 13, 14) did, between neurotic anxiety and objective anxiety. Fear may be thought of as an affective reaction proportionate to some external danger. Anxiety, on the other hand, differs from fear in at least two ways. First, if one asks a "neurotic" patient what he is afraid of, he will admit to being afraid but will generally have no idea of what the source of the possible danger might be. Anxiety may be aptly termed either a fear of "nothing" or a fear of something which is objectively irrelevant. Second, while both fear and anxiety are anticipatory states involving some kind of premonition of danger, the signal to which anxiety is a reaction is usually internal, some impulse to act in a way that has been forbidden. An illustrative case may clarify this point.

E. B., a 24-year-old male undergraduate veteran, despite slightly better than average academic ability, is making poor grades and is in danger of being dismissed from his university. He complains of being "unable" to study, feelings of inferiority in social groups, and serious doubts as to both his intellectual and social adequacy. He has some guilt feelings about having transferred from a pre-medical curriculum to English, because his parents are quite eager for him to become a physician. His father is a farmer who has been quite successful financially and in community politics, and who has been highly ambitious for his son. He has imposed very high standards of attainment on the boy, has been quite strict and stern with him and has had a number of set ideas which he felt that the youngster should accept and act upon "for his own good." Any deviation on the part of the patient from the parentally prescribed ways of doing was met with severe punishment, the verbal part of which usually consisted in a variety of changes rung on the theme of the boy's worthlessness and a series of predictions that he would come to no good end. In short, any self-initiated activity—behavior which the parents themselves did not lay out—was fraught with danger When the boy began counseling, he was squarely on the horns of a dilemma: unable to meet parental demands for a variety of reasons, he was also unable to initiate any divergent plans of his own without experiencing a flood of anxiety, that is, anticipations of parental punishment.

This, if it is acceptable, leads to a general formulation of non-integrative or neurotic behavior. Anxiety has repeatedly been shown to have drive properties (29, 32), and on the basis of the anxiety drive, individuals who are maladjusted seem to develop various overt reaction patterns that become stable according to the degree to which they reduce the anxiety. This statement in terms of contemporary reinforcement theory (19) is quite in keeping with Freud's (12) idea of the interchangeability of anxiety and symptom, by which he means that through the formation of symptoms the patient protects himself from anxiety attacks. Anxiety is allayed by some anxiety-reducing symptom; if the symptomatic behavior is somehow eliminated, the anxiety returns. On the basis of this notion it is possible to define a neurosis or a maladjustment in terms of behavior which serves to reduce anxiety directly *without altering the conditions which produce the anxiety.* Freud consistently refers to anxiety as a signal of impending danger; the maladjusted person is one who either consciously or unconsciously engages in acts which eliminate or neutralize the signal while leaving the objective danger unaffected. He is in the position of the motorist who shuts his eyes to warnings of dangerous curves, thus protecting himself from worry but leaving himself liable to serious accidents.

Such a conception permits an explanation of the curious observation that nonintegrative behavior is at the same time self-defeating and self-perpetuating. It is self-defeating in that such behavior leads inevitably to further punishment: the motorist has accidents; the illustrative case suffers academic failures and social disarticulation through his avoidance of study to protect himself from the anxiety engendered by self-initiated activity and his withdrawal from social affairs to hide his "worthlessness." It is self-perpetuating because of the immediate reinforcement derived from anxiety reduction. Since the occurrence of a reinforcing state of affairs lies on the temporal gradient of reinforcement in greater proximity to the anxiety-reducing behavior than does the more remote punishment, the connection between the external and internal cues of anxiety and the nonintegrative response tends to be strengthened (38).

A necessary concept in a theory of anxiety is that of repression. This notion refers to the exclusion from communicability (consciousness) of an impulse to act which has led to punishment. When a parent punishes a child severely for some tabooed act, the impulse to commit such an act becomes, through its association with the punishment, a stimulus for anxiety. One way by which the anxiety may be avoided is through repression—the exclusion from awareness of the impulse. If the repression is complete, there is a thorough-going allaying of anxiety, and the forbidden impulse no longer constitutes a problem.

Difficulty arises because repression is seldom if ever complete. The individual is constantly threatened by "a return of the repressed" (14) which touches off anxiety without the patient's being able to verbalize the cues for it. In short, the repressed impulse, although excluded from communicability, is still operative at subliminal levels. Why this should be true is something of a psychological mystery, although some light is shed upon it by investigations of punishment. Estes (9), for example, by a series of experiments has shown that punishment does not extinguish a response which has been positively reinforced. He concludes,

> . . . a response cannot be eliminated from an organism's repertoire more rapidly with the aid of punishment than without it. In fact, severe punishment may have precisely the opposite effect. . . . The punished response continues to exist in the organism's repertoire with most of its original latent strength. While it is suppressed, the response is not only protected from extinction, but it also may become a source of conflict. An emotional state, such as "anxiety" or "dread," which has become conditioned to the incipient movements of making the response will be aroused by any stimuli which formerly acted as occasions for the occurrence of the response (pp. 37-38).

This provides a neat parallel to what is implied in the concept of repression.

In summary, then, one might say that clinical cases share in common (a) anxiety touched off by (b) unverbalized, unsuccessfully repressed impulses to act in ways that have met with punishment, and (c) persistent nonintegrative behavior of many kinds, which reduces the anxiety but does nothing about eliminating its objective causes.

Common Goals in Psychotherapy

In spite of its nonintegrative nature, overt neurotic behavior acquires remarkable persistence through anxiety-avoidance. This persistence is probably the factor most responsible for the failure and consequent elimination of clinical techniques aimed at the elimination of symptoms. Such a goal, in effect, defined psychotherapy as a process of robbing the patient of his defenses against anxiety without alleviating the unbearable state of dread. Since such an end is impossible of realization, advice, persuasion, exhortation, and suggestion have largely gone by the board in favor of methods which focus on the client's anxiety itself.

In other words, the goal of most modern psychotherapies is the modification of the emotional determinants of neurotic behavior. Thus, Alexander and French (1) speak of therapy as "a corrective emotional experience," which presumably results in a diminution of anxiety and a consequent elimination of persistent nonintegrative behavior from the patient's repertoire. Likewise, White (64) points out that "Psychotherapy does not take place primarily in the sphere of intellect. . . . Its sphere of operation is the patient's feelings." The kind of learning with which counseling is concerned has to do chiefly with the alteration of motives and affective drives. This does not mean, of course, that the therapist is uninterested in his client's overt behavior; on the contrary, it is his job to help the patient alter it and achieve a repertoire of more integrative habits. But since this goal does not seem attainable through any kind of direct manipulation, the counselor generally works on the elimination of the basic anxieties, implicitly hypothesizing that once the drive conditions are changed, the neurotic behavior will show less strength.

Common Tools in Psychotherapy

From the standpoint of technique, there are two main aspects of the counseling process common to all schools of psychotherapy. One is the unique *relationship* that develops between therapist and patient; the other is the *conversational content,* what they talk about during their sessions together. The proponents of different theories of counseling may emphasize one or the other of these factors, but both figure in their final formulations of therapeutic procedure. Thus, Williamson (66) and Kraines (24) stress the therapist's obtaining personal information from the client so that the counselor may guide him somehow to a higher level of adjustment. In spite of this emphasis, both these clinicians devote a good deal of attention to the necessity of establishing and maintaining rapport or winning and retaining the patient's confidence. On the other hand, therapists like Taft (60), Allen (2), and Rogers (44) play up the quality of the counselor-client relationship and are concerned only secondarily with the conversational content aspect of therapeutic interviews. Nonetheless, they are quite insistent that the proper content of counseling contacts is the "feelings" of the patient rather than his overt behavior or his intellectualized beliefs.

What is this content factor in counseling? What are the areas of discussion between counselor and counselee? In line with the foregoing (although at variance with a widespread belief among laymen), therapeutic conversations are concerned with the patient's overt behavior only insofar as it bears on his covert reactions—the anxieties from which he suffers and against which he so nonintegratively defends himself.

The client's anxiety (guilt feelings, feelings of inferiority, or inadequacy), then, constitutes the central topic of concern in psychotherapeutic interviews. But clinicians are also interested in the occurrences that engender anxiety. Especially are they interested in the formative past experiences[4] which have been associated with anxiety, and they encourage patients to discuss such events and their reactions to them rather fully. Emphasis throughout seems to be more on the way the client feels about his experience rather than on the objective accuracy of his reportage.

Thus the conversational content of counseling consists chiefly in the discussion of the patient's anxieties and the conditions which either currently evoke them or seem to be causally linked in some historical sense to them.

The relationship aspect of therapeutic procedure has been recently most vigorously expounded by Rogers (44), Snyder (54), and other members (3, 6) of the so-called nondirective or client-centered school. Such a notion is, of course, by no means new to counseling technique. Freud (13) in stressing the idea of transference was talking about essentially the same thing: the basic role in psychotherapy of the affective bonds uniting client to counselor. In the case of orthodox psychoanalysis, transference refers to the displacement of childish attitudes from the analysand's past to the analyst, who becomes a substitute for the important previous objects of his patient's loves and hates. That such things do take place in psychotherapy is not questioned, but whether they *must* occur in just such a form for counseling to be successful may be doubted. For present purposes, it is merely necessary to establish the point that the relationship factor is inherent in the psychoanalytic approach to therapy. Cameron (4), writing from a point of view strongly influenced by Adolph Meyer, says,

> . . . the acquisition of normal biosocial behavior may be greatly facilitated by the organization of a permissive situation, in which the patient has maximal opportunity to work through his attitudes and responses overtly in the presence of a skilled therapist. . . . The immediate goal of treatment in the behavior disorders is that of establishing a biosocial interrelationship . . . in which patient and therapist participate. The ultimate goal is that of making this interrelationship unnecessary and terminating it with benefit to the patient (pp. 576-577).

Dejerine and Gauckler (8) warn, "If . . . you have not been able to awaken a reciprocal sympathy in your patient, and if you have not succeeded in gaining his confidence, it is useless to go any further. The

---

[4] Even therapists like Rogers, who verbally disclaim any interest in personal history data, hardly prevent their patients' discussing past experiences. It would be revealing to go systematically through a series of electrically recorded nondirective interviews to see if the data collected fall very far short of affording a relatively complete case history. In a preliminary trial by the writer, using material collected from twelve sessions with one case, the greater part of a typical anamnestic form could be filled out from the transcriptions of the recordings.

result that you will obtain will be worthless. . . ." Sullivan (58) stresses the concept of parataxis and speaks of the psychiatrist's "participating helpfully in the life of the patient."

While there may be some important differences among the various points of view just touched on, it may be pointed out that there is virtually universal agreement among clinicians on the *importance* of the relationship; there is also high agreement on certain of its characteristics.

The most underscored aspect of the therapeutic relationship seems to be its warmth, permissiveness, and complete freedom from moralistic and judgmental attitudes on the part of the counselor. Far from being a coldly objective consideration of the patient's troubles, therapy necessarily involves a highly personal form of interaction in which the counselor is highly acceptant of the client's behavior, both overt and covert, within clearly defined limits.

Just what "acceptance" means has become somewhat clouded, and a word of clarification may throw some light on the dynamics of the counseling relationship generally. As Sullivan (58) points out, anything a patient feels, says, or does constitutes the data of the therapeutic enterprise. As is the case with data of any kind, one's first job is to understand; it is not to condemn, ignore, reject, or judge. Among such data are the feelings and attitudes that the counselee may develop toward the therapist and which, according to most clinical workers of whatever theoretical orientation, are intimately related to the success or failure of therapy. Here again an atmosphere free from censure or judgment but pervaded by sympathetic understanding is provided by the counselor. On the other hand, acceptance does not imply approval of the client's feelings, attitudes, or overt behavior. This is not surprising since most clinical cases hardly approve of themselves, and their self-disapproval provides one of the most important aspects of the discomfort that brings them into therapy.

As can be inferred from the foregoing, the counseling relationship differs importantly from other forms of human interaction. In the first place, it is essentially one-sided in the sense that the therapist ordinarily says little about himself and that the changes effected within the context of the relationship are centered in the client rather than being a mutual modification. The exchange between counselor and patient, then, does not resemble that between friends in spite of the friendliness that generally permeates the relationship. Secondly, it is sharply limited in that the therapist's expressed interest in his client does not extend beyond the confines of the clinic. The two do not mingle socially, the clinician does not usually intercede for the patient in times of stress, and he generally does not become embroiled in attempts to manipulate the patient's environment. The therapist's office is designated as a place where one can come in perfect safety, free from threats and blame, to "think about" one's problems; but it is not a place where dispensations are sold or intercessions granted. Finally, there is a tacit agreement between therapist and patient that their connection is to be severed as soon as the patient feels free to go about his business without the counselor's support. In other words, the interest, acceptance, and "affection" of the therapist is there for the client to make capital of so long as he wishes it. Unlike non-clinical situations, there is no pressure on him to maintain the relationship out of politeness or any of the other social rules that more or less govern intimate relationships in society at large.

All this may be recapitulated by saying that the methods common to the various forms of psychotherapy involve (a) the formation of a special kind of personal relationship and (b) a conversation with the patient about his anxieties and the events which tend to produce them. As Finesinger (10) puts it, "Communication . . . and the physician-patient relation are the tools that must be adapted to the goals of psychotherapy."

The argument thus far, then, runs something like this: The common problem characterizing clinical patients is anxiety and the behavioral defenses built up against it. The goal of psychotherapy, regardless of the therapist's theoretical leanings, is to eliminate the anxiety and thereby to do away with the symptomatic persistent nonintegrative behavior. To accomplish this goal, all therapists use the devices of conversing with the patient about his anxiety and the situations calling it forth both currently and historically, and forming a unique therapeutic relationship. Since all psychotherapies seem to have successes to their credit and since psychotherapy seems to be a process whereby a patient learns to modify his emotional reactions and his overt behavior, it is hypothesized that therapy may be conceptualized from the point of view of general psychology as a problem in learning theory. Such a conceptualization must account for the changes that occur in counselees in terms of these factors that are apparently common to all forms of counseling. Before attempting such a conceptualization, it is necessary briefly to review the situation in learning theory.

MAJOR THEORIES OF LEARNING

One of the major issues with which learning theorists are concerned has to do with the conditions which are necessary if learning is to occur. Two points of view have gained the widest currency with respect to this question.

Reinforcement Theory

The first is that of Clark Hull (19). Within Hull's system, learning is thought to proceed somewhat in this manner: When a motivated organism is subjected to stimulation—from either or both the stimuli associated with the motivating conditions themselves, as in hunger or pain, and those acting on it from the external environment—it tends to respond in a trial-and-error way. If, in the course of its trial-and-error behavior, the organism performs a response which is associated with the reduction of motivation, the probability of that response occurring again under similar stimulus conditions is increased, or—to put it somewhat differently—the connection between the present stimuli and the response is strengthened. The central emphasis here is on the occurrence of drive reduction or a satisfying state of affairs, variously designated as the law of effect or the principle of reinforcement. As Miller and Dollard (31) succinctly sum it up: To learn, an organism must want something (be motivated in some way), notice something (be acted upon by stimulus cues from the external or internal environment), do something (perform a response or response sequence), and get something (experience a reduction in motivation).

Contiguity Theory

Opposed to a reinforcement theory of learning is a point of view which holds that the basic condition necessary for learning is that of contiguity in experience. Tolman and Guthrie are perhaps the outstanding proponents of this theory, although they differ markedly in their conceptions of the nature of learning.

Tolman (61), taking his point of departure essentially from *Gestalt theorie,* conceives of learning as the acquisition of information or cognitions about the environment. Variously referred to as "sign-gestalt expectations," "sign-significate relations," and "hypotheses," these cognitions presumably have reference to knowledge which the organism acquires to the effect that a given stimulus or sign, if reacted to in a given way by the organism, will lead to a spatially or temporally more remote stimulus or significate. The necessary condition for the acquisition of such "cognitive maps," as Tolman (62) has called them, is contiguity, the spatial and temporal patterning of stimulus events from sign to significate in the organism's experience. Aided by such secondary principles as recency, emphasis, and belongingness, the law of association by contiguity governs *learning;* learning—that is, the acquired cognitive maps—together with the organism's needs and skills governs *performance.*

For Guthrie (15) learning is conceived as the acquisition of stimulus-response bonds as is the case with Hull. Unlike Hull, however, he holds that the occurrence of reinforcement is not a necessary condition for learning. Instead, he states that the principle governing learning is association by contiguity: "A stimulus pattern that is acting at the time of a response will, if it recurs, tend to produce that response." Simultaneity of stimulus cues and response is all that is required for the formation of new S-R bonds. Drive states or the existence of unconditioned stimuli are important only as "forcers" of the response to be learned, not as the basis of reinforcement in the Hullian sense.

The behavior with which the various proponents of these points of view have been concerned in their experimentation has consisted for the most part of skeletal muscle acts—maze running, problem-box solutions, conditioned leg flexions, etc. With this fact kept in mind, it seems fair to conclude that the reinforcement point of view seems to have something of an edge in predictive and explanatory utility over contiguity theory. O'Connor (40) has argued rather devastatingly against Guthrie's position by showing that it cannot accommodate the facts of delayed-reward learning. Likewise, Spence and Lippitt (56), Spence and Kendler (55), and Kendler and Mencher (22) have thrown serious doubt on the adequacy of Tolman's notion of contiguity in experience of sign, significate, and response as the essential and sufficient condition for learning.

Reinforcement theory, on the other hand, has demonstrated its utility in a variety of ways. Whiting (65) has conceptualized the socialization process in terms of Hull's notions. Miller and Dollard (31) have made some fruitful incidental remarks on cultural diffusion. Miller (30) has shown the adequacy of the scheme for explaining certain psychopathological phenomena. Loucks (26) and Loucks and Gantt (27) have supplied evidence that strongly supports Hull's contention that the classical conditioning of skeletal muscle responses is merely a special case of learning according to the principle of reinforcement.

It is precisely at this point, however—in the conditioning of defense reactions—that the law of effect runs into difficulties. Hull (18) pointed out this problem as early as 1929, referring to it as "the dilemma of the conditioned defense reaction." He then wrote,

> For a defense reaction to be wholly successful, it should take place so early that the organism will completely escape injury, that is, the impact of the nocuous (unconditioned) stimulus. But in case the unconditioned stimulus fails to impinge upon the organism, there will be no reinforcement of the conditioned tendency, which means one would expect that experimental extinction will set in at once. This will rapidly render the conditioned reflex impotent, which, in turn, will expose the organism to the original injury. This will initiate a second cycle substantially like the first which will be followed by another and another indefinitely, a series of successful escapes [from all contact with the noxious stimulus] always alternating with a series of injuries. From a biological point of view, the picture emerging from the above theoretical considerations is decidedly not an attractive one.
>
> There is thus presented a kind of biological dilemma . . . (p. 511).

In other words, reinforcement theory finds it hard to explain how an organism can learn to avoid painful stimulation entirely, because if the painful stimuli do not act upon the organism's receptors, no drive is aroused to act as a basis for maintaining the defense reaction.

Mowrer and Lamoreaux (36), concerning themselves with this problem, resolved the dilemma by positing a conditioned fear reaction to the conditioned stimulus. According to their formulation, the conditioned stimulus has signal value, signifying to the organism an approaching danger and arousing in it those anticipations of punishment known as the secondary (acquired) drive of fear (anxiety). On the basis of this secondary drive, trial-and-error behavior occurs, out of which is differentiated, according to the principle of reinforcement, a response which reduces the fear and permits the organism to avoid or to minimize the painful unconditioned stimulus.

Such a resolution of the dilemma of the conditioned defense reaction, however, gives rise to another difficulty of comparable magnitude: How is the fear learned? If one holds to a thoroughly monistic reinforcement position, he is forced to say that the drive state of fear or anxiety is somehow "satisfying" or motivation reducing. Baldly, the reinforcement theorist is forced to hold that secondary drive arousal occurs on the basis of drive reduction. That this is certainly contrary to any kind of common sense consideration is immediately apparent, and it is difficult to see how an exchange of one drive for another—the situation which would obtain were the law of effect rigidly adhered to—could be of any biological benefit. This is particularly true when one recalls that many fears, especially neurotic anxiety, are much more debilitating than the objective conditions which generate them—witness the many people who cannot bear to have dental work done or who refuse to see doctors.

Thus, a kind of *impasse* is reached. Reinforcement theory seems to account rather adequately for the acquisition of striped muscle acts; but at least in the conditioned defense situation—most germane to the clinical problems here under scrutiny—its adequacy is dependent on the operation of secondary motivational states, for the acquisition of which it is hard put to it to explain.

Two-Factor Theory

A number of writers have attempted to overcome this obstacle to efficient theorizing by formulating *two principles* to explain *two different kinds of learning*. Schlosberg (48) in 1937 expressed himself, on the basis of a long series of studies in his laboratory, as believing that there were two types of learning. One had to do with the acquisition of "diffuse, preparatory responses," by which he meant such things as changes in breathing, pulse rate, electrical skin resistance, body volume, voice pitch, and tonicity, which proceeds by "simple conditioning" or according to the principle of association by sheer contiguity. It will be recognized that these reactions are essentially those autonomically mediated viscero-vascular reactions usually thought of as the basic physiological concomitants of emotion. The other type of learning which he felt it necessary to distinguish referred to the acquisition of more "precise, adaptive responses," withdrawal, flexion, or more generally defensive reactions, which are governed by the principle of "success" or reinforcement. These, of course, are the skeletal muscle acts which Hull's kind of theorizing seems to account for so admirably, whether the experimental situation be of the classical or instrumental kind of conditioning.

Skinner (53) in his 1938 volume made explicit a point of view at which he had hinted earlier (52). He distinguished between Type S conditioning as preparatory and Type R as consummatory, holding that the fundamental distinction rested on the event with which the unconditioned stimulus was correlated. In Type S the unconditioned stimulus is correlated with the conditioned stimulus, whereas in Type R it is correlated with the response. Skinner further says,

> Most of the experiments upon skeletal behavior which have been offered as paralleling Pavlov's work are capable of interpretation as discriminated operants of Type R. . . . It is quite possible on the existing evidence that a strict topographical separation of types following the skeletal-autonomic distinction may be made (53, p. 112).

In this formulation, the same classification as that suggested by Schlosberg is implied. Autonomically mediated "emotional" reactions are learned on the basis of contiguity, whereas centrally mediated skeletal muscle responses are learned on the basis of reinforcement.

Razran (43) in 1939 offered a somewhat similar formulation, classifying learning according to what he called "quantitative" and "qualitative" conditioning, corresponding to learning without reinforcement and law-of-effect learning. He reports no evidence for the so-called qualitative conditioning of autonomic reactions, but does not say explicitly that quantitative conditioning applies exclusively to the acquisition of viscero-vascular reactions. He does raise the issue of the differential importance of two events, the *application* or onset of the unconditioned stimulus and the *termination* of the unconditioned stimulus, for the conceptualization of types of learning.

More recently, Mowrer (34) has vigorously exploited the idea of a two-factor theory of learning to account not only for the learning of skeletal muscle responses but for the acquisition of secondary drives like fear and anxiety. He fully accepts the notion that striped muscle acts, mediated by the central nervous system, are learned, according to the principle of reinforcement, by virtue of their association with the *termination* of the noxious stimulation identified as motivational states. This is not only fully in keeping with Hull's position but is quite in line with Mowrer's own previous enthusiastic experimentation and theorizing as a monistic member of the reinforcement school (33). His new point of view, however, holds that smooth muscle and glandular "emotional" reactions, automatically mediated, are acquired through their association with the *onset* of the paired unconditioned stimulus of pain and conditioned stimulus or signal. In other words, fear refers to the viscero-vascular components of the pain response, conditioned to a substitute stimulus through the latter's contiguity with the *onset* of the action of a noxious adequate stimulus. He prefers to restrict the term *conditioning* to the learning of "emotional" reactions by contiguity and to use *problem-solving* to designate the learning of skeletal responses which "solve" the "problems" created by drives and which are acquired according to the reinforcement principle.

One of the points which must be made immediately with respect to two-factor theories such as these is aimed at the scotching of the criticism often (and fairly) leveled against attempts to account for learning in terms of multiple principles. Such attempts frequently permit the theorist to invoke whichever notion happens most easily to explain his data; he can explain everything but predict nothing. With the possible exception of Razran's, the two-factor formulations just reviewed are not liable to such an attack. While two principles are postulated, contiguity and reinforcement, two learning processes, one involving the viscero-vascular system and the other the skeletal muscular system, are also suggested. The principle that governs one process may not be invoked to explain what occurs in the other. For either process, the theory is monistic and parsimonious and presumably subject to an *experimentem crucis*.[5]

Direct experimental tests of the two-factor theory are as yet few. One study having an immediate bearing on the issue is that of Mowrer and Suter (37). These researchers argue that if the drive-termination theory of acquiring "conditioned" responses is valid, the response should become more readily connected with those stimuli present at the time of drive reduction. If, on the other hand, the drive-onset interpretation is correct, there should be no difference in the resulting learning curves. The rationale on which this deduction is based, of course, is that a conditioned stimulus (warning signal) *must* coincide with or approximate the

---

[5] The two-factor theories reviewed here may be contrasted with those of Stephens (57) and Maier and Schnierla (28). For a careful and trenchant critique of these points of view, see Kendler and Underwood (23).

turning on of the noxious unconditioned stimulus. If this contiguity with the *onset* of drive is all that is necessary for "conditioning" to occur, it should make no difference whether the conditioned stimulus overlaps with the *termination* of the unconditioned stimulus or not. Using an arbitrary running response as an index of fear and as their criterion of conditioning, Mowrer and Suter obtained experimental results confirmatory of their prediction: there was no difference in the curves of response acquisition between a group of rats trained under conditions where the conditioned stimulus overlapped and terminated with the turning off of the unconditioned stimulus of shock and a group of animals where the conditioned stimulus was turned off at the time of the unconditioned stimulus's onset.

The interpretation of these results is that the animals learned to *fear* the conditioned stimulus by virtue of its contiguity with the onset of·pain. This anticipation of pain gave rise to trial-and-error behavior out of which was differentiated the running response, which was reinforced by fear reduction or the avoidance of pain. The acquisition of the fear reaction was not furthered, as reinforcement theory would predict, by having the warning signal overlap and end in contiguity with the reinforcing state of affairs provided by the termination of the shock.

The more crucial experiment, yet to be done, would involve the testing of the hypothesis that some autonomically mediated reaction, taken as an index of fear, will be attached to some conditioned stimulus by virtue of its association by contiguity with the onset of noxious stimulation, whereas it will not become attached any more effectively under conditions of reinforcement.

Experimentation with viscero-vascular reactions presents many problems, however, and there is little in the literature that can be brought directly to bear on this issue. Indirect evidence is presented in the cited publications of Schlosberg and Skinner and is thoroughly reviewed by Mowrer (34).

While such interpretations are not crucial, much recent experimentation on secondary drives is readily assimilable into two-factor theory. Miller (29), for example, reports having trained rats by means of strong shock to escape from a white compartment with a grid floor through an open door into a black compartment without a grid. Subsequently, the animals, without shock or noxious stimulation of any kind, learned a new habit—rotating a little wheel to open the door, which had been closed, in order to escape from the white compartment to the black one. This was interpreted to mean that the secondary drive of fear had been acquired and that its termination could be used as reinforcement for striped muscle responses. In terms of the two-factor formulation, the rats learned to run into the black box by virtue of the reinforcement provided by pain reduction. At the same time, however, fear or the visceral component of pain became conditioned to the cues of "whiteness and grid floor" associated with the *onset* of shock. The conditioned fear then served as the drive on the basis of which the wheel-rotating habit was learned without benefit of further primary drive arousal through shock.

It would seem, then, that in spite of its present tentative status, a two-factor theory of learning—holding that adaptive, striped muscle habits are built up according to the principle of reinforcement whereas anticipatory, "emotional" reactions, probably viscero-vascular in nature and having drive properties, are acquired according to the principle of contiguity—has the greatest explanatory and predictive power at the moment.

LEARNING THEORY AND PSYCHOTHERAPY

How can such a conception of learning be applied to psychotherapy to cover the elements of the psychotherapeutic process common to all forms of counseling? It will be recalled that the problem of therapy is essentially that of somehow ridding the patient of neurotic anxiety, which supports his persistent nonintegrative defenses and accounts in large measure for his "unhappiness." The tools used by all therapists to accomplish this job are those of conversational content and the therapeutic relationship.

Therapy as the Acquisition of Symbolic Controls

Shaffer (49) suggests that psychotherapy be conceptualized in terms of the patient's acquisition of language symbols by which he can more effectively control his nonintegrative behavior. The rationale of this approach is based on the observation that an outstanding characteristic of the maladjusted is their inability to control their own acts; in their own terms, "I know I should (or shouldn't) do this, but I just can't (or must)." Since "normal" people seem to control their behavior by means of symbols—including subvocal and gestural symbols—Shaffer's notion seems at first blush to follow readily.

Such an idea is also more or less explicit in Shaw's (50) analysis of repression and insight. He argues from Mowrer and Ullman's (38) point that

The common denominator in all . . . forms of nonintegrative behavior seems to be the inability to use symbols appropriately as a means of bringing remote as well as immediate consequences into the present in such a manner that they may exert an influence proportional to their objective importance (p. 81).

Shaw moves from here to the contention that therapy is a process by which nonintegrative behavior is eliminated by the making available of symbols, holding that the symbols become cues for the more remote punishing consequences of neurotic defenses.

It is not quite clear, however, according to either Shaffer or Shaw, what the symbolization at which therapy aims might be. If it is the symbolizing of acts which have been repressed, there is no indication of how such a procedure would accomplish anything more than the release of a flood of anxiety heretofore held in check—albeit imperfectly—by the repression mechanism. On the other hand, if the symbols made available by therapy amount only to accurate predictions of the consequences of the client's nonintegrative behavior, their utility is questionable on several grounds: First, most clinical patients are only too sharply aware of the self-defeating nature of their activity; their complaint is that they don't know why they engage in it and at the same time seem unable to avoid it. Second, some cases (especially those who have been formally psychoanalyzed) demonstrate a remarkable glibness—sometimes quite accurate —about their own defenses and yet are anxiety ridden on the one hand and socially somewhat obnoxious on the other. It is probably these instances which gave rise to H. M. Johnson's (20) rather oversevere recent strictures on psychoanalysis as therapy and as rationale. Third, there is a question as to whether or not simply making available symbols which can arouse at an earlier point in the temporal sequence the anxiety that accrues from future punishment amounts to anything more than a more effective punishment of the already nonintegrative response. In this case, there may be the danger of the repression of one mechanism while another, equally self-defeating, is developed as a defense against a compounded neurotic anxiety, now attached not only to the ineffectively repressed impulses which existed prior to "therapy," but also to those incipient tendencies connected with the defense mechanism which has undergone the "punishment" of having its hurtful ultimate consequences symbolically brought into the psychological present. Thus, if a clinician is dealing with a patient whose anxiety has its origin in the faulty repression of aggressive tendencies and defends himself against it by social withdrawal, the anxiety may be compounded by making the damaging effects of the mechanism more apparent through the providing of symbols within the therapeutic context. All this is not to be construed as an attack on the Shaw-Shaffer hypothesis; as a matter of fact, it seems to describe quite adequately one segment of the therapeutic process. It is merely an effort to point out that such an hypothesis does not seem quite to account for *everything* that happens in psychotherapy.

A somewhat different suggestion, here proposed, is this: If neurotic anxiety is produced by the repression of some unextinguished response, it should follow that the anxiety can be dissipated in one of two ways—either by the elicitation of unreinforced occurrences of the response, thus leading to extinction, or by the connecting of a different affect to response tendencies which have undergone repression. With respect to the illustrative case mentioned above, anxiety could be dispelled either through eliciting self-initiated behavior and failing to reinforce it until extinction occurred, or through forming a bond between the tendencies to self-initiated behavior and some nonanxious visceral reaction which will supplant the connection between anxiety and the repressed activity. In either case, the Shaw-Shaffer notion holds as the first step in therapy, the bringing into communicability (consciousness) of the tendency that has undergone repression.

This lifting of repression is what is usually known as insight. When the patient is able to verbalize the repressed tendencies fundamentally associated with his anxiety, he "sees" or demonstrates insight. It is difficult to understand, however, why this should be equated with cure, regardless of how important it is as a step toward psychological recovery. Merely being able to talk about the cues for anxiety does not make them any less terrifying. Extinction or counterconditioning is still necessary.

Whether the extinction or the counter-conditioning technique is preferable depends in part on the desirability of the repressed behavior. In the case of self-initiated activity, the question seems rather clear. Socialization has been defined (35) as the process of developing from a dependent infant into an independent and dependable adult. The extinction of tendencies toward self-initiated "responsible" behavior would mean the continuation of dependence and infantilism. It seems probable that few clinicians would look upon this as a suitable therapeutic goal. The same thing might well be said of most of the impulses which typically undergo repression, sexuality being a case in point. The frigid wife, raised under conditions of puritanical restrictiveness, might well find some immediate relief from anxiety by having her repressed sexual impulses extinguished (if this is possible); but it is doubtful that such a procedure would be helpful in her marriage.

THE COUNTERCONDITIONING HYPOTHESIS. The hypothesis of counterconditioning is suggested as somewhat more tenable. It involves the following set of notions: The conversational content aspect of counseling consists in the symbolic reinstatement of the stimuli which produce and have produced the patient's anxiety. Through his words to the therapist, the client, on a symbolic level, again "lives through" the stimulus situations which were painful to him, in which he underwent punishment, and which initiated the repression sequence. This constitutes the lifting of repression, the introduction into communicability of the repressed tendencies, the development of insight. This proceeds essentially by the therapist's reinforcing by his acceptance and his sympathetic participation of the patient's self-revelatory behavior. At the same time, the discussion of the client's anxiety is being carried on within the context of the unique patient-therapist relationship. This is conceived as an unconditioned stimulus for feelings of pleasure, acceptance, security—nonanxious affective reactions. The therapeutic process consists in the establishment of a bond between the symbolically reproduced stimuli which evoke and have evoked anxiety—chiefly the cues associated with the incipient movements toward performing some repressed activity—and the nonanxiety, that is, comfort and confidence, reactions made to the counseling relationship.

Such a formulation goes somewhat beyond the bounds of "emotional" learning as accounted for by the two-factor theories briefly discussed above. They are chiefly concerned with the learning of fear or anxiety, basic secondary drives. While the idea presented here may be an extension of the theory that its protagonists would find unacceptable, there seems to be no reason why the principle of contiguity should not apply to viscero-vascular reactions that are "pleasant" as well as to those which are "unpleasant"; as a matter of fact, such an application seems to be demanded if the learning of affects is governed by a single principle. The conceptualization proceeds in this wise: Affects possessing drive value—fear, anxiety, and anger[6]—are learned by virtue of the association by contiguity of the visceral aspects of some primary drive with concurrent external stimuli. The so-called "positive" or "pleasurable" affects are learned by virtue of the association by contiguity of proprioceptive cues set up at the onset of drive *reduction* with concurrent external stimuli. It is quite possible that Murray's (39) scheme for conceptualizing motivation in terms of goals is analyzable on some such basis as this latter notion.

Hull (19) seems to use a similar idea when he defines secondary reinforcement in terms of a stimulus situation which has been closely and consistently associated with the occurrence of need reduction. Experimental animals thus develop "needs" for poker chips, tones of given frequency, black compartments rather than white, etc. Likewise, the judgmental theory of affections, as proposed by Carr (5) and expanded upon and experimentally verified by Peters (41), (42), is fully consonant with the suggestion here proposed as fundamental in therapy. According to these writers, the pleasantness or unpleasantness of objects is a function of their association with "satisfying" or "unsatisfying" events in experience. Integrating this with the aspect of two-factor theory that deals

---

[6] The inclusion of anger in this list of secondary drives is somewhat cavalier. Virtually nothing is known of the conditions under which the learning of anger takes place, and it is certainly not assured that it derives from pain.

with the learning of affects, "satisfying" events in experience are those correlated with drive reduction; "unsatisfying" events in experience are those correlated with drive onset.[7]

To return to the counterconditioning hypothesis in psychotherapy, a rather striking analogy may be pointed out between this formulation and the now famous experiment of Mary Cover Jones (21) with the boy Peter. It will be remembered that Peter was a three-year-old with a number of acquired fears of various objects, including small white furry animals. In an effort to eliminate these fears, Dr. Jones attempted a counterconditioning procedure. At lunch time, just as the child began to eat a meal which included his favorite dishes, a white rabbit was introduced in a wire cage at the end of the room, far enough away not to disturb the boy's eating. Each day the animal was brought a little closer until finally Peter could eat with one hand while stroking the rabbit with the other. Further tests showed that the newly conditioned "comfort" reaction to the rabbit had generalized to a large number of other, formerly fear-evoking stimuli such as rats, frogs, cotton, and fur rugs.

The meaning of these results is that a new connection was formed between the stimuli (rabbit) which produced a fear reaction and the comfort reaction made to the stimulus of the lunch with all its various cues. The necessary condition for the formation of this new connection was contiguity of the noxious stimulus and the comfort reaction aroused by the unconditioned luncheon stimulus situation. The problem of how to pair the stimuli so that those connected with the meal did not come to evoke fear does not affect the fundamental point of contiguity as the basis for the establishment of the new bond, but is merely a matter of the spatial and temporal patterning of stimuli common to most experimentation under the conditions of classical conditioning.

The main objection to this analogy probably rests on the point that Peter was troubled by a fear rather than an anxiety—that is, an affective reaction, uncomplicated by repression, made to external stimuli rather than to some impulse to behave in a tabooed way. The objection is certainly granted and actually implies the basis for the first step in therapy, the uncovering by use of the conversational content of therapeutic interviews of the repressed impulses. Before counterconditioning can occur, the stimuli connected with anxiety must be brought into communicability, where they can be symbolically reinstated at the appropriate times. Insight is a prior condition of counterconditioning.

A second objection that can be raised to the counterconditioning

---

[7] It is interesting to speculate as to whether or not this is the mechanism underlying the acquisition of aesthetic tastes, preferences, and other "likes" and "dislikes." The implications for a psychological approach to valuative behavior are obvious.

notion is this: If therapy is simply a matter of connecting anxiety-provoking stimuli with some comfort reaction, why is it not therapeutically effective to think of one's troubles while lying in a comfortably warm tub? [8] There seem to be three answers to this. First, to a degree it *is* effective. The widespread method of combatting the "blues" by means of a shower is directly in point, as is the use of continuous baths and warm packs in mental hospitals. The real problem is: Why is such a procedure less effective than psychotherapy? This gives rise to the second answer, which is that thinking of one's troubles while lying in a comfortably warm tub is usually of little help in creating insight, symbolically re-introducing the relevant anxiety-producing stimuli. The bath is of little assistance in bringing forbidden impulses into communicability, hence the "therapeutic effects" of the bath are of short duration. The third reply to such an objection is based on the fact that neurotic anxiety is primarily social in its inception. Sullivan (59) insists that this "interpersonal induction of anxiety, and the exclusively interpersonal origin of every instance of its manifestations, is the unique characteristic of anxiety and of the congeries of more complex tensions . . . to which it contributes." This squares perfectly, of course, with the concept of repression and the role it plays in anxiety theory. If neurotic anxiety is an anticipation of punishment for the performance of some tabooed act, it follows that the taboo must have been laid down and enforced through some kind of social medium. Consequently, one would expect in the light of such social origins that the elimination of anxiety would be facilitated by the presence of certain social factors in therapy—provided in this case by the patient-therapist relationship.

This last point also bears on the function of catharsis in psychotherapy. It is a commonplace experience among clinicians to have clients say, after a period of vigorous abreaction, "I've thought about that a lot, but I've never said it to anybody before. I feel a bit better now." This poses something of a conceptual difficulty, since it is hard to understand how the expression of an affect should dissipate an affect unless the expression has some effect on the maintaining stimulus conditions. Such an environmental modification certainly does not occur in counseling; and yet catharsis in the social situation of therapy (and possibly in other social situations) seems to bring some relief, whereas catharsis subvocally or made without the presence of a therapist or therapist-surrogate apparently does not. According to the formulation here offered, *catharsis will be effective when it involves (a) the symbolic reinstatement of the repressed cues for anxiety (b) within the context of a warm, permissive, nonjudgmental social relationship.* Under these conditions the situation

---

[8] This point was raised in a very helpful personal communication from Dr. John P. Seward. The replies offered to the objection, however, are not chargeable to him.

is ripe for counterconditioning to take place, whereby the patient learns to react nonanxiously to the original stimuli.

The counterconditioning hypothesis likewise bears on the problems of technique inherent in the directive-nondirective controversy. This argument can perhaps be more profitably stated this way: How much and what can the therapist do to help reinstate symbolically the anxiety-arousing stimuli acting on the patient without endangering the relationship (that is, weakening the relationship-comfort bond)? Asked in these terms, the question bears on the first step in counseling, that of lifting repressions or developing insight, and becomes the purely empirical matter of determining the categories of counselor response that most effectively further the bringing into communicability of repressed impulses. On somewhat dangerous *a priori* grounds it would seem that interpretation, probing and other more active procedures would be useful unless introduced too peremptorily or too early into therapy, thereby destroying the patient-therapist relationship. That this occurs is not denied, but to attack such techniques as being of no value because they are sometimes misused seems somewhat absurd. The situation is analogous to bringing the rabbit too far into Peter's lunch room too early and connecting the fear reaction to the animal to the stimulus complex of food, room, high chair, and so forth. It seems somewhat nonsensical to argue that the baby should be thrown out with the bath water simply because it is still a bit grimy. One wonders if Peter would have overcome his fear of rabbits had he only been thoroughly "accepted" without ever having any help in reencountering the noxious stimulus in a secure and "pleasant" situation.

The directive-nondirective controversy may well reduce to a consideration of the types of case for which each is best suited. It can be hypothesized that more nondirective approaches will be more likely to succeed with those clients who have few and relatively unsevere repressions, some insight into the sources of their anxiety, and a capacity to relate easily to the therapist. These are cases which do not require much help in *discovering* the anxiety-producing stimuli; they do need assurance from a counselor that they may talk about them in his presence with complete impunity. Conversely, more interpretative methods by hypothesis will be of greater effectiveness with cases characterized by higher defenses, greater repression, and less initial insight. It must be emphasized, however, that all this is a matter of the empirical determination of what techniques work best for given cases so far as the lifting of repressions is concerned. The hypothesis of counterconditioning is still the means of explaining the diminution of anxiety after insight has been developed.

If this formulation is correct, how can various failures of counterconditioning methods in psychological treatment be answered? Voegtlin's (63) work with alcoholics is typical. This clinician attempted to cure his patients of drinking by having them take whiskey so heavily dosed with a powerful emetic that vomiting to the point of pain was immediately induced. Results were disappointing. Most of his cases did not build up more than momentary conditioned aversions to alcohol. Of those few who became conditioned against liquor over a period of time, several showed symptom substitutions, for example, the development of psychosomatic symptoms or neurotic syndromes instead of alcohol addiction.

The first objection to such a procedure is that it consists in a direct attack on the symptomatic mechanism rather than on the underlying anxiety. If the anxiety reduction occurring from drinking were greater than the pain of the treatment, the treatment would have very nearly as little effect as strongly advising the patient "to get on the wagon." The ineffectiveness of "hangovers" is relevant in this connection. Second, if the alcohol addiction were wiped out by virtue of the conditioning procedure, the underlying anxiety would be unaffected, and one would therefore expect that the patient would develop some other persistently nonintegrative way of reducing it. Third, the treatment situation contains too many elements of attempting to eliminate a response by merely punishing it. The inefficacy of such methods has already been discussed. Thus, an objection based on such therapeutic experience fails to carry much weight.

Reeducation in Psychotherapy

Does the point of view developed here overlook this notion in the therapeutic armamentarium? On the contrary, it fully includes it as an important third aspect of counseling, along with the lifting of repression and the counterconditioning of anxiety. Following the development of insight, as anxiety is dissipated through conditioning, the patient typically begins to plan. His first tentative steps in this direction may take the form of asking, "What shall I do?" Or it may be a more vigorous exploration of the possible consequences of projected steps. Here the therapist may be of assistance in helping his client to formulate goals clearly and to consider realistically the various behavioral methods he might employ to reach them. This constitutes a law-of-effect learning situation in which reinforcement is produced through the patient's own verbal self-approval or self-disapproval, based in part on the predictions of consequences which the counselor can help him arrive at. In a sense, this constitutes the "rational" exercise of symbolically mediated self-control of which Shaw and Shaffer may be speaking. It is rational insofar as the behavior selected is founded on some consideration of its probable remote outcomes rather than on its immediate value as an anxiety-reducing agent, and it is "responsible" insofar as it is chosen[9] in terms of the patient's own values as of the moment of choice. The counselor does not direct; he merely helps the client work out relatively accurate estimates of the consequences. If a particular behavior pattern is rejected, it merely undergoes a voluntary suppression or is extinguished through failure of reinforcement without being forced into incommunicability and becoming a stimulus for anxiety, as is the case in the repression of punished tendencies. Through this symbolic trial and error, then, the patient develops, according to the principle of reinforcement, a tentative plan of integrative behavior based on rational considerations to supplant his former pattern of persistent nonintegrative behavior based on the immediate necessity of reducing anxiety regardless of the ultimate cost.

SUMMARY

A learning theory interpretation of psychotherapy must take into account (a) the fact that all forms of psychotherapy are able to claim cures, (b) the similarity of clinical cases in terms of neurotic anxiety and its defenses, (c) the common goal of psychotherapies of the diminution of anxiety, and (d) the fact that all clinicians employ as their chief techniques conversational content and the therapeutic relationship.

It is here proposed that psychotherapy occurs through three interrelated processes: first, the lifting of repression and development of insight through the symbolic reinstating of the stimuli for anxiety; second, the diminution of anxiety by counterconditioning through the attachment of the stimuli for anxiety to the comfort reaction made to the therapeutic relationship; and third, the process of reeducation through the therapist's helping the patient to formulate rational goals and behavioral methods for attaining them.

Such a scheme seems to harmonize most effectively with a two-factor learning theory of the type most recently developed by Mowrer (34). Such a theory conceives of skeletal muscle responses as being acquired through the principle of reinforcement, whereas viscero-vascular, "emotional" reactions are acquired according to the principle of contiguity.

This formulation is certainly not to be regarded as anything final. It leans rather too much on plausible but inadequately tested hypotheses and on scientifically tenuous analogies. It is offered only as a preliminary attempt to effect a *rapprochement* between psychotherapy and general psychology, and to organize some of the phenomena of clinical practice within the framework of systematic behavior theory.

---

[9] Lest the language used here seem flavored too heavily with free will, reference is made to Hall's (16) paper, in which the problem of choice within a deterministic philosophy is discussed.

References

1. Alexander, F., and French, T. *Psychoanalytic therapy*. New York: Ronald, 1946.

2. Allen, F. *Psychotherapy with children*. New York: Norton, 1942.

3. Axline, V. *Play therapy*. Boston: Houghton Mifflin, 1947.

4. Cameron, N. *The psychology of the behavior disorders*. Boston: Houghton Mifflin, 1947.

5. Carr, H. *Psychology*. New York: Longmans, Green, 1925.

6. Combs, A. W. Phenomenological concepts in nondirective therapy. *J. consult. Psychol.*, 1948, *12*, 197-208.

7. Darley, J. Review of *"Counseling and psychotherapy."* *J. abnorm. soc. Psychol.*, 1943, *38*, 199-201.

8. Dejerine, J., and Gauckler, E. *The psychoneuroses and their treatment by psychotherapy*. Philadelphia: J. B. Lippincott, 1913.

9. Estes, W. K. An experimental study of punishment. *Psychol. Monogr.*, 1944, *57*, No. 3.

10. Finesinger, J. E. Psychiatric interviewing. *Amer. J. Psychiat.*, 1948, *105*, 187-195.

11. French, T. Interrelations between psychoanalysis and the experimental work of Pavlov. *Amer. J. Psychiat.*, 1933, *12*, 1165-1203.

12. Freud, S. *New introductory lectures on psychoanalysis*. New York: Norton, 1933.

13. Freud, S. *A general introduction to psychoanalysis*. New York: Liveright, 1935.

14. Freud, S. *The problem of anxiety*. New York: Norton, 1936.

15. Guthrie, E. R. A theory of learning in terms of stimulus, response, and association. *National Society for the Study of Education*, 41st Yearbook. Bloomington: Public School Publ. Co., 1942. Pp. 17-60.

16. Hall, E. W. An ethics for today. *Amer. J. econ. Sociol.*, 1943, *2*, 444-446.

17. Horney, K. *The neurotic personality of our time*. New York: Norton, 1937.

18. Hull, C. A functional interpretation of the conditioned reflex. *Psychol. Rev.*, 1929, *36*, 498-511.

19. Hull, C. *Principles of behavior*. New York: Appleton-Century-Crofts, 1943.

20. Johnson, H. M. Psychoanalytic therapy versus psychoanalytic rationale. *Amer. Psychologist*, 1948, *3*, 337. (Abstract.)

21. Jones, M. C. A laboratory study of fear: the case of Peter. *Ped. Sem.*, 1924, *31*, 308-315.

22. Kendler, H. H., and Mencher, H. C. The ability of rats to learn the location of food when motivated by thirst—an experimental reply to Leeper. *J. exp. Psychol.*, 1948, *38*, 82-88.

23. Kendler, H. H., and Underwood, B. J. The role of reward in conditioning theory. *Psychol. Rev.,* 1948, *55,* 209-215.

24. Kraines, S. *Treatment of the neuroses and psychoses.* (2d ed.) Philadelphia: Lea & Febiger, 1943.

25. Kubie, L. S. Relation of the conditioned reflex to psychoanalytic technique. *Arch. Neurol. Psychiat.,* 1934, *32,* 1137-1142.

26. Loucks, R. B. The experimental delimitation of neural structures necessary for learning: the attempt to condition striped muscle responses with faradization of the sigmoid gyri. *J. Psychol.,* 1935, *1,* 5-44.

27. Loucks, R. B., and Gantt, W. H. The conditioning of striped muscle responses based on faradic stimulation of dorsal roots and dorsal columns of the spinal cord. *J. comp. Psychol.,* 1938, *25,* 415-426.

28. Maier, N. R. F., and Schnierla, T. C. Mechanisms in conditioning. *Psychol. Rev.,* 1942, *49,* 117-134.

29. Miller, N. E. Studies of fear as an acquirable drive. I. Fear as motivation and fear-reduction as reinforcement in the learning of new responses. *J. exp. Psychol.,* 1948, *38,* 89-101.

30. Miller, N. E. Theory and experiment relating psychoanalytic displacement to stimulus-response generalization. *J. abnorm. soc. Psychol.,* 1948, *43,* 155-178.

31. Miller, N. E., and Dollard, J. *Social learning and imitation.* New Haven: Yale Univer. Press, 1941.

32. Mowrer, O. H. A stimulus-response analysis of anxiety and its role as a reinforcing agent. *Psychol. Rev.,* 1939, *46,* 553-565.

33. Mowrer, O. H. The law of effect and ego psychology. *Psychol. Rev.,* 1946, *53,* 321-334.

34. Mowrer, O. H. On the dual nature of learning—A reinterpretation of "conditioning" and "problem-solving." *Harvard educ. Rev.,* 1947, *17,* 102-148.

35. Mowrer, O. H., and Kluckhohn, C. A dynamic theory of personality. In J. McV. Hunt (Ed.), *Personality and the behavior disorders.* New York: Ronald, 1943. Pp. 69-135.

36. Mowrer, O. H., and Lamoreaux, R. R. Fear as an intervening variable in avoidance conditioning. *J. comp. Psychol.,* 1946, *39,* 29-50.

37. Mowrer, O. H., and Suter, J. Further evidence for a two-factor theory of learning. Unpublished study.

38. Mowrer, O. H., and Ullman, A. D. Time as a determinant in integrative learning. *Psychol. Rev.,* 1945, *52,* 61-90.

39. Murray, H. *Explorations in personality.* New York: Oxford Univer. Press, 1938.

40. O'Connor, F. J. Recency or effect? A critical analysis of Guthrie's theory of learning. *Harvard educ. Rev.,* 1946, *16,* 194-206.

41. Peters, H. N. The judgmental theory of pleasantness and unpleasantness. *Psychol. Rev.,* 1935, *42,* 354-386.

42. Peters, H. N. Experimental studies of the judgmental theory of feeling: I. Learning of positive and negative reactions as a determinant of affective judgments. *J. exp. Psychol.*, 1938, *23*, 1-25.

43. Razran, G. S. The law of effect or the law of qualitative conditioning? *Psychol. Rev.*, 1939, *46*, 445-463.

44. Rogers, C. *Counseling and psychotherapy*. Boston: Houghton Mifflin Co., 1942.

45. Rogers, C. Some observations on the organization of personality. *Amer. Psychologist*, 1947, *2*, 358-368.

46. Rosenzweig, S. Some implicit common factors in diverse methods of psychotherapy. *Amer. J. Orthopsychiat.*, 1936, *6*, 412-415.

47. Sanford, R. N. Psychotherapy and counseling: Introduction. *J. consult. Psychol.*, 1948, *12*, 65-67.

48. Schlosberg, H. The relationship between success and the laws of conditioning. *Psychol. Rev.*, 1937, *44*, 379-394.

49. Shaffer, L. The problem of psychotherapy. *Amer. Psychologist*, 1947, *2*, 459-467.

50. Shaw, F. A stimulus-response analysis of repression and insight in psychotherapy. *Psychol. Rev.*, 1946, *53*, 36-42.

51. Shoben, E. J., Jr. A learning-theory interpretation of psychotherapy. *Harvard educ. Rev.*, 1948, *18*, 129-145.

52. Skinner, B. F. Two types of conditioned reflex and a pseudo-type. *J. gen. Psychol.*, 1935, *12*, 66-77.

53. Skinner, B. F., *The behavior of organisms*. New York: Appleton-Century-Crofts, 1938.

54. Snyder, W. U. An investigation of the nature of nondirective counseling. *J. gen. Psychol.*, 1945, *33*, 193-224.

55. Spence, K. W., and Kendler, H. H. The speculations of Leeper with respect to the Iowa tests of the sign-gestalt theory of learning. *J. exp. Psychol.*, 1948, *38*, 106-109.

56. Spence, K. W., and Lippitt, R. An experimental test of the sign-gestalt theory of trial-and-error learning. *J. exp. Psychol.*, 1946, *36*, 491-502.

57. Stephens, J. M. Expectancy vs. effect-substitution as a general principle of reinforcement. *Psychol. Rev.*, 1942, *49*, 102-116.

58. Sullivan, H. S. *Conceptions of modern psychiatry*. Washington: The William Alanson White Memorial Foundation, 1947.

59. Sullivan, H. S. The meaning of anxiety in psychiatry and in life. *Psychiatry*, 1948, *11*, 1-13.

60. Taft, Jessie. *The dynamics of therapy*. New York: Macmillan, 1933.

61. Tolman, E. C. The determiners of behavior at the choice point. *Psychol. Rev.*, 1938, *45*, 1-41.

62. Tolman, E. C. Cognitive maps in rats and men. *Psychol. Rev.*, 1948, *55*, 189-208.

63. Voegtlin, W. L. The treatment of alcoholism by establishing a conditioned reflex. *Amer. J. med. Sci.,* 1940, *109,* 102.

64. White, R. *The abnormal personality.* New York: Ronald, 1948.

65. Whiting, J. W. M. *Becoming a Kwoma.* New Haven: Yale Univer. Press, 1941.

66. Williamson, E. G. *How to counsel students.* New York: McGraw-Hill, 1939.

Relationship Conditions for Effective Counterconditioning

Again we see the point made that psychotherapy must first be viewed as an interpersonal exchange and that "the difficult-to-isolate aspects of the personalities of *both* patient and counselor must be taken into consideration." The therapist is not only "the wielder of some supposedly ameliorative technique but is deeply involved as a personality in the counseling process." Furthermore, Shoben states that "the psychology of the psychologist, as well as the psychology of the patient and the nature of the therapeutic method, enters into the determination of the therapeutic end product."

The efficacy of the counterconditioning rests upon the level and value of the counselor-patient interpersonal relationship. The social-psychological conditions offered by the therapist make it possible for learning to take place. To be ready or "ripe" for relearning, the patient must trust the therapist's motives so that he (the patient) can be open enough to reconsider repressed material. The diminution of anxiety (except in some cases of phobics and compulsions) based on recall of repressed material and counterconditioning takes place only to the extent that the therapist is a person who cares, understands, communicates concretely, and is warm and *honestly* accepting (that is, does not employ acceptance as a technique). Techniques administered in sterile medicinal doses may not only leave the patient the same, but worse.

Another point hinted at, or one that can easily be read into Shoben's discussion, is that with a fuller awareness of each other's worlds, counselors and therapists may develop preferred modes of treatment for different patient populations *based on a relatively small number of dimensions.*

In a selected manner, Krasner's (1962) article is an extension of Shoben's. In contrast to Shoben, however, Krasner considers fully the possibility that to be most effective, the therapist may need to become a depersonalized dispenser of scientifically derived techniques. Both authors share two assumptions: (a) therapy is most profitably viewed as a learning problem, and (b) the variables that prove to be significant contributors to the outcome of therapy apply to a large number of other interpersonal situations.

THE REINFORCEMENT MACHINE*

Leonard Krasner

In recent years the therapist has emerged, reluctantly, from the shadow of the patient to a fuller recognition of the influence of his behavior in the psychotherapy process. Certain assumptions are implicit in the selection of the type of research studies used to illustrate the major issues in research on the therapist variable in the psychotherapy process. These assumptions may be stated as follows: (a) Psychotherapy is a lawful, predictable, and directive process which can be investigated most parsimoniously within the framework of a reinforcement theory of learning. (b) The variables which affect the therapy process are the same as those in other interpersonal situations which involve the reinforcement, control, manipulation, influencing, or redirection of human behavior.

If these general assumptions about psychotherapy are accepted, a number of deductions follow which can guide research programs: (a) The therapist, as the central variable in the therapeutic situation, is a social "reinforcement machine," programmed by prior training and experience. The therapist has been trained to use his behavior as a decisive factor in interpersonal situations with individuals who come to him for assistance. His goal is to influence his patient's behavior in the therapy situation so that certain changes may occur in the patient's total life situation; (b) The therapist has available to him a series of reinforcement techniques to influence the probability of selected behavior change in the patient; (c) The effectiveness of the reinforcement process can be

* The therapist as a social reinforcement machine. In *Research in psychotherapy*, Vol. II. Washington, D.C.: American Psychological Association, 1962, pp. 61-94. Reprinted by permission of author and publisher. This paper is the result of work done at the Behavioral Research Laboratory, VA Hospital, Palo Alto. Its preparation was facilitated by support, in part, from Research Grant M-2458 from the National Institute of Mental Health, Public Health Service, through Stanford University. The author wishes to express his appreciation to his colleagues Leonard Ullmann, Robert Weiss, and Paul Ekman for their valuable assistance in the conception, design, and analysis of data of the various studies in this project.

maximized by appropriate interactions of the therapist, situational, and patient variables.

It is difficult to find an area of human endeavor whose effectiveness is as strongly defended with as little concrete evidence as "psychotherapy" (Eysenck, 1952). It is increasingly difficult for research in this field to break out of the confines of the narrow boundaries of the framework of *traditional* psychotherapeutic interaction. Research in psychotherapy will not be as productive as it could be until the therapist can accept his role as an influencer of behavior and thus permit investigation of the variables of behavior control. Within this concept, new approaches and new techniques can develop. Further, we will be able to develop predictive devices for evaluating the changes in behavior which may result from such techniques.

To put into proper perspective the variables of the therapy process, we must investigate relevant research in a number of related fields, in addition to traditional psychotherapy research. This should include other "influencing" processes such as: "brainwashing," hypnosis, "placebos," role-taking, sensory deprivation, attitude influence, verbal operant conditioning, motor operant conditioning, and subliminal perception. The process of psychotherapy is an integral part of a broader psychology of behavior control (Frank, 1961; McConnell;[1] Meerloo, 1956; Rotter, 1960; Sargant, 1957).

In recent years, this point of view has become increastingly prominent in a wide range of both theoretical and research papers. A series of earlier papers and books had placed psychotherapy within the framework of learning or social reinforcement theory (Dollard and Miller, 1950; Mowrer, 1953; Schaffer and Lazarus, 1952; Shaw, 1948; Shoben, 1949). However, learning theory approaches usually limit themselves to the reinterpretation or translation of the ongoing therapy process into learning theory terminology, and as such, offer little in the way of relevant new research techniques into the process. More recent works (Bachrach, in press; Bandura, 1961; Frank, 1958, 1959a, 1961; Kanfer, 1961; Krasner, 1955; Lunden, 1961; Marmor, 1961; Salzinger, in press; Shaw, 1961) have moved sharply in the direction of interpreting the therapist as one who manipulates and controls the therapy situation by his knowledge and use of learning techniques in a social reinforcement situation. This approach to psychotherapy research is implicit in verbal operant conditioning studies (Krasner, 1958a; Salzinger, 1959) which have been strongly influenced by the work of Skinner (1953a, 1953b, 1957, 1958), and Keller and Schoenfeld (1950). These studies have features in common that distinguish them as a unique body of research. In verbal operant conditioning, S is required to emit verbal behavior as part of a given task, and E rein-

---

[1] McConnell, J. V. Persuasion and behavioral change. Unpublished manuscript, 1960.

forces a preselected class of S's verbal behavior by carefully controlled verbal and/or nonverbal behavioral cues. The conditioning of verbal behavior is developing as a major technique for systematically exploring variables of interpersonal situations. Relevant studies will be cited as they illuminate the psychology of behavior control.

Historically, in the conceptualization of therapy, major emphasis was placed on the role and attributes of the patient, with relatively little regard for the therapist's characteristics, except that he be a well-trained person who was warm and "accepting." If anything, the therapist variable was to be controlled by removing the therapist's personality from the therapy situation by his own analysis, which would clear him of any involvement or "illegal" influence on the patient. Even the seating arrangements, with the therapist located *behind* the patient on the couch, was calculated to take the therapist "out" of the situation. Then, later writers began to push the therapist back into the therapy situation by emphasis on the "relationship," or the therapist role as a "participant observer" (Sullivan, 1947). The current reinforcement viewpoint de-emphasizes the uniqueness of the role of the patient, while pushing to the fore the role of the therapist and his interaction with the patient.

In the literature, there is a growing acceptance of the therapist as being in a controlling role. For example, Rogers (Rogers and Skinner, 1956) is willing to concede, perhaps reluctantly, that "in client-centered therapy, we are deeply engaged in the prediction and influencing of behavior, or even the control of behavior. As therapists, we institute certain attitudinal conditions, and the client has relatively little voice in the establishment of these conditions. We predict that if these conditions are instituted, certain behavioral consequences will ensue in the client." Haley (1959) interprets psychoanalytical psychotherapy as being a "controlling type of therapy." He suggests that "the therapist must take control of what happens in his relationship with the patient," and "to control a relationship a person must be in a position to establish the rules for what is to happen between himself and another person." Haley cites the works of Lindner, Rosen, and Erikson as examples of what he calls "New Style Directive Therapy."

Thus, from two "schools" which might be expected to refuse to acknowledge that all psychotherapy is directive in nature, the "non-directive" and the "psychoanalytical," there is tacit recognition from at least some writers of the controlling aspects of the therapist's behavior (Marmor, 1961). Rogers, however, in his symposium discussion with Skinner (1956), contends that the therapist's goal is to establish a self-directing or self-controlling patient. Skinner, on the other hand, feels that this is unrealistic, and that the controlling forces on the patient will continue to come from the patient's environment.

Gill and Brenman (1948) point out that the "raw data in psychotherapeutic research is inevitably influenced by the therapist's views . . . the subtleties of showing interest in certain kinds of material, often not consciously detected either by therapist or patient, are manifold. This may include a questioning glance, a shifting of visual focus, a well-timed 'mm-hmm,' a scarcely perceptible nod, or even a clearing of the throat. The therapist's conception of what his interpersonal relationship with a patient should be will also seriously influence the kind of material he obtains. If one therapist believes he should be 'friendly' and another that he should be 'distant,' the raw data obtained by each will obviously differ."

Therapists have usually recognized that they are dealing primarily with "talk," "words." Shaffer and Lazarus (1952) point out that "the techniques of getting the patient to talk and to continue to talk must be the real core of the treatment." Verbal behavior can be approached systematically in research with the advent of verbal conditioning techniques and other techniques of analyzing of verbal behavior, such as content analysis (Murray, 1954; Auld and Murray, 1955; Auld and White, 1959); grammatical characterizations (Goldman-Eisler, 1952, 1954; Lorenz and Cobb, 1953); word-counting and verbal input-output procedures (Mowrer, 1953a; Lennard, Calogeras, and Hendin, 1957); interaction chronographs (Saslow and Matarazzo, 1959); and others (Bales, 1950; Dibner, 1956; Dittmann, 1952; Glad, 1959; Grossman, 1952; Leary, 1957; Mahl, 1956, 1959; Palmore, Lennard, and Hendin, 1959; Starkweather, 1956a, 1956b; Whitehorn and Betz, 1954). Further, Skinner's (1957) definition of verbal behavior as "behavior reinforced through the mediation of other persons," points up the social learning involved in verbal behavior and places it squarely within the bounds of a reinforcement approach to psychotherapy research (Bachrach, 1962; Kanfer, 1960; Krasner, 1955; Salzinger, 1962).

If we are to conceive of psychotherapy as a process involving reinforcement procedures, then the major research task is to investigate the conditions under which the reinforcement procedure is most effective. These variables involved can be considered under three categories: (a) variables related directly to therapist characteristics, (b) situational variables, (c) therapist-patient interaction variables.

The "therapist characteristics" variables include: (a) the personal characteristics of the therapist, such as sex, personality, prestige, and socioeconomic status, (b) the specific influences on the therapist's concept of his role, such as his value and ethical system, and his formal and informal training, (c) the special techniques used by the therapist. The situational variables include the environmental setting and "atmosphere" in which the reinforcement process is taking place. The interaction variables are the result of the interaction of the therapist behavior with various characteristics of the patient population, such as diagnostic category, personality, response class, and awareness.

THERAPIST CHARACTERISTICS

Personal

The effectiveness of the interpersonal influencing process is related directly to the personal characteristics of the "influencer." These characteristics include: age, sex, personality, appearance, voice quality, prestige, and socioeconomic status. These are all characteristics that can be varied, and can be interrelated with variables of the situation and of the "influencee" to determine most effective reinforcement combinations.

PERSONALITY. The literature is replete with literally hundreds of adjectives descriptive of the personality of the ideal therapist. However, the number of research studies investigating the influence of therapist personality upon patient behavior is relatively small. The usual approach involves investigation by content analysis of correlational relationships between: (a) therapist personality characteristics, such as "warmth," "conflict," or "anxiety level," and (b) aspects of patient behavior, such as "staying in therapy" or "expressions of hostility" (Aronson, 1953; Bandura, 1956; Cutler, 1958; Fiedler, 1953; Ford, 1959; Hiler, 1958; Parloff, 1956).

Another research approach to the investigation of the interpersonal influencing process has been that of verbal operant conditioning. This approach is potentially more productive than content analysis approaches because of the ability to manipulate experimental variables, and to break out of the confines of the circularity of reasoning inherent in the more traditional "protocol" bound investigations.

For example, verbal conditioning studies have been used to explore the differences in E characteristics as they differentially affect S behavior. Binder, McConnell, and Sjoholm (1957) found differences in the effectiveness of two Es who differed sharply in physical, sexual, and personality characteristics. An attractive-appearing petite female was significantly more effective in conditioning hostile words than a husky, ex-Marine male, although both were able to achieve conditioning. Ferguson and Buss (1960) follow up the study by Binder by using a male and female E reinforcing hostile words. These Es varied their behavior to the Ss and found that it was the aggressiveness, not the sex, of E that led to significant differences in S's responsivity. In both studies the differences in effectiveness were hypothesized to be related to specific differences in physical characteristics of E. In contrast, Matarazzo, Saslow, and Pareis (1960) found that two Es differing in age, professional background, and attitude toward verbal conditioning obtained the same verbal conditioning effects.

Kanfer (1958) approaches this same problem in a slightly different manner. He found that in addition to status and physical characteristics, another source of variability was the *ability* of E to delineate a verbal class and to identify its class members. Since reinforcing operations usually must immediately follow the emitted response, quick decisions by E are required in classifying verbal material. Learning in such situations would thus be more variable than learning of easily discriminable responses which are not subject to interpretation by E. Kanfer suggests that E's role as a reinforcing agent in clinical situations such as therapy interviews, might vary as a function of his *perception* of the client's attitudes as inferred from the client's verbal behavior.

Krasner, Ullmann, Weiss, and Collins (1961) extended these studies by testing two hypotheses: (a) that different Es can obtain the same verbal conditioning effects, and (b) that different Es can obtain similar correlations between S's conditionability and S's response to a personality inventory. Two of the Es used were male Ph.D.s and the third E was a female A.B. The results indicated that all three Es obtained an increase in the use of emotional words from operant to reinforced trials, but this increase was significant only for the two male Ph.D. examiners. Correlations between S's responsivity to verbal conditioning and S's scores on personality measures were obtained for each of the three individual Es. The three Es did not differ significantly in the correlations they obtained, thus pointing up the stability on this type of measure of responsivity to verbal conditioning. A technique is thus being developed which can be used to investigate the effects of E's personality as it interacts both with S responsivity and with S personality measures. Although in this particular study (Krasner *et al.*, 1961) E's attributes of prestige, sex, or personality were not separated, the technique can readily be adapted to exploring the effects of differences in these kinds of E personal attributes.

An important study in this direction is Sapolsky's (1960) use of verbal conditioning to explore systematically the effects of the therapist variable in a factorial design. Sapolsky used the Schutz FIRO-B Scale of interpersonal "needs" to determine the relative "compatibility" of two given individuals. He hypothesized that the influence process in verbal conditioning would be most effective when S's and E's "needs" were compatible with each other. In one study, he assigned students as Ss and as Es, on a basis of compatibility of personality "needs" for one group, and incompatibility of "needs" for another. Results were that during the acquisition period the compatible group conditioned, whereas incompatible Ss–Es did not. During the extinction period (E out of room), compatible Ss did not extinguish in their use of reinforced pronouns, whereas incompatible Ss increased their use of the pronouns to the level obtained by the compatible Ss. A second study, similarly designed, instead of compatibility, used an experimental "set" of high personal "attraction" on the part of the Ss. The resulting curves in this study were almost identical with those in the first study. The implications of these studies for the influencing process are: (a) the influencing process is most effective when the personality of the S and the E are "compatible," (b) the influencing process is most effective when the S expects or has the "set" that he will like the E, (c) the influencing process, even with an incompatible E, is effective when he is physically removed, and (d) the relationship between S and E can be experimentally manipulated.

In a design also investigating the interaction of examiner-subject personality, Sarason[2] found a significant interaction between hostile Es, hostile responses, and hostile Ss. Campbell (1960) also investigated this interaction by using nurses who had previously been exposed to verbal conditioning as examiners with patients as subjects in a verbal conditioning task.

Strupp (1960) expresses the viewpoint that the therapist personality is almost inextricably interwoven with his technique and that it is extremely difficult, if not impossible, to determine the particular antecedent of a given therapeutic result. The kind of conditioning research being described, however, would hold constant the two variables, personality and technique, and enable us to determine antecedents of specific results.

These verbal conditioning studies emphasize earlier findings of the importance of the E variables, and offer techniques for investigating in detailed analysis these variables in interpersonal situations. Implicit in these types of studies is the assumption that various gross therapist variables, such as sex, appearance, and status, can be reduced to a few dimensions of E's influence on S and can be investigated independently or in various combinations. Further, implicit is the belief that there is no aspect of the reinforcement "machine" which cannot be taken apart to see what makes it tick.

"PLACEBO" EFFECTS.   Essential to the most meaningful application of reinforcement theory to psychotherapy is the inclusion of the implications of a phenomenon usually termed the "placebo" effect. Reports on the effects of placebos have culminated in the excellent review by Shapiro (1960) of the history of the placebo effects, and the important studies by Frank (1959a, 1959b), Gliedman, Nash, Imber, Stone, and Frank (1958), and Whitehorn (1958).

Shapiro's (1960) review starts with a definition of the "placebo"

---

[2] Sarason, I. G. Individual difference and situational variables in verbal conditioning. Unpublished manuscript, 1961.

effect as the "psychological, physiological, or psychophysiological effect of any medication or procedure given with therapeutic intent, which is independent of or minimally related to the pharmacological effect of the medication or to the specific effects of the procedure, and which operates through a psychological mechanism." He points out that until recently the majority of the cures effected by physicians were due to this "placebo" effect. He contends that the physician actually helped his patient not through the ritual and drug which he may have given, but rather by something "inherent in the doctor-patient relationship." "The great lesson, then, of medical history is that the placebo has always been the norm of medical practice, and it was only occasionally and at great intervals that anything really serviceable, such as the cure of scurvy by fresh fruits, was introduced into medical practice." In discussing the implications of this "placebo" effect for psychotherapy and psychiatry, Shapiro cites the well known fact that a large variety of different methods have been reported as being successful in bringing about therapeutic behavior changes. This would certainly imply some communality in behavior cutting across all techniques.

Shapiro quotes Janet's views on the factors in the patient, physician, and situation, which underlie therapeutic success: "in the patient—enthusiasm, faith, belief, feelings in general, power of the imagination, expectant attention, faith in authority, the importance to the patient of being the object of investigation; in the physician—undoubting enthusiasm, faith, and belief, the unconscious personality of the healer; in the situation—the ritual, mystery, and strangeness of the proceedings and the situation, changed environment, repetitive education, and suggestibility factors." These variables are similar to those under discussion, but under less specifiable terminology. Shapiro concludes with a suggestion which is of importance in attempting to determine experimentally the influence of the "placebo" effects in a research setting: "the principles underlying the effect of this variable can be extended to non-therapeutic experimental situations which involve an interpersonal relationship with an investigator, or even some symbolic representative of the latter."

Frank (1958, 1959a), Frank, Gliedman, Imber, Stone, and Nash (1959), Rosenthal and Frank (1956), and Whitehorn (1958) stress the role of faith, expectancy, and confidence both in achieving effective results and as basic ingredients for the "placebo" effect. Frank (1959a) says that in seeking communality in the therapy process the "common feature is the patient's reliance on the therapist to relieve his distress." He terms the expectancy of relief to be strong enough to justify the term "faith." He points out that there are two attitudes of the therapist which foster the patient's confidence in him: (a) his faith in the patient's capacity to benefit from treatment, and (b) his confidence in his theory and method of treatment. For example, the replies of psychotherapists to a questionnaire by Wolff (1956) indicated that 70 percent believe their particular form of therapy to be the best. Frank goes on to conclude that there is a good possibility that the emotional state of trust or "faith," in itself, can sometimes produce far-reaching and permanent changes in attitude or body states, although he points out that this phenomenon cannot be predicted or controlled, and cites as evidence religious conversions and miracle cures. Finally, Frank is careful to state that he does not believe that all, or even most, of the process of psychotherapy can be explained on the basis of trust or faith: "there are obviously many important determinants of the processes and outcomes of treatment besides the direct influence of the therapist based on faith and trust in him." Frank contends that the therapist's influence over the patient arises from this strong faith and favorable expectations strengthened by cultural factors, aspects of the referral or intake process, cues in the therapy situation, and the therapist's confidence in his ability to help. Cartwright and Cartwright (1958) take issue with Frank's emphasis on the role of patient's expectancies as a major determinant of the therapist's influence and his concern for the "placebo" effect. They feel that the terms "faith" and "belief" are too nebulous to specify objectively.

The reinforcement approach offers the techniques for translating the concepts of faith, expectancy, and other unknown factors involved in the "placebo" effect into terms which would allow for systematic investigation. The same may also be said for the kinds of therapist personality characteristics discussed by Strupp (1960) as essential in the therapeutic situation—integrity, honesty, and dedication—these are analyzable in terms of behaviors associated with effective reinforcement.

The obvious point generally missed in discussing the "placebo" effect is that one person's behavior is serving as a source of reinforcement for another's behavior. In analyzing the behavior of the therapist, Krasner (1955) has called attention to the one common factor in *all* psychotherapy, the presence of another person listening, paying attention, showing some interest. The therapist focuses more attention on those aspects of the patient's verbal behavior which his particular orientation calls for, but in any case, he displays a generalized form of behavior cues which may be called "attention." In speculating why these behavioral cues should serve as a means of reinforcing behavior, Skinner's (1953a) classification of attention as a generalized reinforcer is appropriate. The attention of other people is reinforcing because it is a necessary condition for receiving other more specific reinforcements from them. Only people who are "attending" reinforce behavior. It is reinforcement of an intermittent nature, not dependent on the momentary condition of the organism and continually being used to shape the behavior of others.

Ferster (1961) develops Skinner's notion about the use of generalized reinforcers in an analysis of the effects of positive reinforcement on autistic children. Ferster points out that parental responses, such as smiling, "good," and "right," can have little effect on the child if there is not a history by which, on these occasions, many different forms of the child's performance have produced various reinforcers. Without the parental generalized reinforcement, educational processes and positive parental control are all but impossible. This control is normally carried out by the use of praise, parental attention, coupled with a mild form of threat of discontinuing the reinforcers.

The therapist or influencer is a "reinforcement machine," which by its very presence is supplying generalized reinforcement at all times in the therapy situation, irrespective of the particular technique or personality involved. In psychotherapy, there is a subtle manipulation of the patient's behavior by the therapist's reinforcing behavior, often without awareness of either person of what is taking place. This is the basic ingredient in the so-called "placebo" effect. There is no need to postulate a mysterious interactional effect, but rather what is taking place are the kinds of behavior control which are being cited throughout this paper. Thus, the "placebo" effect (generalized reinforcement) *is* the common element in all influencing processes. There is reluctance by most researchers to take the final plunge and eliminate the last drop of faith, hope, and warmth, from psychotherapy—that last element of a mysterious unknown, and probably unknowable. But, until the therapist recognizes the full implications and potentialities of a psychology of behavior control, then the aura of mysticism which still clings to psychotherapy will remain.

ROLE-TAKING.   Further conditions affecting reinforcement effectiveness include attitudinal variables such as those of the therapist's and patient's role conceptualizations of themselves and their role expectancies of each other (Krasner, 1959). Psychotherapy studies frequently cite the self-confidence and assurance of the therapist as having an important effect on the patient. The elements that go into producing the therapist "self-assured role," such as personality, physical characteristics, prestige, training techniques, and socioeconomic status, are involved in the building of a particular "reinforcement machine" and determine its effectiveness and the kinds of behavior it will select to reinforce. On the patient's part, Sarbin's (1950) hypothesis about the variables associated with learning of the patient role are relevant. Sarbin feels that this would include favorable motivation, ability to perceive roles, and ability to take roles, all of which are also associated with learning the role of the hypnotic subject. "Role-taking" ability is an important aspect both of patient and therapist personality and, as such, is measurable and manipulatable (Krasner, 1959; Krasner, Weiss, and Ullmann, 1961).

PRESTIGE.   The prestige or status variable readily lends itself to behavioral analysis by conditioning techniques. This can be done by the role expectancies created by instructional set under which E (or therapist) is presented to S (or patient). One difficulty is separating role attributes from other E characteristics, and this can be done by the same E being presented in differing roles, without E knowing what role expectancies S has of him.

As an example of this approach, Ekman and Friesen (1960) investigated the effects of *status* of the E, holding personality constant, as an influence on verbal conditioning effectiveness. They performed a series of studies in which an officer and enlisted man served as Es, both in their own role, and switching roles. They were unable to obtain consistent differences in either conditioning or extinction attributed to either the status or personality of the Es, although both obtained significant conditioning. They concluded that in the particular army setting in which they worked, everyone giving "tests" to recruits had "status" even if he was an enlisted man. This points up the relevance of S's expectancies toward E and E's role. Examiner "status" or lack of it is also considered in the interpretation of the results of other verbal conditioning studies (Daily, 1953; Marion, 1956; Krasner, Ullmann, Weiss, and Collins, 1961).

Influences on Therapist Role

VALUES AND ETHICS.   Most therapists are uncomfortable in a role labeled as a "controller" or "manipulator" of behavior. The evidence, however, is that this is an accurate description of what the therapist role actually is. For example: Sheehan (1953) and Graham (1960) both report studies in which key Rorschach categories of successful patients changed significantly in the direction of those of the therapist. Rosenthal (1955) found that "improved" patients changed their "moral" values in the direction of the therapist. Palmore, Lennard, and Hendin (1959) report increasing similarity in verbal behavior between patients and therapists as therapy proceeds. Stekel (1951) points out that patients' dreams always confirm the theoretical formulations of their therapist. Heine (1953) reports a study of three different approaches to therapy in which the patients' subjective report of the changes which took place within themselves did not differ, while there were sharp differences along "school" lines as to the theoretical explanation of these changes by the patients. Whitehorn (1959) points out that successful psychotherapy involves leadership "toward preferred values, toward the therapist's conception of what constitutes value in life." The evidence is strong that the therapist by virtue of his role has the power to influence and control the behavior and values of other human beings. For the therapist not to accept this situation and to be continually unaware of influencing effects of his behavior on his patients would in itself be "unethical."

Skinner's comments (Rogers and Skinner, 1956) on the general problem of the therapist as a controller are relevant to consideration of the ethical problems involved. Frequently, an important reinforcement for the therapist himself is his success in manipulating human behavior. He may be involved in proving the value of a particular theory of behavior or of psychotherapy. There is always the possibility that the therapist control will be misused. The countercontrol which discourages the misuse of power is represented by the ethical standards and practices of the organized profession of psychotherapy. Skinner feels that it is this danger of misuse which explains the popularity of theories of psychotherapy which deny that human behavior can be controlled and refuse to accept responsibility of control. However, to refuse to accept control is merely to leave control in other hands. Skinner does not agree with Rogers that the individual always holds within himself the solution to his problems. If the individual were the product of training and education which have effectively supplied the inner kinds of solutions which Rogers advocates, then it would be unlikely that the individual would be a therapy candidate. But, as is more likely, if the individual were the product of excessive or damaging kinds of control or extreme deprivation, it is unlikely that an acceptable solution was available within himself, but must come from environmental contacts. Kanfer (1961) also comments on the motivation of the therapist, pointing up the long-range source of reinforcement as lying in the "professional role" and all of its attractions for the therapist. Krasner (1961a) has pointed out that the investigation of "values" of behavior controllers such as psychotherapists as they are related to other variables such as "effectiveness" can, and should be, investigated by experimental techniques.

SOCIOECONOMIC STATUS.   Only brief mention will be made of the by now accepted fact that there are important socioeconomic influences on the social role of the therapist. The New Haven studies (Hollingshead and Redlich, 1958) have pointed out the different social and economic class attitudes toward the importance of psychotherapy and the differential assignment of patients to psychotherapy according to social class. This further emphasizes the cultural conditioning of therapy role expectancies, both in the patient as well as in the therapist. Auld's (1952) study of the influence of social class on personality test responses is also quite relevant to viewing psychotherapy within the context of social role expectancies. This is a variable which is often acknowledged, but to which very little research has been directed.

The reinforcement paradigm enables us to determine how the socio-economic status of the therapist influences his patient interactions. It may be surmised, for example, that the particular response class reinforced or punished will be determined by the therapist's class morality background. Further, the reinforcing value of therapist "prestige" does not exist for all potential patient groups. A group such as delinquents may consider a therapist to be a "square," thus decreasing the likelihood of reinforcement from such a source being effective.

TRAINING AND EXPERIENCE. A major variable which must enter into evaluating the therapist role is that of his background and specific training. This may be put in terms of investigating the information that has been programmed into the "reinforcement machine." It is this information which will determine the probability of the influencer responding to one kind of behavior, rather than another, and the contingencies related to his effectiveness. Training represents the conscious efforts of a profession to "program" future therapists. There has been recent investigation of the effect of training variables as they have influenced the psychotherapist's behavior (Ashby, Ford, Guerney, and Guerney, 1957; Fey, 1958; Fiedler, 1950, 1951; Holt and Luborsky, 1958; Lakin and Lebovitz, 1958; Strupp, 1955a, 1957a). The particular "school" of training, the professional discipline, the presence or absence of personal analysis, and the therapist's experience, have been found to be related to the types of verbal behavior and techniques used by the therapist and his effectiveness in changing patient behavior (Strupp, 1955a, 1955b, 1955c, 1957a, 1957b, 1958a, 1958b, 1960).

Studies on the effects of training highlight the kinds of information that is programmed into the therapist-reinforcer. They also, however, point out that this particular "machine" is self-correcting and continually modifying its own behavior, based on the kinds of feedback or reinforcement received from patients, other therapists, and living experiences.

The verbal conditioning technique offers considerable promise for investigating the influence of training on therapist techniques. Krasner (1958b) reports a technique of selecting a given response class in a story-telling situation and manipulating it with selected cue reinforcement by E. He reported that changes in a preselected class of verbal behavior vary as a function of the systematic applications of behavior cues by E. Using this technique, Dinoff, Rickard, Salzberg, and Sipprelle (1960) developed an experimental design in which categories of verbal behavior comparable to different therapeutic approaches could be observed, reinforced, and measured to determine the effects of the reinforcement.

Dinoff *et al.* demonstrated that varying theoretical positions may direct the verbalizations of *S*s into areas in keeping with *E*'s own "theoretical biases." They found that the frequency of responding was significantly increased as predicted, in the three response categories—"Environment," "Patient," and "Therapist." Further, the authors suggest that their technique is an objective, reliable, and essentially content-free way of manipulating and scoring therapeutic verbal responses. These studies point the way to future research in which therapist behavior can be deliberately programmed and manipulated by the kinds of information and role-sets to which the therapist (*E*) is exposed (Krasner, 1961b).

Winokur (1955) points out the similarity between extracting "confessions," as done in "brainwashing," and certain professional situations such as psychotherapy. He goes further in this direction by interpreting the supervisor-student relationship in psychotherapy as an example of "brainwashing." To reduce anxiety, "prisoners change their thinking to conform with that of their 'captors.'" He feels that the training situation (applicable to psychiatrists, psychologists, and social workers) is a forced modification of both behavior and thinking to conform to that of the teacher-supervisor. The evidence he cites is anecdotal, rather than experimental, but it is quite provocative.

Therapist Techniques

The therapist has a broad spectrum of behavioral techniques available to him, limited only by his ingenuity in varying his behavior and the setting. The traditional way of classifying therapist techniques is by the "schools of therapy" approach. One way of investigating these differences would be to develop a classification of techniques which describe the characteristics of reinforcement.

TYPE OF REINFORCEMENT.   (a) Positive: These are cues controlled by the therapist so as to *reward* specific responses of the patient. These may range from generalized reinforcers, such as head nodding or "mm-hmm," to more specific reinforcement such as tokens (Buss and Gerjuoy, 1958; Buss, Gerjuoy, and Zusman, 1958; Ferguson and Buss, 1960), or candy (Peters and Jenkins, 1954), or cigarettes (Lindsley, 1956, 1960). They may also include specific interpretive statements which expressly verbalize the contingencies in a patient's behavior. Such reinforcements may be difficult to classify as to whether they are rewarding or punishing. (b) Negative (punishing): These may range from verbal admonishments, such as "you are wrong" (Kanfer and Karas, 1959), through subtler head shaking and "huh-huh" (Greenspoon, 1955; Hartman, 1955; Mock, 1957), to actual physical pain-evoking stimuli, such as shock. (c) Negative (withdrawing of positive reinforcement [Ferster, 1957]): Illustrations of this would include techniques which vary "silences" (Saslow and Matarazzo, 1959), and techniques which use extinction (withdrawal of reinforcement) as a deliberate controlling device (Weiss, Krasner, and Ullmann, 1960).

It should be emphasized that the same stimulus is not necessarily reinforcing under all conditions; for example, "good" would appear to be an excellent illustration of a positive verbal reinforcer. However, there is evidence (Cohen and Cohen, 1960) that "good" is not necessarily reinforcing for schizophrenics. The reinforcement history of the schizophrenic is such that "good" may have taken on aversive properties (Atkinson, 1957; Robinson, 1957). "Mm-hmm" is probably a more effective reinforcer with schizophrenics because it does not have the social connotations of "approval" that "good" has acquired for the schizophrenic (Krasner and Ullmann, 1958). On the other hand, Hildum and Brown (1956) found that with a college population, "good" was an effective reinforcer, whereas "mm-hmm" was not. Mandler and Kaplan (1956) found that the effectiveness of a reinforcer such as "mm-hmm" was related to S's subjective interpretation of the stimuli as being either "positive" or "negative."

If generalized reinforcers are effective because of the "need" for them by the patient, then this can be controlled by deprivation procedures (Gewirtz and Baer, 1957, 1958a, 1958b; Peters and Jenkins, 1954; Walters and Karal, 1960). Various "brainwashing" reports (Lifton, 1956, 1957a, 1957b) also illustrate the method of depriving Ss of particular needs so that they may be more amenable to being influenced by techniques designed to meet the artificially created need.

MEDIUM OF EXPRESSION. (a) Verbal: This is the most frequent in therapy and would include the range of cues from "mm-hmm" through "good," "right," "fine," "paraphrasing" (Verplanck, 1955), "repetition" (Fahmy, 1953), to interpretative statements of behavior contingencies. (b) Gestural: These cues include head nodding (Mock, 1957), head shaking (Hartman, 1955), smiling (Verplanck, 1955), and forward movement of body (Ekman, 1958). (c) Mechanical: These may include light flashes (Ball, 1952; Greenspoon, 1954; Nuthmann, 1957), a buzzer (Ball, 1952; Greenspoon, 1954), a bell tone (McNair, 1957), or mechanical gadgets delivering objects such as candy (Lindsley, 1956). In some instances, for example, McNair, the mechanical device was labeled as signifying approval. (d) Symbolic: These include poker chips or tokens to be turned in for cigarettes or candy (Buss, Gerjuoy, and Ferguson, 1958). Various combinations of these mediums of expressing the reinforcement may be explored to determine the most effective combinations.

SCHEDULES OF REINFORCEMENT. In the therapy situation, timing of therapist behavior vis-à-vis patient verbalizations is of major importance. The therapist must make a quick decision whether a response of the patient belongs to the class to be reinforced. If so, is this the time to reinforce it? A failure to do so may extinguish the response, at least for the moment. Thus in an analysis of the effectiveness of the cueing of E, scheduling of this cueing is a major factor. The effectiveness of various intermittent reinforcement schedules has been demonstrated with laboratory animals. Ferster and Skinner (1957) have provided a detailed description of such schedules. There have been successful applications of various schedules to reinforcing of verbal behavior (Bachrach, Candland, and Gibson, 1959; Grossberg, 1956; Kanfer, 1954, 1958; McNair, 1957; O'Donnell, 1959).

Kanfer (1958) compared three types of reinforcement schedules in a verbal conditioning situation and concluded that reinforcing behavior of a therapist, such as agreement, reassurance, or approval, might be regulated to occur on a ratio schedule, if it is desirable that a client continue to make similar responses. On the other hand, he points out, if flexibility in topics were desired, characterized by a high rate of talk about a given topic only when the therapist supplies a cue for its relevance, then an interval schedule would be more effective in controlling the desired behavior pattern.

O'Donnell (1959) obtained significant results in conditioning mildly hostile verbs using "good" as a reinforcement, with a reinforcement ratio of $66\frac{2}{3}$ percent. Bachrach et al. (1960) applied "pseudo-fixed interval schedules" in a verbal conditioning situation. The Ss were reinforced only during the last 30 seconds of each successive 1-minute period. Although their results were somewhat equivocal, they concluded that social behavior may be examined as a function of the schedule of reinforcement, but that a mechanical reinforcer may be necessary to assure accurate programming.

In his review of verbal conditioning studies, Krasner (1958a) divided the response class into four types of tasks demanded of the S: saying words or numbers, storytelling and interviews, completing sentences, and test-like situations. In three of these tasks the responses may be considered to be discrete, whereas in the storytelling and interview type of situation (Dinoff et al., 1960; Krasner, 1958b; Mock, 1957; Pisoni and Salzinger, 1960; Salzinger and Pisoni, 1958, 1960; Salzinger, Pisoni, and Feldman, 1960; Verplanck, 1955; and others), there is a continuous flow of conversation. E must be alert to make a discriminative response and must quickly make a number of decisions as to his own behavior. In such situations, the rate of reinforcement is rarely continuous. This is virtually impossible, and not necessarily desirable. In a storytelling situation, Krasner (1958b) found that approximately 80 percent of reinforceable responses were actually reinforced. Tobias (1960), using the same type of situation, found that only 76 percent of the animal responses which he was reinforcing were actually followed by reinforcing stimuli. What is taking place in situations requiring continuous verbalization, as in psychotherapy, is an intermittent reinforcement schedule, which is more effective, and more realistic, than a continuous reinforcement schedule.

Both the amount and patterning of the reinforcement are also important aspects of the mediating contingencies. Salzinger (in press) reports conditioning with both normal and schizophrenic Ss who receive a *large* amount of reinforcement in contrast to failure to condition in Ss receiving a *small* amount of reinforcement. Patterning of reinforcement can also be used as a controlling technique in itself (Weiss, Krasner, and Ullmann, 1960).

SITUATIONAL VARIABLES

The situation variables are manipulatable environmental and interpersonal *conditions* under which the therapist influences the patient. They include: the "atmosphere" in which therapy takes place; the "set" which is created for the patient; antecedent contacts between the therapist and patient; sensory input permitted the patient; and *"ambiguity."* All are controlled by the therapist, often without awareness of their effect.

Atmosphere

An important element of the situation in which the influencing process occurs may be labeled "atmosphere." This refers to the class of variables dealing with the S's attitude toward the E and/or toward the influencing session itself. These are important in the "rapport" which is so frequently mentioned as a necessary element of psychotherapy. Several studies have attempted to manipulate experimentally the emotional atmosphere of the conditioning session. Kanfer and Karas (1959) provide a success and a failure condition on a preconditioning task. Subsequent conditioning scores were not significantly affected by the success and failure manipulations, even though Ss in the failure condition reported that E had annoyed them and had made them feel tense. They note that their failure condition had the effect of increasing S's motivation to try harder and thus Ss may have been more responsive to the E's directions during the conditioning session. The Sapolsky (1960) study previously described can be seen as manipulating "atmospheres" by instructional set to affect the influencing process.

Weiss, Krasner, and Ullmann (1960) investigated the effects on responsivity of manipulating the atmosphere under which conditioning took place. College students told TAT-like stories during which E verbally reinforced the use of emotional words (Ullmann and McFarland,

1957). Following this, hostile and neutral emotional atmospheres were experimentally induced, after which the verbal conditioning was repeated. The induced hostile atmosphere resulted in a decrease in responsiveness. This study indicated that by using a validated response class and a validated procedure for inducing hostility, atmospheres can have a demonstrable effect on conditioning. Thus "atmosphere" as an important variable in the influencing situation can be manipulated and experimentally investigated.

Antecedent Contacts

Gewirtz and Baer (1957, 1958a, 1958b) report a series of studies with children, investigating the relationship between antecedent social contacts between Es and Ss, and subsequent effectiveness of social reinforcement. Walters and Karal (1960) and Kanfer and Karas (1959) extend this approach with adults. Kanfer and Karas (1959) found that Ss with prior experience with E, irrespective of the type of experience, were more effectively conditioned than Ss having no prior experience with E. The authors suggest that if additional contacts increase the effectiveness of the conditioning process, this may be one source of the increased control by the therapist as the treatment process continues. Solley and Long (1958) also report obtaining significant verbal conditioning effects with "mm-hmm" only when E carries out "chit-chat," or informal "rapport" —getting conversation with S prior to the conditioning sessions. They conclude that conditioning results only when antecedent contacts have been made.

Walters and Karal (1960) report a series of studies investigating the hypotheses of Gewirtz and Baer that social deprivation is a motivating condition and, consequently, social reinforcement cues would be more effective following social deprivation than following social satiation. The results of Walters and Karal are somewhat equivocal, but generally do *not* provide support for the concept of a motivational state resulting from social deprivation. They suggest that social deprivation may be a special case of sensory deprivation in which Ss are deprived of social contact. They point out the possibility that some effects of sensory deprivation studies attributed now primarily to the lack of visual, auditory, and tactual stimulation can actually be attributed to the absence of social contacts, and consequent anxiety. Walters and his colleagues (Walters and Ray, 1960; Walters and Quinn, 1960; Walters, Marshall, and Shooter, 1960) also report a series of other studies relating social isolation, anxiety, and susceptibility to social influence. One conclusion they reach is that social isolation has, in itself, no effect upon susceptibility to social influence, but that under the anxiety-arousing conditions, sometimes produced by social isolation, Ss can be more readily influenced than when anxiety is not present. The implicit relationship between social deprivation studies and sensory deprivation studies is relevant also to the discussion in the next section on sensory deprivation.

Sensory Input

SENSORY DEPRIVATION.   The sensory input variable refers to the amount, variety, and kind of physical stimuli permitted the patient or "influencee." On one extreme, we have the conditions of DDD—debility, dependency, and dread, described by Farber, Harlow, and West (1957), as being a basic ingredient of the thought-reform process used by the Chinese Communists both on prisoners of war and on their own people. Farber *et al.* point out that the conditions of DDD lead to increasing susceptibility to conditioning. The Chinese used the DDD on an intermittent reinforcement schedule to condition prisoner expectancies. Lifton (1956, 1957a, 1957b) also describes what he terms "milieu control" in the Chinese thought-reform process. This is the control and manipulation of all communication and sensory stimulation directed to the "reformee." Lifton compares the effects of the "milieu control" on a prisoner to the effects on the sensory deprived Ss of Lilly (1956). In both processes the S is unable to check on what is reality. Having no other source of verification or information, the S has no alternative but to accept the communications which come to him. In one instance, this is the propaganda of the Chinese Communists; in the other, it is the internal push which manufactures the hallucinations which fill out his environment. The works of Hebb (1958), Heron, Doane, and Scott (1956), Azima and Cramer-Azima (1956b, 1957) and the symposium edited by Solomon (1961) further amplify these points. Hebb (1958) analyzes the effects of perceptual deprivation on human motivation. Since the adult is dependent on his sensory environment, the first approach to him in "brainwashing" is by isolation (others being sleep, fatigue, and hunger). The effects of isolation are hallucinations, disturbances of self-perception, impaired intelligence test score, changes in EEG records, and visual disturbances. Such effects Hebb found to be reversible, disappearing in a few days after the isolation ends. However, after telling Ss "ridiculous" things during their state of isolation, he found that such "propaganda effects" were longer lasting. Thus, it would appear that an individual is more responsive to influence from his environment while under sensory deprivation, and less likely to extinguish behavior learned while under such conditions.

Studies by Adams, Carrera, Cooper, Gibby, and Tobey (1960) and Azima and Cramer-Azima (1956a) also use sensory deprivation procedures as such, to enhance therapeutic change in patients. Azima and

Cramer-Azima (1956a) used sensory isolation as a therapeutic technique in modifying behavior of psychotic patients with problems of depersonalization. They put a variety of patients in a situation of partial sensory and expressive isolation for an average period of four days. Some of the patients appeared to have been helped by this process, others possibly worsened.

The kinds of physical stimuli conditions which the therapist controls may include: couch or easy chairs (face-to-face); room illumination; sound proofing; mood music; heavy carpets; bland clothing. These types of stimuli can be manipulated to make behavior control more effective. It would seem reasonable that cutting down external stimuli would enable the patient to focus on and pay more attention to therapist originated stimuli, making them more effective.

SENSORY ENHANCEMENT. On the opposite side of the sensory input continuum, there are several studies which approach psychotherapy by sensory enhancement. McReynolds, Acker, and Daily (1959) reason that if certain symptoms of schizophrenia, such as hallucinations, feelings of depersonalization, and difficulties in concentration, are the result of functional sensory deprivation, then it would be expected that "perceptual enhancement" in schizophrenics would bring about alleviation of the symptoms indicated. In preliminary work on six patients, each participating in a number of activities designed to enhance rate of perceptual input and assimilation, the evidence points in the direction of their hypothesis. In a verbal conditioning study, Chan (1958) found that the effect of enhancing visual sensory input in the form of geometric forms, colors, algebraic signs, and Chinese characters increased the probability of susceptibility to verbal conditioning.

SUBLIMINAL STIMULATION. Under the heading of sensory input variable should also be included the studies on subliminal stimulation. These studies are relevant for the study of behavior control in at least three ways: they are essentially techniques of behavior control; they are related to learning without awareness; and they raise ethical problems. The excellent reviews by McConnell, Cutler, and McNeil (1958) and Goldiamond (1958) bring the field together in such a way that subliminal stimulation can be incorporated into the more general field of behavioral control.

Set and Ambiguity

A person in an influencing situation is continually seeking cues as to what is expected of him. It does not follow, however, that these cues should be clear cut for maximum effectiveness, as evidenced by studies of the importance of ambiguity in the influencing process. Frank (1959) points out that "it is in the ambiguity of the therapeutic situation, however, that its greatest potentiality for influence probably lies. Like the interrogators in thought reform, some psychotherapists convey to the patient that they know what is wrong with him, but that he must find it out for himself in order to be helped. This is one means of enlisting his participation, but it also gives the patient an ambiguous task." Bordin (1955) also sees ambiguity as part of the stimulus value of the therapist. Dibner (1958) found evidence to confirm the deduction that anxiety is positively related to ambiguity in an interpersonal relationship.

Ambiguity is closely related to the variable of "set" which can be expressed in terms of S's expectancies of what is to occur during a particular influencing session. Asch (1948) reports that in his studies S changes his set from "what differences can I observe between these materials" to "which of these am I expected to like and dislike." Hall (1958) found significant verbal conditioning only in Ss who had become "ego-involved" by the instructional set. In a study by Krasner, Weiss, and Ullmann (1961) the very questioning about awareness influenced S's performance. One effect of the reported awareness interview itself was to change S's definition of the experimental task; that is, E signaled S that the latter's knowledge of what is going on was a part of the experimental situation. Thus, conditioning trials occurring after an awareness interview can be viewed as problem solving trials. This served to decrease the ambiguity for S, and in this study (Krasner et al., 1961) the result was a decrease in responsivity. In his investigation of the psychology of affiliation, Schacter (1959) concludes that ambiguous situations lead to a desire to be with others as a socially evaluating event which helps determine the appropriate and proper reaction. These findings are consistent in interpreting ambiguity as enhancing the reinforcing value of the therapist. The studies of Ekman, Krasner, and Ullmann[3] and Sarason and Ganzer[4] investigated the relationship between instructional set, operant level, and responsivity to reinforcement. In both studies, responsivity was manipulated by the instructional set.

Group Setting

One final note about the situation variable: the influencing process need not be limited to a one-to-one relationship (Asch, 1948; Bachrach, 1960; Cieutat, 1959; Dinoff, Horner, Kurpiewski, and Timmons, 1960; Sidowski, 1959). Asch (1948, 1956) and those using his influencing techniques have investigated the process under simulated group conditions. Bachrach et al. (1960) defined a group setting as using two Es working

[3] Ekman, P., Krasner, L., and Ullmann, L. P. The interaction of set and awareness as determinants of response to verbal conditioning. Unpublished manuscript, 1961.

[4] Sarason, I. G., and Ganzer, V. J. Anxiety, reinforcement, and experimental instructions. Unpublished manuscript, 1961.

as a team of "human programmers" reinforcing the third person in the group, the naive S. Dinoff et al. (1960) investigated the effectiveness of verbal conditioning in a group therapy situation with a schizophrenic population.

THERAPIST-PATIENT INTERACTION VARIABLES

The "therapist variables" cannot be investigated except insofar as they interact with patient characteristics. For maximal effectiveness of the reinforcement process the following manipulable patient characteristics should be considered in the context of therapist and situational variables: type of population; personal characteristics such as age, sex, intelligence, education, personality; and socioeconomic class.

Type of Populations

One of the trends in verbal conditioning studies has been the extension of these techniques to adult populations other than college students and schizophrenics. This has included extension along diagnostic lines: delinquents (Cairns, 1960); mental defectives (Barnett, Pryer, and Ellis, 1959); "neurotics" (Levanthal, 1959; and Johns and Quay[5]); and along education lines: medical students (Krasner, Ullmann, Weiss, and Collins, 1961); high school educated military trainees (Ekman and Friesen, 1960a, 1960b; Friesen and Ekman, 1960). Johns and Quay[5] report failure in conditioning a psychopathic group which was interpreted as evidence of psychopathic resistance to social reward. Systematic attempts at comparing diagnostic group responsivity are necessary as preliminary to predicting reaction to psychotherapy, and some studies have moved in this direction (Campbell, 1960; Franks, 1956; Hagen, 1959; Hartman, 1955; Johns and Quay[5]; Leventhal, 1959; O'Conner and Rawnsley, 1959; Salzinger, 1962).

Although verbal conditioning techniques have been effective with this wide variety of people, there are questions as to the susceptibility of schizophrenics to conditioning procedures (Cohen and Cohen, 1960). However, both Dinoff et al. (1960) and Salzinger and Pisoni (1958) found that they could condition schizophrenics, but the effect is short-lived and extinction is rapid. Dinoff et al. suggest the use of partial reinforcement during conditioning to extend the period of extinction in schizophrenics. The authors suggest that negative findings with schizophrenics (Cohen and Cohen, 1960) may have resulted because the effect was hidden due to its brevity. Others reporting successful conditioning of schizophrenic patients include: Krasner (1958b); Krasner and Ullmann (1958); Mock (1957); Weiss, Krasner, and Ullmann (1961). Specification

---

[5] Johns, J. H., and Quay, H. C. The effect of social reward on verbal conditioning in psychopathic and neurotic military offenders. Unpublished manuscript, 1959.

of type of schizophrenia and severity of illness are essential in these studies as in all research with schizophrenics.

Patient Characteristics

PERSONALITY.   The relationship between S personality and S susceptibility to conditioning techniques has been investigated under a variety of conditioning procedures (Anderson, 1959; Babladelis, 1960; Buss and Gerjuoy, 1958; Cairns, 1960; Campbell, 1960; Cushing, 1957; Daily, 1953; Ekman, 1958; Franks, 1956, 1957; Kirman, 1958; Gelfand and Winder, 1961; Matarazzo *et al.*, 1960; McKee, 1960; Medini, 1958; O'Donnell, 1960; Sarason, 1958; Sarason and Campbell, 1962; Taffel, 1955). Some studies hypothesize differentiations in responsivity along personality dimensions, such as anxiety, whereas others are nosologically oriented. Since the focus of this paper is on the therapist variable as such, we will not go further into the patient personality variables, other than to point to two types of studies which can be used to investigate the effects of the patient variable on the reinforcement process. First, there is manipulation by instruction of the therapist personality-patient personality interaction (Sapolsky, 1960). The second is a manipulation of the patient personality variable by inducing an experimental atmosphere (Weiss, Krasner, and Ullmann, 1960).

In a broader view of a psychology of behavior influence there are other important approaches to investigating the relationship between personality characteristics and susceptibility to the influencing process (Asch, 1948, 1956; Berkowitz and Lundy, 1957; Helson, Blake, Mouton, and Olmstead, 1956; Kelman, 1956; Janis, 1954). All are relevant to a psychology of behavior control and consequently to the psychotherapy process.

SOCIOECONOMIC STATUS.   The factors discussed above affecting the behavior of the therapist as a function of his class identification also hold for the patient, and interaction effects become crucial. Although much lip service is given to the importance of this variable, few research data are available. Imber, Frank, Gliedman, Nash, and Stone (1956) and Imber, Nash, and Stone (1959) investigated the relationship between suggestibility, social class, the acceptance, and duration of psychotherapy. Imber *et al.* (1956) found that suggestible patients, as measured by the Sway Test, tend to remain in psychotherapy. It was postulated that suggestible patients were influenced by the authority of the doctor in his role as expert advisor and the general prestige of the medical setting. No differences in suggestibility were found between middle- and lower-class patients, but middle-class patients who were "suggestible" were most responsive to psychotherapy in terms of rate of "staying in."

RESPONSE CLASS.   The specific point of interaction in the therapist-patient relationship is between the patient response class and the therapist reinforcing cue behavior. That such interaction is lawful and predictable in the therapy situation has been demonstrated in studies such as Murray (1954), Bandura, Lipsher, and Miller (1960), and others. The response class is usually the most important aspect of patient behavior which the therapist influences. Response classes that are influenceable are limited only by E's ingenuity in labeling them. In the verbal conditioning studies alone a whole variety of response classes directly relevant to psychotherapy have been shown to be influenceable under certain specified reinforcement conditions. These are: affect statements (Anderson, 1959; Buss and Durkee, 1958; Cushing, 1957; Doering, 1959; Krasner, Ullmann, Weiss, and Collins, 1961; Pisoni and Salzinger, 1960; Salzinger and Pisoni, 1958, 1960; Salzinger, Pisoni, and Feldman, 1960; Weiss, Ullmann, and Krasner, 1960); self-reference statements (Adams and Hoffman, 1960; Babladelis, 1960; Rogers, 1960); "hallucinations" (Dobie, 1959); "negative words" (Zebek, 1959); "neurotic" verbalizations (Everstine and Bendig, 1960); "early childhood memories" (Quay, 1959); references to "mother" (Krasner, 1958b; Mock, 1957); opinions and attitudes (Verplanck, 1955; Ekman, 1958); "complex" sentences (Barik and Lambert, 1960); "acceptance of self" (Nuthmann, 1957); and "confiding responses" (Cairns, 1960).

Berg (1958) and Bachrach (1962) report work currently in progress by Greenspoon that is even more directly related to psychotherapy. This is being done within the context of a therapy interview with patients. When the patient verbalizes bizarre material, the therapist swivels his chair around, turning his back on the patient, opens his mail, or makes a telephone call. When the patient talks realistically, the therapist reinforces this rational content by leaning forward and nodding or saying "mm-hmm." Irrational material begins to drop out and material such as realistic discussion of illness increases. Greenspoon also reports observations, systematically gathered during regular counseling sessions of the therapist reinforcing patient verbalizations about a response class such as sex by looking interested and leaning forward. The number of sex references then markedly increase during the course of the interview. Rickard, Dignam, and Horner (1960) report the manipulation of verbal behavior in an actual therapeutic treatment case. Rational verbalizations in a 60-year-old delusional patient were positively reinforced, while delusional material was "punished" by the therapist "looking away." A high level of rational speech was obtained, but extinction also was rapid.

Krasner and Ullmann (1958) demonstrated that E could switch from reinforcing one response class to another with a significant increment of the second class. In this study, using storytelling procedures, the response class reinforced was switched from "mother" to "father" references with the same patients, and the new reinforced response class increased significantly as a function of E's behavior.

Studies have also appeared in other areas which have demonstrated the effects of the influencing process on verbal response classes, especially those which may be termed as indicating "attitudes" or "opinions" (Asch, 1948; Back, 1951; Bergin, 1960; Helson, Blake, Mouton, and Olmstead, 1956; Hovland, Janis, and Kelley, 1953; Janis and King, 1954; Kelman, 1950, 1956, 1958; Schacter, 1959; Scott, 1957; Staats, 1959; Staats and Staats, 1958; Staats, Staats, and Heard, 1959). All of these approaches have in common the use of influencing techniques to change verbal behavior. Blake and Mouton (1957), based on their studies of the dynamics of influence and coercion, conclude that the most significant dimensions operating in the exertion of influence under face-to-face conditions are: (a) the properties of the direct influence induction, and (b) the properties of the social background. Their major emphasis is on training in various phases of social science so that the therapist may become aware of the forces within the social situation which must be shifted in order to effect behavior changes.

AWARENESS.   The variable of awareness is crucial to the influencing process. The problem of whether learning without awareness does, or does not, occur has been repeatedly explored under many different guises in laboratories and experimental settings (Adams, 1957; Dulany, 1961; Eriksen, 1961; Kanfer and McBrearty, 1961; Levin, 1960; Sidowski, 1954; Tatz, 1956). In psychotherapy the question is whether you can have behavioral changes in a patient without his verbalizing insight into the relationship between his present behavior and (a) a set of events which have occurred in his past life, and/or (b) the therapist's behavior. As is true of other aspects of psychotherapy, the process of awareness has been difficult to measure. Verbal conditioning studies are faced with the difficulty of an extremely unreliable measure of awareness, namely that of the S's self report. The issue is the same as that found in psychotherapy—self reports are unreliable and also subject to the influencing process. Krasner, Weiss, and Ullmann (1961) investigated relationships between awareness and behavior change in a verbal conditioning situation with college students using "mm-hmm" to reinforce "emotional words." The authors' position was that awareness is not a single phenomenon but refers to a complex of different cognitive events. Therefore, awareness was first investigated as a dependent variable by the technique of reported awareness typical in other verbal conditioning studies. Reported awareness at this point of the study was *not* significantly related to (a) increased responsivity on reinforced trials as compared to operant trials, (b) previously induced emotional atmospheres, either hostile or neutral (Weiss *et al.*, 1960), or (c) previous pattern of reinforced trials. Thus, a typical measure of S's awareness, his self report, was not associated with either responsivity to verbal conditioning or with two experimental manipulations (atmospheres and patterns of reinforcement) which in themselves had significantly decreased responsiveness to verbal conditioning. Awareness was then treated as an independent variable and was manipulated by means of two different sets of instructions. Half the Ss were given cues designed to focus attention on the phenomenon of verbal conditioning. It was found that induced-awareness cues decreased responsiveness on *subsequent* reinforcement trials. The second experimental manipulation of awareness followed one of two sets of instruction: Ss were explicitly informed of the reinforcing contingency and were told that either (a) they had been controlling E, or (b) E had been controlling them. Two reinforcement trials followed these instructions. These resulted in significant heterogeneity of variance. Whether S would respond by increasing or decreasing his "emotional words" was predictable based on the previous experimental conditions to which he had been exposed.

The following conclusions were drawn: (a) Conflicting reports on the relationship between reported awareness and conditioning reflect conceptual confusion with regard to the role of reported awareness in performance. (b) Ss' awareness of the reinforcing contingency will affect performance in verbal conditioning experiments when awareness is made an integral part of Ss' task. (c) The specific effect that awareness will have on performance depends on subject-determined variables, for example, Ss' emotional attitude toward E.

In another study in which "awareness" was experimentally manipulated (Ekman, Krasner, and Ullmann, see Footnote 3) the storytelling task was introduced to half the Ss as a measure of empathy (amount of warmth and feeling towards other people) and was introduced to the other half as a measure of personal problems (difficulties in getting along with other people). Half the Ss in each group were told that "after the first few stories I [E] will let you know that you are revealing your own personal problems (or that you are showing warmth) by going 'mm-hmm' whenever you do this." In this factorial design, there were no differences among the four groups in number of emotional words used during operant trials. However, the groups differed significantly in increase of number of emotional words used during reinforced trials. The groups for whom the task had been structured as a measure of empathy showed significantly greater increase of emotional words during reinforced trials than the group for whom the task had been structured as revealing personal problems. The greatest increase was in the "empathy" group who had been given "awareness" instructions. In short, both the structure given the examiner's reinforcing behavior and the subject's awareness of said behavior were germane to the direction of his verbal behavior. The "personal problem" group who had been given "awareness" instructions *decreased* slightly under reinforcement. Thus, verbal conditioning allows for the manipulation of "awareness" itself in such a way as to permit the measurement of its influence on S's subsequent behavior. Taken by itself, in terms of verbal report, "awareness" is a concept of dubious validity in verbal conditioning studies.

GENERALIZATION AND PREDICTION

Two major problems facing the therapist, as well as E in other influence situations, are those of generalization and prediction: (a) What is the relationship between S's verbalizations in the influencing situation and S's behavior outside of that situation? (b) What are the techniques of predicting those who will be most susceptible to the influencing process?

Prediction

Implicit, of course, in all verbal conditioning studies is the element of determining the most effective influencing conditions for predictive purposes. This is especially so for studies hypothesizing relationships between S personality variables and conditionability, previously discussed. I. G. Sarason (1958) carries this closer to psychotherapy by investigating responsivity to verbal conditioning as it is related to rated behavior in the psychotherapy situation itself. One finding, for example, was that patients compliant in psychotherapy were significantly more conditionable than noncompliant patients. A major assumption still to be demonstrated is that the S who is susceptible to influence in one situation, such as hypnosis or brainwashing, would also be susceptible to influence in other situations, such as verbal conditioning or Asch type procedures.

Weiss, Ullmann, and Krasner (1960) found in a group of college students a positive relationship between responsivity to verbal operant conditioning and an indirect measure of susceptibility to hypnosis—a scale of likelihood of hypnotizability adopted from hypnosis research of Hilgard and Weitzenhoffer. In a later study by Krasner, Ullmann, Weiss, and Collins (1961), this scale was expanded into a more general "Resistance to Conditioning Scale" which includes items from the CPI and MMPI. This scale correlated significantly with responsivity to verbal conditioning (of emotional words) in a group of medical students. Further refinements on this prediction scale are now in progress (Ullmann, Weiss, and Krasner, 1961).

Along similar lines, Crowne and Strickland (1961) found positive and significant relationships between responsivity to verbal conditioning and scores on a social desirability scale. This scale correlated significantly with a tendency to conform as measured by the Barron Scale and performance in a standard Asch conformity situation. Crowne and Strickland found that those Ss (college students) scoring high on this social desirability or need for approval scale were conditionable in the verbal conditioning situation, whereas those scoring low on this scale were not.

Generalization

No other issue is of more concern to the therapist than that of the generalization of behavior change from office to "life outside." Verbal conditioning studies have offered a clear-cut approach to this problem (B. R. Sarason, 1957), although generalization effects have been difficult to demonstrate (Dinoff, Horner, Kurpiewski, Rickard, and Timmons, 1960; Ekman and Friesen, 1960a; Moos, 1961; Rogers, 1960; Sandler, Gersten, and Greenspoon[6], Tobias, 1960; Weide, 1960; Williams, 1958).

Ullmann, Krasner, and Collins (1961) approached the problem of generalization by first isolating the behaviors of the therapist and patient which are characteristic of the psychotherapy situation. Then they systematically manipulated these behaviors to test hypotheses about the psychotherapeutic process. These hypotheses were: (a) a person can influence the behavior of another in a predictable direction, (b) this behavior change has a desirable effect on behavior in a second criterion situation, and (c) the changed behavior in the criterion situation is associated with a specific aspect of the already circumscribed behavior of the therapist.

Neuropsychiatric patients who were receiving group therapy participated in storytelling sessions during which emotional words were reinforced in one of three ways: a positive-personal manner ("mm-hmm" and head nodding); an impersonal-unstructured manner (the click of an electric counter); and no reinforcement at all. Ratings (Finney, 1954) made by the group therapist before and after the experimental storytelling sessions indicated a significant gain in adequacy of interpersonal relationships manifested in group therapy for the group receiving positive-personal reinforcement $(t = 1.83)$. There was no significant gain for the other two groups on this criterion measure $(t = 0.34$ and $t = 0.15)$. The results supported the hypothesis that one person can influence another in a positive way and that this change is measurable by an independent criterion situation. Further, this change in an S's behavior was demonstrated to be associated with specific behavior on the part of the experimenter. The authors point out that the hypothesis of

---

[6] Sandler, J. S., Gersten, C. O., and Greenspoon, J. The effects of behavioral cues on test performance in a clinical setting. Unpublished manuscript, 1960.

the positive correlation between change in use of verbal class during experimental sessions and change in the criterion may be oversimplified. Using a different *E,* new *Ss,* and introducing nonreinforced operant trials, Ullmann, Krasner, and Ekman (1961) found that patients in a positive-personal reinforcement group increased significantly in group therapy scores ($t = 2.25$), while the change of a "no-contact" comparison group approached but did not reach significance ($t = 1.69$). More importantly, when only *Ss* were used whose admission had occurred at least three months prior to the start of the experiment, it was found that the positive-personal reinforcement group gained an average of 9.00 points on Finney's Group Therapy Scale, while no-contact comparison subjects gained only 1.15 points on the average. The difference between the means of the two groups was statistically significant ($t = 1.95$). In this study, the relationship between increased group therapy scores and increased use of emotional words during the first two reinforced trials was insignificant. Thus, it is unlikely that the improvement in rated behavior was due to an increase in the use of emotional words, *per se.* Rather, we would hypothesize that the major element underlying these results was a form of role retraining in terms of learning the appropriateness of spontaneous expression in an interpersonal situation.

It should be pointed out that Rogers (1960) and Williams (1958) both failed to obtain generalization effects after having obtained significant effects of conditioning. It is speculated that the difference in results lies in the different relationship between the response class conditioned and the criterion behavior.

A significant generalization effect (favorable effect on a clinical criterion associated with verbal conditioning) was also obtained in another study with psychiatric patients (Ullmann, Weiss, and Krasner, 1961). A perceptual defense task consisting of matched threatening and neutral words on successive carbons was administered to one group *prior* to verbal conditioning of emotional words and to another group *after* verbal conditioning of emotional words. The latter group had lower defensive scores than the former. Further analysis of the data indicated that the "inhibitors" (repressors) as measured by the MMPI (Ullmann, 1962) showed significant generalization, while "facilitators" (externalizers) showed no significant effect of prior verbal conditioning of emotional words.

PSYCHOTHERAPY RESEARCH—PRESENT AND FUTURE

In his review chapter on "psychotherapy," Rotter (1960) summarizes several current research trends which have been emphasized in this paper: a greater flexibility in techniques; greater appreciation of patient-therapist interaction; greater willingness to challenge old taboos and beliefs in regard to psychotherapy, such as the importance of personal analysis and the "passive, constrained, and nonjudgmental role of the therapist"; more concern with psychotherapeutic procedure and less with outcome; concentration on the therapist and his verbal and non-verbal responses; and the increasing importance of "values" in psychotherapy. Further, Rotter suggests that more attention be paid to conceiving of psychotherapy as "a social interaction which follows the same laws and principles as other social interactions, and in which many different effects can be obtained by a variety of different conditions." He also feels that there is a relative lack of appreciation of the potential for using laboratory analogues in which the principles underlying psychotherapy can be investigated under relatively controlled conditions.

In fully assessing the implications of verbal conditioning studies for investigating psychotherapy, it should be pointed out that a certain percentage of these studies report negative results. In his review of 31 verbal conditioning studies, Krasner (1958a) found that approximately 25 percent of these studies report some aspects of negative results—the "reinforced" behavior either did not increase significantly or its increase was no more than in a control group. A recent study of Sullivan and Calvin (1959) also reports failure to condition "opinions" in a student group. These studies point to the need for investigation of the conditions under which the influencing process is *not* effective. Azrin, Holz, Ulrich, and Goldiamond (1961) report difficulties in replicating Verplanck's (1955) earlier work, and discuss some of the problems involved in adequate measurement of verbal operants and in training examiners. Barik and Fillenbaum (1961) also discuss "failures" to condition as they are related to the use of control groups.

A brief summary of the current trends in verbal operant conditioning studies would point up directions in which this approach to research on interpersonal processes has been headed, as well as offer a guide for future research: (a) an increasing complexity of design which places greater emphasis on the interaction of variables; (b) wider range of types of people being reinforced; (c) wider range of response class being reinforced with more emphasis on using continuous verbal behavior, rather than discrete verbal behavior; (d) explicit use of verbal conditioning as a therapeutic technique; (e) the study of issues which have evolved out of other learning studies, such as scheduling of reinforcement, learning without awareness, and instructional set; (f) the employment of operant conditioning techniques to lead to mechanical *instrumentation* for more effective behavior change; (g) the use of verbal conditioning techniques as stable measures of responsivity as the dependent variable in evaluating personality changes: (h) extension of verbal conditioning techniques to group situations; (i) the construction of predictive personality scales of responsivity to verbal conditioning and other influencing situations; (j) verbal conditioning responsivity as a predictor of success in psychotherapy; (k) verbal conditioning procedures as an experimental "control" on other treatment techniques. Finally, it should be emphasized that this technique of investigation offers opportunities to bring the process of psychotherapy within the framework of a scientific learning theory. Further, these techniques of investigation can fit in with a broader psychology of behavior control by incorporating into their design such techniques as hypnosis, sensory deprivation, isolation, drugs, physiological measurements, and nonverbal behavior. Future research can also use these techniques to investigate the countercontrols exerted by the patient on the therapist. The ideal "reinforcement machine" will have these effects programmed in, just as the experienced therapist is able to recognize and use patient "controlling" behavior.

One of the criticisms leveled against extrapolating the results of "laboratory" studies, such as verbal conditioning, into the "living process" of psychotherapy is that these studies miss many of the subleties and complexities involved in the psychotherapy process and tend to oversimplify the process. Rather than being defensive in interpreting laboratory studies of the influencing process, there is now enough evidence that these techniques can be used not only for research, but as actual therapeutic techniques. The studies by Ullmann, Krasner, and Collins (1961) and by Rickard et al. (1960) were used in psychotherapeutic context to change patient behavior in a desired direction. Other studies (Salzinger and Pisoni, 1958, 1960) take place within the context of ordinary clinical interactions, or were labeled as "psychotherapy" (Williams, 1958). Greenspoon[7] is in the process of developing a modified tape recorder which can be utilized as a mechanical reinforcer in a psychotherapy situation.

As part of an ongoing study by Ullmann, Krasner, and Gelfand,[8] each instance of the reinforced verbal class, emotional words, was scored on a scale of "Pleasantness-Unpleasantness." To eliminate individual differences in *number* of emotional words used, the *average* rating of emotional words determined each S's score. The correlations between pairs of raters for 25 cases were .96, .93, and .93. Comparing these scores for emotional words used during operant and reinforced trials for 80 college Ss (Weiss, Krasner, and Ullmann, 1960), the emotional words used during reinforcement were significantly pleasanter than the emotional words used during operant trials, the critical ratio being 5.27. Similarly,

[7] Greenspoon, J. Personal communication, 1960.

[8] Ullmann, L. P., Krasner, L., and Gelfand, Donna M. Fantasy hostility associated with the attenuation of aggression. Mimeographed manuscript, University of Illinois, 1966.

for another group of 48 college students (Ekman, Krasner, and Ullmann, see Footnote 4) emotional words used during reinforced trials were significantly pleasanter than the emotional words used during operant trials, the critical ratio being 4.84. Aside from the similarity of this score to the Discomfort-Relief Quotient (DRQ) (Mowrer, 1953a), work in progress indicates that "Pleasantness-Unpleasantness" scores are associated with tension measures such as Barron Egostrength (1953) and McReynolds Incongruency Technique (1958).

Krasner and Winder have used role-taking techniques for training schizophrenic patients to take the E role in a verbal conditioning situation with college students as Ss. Preliminary work indicates that this type of training is feasible, and the plan is to gradually extend the kind and complexities of verbal behavior which the schizophrenic patient is trained to reinforce, as well as to increase the complexities of the cues which the schizophrenic patient will use as reinforcers.

The motor operant conditioning studies (Bullock, 1960; Bullock and Brunt, 1959; Driskell and Tremaine, 1960; King, Merrell, Lovinger, and Denny, 1957; Lindsley, 1956, 1960; Lindsley and Skinner, 1954; Peters and Jenkins, 1954; Tilton, 1957; Verplanck, 1956) use as dependent variables changes in behavior which may be termed "therapeutic." An illustration of this is the work of Ferster (1958) and Ferster and De Myer (1961) with autistic children in which the conditioning of motor operants is used to shape up and bring into contact with his environment the behavior of the autistic child. A series of investigations with children as Ss further illustrate the use of motor and verbal operant conditioning techniques in behavioral analysis and in "therapeutic manipulation" of behavior (Azrin and Lindsley, 1956; Baer, 1960, 1961; Bijou, 1955, 1957; Bijou and Baer, 1961; Bijou and Orlando, 1961; Lovaas, 1961; Patterson, 1959; Patterson, Helper and Wilcott, 1960; Warren and Brown, 1943). Other recent developments have included the application of operant conditioning techniques to: the "reinstatement" of verbal behavior in psychotics (Isaacs, Thomas, and Goldiamond, 1960); the control of stuttering (Flanagan, Goldiamond, and Azrin, 1958, 1959); and working with "unreachable cases" (Slack, 1960); and the shaping of a wide range of behaviors in schizophrenics by appropriate "behavioral engineering" techniques (Ayllon, 1960; Ayllon and Michael, 1959).

Viewing research in psychotherapy as part of a broader psychology of behavior control has other implications which must be faced. Many therapists will object to having their sacred healing process identified with concepts such as "brainwashing," sensory deprivation, or "placebos." They will refuse to acknowledge that a therapist can be "programmed" to maximize efficiency in the influencing process. They may contend that this is too mechanical an approach and as such belongs to the science fiction world of Orwell and Huxley (Skinner, 1948; Vandenberg, 1956) but not to the psychotherapy world of Freud. However, the research approaches cited in this paper are investigating a process that occurs every day in the therapist's office. They demonstrate that this process is lawful and amenable to systematic approach as part of the interpersonal influencing process. It is conceivable that future research will find that this process is most effective under certain conditions which may utilize: sensory deprivation; hypnosis; conditioning techniques; subliminal stimuli; manipulation of antecedent contacts, set, awareness, and ambiguity; and "programmed" therapists. With our goal as therapists to better the lives of our patients, to make them more comfortable with themselves, and to better their interpersonal relationships, then we cannot avoid recognition of our use of these techniques, if this is the way people's behavior is influenced. Intrinsically, there is nothing evil or unethical in such techniques. The task for the research investigator is now to determine the most effective techniques of behavior control. He must also give serious consideration to helping develop societal *safeguards* so that these techniques will not be misused or exploited for "nontherapeutic" purposes (Krasner, 1961a). This is a far more difficult task than any discussed in this paper and is worth a "conference" in its own right.

REFERENCES

Aronson, M. A study of the relationships between certain counselor and client characteristics in client-centered therapy. In W. U. Snyder (Ed.), *Group report of a program of research in psychotherapy*. State College, Pa.: Pennsylvania State Univer., 1953. Pp. 39-54.

Adams, H. B., Carrera, R. N., Cooper, G. D., Gibby, R. G., and Tobey, H. R. Personality and intellectual changes in psychiatric patients following brief partial sensory deprivation. *Amer. Psychologist*, 1960, *15*, 448. (Abstract)

Adams, J. K. Laboratory studies of behavior without awareness. *Psychol. Bull.*, 1957, *54*, 383-405.

Adams, J. S., and Hoffman, B. The frequency of self-reference statements as a function of generalized reinforcement. *J. abnorm. soc. Psychol.*, 1960, *60*, 384-389.

Anderson, D. E. Personality variables and verbal conditioning. *Dissertation Abstr.*, 1959, *19*, 1811.

Asch, S. E. The doctrine of suggestion, prestige, and imitation in social psychology. *Psychol. Rev.*, 1948, *55*, 250-277.

Asch, S. E. Studies of independence and conformity: I. A minority of one against a unanimous majority. *Psychol. Monogr.*, 1956, *70* (9, Whole No. 416).

Ashby, J. D., Ford, D. H., Guerney, B. G., Jr., and Guerney, Louise F. Effects on clients of a reflective and a leading type of psychotherapy. *Psychol. Monogr.*, 1957, *71* (24, Whole No. 453).

Atkinson, Rita L. Paired-associate learning by schizophrenic and normal subjects under conditions of verbal reward and verbal punishment. Unpublished doctoral dissertation, Indiana Univer., 1957.

Auld, F., Jr. Influence of social class on personality test responses. *Psychol. Bull.*, 1952, 49, 318-332.

Auld, F., Jr., and Murray, E. J. Content-analysis studies of psychotherapy. *Psychol. Bull.*, 1955, *52*, 377-395.

Auld, F., Jr., and White, Alice. Sequential dependencies in psychotherapy. *J. abnorm. soc. Psychol.*, 1959, *58*, 100-104.

Ayllon, T. Some behavioral problems associated with eating in chronic schizophrenic patients. Paper presented to Amer. Psychol. Association, Chicago, September, 1960.

Ayllon, T., and Michael, J. The psychiatric nurse as a behavioral engineer. *J. exp. Anal. Behav.*, 1959, *2*, 323-334.

Azima, H., and Cramer, Fern J. Effects of partial perceptual isolation in mentally disturbed individuals. *Dis. nerv. Syst.*, 1956, *17*, 117-122. (a)

Azima, H., and Cramer-Azima, Fern J. Effects of the decrease in sensory variability on body scheme. *Canad. Psychiatric Ass. J.*, 1956, *1*, 59-72. (b)

Azima, H., and Cramer-Azima, Fern J. Studies on perceptual isolation. *Dis. nerv. Syst.*, Monogr. Suppl., 1957, *18*, No. 8.

Azrin, N. H., Holz, W., Ulrich, R., and Goldiamond, I. The control of the content of conversation through reinforcement. *J. exp. Anal. Behav.*, 1961, *4*, 25-30.

Azrin, N. H., and Lindsley, O. R. The reinforcement of cooperation between children. *J. abnorm. soc. Psychol.*, 1956, *52*, 100-102.

Babladelis, Georgia. A study of the effects of a personality variable in verbal conditioning. Unpublished doctoral dissertation, Univer. of Colorado, 1960.

Bachrach, A. J. Notes on the experimental analysis of behavior. In H. Lief, N. Lief, and V. Lief (Eds.), *The psychological basis of medical practice*. New York: Hoeber, 1962.

Bachrach, A. J., Candland, D. K., and Gibson, Janice T. Experiments in verbal behavior: I. Group reinforcement of individual response. *Tech. Rep.*, 1960, Contract Nonr. 474 (8).

Back, K. W. Influence through social communication. *J. abnorm. soc. Psychol.*, 1951, *46*, 9-23.

Baer, D. M. Control of thumbsucking in a young child by withdrawal and representation of positive reinforcement. *Amer. Psychologist*, 1960, *15*, 475. (Abstract)

Baer, D. M. Effect of withdrawal of positive reinforcement on an extinguishing response in young children. *Child Develpm.*, 1961, *32*, 67-74.

Bales, R. F. *Interaction process analysis*. Cambridge, Mass.: Addison-Wesley, 1950.

Ball, R. S. Reinforcement conditioning of verbal behavior by verbal and non-verbal stimuli in a situation resembling a clinical interview. Unpublished doctoral dissertation, Indiana Univer., 1952.

Bandura, A. Psychotherapist's anxiety level, self-insight, and psychotherapeutic competence. *J. abnorm. soc. Psychol.*, 1956, *52*, 333-337.

Bandura, A. Psychotherapy as a learning process. *Psychol. Bull.*, 1961, *58*, 143-159.

Bandura, A., Lipsher, D. H., and Miller, Paula E. Psychotherapists' approach-avoidance reactions to patients' expressions of hostility. *J. consult. Psychol.*, 1960, *24*, 1-8.

Barik, H. C., and Fillenbaum, S. Negative reinforcement of two grammatical response classes. *Canad. J. Psychol.*, 1961, *15*, 107-115.

Barik, H. C., and Lambert, W. E. Conditioning of complex verbal sequences. *Canad. J. Psychol.*, 1960, *14*, 87-95.

Barnett, C. D., Pryer, Margaret W., and Ellis, N. R. Experimental manipulation of verbal behavior in defectives. *Psychol. Rep.*, 1959, *5*, 593-596.

Barron, F. An ego-strength scale which predicts response to psychotherapy. *J. consult. Psychol.*, 1953, *17*, 327-333.

Berg, I. A. Comments on current books and the passing scene. *J. counsel. Psychol.*, 1958, *5*, 316-317.

Bergin, A. Personality interpretation as persuasive communication. Unpublished doctoral dissertation, Stanford Univer., 1960.

Berkowitz, L., and Lundy, R. M. Personality characteristics related to suscepti-bility to influence by peers or authority figures. *J. Pers.*, 1957, *25*, 306-316.

Bextion, W. H., Heron, W., and Scott, T. H. Effects of decreased variation in the sensory environment. *Canad. J. Psychol.*, 1954, *8*, 70-76.

Bijou, S. W. A systematic approach to an experimental analysis of young chil-dren. *Child Develpm.*, 1955, *26*, 161-168.

Bijou, S. W. Patterns of reinforcement and resistance to extinction in young children. *Child Develpm.*, 1957, *28*, 47-54.

Bijou, S. W., and Baer, D. M. *Child development: A systematic and empirical theory.* Vol. 1. New York: Appleton-Century-Crofts, 1961.

Bijou, S. W., and Orlando, R. Rapid development of multiple-schedule per-formances with retarded children. *J. exp. Anal. Behav.*, 1961, *4*, 7-16.

Binder, A., McConnell, D., and Sjoholm, Nancy A. Verbal conditioning as a function of experimenter characteristics. *J. abnorm. soc. Psychol.*, 1957, *55*, 309-314.

Blake, R. R., and Mouton, Jane S. The dynamics of influence and coercion. *Int. J. soc. Psychiat.*, 1957, *2*, 263-274.

Bordin, E. S. Ambiguity as a therapeutic variable. *J. consult. Psychol.*, 1955, *19*, 9-15.

Bullock, D. H. Some aspects of human operant behavior. *Psychol. Rec.*, 1960, *10*, 241-258.

Bullock, D. H., and Brunt, M. Y., Jr. The test-ability of psychiatric patients in an operant conditioning situation. *Psychol. Rec.*, 1959, *9*, 165-170.

Buss, A. H., and Durkee, Ann. Conditioning of hostile verbalizations in a situation resembling a clinical interview. *J. consult. Psychol.*, 1958, *6*, 415-418.

Buss, A. H., and Gerjuoy, Irma R. Verbal conditioning and anxiety. *J. abnorm. soc. Psychol.*, 1958, *57*, 249-250.

Buss, A. H., Gerjuoy, Irma R., and Zusman, J. Verbal conditioning and extinction with verbal and nonverbal reinforcers. *J. exp. Psychol.*, 1958, *56*, 139-145.

Cairns, R. B. The influence of dependency-anxiety on the effectiveness of social reinforcers. Unpublished doctoral dissertation, Stanford Univer., 1960.

Campbell, J. M. Verbal conditioning as a function of the personality characteristics of experimenters and subjects. Unpublished doctoral dissertation, Univer. of Washington, 1960.

Cartwright, D. S., and Cartwright, Rosalind D. Faith and improvement in psychotherapy. *J. counsel. Psychol.*, 1958, *5*, 174-177.

Chan, Kathleen Swat Hoon. The effect of enhanced visual sensory input on the probability of verbal response. *Dissertation Abstr.*, 1958, *18*, 283-284.

Cieutat, V. J. Surreptitious modification of verbal behavior during class discussion. *Psychol. Rep.*, 1959, *5*, 648.

Cohen, E., and Cohen, B. D. Verbal reinforcement in schizophrenia. *J. abnorm. soc. Psychol.*, 1960, *60*, 443-446.

Crowne, D. P., and Strickland, Bonnie R. The conditioning of verbal behavior as a function of the need for social approval. *J. abnorm. soc. Psychol.*, 1961, *63*, 395-401.

Cushing, M. C. Affective components of the response class as a factor in verbal conditioning. *Dissertation Abstr.*, 1957, *17*, 2313.

Cutler, R. L. Countertransference effects in psychotherapy. *J. consult. Psychol.*, 1958, *22*, 349-356.

Daily, J. M. Verbal conditioning without awareness. *Dissertation Abstr.*, 1953, *13*, 1247-1248.

Dibner, A. S. Cue-counting: A measure of anxiety in interviews. *J. consult. Psychol.*, 1956, *20*, 475-478.

Dibner, A. S. Ambiguity and anxiety. *J. abnorm. soc. Psychol.*, 1958, *56*, 165-174.

Dinoff, M., Horner, R. F., Kurpiewski, B. S., Rickard, H. C., and Timmons, E. O. Conditioning verbal behavior of a psychiatric population in a group therapy-like situation. *J. clin. Psychol.*, 1960, *16*, 371-371.

Dinoff, M., Horner, R. F., Kurpiewski, B. S., and Timmons, E. O. Conditioning verbal behavior of schizophrenics in a group therapy-like situation. *J. clin. Psychol.*, 1960, *16*, 367-370.

Dinoff, M., Rickard, H. C., Salzberg, H., and Sipprelle, C. N. An experimental analogue of three psychotherapeutic approaches. *J. clin. Psychol.*, 1960, *16*, 70-73.

Dittmann, A. T. The interpersonal process in psychotherapy: Development of a research method. *J. abnorm. soc. Psychol.*, 1952, *17*, 236-244.

Dobie, Shirley I. Operant conditioning of verbal and hallucinatory responses with nonverbal reinforcement. Paper read at Midwestern Psychol. Assoc., Chicago, May, 1959.

Doering, M. F. A test of a training procedure designed to increase the intensity of angry verbalizations. *Dissertation Abstr.*, 1959, *19*, 2144.

Dollard, J., and Miller, N. E. *Personality and psychotherapy.* New York: McGraw-Hill, 1950.

Driskell, Joyce C., and Tremaine, D. L. Operant conditioning of human motor behavior without subjects' awareness. *Amer. Psychologist*, 1960, *7*, 430. (Abstract)

Dulany, D. E., Jr. Hypotheses and habits in verbal "operant conditioning." *J. abnorm. soc. Psychol.*, 1961, *63*, 251-263.

Ekman, P. A comparison of verbal and nonverbal behavior as reinforcing stimuli of opinion responses. Unpublished doctoral dissertation, Adelphi College, 1958.

Ekman, P., and Friesen, W. V. The conditioning of hostile responses to photographs of peers: Three measures of generalization. Paper read at Eastern Psychol. Assoc., New York, April, 1960. (a)

Ekman, P., and Friesen, W. V. Status and personality of the experimenter as a determinant of verbal conditioning. *Amer. Psychologist*, 1960, *15*, 430. (Abstract) (b)

Eriksen, C. W. Discrimination and learning without awareness: A methodological survey and evaluation. *Psychol. Rev.*, 1960, *67*, 279-300.

Everstine, L., and Bendig, A. W. Conditioning neurotic verbalizations. *Amer. Psychologist*, 1960, *15*, 430. (Abstract)

Eysenck, H. J. The effects of psychotherapy: An evaluation. *J. consult. Psychol.*, 1952, *16*, 319-324.

Fahmy, Sumaya A. Conditioning and extinction of a referential verbal response class in a situation resembling a clinical diagnostic interview. *Dissertation Abstr.*, 1953, *13*, 873-874.

Farber, I. E., Harlow, H. F., and West, L. J. Brainwashing, conditioning, and DDD (debility, dependency, and dread). *Sociometry*, 1957, *20*, 271-285.

Ferguson, D. C., and Buss, A. H. Operant conditioning of hostile verbs in relation to experimenter and subject characteristics. *J. consult. Psychol.*, 1960, *24*, 324-327.

Ferster, C. B. Withdrawal of positive reinforcement as punishment. *Science*, 1957, *126*, 509.

Ferster, C. B. Development of normal behavioral processes in austistic children. *Res. relat. Children*, 1958, *9*, 30.

Ferster, C. B. Positive reinforcement and behavioral deficits of autistic children. *Child Develpm.*, 1961, *32*, 437-456.

Ferster, C. B., and De Myer, Marian K. The development of performances in autistic children in an automatically controlled environment. *J. chronic Dis.*, 1961, *13*, 312-345.

Ferster, C. B., and Skinner, B. F. *Schedules of reinforcement.* New York: Appleton-Century-Crofts, 1957.

Fey, W. F. Doctrine and experience: Their influence upon the psychotherapist. *J. consult. Psychol.,* 1958, *22,* 403-409.

Fiedler, F. E. A comparison of therapeutic relationships in psychoanalytic, nondirective, and Adlerian therapy. *J. consult. Psychol.,* 1950, *14,* 436-445.

Fiedler, F. E. Factor analyses of psychoanalytic, nondirective, and Adlerian therapeutic relationships. *J. consult. Psychol.,* 1951, *15,* 32-38.

Fiedler, F. E. Quantitative studies on the role of therapists' feelings toward their patients. In O. H. Mowrer (Ed.), *Psychotherapy: Theory and research.* New York: Ronald, 1953.

Finney, B. C. A scale to measure interpersonal relationships in group therapy. *Group Psychother.,* 1954, *7,* 52-66.

Flanagan, B., Goldiamond, I., and Azrin, N. Operant stuttering: The control of stuttering through response-contingent consequences. *J. exp. Anal. Behav.,* 1958, *1,* 173-177.

Flanagan, B., Goldiamond, I., and Azrin, N. H. Instatement of stuttering in normally fluent individuals through operant procedures. *Science,* 1959, *130,* 979-981.

Ford, D. H. Research approaches to psychotherapy. *J. counsel. Psychol.,* 1959, *6,* 55-60.

Frank, J. D. Some effects of expectancy and influence in psychotherapy. In J. H. Masserman and J. L. Moreno (Eds.), *Progress in psychotherapy.* Vol. III. New York: Grune & Stratton, 1958.

Frank, J. D. The dynamics of the psychotherapeutic relationship: Determinants and effects of the therapist's influence. *Psychiatry,* 1959, *22,* 17-39. (a)

Frank, J. D. Problems of controls in psychotherapy as exemplified by the psychotherapy research project of the Phipps Psychiatric Clinic. In E. A. Rubinstein and M. B. Parloff (Eds.), *Research in psychotherapy.* Washington, D. C.: Amer. Psychol. Assoc., 1959. (b)

Frank, J. D. *Persuasion and healing: A comparative study of psychotherapy.* Baltimore: Johns Hopkins Press, 1961.

Frank, J. D., Gliedman, L. H., Imber, S. D., Stone, A. R., and Nash, E. H. Patients' expectancies and relearning as factors determining improvement in psychotherapy. *Amer. J. Psychiat.,* 1959, *115,* 961-968.

Franks, C. M. Conditioning and personality: A study of normal and neurotic subjects. *J. abnorm. soc. Psychol.,* 1956, *52,* 143-150.

Franks, C. M. Personality factors and the rate of conditioning. *Brit. J. Psychol.,* 1957, *48,* 119-126.

Friesen, W. V., and Ekman, P. Conditioning of hostile and friendly responses to peer photographs. *Amer. Psychologist,* 1960, *15,* 430. (Abstract)

Gelfand, Donna M., and Winder, C. L. Operant conditioning of verbal behavior in dysthymics and hysterics. *J. abnorm. soc. Psychol.,* 1961, *62,* 688-689.

Gewirtz, J. L., and Baer, D. M. The effects of deprivation and satiation on behaviors for a social reinforcer. *Amer. Psychologist*, 1957, *12*, 401. (Abstract)

Gewirtz, J. L., and Baer, D. M. Deprivation and satiation of social reinforcers as drive conditions. *J. abnorm. soc. Psychol.*, 1958, *57*, 165-172. (a)

Gewirtz, J. L., and Baer, D. M. The effect of brief social deprivation on behaviors for a social reinforcer. *J. abnorm. soc. Psychol.*, 1958, *56*, 49-56. (b)

Gill, M. G., and Brenman, Margaret. Research in psychotherapy. *Amer. J. Orthopsychiat.*, 1948, *18*, 100-110.

Glad, D. D. *Operational values in psychotherapy*. New York: Oxford Univer. Press, 1959.

Gliedman, L. H., Nash, E. H., Imber, S. D., Stone, A. R., and Frank, J. D. Reduction of symptoms by pharmacologically inert substances and by short-term psychotherapy. *AMA Arch. Neurol. Psychiat.*, 1958, *79*, 345-351.

Goldiamond, I. Indicators of perception: I. Subliminal perception, subception, unconscious perception: An analysis in terms of psycho-physical indicator methodology. *Psychol. Bull.*, 1958, *55*, 373-411.

Goldman-Eisler, Frieda. Individual differences between interviewers and their effect on interviewees' conversational behavior. *J. ment. Sci.*, 1952, *98*, 660-671.

Goldman-Eisler, Frieda. On the variability of the speed of talking and its relation to the length of utterances in conversations. *Brit. J. Psychol.*, 1954, *45*, 94-107.

Graham, S. R. The influence of therapist character structure upon Rorschach changes in the course of psychotherapy. *Amer. Psychologist*, 1960, *15*, 415. (Abstract)

Greenspoon, J. The effect of two nonverbal stimuli on the frequency of members of two verbal response classes. *Amer. Psychologist*, 1954, *9*, 384. (Abstract)

Greenspoon, J. The reinforcing effect of two spoken sounds on the frequency of two responses. *Amer. J. Psychol.*, 1955, *68*, 409-416.

Grossberg, J. M. The effect of reinforcement schedule and response class on verbal conditioning. *Dissertation Abstr.*, 1956, *16*, 2211.

Grossman, D. An experimental investigation of a psychotherapeutic technique. *J. consult. Psychol.*, 1952, *16*, 325-331.

Hagen, J. The conditioning of verbal affect responses in two hospitalized schizophrenic diagnostic groups during the clinical interview. Unpublished doctoral dissertation, Washington State Univer., 1959.

Haley, J. Control in psychoanalytic psychotherapy. In J. H. Masserman and J. L. Moreno (Eds.), *Progress in psychotherapy*. Vol. IV. New York: Grune & Stratton, 1959.

Hall, W. E. The effects of set and reinforcement in verbal conditioning. *Dissertation Abstr.*, 1958, *19*, 1115-1116.

Hartman, C. H. Verbal behavior of schizophrenic and normal subjects as a function of types of social reinforcement. *Dissertation Abstr.*, 1955, *15*, 1652-1653.

Hebb, D. O. The motivating effects of exteroceptive stimulation. *Amer. Psychologist*, 1958, *13*, 109-113.

Heine, R. W. A comparison of patients' reports on psychotherapeutic experience with psychoanalytic, nondirective, and Adlerian therapists. *Amer. J. Psychother.*, 1953, *7*, 16-23.

Helson, H., Blake, R. R., Mouton, Jane S., and Olmstead, J. A. Attitudes as adjustments to stimulus, background, and residual factors. *J. abnorm. soc. Psychol.*, 1956, *52*, 314-322.

Heron, W., Bexton, W. H., and Hebb, D. O. Cognitive effects of a decreased variation in the sensory environment. *Amer. Psychologist*, 1953, *8*, 366. (Abstract)

Heron, W., Doane, B. K., and Scott, T. H. Visual disturbances after prolonged perceptual isolation. *Canad. J. Psychol.*, 1956, *10*, 13-18.

Hildum, D. C., and Brown, R. W. Verbal reinforcement and interviewer bias. *J. abnorm. soc. Psychol.*, 1956, *53*, 108-111.

Hiler, E. W. An analysis of patient-therapist compatibility. *J. consult. Psychol.*, 1958, *22*, 341-347.

Hollingshead, A. R., and Redlich, F. C. *Social class and mental illness: A community study*. New York: Wiley, 1958.

Holt, R. R., and Luborsky, L. *Personality patterns of psychiatrists*. New York: Basic Books, 1958.

Hovland, C. I., Janis, I. L., and Kelley, H. H. *Communication and persuasion: Psychological studies of opinion change*. New Haven: Yale Univer. Press, 1953.

Imber, S. D., Frank, J. D., Gliedman, L. H., Nash, E. H., Jr., and Stone, A. R. Suggestibility, social class and the acceptance of psychotherapy. *J. clin. Psychol.*, 1956, *12*, 341-344.

Imber, S. D., Nash, E. H., and Stone, A. R. Social class and duration of psychotherapy. *J. clin. Psychol.*, 1955, *11*, 281-284.

Isaacs, W., Thomas, J., and Goldiamond, I. Application of operant conditioning to reinstate verbal behavior in psychotics. *J. speech hear. Dis.*, 1960, *25*, 8-12.

Janis, I. L. Personality correlates of susceptibility to persuasion. *J. Pers.*, 1954, *22*, 504-518.

Janis, I. L., and King, B. T. The influence of role playing on opinion change. *J. abnorm. soc. Psychol.*, 1954, *49*, 211-218.

Kanfer, F. H. The effect of partial reinforcement on acquisition and extinction of a class of verbal responses. *J. exp. Psychol.*, 1954, *48*, 424-432.

Kanfer, F. H. Verbal conditioning: Reinforcement schedules and experimenter influence. *Psychol. Rep.*, 1958, *4*, 443-452.

Kanfer, F. H. Incentive value of generalized reinforcers. *Psychol. Rep.*, 1960, *7*, 531-538.

Kanfer, F. H. Comments on learning in psychotherapy. *Psychol. Rep.*, 1961, *9*, 681-699.

Kanfer, F. H., and Karas, Shirley C. Prior experimenter-subject interaction and verbal conditioning. *Psychol. Rep.,* 1959, *5,* 345-353.

Kanfer, F. H., and McBrearty, J. F. Verbal conditioning: Discrimination and awareness. *J. Psychol.,* 1961, *52,* 115-124.

Keller, F. S., and Schoenfeld, W. N. *Principles of psychology.* New York: Appleton-Century-Crofts, 1950.

Kelman, H. C. Three processes of acceptance of social influence: Compliance, identification, and internalization. *Amer. Psychologist,* 1956, *11,* 361 (Abstract)

King, G. F., Merrell, D. W., Lovinger, E., and Denny, M. R. Operant motor behavior in acute schizophrenics. *J. Pers.,* 1957, *25,* 317-326.

Kirman, W. J. The relationship of learning, with and without awareness, to personality needs. *Dissertation Abstr.,* 1958, *19,* 362-363.

Krasner, L. The use of generalized reinforcers in psychotherapy research. *Psychol. Rep.,* 1955, *1,* 19-25.

Krasner, L. Studies of the conditioning of verbal behavior. *Psychol. Bull.,* 1958, 55, 148-170. (a)

Krasner, L. A technique of investigating the relationships between behavior cues of examiner and verbal behavior of patient. *J. consult. Psychol.,* 1958, *22,* 364-366. (b)

Krasner, L. Role-taking research and psychotherapy. *VA Res. Rept., Palo Alto,* Nov., 1959, No. 5.

Krasner, L. Behavior control and social responsibility. Paper presented at Western Psychol. Assoc., Seattle, June, 1961. (a)

Krasner, L. Behavior control, values and training. In Symposium on predoctoral training, Western Psychol. Assoc., Seattle, June, 1961. (b)

Krasner, L., and Ullmann, L. P. Variables in the verbal conditioning of schizophrenic subjects. *Amer. Psychologist,* 1958, *13,* 358. (Abstract)

Krasner, L., Ullmann, L. P., and Weiss, R. L. Distribution and validation of modal perceptual responses of normal and psychiatric subjects. Paper presented at Amer. Psychol. Assoc., New York, September, 1961.

Krasner, L., Ullmann, L. P., Weiss, R. L., and Collins, Beverly J. Responsivity to verbal conditioning as a function of three different examiners. *J. clin. Psychol.,* 1961, *17,* 411-415.

Krasner, L., Weiss, R. L., and Ullmann, L. P. Responsivity to verbal conditioning as a function of "awareness." *Psychol. Rep.,* 1961, *8,* 523-538.

Lakin, M., and Lebovits, B. Bias in psychotherapists of different orientations. *Amer. J. Psychother.,* 1958, *12,* 79-86.

Leary, T. F. *Interpersonal diagnosis of personality.* New York: Ronald, 1957.

Lennard, H. L., Calogeras, R., and Hendin, Helen. Some relationships between verbal behavior of therapist and patient in psychotherapy. *J. Psychol.,* 1957, *43,* 181-186.

Leventhal, A. M. The effects of diagnostic category and reinforcer on learning without awareness. *J. abnorm. soc. Psychol.*, 1959, *59*, 162-166.

Levin, S. M. The effects of awareness on verbal conditioning. *J. exp. Psychol.*, 1961, *61*, 67-75.

Lifton, R. J. "Thought reform" of western civilians in Chinese communist prisons. *Psychiatry*, 1956, *19*, 173-195.

Lifton, R. J. Chinese communist thought reform. In *Group processes: Transactions of the third Conference*. New York: Josiah Macy, Jr. Foundation, 1957. Pp. 219-311. (a)

Lifton, R. J. Thought reform of Chinese intellectuals: A psychiatric evaluation. *J. soc. Issues*, 1957, *13* (3), 5-10. (b)

Lilly, J. C. Mental effects of reduction of ordinary levels of physical stimuli on intact, healthy persons. *Psychiat. res. Rep.*, 1956, *5*, 1-9.

Lindsley, O. R. Operant conditioning methods applied to research in chronic schizophrenia. *Psychiat. res. Rep.*, 1956, *5*, 118-139.

Lindsley, O. R. Characteristics of the behavior of chronic psychotics as revealed by free-operant conditioning methods. *Dis. nerv. Syst.*, 1960, *21*, 66-78.

Lindsley, O. R., and Skinner, B. F. A method for the experimental analysis of the behavior of psychotic patients. *Amer. Psychologist*, 1954, *9*, 419-420. (Abstract)

Lorenz, Maria, and Cobb, S. Language behavior in psychoneurotic patients. *AMA Arch. Neurol. Psychiat.*, 1953, *69*, 684-694.

Lovaas, O. I. The control of operant responding by rate and content of verbal operants. Paper presented at Western Psychol. Assoc., Seattle, June, 1961.

Luchins, A. S., and Luchins, Edith H. On conformity with true and false communications. *J. soc. Psychol.*, 1955, *42*, 283-303.

Lundin, R. W. *Personality: An experimental approach*. New York: Macmillan, 1961.

Mahl, G. F. Disturbances and silences in the patient's speech in psychotherapy. *J. abnorm. soc. Psychol.*, 1956, *53*, 1-15.

Mahl, G. F. Measuring the patient's anxiety during interviews from "expressive" aspects of his speech. *Trans. New York Acad. Sci.*, 1959, *21*, 249-257.

Mandler, G., and Kaplan, W. K. Subjective evaluation and reinforcing effect of a verbal stimulus. *Science*, 1956, *124*, 582-583.

Marion, A. J. The influence of experimenter status upon verbal conditioning. Unpublished doctoral dissertation, Univer. of California, Los Angeles, 1956.

Marmor, J. Psychoanalytic therapy as an educational process: Common denominators in the therapeutic approaches of different psychoanalytic "schools." Paper presented at Academy of Psychoanalysis, Chicago, May, 1961.

Matarazzo, J. D., Saslow, G., and Pareis, E. N. Verbal conditioning of two response classes: Some methodological considerations. *J. abnorm. soc. Psychol.*, 1960, *61*, 190-206.

McConnell, J. V., Cutler, R. L., and McNeil, E. B. Subliminal stimulation: An overview. *Amer. Psychologist*, 1958, *13*, 229-242.

McKee, M. G. Examiner-subject relationship in verbal conditioning. Unpublished doctoral dissertation, Univer. of California, 1960.

McNair, D. M. Reinforcement of verbal behavior. *J. exp. Psychol.*, 1957, *53*, 40-46.

McReynolds, P. Anxiety as related to incongruencies between values and feelings. *Psychol. Rec.*, 1958, *8*, 57-66.

McReynolds, P., Acker, M., and Daily, J. On the effects of perceptual enhancement on certain schizophrenic symptoms. *VA Res. Rept., Palo Alto*, 1959, No. 1.

Medini, G. J. Learning without awareness and its relationship to insight and the hysteric-obsessive dimension. *Dissertation Abstr.*, 1958, *18*, 666.

Meerloo, J. A. M. *The rape of the mind: The psychology of thought control, menticide and brain-washing.* New York: World Publishing, 1956.

Mock, J. F. The influence of verbal and behavioral cues of a listener on the verbal productions of the speaker. Unpublished doctoral dissertation, Univer. of Kentucky, 1957.

Moos, R. H. The retention and generalization of operant conditioning effects in a free interview situation. Paper presented at Western Psychol. Assoc., Seattle, June, 1961.

Mowrer, O. H. Changes in verbal behavior during psychotherapy. In O. H. Mowrer (Ed.), *Psychotherapy: Theory and research.* New York: Ronald, 1953. (a)

Mowrer, O. H. (Ed.) *Psychotherapy: Theory and research.* New York: Ronald, 1953. (b)

Mowrer, O. H., Hunt, J. McV., and Kogan, L. S. Further studies utilizing the Discomfort-Relief Quotient. In O. H. Mowrer (Ed.), *Psychotherapy: Theory and research.* New York: Ronald, 1953.

Murray, E. J. A case study in a behavioral analysis of psychotherapy. *J. abnorm. soc. Psychol.*, 1954, *49*, 305-310.

Murray, E. J. A content-analysis method for studying psychotherapy. *Psychol. Monogr.*, 1956, *70* (13, Whole No. 420).

Nuthmann, Anne M. Conditioning of a response class on a personality test. *J. abnorm. soc. Psychol.*, 1957, *54*, 19-23.

O'Connor, N., and Rawnsley, K. Two types of conditioning in psychotics and normals. *J. abnorm. soc. Psychol.*, 1959, *58*, 157-161.

O'Donnell, W. F., Jr. The effects of individual differences and hostility arousal on the expression of hostility in a verbal conditioning situation. Unpublished doctoral dissertation, Univer. of Washington, 1959.

Palmore, E., Leonard, H. L., and Hendin, Helen. Similarities of therapist and patient verbal behavior in psychotherapy. *Sociometry*, 1959, *22*, 12-22.

Parloff, M. B. Some factors affecting the quality of therapeutic relationships. *J. abnorm. soc. Psychol.*, 1956, *52*, 5-10.

Patterson, G. R. Fathers as reinforcing agents. Paper read at Western Psychol. Assoc., San Diego, April, 1959.

Patterson, G. R., Helper, M. E., and Wilcott, R. C. Anxiety and verbal conditioning in children. *Child Develpm.*, 1960, *31*, 101-108.

Peters, H. N., and Jenkins, R. L. Improvement of chronic schizophrenic patients with guided problem-solving motivated by hunger. *Psychiat. quart. Suppl.*, 1954, *28*, 84-101.

Pisoni, Stephanie, and Salzinger, K. The unidimensionality of verbal affect and its distinctiveness from verbal nonaffect. *Amer. Psychologist*, 1960, *15*, 431. (Abstract)

Quay, H. C. The effect of verbal reinforcement on the recall of early memories. *J. abnorm. soc. Psychol.*, 1959, *59*, 254-257.

Rickard, H. C., Dignam, P. J., and Horner, R. F. Verbal manipulation in a psychotherapeutic relationship. *J. clin. Psychol.*, 1960, *16*, 364-367.

Robinson, Nancy M. Paired-associate learning by schizophrenic subjects under conditions of personal and impersonal reward and punishment. Unpublished doctoral dissertation, Stanford Univer., 1957.

Rogers, C. R., and Skinner, B. F. Some issues concerning the control of human behavior: A symposium. *Science*, 1956, *124*, 1057-1066.

Rogers, J. M. Operant conditioning in a quasi-therapy setting. *J. abnorm. soc. Psychol.*, 1960, *60*, 247-252.

Rosenthal, D. Changes in some moral values following psychotherapy. *J. consult. Psychol.*, 1955, *19*, 431-436.

Rosenthal, D., and Frank, J. D. Psychotherapy and the placebo effect. *Psychol. Bull.*, 1956, *53*, 294-302.

Rotter, J. B. *Social learning and clinical psychology*. New York: Prentice-Hall, 1954.

Rotter, J. B. Psychotherapy. In P. R. Farnsworth (Ed.), *Annual review of psychology*. Vol. 11, Palo Alto: Annual Reviews, 1960. Pp. 381-414.

Salzinger, K. Experimental manipulation of verbal behavior: A review. *J. gen. Psychol.*, 1959, *61*, 65-94.

Salzinger, K. The experimental analysis of the interview. In J. Zubin (Ed.), *Experimental abnormal psychology*, 1962.

Salzinger, K., and Pisoni, Stephanie. Reinforcement of affect responses of schizophrenics during the clinical interview. *J. abnorm. soc. Psychol.*, 1958, *57*, 84-90.

Salzinger, K., and Pisoni, Stephanie. Reinforcement of verbal affect responses of normal subjects during the interview. *J. abnorm. soc. Psychol.*, 1960, *60*, 127-130.

Salzinger, K., Pisoni, Stephanie, and Feldman, R. S. The experimental manipulation of continuous speech in schizophrenic patients. *Amer. Psychologist*, 1960, *15*, 430. (Abstract)

Sapolsky, A. Effect of interpersonal relationships upon verbal conditioning. *J. abnorm. soc. Psychol.*, 1960, *60*, 241-246.

Sarason, Barbara R. The effects of verbally conditioned response classes on post-conditioning tasks. *Dissertation Abstr.*, 1957, *17*, 679.

Sarason, I. G. Interrelationships among individual difference variables, behavior in psychotherapy, and verbal conditioning. *J. abnorm. soc. Psychol.*, 1958, *56*, 339-344.

Sarason, I. G., and Campbell, J. M. Anxiety and the verbal conditioning of mildly hostile verbs. *J. consult. Psychol.*, 1962, *26*, 213-216.

Sarbin, T. R. Contributions to role taking theory: I. Hypnotic behavior. *Psychol. Rev.*, 1950, *57*, 255-270.

Sargant, W. *Battle for the mind.* Garden City, N. Y.: Doubleday, 1957.

Saslow, G., and Matarazzo, J. D. A technique for studying changes in interview behavior. In E. A. Rubinstein and M. B. Parloff (Eds.), *Research in psychotherapy.* Washington: Amer. Psychol. Assoc., 1959.

Schacter, S. *The psychology of affiliation.* Stanford: Stanford Univer. Press, 1959.

Scott, W. A. Attitude change through reward of verbal behavior. *J. abnorm. soc. Psychol.*, 1957, *55*, 72-75.

Shaffer, G. W., and Lazarus, R. S. *Fundamental concepts in clinical psychology.* New York: McGraw-Hill, 1952.

Shapiro, A. K. A contribution to a history of the placebo effect. *Behav. Sci.*, 1960, *5*, 109-135.

Shaw, F. J. Some postulates concerning psychotherapy. *J. consult. Psychol.*, 1948, *12*, 426-431.

Shaw, F. J. (Ed.) Behavioristic approaches to counseling and psychotherapy. *Univer. of Alabama Studies No. 13*, 1961, Southeastern Psychological Association Symposium.

Sheehan, J. G. Rorschach changes during psychotherapy in relation to personality of the therapist. *Amer. Psychologist*, 1953, *8*, 434. (Abstract)

Shoben, E. J., Jr. Psychotherapy as a problem in learning theory. *Psychol. Bull.*, 1949, *46*, 366-392.

Sidowski, J. B. Influence of awareness of reinforcement on verbal conditioning. *J. exp. Psychol.*, 1954, *48*, 355-360.

Sidowski, J. Reinforcement in social situations. Paper read at Western Psychol. Assoc., San Diego, April, 1959.

Skinner, B. F. *Walden two.* New York: Macmillan, 1948.

Skinner, B. F. *Science and human behavior.* New York: Macmillan, 1953. (a)

Skinner, B. F. Some contributions of an experimental analysis of behavior to psychology as a whole. *Amer. Psychologist*, 1953, *8*, 69-78. (b)

Skinner, B. F. *Verbal behavior.* New York: Appleton-Century-Crofts, 1957.

Skinner, B. F. Reinforcement today. *Amer. Psychologist*, 1958, *13*, 94-99.

Slack, C. W. Experimenter-subject psychotherapy: A new method of introducing intensive office treatment for unreachable cases. *Ment. Hyg. N. Y.*, 1960, *44*, 238-256.

Solley, C. M., and Long, J. When is "uh-huh" reinforcing? *Percept. mot. Skills*, 1958, *8*, 277.

Solomon, P. (Ed.) *Sensory deprivation*. Cambridge: Harvard Univer. Press, 1961.

Staats, A. W. Verbal habit-families, concepts and the operant conditioning of word classes. *Tech Rep. No. 10*, 1959 (Aug.), Contract Nonr. 2794(02).

Staats, A. W., and Staats, Carolyn K. Attitudes established by classical conditioning. *J. abnorm. soc. Psychol.*, 1958, *57*, 37-40.

Staats, Carolyn K., Staats, A. W., and Heard, W. G. Attitude development and ratio of reinforcement. *Tech. Rep. No. 9*, 1959 (June), Contract Nonr. 2305(00).

Starkweather, J. A. The communication-value of content-free speech. *Amer. J. Psychol.*, 1956, *69*, 121-123. (a)

Starkweather, J. A. Content-free speech as a source of information about the speaker. *J. abnorm. soc. Psychol.*, 1956, *52*, 394-402. (b)

Stekel, W. *How to understand your dreams*. New York: Eton, 1951.

Strupp, H. H. The effect of the psychotherapist's personal analysis upon his techniques. *J. consult. Psychol.*, 1955, 19, 197-204. (a)

Strupp, H. H. An objective comparison of Rogerian and psychoanalytic techniques. *J. consult. Psychol.*, 1955, *19*, 1-7. (b)

Strupp, H. H. Psychotherapeutic technique, professional affiliation, and experience level. *J. consult. Psychol.*, 1955, *19*, 97-102. (c)

Strupp, H. H. A multidimensional comparison of therapist activity in analytic and client-centered therapy. *J. consult. Psychol.*, 1957, *21*, 301-308. (a)

Strupp, H. H. A multidimensional system for analyzing psychotherapeutic techniques. *Psychiatry*, 1957, *20*, 293-306. (b)

Strupp, H. H. The nature of the psychotherapist's contribution to the treatment process: Some research results and speculations. Lasker Memorial Lecture, Michael Reese Hospital, April, 1960.

Strupp, H. H. The performance of psychiatrists and psychologists in a therapeutic interview. *J. clin. Psychol.*, 1958, *14*, 219-226. (a)

Strupp, H. H. The psychotherapist's contribution to the treatment process. *Behav. Sci.*, 1958, *3*, 34-37. (b)

Sullivan, H. S. *Conceptions of modern psychiatry*. Washington: William Alanson White Psychiatric Foundation, 1947.

Sullivan, M. W., and Calvin, A. D. Further investigation of verbal conditioning. *Psychol. Rep.*, 1959, *5*, 79-82.

Taffel, C. Anxiety and the conditioning of verbal behavior. *J. abnorm. soc. Psychol.*, 1955, *51*, 496-501.

Tatz, S. J. Symbolic mediation in "learning without awareness." Paper read at Eastern Psychol. Assoc., Atlantic City, March, 1956.

Tilton, J. R. The use of instrumental motor and verbal learning techniques in the treatment of chronic schizophrenics. Unpublished doctoral dissertation, Michigan State Univer., 1957.

Tobias, S. Effects of verbal reinforcement on response changes in a nonreinforced situation. *Amer. Psychologist*, 1960, *15*, 390. (Abstract)

Ullmann, L. P. An empirically derived MMPI scale which measures facilitation-inhibition of recognition of threatening stimuli. *J. clin. Psychol.*, 1962, *18*, 127-132.

Ullmann, L. P., Krasner, L., and Collins, Beverly J. Modification of behavior through verbal conditioning. *J. abnorm. soc. Psychol.*, 1961, *62*, 128-132.

Ullmann, L. P., Krasner, L., and Ekman, P. Verbal conditioning of emotional words: Effects on behavior in group therapy. *VA Res. Rept., Palo Alto*, 1961, No. 15.

Ullmann, L. P., Weiss, R. L., and Krasner, L. Verbal conditioning of emotional words: Effects of recognition of threatening stimuli. Paper presented at Amer. Psychol. Assoc., New York, September, 1961.

Ullmann, L. P., and McFarland, R. L. Productivity as a variable in TAT protocols: A methodological study. *J. proj. Tech.*, 1957, *21*, 80-87.

Vandenberg, S. G. Great expectations or the future of psychology (as seen in science fiction). *Amer. Psychologist*, 1956, *11*, 339-342.

Verplanck, W. S. The control of the content of conversation: Reinforcement of statements of opinion. *J. abnorm. soc. Psychol.*, 1955, *51*, 668-676.

Verplanck, W. S. The operant conditioning of human motor behavior. *Psychol. Bull.*, 1956, *53*, 70-83.

Walters, R. H., and Karal, Pearl. Social deprivation and verbal behavior. *J. Pers.*, 1960, *28*, 89-107.

Walters, R. H., Marshall, W. E., and Shooter, J. R. Anxiety, isolation and susceptibility to social influence. *J. Pers.*, 1960, *28*, 518-529.

Walters, R. H., and Quinn, M. J. The effects of sensory and social deprivation on autokinetic judgments. *J. Pers.*, 1960, *28*, 210-220.

Walters, R. H., and Ray, E. Anxiety, isolation and reinforcer effectiveness. *J. Pers.*, 1960, *28*, 358-367.

Warren, A. B., and Brown, R. H. Conditioned operant response phenomenon in children. *J. gen. Psychol.*, 1943, *28*, 181-207.

Weide, T. N. Conditioning and generalization of the use of affect-relevant words. Unpublished doctoral dissertation, Stanford Univer., 1960.

Weiss, R. L., Krasner, L., and Ullmann, L. P. Responsivity to verbal conditioning as a function of emotional atmosphere and pattern of reinforcement. *Psychol. Rep.*, 1960, *6*, 415-426.

Weiss, R. L., Krasner, L., and Ullmann, L. P. Responsivity of psychiatric patients to verbal conditioning: "Success" and "failure" conditions and pattern of reinforced trials. Paper presented at Amer. Psychol. Assoc., New York, September, 1961.

Weiss, R. L., Ullmann, L. P., and Krasner, L. On the relationship between hypnotizability and response to verbal operant conditioning. *Psychol. Rep.*, 1960, *6*, 59-60.

Whitehorn, J. C. Psychiatric implications of the "placebo effect." *Amer. J. Psychiat.*, 1958, *114*, 662-664.

Whitehorn, J. C. Goals of psychotherapy. In E. A. Rubinstein and M. B. Parloff (Eds.), *Research in psychotherapy*, Washington: Amer. Psychol. Assoc., 1959.

Williams, R. I. Verbal conditioning in psychotherapy. *Amer. Psychologist*, 1958, *14*, 388. (Abstract)

Winokur, G. "Brainwashing": A social phenomenon of our time. *Hum. Organization*, 1955, *13*, 16-18.

Wolff, W. *Contemporary psychotherapists examine themselves*. Springfield, Ill.: Charles C Thomas, 1956.

Zedek, Meira E. The conditioning of verbal behavior with negative cultural connotations. *J. Pers.*, 1959, *27*, 477-486.

The Final Plunge

Krasner identifies a major factor that has held back research in therapy and counseling: "Research in psychotherapy will not be as productive as it could be until the therapist can accept his role as an influencer of behavior and thus permit investigation of the variables of behavior control."

However, although we agree with Krasner that the therapist must have an objective view of his role, we wonder whether a scientific attitude in psychotherapy is possible. Psychotherapists would have to "take the final plunge and eliminate the last drop of faith, hope, and warmth from psychotherapy. . . ." They would have to be unfeeling Es who administered only techniques. Their opposites would be unthinking Es who administered only warmth.

We do not think it is possible for human beings to take either extreme position. What therapist, *over a period of time,* can be permissive and warm throughout? What therapist can administer a programmed set of techniques day after day without either being incongruent (living a lie) or totally bored?

The major question Krasner's stance leads to is: Is therapy a set of techniques designed to control behavior, or a genuinely open, human encounter? Again, the answer is not simple, because in any given case it depends upon the unique interaction of patient, therapist, and situational variables and *may change even within the same therapy hour.*

We believe that there is room for techniques *and* a client-centered atmosphere in the therapy process; but in addition, there must be room for the therapist as a person, and for consideration of the changing interactions among the critical sets of variables (patient, therapist, and contextual) contributing to process and outcome.

Krasner's model for therapy is most strongly influenced by the physical sciences. Others, representing a similar behavioral stance, imply that the therapist should follow a medical model. For example, Goodstein (1964) writes about "dosing of anxiety" and the application of techniques to extinguish symptoms.

Krasner points to a formidable body of literature demonstrating the efficacy of objectifying research in the area of psychotherapy. Rachman (1963) applies this literature to behavior therapy, and applies his theory to patients.

BEHAVIOR THERAPY*
S. Rachman

Behavior therapy is a term used to describe a number of new psychotherapeutic methods which have been developed in recent years. Although the actual procedures vary from aversion conditioning to desensitization they all have a common theoretical basis (Wolpe, 1958; Eysenck, 1960 a, b; Jones, 1960; Metzner, 1961).

Behavior therapy derives its impetus from experimental psychology and is essentially an attempt to apply the findings and methods of this discipline to disorders of human behavior. The area of experimental psychology which has the most immediate and obvious value for psychotherapy is the study of learning processes. The early experience of behavior therapy seems to vindicate these attempts and one can draw further encouragement from the very extensive information about learning processes which has yet to be tapped by therapists. The literature of experimental psychology provides a firm foundation for the development of scientific methods of psychotherapy.

A brief account of the rationale of behavior therapy may be stated as follows. The position adapted by behavior therapists is that neurotic behavior is acquired. If neurotic behavior is regarded as being acquired, then it must follow that such behavior will be subject to the established laws of learning. Current knowledge about the learning process concerns not only the acquisition of new habit patterns, but also how habits are

* Introduction to behaviour therapy. *Behaviour Research and Therapy*, 1963, *1*, 1-15. Reprinted by permission of author and publisher.

eliminated. The elimination of learned responses occurs either by a process of extinction, or by inhibition.

Wolpe (1961) has defined neurotic behavior as "any persistent habit of unadaptive behaviour acquired by learning in a physiologically normal organism." Anxiety is "usually the central constituent of this behavior, being invariably present in the causal situation." Similarly, Eysenck (1960a) postulates that "neurotic symptoms are learned patterns of behaviour which for some reason or another are unadaptive." It should be noted, however, that neurotic symptoms may under certain circumstances result "not only from the learning of an unadaptive response, but from the failure to learn an adaptive response" (Eysenck, 1960a; Jones, 1960). A common example of this type is enuresis. The re-learning and unlearning techniques which have been used therapeutically include:

1. Desensitization based on relaxation (Wolpe, 1954, 1958 and 1961; Bond and Hutchison, 1960; Lazarus, 1963; Rachman, 1959; Hussain, 1963; Clarke, 1963; Walton, 1960 and 1963; Meyer, 1958).
2. Operant conditioning (Ayllon, 1960 and 1963; Lindsley, 1956 and 1961; King et al., 1960; Brady and Lind, 1961; Ferster and De Myer, 1961).
3. Aversion conditioning—chemical or electrical (Wolpe, 1958; Blakemore et al., 1963; Freund, 1960; Raymond, 1956; Franks, 1960; Max, 1935).
4. Training in assertive behavior (Salter, 1950; Wolpe, 1958; Lazarus, 1963).
5. Use of sexual responses (Wolpe, 1958; Lazarus, 1963).
6. Use of feeding responses (Jones, 1924a, b; Lazarus, 1960).
7. Extinction based on negative practice (Yates, 1960; Jones, 1960; Williams, 1959).
8. Anxiety-relief responses (Wolpe, 1958).
9. Avoidance learning (Lovibond, 1963; Jones, 1960).

Behavior therapy has been successfully used in the treatment of a wide range of neurotic conditions including: *Phobias* (for example, Wolpe, 1958; Lazarus, 1963; Meyer, 1958; Eysenck, 1960), *hysteria* (for example, Brady and Lind, 1961; Sylvester and Liversedge, 1960; Wolpe, 1958), *enuresis* (for example, Jones, 1960; Mowrer, 1939; Lovibond, 1963), *sexual disorders* (for example, Blakemore et al., 1963; Rachman, 1961), *tics* (for example, Yates, 1958; Walton, 1961; Barrett, 1962), *tension states* (for example, Wolpe, 1958; Eysenck, 1960), *children's disorders* (for example, Rachman, 1963). Recently, some limited improvements have been obtained even in psychotic illnesses (for example, Cowden and Ford, 1962; King et al., 1960; Ayllon, 1963).

ORIGINS

Modern psychology is dominated by what are known as "theories of learning." The two theories of learning which are of direct relevance to psychotherapy are those of Hull (reinforcement theory) and Skinner (operant conditioning). These theories are in a sense, modern versions of Behaviorism. Some of the most significant improvements are the insistence on quantitative studies, increasingly flexible methods and theorizing, and in the case of Hull, the use of the hypothetico-deductive method. In the past thirty years, psychologists have acquired a considerable amount of quantitative information concerning various human processes, particularly in the field of learning. The word 'learning' it should be noted is used in an extremely broad manner and includes any aspect of behavior which is 'acquired' by experience. This excludes changes in behavior which result from maturation or by direct intervention in the functioning of the nervous system.

Behavior therapy has developed partly as a consequence of these advances in psychology and partly as a reaction to psychoanalysis and its derivatives (for example, Wolpe and Rachman (1960) and Rachman and Costello (1961)). The need for a new approach to psychotherapy is emphasized by the disappointing results obtained with prevailing techniques (Eysenck, 1960c; Levitt, 1957; Bailey, 1956). Since 1948 systematic attempts have been made to apply the facts, theories, and methods of learning theory to the practice of psychotherapy.

Before dealing with these more recent developments, two earlier investigations should be mentioned. The first is the case of Albert reported by Watson and Rayner (1920). They provided a classical demonstration of the development of a phobia in a young child. Having first ascertained that it was a neutral object, they presented an 11-month-old boy, Albert, with a white rat to play with. Whenever he reached for the animal the experimenters made a loud noise behind the boy. After only five trials Albert began showing signs of fear in the presence of the white rat. This fear then generalized to similar stimuli such as furry objects, cotton wool, white rabbits. These phobic reactions were still present when Albert was tested 4 months later. The process involved in this demonstration provides a striking illustration of the way in which phobias can develop. The implications of this work are discussed in detail elsewhere (Wolpe and Rachman, 1960). It is sufficient for present purposes to note that this demonstration provided the first model of a human neurosis.

The second investigation of importance was that reported by Mary Cover Jones in 1924:

A 3-year-old boy, Peter, showed fear of white rats, rabbits, fur, cotton wool and other similar objects. Jones treated Peter by de-conditioning methods. It was decided to start on the rabbit phobia as this seemed to be a focus of Peter's fears.

Peter was gradually introduced to contacts with a rabbit during his daily play period. He was placed in a play group with 3 fearless children and the rabbit was brought into the room for short periods each day. Peter's toleration of the rabbit was gradually improved. The progressive steps observed in the process included: "rabbit in cage 12 feet away tolerated . . . in cage 4 feet away tolerated . . . close by in cage tolerated . . . free in room tolerated . . . eventually, fondling rabbit affectionately." Another measure employed by Jones involved the use of feeding responses. "Through the presence of the pleasant stimulus (food) whenever the rabbit was shown, the fear was eliminated gradually in favour of a positive response."

Using these techniques Jones overcame not only Peter's fear of rabbits but all his associated fears. The follow-up of this case showed no resurgence of the phobia.

The next important advance in behavior therapy occurred in 1948. On the basis of the evidence accumulated on experimental neuroses in animals (dating back to Pavlov's work) and on his own experiments, Wolpe (1954, 1958 and 1962a) constructed a systematic theory of neurosis and psychotherapy. Merging the experimental evidence[1] with Hull's theory of learning, Wolpe elaborated the principle of reciprocal inhibition as the main basis of psychotherapeutic effects. Wolpe provided evidence that neurotic behavior is acquired in anxiety-generating situations and that anxiety is always prominent in these conditions. Successful treatment of a neurosis, therefore, would depend on the reciprocal inhibition of neurotic anxiety responses, that is, the suppression of the anxiety responses as a consequence of the simultaneous evocation of other responses which are physiologically antagonistic to anxiety. If a response which is incompatible with anxiety can be made to occur in the presence of anxiety-producing stimuli it will weaken the bond between these stimuli and the anxiety responses. Whereas most psychotherapists report cured or improved cases in the vicinity of 60 percent, Wolpe claims a 90 percent level of cures or 'marked improvements' with his methods. Wolpe compared his results with those obtained by other methods and by applying the x^2 test for significance, showed that it is highly improbable that his higher proportion of successes can be accounted for by chance.

---

[1] Papers dealing with the background evidence include those of Gantt (1944), Liddell (1944), Lazovik and Lang (1960), Metzner (1961), Bandura (1961), Eysenck (1960b, c), Bachrach (1961), and Broadhurst (1960) .

Wolpe developed several therapeutic techniques on the basis of learning theory and the most prominent of these is 'systematic desensitization.' This method will be described and then illustrated by case histories.

An inquiry is first conducted in order to ascertain which stimulus situations provoke anxiety in the patient. The patient is told that he can add to or modify this list at any time. The stimuli are then categorized by the therapist and the patient is asked to rank the stimuli in order, from the most to the least disturbing. This ranked list of noxious stimulus conditions is referred to as the hierarchy. In the first case discussed below for example, one would refer to the 'ambulance hierarchy' and the 'hospital hierarchy.' Hierarchies can contain from 5 to 25 items. The hospital hierarchy mentioned above consisted of the following stimulus situations; a hospital in the distance, a hospital ten corners away, walking past the hospital, standing outside the gates, walking in the grounds, standing outside the foyer, in the foyer, walking in the corridors, standing in a small ward of 4 beds, in a larger ward and in a surgical ward with a few bandaged people in bed. The construction of the relevant hierarchies generally takes 1-3 interviews and the patient is concurrently given practice in hypnotic and relaxation procedures. Hypnosis is not an essential requirement, and in these cases where the patient refuses to be hypnotized or requires prolonged practice the procedure can be omitted and deep nonhypnotic relaxation employed instead.

When the hierarchies have been worked out, the subject is told which stimuli are to be presented in each session and is advised to signal with his hand if a stimulus presentation disturbs him unduly. This is an important instruction and should on no account be omitted, for the arousing of anxiety during the session can be damaging. In our experience it has been found that with most patients it is possible by observing his facial expressions, bodily tension, respiration and so forth, to perceive such disturbances before the patient actually signals. When such disturbances occur the therapist immediately 'withdraws' the stimulus and calms the patient. No session should be concluded when a disturbance occurs, but before rousing the patient the therapist should continue and present a further 'easy' stimulus which has already been successfully overcome. The reason for this is to be found in the commonly observed fact that the last item of any learning series is well retained. Anxiety which occurs at the end of a session is likely to require a longer period before dissipating.

When the preliminary instructions have been given, the patient is relaxed (hypnotically or otherwise) and then told to visualize the various stimuli, for example, 'Picture a hospital in the distance. . . . Now stop picturing that and go on relaxing.' Each stimulus is visualized for 5-10 seconds and 2-4 different items are presented each session. Each item is generally presented twice. When the requisite number of stimuli have been presented the patient is slowly roused and then asked for a report on his reactions. If the items were visualized vividly and without undue disturbance, the therapist then proceeds to the next items in the following session. The items lowest in the hierarchy (that is, the least disturbing ones) are introduced first and the therapist proceeds slowly up the list depending on the progress achieved and the patient's reactions. In this way, it is possible for the patient to eventually picture formerly noxious stimuli without any anxiety whatever. This ability to imagine the noxious stimulus with tranquility then transfers to the real-life situation (see below).

ILLUSTRATIVE CASES

Case 1. A 14-year-old boy was referred for treatment of a phobia. He had suffered from a fear of ambulances and hospitals for a period of 4 years. He stated that he was frightened by the sight of ambulances and avoided them wherever and however possible, for example, by planning his journeys in advance and changing direction when an ambulance was sighted. He reported having fainted on several occasions when an ambulance was nearby. He was also scared of hospitals and nursing homes and refused to visit these institutions. His social and scholastic adjustments were both satisfactory and systematic desensitization was commenced after an initial period of training in relaxation. Separate hierarchies of noxious situations were constructed for the ambulance and hospital phobias. The ambulance-hierarchy ranged from easy (non-disturbing) stimuli such as a parked ambulance in the distance and a derelict ambulance in a scrap-yard, to difficult ones like sitting in an ambulance (a) next to the driver or (b) in the back. In the hospital-hierarchy the first easy situation was a distant hospital which could be barely seen and the final one, a surgical ward. Three days after the third desensitization session the subject walked past a parked ambulance with its rear doors open and experienced no anxiety. Two further situations of a similar nature occurred during the course of therapy and neither of these evoked fear. After 10 interviews he was much improved and was able to visit the hospital and approach ambulances without difficulty. After a 3-month period there has been no recurrence of the earlier fears.

Case 2. A married woman of 34 was referred for treatment of an anxiety neurosis of 5 years' duration. She had received intermittent treatment during this period, including a brief spell of psychoanalysis, without apparent success. Two weeks before her first interview she had been advised to consider the possibility of undergoing a leucotomy.

She complained of attacks of fear with sweating, trembling and severe headaches. A wide variety of situations appeared to provoke these attacks, which tended to occur most severely and frequently in the late afternoon and in dull, overcast weather. The anxiety-producing situations included walking in the street, being outdoors in the afternoon, shopping, telephoning, crowds of people and places of public amenity. She also reported an inability to cope in social situations and disturbing feelings of inadequacy and inferiority. Her sexual activity had been disrupted in recent months as the anxiety had increased and was unsatisfactory. She had been taking 2-3 tranquillizing tablets per day for a short period with slight, variable results.

Application of the Thematic Apperception Test and the Willoughby neurotic tendency inventory revealed neurotic trends such as guilt, hypersensitivity and a marked lack of confidence (the Willoughby score was extremely high, 87, indicating severe neurotic disturbance).

The patient was instructed in the use of assertive responses and deep (nonhypnotic) relaxation. The first anxiety hierarchy dealt with was that of dull weather. Starting from 'a bright sunny day' it was possible for the subject to visualize 'damp overcast weather' without anxiety after 21 desensitization sessions, and 10 days after the completion of this hierarchy she was able to report that, "The weather is much better, it doesn't even bother me to look at the weather when I wake up in the morning" (previously depressing). In addition to this improvement, she was also able to go out for short periods during the afternoon. The following hierarchies were then dealt with: telephoning, shopping, having guests at the house, walking in the street, going to places of public entertainment, sitting in the garden in the afternoon.

Two weeks after the completion of the last hierarchy, the patient was given the Willoughby test again. Her score had dropped 40 points to the slightly inflated score of 47. She also reported increased sexual responsiveness, a slight improvement in interpersonal relationships and increased self-confidence. The patient commenced a refresher course in stenography with the intention of obtaining employment. She had not worked for 7 years. She voluntarily reduced her dose of tranquillizers to one a day and dispensed with them completely 1 week later.

At this stage the patient's husband fell seriously ill and she was able to support him emotionally despite the considerable effort involved. As her husband's health improved, she suffered a minor relapse for 2 weeks and then returned to her improved state spontaneously.

After 8 months of treatment, comprising 65 interviews devoted largely to systematic desensitization, this patient was 'much improved' in terms of Knight's criteria (symptom improvement, increased productivity, improved sexual relations, improved interpersonal relations, increased stress tolerance).

During the course of therapy, part of the reason for the development of the anxiety state in this patient was unearthed. When she was 17 years old she had become involved in a love affair with a married man 12 years her senior. This affair had been conducted in an extremely secretive manner for 4 years, during which time she had suffered from recurrent guilt feelings and shame, so much so, that on one occasion she had attempted suicide by throwing herself into a river. It was her custom to meet her lover after work in the later afternoon. The dull weather can be accounted for, as this affair took place in London.

Case 3. Bond and Hutchison (1960) obtained marked improvement in a patient with a severe and long-standing case of exhibitionism by using the reciprocal inhibition technique. The patient was a 25-year-old married man of average intelligence. His first exposure occurred at age 13 following sex play with a younger girl. His exhibitionism continued throughout adolescence and had reached "bizarre proportions" by the time he reached adulthood. The attacks of exhibitionism were preceded by tension, dread and sexual excitement. Attacks were often provoked by the perception of attractive young women.

The antecedent tension was constant and the patient often exposed several times a day. He had been convicted for indecent exposure on 11 occasions and had as a result spent a considerable amount of time in detention. The severity of his condition is best illustrated by the author's account. "A frequent practice was to hide completely nude in a small wooded area in the centre of the town where he then lived and spring out and expose himself to the first woman who passed." Various types of therapy had failed to relieve his condition.

It was decided to attempt Wolpe's desensitization procedure and the patient was accordingly trained to relax. A hierarchy of exposure-provoking stimuli was constructed and the patient gradually desensitized over a period of 30 sessions. By the eighth interview the patient evidenced distinct improvements. He was less tense, less prone to expose himself and able to venture out unaccompanied. As the desensitizing therapy continued, further evidences of progress appeared. His exhibitionist urges declined in frequency and strength, his sexual fantasies diminished and he reported an improvement in his sexual relations with his wife.

Therapy had to be discontinued after 29 sessions but the patient reported in succeeding months that he was much improved. He then exposed himself in a feeble and uncharacteristic manner in a store. The patient was returned for treatment on a weekly basis and two months later no relapse had occurred.

A full description of these and other methods developed by Wolpe (1958) is given in his book "Psychotherapy by Reciprocal Inhibition." He also describes the treatment of a wide range of cases, including anxiety states, phobias, compulsions and sexual disorders. Additional case material is provided in "Behavior Therapy and the Neuroses" edited by Eysenck (1960b). This text also contains several important papers on theory and methodology.

Inhibition and Extinction

Neurotic behavior has been defined as "persistent unadaptive learned behavior in which anxiety is almost always prominent and which is acquired in anxiety-generating situations." Behavior which is learned can also be 'un-learned.' The processes by which responses are ordinarily diminished in magnitude and frequency of occurrence are 'extinction' and 'inhibition.'

Similarly neurotic behavior is open to modification and elimination by the process of inhibition and extinction. The numerous types of psychological inhibition which have been observed or postulated include proactive, retroactive, external, reciprocal, reactive and conditioned inhibition. For several reasons, mainly of a practical nature, conditioned inhibition has received the greatest amount of attention in psychotherapy. Conditioned inhibition is generated when stimuli are associated with the cessation of a response in the presence of reactive inhibition (a negative drive tending to cause cessation of activity). Conditioned inhibition is acquired in the same way as positive behavior patterns are learnt. It increases progressively as a function of the number of rewarded or reinforced trials and like all habit patterns is relatively permanent. It does not dissipate spontaneously even over long periods of time. Because of these characteristics, conditioned inhibition has been widely employed by psychotherapists in their attempts to eradicate neurotic behavior.

Wolpe's technique of psychotherapy is an attempt to produce a conditioned inhibition of neurotic behavior by the repeated simultaneous presentation of incompatible response tendencies (reciprocal inhibition). In this way, the tendency to respond anxiously to the noxious stimulus (for example, blood) is superseded by the stronger and incompatible relaxation response. Repeated doses of this reciprocal inhibition (which is by itself temporary in effect) in the consulting room will steadily build up a permanent 'conditioned' inhibition of the neurotic behavior.

For every behavior pattern there is another type of behavior which is incompatible with the first. The task of the therapist is to find an acceptable response pattern which is antagonistic to the neurotic activity of the patient and to substitute this adaptive behavior for the non-adaptive, neurotic behavior. Wolpe has proposed relaxation or feeding or avoidance or sexual or assertive responses as possible substitutes for neurotic behavior, according to the requirements of the case.

Operant Conditioning

The work of Skinner on operant conditioning has recently been applied to problems of psychotherapy. Although Skinner's theoretical views differ from those of Hull, the practical application of his work to psychotherapy involves a similar rationale. Behavior disturbances are regarded as problems in the acquisition and retention of complex responses. Consequently, these disturbances are open to manipulation and modification by the recognized processes of learning. Skinner (1953, 1959) argues that the use of appropriate learning techniques should enable the therapist to shape human behavior in the desired direction of improved mental health. Operant conditioning has been the subject of intensive research and the information which has been collected can be fruitfully applied to the training and re-training of maladjusted behavior.

From the therapeutic point of view, the four most significant concepts are reinforcement, intermittent reinforcement, selective reinforcement and successive approximation. In operant conditioning, the strengthening of the response (reinforcement) is dependent on the response itself. Reinforcement cannot follow unless the response appears. It is the response which causes the reward to arrive and this reinforces (strengthens) the responses. This process is of course different from that described by Pavlov (classical conditioning). It will be noticed that the subject in an operant conditioning situation plays an active role in the learning process whereas the subject's part in classical conditioning is a relatively passive one.

Considerable research has been devoted to the analysis of rewards (reinforcers) in the operant conditioning situation. A highly significant finding is that if reinforcers are presented irregularly (in time or sequence) they are more effective. This intermittent reinforcement produces stronger responses than can be obtained by rewards presented on a regular basis. Apart from its value for the therapist, this observation is useful in the analysis of many aspects of human behavior (Ferster, 1958). For example, it helps to account for the often surprising effects of inconsistent parental care on the behavior of children.

Experimental work has led to the development of the technique known as selective reinforcement. The use of this method enables one to simultaneously strengthen a desirable response and extinguish an undesirable one. Briefly, this method involves rewarding the appearance of the selected response and withholding rewards when the undesired response appears. In this way, the person's behavior can be shaped in the desired direction. The skilful use of this method coupled with 'successive approximation' brings a wide variety of human behavior into the range of therapeutic manipulation. 'Successive approximation' refers to the gradual and graduated building up of a new response on the basis of the person's existing repertoire of responses. By careful planning it is possible to build up the person's simple responses (such as pressing a lever) into complex patterns of socially co-operative behavior. This process is illustrated by the work of King *et al.* (1957, 1960) on schizophrenic patients.

To date, most of the research on operant conditioning has been concerned with the development of new techniques and the refinement of existing ones. Some examples from case material will, however, illustrate the therapeutic possibilities of operant conditioning.

Case 4. Brady and Lind (1961) were able to cure a patient suffering from hysterical blindness with this method. The patient had lost his sight after being involved in an accident. No organic basis for this loss of vision could be found and he received various types of psychotherapy without success. Two years after the onset of the illness he was treated by a conditioning technique. He was conditioned to respond to the presence of a light in the following way. The patient was informed that he would be rewarded with tokens when he pressed a small lever. These tokens could be exchanged at the hospital canteen for various articles. The light was switched on at irregular intervals and when a lever-pressing response followed the presentation of the light, the patient was given a token. He gradually learnt to respond to the light. This conditioned response was accompanied by vague visual sensations until he eventually reported that he could see the light. After regaining this visual ability he progressed further and full vision was restored.

Numerous studies of the behavior of psychotic patients raise the possibility of obtaining limited improvements in these cases by the methods of operant conditioning. King, Armitage and Tilton (1960) conditioned 12 schizophrenic patients to operate a lever using food, cigarettes and other items as rewards or reinforcers. When the patients reached a stable rate of responding, they were conditioned to more complex tasks involving verbal behavior and even social co-operation. By comparison with 3 matched groups comprising 12 schizophrenics each, the conditioned group showed the greatest over-all improvement. The patients in the conditioned group improved in "level of verbalization, motivation to leave the ward, more interest in occupational therapy, decreased enuresis."

Other investigations of psychotic patients include those of Lindsley (1956, 1960) and Ayllon and Michael (1959, 1963). Some promising work on the treatment of children has also been reported by Baer (1962) and Bijou and Orlando (1961) among others.

It would be unwise to offer dogmatic assertions until more research work has been conducted but the following assessments are proposed on the basis of the available information. Firstly, operant conditioning methods are likely to prove of particular value in the treatment of what may be called deficit behavior disorders. This would encompass disorders which arise out of a failure to develop adequate behavior, such as aphemia, alexia, anorexia and so forth. It could also be used in developing psychological functions which are only partially or improperly operative. Secondly, operant conditioning is likely to prove extremely valuable in the treatment of children's disorders. Many of these disorders are of the deficit variety discussed above and in addition, the technique itself seems to be admirably suited for use with children (Rachman, 1963). It is simple, the control of rewards is easier with children and it can be conducted with a minimum reliance on language.

SOME THEORETICAL CONSIDERATIONS

An objection which is frequently presented by critics of behavior therapy is the concept of 'basic causes.' They argue that this therapy deals only with symptoms and leaves the basic cause or causes of the neurosis untouched; that this 'superficial approach' to the treatment of neurotic behavior is destined to bring about only temporary alleviation of symptoms (at best) and may well aggravate the patient's condition. They claim that it is only when the 'inner forces of the psyche' have been restored to harmony by free association, transference and interpretation that the person is normal again. The major objections may be summarized as follows: Behavior therapy (a) is superficial, (b) is symptom-oriented, (c) ignores the deep inner causes of the neuroses, (d) can effect only temporary improvements, and (e) smothers certain symptoms only to provoke new ones.

Behavior therapy is not superficial if this implies either that such treatment is 'not complete' or that it can be applied with success only in certain minor types of behavior disorders. There is considerable clinical and experimental evidence which shows, on the contrary, that such therapy is both complete and capable of being applied in many types of disorder, including those which are regarded as 'deep-seated,' for example, phobic states and anxiety neuroses of longstanding. Examples of therapeutic successes with enuretics, hysterics, stutterers, drug-addicts, homosexuals, phobic states, alcoholics, and tension-states, have been reported in which the 'superficial approach' has provided complete or near-complete recovery. In many of the cases referred to here, the improvement has been obtained without either therapist or patient knowing what the 'basic cause' of the illness was. A particularly striking example of such a case is provided by Wolpe (1958):

A 37-year-old miner was seen in a state of intense anxiety. He had a very marked tremor and a total amnesia for the previous 4 days. He said that his wife, on whom he was greatly dependent, had cunningly got him to agree to "temporary divorce" 6 months before and was now going to marry a friend of his. No attempt was made at this juncture to recall the lost memories. The patient was made to realize how ineffectual his previous attitudes had been and how he had been deceived. As a result he angrily "had it out" with his wife and a few others. The anxiety rapidly decreased and he soon felt sufficiently motivated to organize his whole life differently. At his fifth interview (10 days after treatment began) he said that he felt "a hundred percent" and was full of plans for the future. Yet he had still recalled nothing whatever of the forgotten 4 days. The patient later recalled the lost memories under hypnosis. No important consequences ensued. A few months later he married another woman and was apparently very well adjusted generally.

Other examples are provided by Lazarus and Rachman (1957), Lovibond (1963) and Salter (1950).

Can this evidence be taken to mean that a knowledge of the causative factors is unnecessary? The answer to this problem would appear to be a qualified affirmative. In some instances it seems unlikely that improvement in the patient's condition can be effected without such knowledge. On the other hand it would appear from the numerous therapeutic failures reported by analysts and other therapists, that in certain cases insight and interpretation do not assist. A very obvious example of such a state of affairs can be observed in the treatment of psychopathy. An appraisal of the data leads us to the conclusion that while a knowledge of the causative process and genesis of the individual neurosis can be of considerable value in therapy, improvement can nevertheless be obtained in many cases without such knowledge.

Too great a concern with 'underlying causes' may under certain circumstances even impede therapeutic progress. The case of the miner treated by Wolpe and quoted above is one such instance. The 'forward-looking approach' as opposed to the historical technique has much to recommend it. It is quite conceivable that a patient with some pressing, immediate problem (for example, pending divorce) may receive a severe and unnecessary jolt from the apparent lack of concern of the nondirective therapist.

With regard to the observation that objective psychotherapy is symptom-oriented, this is generally true. The treatment of the symptom or symptoms is quite logically one of the first considerations of the psychotherapist. In numerous cases there is little else that is required as 'the deep inner causes,' if they exist, cease to be relevant (Mowrer, 1950). The five cases reported by Lazarus and Rachman (1957) all bear this contention out. In Case 1 above, the precise reason or reasons for the ambulance-phobia developing in this 14-year-old boy were never discovered. The fear was inhibited and extinguished by systematic desensitization and this removal of the symptom was sufficient.

Does behavior therapy effect only temporary improvement? There is some evidence that improvements obtained by these techniques are long-lasting or permanent, but it must be admitted that the design of research work in the field of therapy, both objective and psychoanalytic, has been inadequate in this respect.

Behavior therapy has also been criticized on the grounds that it merely smothers the neurotic symptoms. Because the 'basic causes' of the maladaptive behavior have not been treated, it is said that new symptoms will necessarily arise to replace the extinguished behavior patterns. For example, training an enuretic to relieve himself in the lavatory or teaching a stutterer to speak fluently will merely result in the patient 'adopting' some new deviant response. While such 'transfer' of symptoms can occur, its frequency has probably been unduly exaggerated (Wolpe, 1958; Yates, 1958). In those cases where transferred symptoms arise the therapeutic procedure is quite uncomplicated. The therapist after having desensitized the patient to the original noxious stimulus situations, if confronted with a so-called 'substitute-symptom' would proceed to desensitize this new symptom in turn. When this treatment has been successfully completed, the probability of recurrence is slight. It will be agreed that all neurotic symptoms in the patient have some degree of interdependence and that the weakening or extinction of any one symptom is likely to affect all the others in like manner. The symptom which is treated first is usually the most resistant. Behavior patterns treated subsequently are more easily modified. If a new symptom arises it can be expected to be of rather weaker strength and hence readily amenable to inhibition or extinction. This symptom-substitution phenomenon and its treatment has been described by Lazarus and Rachman (1957). One of their cases, a married woman of 29, had developed a phobic reaction to dogs as the result of a traumatic incident 5 years earlier. After 3 years of psychoanalysis, her fear of dogs had disappeared but instead she had developed a chronic anxiety state with numerous, varied phobias (symptom-substitution). After 6 weeks of intensive psychotherapy (28 sessions) she was much improved, but her dog-phobia returned. After a further 28 sessions devoted mainly to the inhibition of this phobia, she was discharged as 'much improved.' A year later she was still healthy and the extinction of the dog-phobia had been maintained. This case-history illustrates the treatment of symptom-substitution by objective psychotherapy and also the development of a substitute symptom under psychoanalysis.

Reservations about the improvements obtained with behavior therapy are sometimes based on the claim that the effective mechanism is not the re-learning process but rather, some aspect of the patient-therapist relationship, for example transference, insight, derepression. Such introductions are unnecessary and in a neat demonstration Wolpe (1962b) was able to isolate the effective agent in the treatment of a woman with a traffic phobia. The therapeutic sessions were restricted to conditioning practice only and it was shown that the time and amount of the patient's improvements were directly related to the conditioning sessions. Furthermore, a change of therapist failed to disturb the direct relationship between conditioning treatment and actual improvements.

PROSPECT

Behavior therapy has now developed to the point where large scale field trials with adequate controls can be carried out. The evaluation studies which are presently available can at best be regarded as highly suggestive and encouraging. Wolpe (1958) has reported that nearly 90 percent of 210 patients had either been much improved or apparently recovered after a median number of 23 interviews. Lazarus (1963) states that 78 percent of the 408 patients who consulted him derived marked benefit. Of these 408 patients, Lazarus classified 126 as suffering from severe disturbances and in this sub-group the improvement rate was 62 percent. Hussain (1963) reported that 95 percent of his 105 patients were much improved by behavior therapy which generally lasted less than three months. In addition to these reports on the effects of behavior therapy with large groups of patients, there are numerous accounts of successes claimed with small numbers of patients (for example, Eysenck, 1960). On the other hand, a small retrospective survey conducted by Cooper (1962) suggested that some phobic cases treated by behavior therapy tended to relapse. Clearly, the effectiveness of behavior therapy needs to be determined by strict, highly controlled experiments.

As the recent developments in operant conditioning procedures demonstrate, there are many more therapeutic procedures which can be derived from experimental psychology. It is to be hoped that new clinical methods will continue to increase the scope and effectiveness of behavior therapy. The high rate of spontaneous remissions in neurotic illnesses constitutes a problem of considerable theoretical and practical importance (Eysenck, 1962) and research in this area would also be most valuable.

CONCLUSIONS

Behavior therapy offers substantial advantages as a method of treating disorders of behavior. It has developed out of established psychological theories and has a large body of experimental evidence on which to proceed. The therapeutic process and its outcome are both open to quantification. It permits precision and a systematic planning of the treatment required in individual cases. Behavior therapy has now reached the point where large-scale field tests are possible and indeed, necessary.

REFERENCES

Ayllon, T. Some behavioral problems associated with eating in chronic schizophrenic patients. Read at an APA meeting, Chicago, 1960.

Ayllon, T. Intensive treatment of psychotic behavior by stimulus satiation and food reinforcement. *Behav. Res. Ther.*, 1963, *1*, 53-61.

Ayllon, T., and Michael, J. The psychiatric nurse as a behavioral engineer. *J. exp. Anal. Behav.*, 1959, *2*, 323-334.

Bachrach, A. L. *Experimental foundations of clinical psychology*. New York: Basic Books, 1962.

Baer, D. M. Laboratory control of thumbsucking in three young children by withdrawal and representation of positive reinforcement. *J. exp. Anal. Behav.*, 1962, *5*, 525-528.

Bailey, P. B. The great psychiatric revolution. *Amer. J. Psychiat.*, 1956, *113*, 147-168.

Bandura, A. Psychotherapy as a learning process. *Psychol. Bull.*, 1961, *58*, 144-159.

Barrett, B. H. Reduction in rate of multiple tics by free-operant conditioning methods. Unpublished paper, 1961.

Blakemore, C. *et al.* Application of faradic aversion conditioning in a case of transvestism. *Behav. Res. Ther.*, 1963, *1*, 29-34.

Bond, J., and Hutchison, H. C. Application of reciprocal inhibition therapy to exhibitionism. *Canad. Med. Ass. J.*, 1960, *83*, 122-128.

Brady, J., and Lind, D. L. Experimental analysis of hysterical blindness. *Arch. Gen. Psychiat.*, 1961, *4*, 331-339.

Broadhurst, P. Abnormal animal behavior. In *Handbook of abnormal psychology*, Ed. H. J. Eysenck. London: Pitmans, 1960.

Clarke, D. F. Treatment of a monosymptomatic phobia by systematic desensitization. *Behav. Res. Ther.*, 1963, *1*, 63-68.

Cooper, J. E. Some aspects of the use of behavior therapy in psychiatry. Dissertation, Univer. of London, 1961.

Cowden, R., and Ford, L. Systematic desensitization with phobic schizophrenics. *Amer. J. Psychiat.*, 1962, *119*, 241-245.

Eysenck, H. J. Personality and behavior therapy. *Proc. royal Soc. Med.*, 1960, *53*, 504-508. (a)

Eysenck, H. J. *Behavior therapy and the neuroses*. Oxford: Pergamon Press, 1960. (b)

Eysenck, H. J., Ed. *Handbook of abnormal psychology*. London: Pitmans, 1960. (c)

Ferster, C. B. Reinforcement and punishment in the control of human behavior in social agencies. *Psychiat. Res. Rep. Amer. psychiat. Assoc.*, 1958, *10*, 101-118.

Ferster, C. B., and De Myer, M. The development of performances in autistic children in an automatically controlled environment. *J. chron. Dis.*, 1961, *13*, 312-345.

Franks, C. Alcohol, alcoholism, and conditioning. *J. ment. Sci.*, 1958, *104*, 14-33.

Freund, K. Problems in the treatment of homosexuality. In *Behavior therapy and the neuroses.* Ed. H. J. Eysenck. Oxford: Pergamon Press, 1960.

Gantt, W. H. Experimental basis for neurotic behavior. *Psychosom. Med. Monog. Suppl.*, 1944, *3*, Nos. 3 and 4.

Hussain, A. Unpublished paper, 1962.

Jones, H. G. The behavioral treatment of enuresis nocturna. In *Behavior therapy and the neuroses.* Ed. H. J. Eysenck. Oxford: Pergamon Press, 1960. (a)

Jones, M. C. The elimination of children's fears. *J. exp. Psychol.*, 1924a, *7*, 383-390.

Jones, M. C. A laboratory study of fear: The case of Peter. *Pedagog. Sem.*, 1924b, *31*, 308-315.

King, G. F., Armitage, S., and Tilton, J. A therapeutic approach to schizophrenics of extreme pathology. *J. abnorm. soc. Psychol.*, 1960, *61*, 276-286.

King, G. F., Merrell, D., Lovinger, E., and Denny, M. Operant motor behavior in acute schizophrenics. *J. Personality*, 1957, *25*, 317-326.

Lazarus, A. The elimination of children's phobias by deconditioning. In *Behavior therapy and the neuroses.* Ed. H. J. Eysenck. Oxford: Pergamon Press, 1960.

Lazarus, A. The results of behavior therapy in 126 cases of severe neuroses. *Behav. Res. Ther.*, 1963, *1*, 69-79.

Lazarus, A., and Abramovitz, A. The use of "emotive imagery" in the treatment of children's phobias. *J. ment. Sci.*, 1962, *108*, 191-195.

Lazarus, A., and Rachman, S. The use of systematic desensitization psychotherapy. In *Behavior therapy and the neuroses.* Ed. H. J. Eysenck. Oxford: Pergamon Press, 1960.

Lazovik, A. D., and Lang, P. J. A laboratory demonstration of systematic desensitization psychotherapy. *J. Psychol. Stud.*, 1960, *11*, 238-242.

Levitt, E. E. The results of psychotherapy with children. *J. consult. Psychol.*, 1957, *21*, 189-196.

Liddell, H. S. Conditioned reflex method and experimental neurosis. In *Personality and the behavior disorders.* Ed. J. McV. Hunt. New York: Ronald, 1944.

Lindsley, O. R. Operant conditioning methods applied to research in chronic schizophrenia. *Psychiat. Res. Rep. Amer. psychiat. Assoc.*, 1956, *5*, 118-139.

Lindsley, O. R. Characteristics of the behavior of chronic psychotics as revealed by free-operant conditioning methods. *Dis. nerv. Syst.*, 1960, *21*, 66-78.

Lovibond, S. H. Conditioning and enuresis. Thesis, Univer. of Adelaide, 1961.

Lovibond, S. H. The mechanism of conditioning treatment of enuresis. *Behav. Res. Ther.* 1963, *1*, 17-21.

Max, L. Breaking a homosexual fixation by the conditioned reflex technique. *Psychol. Bull.*, 1935, *32*, 734.

Metzner, R. Learning theory and the therapy of the neuroses. *Brit. J. Psychol.,* Monogr. Suppl., 33, 1961.

Meyer, V. The treatment of two phobic patients on the basis of learning theory. *J. abnorm. soc. Psychol.,* 1957, *55,* 261-265.

Mowrer, O. H., and Mowrer, W. Enuresis: A method for its study and treatment. *Amer. J. Orthopsychiat.,* 1938, *8,* 436-459.

Orlando, R., and Bijou, S. W. Single and multiple schedules of reinforcement in developmentally retarded children. *J. exper. Anal. Behav.,* 1960, *3,* 339-348.

Rachman, S. Treatment of anxiety and phobic reactions by desensitization. *J. abnorm. soc. Psychol.,* 1959, *102,* 421-427.

Rachman, S. Sexual disorders and behavior therapy. *Amer. J. Psychiat,* 1961, *46,* 57-70.

Rachman, S. Child psychology and learning theory. *J. child Psychol. Psychiat.,* 1962, *3,* 149-163.

Rachman, S., and Costello, C. G. The aetiology and treatment of children's phobias: A review. *Amer. J. Psychiat.,* 1961, *118,* 97-105.

Raymond, M. J. Case of fetishism treated by aversion therapy. *Brit. Med. J.,* 1956, *2,* 854-856.

Salter, A. *Conditioned reflex therapy.* New York: Creative Age Press, 1950.

Skinner, B. F. *Science and human behavior.* New York: Macmillan, 1953.

Skinner, B. F. *Cumulative record.* New York: Appleton-Century-Crofts, 1959.

Sylvester, J., and Liversedge, L. A. Conditioning and the occupational cramps. In *Behavior therapy and the neuroses,* Ed. H. J. Eysenck. Oxford: Pergamon Press, 1960.

Walton, D. Experimental psychology and the treatment of a tiqueur, *J. child Psychol. Psychiat.,* 1961, *2,* 148-155.

Walton, D. The interaction effects of drive, reactive, and conditioned inhibition. *Behav. Res. Ther.,* 1963, *1,* 35-43.

Watson, J. B., and Rayner, R. Conditioned emotional reactions. *J. exp. Psychol.,* 1920, *3,* 1-14.

Williams, C. D. The elimination of tantrum behavior by extinction procedures. *J. abnorm. soc. Psychol.,* 59, 269-270.

Wolpe, J. *Psychotherapy by reciprocal inhibition.* Stanford, Calif.: Stanford Univer. Press, 1958.

Wolpe, J. The systematic desensitization treatment of neuroses. *J. nerv. ment. Dis.,* 1961, *132,* 189-203.

Wolpe, J., and Rachman, S. Psychoanalytic evidence: A critique based on Freud's case of Little Hans. *J. nerv. ment. Dis.,* 1961, *131,* 135-143.

Wolpe, J. Experimental foundations of some new psychotherapeutic methods. In *Experimental foundations in clinical psychology,* Ed. A. J. Bachrach. New York: Basic Books, 1962. (a)

Wolpe, J. Isolation of a conditioning procedure as the crucial psychotherapeutic factor: A case study. *J. nerv. ment. Dis.,* 1962 (b), *134,* 316-329.

Yates, A. J. The application of learning theory to the treatment of tics. *J. abnorm. soc. Psychol.,* 1958, *56,* 175-182.

A Bagful of Techniques

Rachman shows that exciting results and dramatic changes in patient behaviors can take place when the patient *and* the therapist are unaware of the "basic cause," thus pointing to the possibly superfluous role of understanding or insight. The outcomes reported were brought about by treatment of behavior, not dynamics.

Nevertheless, the article does not prove that desensitization, operant conditioning, training assertive behavior, and other techniques account for most of the significant variance observed in the outcome. Other factors, such as therapist-patient interaction, may have been involved but not noted. The question of control of the environment is also not fully raised. What happens when we change important aspects of the stimulus complex? We are reminded of the story of the dog in Pavlov's laboratory, a dog which was allegedly aversively conditioned to a circular stairway. Upon *E*'s exit, questioning American visitors walked the dog down the stairway—readily and easily. To be sure, conditioning had taken place —the dog was conditioned to its conditioner. Will similar changes take place when the client leaves the experimental clinician to return to his intimates?

PART THREE

*"The final good
must be a thing
sufficient in itself."*

ARISTOTLE

Out of the Darkness

RESEARCH DEVELOPMENTS AND DIRECTIONS

If Eysenck and Levitt's challenge is ever to be answered, psychotherapy requires more than the traditional defenses and more than the exciting but somewhat limited views of experimental approaches. The need is for a more *open* perspective pointing to *new* directions.

The following collection of readings offers not only hope for the future of psychotherapy but a new challenge. These authors go beyond the support of a particular orientation and bring together a mass of literature that puts people back into the therapeutic process, identifying three major steps forward: (a) the effective ingredients of a facilitative interpersonal relationship; (b) the possibility of utilizing preferred modes of treatment; and (c) a complete revamping of our training programs as well as of our professional roles.

Bandura (1961) introduces social learning theory as a basis for a more comprehensive view of psychotherapy.

PSYCHOTHERAPY AS SOCIAL LEARNING*
Albert Bandura

While it is customary to conceptualize psychotherapy as a learning process, few therapists accept the full implications of this position. Indeed, this is best illustrated by the writings of the learning theorists themselves. Most of our current methods of psychotherapy represent an accumulation of more or less uncontrolled clinical experiences and, in many instances, those who have written about psychotherapy in terms of learning theory have merely substituted a new language; the practice remains essentially unchanged (Dollard, Auld, and White, 1954; Dollard and Miller, 1950; Shoben, 1949).

If one seriously subscribes to the view that psychotherapy is a learning process, the methods of treatment should be derived from our knowledge of learning and motivation. Such an orientation is likely to yield new techniques of treatment which, in many respects, may differ markedly from the procedures currently in use.

Psychotherapy rests on a very simple but fundamental assumption, that is, human behavior is modifiable through psychological procedures. When skeptics raise the question, "Does psychotherapy work?" they may be responding in part to the mysticism that has come to surround the term. Perhaps the more meaningful question, and one which avoids the surplus meanings associated with the term "psychotherapy," is as follows: Can human behavior be modified through psychological means and if so, what are the learning mechanisms that mediate behavior change?

In the sections that follow, some of these learning mechanisms will be discussed, and studies in which systematic attempts have been made to apply these principles of learning to the area of psychotherapy will be reviewed. Since learning theory itself is still somewhat incomplete, the list of psychological processes by which changes in behavior can occur should not be regarded as exhaustive, nor are they necessarily without overlap.

COUNTERCONDITIONING

Of the various treatment methods derived from learning theory, those based on the principle of counterconditioning have been elaborated in greatest detail. Wolpe (1954, 1958, 1959) gives a thorough account of this method, and additional examples of cases treated in this manner are

* Psychotherapy as a learning process. *Psychological Bulletin*, 1961, *58*, 143-159. Reprinted by permission of author and publisher.

provided by Jones (1956), Lazarus and Rachman (1957), Meyer (1957), and Rachman (1959). Briefly, the principle involved is as follows: if strong responses which are incompatible with anxiety reactions can be made to occur in the presence of anxiety evoking cues, the incompatible responses will become attached to these cues and thereby weaken or eliminate the anxiety responses.

The first systematic psychotherapeutic application of this method was reported by Jones (1924b) in the treatment of Peter, a boy who showed severe phobic reactions to animals, fur objects, cotton, hair, and mechanical toys. Counterconditioning was achieved by feeding the child in the presence of initially small but gradually increasing anxiety-arousing stimuli. A rabbit in a cage was placed in the room at some distance so as not to disturb the boy's eating. Each day the rabbit was brought nearer to the table and eventually removed from the cage. During the final stage of treatment, the rabbit was placed on the feeding table and even in Peter's lap. Tests of generalization revealed that the fear responses had been effectively eliminated, not only toward the rabbit, but toward the previously feared furry objects as well.

In this connection, it would be interesting to speculate on the diagnosis and treatment Peter would have received had he been seen by Melanie Klein (1949) rather than by Mary Cover Jones!

It is interesting to note that while both Shoben (1949) and Wolpe (1958) propose a therapy based on the principle of counterconditioning, their treatment methods are radically different. According to Shoben, the patient discusses and thinks about stimulus situations that are anxiety provoking in the context of an interpersonal situation which simultaneously elicits positive affective responses from the patient. The therapeutic process consists in connecting the anxiety-provoking stimuli, which are symbolically reproduced, with the comfort reaction made to the therapeutic relationshp.

Shoben's paper represents primarily a counterconditioning interpretation of the behavior changes brought about through conventional forms of psychotherapy since, apart from highlighting the role of positive emotional reactions in the treatment process, no new techniques deliberately designed to facilitate relearning through counterconditioning are proposed.

This is not the case with Wolpe, who has made a radical departure from tradition. In his treatment, which he calls reciprocal inhibition, Wolpe makes systematic use of three types of responses which are antagonistic to, and therefore inhibitory of, anxiety. These are: assertive or approach responses, sexual responses, and relaxation responses.

On the basis of historical information, interview data, and psychological test responses, the therapist constructs an anxiety hierarchy, a ranked list of stimuli to which the patient reacts with anxiety. In the case of desensitization based on relaxation, the patient is hypnotized and given relaxation suggestions. He is then asked to imagine a scene representing the weakest item on the anxiety hierarchy and, if the relaxation is unimpaired, this is followed by having the patient imagine the next item on the list, and so on. Thus, the anxiety cues are gradually increased from session to session until the last phobic stimulus can be presented without impairing the relaxed state. Through this procedure, relaxation responses eventually come to be attached to the anxiety-evoking stimuli.

Wolpe reports remarkable therapeutic success with a wide range of neurotic reactions treated on this counterconditioning principle. He also contends that the favorable outcomes achieved by the more conventional psychotherapeutic methods may result from the reciprocal inhibition of anxiety by strong positive responses evoked in the patient-therapist relationship.

Although the counterconditioning method has been employed most extensively in eliminating anxiety-motivated avoidance reactions and inhibitions, it has been used with some success in reducing maladaptive approach responses as well. In the latter case, the goal object is repeatedly associated with some form of aversive stimulus.

Raymond (1956), for example, used nausea as the aversion experience in the treatment of a patient who presented a fetish for handbags and perambulators which brought him into frequent contact with the law in that he repeatedly smeared mucus on ladies' handbags and destroyed perambulators by running into them with his motorcycle. Though the patient had undergone psychoanalytic treatment, and was fully aware of the origin and the sexual significance of his behavior, nevertheless, the fetish persisted.

The treatment consisted of showing the patient a collection of handbags, perambulators, and colored illustrations just before the onset of nausea produced by injections of apomorphine. The conditioning was repeated every 2 hours day and night for 1 week plus additional sessions 8 days and 6 months later.

Raymond reports that, not only was the fetish successfully eliminated, but also the patient showed a vast improvement in his social (and legal) relationships, was promoted to a more responsible position in his work, and no longer required the fetish fantasies to enable him to have sexual intercourse.

Nauseant drugs, especially emetine, have also been utilized as the unconditioned stimulus in the aversion treatment of alcoholism (Thirmann, 1949; Thompson and Bielinski, 1953; Voegtlen, 1940; Wallace, 1949). Usually 8 to 10 treatments in which the sight, smell, and taste of alcohol is associated with the onset of nausea is sufficient to produce abstinence. Of 1000 or more cases on whom adequate follow-up data are reported, approximately 60 percent of the patients have been totally abstinent following the treatment. Voegtlen (1940) suggests that a few preventive treatments given at an interval of about 6 months may further improve the results yielded by this method.

Despite these encouraging findings, most psychotherapists are unlikely to be impressed since, in their opinion, the underlying causes for the alcoholism have in no way been modified by the conditioning procedure and, if anything, the mere removal of the alcoholism would tend to produce symptom substitution or other adverse effects. A full discussion of this issue will be presented later. In this particular context, however, several aspects of the Thompson and Bielinski (1953) data are worth noting. Among the alcoholic patients whom they treated, six "suffered from mental disorders not due to alcohol or associated deficiency states." It was planned, by the authors, to follow up the aversion treatment with psychotherapy for the underlying psychosis. This, however, proved unnecessary since all but one of the patients, a case of chronic mental deterioration, showed marked improvement and were in a state of remission.

Max (1935) employed a strong electric shock as the aversive stimulus in treating a patient who tended to display homosexual behavior following exposure to a fetishistic stimulus. Both the fetish and the homosexual behavior were removed through a series of avoidance conditioning sessions in which the patient was administered shock in the presence of the fetishistic object.

Wolpe (1958) has also reported favorable results with a similar procedure in the treatment of obsessions.

A further variation of the counterconditioning procedure has been developed by Mowrer and Mowrer (1938) for use with enuretic patients. The device consists of a wired bed pad which sets off a loud buzzer and awakens the child as soon as micturition begins. Bladder tension thus becomes a cue for waking up which, in turn, is followed by sphincter contraction. Once bladder pressure becomes a stimulus for the more remote sphincter control response, the child is able to remain dry for relatively long periods of time without wakening.

Mowrer and Mowrer (1938) report complete success with 30 children treated by this method; similarly, Davidson and Douglass (1950) achieved highly successful results with 20 chronic enuretic children (15 cured, 5 markedly improved); of 5 cases treated by Morgan and Witmer (1939), 4 of the children not only gained full sphincter control, but also made a significant improvement in their social behavior. The one child with whom the conditioning approach had failed was later found to have bladder difficulties which required medical attention.

Some additional evidence for the efficacy of this method is provided by Martin and Kubly (1955) who obtained follow-up information from 118 of 220 parents who had treated their children at home with this type of conditioning apparatus. In 74 percent of the cases, according to the parents' replies, the treatment was successful.

EXTINCTION

"When a learned response is repeated without reinforcement the strength of the tendency to perform that response undergoes a progressive decrease" (Dollard and Miller, 1950). Extinction involves the development of inhibitory potential which is composed of two components. The evocation of any reaction generates reactive inhibition (I_r) which presumably dissipates with time. When reactive inhibition (fatigue, etc.) reaches a high point, the cessation of activity alleviates this negative motivational state and any stimuli associated with the cessation of the response become conditioned inhibitors $(_sI_r)$.

One factor that has been shown to influence the rate of extinction of maladaptive and anxiety-motivated behavior is the interval between extinction trials. In general, there tends to be little diminution in the strength of fear-motivated behavior when extinction trials are widely distributed, whereas under massed trials, reactive inhibition builds up rapidly and consequently extinction is accelerated (Calvin, Clifford, Clifford, Bolden, and Harvey, 1956; Edmonson and Amsel, 1954).

An illustration of the application of this principle is provided by Yates (1958) in the treatment of tics. Yates demonstrated, in line with the findings from laboratory studies of extinction under massed and distributed practice, that massed sessions in which the patient performed tics voluntarily followed by prolonged rest to allow for the dissipation of reactive inhibition was the most effective procedure for extinguishing the tics.

It should be noted that the extinction procedure employed by Yates is very similar to Dunlap's method of negative practice, in which the subject reproduces the negative behaviors voluntarily without reinforcement (Dunlap, 1932; Lehner, 1954). This method has been applied most frequently, with varying degrees of success, to the treatment of speech disorders (Fishman, 1937; Meissner, 1946; Rutherford, 1940; Sheehan, 1951; Sheehan and Voas, 1957). If the effectiveness of this psychotherapeutic technique is due primarily to extinction, as suggested by Yates' study, the usual practice of terminating a treatment session before the subject becomes fatigued (Lehner, 1954), would have the effect of reducing the rate of extinction, and may in part account for the divergent results yielded by this method.

Additional examples of the therapeutic application of extinction procedures are provided by Jones (1955), and most recently by C. D. Williams (1959).

Most of the conventional forms of psychotherapy rely heavily on extinction effects although the therapist may not label these as such. For example, many therapists consider *permissiveness* to be a necessary condition of therapeutic change (Alexander, 1956; Dollard and Miller, 1950; Rogers, 1951). It is expected that when a patient expresses thoughts or feelings that provoke anxiety or guilt and the therapist does not disapprove, criticize, or withdraw interest, the fear or guilt will be gradually weakened or extinguished. The extinction effects are believed to generalize to thoughts concerning related topics that were originally inhibited, and to verbal and physical forms of behavior as well (Dollard and Miller, 1950).

Some evidence for the relationship between permissiveness and the extinction of anxiety is provided in two studies recently reported by Dittes (1957a, 1957b). In one study (1957b) involving an analysis of patient-therapist interaction sequences, Dittes found that permissive responses on the part of the therapist were followed by a corresponding decrease in the patient's anxiety (as measured by the GSR) and the occurrence of avoidance behaviors. A sequential analysis of the therapeutic sessions (Dittes, 1957a), revealed that, at the onset of treatment, sex expressions were accompanied by strong anxiety reactions; under the cumulative effects of permissiveness, the anxiety gradually extinguished.

In contrast to counterconditioning, extinction is likely to be a less effective and a more time consuming method for eliminating maladaptive behavior (Jones, 1924a; Dollard and Miller, 1950); in the case of conventional interview therapy, the relatively long intervals between interview sessions, and the ritualistic adherence to the 50-minute hour may further reduce the occurrence of extinction effects.

DISCRIMINATION LEARNING

Human functioning would be extremely difficult and inefficient if a person had to learn appropriate behavior for every specific situation he encountered. Fortunately, patterns of behavior learned in one situation will transfer or generalize to other similar situations. On the other hand, if a person overgeneralizes from one situation to another, or if the generalization is based on superficial or irrelevant cues, behavior becomes inappropriate and maladaptive.

In most theories of psychotherapy, therefore, discrimination learning, believed to be accomplished through the gaining of awareness or insight, receives emphasis (Dollard and Miller, 1950; Fenichel, 1941; Rogers, 1951; Sullivan, 1953). It is generally assumed that if a patient is aware of the cues producing his behavior, of the responses he is making, and of the reasons that he responds the way he does, his behavior will become more susceptible to verbally-mediated control. Voluntarily guided, discriminative behavior will replace the automatic, overgeneralized reactions.

While this view is widely accepted, as evidenced in the almost exclusive reliance on interview procedures and on interpretative or labeling techniques, a few therapists (Alexander and French, 1946) have questioned the importance attached to awareness in producing modifications in behavior. Whereas most psychoanalysts (Fenichel, 1941), as well as therapists representing other points of view (Fromm-Reichmann, 1950; Sullivan, 1953) consider insight a precondition of behavior change, Alexander and French consider insight or awareness a result of change rather than its cause. That is, as the patient's anxieties are gradually reduced through the permissive conditions of treatment, formerly inhibited thoughts are gradually restored to awareness.

Evidence obtained through controlled laboratory studies concerning the value of awareness in increasing the precision of discrimination has so far been largely negative or at least equivocal (Adams, 1957; Erikson, 1958; Razran, 1949). A study by Lacy and Smith (1954), in which they found aware subjects generalized anxiety reactions less extensively than did subjects who were unaware of the conditioned stimulus provides evidence that awareness may aid discrimination. However, other aspects of their findings (for example, the magnitude of the anxiety reactions to the generalization stimuli were greater than they were to the conditioned stimulus itself) indicate the need for replication.

If future research continues to demonstrate that awareness exerts little influence on the acquisition, generalization, and modification of behavior, such negative results would cast serious doubt on the value of currently popular psychotherapeutic procedures whose primary aim is the development of insight.

METHODS OF REWARD

Most theories of psychotherapy are based on the assumption that the patient has a repertoire of previously learned positive habits available to him, but that these adaptive patterns are inhibited or blocked by competing responses motivated by anxiety or guilt. The goal of therapy, then, is to reduce the severity of the internal inhibitory controls, thus allowing the healthy patterns of behavior to emerge. Hence, the role of the therapist is to create permissive conditions under which the patient's "normal growth potentialities" are set free (Rogers, 1951). The fact that most of our theories of personality and therapeutic procedures have been developed primarily through work with oversocialized, neurotic patients may account in part for the prevalence of this view.

There is a large class of disorders (the undersocialized, antisocial personalities whose behavior reflects a failure of the socialization process) for whom this model of personality and accompanying techniques of treatment are quite inappropriate (Bandura and Walters, 1959; Schmideberg, 1959). Such antisocial personalities are likely to present *learning deficits,* consequently the goal of therapy is the acquisition of secondary motives and the development of internal restraint habits. That antisocial patients prove unresponsive to psychotherapeutic methods developed for the treatment of oversocialized neurotics has been demonstrated in a number of studies comparing patients who remain in treatment with those who terminate treatment prematurely (Rubenstein and Lorr, 1956). It is for this class of patients that the greatest departures from traditional treatment methods is needed.

While counterconditioning, extinction, and discrimination learning may be effective ways of removing neurotic inhibitions, these methods may be of relatively little value in developing new positive habits. Primary and secondary rewards in the form of the therapist's interest and approval may play an important, if not indispensable, role in the treatment process. Once the patient has learned to want the interest and approval of the therapist, these rewards may then be used to promote the acquisition of new patterns of behavior. For certain classes of patients such as schizophrenics (Atkinson, 1957; Peters, 1953; Robinson, 1957) and delinquents (Cairns, 1959), who are either unresponsive to, or fearful of, social rewards, the therapist may have to rely initially on primary rewards in the treatment process.

An ingenious study by Peters and Jenkins (1954) illustrates the application of this principle in the treatment of schizophrenic patients. Chronic patients from closed wards were administered subshock injections of insulin designed to induce the hunger drive. The patients were then encouraged to solve a series of graded problem tasks with fudge as the reward. This program was followed 5 days a week for 3 months.

Initially the tasks involved simple mazes and obstruction problems in which the patients obtained the food reward directly upon successful completion of the problem. Tasks of gradually increasing difficulty were then administered involving multiple-choice learning and verbal-reasoning problems in which the experimenter personally mediated the primary rewards. After several weeks of such problem solving activities the insulin injections were discontinued and social rewards, which by this time had become more effective, were used in solving interpersonal problems that the patients were likely to encounter in their daily activities both inside and outside the hospital setting.

Comparison of the treated group with control groups, designed to isolate the effects of insulin and special attention, revealed that the patients in the reward group improved significantly in their social relationships in the hospital, whereas the patients in the control groups showed no such change.

King and Armitage (1958) report a somewhat similar study in which severely withdrawn schizophrenic patients were treated with operant conditioning methods; candy and cigarettes served as the primary rewards for eliciting and maintaining increasingly complex forms of behavior, that is, psychomotor, verbal, and interpersonal responses. Unlike the Peters and Jenkins study, no attempt was made to manipulate the level of primary motivation.

An interesting feature of the experimental design was the inclusion of a group of patients who were treated with conventional interview therapy, as well as a recreational therapy and a no-therapy control group. It was found that the operant group, in relation to similar patients in the three control groups, made significantly more clinical improvement.

Skinner (1956b) and Lindsley (1956) working with adult psychotics, and Ferster (1959) working with autistic children, have been successful in developing substantial amounts of reality-oriented behavior in their patients through the use of reward. So far their work has been concerned primarily with the effect of schedules of reinforcement on the rate of evocation of simple impersonal reactions. There is every indication, however, that by varying the contingency of the reward (for example, the patient must respond in certain specified ways to the behavior of another individual in order to produce the reward) adaptive interpersonal behaviors can be developed as well (Azran and Lindsley, 1956).

The effectiveness of social reinforcers in modifying behavior has been demonstrated repeatedly in verbal conditioning experiments (Krasner, 1958; Salzinger, 1959). Encouraged by these findings, several therapists have begun to experiment with operant conditioning as a method of treatment in its own right (Tilton, 1956; Ullmann, Krasner, and Collins, 1961; R. I. Williams, 1959); the operant conditioning studies cited earlier are also illustrative of this trend.

So far the study of generalization and permanence of behavior changes brought about through operant conditioning methods has received relatively little attention and the scanty data available are equivocal (Rogers, 1960; Sarason, 1957; Weide, 1959). The lack of consistency in results is hardly surprising considering that the experimental manipulations in many of the conditioning studies are barely sufficient to demonstrate conditioning effects, let alone generalization of changes to new situations. On the other hand, investigators who have conducted more intensive reinforcement sessions, in an effort to test the efficacy of operant conditioning methods as a therapeutic technique, have found significant changes in patients' interpersonal behavior in extra-experimental situations (King and Armitage, 1958; Peters and Jenkins, 1954; Ullmann *et al.*, 1961). These findings are particularly noteworthy since the response classes involved are similar to those psychotherapists are primarily concerned in modifying through interview forms of treatment. If the favorable results yielded by these studies are replicated in future investigations, it is likely that the next few years will witness an increasing reliance on conditioning forms of psychotherapy, particularly in the treatment of psychotic patients.

At this point it might also be noted that, consistent with the results from verbal conditioning experiments, content analyses of psychotherapeutic interviews (Bandura, Lipsher, and Miller, 1960; Murray, 1956) suggest that many of the changes observed in psychotherapy, at least insofar as the patients' verbal behavior is concerned, can be accounted for in terms of the therapists' direct, although usually unwitting, reward and punishment of the patients' expressions.

PUNISHMENT

While positive habits can be readily developed through reward, the elimination of socially disapproved habits, which becomes very much an issue in the treatment of antisocial personalities, poses a far more complex problem.

The elimination of socially disapproved behaviors can be accomplished in several ways. They may be consistently unrewarded and thus extinguished. However, antisocial behavior, particularly of an extreme form, cannot simply be ignored in the hope that it will gradually extinguish. Furthermore, since the successful execution of antisocial acts may bring substantial material rewards as well as the approval and admiration of associates, it is extremely unlikely that such behavior would ever extinguish.

Although punishment may lead to the rapid disappearance of socially disapproved behavior, its effects are far more complex (Estes, 1944; Solomon, Kamin, and Wynne, 1953). If a person is punished for some socially disapproved habit, the impulse to perform the act becomes, through its association with punishment, a stimulus for anxiety. This anxiety then motivates competing responses which, if sufficiently strong, prevent the occurrence of, or inhibit, the disapproved behavior. Inhibited responses may not, however, thereby lose their strength, and may reappear in situations where the threat of punishment is weaker. Punishment may, in fact, prevent the extinction of a habit; if a habit is completely inhibited, it cannot occur and therefore cannot go unrewarded.

Several other factors point to the futility of punishment as a means of correcting many antisocial patterns. The threat of punishment is very likely to elicit conformity; indeed, the patient may obligingly do whatever he is told to do in order to avoid immediate difficulties. This does not mean, however, that he has acquired a set of sanctions that will be of service to him once he is outside the treatment situation. In fact, rather than leading to the development of internal controls, such methods are likely only to increase the patient's reliance on external restraints. Moreover, under these conditions, the majority of patients will develop the attitude that they will do only what they are told to do —and then often only half-heartedly—and that they will do as they please once they are free from the therapist's supervision (Bandura and Walters, 1959).

In addition, punishment may serve only to intensify hostility and other negative motivations and thus may further instigate the antisocial person to display the very behaviors that the punishment was intended to bring under control.

Mild aversive stimuli have been utilized, of course, in the treatment of voluntary patients who express a desire to rid themselves of specific debilitating conditions.

Liversedge and Sylvester (1955), for example, successfully treated seven cases of writer's cramp by means of a retraining procedure involving electric shock. In order to remove tremors, one component of the motor disorder, the patients were required to insert a stylus into a series of progressively smaller holes; each time the stylus made contact with the side of the hole the patients received a mild shock. The removal of the spasm component of the disorder was obtained in two ways. First, the patients traced various line patterns (similar to the movements required in writing) on a metal plate with a stylus, and any deviation from the path produced a shock. Following training on the apparatus, the subjects then wrote with an electrified pen which delivered a shock whenever excessive thumb pressure was applied.

Liversedge and Sylvester report that following the retraining the patients were able to resume work; a follow-up several months later indicated that the improvement was being maintained.

The aversive forms of therapy, described earlier in the section on counterconditioning procedures, also make use of mild punishment.

SOCIAL IMITATION

Although a certain amount of learning takes place through direct training and reward, a good deal of a person's behavior repertoire may be acquired through imitation of what he observes in others. If this is the case, social imitation may serve as an effective vehicle for the transmission of prosocial behavior patterns in the treatment of antisocial patients.

Merely providing a model for imitation is not, however, sufficient.

Even though the therapist exhibits the kinds of behaviors that he wants the patient to learn, this is likely to have little influence on him if he rejects the therapist as a model. Affectional nurturance is believed to be an important precondition for imitative learning to occur, in that affectional rewards increase the secondary reinforcing properties of the model, and thus predispose the imitator to pattern his behavior after the rewarding person (Mowrer, 1950; Sears, 1957; Whiting, 1954). Some positive evidence for the influence of social rewards on imitation is provided by Bandura and Huston (1961) in a recent study of identification as a process of incidental imitation.

In this investigation preschool children performed an orienting task but, unlike most incidental learning studies, the experimenter performed the diverting task as well, and the extent to which the subjects patterned their behavior after that of the experimenter-model was measured.

A two-choice discrimination problem similar to the one employed by Miller and Dollard (1941) in their experiments of social imitation was used as the diverting task. On each trial, one of two boxes was loaded with two rewards (small multicolor pictures of animals) and the object of the game was to guess which box contained the stickers. The experimenter-model (M) always had her turn first and in each instance chose the reward box. During M's trial, the subject remained at the starting point where he could observe the M's behavior. On each discrimination trial M exhibited certain verbal, motor, and aggressive patterns of behavior that were totally irrelevant to the task to which the subject's attention was directed. At the starting point, for example, M made a verbal response and then marched slowly toward the box containing the stickers, repeating, "March, march, march." On the lid of each box was a rubber doll which M knocked off aggressively when she reached the designated box. She then paused briefly, remarked, "Open the box," removed one sticker, and pasted it on a pastoral scene which hung on the wall immediately behind the boxes. The subject then took his turn and the number of M's behaviors performed by the subject was recorded.

A control group was included in order to, (a) provide a check on whether the subjects' performances reflected genuine imitative learning or merely the chance occurrence of behaviors high in the subjects' response hierarchies, and (b) to determine whether subjects would adopt certain aspects of M's behavior which involved considerable delay in reward. With the controls, therefore, M walked to the box, choosing a highly circuitous route along the sides of the experimental room; instead of aggressing toward the doll, she lifted it gently off the container.

The results of this study indicate that, insofar as preschool children are concerned, a good deal of incidental imitation of the behaviors displayed by an adult model does occur. Of the subjects in the experimental group, 88 percent adopted the M's aggressive behavior, 44 percent imitated the marching, and 28 percent reproduced M's verbalizations. In contrast, none of the control subjects behaved aggressively, marched, or verbalized, while 75 percent of the controls imitated the circuitous route to the containers.

In order to test the hypothesis that children who experience a rewarding relationship with an adult model adopt more of the model's behavior than do children who experience a relatively distant and cold relationship, half the subjects in the experiment were assigned to a nurturant condition; the other half of the subjects to a nonnurturant condition. During the nurturant sessions, which preceded the incidental learning, M played with subject, she responded readily to the subject's bids for attention, and in other ways fostered a consistently warm and rewarding interaction with the child. In contrast, during the nonnurturant sessions, the subject played alone while M busied herself with paperwork at a desk in the far corner of the room.

Consistent with the hypothesis, it was found that subjects who experienced the rewarding interaction with M adopted significantly more of M's behavior than did subjects who were in the nonnurturance condition.

A more crucial test of the transmission of behavior patterns through the process of social imitation involves the delayed generalization of imitative responses to new situations in which the model is absent. A study of this type just completed, provides strong evidence that observation of the cues produced by the behavior of others is an effective means of eliciting responses for which the original probability is very low (Bandura, Ross, and Ross, 1961).

Empirical studies of the correlates of strong and weak identification with parents, lend additional support to the theory that rewards promote imitative learning. Boys whose fathers are highly rewarding and affectionate have been found to adopt the father-role in doll-play activities (Sears, 1953), to show father-son similarity in response to items on a personality questionnaire (Payne and Mussen, 1956), and to display masculine behaviors (Mussen and Distler, 1956, 1960) to a greater extent than boys whose fathers are relatively cold and nonrewarding.

The treatment of older unsocialized delinquents is a difficult task, since they are relatively self-sufficient and do not readily seek involvement with a therapist. In many cases, socialization can be accomplished only through residential care and treatment. In the treatment home, the therapist can personally administer many of the primary rewards and mediate between the boys' needs and gratifications. Through the repeated association with rewarding experiences for the boy, many of the therapist's attitudes and actions will acquire secondary reward value, and thus the patient will be motivated to reproduce these attitudes and actions in himself. Once these attitudes and values have been thus accepted, the boy's inhibition of antisocial tendencies will function independently of the therapist.

While treatment through social imitation has been suggested as a method for modifying antisocial patterns, it can be an effective procedure for the treatment of other forms of disorders as well. Jones (1924a), for example, found that the social example of children reacting normally to stimuli feared by another child was effective, in some instances, in eliminating such phobic reactions. In fact, next to counterconditioning, the method of social imitation proved to be most effective in eliminating inappropriate fears.

There is some suggestive evidence that by providing high prestige models and thus increasing the reinforcement value of the imitatee's behavior, the effectiveness of this method in promoting favorable adjustive patterns of behavior may be further increased (Jones, 1924a; Mausner, 1953, 1954; Miller and Dollard, 1941).

During the course of conventional psychotherapy, the patient is exposed to many incidental cues involving the therapist's values, attitudes, and patterns of behavior. They are incidental only because they are usually considered secondary or irrelevant to the task of resolving the patient's problems. Nevertheless, some of the changes observed in the patient's behavior may result, not so much from the intentional interaction between the patient and the therapist, but rather from active learning by the patient of the therapist's attitudes and values which the therapist never directly attempted to transmit. This is partially corroborated by Rosenthal (1955) who found that, in spite of the usual precautions taken by therapists to avoid imposing their values on their clients, the patients who were judged as showing the greatest improvement changed their moral values (in the areas of sex, aggression, and authority) in the direction of the values of their therapists, whereas patients who were unimproved became less like the therapist in values.

FACTORS IMPEDING INTEGRATION

In reviewing the literature on psychotherapy, it becomes clearly evident that learning theory and general psychology have exerted a remarkably minor influence on the practice of psychotherapy and, apart from the recent interest in Skinner's operant conditioning methods (Krasner, 1955; Skinner, 1953), most of the recent serious attempts to apply learning principles to clinical practice have been made by European psychotherapists (Jones, 1956; Lazarus and Rachman, 1957; Liversedge and Sylvester, 1955; Meyer, 1957; Rachman, 1959; Raymond, 1956;

Wolpe, 1958; Yates, 1958). This isolation of the methods of treatment from our knowledge of learning and motivation will continue to exist for some time since there are several prevalent attitudes that impede adequate integration.

In the first place, the deliberate use of the principles of learning in the modification of human behavior implies, for most psychotherapists, manipulation and control of the patient, and control is seen by them as antihumanistic and, therefore, bad. Thus, advocates of a learning approach to psychotherapy are often charged with treating human beings as though they were rats or pigeons and of leading on the road to Orwell's *1984*.

This does not mean that psychotherapists do not influence and control their patients' behavior. On the contrary. In any interpersonal interaction, and psychotherapy is no exception, people influence and control one another (Frank, 1959; Skinner, 1956a). Although the patient's control of the therapist has not as yet been studied (such control is evident when patients subtly reward the therapist with interesting historical material and thereby avoid the discussion of their current interpersonal problems), there is considerable evidence that the therapist exercises personal control over his patients. A brief examination of interview protocols of patients treated by therapists representing differing theoretical orientations, clearly reveals that the patients have been thoroughly conditioned in their therapists' idiosyncratic languages. Client-centered patients, for example, tend to produce the client-centered terminology, theory, and goals, and their interview content shows little or no overlap with that of patients seen in psychoanalysis who, in turn, tend to speak the language of psychoanalytic theory (Heine, 1950). Even more direct evidence of the therapists' controlling influence is provided in studies of patient-therapist interactions (Bandura *et al.*, 1960; Murray, 1956; Rogers, 1960). The results of these studies show that the therapist not only controls the patient by rewarding him with interest and approval when the patient behaves in a fashion the therapist desires, but that he also controls through punishment, in the form of mild disapproval and withdrawal of interest, when the patient behaves in ways that are threatening to the therapist or run counter to his goals.

One difficulty in understanding the changes that occur in the course of psychotherapy is that the independent variable, that is, the therapist's behavior, is often vaguely or only partially defined. In an effort to minimize or to deny the therapist's directive influence on the patient, the therapist is typically depicted as a "catalyst" who, in some mysterious way, sets free positive adjustive patterns of behavior or similar outcomes usually described in very general and highly socially desirable terms.

It has been suggested, in the material presented in the preceding sections, that many of the changes that occur in psychotherapy derive from the unwitting application of well-known principles of learning. However, the occurrence of the necessary conditions for learning is more by accident than by intent and, perhaps, a more deliberate application of our knowledge of the learning process to psychotherapy would yield far more effective results.

The predominant approach in the development of psychotherapeutic procedures has been the "school" approach. A similar trend is noted in the treatment methods being derived from learning theory. Wolpe, for example, has selected the principle of counterconditioning and built a "school" of psychotherapy around it; Dollard and Miller have focused on extinction and discrimination learning; and the followers of Skinner rely almost entirely on methods of reward. This stress on a few learning principles at the expense of neglecting other relevant ones will serve only to limit the effectiveness of psychotherapy.

A second factor that may account for the discontinuity between general psychology and psychotherapeutic practice is that the model of personality to which most therapists subscribe is somewhat dissonant with the currently developing principles of behavior.

In their formulations of personality functioning, psychotherapists are inclined to appeal to a variety of inner explanatory processes. In contrast, learning theorists view the organism as a far more mechanistic and simpler system, and consequently their formulations tend to be expressed for the most part in terms of antecedent-consequent relationships without reference to inner states.

> Symptoms are learned S-R connections; once they are extinguished or deconditioned treatment is complete. Such treatment is based exclusively on present factors; like Lewin's theory, this one is a-historical. Nonverbal methods are favored over verbal ones, although a minor place is reserved for verbal methods of extinction and reconditioning. Concern is with *function,* not with *content.* The main difference between the two theories arises over the question of "symptomatic" treatment. According to orthodox theory, this is useless unless the underlying complexes are attacked. According to the present theory, there is no evidence for these putative complexes, and symptomatic treatment is all that is required (Eysenck, 1957, pp. 267-268). (Quoted by permission of Frederick A. Praeger, Inc.)

Changes in behavior brought about through such methods as counterconditioning are apt to be viewed by the "dynamically-oriented" therapist, as being not only superficial, "symptomatic" treatment, in that the basic underlying instigators of the behavior remain unchanged, but also potentially dangerous, since the direct elimination of a symptom may precipitate more seriously disturbed behavior.

This expectation receives little support from the generally favorable outcomes reported in the studies reviewed in this paper. In most cases where follow-up data were available to assess the long-term effects of the therapy, the patients, many of whom had been treated by conventional methods with little benefit, had evidently become considerably more effective in their social, vocational, and psychosexual adjustment. On the whole the evidence, while open to error, suggests that no matter what the origin of the maladaptive behavior may be, a change in behavior brought about through learning procedures may be all that is necessary for the alleviation of most forms of emotional disorders.

As Mowrer (1950) very aptly points out, the "symptom-underlying cause" formulation may represent inappropriate medical analogizing. Whether or not a given behavior will be considered normal or a symptom of an underlying disturbance will depend on whether or not somebody objects to the behavior. For example, aggressiveness on the part of children may be encouraged and considered a sign of healthy development by the parents, while the same behavior is viewed by school authorities and society as a symptom of a personality disorder (Bandura and Walters, 1959). Furthermore, behavior considered to be normal at one stage in development may be regarded as a "symptom of a personality disturbance" at a later period. In this connection it is very appropriate to repeat Mowrer's (1950) query: "And when does persisting behavior of this kind suddenly cease to be normal and become a symptom" (p. 474).

Thus, while a high fever is generally considered a sign of an underlying disease process regardless of when or where it occurs, whether a specific behavior will be viewed as normal or as a symptom of an underlying pathology is not independent of who makes the judgement, the social context in which the behavior occurs, the age of the person, as well as many other factors.

Another important difference between physical pathology and behavior pathology usually overlooked is that, in the case of most behavior disorders, it is not the underlying motivations that need to be altered or removed, but rather the ways in which the patient has learned to gratify his needs (Rotter, 1954). Thus, for example, if a patient displays deviant sexual behavior, the goal is not the removal of the underlying causes, that is, sexual motivation, but rather the substitution of more socially approved instrumental and goal responses.

It might also be mentioned in passing, that, in the currently popular forms of psychotherapy, the role assumed by the therapist may bring him a good many direct or fantasied personal gratifications. In the course of treatment the patient may express considerable affection and admiration for the therapist, he may assign the therapist an omniscient status, and the reconstruction of the patient's history may be an intellectually stimulating activity. On the other hand, the methods derived from learning theory place the therapist in a less glamorous role, and this in itself may create some reluctance on the part of psychotherapists to part with the procedures currently in use.

Which of the two conceptual theories of personality—the psychodynamic or the social learning theory—is the more useful in generating effective procedures for the modification of human behavior remains to be demonstrated. While it is possible to present logical arguments and impressive clinical evidence for the efficiency of either approach, the best proving ground is the laboratory.

In evaluating psychotherapeutic methods, the common practice is to compare changes in a treated group with those of a nontreated control group. One drawback of this approach is that, while it answers the question as to whether or not a particular treatment is more effective than no intervention in producing changes along specific dimensions for certain classes of patients, it does not provide evidence concerning the relative effectiveness of alternative forms of psychotherapy.

It would be far more informative if, in future psychotherapy research, radically different forms of treatment were compared (King and Armitage, 1958; Rogers, 1959), since this approach would lead to a more rapid discarding of those of our cherished psychotherapeutic rituals that prove to be ineffective in, or even a handicap to, the successful treatment of emotional disorders.

REFERENCES

Adams, J. K. Laboratory studies of behavior without awareness. *Psychol. Bull.*, 1957, *54*, 393-405.

Alexander, F. *Psychoanalysis and psychotherapy*. New York: Norton, 1956.

Alexander, F., and French, M. T. *Psychoanalytic therapy*. New York: Ronald, 1946.

Atkinson, Rita L. Paired-associate learning by schizophrenic and normal subjects under conditions of verbal reward and verbal punishment. Unpublished doctoral dissertation, Indiana Univer., 1957.

Azran, N. H., and Lindsley, O. R. The reinforcement of cooperation between children. *J. abnorm. soc. Psychol.*, 1956, *52*, 100-102.

Bandura, A., and Huston, Aletha C. Identification as a process of incidental learning. *J. abnorm. soc. Psychol.*, 1961, *63*, 311-318.

Bandura, A., Lipsher, D. H., and Miller, Paula, E. Psychotherapists' approach-avoidance reactions to patients' expressions of hostility. *J. consult. Psychol.*, 1960, *24*, 1-8.

Bandura, A., Ross, Dorothea, and Ross, Sheila A. Transmission of aggression through imitation of aggressive models. *J. abnorm. soc. Psychol.*, 1961, *63*, 575-582.

Bandura, A., and Walters, R. H. *Adolescent aggression*. New York: Ronald, 1959.

Cairns, R. B. The influence of dependency-anxiety on the effectiveness of social reinforcers. Unpublished doctoral dissertation, Stanford Univer., 1959.

Calvin, A. D., Clifford, L. T., Clifford, B., Bolden, L., and Harvey, J. Experimental validation of conditioned inhibition. *Psychol. Rep.*, 1956, *2*, 51-56.

Davidson, J. R., and Douglass, E. Nocturnal enuresis: A special approach to treatment. *British med. J.*, 1950, *1*, 1345-1347.

Dittes, J. E. Extinction during psychotherapy of GSR accompanying "embarrassing" statements. *J. abnorm. soc. Psychol.*, 1957, *54*, 187-191. (a)

Dittes, J. E. Galvanic skin responses as a measure of patient's reaction to therapist's permissiveness. *J. abnorm. soc. Psychol.*, 1957, *55*, 295-303. (b)

Dollard, J., Auld, F., and White, A. M. *Steps in psychotherapy*. New York: Macmillan, 1954.

Dollard, J., and Miller, N. E. *Personality and psychotherapy*. New York: McGraw-Hill, 1950.

Dunlap, K. *Habits, their making and unmaking*. New York: Liveright, 1932.

Edmonson, B. W., and Amsel, A. The effects of massing and distribution of extinction trials on the persistence of a fear-motivated instrumental response. *J. comp. physiol. Psychol.*, 1954, *47*, 117-123.

Erikson, C. W. Unconscious processes. In M. R. Jones (Ed.), *Nebraska symposium on motivation*. Lincoln: Univer. of Nebraska Press, 1958.

Estes, W. K. An experimental study of punishment. *Psychol. Monogr.*, 1944, *57* (3, Whole No. 363).

Eysenck, H. J. *The dynamics of anxiety and hysteria*. New York: Praeger, 1957.

Fenichel, O. *Problems of psychoanalytic technique*. (Trans. by D. Brunswick) New York: Psychoanalytic Quarterly, 1941.

Ferster, C. B. Development of normal behavioral processes in autistic children. *Res. relat. Child.*, 1959, No. 9, 30. (Abstract)

Fishman, H. C. A study of the efficiency of negative practice as a corrective for stammering. *J. speech Dis.*, 1937, *2*, 67-72.

Frank, J. D. The dynamics of the psychotherapeutic relationship. *Psychiatry*, 1959, *22*, 17-39.

Fromm-Reichmann, Frieda. *Principles of intensive psychotherapy*. Chicago: Univer. of Chicago Press, 1950.

Heine, R. W. An investigation of the relationship between change in personality from psychotherapy as reported by patients and the factors seen by patients as producing change. Unpublished doctoral dissertation, Univer. of Chicago, 1950.

Jones, E. L. Exploration of experimental extinction and spontaneous recovery in stuttering. In W. Johnson (Ed.), *Stuttering in children and adults*. Minneapolis: Univer. of Minnesota Press, 1955.

Jones, H. G. The application of conditioning and learning techniques to the treatment of a psychiatric patient. *J. abnorm. soc. Psychol.*, 1956, *52*, 414-419.

Jones, Mary C. The elimination of children's fears. *J. exp. Psychol.*, 1924, *7*, 382-390. (a)

Jones, Mary C. A laboratory study of fear: The case of Peter. *J. genet. Psychol.*, 1924, *31*, 308-315. (b)

King, G. F., and Armitage, S. G. An operant-interpersonal therapeutic approach to schizophrenics of extreme pathology. *Amer. Psychologist*, 1958, *13*, 358. (Abstract)

Klein, Melanie. *The psychoanalysis of children*, London: Hogarth, 1949.

Krasner, L. The use of generalized reinforcers in psychotherapy research. *Psychol. Rep.*, 1955, *1*, 19-25.

Krasner, L. Studies of the conditioning of verbal behavior. *Psychol. Bull.*, 1958, *55*, 148-170.

Lacey, J. I., and Smith, R. I. Conditioning and generalization of unconscious anxiety. *Science*, 1954, *120*, 1-8.

Lazarus, A. A., and Rachman, S. The use of systematic desensitization in psychotherapy. *S. Afr. med. J.*, 1957, *32*, 934-937.

Lehner, G. F. J. Negative practice as a psychotherapeutic technique. *J. gen. Psychol.*, 1954, *51*, 69-82.

Lindsley, O. R. Operant conditioning methods applied to research in chronic schizophrenia. *Psychiat. res. Rep.*, 1956, *5*, 118-138.

Liversedge, L. A., and Sylvester, J. D. Conditioning techniques in the treatment of writer's cramp. *Lancet*, 1955, *1*, 1147-1149.

Martin, B., and Kubly, Delores. Results of treatment of enuresis by a conditioned response method. *J. consult. Psychol.*, 1955, *19*, 71-73.

Mausner, B. Studies in social interaction: III. The effect of variation in one partner's prestige on the interaction of observer pairs. *J. appl. Psychol.*, 1953, *37*, 391-393.

Mausner, B. The effect of one partner's success in a relevant task on the interaction of observer pairs. *J. abnorm. soc. Psychol.*, 1954, *49*, 557-560.

Max, L. W. Breaking up a homosexual fixation by the conditioned reaction technique: A case study. *Psychol. Bull.*, 1935, *32*, 734.

Meissner, J. H. The relationship between voluntary nonfluency and stuttering. *J. speech Dis.*, 1946, *11*, 13-33.

Meyer, V. The treatment of two phobic patients on the basis of learning principles: Case report. *J. abnorm. soc. Psychol.*, 1957, *55*, 261-266.

Miller, N. E., and Dollard, J. *Social learning and imitation*. New Haven: Yale Univer. Press, 1941.

Morgan, J. J. B., and Witmer, F. J. The treatment of enuresis by the conditioned reaction technique. *J. genet. Psychol.*, 1939, *55*, 59-65.

Mowrer, O. H. *Learning theory and personality dynamics*. New York: Ronald, 1950.

Mowrer, O. H., and Mowrer, W. M. Enuresis—a method for its study and treatment. *Amer. J. Orthopsychiat.*, 1938, *8*, 436-459.

Murray, E. J. The content-analysis method of studying psychotherapy. *Psychol. Monogr.*, 1956, *70* (13, Whole No. 420).

Mussen, P., and Distler, L. M. Masculinity, identification, and father-son relationships. *J. abnorm. soc. Psychol.*, 1959, *59*, 350-356.

Mussen, P., and Distler, L. M. Child-rearing antecedents of masculine identification in kindergarten boys. *Child Develpm.*, 1960, *31*, 89-100.

Payne, D. E., and Mussen, P. H. Parent-child relationships and father identification among adolescent boys. *J. abnorm. soc. Psychol.*, 1956, *52*, 358-362.

Peters, H. N. Multiple choice learning in the chronic schizophrenic. *J. clin. Psychol.*, 1953, *9*, 328-333.

Peters, H. N., and Jenkins, R. L. Improvement of chronic schizophrenic patients with guided problem-solving motivated by hunger. *Psychiat. Quart. Suppl.*, 1954, *28*, 84-101.

Rachman, S. The treatment of anxiety and phobic reactions by systematic desensitization psychotherapy. *J. abnorm. soc. Psychol.*, 1959, *58*, 259-263.

Raymond, M. S. Case of fetishism treated by aversion therapy. *Brit. med. J.*, 1956, *2*, 854-857.

Razran, G. Stimulus generalization of conditioned responses. *Psychol. Bull.*, 1949, *46*, 337-365.

Robinson, Nancy M. Paired-associate learning by schizophrenic subjects under conditions of personal and impersonal reward and punishment. Unpublished doctoral dissertation, Stanford Univer., 1957.

Rogers, C. R. *Client-centered therapy*. Boston: Houghton Mifflin, 1951.

Rogers, C. R. Group discussion: Problems of controls. In E. H. Rubinstein and M. B. Parloff (Eds.), *Research in psychotherapy*. Washington, D. C.: Amer. Psych. Assoc., 1959.

Rogers, J. M. Operant conditioning in a quasi-therapy setting. *J. abnorm. soc. Psychol.*, 1960, *60*, 247-252.

Rosenthal, D. Changes in some moral values following psychotherapy. *J. consult. Psychol.*, 1955, *19*, 431-436.

Rotter, J. B. *Social learning and clinical psychology*. Englewood Cliffs, N. J.: Prentice-Hall, 1954.

Rubenstein, E. A., and Lorr, M. A comparison of terminators and remainers in out-patient psychotherapy. *J. clin. Psychol.*, 1956, *12*, 345-349.

Rutherford, B. R. The use of negative practice in speech therapy with children handicapped by cerebral palsy, athetoid type. *J. speech Dis.*, 1940, *5*, 259-264.

Salzinger, K. Experimental manipulation of verbal behavior: A review. *J. gen. Psychol.*, 1959, *61*, 65-94.

Sarason, Barbara R. The effects of verbally conditioned response classes on post-conditioning tasks. *Dissertation Abstr.*, 1957, *12*, 697.

Schmidberg, Melitta. Psychotherapy of juvenile delinquents. *Int. ment. hlth. res. Newsltr.*, 1959, *1*, 1-2.

Sears, Pauline S. Child-rearing factors related to playing of sex-typed roles. *Amer. Psychologist*, 1953, *8*, 431. (Abstract)

Sears, R. R. Identification as a form of behavioral development. In D. B. Harris (Ed.), *The concept of development: An issue in the study of human behavior*. Minneapolis: Univer. of Minnesota Press, 1957.

Sheehan, J. G. The modification of stuttering through non-reinforcement. *J. abnorm. soc. Psychol.*, 1951, *46*, 51-63.

Sheehan, J. G., and Voas, R. B. Stuttering as conflict: I. Comparison of therapy techniques involving approach and avoidance. *J. speech Dis.*, 1957, *22*, 714-723.

Shoben, E. J. Psychotherapy as a problem in learning theory. *Psychol. Bull.*, 1949, *46*, 366-392.

Skinner, B. F. *Science and human behavior*. New York: Macmillan, 1953.

Skinner, B. F. Some issues concerning the control of human behavior. *Science*, 1956, *124*, 1057-1066. (a)

Skinner, B. F. What is psychotic behavior? In *Theory and treatment of psychosis: Some newer aspects*. St. Louis: Washington Univer. Stud., 1956. (b)

Solomon, R. L., Kamin, L. J., and Wynne, L. C. Traumatic avoidance learning: The outcomes of several extinction procedures with dogs. *J. abnorm. soc. Psychol.*, 1953, *48*, 291-302.

Sullivan, H. S. *The interpersonal theory of psychiatry*. New York: Norton, 1953.

Thirmann, J. Conditioned-reflex treatment of alcoholism. *New Engl. J. Med.*, 1949, *241*, 368-370, 406-410.

Thompson, G. N., and Bielinski, B. Improvement in psychosis following conditioned reflex treatment in alcoholism. *J. nerv. ment. Dis.*, 1953, *117*, 537-543.

Tilton, J. R. The use of instrumental motor and verbal learning techniques in the treatment of chronic schizophrenics. Unpublished doctoral dissertation, Michigan State Univer., 1956.

Ullmann, L. P., Krasner, L., and Collins, Beverly J. Modification of behavior in group therapy associated with verbal conditioning. *J. abnorm. soc. Psychol.*, 1961, *63*, 128-132.

Voegtlen, W. L. The treatment of alcoholism by establishing a conditioned reflex. *Amer. J. med. Sci.*, 1940, *119*, 802-810.

Wallace, J. A. The treatment of alcoholics by the conditioned reflex method. *J. Tenn. med. Ass.*, 1949, *42*, 125-128.

Weide, T. N. Conditioning and generalization of the use of affect-relevant words. Unpublished doctoral dissertation, Stanford Univer., 1959.

Whiting, J. W. M. The research program of the Laboratory of Human Development: The development of self-control. Cambridge: Harvard Univer., 1954. (Mimeo)

Williams, C. D. The elimination of tantrum behaviors by extinction procedures. *J. abnorm. soc. Psychol.*, 1959, *59*, 269.

Williams, R. I. Verbal conditioning in psychotherapy. *Amer. Psychologist*, 1959, *14*, 388. (Abstract)

Wolpe, J. Reciprocal inhibition as the main basis of psychotherapeutic effects. *AMA Arch. Neurol. Psychiat.*, 1954, *72*, 205-226.

Wolpe, J. *Psychotherapy by reciprocal inhibition.* Stanford: Stanford Univer. Press, 1958.

Wolpe, J. Psychotherapy based on the principle of reciprocal inhibition. In A. Burton (Ed.), *Case studies in counseling and psychotherapy.* Englewood Cliffs, N. J.: Prentice-Hall, 1959.

Yates, A. J. The application of learning theory to the treatment of tics. *J. abnorm. soc. Psychol.*, 1958, *56*, 175-182.

People Can Learn from People

Within the social context the specialized techniques based on learning mechanisms are most effective.

Bandura does more than put together a summary of the literature. He focuses on several learning processes and places them (and those yet to be developed) into a useful and workable framework. By integrating these techniques within the structure of social learning, Bandura defines a position that should serve the needs of the clinician as well as the general psychologist.

With impressive evidence, he again makes us face the issue that therapists and counselors influence and control their patients' behavior. This article also brings into sharper focus the role of discrimination learning and translates the function of the therapist as a model into learning terms. However, unlike Bandura, who feels that the role he assigns to the therapist is smaller and less glamorous than the one prescribed by the currently popular forms of therapy, we feel that *it is an expanded role.*

Working within the framework of social learning, the therapist is now compelled to see therapy as a part of life rather than as an isolated, mystical communication, which no one other than the chosen few can fully understand or appreciate. This framework also saves the therapist from buying one creative insight (for example, acceptance) and turning it into an aspirin he prescribes for all patients. On a more compelling level, Bandura supplies the background and perspective to go beyond therapy and apply our learnings to other interpersonal problems.

Researchers have for decades studied the therapeutic process in order to learn more about effective therapy. Real movement took place when researchers began to examine the principles of life itself. We would like to add one word to one of Bandura's closing paragraphs so that it reads, "While it is possible to present logical arguments and impressive clinical evidence for the efficiency of either approach (psychodynamic or social learning theory), the best proving ground is the laboratory" (*life*).

Gardner (1964) reviews the one aspect of psychotherapy that cannot be ignored unless the therapist does, in reality, become a machine. Her summary of the literature dealing with the psychotherapeutic relationship is a logical and necessary extension of Bandura's classical contribution.

THE FACILITATIVE RELATIONSHIP*[1]

G. Gail Gardner

Psychotherapy has been variously defined. In this paper, it will refer to

a warm, permissive, safe, understanding, but limited social relationship within which therapist and patient discuss the affective behavior of the latter, including his ways of dealing with his emotionally toned needs and the situations that give rise to them (Shoben, 1953, p. 127).

Some writers on the subject of psychotherapy have focused on the "within which" aspects, citing numerous techniques as being more or less beneficial. Others have focused on the fact that psychotherapy is a relationship, and they have asserted that factors directly associated with this phenomenon contribute significantly to success or failure. This paper addresses itself to the validity of the latter assertion. The literature cited covers the period 1946-1962.

CONCEPTIONS OF THE IDEAL THERAPEUTIC RELATIONSHIP

Since a relationship may be characterized in a myriad of ways, anyone who asserts that the relationship itself is important in psychotherapy

* The psychotherapeutic relationship. *Psychological Bulletin*, 1964, *61*, 426-437. Reprinted by permission of author and publisher.

[1] The author wishes to express gratitude to Allen E. Bergin, Rosalea A. Schonbar, and Laurance F. Shaffer for their helpful comments and criticism during the preparation of this paper.

must state which sorts of relationship are desirable and which not. As Shoben (1949) pointed out, there is considerable agreement on this issue. The characteristics most frequently cited as desirable are the therapist's warmth, acceptance, permissiveness, respect for the patient, understanding, interest in the patient, and liking for the patient. Rogers (1957, 1959) made the additional stipulation that, in successful therapy, the patient must be able to perceive these therapist qualities, and he also asserted (Rogers, 1954) that the patient must like and respect the therapist.

A number of scales which have been constructed (Anderson and Anderson, 1954; Apfelbaum, 1958; Chase, 1946; Fiedler, 1950b; McClelland and Sinaiko, 1950; Sundland and Barker, 1962) for the purpose of defining the ideal relationship indicate that, while the factors cited above are the modal conception, agreement is far from perfect. Thus the issue is raised as to what factors are related to agreement with the modal conception.

Chase (1946) derived his scale from statements about counseling procedure which were endorsed by a majority of "expert" counselors. Counseling students' attitudes generally did not agree with those of the experts and did not correlate either with grades in the counseling course or with Army General Classification Test scores. Chase concluded that acquisition of effective counseling attitudes was not related to scholastic achievement and probably was a function of actual experience in the counseling situation.

McClelland and Sinaiko (1950) refined the Chase scale and administered it to undergraduate and graduate psychology students. Comparisons within each of the two levels confirmed Chase's finding regarding scholastic achievement. Between-group comparisons, however, showed higher scores for the graduate students, and the authors concluded that training helped the students to acquire their instructors' attitudes. Of course this discrimination may have been more a function of self-selection of graduate students than of the training itself. Arbuckle (1956) found high agreement among graduate students' descriptions of the ideal counselor. In both studies, however, it is a moot question whether the graduate students actually believed in the attitudes they professed or merely were more adept at judging what answer was expected.

Fiedler (1950b), using a Q-sort technique, found for seven therapists representing three schools that there were no significant differences in conception of the ideal therapeutic relationship between therapists of different schools, but that experienced and inexperienced therapists of the same school did differ significantly from each other. He argued that ability to describe the ideal therapeutic relationship was a function of experience rather than of theoretical allegiance. Though Fiedler's evidence has often been cited as conclusive, it has not gone unchallenged. Apfelbaum (1958) criticized Fiedler's Q deck on the grounds that the items reflected extreme positions and thus tended to compel agreement among sorters, resulting in spuriously high intersorter correlations.

Behar and Altrocci (1961), using a scale constructed by Apfelbaum, asked nursing students to describe the ideal psychiatric nurse. Participation in psychiatric nursing courses seemed to produce high agreement, whereas actual experience with psychiatric patients did not. The authors concluded that they had refuted Fiedler's (1950b) hypothesis concerning experience, and that training instead was the critical variable. However, they failed to note that the high-agreement groups had had considerable experience with nonpsychiatric patients. Since it is quite doubtful that student nurses are taught to hold significantly different attitudes toward psychiatric patients as opposed to patients in general, the authors' conclusions are questionable. The training and experience variables were not properly controlled in either this study or Fiedler's (1950b); thus the issue remains unresolved as to which contributes more to agreement on good therapeutic attitudes.

Sundland and Barker (1962) constructed a scale which did differentiate between therapeutic schools in terms of therapeutic attitudes. The criterion for item selection was that the items described points of controversy between schools; thus all that can be concluded is that the authors successfully validated their scale. In comparing their results to Fiedler's the authors recognized that different attitudes were measured, and they properly raised the issue of the extent to which differential responses to a scale may be a function of its content rather than of the persons responding. A related issue concerns the appropriate degree of specificity of items in an attitude scale. While everyone may agree that a therapist should be warm and accepting, there may be considerable disagreement as to what these terms actually imply. Sundland and Barker (1962) found, contrary to Fiedler's (1950b) results, that experienced and inexperienced therapists did not differ in their responses. But it must be noted that if a therapist is trained in a given school of thought, he does not need much experience to learn his school's position on the more controversial issues. Thus Fiedler's findings regarding experience and schools have still not been conclusively refuted.

Three studies (Anderson and Anderson, 1954; Fiedler, 1950b; Thomas, Polansky, and Kounin, 1955) noted that persons with no professional experience or training could describe the ideal therapeutic relationship about as well as therapists. Fiedler hypothesized that the therapeutic relationship may be only a variation of good interpersonal relationships in general.

Soper and Combs (1962), using a modification of Fiedler's (1950b)

Q deck, found that teachers described the ideal teacher in much the same way that expert therapists described the ideal therapist. These data cannot be said to confirm Fiedler's hypothesis that the therapeutic relationship is only a paradigm of good human relationships generally, but they do support the notion of commonality among helping relationships, at least as described in Fiedler's terms by experts in the respective fields.

About the most that can be concluded from these various scales and samples is that the ideal therapeutic relationship may be as uniformly described as the scale provided permits. It is probably a variant of helping relationships in general and can probably be reasonably well described by anyone who considers it important. This latter hypothesis might explain the fact that Anderson and Anderson's (1954) patients were successful in the task while Behar and Altrocci's (1961) nonnursing students failed. Personal commitment to the significance of helping relationships may be a more pertinent variable than experience per se. Professional training does not seem to be especially relevant.

RELATIONSHIP FACTORS AND THERAPEUTIC CHANGE

We now consider studies in which aspects of the patient-therapist relationship are related to therapeutic change. The studies will be discussed in blocks according to the way in which the relationship variable is measured.

Therapist Ratings

It is difficult to obtain independent measures of the two variables under consideration. When one judges a helping relationship to be good in that it satisfies the conditions outlined above, one tends to experience a feeling of satisfaction which in turn acts as a set for perceiving progress toward therapeutic goals. Similarly, the converse is true. Even when one variable is measured alone, it is difficult not to get cues regarding the other. Given this inherent contamination, it only adds fuel to the fire to propose a design in which the same people rate both variables. The following two studies suffer from this error, and their results should be interpreted with caution.

Gorlow, Hoch, and Telschow (1952) studied therapy groups and found that the therapists had greatest liking for the most profited group. Since no statistical data were provided, it cannot be ascertained how strong the relationship was between liking and progress. Seeman (1954) found that therapist ratings of liking for their patients correlated .65 with therapist ratings of therapeutic success ($N = 23$). Retest reliability of the ratings was satisfactory. Since both ratings were made at the end of therapy, contamination is very likely. Therapist ratings of the degree to which the patient used his relationship to the therapist as a focus for therapy were not related to success. This finding casts doubt on the validity of notions to the contrary held by many therapists.

Snyder (1961) had significantly more positive affect toward his more improved patients. But the facts that his relationship and progress measures overlapped and that the patients were also his students suggest caution in interpreting these data and others from the same research to be reported below.

Two studies (Coons, 1957; Lesser, 1961) utilized projective and other personality tests to measure therapeutic change and thereby minimized the possibility of contamination. Coons (1957) found that a therapy group which focused on interaction showed significantly more improvement than either a group that stressed insight into psychological problems or a no-therapy control group. The latter two groups did not differ from each other. Coons concluded that interaction is the essential condition for therapeutic change. These findings contradict those of Seeman (1954). The difference may be due to the fact that Coons' patients were hospitalized schizophrenics and Seeman's were neurotics. Since withdrawal from interpersonal interaction is a major symptom of schizophrenia, whereas it may or may not be a central issue in neurosis, it seems entirely reasonable that measures of improvement would be more closely related to interaction in the former case than in the latter. The fact that Seeman's patients were in individual therapy and Coons' were in group therapy may also contribute to the difference in results.

Lesser (1961) found no relationship between therapists' ratings of their own empathic understanding and differences in patients' self-ideal discrepancies (Butler and Haigh, 1954) before and after therapy. It should be noted, however, that the number of hours of therapy varied from 3 to 12. For most patients in treatment for this short a period, even the most expert therapists cannot hope to effect significant changes in the more permanent personality constructs measured by the Butler and Haigh Q sort.

In all these studies, of course, the problems inherent in self-reports are relevant.

Patient Ratings

Studies in which patients made both judgments (Feifel and Eells, 1962; Grigg and Goodstein, 1957; Lipkin, 1948) also suffer from interdependent measures and must therefore be interpreted with caution. A patient who feels warmly toward his therapist has more reason to judge himself improved; conversely, one who feels himself improved is more likely to have positive feelings toward his therapist, especially in retrospect.

Lipkin (1948) found that patients who mentioned the counselor's permissive attitude in posttherapy evaluations usually felt that it helped them to achieve insight into their problems. Though the length of treatment was no greater than that employed by Lesser (1961), the improvement criteria were much more situational; this difference probably explains the discrepant results. Grigg and Goodstein (1957), using a follow-up questionnaire, found that clients who felt a close relationship with their counselor reported significantly more favorable outcomes than did clients who felt a more distant relationship. Feifel and Eells (1962) obtained similar results.

Van der Veen (1961) utilized ratings by outside judges as the measure of improvement. He found significant positive correlations between patient ratings of the degree to which therapists provided a positive relationship and judges' process ratings.

A few studies have relied on test scores as the measure of progress in therapy. Lipkin (1954) measured therapy change by global judgments of Thematic Apperception Test protocols. He found that successful patients focused less than unsuccessful patients on their willingness to confide in the therapist, and when they did so focus, it was in a more positive way. The unsuccessful patients focused on mistrust. Lesser (1961) found no relationship between client ratings of therapist empathy and changes in self-ideal discrepancies. These negative results have been explained in the section on therapist ratings. Snyder (1961) reported a significant positive relationship between patients' attitudes toward the therapist and their classification as better or worse patients. Since, however, the measure of the two variables overlapped, the results are contaminated.

Ratings by Outside Judges

In studies in which judges rated both therapeutic change and the quality of the therapeutic relationship, it is not always clear whether or not the same judges made both ratings. Even if they did, these studies have merit over those described above in that the patient-therapist relationship is now rated by people who are not personally involved in the outcome of therapy.

Holt and Luborsky (1952) found that resident psychiatrists rated by their supervisors as successful were also rated as having better relationships with patients than were residents rated as unsuccessful. Unfortunately, the ratings were contaminated by the fact that the supervisors themselves had better relationships with the residents they judged to be successful. Luborsky (1952) noted that the successful residents were more flexible with respect to the range of behavior which they felt appropriate for their patients. Apparently the less successful residents tended to try to cast their patients into a preconceived mold. The finding that the successful residents had better relationships with ward personnel and fellow residents as well as with supervisors and patients lends some support to Fiedler's (1950b) hypothesis that good therapy relationships are not unique entities but rather instances of good relationships in general. Parloff's (1956) findings further support this notion.

Knupfer, Jackson, and Krieger (1959) noted the authoritarian nature of the relationship between the supervisor and the beginning therapist, and argued that supervisors' ratings may be heavily weighted with evaluations of the therapists' attitudes toward authority. Nevertheless, such ratings are probably more valid than the therapists' own ratings.

Van der Veen (1961) reported greater process-movement scores for clients whose therapists were judged to create better relationships. Truax (1961a) reported similar results and properly pointed out that causality had not been demonstrated. One study (Parloff, 1961), in which it was made clear that the judges of the relationship were different from the judges of therapeutic change, reported significant positive correlations between the two variables for patients in group therapy.

Two studies (Hiler, 1958; Parloff, 1961) relied on patient reports and behavior as the measure of change. Parloff (1961) noted a positive correlation between judged quality of the therapeutic relationship and patient reports of relief from symptomatic discomfort. In Hiler's (1958) study, therapists rated by staff psychologists as warm were better able to keep unproductive patients in treatment.

Truax (1961b, 1962) measured change by various test scores, including the Minnesota Multiphasic Personality Inventory (MMPI), and reported that, for two samples of schizophrenic patients, judged therapist empathy was positively related to improvement.

Three studies measured therapy change with a combination of ratings and test scores. Aronson (1953) reported no differences in improvement for clients of four therapists who were judged by their peers to have significantly different degrees of ability for warm interpersonal relationships. The fact that both therapists and judges were graduate students and that the judgments were not limited to therapist-patient relationships may have contributed to the null results. Truax (1961b), in a similarly designed study, obtained positive results for both neurotic and schizophrenic samples. His research differed from Aronson's primarily in that his relationship judgments were based on actual therapy sessions. Stoler's (1961) judges did not concern themselves with the therapists, but rather rated the likability of the patients on the basis of tape-recorded segments of therapy. Patients identified as more likable were more often identified as improved.

In evaluating all these studies, one must consider that, when there is little agreement as to the nature of improvement and no conclusive evidence that any form of change occurs as a result of psychotherapy, it seems premature blithely to examine the correlates of therapeutic change. Yet there seems to be no other appropriate course of action.

The evidence that the quality of the therapeutic relationship is a correlate of therapeutic change lies not in the conclusive results of any one study but rather in the repeated findings of a series of studies, most of which contain one or more serious defects. Methodology varies greatly, and absence of precise definitions often makes it difficult to discern whether the "good relationship" of one study contains the same elements as that of another study or different. In a sense, the diversity of procedure strengthens the force of the conclusion. Null results do not cluster in any one methodological cell, and, in all types of design, positive results occur far more frequently. Further support derives from the high agreement among different types of raters regarding the nature of the relationship between a given therapist and patient. Miller (1949) reported non-significant differences between the judgments of four raters with widely varying amounts of training. Parloff (1961) and Snyder (1961) reported correlations of .79 and .70, respectively, between patients' and judges' or therapists' descriptions of the patient-therapist relationship.

OTHER FACTORS RELATED TO THE PSYCHOTHERAPEUTIC RELATIONSHIP

Patient Variables

DIAGNOSIS.   Parloff (1961) found no correlation between initial patient evaluations and subsequent measures of the quality of the therapeutic relationship. Since the patients were all neurotic, the range of maladjustment probably was not very great. Hollingshead and Redlich (1958) reported an inverse relationship between patient maladjustment and therapist liking for patients ranging over the whole gamut of disturbance. However, since maladjustment was also inversely related to social class, and since liking was positively related to social class, the results may be an artifact. Snyder (1961) indicated that the patients toward whom he felt most friendly were relatively more energetic, uninhibited, and suggestible. On the pretherapy MMPI, these patients were more hypomanic and obsessive; the least-liked patients tended to be more schizoid and depressive.

PROGNOSIS.   Since diagnosis and prognosis are usually themselves related, it should follow that prognosis is correlated with therapists' affective attitudes. Strupp (1958, 1960) and Wallach and Strupp (1960) found this to be true. Strupp (1960) commented on "the ubiquitous but insufficiently realized effects of the therapists' attitudes as they permeate and color his clinical observations and judgments" (p. 28). Of course it must be realized that the direction of influence may also be the other way.

MOTIVATION FOR THERAPY. In three studies (Raskin, 1961; Strupp, 1960; Wallach and Strupp, 1960), therapists had greater liking for patients who evidenced a desire to change and improve. This is hardly surprising since motivation for therapy is usually a central consideration in making a prognosis. Wallach and Strupp inferred from their data that the patient's motivation probably influences the therapist's attitude only when the degree of maladjustment is not too great. Raskin (1961) noted that liking was more effective as a predictor of high- than of low-motivation ratings. Considering the correlational design of his research, the use of the word "predictor" seems inappropriate. Still the finding warrants further study.

CAPACITY FOR FRIENDLINESS. In two studies (Heller, Myers, and Kline, 1962; Snyder, 1961) therapists had warmer feelings for patients who were themselves more friendly.

DEPENDENCY. Heller *et al.* (1962) also noted that dependent clients evoked more interviewer friendliness than did more dominant clients. It seems that, at least for therapists judging clients at the outset of therapy, friendliness and dependency are interdependent variables. Presumably this would not hold true at the later stages of therapy.

ETHICAL VALUES. Snyder (1961) developed a warmer relationship with patients whom he rated as relatively more idealistic and altruistic.

SOCIAL CLASS. Hollingshead and Redlich (1958) observed that therapists' attitudes toward their patients were positively related to the patients' social class. This was true even when the range of maladjustment was curtailed by studying only the neurotic sample. The authors felt that therapists generally are unable to understand lower-class values and hence are less prone to like persons holding such values. Furthermore, the therapist's technical skill is threatened by the lower-class patient's tendency to demand that the therapist behave in an authoritarian manner.

EXPECTATIONS REGARDING THE THERAPIST. Apfelbaum (1958) found that patients who expected a high degree of warmth from the therapist did not differ on pretherapy MMPI scores from patients who expected a low degree, and that both these groups had more maladjusted MMPI scores than a group which expected a moderate degree of warmth. It could be hypothesized that therapists would have the most positive feelings for this middle group.

That therapist liking results from perceiving a "good patient" rather than the reverse was indicated by Strupp and Williams (1960) who found that two therapists' ratings of the following variables were all highly intercorrelated: patients' defensiveness, patients' capacity for insight, patients' motivation for therapy, patients' prognosis, and therapists' liking for the patients. When therapist liking was partialed out, there was no change in the magnitude of the other coefficients. Two writers (Fiedler, 1953; Truax, 1961b) reported contradictory data. In each of these studies, a given therapist's attitudes were found not to vary across different patients. Homogeneity of sampling may account for the null results in both cases.

While it appears that warm relationships can best be established with "good" patients who are motivated for therapy, only moderately maladjusted, friendly, submissive, and who represent the middle or upper social classes, persons who do not fit into this category can sometimes be treated successfully. In order to raise this success rate, it would probably be fruitful to investigate which sorts of therapists are most capable of forming positive relationships with persons who are not good patients.

Therapist Variables

PERSONALITY CHARACTERISTICS.   Three studies (Ashby, Ford, Guerney, and Guerney, 1957; Brams, 1961; Fiedler and Senior, 1952) correlated a large number of therapist personality variables with measures of the quality of the therapeutic relationship. Positive results occurred no more often than would be expected by chance.

Holt and Luborsky (1952) reported that their successful psychiatrists —who maintained better patient-therapist relationships—were in the middle of the range on dimensions of control of affect and emotional impulsivity. Unsuccessful psychiatrists tended to be either impulsively expressive with their patients or overcontrolled with no expression of feeling. It may be that other therapist qualities have a curvilinear relationship with attitudinal variables and that their relevance has been refuted because only linear relationships were investigated.

Streitfeld (1959) found that ratings of self-acceptance (SA) and acceptance of others (AO) were not related to ratings of therapeutic competence. He concluded that, while general acceptance of others is not related to psychotherapeutic ability, acceptance of specific patients probably is related. The null results might also be explained by the fact that the therapists were all graduate students. Interestingly, therapists who obtained low scores on SA and AO rated their therapeutic ability similarly to the way in which their supervisors rated it, whereas this was not true for therapists high on SA and AO. The author suggested that high SA and AO therapists may be defensive and immature. A similar conclusion may be drawn from data reported by Fiedler and Senior (1952). Correlational techniques which are sensitive to curvilinearity may be most appropriate for studying the self-acceptance variable.

FAMILIARITY WITH THE PATIENT.   Stoler (1961) found that raters who were familiar with patients' cases judged the patients as more likable than did raters reviewing the cases for the first time.

ABILITY TO PREDICT PATIENT BEHAVIOR.   A number of studies (Affleck and Garfield, 1961; Chance, 1959; Dymond, 1953; Fiedler, 1953; Luft, 1950; Melton, 1952) have found therapists' predictive ability to be quite poor and generally no better than that of persons who are not therapists. Correlations of this ability, such as it is, with relationship factors have variously been described as positive (Kahn, 1957), negative (Smith, 1960), and zero (Mellinger, 1956). Snyder (1961) reported positive but nonsignificant differences in his ability to predict questionnaire responses of his better and poorer clients.

Fiedler (1953) commented that therapeutic understanding refers primarily to making the patient feel understood and not to any objective diagnostic or predictive ability. The evidence is generally in support of his implication, namely, that predictive ability is not a relevant therapist variable.

EXPERIENCE.   Parloff (1956) reported that, for two experienced therapists, judges agreed that one created better therapeutic relationships than the other. Fiedler (1950a, 1951a) found that expert therapists were judged better able to approximate the ideal relationship than were novices. A major weakness in the study was that the judges could distinguish the experts—who were nationally known—from the novices on the basis of their voices. It is impossible to estimate the extent to which halo and "pitchfork" effects, respectively, were operating. Three other studies (Chance, 1959; McGowan, 1954; Strupp, 1958), in which this defect was avoided, obtained similar results. Hollingshead and Redlich (1958) found that inexperienced therapists tended more to dislike lower-class patients than did experienced therapists. It may be that the experience variable is most relevant in the case of patients who do not fit into the "good patient" category.

Therapist-Patient Similarity

ASSUMED SIMILARITY (AS).   This construct (Fiedler, 1951b) refers to the degree to which a therapist believes that his own personality is similar to his patient's personality. Hunt, Ewing, LaForge, and Gilbert (1959) reported a positive correlation between AS scores and the degree to which therapists liked their clients.

REAL SIMILARITY.   Lesser (1961) found that similarity of self-concept between therapist and patient was not related to empathy scores. Vogel (1961) reported no correlation between judged quality of the therapeutic relationship and patient-therapist similarity on the California F Scale. However, there was a significant correlation between relationship ratings and similarity between patient and therapist ratings of the extent to which the therapist should behave in an authoritarian manner. It should be noted that, in this case, similar opinions would reflect complementary need patterns. Snyder (1961) also reported that patients with whom he had better relationships had need profiles (Edwards Personal Preference Schedule) which complemented, rather than reflected, his own. In this research also, *n* Dominance was the primary factor. Hollingshead and Redlich (1958) noted that therapists had more positive feelings toward patients whose social-class backgrounds were similar to their own.

Carson and Heine (1962) found a curvilinear relationship between therapist-patient similarity on the MMPI and therapeutic success ratings. That is, patients whose profiles were moderately similar to their therapists' were judged most improved. The authors reasoned that high similarity prevents the therapist from maintaining suitable distance and objectivity whereas high dissimilarity prevents him from being able to emphasize with or understand his patient's problems.

These studies strongly support Levinson's (1961) thesis that patient-therapist similarity cannot be thought of as a unitary trait. Some similarities may facilitate good relationships and therapeutic progress, while others may be sources of impasses.

Technique Variables

RELATIVE IMPORTANCE OF RELATIONSHIP AND TECHNIQUE.   Shortly before relationship variables came into vogue, Seeman (1949) studied reactions of clients who had been counseled by directive and nondirective methods. He found significantly different client reactions for pairs of counselors whose techniques were similar and nonsignificant differences where techniques were different. He concluded that some factor other than therapeutic method was producing differences in client reactions.

Fiedler (1950a, 1951a, 1953) rushed in to fill the vacuum, affirming Seeman's (1949) conclusion and stating that the therapeutic relationship is the critical variable in successful therapy. Fiedler (1953) commented, however, that a given technique might serve to make a therapist feel more secure and thus indirectly affect the course of therapy.

More recent research (Ford, 1956; Forgy and Black, 1954; Snyder, 1957) has placed technique in a somewhat more favorable light. These writers have concluded that relationship and success vary not as a function of technique alone, but rather as a function of a particular therapist using a particular technique. They feel that the therapist and his method must be viewed as a single unit.

Strupp (1958) concurred that both relationship and technique factors are important in successful therapy. Interestingly, in a later article (Strupp, 1962), he was not so willing to commit himself and stated:

For some years it has been held that the quality of the therapeutic relationship is more basic to therapeutic success than the therapist's specific
methods and techniques. . . . It may be predicted that the issue will
remain alive for some time (p. 452).

COVARIANCE OF RELATIONSHIP AND TECHNIQUE FACTORS.   TWO
studies (Aronson, 1953; Strupp, 1958) reported a negative correlation
between the degree of warmth in therapists' attitudes toward their patients and the extent to which they used directive techniques. Apfelbaum
(1958) studied patients' pretherapy expectations of their therapists' behavior and reported a curvilinear relationship between the two variables.
Therapists expected to be at the extremes of the warmth dimension
were expected to employ directive techniques; therapists expected to
exhibit a moderate amount of warmth were expected to be relatively
more nondirective. The discrepancy between these data and those of
Strupp (1958) and Aronson (1953) may be explained in two ways: either
therapists do not exist who are as warm as some patients expect or such
therapists do exist but were not represented in Strupp's and Aronson's
samples. Of course variations in measuring instruments may also account for the differences.

Throughout this paper, considerable weight has been given to
methodological issues. It is indeed a pity that research findings must so
often be questioned because of methodological defects. Not only the
nature of the measurements but also the point at which they are made
should be considered, especially in the case of patients' and therapists'
self-reports. While time may dim the memory, it may also extinguish inhibitions and thus allow greater honesty as regards negative feelings and
evaluations (Feifel and Eells, 1962).

REFERENCES

Affleck, D. C., and Garfield, S. L. Predictive judgments of therapists and duration of stay in psychotherapy. *J. clin. Psychol.,* 1961, *17,* 134-137.

Anderson, R. P., and Anderson, G. V. The development of an instrument for
measuring rapport. In *Occasional papers in testing and guidance.* Austin:
Univer. of Texas, Testing and Guidance Bureau, 1954.

Apfelbaum, B. *Dimensions of transference in psychotherapy.* (Publications in
Personality Assessment and Research, No. 2) Berkeley: Univer. of California
Publications, 1958.

Arbuckle, D. S. Client perception of counselor personality. *J. counsel. Psychol.,*
1956, *3,* 93-96.

Aronson, M. A study of the relationships between certain counselor and client
characteristics in client-centered therapy. In W. U. Snyder (Ed.), *Group
report of a program of research in psychotherapy.* State College: Pennsylvania State College, 1953. Pp. 39-54.

Ashby, J. D., Ford, D. H., Guerney, B. G., Jr., and Guerney, Louise F. Effects on clients of a reflective and a leading type of psychotherapy. *Psychol. Monogr.*, 1957, *71* (24, Whole No. 453).

Behar, Lenore, and Altrocci, J. Agreement on the concept of the ideal therapist as a function of experience. *J. clin. Psychol.*, 1961, *17*, 66-69.

Brams, J. M. Counselor characteristics and effective communication in counseling. *J. counsel. Psychol.*, 1961, *8*, 25-30.

Butler, J. M., and Haigh, G. V. Changes in the relation between self-concepts and ideal concepts consequent upon client-centered counseling. In C. R. Rogers and Rosalind F. Dymond (Eds.), *Psychotherapy and personality change*. Chicago: Univer. of Chicago Press, 1954. Pp. 55-75.

Carson, R. C., and Heine, R. W. Similarity and success in therapeutic dyads. *J. consult. Psychol.*, 1962, *26*, 38-43.

Chance, Erika. *Families in treatment*. New York: Basic Books, 1959.

Chase, W. P. Measurement of attitudes toward counseling. *Educ. psychol. Measmt.*, 1946, *6*, 467-473.

Coons, W. H. Interaction and insight in group psychotherapy. *Canad. J. Psychol.*, 1957, *11*, 1-8.

Dymond, Rosalind F. Can clinicians predict individual behavior? *J. Pers.*, 1953, *22*, 151-161.

Feifel, H., and Eells, Janet. Patients and therapists assess the same psychotherapy. Paper read at Amer. Psychol. Assoc., St. Louis, September 1962.

Fiedler, F. E. A comparison of therapeutic relationships in psychoanalytic, nondirective, and Adlerian therapy. *J. consult. Psychol.*, 1950, *14*, 436-445. (a)

Fiedler, F. E. The concept of an ideal therapeutic relationship. *J. consult. Psychol.*, 1950, *14*, 239-245. (b)

Fiedler, F. E. Factor analyses of psychoanalytic, nondirective, and Adlerian therapeutic relationships. *J. consult. Psychol.*, 1951, *15*, 32-38. (a)

Fiedler, F. E. A method of objective quantification of certain countertransference attitudes. *J. clin. Psychol.*, 1951, *7*, 101-107. (b)

Fiedler, F. E. Quantitative studies on the role of therapists' feelings toward their patients. In O. H. Mowrer (Ed.), *Psychotherapy: Theory and research*. New York: Ronald, 1953. Pp. 296-315.

Fiedler, F. E., and Senior, K. An exploratory study of unconscious feeling reactions in 15 patient-therapist pairs. *J. abnorm. soc. Psychol.*, 1952, *47*, 446-453.

Ford, D. H. An experimental comparison of the relationship between client and therapist in a reflective and a leading type of psychotherapy. Unpublished doctoral dissertation, Pennsylvania State Univer., 1956. (*Dissert. Abstr.*, 1956, *16*, 1490-1491.)

Forgy, E. W., and Black, J. D. A follow-up after three years of clients counseled by two methods. *J. counsel. Psychol.*, 1954, *1*, 1-8.

Gorlow, L., Hoch, E. L., and Telschow, E. F. *The nature of nondirective group psychotherapy: An experimental investigation*. New York: Teachers College, Columbia Univer., 1952.

Grigg, A. E., and Goodstein, L. D. The use of clients as judges of the counselor's performance. *J. counsel. Psychol.*, 1957, *4*, 31-36.

Heller, K., Myers, R. A., and Kline, Linda V. Interviewer behavior as a function of standardized client roles. Paper read at Amer. Psychol. Assoc., St. Louis, September 1962.

Hiler, E. W. An analysis of patient-therapist compatibility. *J. consult. Psychol.*, 1958, *22*, 341-347.

Hollingshead, A. B., and Redlich, F. C. *Social class and mental illness.* New York: Wiley, 1958.

Holt, R. R., and Luborsky, L. Research in the selection of psychiatrists: A second interim report. *Bull. Menninger Clin.*, 1952, *16*, 125-135.

Hunt, J. McV., Ewing, T. N., LaForge, R., and Gilbert, W. M. An integrated approach to research on therapeutic counseling with samples of results. *J. counsel. Psychol.*, 1959, *6*, 46-54.

Kahn, R. K. Therapist discomfort in two psychotherapies. Unpublished doctoral dissertation, Pennsylvania State Univer., 1957. Cited by W. U. Snyder, Some investigations of relationship in psychotherapy. In E. A. Rubinstein and M. B. Parloff (Eds.), *Research in psychotherapy.* Washington, D. C.: National Publishing, 1959. P. 252.

Knupfer, Genevieve, Jackson, D. D., and Krieger, G. Personality differences between more and less competent psychotherapists as a function of criteria of competence. *J. nerv. ment. Dis.*, 1959, *129*, 375-384.

Lesser, W. M. The relationship between counseling progress and empathic understanding. *J. counsel. Psychol.*, 1961, *8*, 330-336.

Levinson, D. J. The psychotherapist's contribution to the patient's treatment career. Paper read at Conference on Psychotherapy Research, Chapel Hill, North Carolina, 1961.

Lipkin, S. The client evaluates nondirective psychotherapy. *J. consult. Psychol.*, 1948, *12*, 137-146.

Lipkin, S. Clients' feelings and attitudes in relation to the outcome of client-centered therapy. *Psychol. Monogr.*, 1954, *68* (1, Whole No. 372).

Luborsky, L. B. The personalities of successful and less successful psychotherapists. *Amer. Psychologist*, 1952, *7*, 337. (Abstract)

Luft, J. Implicit hypotheses and clinical predictions. *J. abnorm. soc. Psychol.*, 1950, *45*, 756-759.

McClelland, W. A., and Sinaiko, H. W. An investigation of a counselor attitude questionnaire. *Educ. psychol. Measmt.*, 1950, *10*, 128-133.

McGowan, J. F. Client anticipations and expectancies as related to initial interview performance and perceptions. Unpublished doctoral dissertation, Univer. of Missouri, 1954. (*Dissert. Abstr.*, 1955, *15*, 228-229.)

Mellinger, G. D. Interpersonal trust as a factor in communication. *J. abnorm. soc. Psychol.*, 1956, *52*, 304-309.

Melton, R. S. A comparison of clinical and actuarial methods of prediction with an assessment of the relative accuracy of different clinicians. Unpublished doctoral dissertation, Univer. of Minnesota, 1952.

Miller, Helen E. "Acceptance" and related attributes as demonstrated in psychotherapeutic interviews. *J. clin. Psychol.,* 1949, *5,* 83-87.

Parloff, M. B. Some factors affecting the quality of therapeutic relationships. *J. abnorm. soc. Psychol.,* 1956, *52,* 5-10.

Parloff, M. B. Therapist-patient relationships and outcome of psychotherapy. *J. consult. Psychol.,* 1961, *25,* 29-38.

Raskin, A. Factors therapists associate with motivation to enter psychotherapy. *J. clin. Psychol.,* 1961, *17,* 62-65.

Rogers, C. R. An overview of the research and some questions for the future. In C. R. Rogers and Rosalind F. Dymond (Eds.), *Psychotherapy and personality change.* Chicago: Univer. of Chicago Press, 1954. Pp. 413-430.

Rogers, C. R. The necessary and sufficient conditions of therapeutic personality change. *J. consult. Psychol.,* 1957, *21,* 95-103.

Rogers, C. R. Therapist-patient relationship. In E. A. Rubinstein and M. B. Parloff (Eds.), *Research in psychotherapy.* Washington, D. C.: National Publishing, 1959. P. 273.

Seeman, J. An investigation of client reactions to vocational counseling. *J. consult. Psychol.,* 1949, *13,* 95-104.

Seeman, J. Counselor judgments of therapeutic process and outcome. In C. R. Rogers and Rosalind F. Dymond (Eds.), *Psychotherapy and personality change.* Chicago: Univer. of Chicago Press, 1954. Pp. 99-108.

Shoben, E. J., Jr. Psychotherapy as a problem in learning theory. *Psychol. Bull.,* 1949, *46,* 366-392.

Shoben, E. J., Jr. Some observations on psychotherapy and the learning process. In O. H. Mowrer (Ed.), *Psychotherapy: Theory and research.* New York: Ronald, 1953. Pp. 120-139.

Smith, W. Social adjustment and interpersonal perception. In J. McV. Hunt (Ed.), Interpersonal perception and interpersonal relationships in therapeutic counseling. Technical Report No. 1, 1960, Univer. of Illinois, ONR Contract Nonr-1834 (11), Office of Naval Research.

Snyder, W. U. The psychotherapy research program at the Pennsylvania State University. *J. counsel. Psychol.,* 1957, *4,* 9-14.

Snyder, W. U. *The psychotherapy relationship.* New York: Macmillan, 1961.

Soper, D. W., and Combs, A. W. The helping relationship as seen by teachers and therapists. *J. consult. Psychol.,* 1962, *26,* 288.

Stoler, N. Client likability as a variable in the study of psychotherapy. *U. Wisc. Psychiat. Inst. Bull.,* 1961, *1* (No. 11).

Streitfeld, J. W. Expressed acceptance of self and others by psychotherapists. *J. consult. Psychol.,* 1959, *23,* 435-441.

Strupp, H. H. The psychotherapist's contribution to the treatment process. *Behav. Sci.,* 1958, *3,* 34-67.

Strupp, H. H. *Psychotherapists in action.* New York: Grune & Stratton, 1960.

Strupp, H. H. Psychotherapy. *Annu. Rev. Psychol.,* 1962, *13,* 445-478.

Strupp, H. H., and Williams, J. V. Some determinants of clinical evaluations of different psychiatrists. *Arch. gen. Psychiat.,* 1960, *2,* 434-440.

Sundland, D. H., and Barker, E. N. The orientation of psychotherapists. *J. consult. Psychol.,* 1962, *26,* 201-212.

Thomas, E., Polansky, N., and Kounin, J. The expected behavior of a potentially helpful person. *Hum. Relat.,* 1955, *8,* 165-174.

Truax, C. B. The process of group psychotherapy: Relationships between hypothesized therapeutic conditions and interpersonal exploration. *Psychol. Monogr.,* 1961, *75* (7, Whole No. 511). (a)

Truax, C. B. Therapeutic conditions. *U. Wisc. Psychiat. Inst. Bull.,* 1961, *1* (No. 10c). (b)

Truax, C. B. Constructive personality change in schizophrenic patients receiving high-condition therapy, low-condition therapy, and no therapy. Unpublished manuscript, Univer. of Wisconsin, Wisconsin Psychiatric Institute, 1962.

Van der Veen, F. The perception by clients and by judges of the conditions offered by the therapist in the therapy relationship. *U. Wisc. Psychiat. Inst. Bull.,* 1961, *1* (No. 10).

Vogel, J. L. Authoritarianism in the therapeutic relationship. *J. consult. Psychol.,* 1961, *25,* 102-108.

Wallach, M. S., and Strupp, H. H. Psychotherapists' clinical judgments and attitudes toward patients. *J. consult. Psychol.,* 1960, *24,* 316-323.

To Care or Not To Care

It is not a question of choosing between an objective set of techniques and a significantly meaningful therapeutic relationship. Rather, they should come together as a dynamic unit. Although the research literature dealing with the psychotherapeutic relationship has yielded results of questionable validity, in general it shows that it does not appear to be useful to separate the technique from the particular therapist.

Of special interest is Gardner's statement that *"personal commitment to the significance of helping relationships may be a more pertinent variable than experiences per se. Professional training does not seem to be especially relevant."* Professional training *adds nothing* to an ability to create a helping relationship. It is the personal commitment that proves to be important. If we do not believe in the possibility of constructive personality change, therapy must be a situation in which the "blind are leading the blind."

Another point continues to emerge: "Psychotherapy may be only a variation of good interpersonal relationships in general." This may account for (as was mentioned earlier) the facts that so many people get by without formal therapy, and that control groups improve at a rate equal to, or better than, treatment groups. However, this point should not be interpreted to mean that the relationship ought to be the sole focal point of therapy. On the contrary, it would appear that there are two phases in therapy: the first phase, in which the goal is client self-exploration, and the means for reaching it is the therapeutic relationship; and the second phase, in which the therapist seeks a direction out of the client's difficulty, a direction which hopefully translates to action on the part of the client.

Grossberg (1964) in the following article reviews the nonrelationship area of systematic techniques and gathers a large body of evidence to support the joining of clinical practice with basic science.

BEHAVIOR THERAPY: MORE OR LESS *

John M. Grossberg

Serious efforts by psychologists to apply the rigorous standards of science to the study of psychotherapy have increased since World War II. The use of clinical and other psychologists in clinical capacities during the war due to the pressing need for therapeutic assistance may have instigated this interest.

Earlier attempts to integrate Watsonian behaviorism and the Pavlovian position with personality variables were essentially translations of the facts of personality behavior into the new language of conditioning. This "dictionary construction" (Eysenck, 1957) has moved ahead rapidly in the last 15 years, although the Russian position that neurosis was caused by actual cerebral pathology (Pavlov, 1941) did not retain many influential adherents among English-speaking psychologists. How-

* Behavior therapy: *A review. Psychological Bulletin,* 1964, *62,* 73-88. Reprinted by permission of author and publisher. This paper is a portion of Technical Report No. 1, Grant RD-892P-63 from the Vocational Rehabilitation Administration, United States Department of Health, Education, and Welfare, to the Western Behavioral Sciences Institute, La Jolla, California.

The author wishes to thank E. G. Aiken for his helpful comments during the preparation of this paper.

ever, many accepted and retained the concept of a disturbed central state which was manifested in observable neurotic behavior. This notion is also basic to psychodynamic personality theories, as exemplified by Dollard and Miller's (1950) comprehensive translation of psychoanalysis in terms of Hull's behavior theory, where internal drives in conflict are said to produce a variety of maladaptive behaviors called symptoms. Translations such as this have helped to reduce vague psychodynamic terms to behavioral language, furnishing a common ground for practitioners and experimenters. However, they have also served to perpetuate psychodynamic therapies unchanged and have failed to provide new or more effective therapeutic procedures.

Recent investigators (Kanfer, 1961; Krasner, 1958) have regarded psychotherapy as a verbal interaction process in which verbal inter-behavior is subject to lawful modification by appropriate reinforcing operations, extinction procedures, and the like, in no way qualitatively different from other behavior. However, while generally rejecting a dualistic central conflict-peripheral symptom model, some dubious relics of psychodynamic thinking remain. These include the assumption that changes in verbal behavior are necessary prerequisites for improvements in other maladaptive behaviors (Krasner, 1955; Metzner, 1961), or that it is important to talk about things you do not want to, make more affect statements, or recall early memories (Greenspoon, 1962). Although it is well established that there is systematic modification of verbal behavior in psychotherapy (Bandura, 1961; Frank, 1961) and experimental verbal conditioning analogues of psychotherapy (Greenspoon, 1962), both Greenspoon and Kanfer (1961) have concluded that there is very little evidence for the transfer of interview effects to other behaviors. Zax and Klein (1960) reviewed the literature on behavior changes following psychotherapy and concluded that there was no good evidence relating verbal behavior changes during therapy to behavioral changes in the family and community. Bandura (1961) indicated that current research on verbal conditioning without awareness casts serious doubt on the value of therapies whose primary aim was the development of insight, and Hobbs (1962) concluded that insight is either independent of personality change or an occasional by-product of such change.

Although investigators in this area have focused on the direct effects of therapist verbalizations on patient behavior rather than on some central process, we have seen that elaborate verbal exchange is often assumed to be an important part of treating maladaptive behavior, without strong supporting evidence. In the last 15 years, Eysenck, Wolpe, and their students have departed radically from psychodynamic and verbal insight assumptions and their related procedures for modifying maladaptive behavior. Eysenck (1952, 1961) reviewed studies of the recovery rate from neurotic disorders claimed for psychoanalysis and other dynamic psychotherapies as compared with custodial treatment and/or nonspecific treatment. He concluded that psychodynamic therapies were no more successful than the comparison control procedures, and questioned the effectiveness of traditional therapy in producing beneficial behavior changes, stating in effect that he failed to see the Emperor's new clothes. Levitt (1957) reached a similar conclusion after evaluating outpatient child psychotherapy studies.

These findings led Eysenck and Wolpe to reject traditional psychodynamic approaches to treatment. Instead Eysenck (1960b) defined neurotic behavior as maladaptive habits formed through a process of conditioning and capable of being extinguished through several techniques of demonstrated effectiveness in the laboratory. There is no complex, no illness, and treatment is directed entirely to the symptoms, as distinguished from psychotherapy with its stress on hypothetical underlying complexes and disease processes. Wolpe (1958) proposed a similar view, that neurosis is persistent maladaptive learned behavior with a prominent anxiety component, acquired in anxiety-generating circumstances.

Skinner (1953) also attacked the assumption that behavior disorders were a reflection of some internal conflict or sickness. He termed the conversion of disordered behavior into a thing labeled "neurosis" an explanatory fiction, which has had several unfortunate consequences. It has encouraged the therapist to avoid specifying the behavior to be corrected, and by suggesting a single cause for a variety of maladaptive behaviors it has implied a uniformity not to be found in the data. More serious from a humanitarian viewpoint, it has fostered the belief that inner causes must be extirpated or purged, leading to electrical, surgical, or pharmacological assaults of questionable benefit to the person (Gordon, 1948; Reider, 1955). In Skinner's view, motivation does not reside in the person, so that conceptions such as insight, the lifting of repressions, making the unconscious conscious, etc., are unnecessary for behavior change. The idea that people learn to do things because they "want to" is discarded, and the problem becomes one of altering the reinforcing environment so that adequate behaviors are maintained, effective new behaviors learned, and inadequate behaviors extinguished (Michael and Meyerson, 1962).

While Eysenck, Wolpe, and Skinner are in accord with respect to the emphasis on direct behavior modification as the focus of remedial efforts, Eysenck and Wolpe employ a Hullian behavior theory with constructs such as inhibition and drive which are rejected by Skinner. Although this theoretical divergence is of great importance, it is beyond the scope of this paper.

Behavior therapy is derived from the rejection of traditional psychodynamic personality theories, and consists of the application of the principles of modern learning theory to the treatment of behavior disorders. Theorists who have described behavior therapies (Bandura, 1961; Dunlap, 1932; Eysenck, 1960a; Metzner, 1961; Skinner, 1953; Wolpe, 1958) have often used different terms for similar procedures. Descriptive terms for treatment procedures tend to be confounded with the learning mechanisms involved in behavior modification. In this paper, the following classification is used:

1. Aversion therapy. (a) Aversive stimuli are presented in conjunction with the elicitation of a maladaptive response (counterconditioning or punishment, Bandura; aversion therapy, Eysenck; conditioning avoidance response, Wolpe). (b) Aversive stimuli are reduced or terminated upon the occurrence of a response whose low frequency constitutes a behavior deficit (negative reinforcement, Skinner; conditioned anxiety-relief responses, Wolpe).
2. Negative practice. The maladaptive response is elicited repeatedly and frequently (extinction, Bandura; negative practice, Dunlap; conditioned inhibition, Eysenck; reactive inhibition, Metzner).
3. Operant conditioning. Reinforcing stimuli are presented which increase the frequency of responses whose low frequency constitutes a behavior deficit (reward, Bandura; positive conditioning, Eysenck; operant conditioning, Skinner).
4. Reinforcement withdrawal. Positive reinforcing stimuli are withdrawn following the occurrence of a maladaptive response (extinction, Bandura).
5. Desensitization. Stimuli evoking maladaptive responses are repeatedly presented at low intensities which do not provoke a full-blown response. Stimulus intensity is systematically increased until even high intensities no longer evoke maladaptive responses (counterconditioning, Bandura; reciprocal inhibition, Eysenck; graded stimulus situations, Metzner; reciprocal inhibition with systematic desensitization, Wolpe).

In this review, maladaptive behaviors are divided into neurotic and psychotic disorders for purposes of convenient communication. Within these broad categories, the cases are organized around the dominant maladaptive behavior treated by behavior therapy. Wherever possible, such clusters of cases are grouped according to standard psychiatric nomenclature. The terms *fear* and *anxiety* are used interchangeably.

NEUROTIC DISORDERS

Phobic Reaction

The most widely used and successful behavior therapy for phobias was developed by Wolpe (1958). It is a desensitization procedure based on the assumption that relaxation responses are antagonistic to fear. Therapist and patient construct a ranked list of fear-evoking stimulus situations. The patient is then trained to relax, often while hypnotized. He is then told to visualize the weakest fear situation on the list. After a few trials it can usually be visualized without fear, whereupon the next situation in the hierarchy is visualized. Eventually relaxation responses come to be attached not only to all visualized situations on the list but also to their real-life counterparts. The induced relaxation is said to reciprocally inhibit the fear, which extinguishes upon repetitions of the procedure. Wolpe occasionally used an anxiety-relief procedure in which he administered an electric shock to the forearm which the patient terminated by saying "calm" when it reached unbearable intensity. Patients reported that the repetition of calm, which had been associated with fear/pain cessation, was often helpful in reducing fears. Wolpe reported that 90 percent of 210 patients treated by such methods were cured or much improved. Of the 210 cases, 135 were termed anxiety reactions, including phobias, so the exact number of cured phobics is unknown.

Desensitization methods similar to this have been very successful in treating fear of small animals (Freeman and Kendrick, 1960; Jones, 1924a, 1924b; Lang and Lazovik, 1963; Lazarus, 1959; Lazarus and Abramovitz, 1962; Lazarus and Rachman, 1957; Weinberg and Zaslove, 1963), fear of the dark (Holmes, 1936), fear of height (Holmes, 1936; Lazarus, 1961), fear of cars (Lazarus, 1959; Wolpe, 1962a, 1962b), agoraphobia (Meyer, 1957; Terhune, 1949; Wolpe, 1958), fear of hospitals and injections (Lazarus and Rachman, 1957; Rachman, 1959), and fear of public speaking (Grossberg, 1963). Meyer and Gelder (1963), however, were unsuccessful with agoraphobics and reported one of the few instances of symptom substitution in the behavior therapy literature. Malleson (1959) reported that instructions to practice an examination fear led to its rapid extinction.

Anxiety Reaction

Many patients Wolpe (1958) cured with desensitization complained of pervasive rather than specific anxiety. Wolpe (1961) described the successful extension of desensitization therapy to problems such as feelings of guilt and devaluation. Other cures of anxiety reactions by desensitization and relaxation were reported by Haugen, Dixon, and Dickel (1958) and Lazarus and Rachman (1957).

Gross Stress Reaction (Combat)

During World War II desensitization was successfully used to reduce exaggerated startle responses to noise, with the presentation of low intensity sounds which were gradually made louder until maladaptive responses extinguished (McLaughlin and Millar, 1941; Rudolf, 1961; Saul, Rome, and Leuser, 1946; Schwartz, 1945).

Sexual Disorders

Rachman (1961) reviewed the recent literature on behavior therapies for sexual disorders and his data are included in this section. Freund (1960) reported that aversion therapy with the nauseant drugs, apomorphine and emetine, was no more successful than conventional psychotherapy with 67 male homosexuals. Oswald (1962) failed to help another homosexual with these drugs, although Max (1935) reported a cure with electric shock as the aversive stimulus. Clark (1963), Oswald (1962), and Raymond (1956) used apomorphine successfully to cure four of five fetishists. Glynn and Harper (1961) and Lavin, Thorpe, Barker, Blakemore, and Conway (1961) used apomorphine aversion conditioning to cure male transvestites although Oswald (1962) reported a failure with this procedure. Aversion procedures apparently yield equivocal results, and the picture is further complicated by the fact that apomorphine alone, without aversion conditioning trials, is used to treat neuroses (Kalinowsky and Hoch, 1961).

Dunlap (1928, 1932) reported that negative practice procedures had cured homosexuality but furnished no details. Stevenson and Wolpe (1960) cured two homosexual men by verbally reinforcing assertiveness which aided them in becoming more aggressive with women. Wolpe's systematic desensitization seems to be more successful than aversion methods, with many cures reported for impotence and frigidity (Lazarus, 1963; Lazarus and Rachman, 1957; Wolpe, 1960), and voyeurism and exhibitionism (Wolpe, 1958), although Bond and Hutchison (1960) were only partly successful in treating a chronic exhibitionist.

Conversion Reactions

SENSORIMOTOR DISORDERS. Hilgard and Marquis (1940) and Sears and Cohen (1933) used classical conditioning methods to reinstate feeling and movement in two women with functional disorders of the arm and hand. Cohen, Hilgard, and Wendt (1933) and Malmo, Davis, and Barza (1952) reinstated seeing and hearing, respectively, by similar procedures. Brady and Lind (1961) cured a functionally blind man by operant conditioning in which his use of visual cues was systematically reinforced. However, the role of conditioning seems confounded with suggestion effects in these cases. For example, in the Malmo, Davis, and Barza case the patient was emphatically told that the conditioning procedure would restore her hearing, and there were distinct opportunities for such effects in the other cases.

ANOREXIA NERVOSA.   White (1959) cured a 5-year-old girl who stopped eating following the death of her father who used to help feed her. Successive approximations to independent eating were instituted during play therapy, beginning with sham eating at doll tea parties, followed by the eating of doll portions of food. Bachrach, Erwin, and Mohr (1965) reinstated eating in a woman whose weight had fallen from 118 to 47 pounds by making reinforcements such as visits, books, music, and TV viewing contingent upon her eating.

Obsessive Compulsive Reaction

Dunlap (1930) and Walton (1960c) used negative practice to cure obsessive thoughts of illness and compulsive handwashing. Bevan (1960) used desensitization to eliminate obsessive thoughts of world destruction in a housewife. Lazarus (1958) cured a man with a handicapping compulsion to recheck his work by suggesting under hypnosis that rechecking aroused great fear which was immediately reduced by leaving the task to go on to another. Wolpe (1958) reported two effective "thought stopping" procedures based on the therapist's shouting, "Stop!" whenever the patient signaled that he was experiencing an obsessive thought.

Enuresis

Jones (1960a) reviewed the physiology, psychology, and treatment of nocturnal enuresis, with emphasis on the bell conditioning treatment devised by Mowrer (1938). Jones cited 15 studies in which this treatment was applied to 1446 enuretics, with a total of 76 percent cures and 14 percent failures. Data for "markedly improved" cases are not included since some authors classified these as cures while others retained this as a separate category. There were no reports of symptom substitution, although most investigators reported beneficial personality changes. This suggests that the other adjustment difficulties often mentioned in conjunction with enuresis are probably secondary to the enuresis. The conditioning procedure appears to be very successful, especially in view of the fact that many of the cases were hard core enuretics who had failed to respond to other treatments. There is some evidence that the cure rate could be further improved by using partial reinforcement, more widely spaced trials, and overlearning (Eysenck, 1963).

Jones (1956) cured a woman with excessive urinary frequency by allowing her to observe her own bladder pressure reading which preceded the urge to urinate. He then introduced increasing amounts of liquid directly into her bladder while manipulating the pressure gauge so that it always read below her urinary threshold.

Alcoholism

To date, some form of aversive procedure has been the sole behavior therapy for alcoholism. Franks (1958), in a comprehensive review of the literature, criticized those who have used aversive methods for their ignorance of learning theory, especially the facts regarding the necessary relationships between conditioned and unconditioned stimuli and responses. In addition, he cited the lack of uniformity of procedures, the dearth of technical details, and general failure to use noxious stimuli other than nauseant drugs, such as electric shock, which would afford more stimulus control and has fewer side effects. The large sample studies cited by Franks reported average total abstinence rates of approximately 50 percent several years after treatment, which is no better than the recovery rate reported for religious conversion, social therapy, or standard psychotherapy (Carlson, 1944). However, aversion therapy seems to be shorter and less expensive than many of these other treatments.

Speech Disorders

The unsystematic use of gradual approximations to adequate speaking is very common in many areas of speech retraining. With stuttering, most behavioral approaches have used some form of negative practice. Lehner (1954), in a review of negative practice methods, concluded that results were best in habit residual cases where the pressures that originally produced stuttering are absent, and where the patient wants speech improvement without more general behavior modification. Jones (1955) demonstrated that decreases in stuttering with repetition was a form of experimental extinction, opening the way for learning interpretations of this behavior. Sheehan (1951) and Wischner (1950) proposed similar learning theories of stuttering based on a response conflict model, and Goldiamond (1962) presented an operant conditioning theory. Shane (1955) found that a loud masking noise decreased ongoing stuttering. Cherry and Sayers (1956) and Cherry, Sayers, and Marland (1955) confirmed this and reported that "speech shadowing" practice in which the patient parroted material read or spoken by the therapist led to clinical improvement. Walton and Black (1958) cured a man who stuttered severely during telephone calls, using the shadowing method. Lazarus and Rachman (1957) reported a cure with systematic desensitization, and Flanagan, Goldiamond, and Azrin (1958) decreased stuttering frequency by having each stuttered word produce a brief blast of loud noise. Bloodstein (1949) reviewed and classified the many diverse techniques which successfully reduced stuttering. His paper clearly illustrates the dangers of using therapeutic effectiveness to verify theoretical formulations. He reported that stuttering is often reduced or abolished when the communicative aspects of speech are reduced, as in speech shadowing; when the patient talks to an understanding or helpful person; or with therapists who have a sincere and unbounded faith in their own particular method, whatever it is.

APHONIA. Bangs and Freidinger (1949, 1950) cured an aphonic girl and a woman by requiring graded vocal activities that were made more and more similar to voiced social speaking. Walton and Black (1960) cured an aphonic woman by changing the length of vocal practice sessions to reward voice volume increases and punish volume decreases, and by practice in vocal tasks approximating everyday life conversation.

Special Symptom Reactions

Dunlap (1932) first reported that the negative practice of tics led to their abolition, and this method was successfully employed by Ernest and Jones (Jones, 1960b), Walton (1961), and Yates (1958a). Barrett (1962) reduced tic frequency by having a patient listen to recorded music which was automatically interrupted by each tic movement.

Liversedge and Sylvester (1955; Sylvester and Liversedge, 1960) reviewed history and treatment of occupational cramps, primarily writer's cramp, and built several retraining devices which delivered an electric shock whenever writing practice was disrupted by spasms or tremor. With this form of aversion therapy they cured 24 of 39 patients. Beech (1960) cured three of four patients with negative practice of the cramp or systematic desensitization.

Dunlap (1930, 1932) reduced the frequency of nailbiting and thumbsucking in "many" cases with negative practice although complete extinction was rare since motivation declined along with habit frequency. Baer (1962) reduced thumbsucking frequency in three boys by interrupting movie cartoons each time the thumb was sucked.

Kuehner (1956) cured "several" cases of teeth gnashing during sleep by a posthypnotic suggestion that the patient would awaken when the mastication muscles contracted strongly. Williams (1959) extinguished bedtime screaming tantrums in a 21-month-old boy by leaving the boy's room and shutting the bedroom door. Zimmerman and Zimmerman (1962) used operant conditioning to eliminate maladaptive classroom behavior in two psychiatric inpatient boys. The teacher withheld attention until adaptive behavior was emitted, and then gave generous social reinforcement, resulting in marked academic and social improvements. While these last two reports seem to describe nothing other than what some parents and teachers have done for generations, nevertheless it is important to demonstrate that there are general psychological principles underlying successful behavior modifications.

Slack (1960) used an operant procedure to establish and maintain regular therapy contacts with highly resistant juvenile delinquents. Initially he tolerated irregular attendance and then gradually shaped regular punctual attendance by reinforcing it with money, food, cigarettes, and occasional bonuses. Slack does not regard this method as therapy but rather as a means of establishing sufficient contact so that the patient can learn that help is available if he wants it.

Miscellaneous Disorders

Walton (1960b) cured a woman whose excessive scratching aggravated a severe skin rash by instructing her fiance and family to omit the excessive attention which seemed to reinforce this response. Walton (1960a) relieved a case of bronchial asthma in an inhibited man whose attacks seemed related to a demanding wife, family, and business associates. After desensitization and assertiveness training, social relationships and asthma improved markedly.

Efron (1957) used stimulus substitution therapeutically to eliminate chronic uncinate grand mal convulsions. After Efron discovered that an aromatic odor inhibited the woman's fits, he was able to train her to substitute looking at a bracelet for sniffing the aromatic substance, thus effecting a conditioned inhibition of the fits. Rubinstein (1931) cured two morphine addicts by associating a neutral stimulus with daily morphine injections, and then gradually reducing the concentration of drug in the injections. Kalinowsky and Hoch (1961, p. 214) reported that Soviet psychiatrists had been moderately successful using a similar stimulus substitution procedure to reduce the amount of insulin required to induce coma in treating schizophrenics.

PSYCHOTIC DISORDERS

Adult Psychosis

Although behavior therapy applied to psychotics has resulted in beneficial behavior changes such as increasing sociability, decreased delusional talk, etc., few investigators have reported hospital discharges attributable to treatment. Operant conditioning procedures were used in the majority of studies.

Fuller (1949) operantly conditioned and extinguished an arm-raising response in a bedfast vegetative idiot, using a sugar-milk solution as reinforcement. Peters and Jenkins (1954) used fudge to reinforce the solving of increasingly complex problems, in an attempt to alter schizophrenic rigidity, and found that their experimental group was granted significantly more hospital privileges. Lindsley (1956, 1960) devised an apparatus and procedure for the experimental analysis and control of psychotic behavior. The patient was seated before a sort of vending machine containing a plunger which, when manipulated, could be made to deliver various reinforcing stimuli. In this way Lindsley studied the behavioral effects of different reinforcing stimuli, reinforcement schedules, drugs, hallucinations, and psychotherapy. King, Armitage, and Tilton (1960) used a similar apparatus with withdrawn schizophrenics in an attempt to elicit more social behavior and environmental interest, and noted significant improvements in ward behavior ratings.

Ayllon and Michael (1959) successfully used operant conditioning and extinction procedures to eliminate specific disruptive behaviors such as excessive floor scrubbing, newspaper hoarding, and pestering visits to the nurses' station. Ayllon and Haughton (1962) eliminated eating problems requiring excessive staff time and effort in 30 of 32 patients by denying access to the dining hall to patients who did not enter during a brief time period. Ayllon (1963) used similar procedures to eliminate food stealing, towel hoarding, and wearing excessive clothing in another psychotic patient. Isaacs, Thomas, and Goldiamond (1960) reinstated talking in two mute catatonics by reinforcing successive approximations to speech with chewing gum. Rickard, Dignan, and Horner (1960) increased the amount of rational speech in a verbose psychotic man by systematically manipulating the therapist's interest responses to his speech content. This man's improvement was still evident 2 years later (Rickard and Dinoff, 1962). Wickland (1963) assigned his patients tasks which more and more closely approximated independent living and working, and found that 40 of 41 chronic schizophrenic women in this progam were released from the hospital and were supporting themselves adequately.

Cowden and Ford (1962) found systematic desensitization successful in helping one of two phobic paranoid schizophrenics. Walton (1960d) cured a schizophrenic man with exaggerated fears of women and social relationships by practice in tasks requiring increasing social contacts with women and others, although the patient's history of relapses suggested that his cure might be short-lived. Thompson and Bielinski (1953) reported that six alcoholics whose psychosis preceded their alcoholism were cured of both disorders after drug aversion therapy.

Child Psychosis

Ferster and DeMyer (1961, 1962) described an operant conditioning apparatus and procedure similar to Lindsley's, consisting of many coin-operated vending machines, which they used to analyze and control autistic children's behavior. They reported that these children did the same things as normal children but much less frequently. Various reinforcing operations were successful in widening the children's narrow behavior repertoires. Ferster (1961) presented a detailed analysis of autistic behavior and those factors relevant to its acquisition and maintenance. Wolf, Mees, and Risley (1963) used operant conditioning methods with a 3-year-old boy to eliminate injurious tantrums and bedtime disturbances, and to train him to wear eyeglasses which were needed to prevent permanent eye damage.

DISCUSSION

Behavior therapies have been most successful when applied to neurotic disorders with specific behavioral manifestations. Desensitization procedures have been successfully applied to the greatest variety of neurotic problems, while therapeutic stimulus substitution has rarely been used. Aversion therapy has produced disappointing results in alcoholism and sexual disorders, although more successful in treating occupational cramps. Negative practice procedures have proven most helpful in treating stuttering and tics. Operant conditioning procedures have been used most frequently with psychotics but as yet there are few reports of clinical recoveries. On the basis of current evidence, behavior therapy appears to be a superior treatment for phobic reactions and enuresis, and definitely worthwhile with selected individual cases of other disorders.

Many psychologists who are interested in behavior therapy have abandoned traditional depth psychotherapies because of their questionable effectiveness (Astin, 1961; Eysenck, 1952, 1961; Levitt, 1957), their basic assumption of a scientifically unacceptable mind-body dualism (Kantor, 1953; Rotter, 1954; Skinner, 1953), and their tenacious devotion to a poorly defined explanatory system which is made to encompass all past, present, and future human experience. Many advocates of the psychodynamic viewpoint, on the other hand, regard behavior therapy as the result of a naive pragmatism which overlooks or ignores the basic therapeutic agent in its procedures, suggestion, and transference (Rosenzweig, 1954). Successful behavior therapy is criticized as palliative and superficial at best, and possibly harmful through symptom substitution (Bookbinder, 1962). There are also objections to the direct, deliberate, and systematic manipulation of the patient's behavior as authoritarian and antihumanistic (for a discussion of this issue, see Bandura, 1961). These criticisms are discussed below.

SUGGESTION-TRANSFERENCE. It is not logically possible to prove the absence of an effect such as suggestion in eliminating maladaptive behavior, or that substitute symptoms do not occur. However, assuming that suggestion-transference effects are behavior modifications resulting from some aspect of the therapist-patient interaction and patient expectations, rather than the specific treatment procedure, we can then discuss behavior therapy procedures to see what opportunities they afford for such effects. Carlson (1944) discussed the many opportunities for suggestion effects in the ritualistic aversion therapy seances for alcoholism, and his criticism is supported by the finding that outcome rates are approximately the same for widely different treatment methods. Bloodstein (1949) indicated that stuttering frequency may be reduced effectively by numerous novel procedures, complicating the role of behavior therapy in this disorder. Classical conditioning methods applied to conversion reactions also offered many opportunities for suggestion. However, the suggestion-transference hypothesis receives little support in the remaining studies, particularly the desensitization literature. Behavior therapy has often been a last resort, and since patients have previously received psychotherapy or other treatment, there would have been ample prior opportunity for flight into health. Some of the successes reported for various therapies probably represent such suggestion cures. Behavior therapies are generally brief and straightforward, with fewer departures from conventional social interaction than traditional psychotherapies, offering a less awesome atmosphere for suggestion cures. Modifications in maladaptive behavior during behavior therapy are generally gradual and regular rather than sudden and dramatic, and resemble the response curves obtained during acquisition or extinction of conditioned responses. Wolpe (1962b), in treating a phobic patient, attempted to omit all activities which might give grounds for a suggestion interpretation. He substituted a medical student therapist for himself for five sessions with no disruption of desensitization, and cited the fact that decreases in fear only occurred during desensitization sessions but not in the long intervals between sessions. Meyer and Gelder (1963) and Wolpe (1958, 1961) make the important point that desensitization only alleviates those phobias that are being treated, but other coexisting phobias remain at high strength, indicating a specific treatment effect. Controlled studies by Lang and Lazovik (1963) and Lazarus (1961) contribute additional evidence that desensitization rather than hypnosis or relaxation alone led to improvements. Thus, general consideration of behavior therapy procedures as well as specific investigations of the role of suggestion in behavior therapy support the conclusion that elimination of maladaptive behavior is probably related to the specific method of treatment.

SYMPTOM SUBSTITUTION.   According to psychoanalytic formulations, maladaptive behavior is a derivative of the conflict between the contradictory impulses striving for discharge and defensive forces. This makes it impossible to discharge tension in the usual way, so tension accumulates, and the defensive system is overpowered by excitation, producing distorted discharges which are symptoms. It follows that treatment which leaves the central conflict unresolved will be unsuccessful, and substitute symptoms are expected. This issue is important not only because of the empirical question of the effectiveness of symptomatic treatment and patient welfare, but because it tests a hypothesis directly derived from psychoanalytic theory, thus bearing on the utility of this aspect of the theory (Eysenck, 1960a; Yates, 1958b). The overwhelming evidence of the present review is that therapy directed at elimination of maladaptive behavior ("symptoms") is successful and long-lasting. Substitute symptoms were reported in two cases of all those surveyed (Lazarus and Rachman, 1957; Meyer and Gelder, 1963), although a number of investigators with psychoanalytic backgrounds were particularly sensitive to this problem. Unfortunately, psychotherapists seem to have stressed the hypothetical dangers of only curing the symptoms, while ignoring the very real dangers of the harm that is done by not curing them.

Bookbinder (1962), in a discussion of this issue from a psychodynamic viewpoint, stated that depth psychotherapy treats neurotic predispositions and reorganizes the character structure, rather than manipulating individual symptoms, and is therefore of wider and more permanent benefit. He also criticized behavior therapists for an overly narrow definition of symptoms, and suggested that subtle substitute symptoms such as ways of relating to others, undesirable mood states, and pathological ways of handling one's internal life may be overlooked. He cited several studies in which severe pathological reactions were precipitated by experimental hypnotic symptom removal or medical treatment of ulcers, ulcerative colitis, and asthma. Bookbinder suggested that since most behavior therapists have dealt with neurotic disorders which are painful or inconvenient, perhaps substitution is more likely in severe conditions which pose a danger to life. This is an interesting empirical question, but present evidence indicates that behavior therapy is seldom followed by additional behavior problems or relapse, although symptom substitution may be a danger in inadequate or improper psychodynamic psychotherapy or the medical treatment of psychosomatic disorders.

MANIPULATION OF THE PATIENT. Behavior therapy has been criticized for mechanical manipulation of the patient, but there is abundant research evidence of subtle, unintentional therapist manipulation, especially of verbal behavior in dynamic psychotherapies (Bandura, 1961; Frank, 1961; Greenspoon, 1962). If there is agreement that all psychological treatment involves a lawful interpersonal influence process, then objections must be to the kind of manipulation or influence involved in behavior therapy, rather than to manipulation per se.

It is unlikely that substantial numbers of traditional psychotherapists will begin to apply behavior therapies, regardless of their demonstrated economy or success. Many mature psychotherapists are personally and professionally committed to personality theories and treatment methods diametrically opposed to those of behavior therapy. According to Frank (1961), evocative therapies which stress self-knowledge and insight appeal to well-educated people who place a high value on self-knowledge and verbal skill, while directive methods have low status for this group. Hobbs (1962) pointed out that insight and understanding appeal to us as central mechanisms in psychotherapy because of our culture's strong commitment to rationality in problem solving. Behavior therapists do not subscribe to a central conflict, symptom derivative model, and therefore insight or the patient's knowledge of the origin of his problems are extraneous to treatment. It is on the proving grounds of the training institutions and laboratories that behavior therapy will compete with traditional theories and practices for the interest of critical young psychologists. Its initial successes will probably be tempered by later reports, as is so often the case with any treatment innovation. There are too few controlled studies in the behavior therapy literature, and there is an obvious need for comparing directly the effectiveness of traditional therapies and behavior therapy with various kinds of maladaptive behaviors. Behavior therapists too often seem prematurely committed to outmoded or oversimplified versions of learning theory, with little clear connection between the theory and practice (Rotter, 1960). Meanwhile, this continues to be an extremely active research area. A new journal has been launched to report work in this field, Wolpe (1961) has been working at the extension of behavior therapy to additional less circumscribed behavior disorders, and others[1] (Lang and Lazovik, 1963) are investigating confounded variables in the desensitization procedure. The demonstrated success of behavior therapy has created challenging new possibilities for the highly effective treatment of behavior disorders and the fruitful marriage of basic science and practice in psychology.

REFERENCES

Astin, A. The functional autonomy of psychotherapy. *Amer. Psychologist,* 1961, *16,* 75-79.

Ayllon, T. Intensive treatment of psychotic behavior by stimulus satiation and food reinforcement. *Behav. Res. Ther.,* 1963, *1,* 53-61.

Ayllon, T., and Haughton, E. Control of the behavior of schizophrenic patients by food. *J. exp. Anal. Behav.,* 1962, *5,* 343-352.

Ayllon, T., and Michael, J. The psychiatric nurse as a behavioral engineer. *J. exp. Anal. Behav.,* 1959, *2,* 323-334.

Bachrach, A. J., Erwin, W., and Mohr, J. P. The control of eating behavior

[1] Beatrice Ashem, personal communication, 1963.

in an anorexic by operant conditioning techniques. In L. Ullmann and L. Krasner (Eds.), *Case studies in behavior modification.* New York: Holt, Rinehart & Winston, 1965.

Baer, D. M. Laboratory control of thumbsucking by withdrawal and re-presentation of reinforcement. *J. exp. Anal. Behav.,* 1962, *5,* 525-528.

Bandura, A. Psychotherapy as a learning process. *Psychol. Bull.,* 1961, *58,* 143-157.

Bangs, J. L., and Freidinger, A. Diagnosis and treatment of a case of hysterical aphonia in a thirteen-year-old girl. *J. speech hear. Disord.,* 1949, *14,* 312-317.

Bangs, J. L., and Freidinger, A. A case of hysterical dysphonia in an adult. *J. speech hear. Disord.,* 1950, *15,* 316-323.

Barrett, Beatrice. Reduction in rate of multiple tics by free operant conditioning methods. *J. nerv. ment. Dis.,* 1962, *135,* 187-195.

Beech, H. R. The symptomatic treatment of writer's cramp. In H. J. Eysenck (Ed.), *Behavior therapy and the neuroses.* New York: Pergamon Press, 1960. Pp. 349-376.

Bevan, J. R. Learning theory applied to the treatment of a patient with obsessional ruminations. In H. J. Eysenck (Ed.), *Behavior therapy and the neuroses.* New York: Pergamon Press, 1960. Pp. 165-169.

Bloodstein, O. Conditions under which stuttering is reduced or absent: A review of literature. *J. speech hear. Disord.,* 1949, *14,* 295-302.

Bond, I. K., and Hutchison, H. C. Application of reciprocal inhibition therapy to exhibitionism. *Canad. Med. Ass. J.,* 1960, *83,* 23-25.

Bookbinder, L. J. Simple conditioning vs. the dynamic approach to symptoms and symptom substitution: A reply to Yates. *Psychol. Rep.,* 1962, *10,* 71-77.

Brady, J. P., and Lind, D. L. Experimental analysis of hysterical blindness. *AMA Arch. gen. Psychiat.,* 1961, *4,* 331-339.

Carlson, A. J. The conditioned reflex therapy of alcohol addiction. *Quart. J. Stud. Alcohol,* 1944, *5,* 212-215.

Cherry, C., and Sayers, B. Experiments upon the total inhibition of stammering by external control, and some clinical results. *J. psychosom. Res.,* 1956, *1,* 233-246.

Cherry, C., Sayers, B., and Marland, P. M. Experiments on the complete suppression of stammering. *Nature, London,* 1955, *176,* 874-875.

Clark, D. F. Fetishism treated by negative conditioning. *Brit. J. Psychiat.,* 1963, *109,* 404-407.

Cohen, L. H., Hilgard, E. R., and Wendt, G. R. Sensitivity to light in a case of hysterical blindness studied by reinforcement-inhibition and conditioning methods. *Yale J. Biol. Med.,* 1933, *6,* 61-67.

Cowden, R. C., and Ford, L. I. Systematic desensitization with phobic schizophrenics. *Amer. J. Psychiat.,* 1962, *119,* 241-245.

Dollard, J., and Miller, N. E. *Personality and psychotherapy.* New York: McGraw-Hill, 1950.

Dunlap, K. A revision of the fundamental law of habit formation. *Science,* 1928, *67,* 360-362.

Dunlap, K. Repetition in the breaking of habits. *Scient. Mon.,* 1930, *30,* 66-70.

Dunlap, K. *Habits: Their making and unmaking.* New York: Liveright, 1932.

Efron, R. The conditioned inhibition of uncinate fits. *Brain,* 1957, *80,* 251-262.

Eysenck, H. J. The effects of psychotherapy: An evaluation. *J. consult. Psychol.,* 1952, *16,* 319-324.

Eysenck, H. J. *The dynamics of anxiety and hysteria.* New York: Praeger, 1957.

Eysenck, H. J. (Ed.) *Behavior therapy and the neuroses.* New York: Pergamon Press, 1960. (a)

Eysenck, H. J. Personality and behavior therapy. *Proc. Roy. Soc. Med.,* 1960, *53,* 504-508. (b)

Eysenck, H. J. The effects of psychotherapy. In H. J. Eysenck (Ed.), *Handbook of abnormal psychology.* New York: Basic Books, 1961. Pp. 697-725.

Eysenck, H. J. Behavior therapy, extinction, and relapse in neurosis. *Brit. J. Psychol.,* 1963, *109,* 12-18.

Ferster, C. B. Positive reinforcement and behavioral deficits of autistic children. *Child Develpm.,* 1961, *32,* 437-456.

Ferster, C. B., and DeMyer, M. K. The development of performance in autistic children in an automatically controlled environment. *J. chron. Dis.,* 1961, *13,* 312-345.

Ferster, C. B., and DeMyer, M. K. A method for the experimental analysis of the behavior of autistic children. *Amer. J. Orthopsychiat.,* 1962, *32,* 89-98.

Flanagan, B., Goldiamond, I., and Azrin, N. Operant stuttering: The control of stuttering behavior through response-contingent consequences. *J. exp. Anal. Behav.,* 1958, *1,* 173-178.

Frank, J. D. *Persuasion and healing.* Baltimore, Md.: Johns Hopkins Press, 1961.

Franks, C. M. Alcohol, alcoholism, and conditioning: A review of the literature and some theoretical considerations. *J. ment. Sci.,* 1958, *104,* 14-33.

Freeman, H. L., and Kendrick, D. C. A case of cat phobia. *Brit. med. J.,* 1960, *2,* 497-502.

Freund, K. Some problems in the treatment of homosexuality. In H. J. Eysenck (Ed.), *Behavior therapy and the neuroses.* New York: Pergamon Press, 1960. Pp. 312-326.

Fuller, P. R. Operant conditioning of a vegetative human organism. *Amer. J. Psychol.,* 1949, *62,* 587-590.

Glynn, J. D., and Harper, P. Behavior therapy in transvestism. *Lancet,* 1961, *1,* 619.

Goldiamond, I. The maintenance of ongoing fluent verbal behavior and stuttering. *J. Mathetics,* 1962, *1,* 57-95.

Gordon, H. L. Fifty shock therapy theories. *Milit. Surgeon,* 1948, *103,* 397-401.

Greenspoon, J. Verbal conditioning and clinical psychology. In A. J. Bachrach (Ed.), *Experimental foundations of clinical psychology*. New York: Basic Books, 1962.

Grossberg, J. M. Behavior therapy in a case of speech phobia ("stage fright"). Technical Report No. 3, 1963, Grant RD-892P-63, U. S. Dept. of Health, Education, and Welfare, Vocational Rehabilitation Administration.

Haugen, G. B., Dixon, H. H., and Dickel, H. A. *A therapy for anxiety tension reactions*. New York: Macmillan, 1958.

Hilgard, E. R., and Marquis, D. M. *Conditioning and learning*. New York: Appleton-Century-Crofts, 1940. Pp. 297-298.

Hobbs, N. Sources of gain in psychotherapy. *Amer. Psychologist*, 1962, *17*, 741-747.

Holmes, Florence B. An experimental investigation of a method of overcoming children's fears. *Child Develpm.*, 1936, *7*, 6-30.

Isaacs, W., Thomas, J., and Goldiamond, I. Application of operant conditioning to reinstate verbal behavior in psychotics. *J. speech hear. Disord.*, 1960, *25*, 8-12.

Jones, E. L. Explorations of experimental extinction and spontaneous recovery in stuttering. In W. Johnson (Ed.), *Stuttering in children and adults*. Minneapolis: Univer. of Minnesota Press, 1955. Pp. 226-231.

Jones, H. G. The application of conditioning and learning techniques to the treatment of a psychiatric patient. *J. abnorm. soc. Psychol.*, 1956, *52*, 414-420.

Jones, H. G. The behavioral treatment of enuresis nocturna. In H. J. Eysenck (Ed.), *Behavior therapy and the neuroses*. New York: Pergamon Press, 1960. Pp. 377-403. (a)

Jones, H. G. Continuation of Yates' treatment of a tiqueur. In H. J. Eysenck (Ed.), *Behavior therapy and the neuroses*. New York: Pergamon Press, 1960. Pp. 250-258. (b)

Jones, Mary C. The elimination of children's fears. *J. exp. Psychol.*, 1924, *7*, 382-390. (a)

Jones, Mary C. A laboratory study of fear: The case of Peter. *Pedag. Seminary*, 1924, *31*, 308-315. (b)

Kalinowsky, L. B., and Hoch, P. B. *Somatic treatments in psychiatry*. New York: Grune & Stratton, 1961.

Kanfer, F. H. Comments on learning in psychotherapy. *Psychol. Rep.*, 1961, 9 (Monogr. Suppl. No. 6), 681-699.

Kantor, J. R. *The logic of modern science*. Bloomington, Ind.: Principia Press, 1953.

King, G. F., Armitage, S. G., and Tilton, J. R. A therapeutic approach to schizophrenics of extreme pathology: An operant-interpersonal method. *J. abnorm. soc. Psychol.*, 1960, *61*, 276-286.

Krasner, L. The use of generalized reinforcers in psychotherapy research. *Psychol. Rep.*, 1955, *1*, 19-25.

Krasner, L. Studies of the conditioning of verbal behavior. *Psychol. Bull.*, 1958, *55*, 148-170.

Kuehner, G. F. Hypnosis in dentistry. In R. M. Dorcus (Ed.), *Hypnosis and its therapeutic applications.* New York: McGraw-Hill, 1956.

Lang, P. J., and Lazovik, A. D. Experimental desensitization of a phobia. *J. abnorm. soc. Psychol.*, 1963, *66*, 519-525.

Lavin, N., Thorpe, J. G., Barker, J., Blakemore, C., and Conway, C. Behavior therapy in a case of transvestism. *J. nerv. ment. Dis.*, 1961, *133*, 346-353.

Lazarus, A. A. New methods in psychotherapy: A case study. *S. Afr. med. J.*, 1958, *33*, 660-663.

Lazarus, A. A. The elimination of children's phobias by deconditioning. *Med. Proc. S. Afr.*, 1959.

Lazarus, A. A. Group therapy of phobic disorders by systematic desensitization. *J. abnorm. soc. Psychol.*, 1961, *63*, 504-510.

Lazarus, A. A. The treatment of chronic frigidity by systematic desensitization. *J. nerv. ment. Dis.*, 1963, *136*, 272-278.

Lazarus, A. A., and Abramovitz, A. The use of "emotive imagery" in the treatment of children's phobias. *J. ment. Sci.*, 1962, *108*, 191-195.

Lazarus, A. A., and Rachman, S. The use of systematic desensitization in psychotherapy. *S. Afr. med. J.*, 1957, *31*, 934-937.

Lehner, G. F. J. Negative practice as a psychotherapeutic technique. *J. gen. Psychol.*, 1954, *51*, 69-82.

Levitt, E. E. The results of psychotherapy with children: An evaluation. *J. consult. Psychol.*, 1957, *21*, 189-196.

Lindsley, O. R. Operant conditioning methods applied to research in chronic schizophrenia. *Psychiat. res. Rep.*, 1956, *5*, 118-139.

Lindsley, O. R. Characteristics of the behavior of chronic psychotics as revealed by free operant conditioning methods. *Dis. nerv. Syst. monogr. Suppl.*, 1960, *21*, 66-78.

Liversedge, L. A., and Sylvester, J. D. Conditioning techniques in the treatment of writer's cramp. *Lancet*, 1955, *2*, 1147-1149.

McLaughlin, F. L., and Millar, W. M. Employment of air-raid noises in psychotherapy. *Brit. med. J.*, 1941, *2*, 158-159.

Malleson, N. Panic and phobia. *Lancet*, 1959, *1*, 225-227.

Malmo, R. B., Davis, J. F., and Barza, S. Total hysterical deafness: An experimental case study. *J. Pers.*, 1952, *21*, 188-204.

Max, L. W. Breaking up a homosexual fixation by the conditioned reaction technique: A case study. *Psychol. Bull.*, 1935, *32*, 734. (Abstract)

Metzner, R. Learning theory and the therapy of neurosis. *Brit. J. Psychol.*, 1961, Monogr. Suppl. No. 33.

Meyer, V. The treatment of two phobic patients on the basis of learning principles. *J. abnorm. soc. Psychol.*, 1957, *55*, 261-266.

Meyer, V., and Gelder, M. G. Behavior therapy and phobic disorders. *Brit. J. Psychiat.*, 1963, *109*, 19-28.

Michael, J., and Meyerson, L. A behavioral approach to counseling and guidance. *Harv. educ. Rev.*, 1962, *32*, 382-402.

Mowrer, O. H. Apparatus for the study and treatment of enuresis. *Amer. J. Psychol.*, 1938, *51*, 163-165.

Oswald, I. Induction of illusory and hallucinatory voices with considerations of behavior therapy. *J. ment. Sci.*, 1962, *108*, 196-212.

Pavlov, I. P. *Lectures on conditioned reflexes.* Vol. 2. *Conditioned reflexes and psychiatry.* (Trans. and ed. by W. H. Gantt.) New York: International Univer. Press, 1941.

Peters, H. N., and Jenkins, R. L. Improvement of chronic schizophrenic patients with guided problem-solving motivated by hunger. *Psychiat. Quart. Suppl.*, 1954, *28*, 84-101.

Rachman, S. The treatment of anxiety and phobic reactions by systematic desensitization psychotherapy. *J. abnorm. soc. Psychol.*, 1959, *58*, 259-263.

Rachman, S. Sexual disorders and behavior therapy. *Amer. J. Psychiat.*, 1961, *118*, 235-240.

Raymond, M. J. Case of fetishism treated by aversion therapy. *Brit. med. J.*, 1956, *2*, 854-856.

Reider, N. The demonology of modern psychiatry. *Amer. J. Psychiat.*, 1955, *111*, 851-856.

Rickard, H. C., Dignan, P. J., and Horner, R. F. Verbal manipulation in a psychotherapeutic relationship. *J. clin. Psychol.*, 1960, *16*, 364-367.

Rickard, H. C., and Dinoff, M. A follow-up note on "Verbal manipulation in a psychotherapeutic relationship." *Psychol. Rep.*, 1962, *11*, 506.

Rosenzweig, S. A transvaluation of psychotherapy: A reply to Hans Eysenck. *J. abnorm. soc. Psychol.*, 1954, *49*, 298-304.

Rotter, J. B. *Social learning and clinical psychology.* Englewood Cliffs, N. J.: Prentice- Hall, 1954.

Rotter, J. B. Psychotherapy. *Annu. Rev. Psychol.*, 1960, *11*, 381-414.

Rubinstein, C. The treatment of morphine addiction in tuberculosis by Pawlow's conditioning method. *Amer. Rev. Tuberc.*, 1931, *24*, 682-685.

Rudolf, G. Deconditioning and time therapy. *J. ment. Sci.*, 1961, *107*, 1097-1101.

Saul, L. J., Rome, H., and Leuser, E. Desensitization of combat fatigue patients. *Amer. J. Psychiat.*, 1946, *102*, 476-478.

Schwartz, L. A. Group psychotherapy in the war neuroses. *Amer. J. Psychiat.*, 1945, *101*, 498-500.

Sears, R. R., and Cohen, L. H. Hysterical anesthesia, analgesia, and astereognosis. *AMA Arch. Neurol. Psychiat.*, 1933, *29*, 260-271.

Shane, Mary Lou. Effect on stuttering of alteration in auditory feedback. In W. Johnson (Ed.), *Stuttering in children and adults.* Minneapolis: Univer. of Minnesota Press, 1955.

Sheehan, J. G. The modification of stuttering through nonreinforcement. *J. abnorm. soc. Psychol.,* 1951, *46,* 51-63.

Skinner, B. F. *Science and human behavior.* New York: Macmillan, 1953.

Slack, C. W. Experimenter-subject psychotherapy: A new method of introducing intensive office treatment for unreachable cases. *Ment. Hyg., N. Y.,* 1960, *44,* 238-256.

Stevenson, I., and Wolpe, J. Recovery from sexual deviations through overcoming nonsexual neurotic responses. *Amer. J. Psychiat.,* 1960, *116,* 737-742.

Sylvester, J. D., and Liversedge, L. A. Conditioning and the occupational cramps. In H. J. Eysenck (Ed.), *Behavior therapy and the neuroses.* New York: Pergamon Press, 1960.

Terhune, W. B. The phobic syndrome. *AMA Arch. Neurol. Psychiat.,* 1949, *62,* 162-172.

Thompson, G., and Bielinski, B. Improvement in psychosis following conditioned-reflex treatment for alcoholism. *J. nerv. ment. Dis.,* 1953, *117,* 537-543.

Walton, D. The application of learning theory to the treatment of a case of bronchial asthma. In H. J. Eysenck (Ed.), *Behavior therapy and the neuroses.* New York: Pergamon Press, 1960. Pp. 188-189. (a)

Walton, D. The application of learning theory to the treatment of a case of neurodermatitis. In H. J. Eysenck (Ed.), *Behavior therapy and the neuroses.* New York: Pergamon Press, 1960. Pp. 272-274. (b)

Walton, D. The relevance of learning theory to the treatment of an obsessive-compulsive state. In H. J. Eysenck (Ed.), *Behavior therapy and the neuroses.* New York: Pergamon Press, 1960. Pp. 153-164. (c)

Walton, D. Strengthening of incompatible reactions and the treatment of a phobic state in a schizophrenic patient. In H. J. Eysenck (Ed.), *Behavior therapy and the neuroses.* New York: Pergamon Press, 1960. Pp. 170-180. (d)

Walton, D. Experimental psychology and the treatment of a ticqueur. *J. child Psychol. Psychiat.,* 1961, *2,* 148-155.

Walton, D., and Black, D. A. The application of learning theory to the treatment of stammering. *J. psychosom. Res.,* 1958, *3,* 170-179.

Walton, D., and Black, D. A. The application of modern learning theory to the treatment of chronic hysterical aphonia. In H. J. Eysenck (Ed.), *Behavior therapy and the neuroses.* New York: Pergamon Press, 1960. Pp. 259-271.

Weinberg, N. H., and Zaslove, M. "Resistance" to systematic desensitization of phobias. *J. clin. Psychol.,* 1963, *19,* 179-181.

White, J. G. The use of learning theory in the psychological treatment of children. *J. clin. Psychol.,* 1959, *15,* 227-229.

Wickland, R. F. A new approach to the treatment and rehabilitation of hospitalized chronic schizophrenics. Paper read at West. Psychol. Assoc., Santa Monica, May 1963. (Mimeo)

Williams, C. D. The elimination of tantrum behavior by extinction procedures. *J. abnorm. soc. Psychol.,* 1959, *59,* 269.

Wischner, G. J. Stuttering behavior and learning: A preliminary theoretical formulation. *J. speech hear. Disord.*, 1950, *15*, 324-335.

Wolf, M., Mees, H., and Risley, T. Application of operant conditioning procedures to the behavior problems of an autistic child. Paper read at West. Psychol. Assoc., Santa Monica, May 1963. (Mimeo)

Wolpe, J. *Psychotherapy by reciprocal inhibition.* Stanford: Stanford Univer. Press, 1958.

Wolpe, J. Reciprocal inhibition as the main basis of psychotherapeutic effects. In H. J. Eysenck (Ed.), *Behavior therapy and the neuroses.* New York: Pergamon Press, 1960. Pp. 88-113.

Wolpe, J. The systematic desensitization treatment of neuroses. *J. nerv. ment. Dis.*, 1961, *132*, 189-203.

Wolpe, J. The experimental foundations of some new psychotherapeutic methods. In A. J. Bachrach (Ed.), *Experimental foundations of clinical psychology.* New York: Basic Books, 1962. Pp. 554-575. (a)

Wolpe, J. Isolation of a conditioning procedure as the crucial psychotherapeutic factor: A case study. *J. nerv. ment. Dis.*, 1962, *134*, 316-329. (b)

Yates, A. J. The application of learning theory to the treatment of tics. *J. abnorm. soc. Psychol.*, 1958, *56*, 175-182. (a)

Yates, A. J. Symptoms and symptom substitution. *Psychol. Rev.*, 1958, *65*, 371-374. (b)

Zax, M., and Klein, A. Measurement of personality and behavior changes following psychotherapy. *Psychol. Bull.*, 1960, *57*, 435-448.

Zimmerman, Elaine H., and Zimmerman, J. The alteration of behavior in a special classroom situation. *J. exp. Anal. Behav.*, 1962, *5*, 59-60.

Compatible Partners

The development of preferred modes of treatment emerges as a real possibility and "psychodynamic depth theories" are dealt another blow. Yet are the learning mechanics of behavior therapy really new? As we talk with experienced and effective therapists, we find that they have been employing these mechanisms for a long time using different terms or no labels at all.

Wolpe's 90 percent rate of cure or improvement is impressive indeed. This statistic may be largely responsible for the fact that behavior therapy has become a "wave of the future." *Yet Wolpe himself reports that the 90 percent figure is based on those patients who have "given behavior therapy a fair chance."* When the others are included, the behavior therapist enjoys little more success than other therapists. The writers supporting this approach rarely include this most important qualifying statement. How many readers have been misled?

In spite of reports of early successes, Grossberg's review suggests that the answers we seek are not to be found in science alone, apart from clinical practice. While at this point in time it is apparent that the techniques derived from learning theory may constitute substantial contributions to effective processes, these techniques have not been adequately tested. For example, comparative studies have not employed interview-oriented therapy control groups that focus exclusively upon a specific set of symptoms, nor have they adequately compared impersonal programmed conditioning with more personal, manipulative processes. Instead, they have incorporated the best relationship conditions that the more traditional orientations have to offer. Typical studies employ a therapeutic relationship control, where the therapist acts as if he were an unthinking, unreinforcing, affective machine; in addition, we are often left without the knowledge of whether the conditioning processes translate to benefits in other aspects of the client's life.

The traditional forms of therapy have attempted to elicit constructive change or gain in more effective living in all aspects of the client's life, such as those suggested by Knight. While the interview-oriented schools have not by themselves satisfactorily achieved these goals, we do not believe that behavior therapy has achieved them either. In sum, while Grossberg's review is an important description of potentially useful techniques, let us not neglect other sources of effect in counseling and therapy.

Implicit and explicit in Grossberg's discussion is the implication that the assumptions, practices, and methods of counseling and psychotherapy need to be re-evaluated. In the next article Breger and McGaugh (1965) reassess behavioristic techniques, and caution about the bases and claims of the learning theory therapists.

ANOTHER VIEW OF BEHAVIOR THERAPY*

Louis Breger

and

James L. McGaugh

A careful look at the heterogeneous problems that are brought to psychotherapy points up the urgent need for new and varied theories and techniques. While some new methods have been developed in recent

* Critique and reformulation of "learning theory" approaches to psychotherapy and neuroses. *Psychological Bulletin*, 1965, *63*, 338-358. Reprinted by permission.

years, the field is still characterized by "schools"—groups who adhere to a particular set of ideas and techniques to the exclusion of others. Thus, there are dogmatic psychoanalysts, Adlerians, Rogerians, and, most recently, dogmatic behaviorists.

It is unfortunate that the techniques used by the behavior-therapy group (Bandura, 1961; Eysenck, 1960; Grossberg, 1964; Wolpe, 1958) have so quickly become encapsulated in a dogmatic "school," but this seems to be the case. Before examining the theory and practice of behavior therapy, let us first distinguish three different positions, all of which are associated with the behaviorism or "learning-theory" label. These are: (a) Dollard and Miller (1950) as represented in their book, (b) the Wolpe-Eysenck position as represented in Wolpe's work (1958; Wolpe, Salter, and Reyna, 1964) and in the volume edited by Eysenck (1960), and (c) the Skinnerian position as seen in Krasner (1961) and the work that appears in the *Journal of the Experimental Analysis of Behavior.*

Dollard and Miller present an attempt to translate psychoanalytic concepts into the terminology of Hullian learning theory. While many recent behavior therapists reject Dollard and Miller because of their identification with psychoanalysis and their failure to provide techniques distinct from psychoanalytic therapy, the Dollard-Miller explanation of neurotic symptoms in terms of conditioning and secondary anxiety drive is utilized extensively by Wolpe and his followers. Wolpe's position seems to be a combination of early Hullian learning theory and various active therapy techniques. He relies heavily on the idea of reciprocal inhibition, which is best exemplified by the technique of counterconditioning. In line with this Hullian background, Wolpe, Eysenck, and others in this group use explanations based on Pavlovian conditioning. They define neurosis as "persistent unadaptive habits that have been conditioned (that is, learned)" (Wolpe *et al.,* 1964, p. 9), and their explanation of neurosis stresses the persistence of "maladaptive habits" which are anxiety reducing.

The Skinnerian group (see Bachrach in Wolpe *et al.,* 1964) have no special theory of neurosis; in fact, following Skinner, they tend to disavow the necessity of theory. Their approach rests heavily on *techniques* of operant conditioning, on the use of "reinforcement" to control and shape behavior, and on the related notion that "symptoms," like all other "behaviors," are maintained by their effects.

Our discussion will be directed to the Wolpe-Eysenck group and the Skinnerians, keeping in mind that some of the points we will raise are not equally applicable to both. Insofar as the Skinnerians disavow a theory of neurosis, for example, they are not open to criticism in this area.

It is our opinion that the current arguments supporting a learning-theory approach to psychotherapy and neurosis are deficient on a number of grounds. First, we question whether the broad claims they make rest on a foundation of accurate and complete description of the basic data of neurosis and psychotherapy. The process of selecting among the data for those examples fitting the theory and techniques while ignoring a large amount of relevant data seriously undermines the strength and generality of the position. Second, claims for the efficacy of methods should be based on adequately controlled and accurately described evidence. And, finally, when over-all claims for the superiority of behavioral therapies are based on alleged similarity to laboratory experiments and alleged derivation from "well-established laws of learning," the relevance of the laboratory experimental findings for psychotherapy data should be justified and the laws of learning should be shown to be both relevant and valid.

In what follows we will consider these issues in detail, beginning with the frequently voiced claim that behavior therapy rests on a solid "scientific" base. Next, we will examine the nature and adequacy of the learning-theory principles which they advocate. We will point out how their learning theory is unable to account for the evidence from laboratory studies of learning. That is to say, the laws or principles of conditioning and reinforcement which form the basis of their learning theory are insufficient explanations for the findings from laboratory experiments, let alone the complex learning phenomena that are encountered in psychotherapy. Then we will discuss how the inadequate conception of learning phenomena in terms of conditioned responses is paralleled by an equally inadequate conception of neurosis in terms of discrete symptoms. Within learning theory, conceptions of habit and response have been shown to be inadequate and are giving way to conceptions emphasizing "strategies," "plans," "programs," "schemata," or other complex central mediators. A central point of this paper is that conceptions of habit and response are also inadequate to account for neuroses and the learning that goes on in psychotherapy and must here too be replaced with conceptions analogous to strategies. Next we will turn our attention to an evaluation of the claims of success put forth by the proponents of behavior therapy. Regardless of the adequacy of their theory, the claims that the methods work are deserving of careful scrutiny. Here we shall raise a number of questions centering around the issue of adequate controls. Finally, we shall attempt a reformulation in terms of more recent developments within learning, emphasizing the role of central processes.

SCIENCE ISSUE

Claims of scientific respectability are made with great frequency by the behavior therapists. Terms such as laboratory based, experimental, behavioral, systematic, and control are continually used to support their position. The validity of a theory or method must rest on empirical evidence, however. Thus, their use of scientific sounding terminology does not make their approach scientific, but rather seems to obscure an examination of the evidence on which their claims are based.

Let us examine some of this evidence. Bandura (1961) provides the following account of a typical behavior-therapy method (Wolpe's counterconditioning):

> On the basis of historical information, interview data, and psychological test responses, the therapist constructs an anxiety hierarchy, a ranked list of stimuli to which the patient reacts with anxiety. In the case of desensitization based on relaxation, the patient is hypnotized, and is given relaxation suggestions. He is then asked to imagine a scene representing the weakest item on the anxiety hierarchy and, if the relaxation is unimpaired, this is followed by having the patient imagine the next item on the list, and so on. Thus, the anxiety cues are gradually increased from session to session until the last phobic stimulus can be presented without impairing the relaxed state. Through this procedure, relaxation responses eventually come to be attached to the anxiety evoking stimuli (p. 144).

Without going into great detail, it should be clear from this example that the use of the terms stimulus and response are only remotely allegorical to the traditional use of these terms in psychology. The "imagination of a scene" is hardly an objectively defined stimulus, nor is something as general as "relaxation" a specifiable or clearly observable response. What the example shows is that counterconditioning is no more objective, no more controlled, and no more scientific than classical psychoanalysis, hypnotherapy, or treatment with tranquilizers. The claim to scientific respectability rests on the misleading use of terms such as stimulus, response, and conditioning, which have become associated with some of the methods of science because of their place in experimental psychology. But this implied association rests on the use of the same *words* and not on the use of the same *methods*.

We should stress that our quarrel is not with the techniques themselves but with the attempt to tie these techniques to principles and concepts from the field of learning. The techniques go back at least as far as Bagby (1928), indicating their independence from "modern learning theory." Although techniques such as these have received little attention in recent years (except from the behavior therapists) they are certainly worth further consideration as potentially useful techniques.[1]

---

[1] Another early application of behavioral techniques has recently been brought to our attention: Stevenson Smith's use of the Guthrie approach to learning in his work

The use of the term conditioning brings us to a second point, that the claims to scientific respectability rest heavily on the attempts of these writers to associate their work with the prestigious field of learning. They speak of something called modern learning theory, implying that psychologists in the area of learning have generally agreed upon a large number of basic principles and laws which can be taken as the foundation for a "scientific" approach to psychotherapy. For example, Eysenck (1960) states:

> Behavior therapy . . . began with the thorough experimental study of the laws of learning and conditioning in normal people and in animals; these well-established principles were then applied to neurotic disorders. . . . It may be objected that learning theorists are not always in agreement with each other and that it is difficult to apply principles about which there is still so much argument. This is only very partially true; those points about which argument rages are usually of academic interest rather than of practical importance. . . . The 10 percent which is in dispute should not blind us to the 90 percent which is not—disagreements and disputes naturally attract more attention, but agreements on facts and principles are actually much more common. Greater familiarity with the large and rapidly growing literature will quickly substantiate this statement (pp. 14-15).

As we shall show in the next section, this assertion is untenable. "Greater familiarity with the large and rapidly growing literature" shows that the very core of "modern learning theory," as Eysenck describes it, has been seriously questioned or abandoned in favor of alternative conceptualizations. For example, the notion that the discrete response provides an adequate unit of analysis, or that reinforcement can be widely used as an explanation of both learning and performance, or that mediational processes can be ignored are being or have been rejected. Eysenck's picture of the field as one with 90 percent agreement about basic principles is quite simply untrue. The references that Eysenck himself give for this statement (Hilgard, 1956; Osgood, 1953) do not support the claim. Hilgard presented many theories, not one "modern learning theory," some of which (Gestalt, Tolman, Lewin) might just as easily be said to be in 90 percent disagreement with behavioristic conditioning approaches. In the same vein, Osgood's text was one of the first to give heavy emphasis to the role of mediation, in an attempt to compensate for the inadequacies of a simple conditioning or one-stage S-R approach. Eysenck seems largely unaware of the very problems within the field of

---

at the children's clinic at the University of Washington. Guthrie's interpretation of reinforcement avoids the pitfalls we discuss shortly, and contemporary behaviorists might learn something from a review of his work (see Guthrie, 1935).

learning which necessitated the introduction of mediational concepts, even by S-R theorists such as Osgood.

These inadequacies center, in part, around the problem of generalization. The problem of generalizing from the level of conditioning to the level of complex human behavior has been recognized for a long time (Lewin, 1951; Tolman, 1933). It is a problem that is crucial in simple laboratory phenomena such as maze learning where it has resulted in the introduction of a variety of mediational concepts, and it is certainly a problem when complex human behavior is being dealt with. For example, Dollard and Miller (1950) began their book with an attempt to explain neurosis with simple conditioning principles. A careful reading of the book reveals, however, that as the behavior to be explained became more and more complex, their explanations relied more and more on mediational concepts, including language. The necessity for these mediators arises from the inadequacy of a simple *peripheral* S-R model to account for the generality of learning, the equivalence of responses, and the adaptive application of behavior in novel situations. We shall return to these points shortly; here we just wish to emphasize that the field of learning is not "one big happy family" whose problems have been solved by the widespread acceptance of a simple conditioning model. The claim to scientific respectability by reference back to established laws of learning is, thus, illusory.

LEARNING AND LEARNING THEORIES

We have already noted the differences between the Wolpe-Eysenck and the Skinnerian approaches; let us now examine the similarities. Three things stand out: the focus on the overt response, the reliance on a conditioning model, and the notion of reinforcement. First, there is the belief that the response, consisting of some discrete aspect of overt behavior, is the most meaningful unit of human behavior. While this should ideally refer to a specific contraction of muscles or secretion of glands, with the possible exception of Guthrie (1935), traditional S-R theorists have tended to define response in terms of an effect on the environment rather than as a specific movement of the organism. The problems raised by the use of the response as a basic unit, both in traditional learning phenomena and in the areas of neuroses and psychotherapy will be discussed in the section entitled What Is Learned? A second common assumption is that the concepts taken from conditioning, either as described by Pavlov or the operant conditioning of Skinner, can be used as explanatory principles. The assumption in question here is that conditioning phenomena are the simplest kinds of learning and that all other behavior can be explained in terms of these "simple" principles. We shall deal with the problems that arise from this source in a second section. The third assumption is that rewards play an essential role in all learning phenomena. We shall consider the problems that stem from this assumption in a third section.

WHAT IS LEARNED?

Since its inception in the early twentieth century, behaviorism has taken overt stimuli and responses as its core units of analysis. Learning, as the behaviorist views it, is defined as the tendency to make a *particular response* in the presence of a *particular stimulus;* what is learned is a discrete response. Almost from its inception, however, this view has been plagued by a number of problems.

First, findings from studies of perception, particularly the fact of perceptual constancy, provide embarrassment for a peripheral S-R theory. Perceptual constancy findings show, for example, that the stimulus is much more than peripheral receptor stimulation. For example, once we have learned a song in a particular key (that is, particular stimulus elements), we can readily recognize it or sing it in other keys. We are amazingly accurate in recognizing objects and events as being "the same" or equivalent, even though the particular stimulation they provide varies considerably on different occasions (Gibson, 1950). Although the bases of perceptual constancies (size, shapes, brightness, etc.) are not yet well understood, the facts of perceptual constancy—invariance in percept with variation in perceptual stimulation—are not in question. The related phenomenon of transposition has received considerable attention in animal experimentation. Animals, infrahuman as well as human, respond to relations among stimuli (Köhler, 1929). For a number of years, transposition was not considered to pose a serious problem for a peripheral S-R theory since it was thought that it could be adequately handled by principles of conditioning and stimulus generalization (Spence, 1937). This view has not been supported by later experiments, however (Lawrence and DeRivera, 1954; Riley, 1958). It now appears more likely that stimulus generalization is but a special case of the more general complex phenomenon of stimulus equivalence. The absolute theory of transposition was important and instructive because it revealed in clear relief the nature and limitations of a peripheral S-R approach to behavior. The effective stimulus is clearly more "central" than receptor excitation. The chapters on learning in the recent Koch series make it clear that workers in this area have seen the need for coming to terms with the facts of perception (Guttman, 1963; Lawrence, 1963; Leeper, 1963; Postman, 1963).

Second, the facts of response equivalence or response transfer posed the same kind of problem for a peripheral S-R view. A learned response does not consist merely of a stereotyped pattern of muscular contraction or glandular secretion. Even within the S-R tradition (for example, Hull, Skinner) there has been a tendency to define responses in terms of environmental achievements. Anyone who has trained animals has recognized that animals can achieve the same general response, that is, make the same environmental change, in a variety of different ways once the response is learned. "What is learned," then, is not a mechanical sequence of responses but rather, *what needs to be done in order to achieve some final event.* This notion is not new; Tolman stressed it as early as 1932 when he wrote of "purposive behavior," and it has been strongly supported by a variety of experimental findings (for example, Beach, Hebb, Morgan, and Nissen, 1960; Ritchie, Aeschliman, and Peirce, 1950). As this work shows, animals somehow seem to be able to bypass the execution of specific responses in reaching an environmental achievement. They can learn to go to particular places in the environment in spite of the fact that to do so requires them to make different responses from trial to trial. The learning of relatively specific responses to specific stimuli appears to be a special case which might be called stereotyped learning (canalization) rather than a basic prototype on the basis of which all other learning may be explained.

It should be noted further that even the stereotyped learning that forms the basic model of S-R conditioning does not hold up under closer scrutiny. First, once a subject has learned a stereotyped movement or response, he is still capable of achieving a goal in other ways when the situation requires it. Thus, while we have all learned to write our names with a particular hand in a relatively stereotyped fashion, we can switch to the other hand, or even write our name with a pencil gripped in our teeth if we have to, in spite of the fact that we may not have made this specific response in this way before. Second, even a response that is grossly defined as constant, stable, or stereotyped does not appear as such a stereotyped pattern of muscular contractions when it is closely observed.[2] These findings in the area of response transfer indicate that a response seems to be highly variable and equipotential. This notion is, of course, quite old in the history of psychology, and it has been stressed repeatedly by numerous investigators including Lashley (see Beach *et al.*, 1960), Osgood (1953), Tolman (1932), and Woodworth (1958).

The facts of both response transfer and stimulus equivalence seem much more adequately handled if we assume that what is learned is a *strategy* (alternatively called cognitive maps, programs, plans, schemata, hypotheses, for example, Krechevsky, 1932) for obtaining environmental achievements. When we take this view, habits, in the traditional behaviorist sense, become a later stage of response learning rather than a basic explanation (building block) for later, more complex learning.

---

[2] G. Hoyle, personal communication, 1963.

Perhaps this whole problem can be clarified if we look at a specific example such as language learning. As Chomsky (1959) has demonstrated in his excellent critique of Skinner's *Verbal Behavior* (1957), the basic facts of language learning and usage simply cannot be handled within an S-R approach. It seems clear that an adequate view of language must account for the fact that humans, at a rather early age, internalize a complex set of rules (grammar) which enable them to both recognize and generate meaningful sentences involving patterns of words that they may never have used before. Thus, in language learning, what is learned are not only sets of responses (words and sentences) but, in addition, some form of internal strategies or plans (grammar). We learn a grammar which enables us to generate a variety of English sentences. We do not merely learn specific English sentence habits. How this grammar or set of strategies is acquired, retained, and used in language comprehension and generation is a matter for serious research effort; but, it is clear that attempts to understand language learning on the basis of analogies from bar-pressing experiments are doomed before they start. To anticipate, we will argue shortly that if we are to make an attempt to understand the phenomena of neurosis, using analogies from the area of learning, it will be much more appropriate to take these analogies from the area of psycholinguistics and language learning rather than, as has typically been done, from studies of classical and operant conditioning. That is, the focus will have to be on response transfer, equipotentiality, and the learning of plans and strategies rather than on stereotyped response learning or habituation.

USE OF A CONDITIONING MODEL

As we indicated earlier, when writers in the behaviorist tradition say "learning theory," they probably mean a conditioning theory; most of the interpretations of clinical phenomena are reinterpretations in terms of the principles of conditioning. Thus, a phobic symptom is viewed as a conditioned response, maintained by the reinforcement of a secondary fear drive or by a Skinnerian as a single operant maintained by reinforcement. Two types of conditioning are involved in these explanations by reduction. The first is Pavlovian or classical conditioning, frequently used in conjunction with later Hullian concepts such as secondary drive; the second is operant conditioning of the kind proposed by Skinner. The use of both of these models to explain more complex phenomena such as transposition, response transfer, problem solving, language learning, or neurosis and psychotherapy poses a number of difficulties.

The basic assumption that underlies the use of either kind of conditioning as an explanation for more complex phenomena is that basic laws of behavior have been established in the highly controlled laboratory situation and may thus be applied to behavior of a more complex variety. When we look at the way conditioning principles are applied in the explanation of more complex phenomena, we see that only a rather flimsy analogy bridges the gap between such laboratory defined terms as stimulus, response, and reinforcement and their referents in the case of complex behavior. Thus, while a stimulus may be defined as an electric shock or a light of a certain intensity in a classical conditioning experiment, Bandura (1961) speaks of the "imagination of a scene"; or, while a response may consist of salivation or a barpress in a conditioning experiment, behavior therapists speak of anxiety as a response. As Chomsky (1959) puts it, with regard to this same problem in the area of language:

> He [Skinner in *Verbal Behavior*] utilizes the experimental results as evidence for the scientific character of his system of behavior, and analogic guesses (formulated in terms of a metaphoric extension of the technical vocabulary of the laboratory) as evidence for its scope. This creates the illusion of a rigorous scientific theory with a very broad scope, although in fact the terms used in the description of real-life and of laboratory behavior may be mere homonyms, with at most a vague similarity of meaning (p. 30).

A second and related problem stems from the fact that the behavior-therapy workers accept the findings of conditioning experiments as basic principles or laws of learning. Unfortunately, there is now good reason to believe that classical conditioning is no more simple or basic than other forms of learning. Rather, it seems to be a form of learning that is in itself in need of explanation in terms of more general principles. For example, a popular but naive view of conditioning is that of stimulus substitution—the view that conditioning consists merely of the substitution of a conditioned stimulus for an unconditioned stimulus. Close examination of conditioning experiments reveals that this is not the case, however, for the conditioned response is typically *unlike* the unconditioned response (Zener, 1937). Apparently, in conditioning, a new response is learned. Most of the major learning theorists have taken this fact into account in abandoning the notion of conditioning as mere stimulus substitution.

More than this, the most important theoretical developments using essentially Pavlovian conditioning principles have not even stressed overt behavior (Osgood, 1953). Hull and the neo-Hullians, for example, have relied quite heavily on Tolman's (1932) distinction between learning and performance, performance being what is observed while learning (conditioning) is but one essential ingredient contributing to any instance of observed performance. The most important, and perhaps the most sophisticated, developments in Hullian and neo-Hullian theory concern the attempts to explain complicated goal-directed behavior in terms of the conditioning of fractional responses. Unobserved, fractional responses (already we see the drift away from the overt behavior criteria of response) are assumed to serve a mediating role in behavior. Once a fractional response is conditioned in a particular situation, it is assumed to occur to the stimuli in that situation when those stimuli recur. The stimulus consequences of the fractional response referred to as the r_g are assumed to serve as guides to behavior either by serving as a cue or by activating responses or by serving to reinforce other responses by secondary reinforcement. The latter-day proponents of a conditioning point of view (Bugelski, 1956; Osgood, 1953) have come to rely more and more heavily on concepts like the fractional response to bridge the gap between stimulus and overt behavior and to account for the facts of response transfer, environmental achievements, and equipotentiality. What this indicates is that a simple conditioning paradigm which rests solely on observable stimuli and responses has proved inadequate even to the task of encompassing simple conditioning and maze-learning phenomena, and the workers within this tradition have come to rely more and more heavily on mediational (central, cognitive, etc.) concepts, although they still attempt to clothe these concepts in traditional conditioning garb. To add to the problem, a number of recent papers (Deutsch, 1956; Gonzales and Diamond, 1960) have indicated that the r_g interpretations of complex behavior are neither simple nor adequate.

When we look again at the way conditioning principles have been applied to clinical phenomena, we see an amazing unawareness of these problems that have been so salient to experimental and animal psychologists working with conditioning.

While the above discussion has been oriented primarily to classical conditioning, the general argument would apply equally well to those attempts to make the principles of learning derived from operant conditioning the basis of an explanation of neurosis and psychotherapy (as in Krasner, 1961). The Skinnerians have been particularly oblivious to the wide variety of problems that are entailed when one attempts to apply concepts and findings from laboratory learning experiments to other, and particularly more complex, phenomena. While we will deal more directly with their point of view shortly, a few comments might be in order now concerning their use of the operant-conditioning paradigm as a basis for the handling of more complex data. When Skinnerians speak of laws of learning, they have reference to the curves representing rate of responding of rats pressing bars (Skinner, 1938), and pigeons pecking (Ferster and Skinner, 1957) which are, in fact, a function of certain highly controlled contingencies such as the schedule of reinforcement, the amount of deprivation, the experimental situation itself (there is very little else to do in a Skinner box), and the species of animals involved. These experiments are of some interest, both as exercises in animal training under highly restricted conditions, and for what light they may shed on the more general question of partial reinforcement. It is dubious that these findings constitute laws of learning that can be applied across species (see Breland and Breland, 1961) or even to situations that differ in any significant way from the Skinner box.

USE OF REINFORCEMENT

Advocates of the application of learning theory to clinical phenomena have relied heavily on the "law of effect" as perhaps their foremost established principle of learning. We shall attempt to point out that a good deal of evidence from experimental animal studies argues strongly that, at the most, the law of effect is a weak law of performance.

Essentially, the controversy can be reduced to the question of whether or not reward is necessary for learning. The initial source of evidence indicating that it was not came from the findings of latent learning studies (Blodgett, 1929; Tolman and Honzik, 1930) in which it was found, for example, that rats who were allowed to explore a maze without reward made fewer errors when learning the maze than controls who had no opportunity for exploration. Thus, these early latent learning studies, as well as a variety of more recent ones (Thistlethwaite, 1951) indicate that learning can take place without reward but may not be revealed until a reward situation makes it appropriate to do so (or to put it another way, the reward elicits the performance but plays little role during learning). Other sources which point to learning without reward come from studies of perceptual learning (Hebb, 1949), imitation (Herbert and Harsh, 1944), language learning (Chomsky, 1959), and imprinting (Moltz, 1960).

Defenders of the point of view that reinforcement is necessary for learning have attempted to handle results such as these in a variety of ways. One has been by appealing to the concept of secondary reinforcement (for example, a maze has secondary reinforcing properties which account for the learning during exploration). When this sort of thing is done, even with respect to experiments where attempts were made to minimize secondary reinforcements (Thistlethwaite, 1951), it seems clear that this particular notion of reinforcement has become incapable of disproof. Another way of handling these potentially embarrassing results has been by the invention of a new set of drives (curiosity drive, exploratory drive, etc.) but this too has a post hoc flavor to it, and one wonders what kind of explanation is achieved by postulating an "exploratory drive" to account for the fact that animals and humans engage in exploration. In fact, the assumption that exploration reduces an exploratory drive makes it difficult to explain why a rat's tendency to enter an alley of a maze *decreases* after he has explored the alley (Watson, 1961). Finally, there are those (particularly the Skinnerians) who tend to define reinforcement so broadly that neither the findings from latent learning nor any other source can prove embarrassing, since whenever learning has taken place this "proves" that there has been reinforcement. To better understand this problem, however, we had best look for a moment at the general problem of defining reinforcement in a meaningful way.

Obviously, if the view that reinforcement is necessary for learning is to have any meaning, what constitutes a reinforcement must be defined independently from the learning situation itself. There has been a great deal of difficulty in getting around a circular definition of the law of effect, and it might be worthwhile to examine some of the attempts that have been made in the past.

One of the best known was the attempt to relate the reinforcing properties of stimuli to their drive-reducing characteristics (Hull, 1951). The drive-reduction model has had to be abandoned, however, because of evidence from a variety of areas including latent learning, sensory preconditioning (Brogden, 1939), and novelty and curiosity (Berlyne, 1960). Other evidence such as that of Olds and Milner (1954) on the effect of direct brain stimulation have strengthened the conviction that the drive-reduction interpretation of reinforcement is inadequate; and, in fact, original adherents of this view have begun to abandon it (for example, Miller, 1959).

The other most frequent solution to the circularity problem has been by way of the "empirical law of effect," an approach typified by Skinner's definition of reinforcement as any stimulus that can be demonstrated to produce a change in response strength. Skinner argues that this is not circular since some stimuli are found to produce changes and others are not, and they can subsequently be classified on that basis. This seems to be a reasonable position if it is adhered to; that is, if care is taken to define reinforcement in terms of class membership *independently* of the observations that show that learning has taken place. When we examine the actual use of the term reinforcement by Skinner (see especially *Verbal Behavior,* 1957) and by other Skinnerians (Lundin, 1961), we find that care is only taken in this regard within the context of animal experiments, but that when the jumps are made to other phenomena, such as language and psychotherapy, care is usually *not* taken to define reinforcement independently from learning as indicated by response strength. This leads to a state of affairs where any observed change in behavior is said to occur *because* of reinforcement, when, in fact, the change in behavior is itself the only indicator of what the reinforcement has been. Chomsky (1959) reviews the use of the concept of reinforcement by Skinner with regard to language and reaches the following conclusion:

> From this sample, it can be seen that the notion of reinforcement has totally lost whatever objective meaning it may ever have had. Running through these examples, we see that a person can be reinforced though he emits no response at all, and the reinforcing "stimulus" need not impinge on the reinforced person or need not even exist (it is sufficient that it be imagined or hoped for). When we read that a person plays what music he likes (165), says what he likes (165), thinks what he likes (438-439), reads what books he likes (163), etc., *because* he finds it reinforcing to do so, or that we write books or inform others of facts *because* we are reinforced by what we hope will be the ultimate behavior of reader or listener, we can only conclude that the term "reinforcement" has a purely ritual function. The phrase "X is reinforced by Y (stimulus, state of affairs, event, etc.)" is being used as a cover term for "X wants Y," "X likes Y," "X wishes that Y were the case," etc. Invoking the term "reinforcement" has no explanatory force, and any idea that this paraphrase introduces any new clarity or objectivity into the description of wishing, liking, etc., is a serious delusion (pp. 37-38).

This problem is exemplified in the area of psychotherapy by the attempts to use the studies of verbal conditioning (Krasner, 1958) as analogues to psychotherapy. First we should note that if these studies are taken at face value (that is, if subjects are conditioned to increase the emission of certain responses because of reinforcement, without their awareness of this fact) it appears that a simple conditioning model is inadequate since subjects are presumably responding in terms of a class of responses (for example, plural nouns, etc.) rather than in terms of a specific response (for example, bar press), such classes implying response transfer and mediation. Second, and more to the point, a number of recent investigators (Eriksen, 1962) have begun to question whether verbal conditioning does occur without the subject's awareness. If it does not, the whole phenomenon begins to look like nothing more than a rather inefficient way to get subjects to figure out what the experimenter wants them to do (telling them directly to emit plural nouns would probably be much more efficient) after which they can decide whether they want to do it or not. In any case, there seems to be enough question about what goes on in verbal conditioning itself to indicate that it cannot be utilized as a more basic explanation for complex phenomena such as psychotherapy. Psychotherapists of many persuasions would agree that rewards of some kind are important in work with patients. Thus, the view that the psychotherapist is a "reinforcement machine" is trivial. The difficult problems are in specifying just what therapist activities are rewarding, in what ways, to what sorts of patients, and with what effects.

The above discussion should make clear that the use of the concept of reinforcement is only of explanatory usefulness when it is specified in some delimited fashion. As an empirical law of performance almost everyone in and out of psychology would accept it, including Lewin, Freud, Tolman, and others outside the traditional S-R movement. But this amounts to saying nothing more than that some events, when presented, tend to increase the probability of responses that they have followed. The hard job, but the only one that will lead to any meaningful use of the concept of reinforcement, is specifying what the various events called reinforcers have in common. Some have argued that since this is such a difficult task, we should restrict ourselves to listing and cataloging so-called reinforcers. But this is nearly impossible, in a general way, because reinforcers differ from individual to individual, from species to species, from situation to situation, and from time to time (the saying "one man's meat is another man's poison" is trite but true). Meaningful analysis must stem from a comprehensive study of the particular learning phenomena in question, whether it is language learning, the development of perceptual and perceptual-motor skills (Fitts, 1964; Hebb, 1949), the acquisition of particular species behavior patterns during critical periods of development (Scott, 1962), the learning of a neurosis, or the learning that takes place during psychotherapy. Experience with all of these phenomena has revealed that different kinds of events seem to be involved and that these can only be understood in the context of the phenomena in question. Lumping all these events together under the single term reinforcement serves to muddle rather than to clarify understanding.

The staunch reinforcement adherent might respond that all these complicated arguments may be true but we can ignore them, since all we are really interested in is predicting what the organism will do, and we can do this when we know the organism's reinforcement history. The answer to this is that the experimental literature does not support such a claim; rather, it shows that, in many instances, performance *cannot* be predicted on the basis of a knowledge of the history of reinforcement.

Latent learning studies indicate this quite clearly. Perhaps of more interest are the findings of discrimination-reversal learning studies (Goodwin and Lawrence, 1955; Mackintosh, 1963). Here we find that subjects that have been trained on a series of discrimination reversals learn to select the correct stimulus with very few errors even though they may have been rewarded *much more frequently and more recently for re-*

sponding to another stimulus. Similarly, in the double drive discrimination studies (Thistlethwaite, 1951) animals chose alleys leading to food when they were hungry and water when they were thirsty, even though they have been rewarded equally frequently on the alleys on previous trials. In other words, "what is learned" was not equivalent with "reinforcement history." The law of effect is not disproved by these studies; it is merely shown to be irrelevant.

To summarize: The "law of effect," or reinforcement, conceived as a *"law of learning,"* occupies a very dubious status. Like the principles of conditioning, it appears to be an unlikely candidate as an explanatory principle of learning. As a strong law of learning it has already been rejected by many of the theorists who previously relied on it. As an empirical "law of *performance"* it is noncontroversial, but usually so generally stated as to be of little explanatory value.

CONCEPTION OF NEUROSIS

In this section we will explicate the conception of neurosis that forms the basis of the behavior-therapy approach (particularly of the Wolpe-Eysenck group) and attempt to demonstrate its inadequacies both in terms of learning theory and as a way of accounting for the observed facts of neurosis. Our argument in the first instance will be that the conception of neurosis in terms of symptoms and anxiety parallels the general conception of learning in terms of overt responses, conditioning, and secondary drives, and suffers from the same inadequacies that we have outlined in the preceding section. With regard to the facts of neurosis, we will argue that the behavior-therapy position is inadequate at a descriptive level as well as being conceptually incorrect. It should be pointed out again that we are discussing the explanation or theory of neurosis here and not the techniques used by the behavior therapists. The strict Skinnerian may excuse himself at this point if he adheres to a "no-theory" position and is only concerned with the effects of environmental manipulation. Furthermore, certain techniques themselves may be useful and have some of the effects attributed to them regardless of the theory.

In its essence, the conception of neurosis put forth by the behavior therapists is that neuroses are conditioned responses or habits (including conditioned anxiety) and *nothing else,* though it should be noted that they do not adhere to this argument when they describe the success of their methods. Wolpe, for example, while ostensibly treating overt symptoms, describes his patients as becoming more productive, having improved adjustment and pleasure in sex, improved interpersonal relationships, and so forth. The argument that removal of a troublesome symptom somewhow "generalizes" to all of these other areas begs the question.

Their conception is typically put forth as an alternative to a psycho-dynamic viewpoint, which they characterize as resting on a distinction between symptoms and underlying causes (unconscious conflicts, im-pulses, defenses, etc.). They stress the point that inferences about under-lying factors of this sort are unnecessary and misleading and that a more parsimonious explanation treats symptoms (which are typically equated with behavior or that which can be objectively observed) as the neurosis per se. They argue that by equating neurosis with symptoms, and symp-toms, in turn, with habits (conditioned responses), they are able to bring "modern learning theory" with its "well-established laws" to bear on the understanding and treatment of neurosis.

As we have labored to show in the preceding section, the well-established laws of learning to which they refer have considerable diffi-culty within the area of simple animal behavior. More specifically, it seems clear that a wide variety of behaviors (from maze learning to more complex forms) cannot be adequately dealt with when the overt response and conditioned habit are the units of analysis. Furthermore, their learn-ing position leads the behavior therapists into postulating an isomorphic relationship between antecedent learning and present behavior in which observed differences are accounted for in terms of principles of generaliza-tion. This is a key issue, and we shall explore it a little further at this time.

Much of the behaviorist conception of neurosis rests on a rejection of the distinction between symptoms and underlying causes (Eysenck, 1960) as typified by Yates' (1958) argument against "symptom substitu-tion." By focusing attention on overt symptoms and banishing all under-lying causes, however, the behavior therapists are faced with the same problem that has long confronted behaviorism; namely, the difficulty of explaining how *generality* of behavior results from specific learning experiences. The problem of *generality* (that is, as exemplified by the facts of transposition and response transfer) has, in fact, brought about the downfall of peripheral S-R learning, of the conditioned habit as a basic unit, and tangentially, is leading to the dethroning of the law of effect. With regard to neurosis, this view has led the behavior therapists into the position where they must posit a specific learning experience for each symptom of a neursosis. They have partly avoided this problem by focusing their attention on those neuroses that can be described in terms of specific symptoms (bedwetting, if this is a neurosis, tics, specific phobias, etc.) and have tended to ignore those conditions which do not fit their model, such as neurotic depressions, general unhappiness, obsessional disorders, and the kinds of persistent interpersonal entangle-ments that characterize so many neurotics. This leaves them free to explain the specific symptom in terms of a specific learning experience, as, for example, when a fear of going outdoors is explained in terms of some previous experience in which the stimulus (outdoors) has been associated with (conditioned to) something unpleasant or painful and has now, through generalization, spread to any response of going outdoors. As our previous analysis should make clear, however, even a simple conceptualization such as this, in terms of stimuli, responses, and conditioning is extremely cumbersome and begs the important questions. Within an S-R framework, in which generalization occurs along the dimension of physical stimulus similarity, it is difficult, if not impossible, to show how a previous experience such as being frightened in the country as a child could generalize to the "stimulus" outdoors without a great deal of *mediation* in which the concept of "outdoors" carried most of the burden of generalization. As we have pointed out, most workers in the field of learning recognize this and rely heavily on mediational concepts in their explanations of complex behavior. Dollard and Miller (1950), for example, return again and again to mediational explanations once they move beyond the "combat neuroses" which lend themselves more readily to a simple isomorphic explanation.

A second important facet of the behaviorist conception of neurosis is the use of the concept of anxiety as a secondary drive. Here, Wolpe and Eysenck and some others seem to follow the explanatory model laid down by Dollard and Miller. Anxiety is viewed as the main motivating force for symptoms and, in general, occupies a central place in their thinking. Briefly, it is worth pointing out that the concept of drive reduction, the distinction between primary drives and secondary drives, as well as the early thinking about the uniquely persistent qualities of fear-motivated behavior have had serious difficulty within learning theory (Watson, 1961; Solomon, 1964). The use of these concepts to explain clinical phenomena thus rests on an exceedingly shaky foundation.

Let us turn our attention now to the phenomena of neuroses. We shall try to point out that underlying the dispute over symptoms versus underlying causes is a real difference in definition that arises at the descriptive level, which, in a sense, antedates disagreements at the level of theory and explanation.

To keep the presentation simple, we will adopt the terms psychodynamic to refer to all those theorists and therapists, following Freud, whose view of neurosis and its treatment deals with motives (conscious and unconscious), conflict, etc. This covers a wide variety of workers, in addition to the more or less traditional followers of Freud, including Sullivan and his adherents (Fromm-Reichman, 1950), other neo-Freudians, and that broad group of psychiatrists and clinical psychologists who have been strongly influenced by the Freudian and neo-Freudian viewpoints even though they may not claim allegiance to any of the formal schools.

The point we wish to make here is that disagreement between the behaviorist and psychodynamic viewpoints seems to rest on a very real difference at the purely descriptive or observational level. The behaviorist looks at a neurotic and sees specific symptoms and anxiety. The psychodynamicist looks at the same individual and sees a complex intra- and interpersonal mode of functioning which may or may not contain certain observable fears[3] or certain behavioral symptoms such as compulsive motor acts. When the psychodynamicist describes a neurosis, his referent is a cohering component of the individual's functioning, including his characteristic ways of interacting with other people (for example, sweet and self-effacing on the surface but hostile in covert ways), his characteristic modes of thinking and perceiving (for example, the hysteric who never "remembers" anything unpleasant, the obsessive whose memories are overelaborated and circumstantial, etc.), characteristic modes of fantasy and dreaming, a variety of secondary gain features, and the like. Specific or isolatable symptoms may sometimes be a part of such an integrated neurotic pattern, but, even viewed descriptively, they in no sense constitute the neurosis per se.

So far, we have considered the behavior therapists' position at face value. In actuality, a good case can be made that they *behave* in a way which is quite inconsistent with their own position. A specific example, taken from one of Wolpe's own case descriptions, will illustrate this point, and, at the same time, show what the psychodynamicist sees when he looks at a neurotic. Wolpe (1960) presents the following case:

> *Case 5.* An attractive woman of 28 came for treatment because she was in acute distress as a result of her lovers' casual treatment of her. Everyone of very numerous love affairs had followed a similar pattern —first she would attract the man, then she would offer herself on a platter. He would soon treat her with contempt and after a time leave her. In general she lacked assurance, was very dependent, and was practically never free from feelings of tension and anxiety.

What is described here is a complex pattern of interpersonal relationships, psychological strategies, and misunderstandings (such as the way she became involved with men, the way she communicated her availability to them, her dependency, etc.), expectations that she had

---

[3] The term anxiety is frequently used as a theoretical inference, that is, a patient deals with personal material in any overly intellectual fashion, and this is described as a defense mechanism—intellectualization—whose purpose is to ward off anxiety.

(presumably that men would not react with contempt to her generosity, that being dependent might lead to being taken care of, etc.), and thoughts and feelings about herself (lack of assurance, acute distress, etc.). Many of the statements about her (for example, the description of the course of her love affairs) are abbreviations for very complex and involved processes involving two people interacting over a period of time. It is this, the psychodynamicist would argue, that *is* the neurosis. The tension and anxiety may be a part of it in this particular case (though there might be other cases in which there is no complaint of anxiety but, rather, its reverse—seeming inability to "feel" anything)—but it is secondary and can be understood only in relation to the other aspects of the patient's functioning. Wolpe's case histories are classic testaments to the fact that he cannot, and does not, apply the symptom approach when working with actual data. As a further example, consider the argument against a symptom-substitution point of view (Yates, 1958) in which it is implied that anything other than symptoms is some sort of metaphysical inference. While it may be true that theories such as psychoanalysis deal with a number of inferential and higher-order constructs in their attempts to integrate the complex mass of data that constitutes a neurosis, it is also true that much more than symptoms exist at the level of observation. Secondary-gain features of a neurosis, in which it is apparent that a variety of goals may be served by a set of interchangeable symptoms are the rule in most neurotic individuals. We are not defending the view (attributed to psychoanalysis by Yates) that if one symptom is removed another pops up to take its place; rather, we are arguing that the empirical phenomena of neurosis does not fit the symptom or response theory, but is much more compatible with a theory built around central mediators. Whether unconscious conflicts and defense mechanisms are adequate ways of conceptualizing the problem is an entirely separate question. What is clear is that a view stressing central mediators in which specific responses are seen as equipotential means of reaching certain goals is necessary to encompass the data of neurosis just as it has proven necessary to encompass the phenomena of animal learning.

To sum up, it would seem that the behaviorists have reached a position where an inadequate conceptual framework forces them to adopt an inadequate and superficial view of the very data that they are concerned with. They are then forced to slip many of the key facts in the back door, so to speak, for example, when all sorts of fantasy, imaginary, and thought processes are blithley called responses. This process is, of course, parallel to what has gone on within S-R learning theory where all sorts of central and mediational processes have been cumbersomely handled with S-R terminology (for example, Deutsch, 1956). Thus, we have a situation where the behavior therapists argue strongly against a dynamic interpretation of neurosis at some points and at other points behave as if they had adopted such a point of view. Thus inconsistency should be kept in mind in reading the next section in which we evaluate the claims of success put forth by the behaviorist group. Insofar as there is disagreement as to what constitutes the descriptive facts of neurosis, it makes little sense to compare the effectiveness of different methods. However, since the behaviorist group adopts very broad (or psychodynamic, if you will) criteria for improvement, and since their *techniques* may have some effectiveness, in spite of theoretical and conceptual inadequacies, it is crucial that we look carefully at the empirical results that they lay claim to.

CLAIMS OF SUCCESS

While much of the writing of the behavior therapists consists of arguments and appeals to principles of science and learning, the claims that are made for the success of the methods seem open to empirical analysis. No doubt a great deal of the appeal of behavior therapy lies right here. Here seem to be methods whose application can be clearly described (unlike such messy psychodynamic methods as "handling countertransference" or "interpreting resistance"), whose course is relatively short, and which seem to achieve a large number of practical results in the form of removal of symptoms. Wolpe (1960), for example, presents the following data: of 122 cases treated with behavioral techniques, 44 percent were "apparently cured," 46 percent were "much improved," 7 percent were "slightly or moderately improved," and 3 percent were "unimproved." Combining categories, he claims 90 percent "apparently cured or much improved," and 10 percent "improvement moderate, slight or nil." (Criteria of improvement consists of "symptomatic improvement, increased productiveness, improved adjustment and pleasure in sex, improved interpersonal relationships and ability to handle ordinary psychological conflicts and reasonable reality stresses.")

He compares this with data from the Berlin Psychoanalytic Institute (Knight, 1941) which shows 62-40.5 percent in the first category and 38-59.5 percent in the second. Wolpe concludes, as have others (Bandura, 1961; Eysenck, 1960; Lazarus, 1963), that this demonstrates the superiority of the behavior therapy methods. The fact that the psychoanalytic method showed as much as 62 percent improvement is explained as being due to whatever accidental "reciprocal inhibition" occurred during the therapy. (There is, however, no analysis or description of how this might have happened.) The behavioral methods achieve superior results presumably because of the more explicit application of these techniques.

It is fair to say that if these results can be substantiated they present a very strong argument in favor of behavioral *techniques*—even granting the theoretical and empirical inconsistencies we have discussed. However, we must ask if these claims are any better substantiated than those made by the practitioners of other methods of psychotherapy. Insofar as claims such as Wolpe's are based on uncontrolled case histories, they may reflect the enthusiasm of the practitioner as much as the effect of the method. History shows that new methods of therapy (ECS, tranquilizing drugs, as well as various schools of psychotherapy) have been oversold by their original proponents. Thus, a careful look at what lies behind the claims of the behavior-therapy group is in order.

The following does not purport to be a comprehensive review of the behavior-therapy literature. Rather, it is based on a survey of all the studies reported in the two reviews that have appeared (Bandura, 1961; Grossberg, 1964). The most striking thing about this large body of studies is that they are almost all case studies. A careful reading of the original sources reveals that only one study (Lang and Lazovik, 1963) is a controlled experiment, and here the subjects were not neurotics but normal college students. Thus, most of the claims (including those of Wolpe which have been widely quoted) must be regarded as no better substantiated than those of any other enthusiastic school of psychotherapy whose practitioners claim that their patients get better. Behavior therapy has appeared to differ on this score because of its identification with experimental psychology and with "well-established laws of learning." We have already dealt with this issue, so let us now turn to some problems in evaluating psychotherapy as a technique.

The problems here are essentially those of control, and they may be broken down into three areas: (a) sampling biases, (b) observer bias, and (c) problems of experimental control. While research in psychotherapy presents particular difficulties in controlling "experimental input," more sophisticated workers (Frank, 1959) have attempted to deal with at least the sampling and observer problems. It thus comes as somewhat of a surprise that the behavior-therapy workers, despite their identification with experimental psychology, base their claims on evidence which is almost totally lacking in any form of control. Let us examine these issues in greater detail.

Sampling Biases

Obviously a claim such as Wolpe's of 90 percent success has meaning only when we know the population from which the sample of patients was drawn and the way in which they were selected. Ideally, a comparison of treatment techniques would involve the random assignment of patient from a common population pool to alternative treatments. Since, in practice, this is rarely feasible, it is essential for anyone making comparisons of different treatment methods to, at the very least, examine the comparability of the populations *and* of the methods used in selecting from these populations. Neither Wolpe's data nor that of Lazarus (1963) contains this evidence. Wolpe reports, for example, that:

> Both series (70 patients reported on in 1952 and 52 patients reported on in 1954 on which the 90 percent figure is based) include only patients whose treatment has ceased after they have been afforded a reasonable opportunity for the application of the available methods; that is, they have had as a minimum both a course of instruction on the changing of behavior in the life situation and a proper initiation of a course of relaxation-desensitization. This minimum takes up to about 15 interviews, including anamestic interviews and *no patient who has had 15 or more interviews has been omitted from the series* [emphasis added].

We may conclude from this that some patients (how many we do not know) having up to 14 interviews have been excluded from the sample—a procedure highly favorable to the success of the method but which violates the simplest canons of sampling. Wolpe's final sample of 122 consists of those patients most likely to show improvement, since both they and he were satisfied enough with the first 14 (or less) interviews to warrant proceeding further. Those patients least likely to improve are those most likely to drop out early (14 sessions or less) and not be included in the computation of success rate. The fact that a large number of poor-prognosis patients would very likely be eliminated during these early sessions is supported by a variety of research findings (Strickland and Crowne, 1963), which show that most dropping-out of untreatable or unsuccessful cases occurs during the first 10 sessions. This serious sampling bias would be expected to spuriously inflate the percent showing improvement.

When we add this to whatever unknown factors operate to delimit the original population (presumably there is some self-selection of patients who seek out this form of treatment), it becomes apparent that little confidence can be given to the reports of success.

Observer Bias

Psychologists have long been aware that human beings are fallible observers, particularly when they have predispositions or vested interests to protect. In controlled studies, we try to protect judges from their own biases by not acquainting them with the hypotheses, or with the nature of the groups they are judging, or by using blind and double-blind designs. This problem is particularly acute with regard to psychotherapy because both therapist and patient have investments of time, involvement, competence, and reputation to protect. For these reasons, workers in the area have become extremely skeptical of claims put forth for any method which rests on the uncontrolled observation of the person administering the treatment. At a minimum we expect some sort of external evidence. Beyond this minimum we hope for an independent judge who can compare differentially treated groups without knowing which is which.

In addition, there is the problem of the patient's freedom to report effects which may be seriously curtailed when all his reports go directly to the person who has treated him. It seems reasonable to assume that some patients are prevented from expressing dissatisfaction with treatment when they must report directly to the therapist, either because they do not want to hurt his feelings, or are afraid, or are just saying what they think is being demanded of them, or are being polite, or for some other reason. Again, it would be highly appropriate to provide the patients with the opportunity of reporting results in a situation as free from such pressure as possible.

Examination of the 26 studies reviewed by Bandura reveals a surprising lack of concern with these problems. Of the 26 studies sampled, only 12 report evaluation of results by persons other than the treating therapist; four of these use ratings of the hospital staff (who may be acquainted with the treatment), four use mothers or parents reporting on their children to the treating therapist, one is a wife reporting on her husband to the therapist, and three use a second observer. Obviously, whatever factors enter in to cause observer and reporter biases are allowed full reign in most of these cases. While we cannot conclude from this that the reported results are *due to* observer and reporter biases (as is clearly indicated with the sampling biases), it is impossible to rule them out. Furthermore, a great deal of evidence from many areas of psychology leads us to be very skeptical of claims in which biases of this sort go uncontrolled.

Experimental Control

While control of sampling and observer effects are basic to a wide variety of research activities, including field and clinical research, more exacting control over experimental conditions has long been the sine qua non of the laboratory methods of experimental psychology. The power of the experimental method stems, in part, from keeping careful control over all but a few conditions, which are experimentally varied, with the subsequent effects of these variations being observed. Since psychotherapy is not a controlled experiment, it is probably unfair to expect this type of control. However, there are more and less accurate descriptions of what goes on during any form of therapy, and we can demand as accurate a description as possible in lieu of experimental control. Thus, while we are led to believe that methods, such as counterconditioning, extinction of maladaptive responses, methods of reward, and the like, are applied in a manner analogous to their laboratory counterparts—examination of what is *actually done* reveals that the application of the learning techniques is embedded in a wide variety of activities (including many of the traditional therapy and interview techniques) which make any attribution of effect to the specific learning techniques impossible. Let us consider a few examples. From Wolpe (1960):

> *Case 4.* The patient had 65 therapeutic interviews, unevenly distributed over 27 months. The greater part of the time was devoted to discussions of how to gain control of her interpersonal relationships and stand up for herself. She had considerable difficulty with this at first, even though it had early become emotionally important to her to please the therapist. But she gradually mastered the assertive behavior required of her, overcame her anxieties and became exceedingly self-reliant in all interpersonal dealings, including those with her mother-in-law.

From Lazarus and Rachman (1957) on systematic desensitization:

> *Case 1.* The patient was instructed in the use of assertive responses and deep (nonhypnotic) relaxation. The first anxiety hierarchy dealt with was that of dull weather. Starting from "a bright sunny day" it was possible for the subject to visualize "damp overcast weather" without anxiety after 21 densensitization sessions, and 10 days after the completion of this hierarchy, she was able to report that, "the weather is much better, it doesn't even bother me to look at the weather when I wake up in the morning" (previously depressing). . . . During the course of therapy, part of the reason for the development of the anxiety state in this patient was unearthed. When she was 17 years old she had become involved in a love affair with a married man 12 years her senior. This affair had been conducted in an extremely discreet manner for 4 years, during which time she had suffered from recurrent guilt feelings and shame—so much so, that on one occasion she had attempted suicide by throwing herself into a river. It was her custom to meet her lover after work *in the late afternoon*. The dull weather can be accounted for, as this affair took place in London.

From Rachman (1959):

> *Interview No. 12.* The patient having received a jolt in her love
> relationship, this session was restricted to a sort of nondirective, cathar-
> tic discussion. No desensitizing was undertaken because of A.G.'s de-
> pressed mood and obvious desire to "just talk."

These excerpts have been presented because they seem representative of the practices of the behavioral therapists. As can be seen, the
number and variety of activities that go on during these treatment
sessions is great, including, in these few examples, discussions, explanations of techniques and principles, explanations of the unadaptiveness
of anxiety and symptoms, hypnosis of various sorts, relaxation practice
and training with and without hypnosis, "nondirective cathartic discussions," "obtaining an understanding of the patient's personality and
background," and the "unearthing" of a 17-year-old memory of an illicit
affair. The case reports are brief and presented anecdotally so that
it is really impossible to know what else went on in addition to those
things described. What should be abundantly clear from these examples is that there is no attempt to restrict what goes on to learning
techniques. Since it seems clear that a great variety of things do go on,
any attribution of behavior change to specific learning techniques is
entirely unwarranted.

In summary, there are several important issues that must be differentiated. First, a review of both learning theory and of the empirical
results of behavior therapy demonstrates that they can claim no special
scientific status for their work on either ground. Second, there are important differences of opinion concerning the type of patient likely to be
affected by behavior therapy. Grossberg (1964), for example, states that:
"Behavior therapies have been most successful when applied to neurotic
disorders with specific behavioral manifestations" (p. 81). He goes on to
point out that the results with alcoholism and sexual disorders have been
disappointing and that the best results are achieved with phobias and
enuresis. He later states that "desensitization only alleviates those
phobias that are being treated, but other coexisting phobias remain at
high strength, indicating a specific treatment effect" (p. 83). Wolpe *et al.*
(1964), on the other hand, argues that: "The conditioning therapist
differs from his colleagues in that he *seeks out* the precise stimuli to
anxiety, and finds himself able to break down almost every neurosis into
what are essentially *phobic systems*" (p. 11). The best controlled study
(Lang and Lazovik, 1963) indicates that "desensitization is very effective
in reducing the intense fear of snakes held by normal subjects, though it
can be questioned whether this is a phobia in the clinical sense."

Thus, there seems to be some evidence that these *techniques* (as techniques and not as learning theory) are effective with certain conditions.[4] We feel that this bears stressing because psychotherapy has come to be narrowly defined in terms of dynamic, evocative, and nondirective methods, placing unnecessary limitations on the kind of patient suitable for psychotherapy. First, we must note that behavior techniques are not new (as Murray, 1964, points out). Freud and Breuer used similar techniques prior to the development of psychoanalysis, Bagby described a number of these methods in 1928, and therapy based on techniques designed to eliminate undesirable responses was used for many years by Stevenson Smith at the University of Washington Clinic. While most of these techniques have been superseded by the various forms of dynamic psychotherapy, recent work (Frank, 1961) suggests that the time may be ripe for taking a fresh look at a variety of methods such as hypnosis, suggestion, relaxation, and other approaches of a more *structured nature* in which the therapist takes a *more active role*. Needless to say, this fresh look would best proceed unencumbered by an inadequate learning theory and with some minimal concern for control. As an example of a nondynamic approach to patient management, we refer to the work of Fairweather (1964) and his colleagues.

REFORMULATION

Up to this point our analysis has been primarily critical. We have tried to show that many of the so-called principles of learning employed by workers with a behaviorist orientation are inadequate and are not likely to provide useful explanations for clinical phenomena. In this section we will examine the potential value of ideas from different learning conceptions. Before proceeding, however, we would like to discuss briefly the issue of the application of "laws," principles, and findings from one area (such as animal experimentation) to another (such as neurosis and psychotherapy). The behaviorists have traditionally assumed that principles established under highly controlled conditions, usually with animal subjects, form a scientific foundation for a psychology of learning. Yet when they come to apply these principles to human learning situations, the transition is typically bridged by rather flimsy analogies which ignore crucial differences between the situations, the species, etc. Recently, Underwood (1964) has made the following comments concerning this problem:

---

[4] Just how many neurotics fit the phobia and/or specific symptom model is a complicated question, the answer to which depends in part on what one's own point of view leads one to look for. For example, an informal census of the first 81 admissions to the University of Oregon Psychology Clinic in 1964 revealed only 2 patients who could be so classified.

Learning theories as developed in the animal-learning laboratory, have never seemed . . . to have relevance to the behavior of a subject in learning a list of paired associates. The emphasis upon the role of a pellet of food or a sip of water in the white rat's acquiring a response somehow never seemed to make contact with the human S learning to say VXK when the stimulus DOF was presented (p. 74).

We would add that the relevance is at least equally obscure in applications of traditional S-R reinforcement theory to clinical phenomena.

We do *not* wish, however, to damn any and all attempts to conceptualize clinical phenomena in terms of principles of learning developed outside the clinic. On the contrary, recent work in learning may suggest certain theoretical models which may prove useful in conceptualizing the learning processes involved in psychotherapy and the development of neuroses. Whether these notions can form the basis for a useful learning conceptualization of clinical phenomena will depend upon the ingenuity with which they are subsequently developed and upon their adequacy in encompassing the facts of neurosis and psychotherapy. Further, we would like to stress that their association with experimental work in the field of learning does not give them any a priori scientific status. Their status as explanatory principles in the clinical area must be empirically established within that area. In what follows, then, we will outline some ideas about learning and make some suggestions concerning their relevance to clinical problems.

Our view of learning centers around the concepts of information storage and retrieval. Learning is viewed as the process by which information about the environment is acquired, stored, and categorized. This cognitive view is, of course, quite contrary to the view that learning consists of the acquisition of specific responses; responses, according to our view, are mediated by the nature of the stored information, which may consist of facts or of strategies or programs analogous to the grammar that is acquired in the learning of a language. Thus, "what is learned" may be a system for generating responses as a consequence of the specific information that is stored. This general point of view has been emphasized by Lashley (see Beach *et al.*, 1960), by Miller, Galenter, and Pribram (1960), in the form of the TOTE hypothesis, and by a number of workers in the cognitive learning tradition (Tolman, 1951; Woodworth, 1958). Recently it has even been suggested as a necessary formulation for dealing with that eminently S-R area, motor skills (Adams, 1964; Fitts, 1964).

This conception of learning may be useful in the clinical area in two ways: one, in formulating a theoretical explanation for the acquisition or development of neurosis, symptoms, behavior pathology, and the like, and, two, in conceptualizing psychotherapy as a learning process, and suggesting new methods stemming from this learning model.

A conceptualization of the problem of neurosis in terms of information storage and retrieval is based on the fundamental idea that what is learned in a neurosis is a set of central strategies (or a program) which guide the individual's adaptation to his environment. Neuroses are not symptoms (responses) but are strategies of a particular kind which lead to certain observable (tics, compulsive acts, etc.) and certain other less observable, phenomena (fears, feelings of depression, etc.). The whole problem of symptom substitution is thus seen as an instance of response substitution or response equipotentiality, concepts which are supported by abundant laboratory evidence.

Similarly, the problem of a learning conceptualization of unconscious phenomena may be reopened. Traditional S-R approaches have equated the unconscious with some kind of avoidance of a verbalization response. From our point of view, there is no reason to assume that people can give accurate descriptions of the central strategies mediating much of their behavior any more than a child can give a description of the grammatical rules which govern the understanding and production of his language. As a matter of fact, consciousness may very well be a special or extraordinary case—the rule being "unawareness" of the mediating strategies—which is in need of special explanation, rather than the reverse. This view avoids the cumbersome necessity of having to postulate specific fear experiences or the persistence of anxiety-motivated behavior, as has typically been done by S-R theorists with regard to unconscious phenomena. It also avoids equating the unconscious with the neurotic, which is a virtue since there is so much that goes on within "normal" individuals that they are unaware of. It further avoids the trap of attributing especially persistent and maladaptive consequences to painful experiences. As Solomon (1964) points out, the existing evidence does not support the view that punishment and pain lead unequivocally to anxiety and maladaptive consequences.

The view of learning we have outlined does not supply a set of ready-made answers to clinical problems that can be applied from the laboratory, but it indicates what sort of questions will have to be answered to achieve a meaningful learning conceptualization of neurosis and symptoms. Questions such as "What are the conditions under which strategies are acquired or developed?" stress the fact that these conditions may be quite different from the final observed behavior. That is to say, a particular symptom is not necessarily acquired because of some learning experience in which its stimulus components were associated with pains or fear-producing stimuli. Rather, a symptom may function as an equipotential response, mediated by a central strategy acquired under different circumstances. As an example, consider Harlow's (1958, 1962) monkeys who developed a number of symptoms, the most striking being sexual impotence (a much better animal analogue of human neurosis than those typically cited as experimental neuroses [Liddell, 1944]). Their longitudinal record, or "learning history," indicates that the development of this abnormal "affectional system," as Harlow terms it, is dependent on a variety of nonisomorphic experiences, including the lack of a mother-infant relationship and the lack of a variety of peer-play experiences.

These brief examples are only meant to give a flavor of where a learning conception of neurosis which stresses the acquisition of strategies will lead. A chief advantage of this view is that it has *generality* built in at the core, rather than imported secondarily, as is the case with S-R concepts of stimulus and response generalization.

Let us now turn our attention to the very difficult problem of applying learning concepts to psychotherapy. Basically, we would argue that the development of methods and techniques is largely a function of the empirical skill and ingenuity of the individual-craftsman-therapist. Even a carefully worked-out and well-established set of learning principles (which we do not have at this time) would not necessarily tell us how to modify acquired strategies in the individual case—just as the generally agreed-upon idea that rewards affect performance does not tell us what will be an effective reward in any specific instance.

Bearing these cautions in mind, we might still address ourselves to the question of what applications are suggested by the learning approach we have presented. As a first suggestion, we might consider the analogy of learning a new language. Here we see a process that parallels psychotherapy insofar as it involves modifying or developing a new set of strategies of a pervasive nature. A careful study of the most effective techniques for the learning of a new language might yield some interesting suggestions for psychotherapy. Learning a new language involves the development of a new set of strategies for responding—new syntax as well as new vocabulary. Language learning *may or may not* be facilitated by an intensive attempt to make the individual *aware* of the strategies used, as is done in traditional language instruction which teaches old-fashioned grammar, and as is done, analogously, in those psychotherapies which stress insight. Alternatively, language learning sometimes seems most rapid when the individual is immersed in surroundings (such as a foreign country) where he hears nothing but the new language and where his old strategies and responses are totally ineffective.

Using this as a model for psychotherapy, we might suggest something like the following process: First, a careful study should be done to delineate the "neurotic language," both its vocabulary and its grammar, of the individual. Then a situation might be constructed (for example, a group therapy situation) in which the individual's existing neurotic language is not understood and in which the individual must develop a new "language," a new set of central strategies, in order to be understood. The detailed working out of such a procedure might very well utilize a number of the techniques that have been found effective in existing therapies, both group and individual, and in addition draw on some new techniques from the fields of psycholinguistics and language learning.

These are, of course, but initial fragmentary guesses, and they may be wrong ones. But we believe that the conceptions on which these guesses are based are sufficiently supported by recent learning research to warrant serious attention. Although this reconceptualization may not lead immediately to the development of effective psychotherapeutic techniques, it may at least provide a first step in that direction.

REFERENCES

Adams, J. A. Motor skills. In P. R. Farnsworth (Ed.), *Annual Review of Psychology*, 1964, *15*, 181-202.

Bagby, E. *The psychology of personality.* New York: Holt, 1928.

Bandura, A. Psychotherapy as a learning process. *Psychol. Bull.*, 1961, *58*, 143-159.

Beach, F. A., Hebb, D. O., Morgan, C. T., and Nissen, H. W. *The neuropsychology of Lashley.* New York: McGraw-Hill, 1960.

Berlyne, D. E. *Conflict, arousal, and curiosity.* New York: McGraw-Hill, 1960.

Blodgett, H. C. The effect of introduction of reward upon the maze performance of rats. *Univer. of California Publications in Psychology*, 1929, *4*, 113-134.

Breland, K., and Breland, M. The misbehavior of organisms. *Amer. Psychol.*, 1961, *16*, 681-684.

Brogden, W. J. Sensory preconditioning. *J. exp. Psychol.*, 1939, *25*, 323-332.

Bugelski, B. R. *The psychology of learning.* New York: Holt, Rinehart & Winston, 1956.

Chomsky, N. Review of B. F. Skinner, *Verbal behavior. Language*, 1959, *35*, 26-58.

Deutsch, J. A. The inadequacy of Hullian derivations of reasoning and latent learning. *Psychol. Rev.*, 1956, *63*, 389-399.

Dollard, J., and Miller, N. E. *Personality and psychotherapy.* New York: McGraw-Hill, 1950.

Eriksen, C. W. (Ed.) *Behavior and awareness.* Durham, N. C.: Duke Univer. Press, 1962.

Eysenck, H. J. (Ed.) *Behavior therapy and the neuroses.* New York: Pergamon Press, 1960.

Fairweather, G. W. *Social psychology in treating mental illness: An experimental approach.* New York: Wiley, 1964.

Ferster, C. B., and Skinner, B. F. *Schedules of reinforcement.* New York: Appleton-Century-Crofts, 1957.

Fitts, P. M. Perceptual-motor skill learning. In A. W. Melton (Ed.), *Categories of human learning.* New York: Academic Press, 1964. Pp. 244-285.

Frank, J. D. Problems of controls in psychotherapy as exemplified by the psychotherapy research project of the Phipps Psychiatric Clinic. In E. A. Rubenstein and M. B. Parloff (Eds.), *Research in psychotherapy.* Washington, D. C.: Amer. Psychol. Assoc., 1959.

Frank, J. D. *Persuasion and healing: A comparative study of psychotherapy.* Baltimore: Johns Hopkins Press, 1961.

Fromm-Reichmann, Frieda. *Principles of intensive psychotherapy.* Chicago: Univer. of Chicago Press, 1950.

Gibson, J. J. *The perception of the visual world.* Boston: Houghton Mifflin, 1950.

Gonzales, R. C., and Diamond, L. A test of Spence's theory of incentive motivation. *Amer. J. Psychol.,* 1960, *73,* 396-403.

Goodwin, W. R., and Lawrence, D. H. The functional independence of two discrimination habits associated with a constant stimulus situation. *J. comp. physiol. Psychol.,* 1955, *48,* 437-443.

Grossberg, J. M. Behavior therapy: A review. *Psychol. Bull.,* 1964, *62,* 73-88.

Guthrie, E. R. *The psychology of learning.* New York: Harper, 1935.

Guttman, N. Laws of behavior and facts of perception. In S. Koch (Ed.), *Psychology: A study of a science.* Vol. 5. New York: McGraw-Hill, 1963. Pp. 114-179.

Harlow, H. F. The nature of love. *Amer. Psychol.,* 1958, *13,* 673-685.

Harlow, H. F. The heterosexual affectional system in monkeys. *Amer. Psychol.,* 1962, *17,* 1-9.

Hebb, D. O. *The organization of behavior: A neurophysiological theory.* New York: Wiley, 1949.

Herbert, M. J., and Harsh, C. M. Observational learning by cats. *J. comp. Psychol.,* 1944, *37,* 81-95.

Hilgard, E. R. *Theories of learning.* New York: Appleton-Century-Crofts, 1956.

Hull, C. L. *Essentials of behavior.* New Haven: Yale Univer. Press, 1951.

Knight, R. P. Evaluation of the results of psychoanalytic therapy. *Amer. J. Psychiat.,* 1941, *98,* 434.

Kohler, W. *Gestalt psychology.* New York: Liveright, 1929.

Krasner, L. Studies of the conditioning of verbal behavior. *Psychol. Bull.,* 1958, *55,* 148-170.

Krasner, L. The therapist as a social reinforcement machine. In H. H. Strupp (Ed.), *Second research conference on psychotherapy.* Chapel Hill, N. C.: Amer. Psychol. Assoc., 1961.

Krechevsky, I. The genesis of "hypotheses" in rats. *Univer. of California Publications in Psychology*, 1932, *6*, 45-64.

Lang, P. J., and Lazovik, A. D. Experimental desensitization of a phobia. *J. abnorm. soc. Psychol.*, 1963, *66*, 519-525.

Lawrence, D. H. The nature of a stimulus: Some relationships between learning and perception. In S. Koch (Ed.), *Psychology: A study of a science*. Vol. 5. New York: McGraw-Hill, 1963, Pp. 179-212.

Lawrence, D. H., and DeRivera, J. Evidence for relational transposition. *J. comp. physiol. Psychol.*, 1954, *47*, 465-471.

Lazarus, A. A. The results of behavior therapy in 126 cases of severe neurosis. *Behav. Res. Ther.*, 1963, *1*, 69-80.

Lazarus, A. A., and Rachman, S. The use of systematic desensitization in psychotherapy. *So. Afr. med. J.*, 1957, *32*, 934-937.

Leeper, R. L. Learning and the fields of perception, motivation, and personality. In S. Koch (Ed.), *Psychology: A study of a science*. Vol. 5. New York: McGraw-Hill, 1963. Pp. 365-487.

Lewin, K. *Field theory in social science*. New York: Harper & Row, 1951. Ch. 4, pp. 60-86.

Liddell, H. S. Conditioned reflex method and experimental neurosis. In J. McV. Hunt (Ed.), *Personality and the behavior disorders*. New York: Ronald, 1944. Ch. 12.

Lundin, R. W. *Personality: An experimental approach*. New York: Macmillan, 1961.

Mackintosh, N. J. Extinction of a discrimination habit as a function of overtraining. *J. comp. physiol. Psychol.*, 1963, *56*, 842-847.

Miller, G. A., Galanter, E. H., and Pribram, K. H. *Plans and the structure of behavior*. New York: Holt, Rinehart & Winston, 1960.

Miller, N. E. Liberalization of basic S-R concepts: Extension to conflict behavior, motivation, and social learning. In S. Koch (Ed.), *Psychology: A study of a science*. Vol. 2. New York: McGraw-Hill, 1959. Pp. 196-292.

Moltz, H. Imprinting, empirical basis, and theoretical significance. *Psychol. Bull.*, 1960, *57*, 291-314.

Murray, E. J. Sociotropic learning approach to psychotherapy. In P. Worchel and D. Byrne (Eds.), *Personality change*. New York: Wiley, 1964. Pp. 249-288.

Olds, J., and Milner, P. Positive reinforcement produced by electrical stimulation of septal area and other regions of rat brain. *J. comp. physiol. Psychol.*, 1954, *47*, 419-427.

Osgood, C. E. *Method and theory in experimental psychology*. New York: Oxford Univer. Press, 1953.

Postman, L. Perception and learning. In S. Koch (Ed.), *Psychology: A study of a science*. Vol. 5. New York: McGraw-Hill, 1963. Pp. 30-113.

Rachman, S. The treatment of anxiety and phobic reactions by systematic desensitization psychotherapy. *J. abnorm. soc. Psychol.*, 1959, *58*, 259-263.

Riley, D. A. The nature of the effective stimulus in animal discrimination learning: Transposition reconsidered. *Psychological Review*, 1958, *65*, 1-7.

Ritchie, B. F., Aeschliman, B., and Peirce, P. Studies in spatial learning. VIII. Place performance and the acquisition of place dispositions. *J. comp. physiol. Psychol.*, 1950, *43*, 73-85.

Rotter, J. B. *Social learning and clinical psychology*. Englewood Cliffs, N. J.: Prentice-Hall, 1954.

Scott, J. P. Critical periods in behavioral development. *Science*, 1962, *138*, 949-958.

Skinner, B. F. *The behavior of organisms: An experimental analysis*. New York: Appleton-Century-Crofts, 1938.

Skinner, B. F. *Verbal behavior*. New York: Appleton-Century-Crofts, 1957.

Solomon, R. L. Punishment. *Amer. Psychol.*, 1964, *19*, 239-253.

Spence, K. W. The differential response in animals to stimuli varying within a single dimension. *Psychol. Rev.*, 1937, *44*, 430-440.

Strickland, Bonnie R., and Crowne, D. P. The need for approval and the premature termination of psychotherapy. *J. consult. Psychol.*, 1963, 27, 95-101.

Thistlethwaite, D. A critical review of latent learning and related experiments. *Psychol. Bull.*, 1951, 48, 97-129.

Tolman, E. C. *Purposive behavior in animals and men*. New York: Appleton-Century, 1932.

Tolman, E. C. Sign gestalt or conditioned reflex? *Psychol. Review*, 1933, *40*, 391-411.

Tolman, E. C. *Collected papers in psychology*. Berkeley: Univer. California Press, 1951.

Tolman, E. C., and Honzik, C. H. Introduction and removal of reward and maze performance in rats. *Univer. of California Publications in Psychology*, 1930, *4*, 257-275.

Underwood, B. J. The representativeness of rote verbal learning. In A. W. Melton (Ed.), *Categories of human learning*. New York: Academic Press, 1964. Pp. 47-78.

Watson, A. J. The place of reinforcement in the explanation of behavior. In W. H. Thorpe and O. L. Zangwill, *Current problems in animal behavior*. Cambridge: Cambridge Univer. Press, 1961.

Wolpe, J. *Psychotherapy by reciprocal inhibition*. Palo Alto: Stanford Univer. Press, 1958.

Wolpe, J. Reciprocal inhibition as the main basis of psychotherapeutic effects. In H. J. Eysenck (Ed.), *Behavior therapy and the neuroses*. New York: Pergamon Press, 1960. Pp. 88-113.

Wolpe, J., Salter, A., and Reyna, L. J. (Eds.) *The conditioning therapies*. New York: Holt, Rinehart & Winston, 1964.

Woodworth, R. S. *Dynamics of behavior*. New York: Holt, Rinehart & Winston, 1958.

Yates, A. J. Symptoms and symptom substitution. *Psychol. Rev.*, 1958, *65*, 371-374.

Zener, K. The significance of behavior accompanying conditioned salivary secretion for theories of the conditioned response. *Amer. J. Psychol.*, 1937, *50*, 384-403.

Errors in Programs: Stops and Checks

The advocates of rigor are called to task on their own terms. At best, our present state of knowledge about learning processes serves as an analogy for real life and, at worst, an intellectual game with some relevance for the laboratory and little for the consulting room.

This reading reminds us of the dubious value of the laws of conditioning and reinforcement when applied to the results of laboratory studies, and the seemingly unquestioned application of these same laws to problems and processes in therapy. Perhaps there is the further suggestion that the issues encountered by our more "rigorous" colleagues are not at their core very different from those encountered by we who identify with applied aspects.

Breger and McGaugh present a tentative direction and constructs that may prove to be acceptable to the more tender-minded among us. The broad and general use of computer language is less demanding than traditional learning constructs. Yet when translated into answers for the therapist or counselor, these authors appear to be proposing a social learning theory. Their model has several advantages: the constructs are easily understood, and it draws heavily on communication networks, language behavior, isolation, and social facilitation, all of which have never before been fully understood or exploited by the clinician.

We are, however, left with the same basic questions. What conditions allow for the acquisition of new and more adaptive strategies? How can the therapist aid the process? What outcome indices would prove to be most useful in evaluating the outcome of such a therapy if it were to be developed, and would we need new criteria?

In the following article, several ambitious tasks are attempted: (a) the evaluation of the present level of knowledge about what works in counseling and psychotherapy; (b) the identification of significant sources of variance; (c) the presentation of a model for future research; and (d) a consideration of the implications for therapy and its training.

NEW DIRECTIONS IN CLINICAL RESEARCH *
Charles B. Truax
and
Robert R. Carkhuff

INTRODUCTION

The developments of techniques and theories of psychotherapy have not grown out of the research soil but have instead emerged from clinical practice. It is difficult, if not impossible, to point to a single psychotherapeutic approach or innovation that has grown out of psychotherapy research. Science has in the past failed to contribute substantially to the practice of psychotherapy. This is a most sobering acknowledgement: but one which we must face—and change!

Brayfield (13) notes that past research dealing with the counseling process and outcome has been largely either trivial or nonexistent. The same could be said of much of psychotherapy research. In the research reported from the 1960s it is quite clear that a great deal of time, money, creative energy, and even scientific brilliance has been tragically wasted. The obvious question is why? The answer seems to lie in the way researchers have asked their questions.

The literature focuses primarily upon two kinds of questions: (1) what are the effects of psychotherapy? and (2) *what* is related to *what* within the momentary process of psychotherapy itself? The recent convergence of research efforts upon the second question has grown out of repeated failures to discover the predictable effects of psychotherapy. Thus, Eysenck, who over ten years ago (25) questioned the efficacy of psychotherapy, is now (26) able to conclude that psychotherapy is not effective in producing therapeutic results.

Eysenck's questioning of the efficacy of therapy is, in the first place, inappropriate. "Psychotherapy" is hardly a unitary phenomenon. It contains within it a variety of both positive and negative experiences. To ask the question, "Is psychotherapy indeed therapeutic?", and to then go

* Significant developments in psychotherapy research. In *Progress in clinical psychology*. New York: Grune & Stratton, 1964, pp. 124-155. Reprinted by permission. This work was supported in part by a grant from the Office of Vocational Rehabilitation, Number RD-906-PM. Carkhuff's work was supported by Public Health Fellowship Number 7 F2 MH-19, 912-02 from the National Institute of Mental Health, Public Health Service.

about answering such a question in the traditional way, is very much like the pharmacologist's asking the question, "Is chemotherapy or drug therapy therapeutic?", and then proceeding to conduct his research by randomly giving unknown kinds of drugs in unknown quantities to one group of patients with various complaints and no drugs to another similar group. To be sure, he would have both treatment and control groups. However, it is difficult indeed to determine what these data might mean. In effect, such an approach is all too often precisely the way intelligent researchers in the field of psychotherapy have proceeded: one group of patients has been given random and unknown amounts of various psychological "conditions" labeled psychotherapy, while another group has received no therapy. Attempts have then been made to show reliable differences between the "experimental" patients and the "control" patients. Fortunately, we are now learning to ask better questions. In part we have learned from what at first view seemed our failures.

Bergin (8), in a scholarly review of studies of effect of psychotherapy, notes that in the results of the Barron and Leary (7) and the Cartwright and Vogel (20) studies, which show no over-all difference between therapy and control groups, one critical finding emerges: patients receiving psychotherapy show significantly greater variability in personality change indices at the conclusion of psychotherapy than did the controls. We might have expected similar findings in other studies, but most often such analyses were not conducted. The Cartwright and Vogel study went further to demonstrate that patients of the experienced therapists tended to show more improvement when compared to patients seen by the inexperienced therapists. Thus, the evidence was clear that this generic experience of "psychotherapy" must have been different for the inexperienced therapists than for the experienced therapists since the outcomes were different.

More recently, our findings from a program of intensive research with schizophrenics (62, 80, 81) have indicated again no over-all difference in outcome between patients receiving psychotherapy and matched control patients. However, when we divided therapy patients according to the level of therapeutic conditions provided to the patients by the therapist—high accurate empathy and unconditional positive regard for the patient and therapist authenticity or congruence—patients receiving high conditions showed significant constructive personality change, whereas patients who received low therapeutic conditions became significantly worse. These later findings, in confirming what was suggested in the Barron and Leary, and the Cartwright and Vogel studies, seem to offer an explanation for the puzzling mass of data concerning the over-all lack of efficacy of psychotherapy. In Bergin's terms, "this clearly shown result is an exciting breakthrough." These findings point the way for future research to ask the more meaningful question of *what* levels of *what* ingredients of psychotherapy produce positive personality and behavioral change?

Pursuing our analogy with the pharmacologist, the psychotherapy researcher would now in effect be asking *what* dosage levels of *what* drugs produce therapeutic effects? The suggestion here is that the psychotherapy researcher need no longer retreat into studies of the momentary process of therapy which may or may not be related to therapeutic outcomes; instead, he can focus upon relating the antecedents and process ingredients of psychotherapy to outcome itself.

Such a step brings psychotherapy research into greater intimacy with the mainstream of psychotherapy practice. As psychotherapists we share a common core of agreement in goals: making unhappy people happy or the malfunctioning people functioning. Psychotherapy research can converge on this goal of practice by focusing its effort upon discovering and isolating the effective elements in the psychotherapeutic process which lead to constructive change in the patient. That is, we can attempt to discover what elements, among all that occur during psychotherapy, contribute to the patient's constructive change. Further, we must attempt to discern the elements that inhibit such constructive change. It has been clear to the clinician, as it is now becoming clear to the researcher, that not all that happens in psychotherapy is indeed beneficial or even relevant to constructive change in the patient.

In this context, even the therapeutic relationship, which so often appears as an end in itself, is not the goal of psychotherapy: it may turn out to be a means in the process of achieving a given end but it is clearly not the goal per se.

If, as researchers and as clinicians, we seriously attempt to account for and predict constructive personality change by discovering, isolating, and measuring the effective ingredients or variables in psychotherapy, it will become increasingly clear that current theoretical models are grossly inadequate. While many of these theoretic models have given both impetus and directionality to research and will continue to do so, each has its own limitations. It is already becoming increasingly apparent that our present models must be modified and expanded to include a multitude of therapists, patients, processes, and contextual variables, alone and in their various interactions, if we are ever to even hope to understand the process of psychotherapy.

Therapist characteristics, such as personality, attitudinal, and other personal variables, influences upon the therapist's role concept, and specialized techniques employed by the therapist must all be taken into consideration. The therapist variables, in turn, may have an impact only insofar as they interact with patient variables, such as the degree of initial disturbance, personality structure, initial expectations, and perhaps demographic characteristics. In addition, situational variables such as the atmosphere in which therapy takes place and the "set" which is created for the patient must be considered. (49) How can we incorporate such an overwhelming number of variables into some kind of meaningful system?

A verbal theory even in skeletal form (which has been the vogue since the beginning of psychotherapy with its fascinating and often creative description of patient-therapist interplays) would at this point indeed leave us overwhelmed.

The essential question, "What are the effective elements in psychotherapy that produce constructive behavioral and personality change?", leads quite naturally to the theory of the general linear equation, as the most simple and useful available model (79, 82). Using this model, we may set the task for clinical theory and research as that of specifying the variables in psychotherapy which successfully predict observed constructive behavioral or personality change in patients. Once the variables are successfully discovered and measured, the problem becomes the empirical one of establishing by the usual statistical procedures the relative importance (or weights) of the known variables that most successfully predict personality or behavioral change.

The proposed model can be stated as:

$$CPC = K + TV_1 + \ldots + TV_n + PV_1 + \ldots + PV_n + SV_1 + \ldots + SV_n + IV^1 + \ldots + IV_n + e$$

Where: CPC = Index of Constructive Personality Change
K = Constant
TV^{1-p} = Therapist Variables 1 to N
PV^{1-p} = Patient Variables, 1 to N
SV^{1-p} = Situational or Contextual Variables, 1 to N
IV^{1-p} = Interaction or Process Variables, 1 to N
e = Error

The general linear equation will yield the fewest elements of psychotherapy possible: the criterion measure of constructive change in the patient can be expressed as a linear function of the psychotherapy variables, and each psychotherapy variable can then be tested for the significance or importance of its effect in the resulting equation. This formulation simply asks the basic question of whether or not a given variable has a significant effect, and whether that variable continues to have an effect when other variables are included in the same linear equation. This is indeed a major question in the field of psychotherapy, especially in view of the present proliferation of concepts: if, for example, the activity level of the therapist were found to be a significant predictor of personality change in psychotherapy, would it still make a difference in outcome if high levels of therapist authenticity and accurate empathic understanding were also present?

It could be argued that the real world is not so simply constructed that linear relationships will always be found. Curvilinear relationships seem inevitable. However, the model is still appropriately useful: we might, for example, transform some of the quantitative measures of the effective therapy variables so that one would be expressed, as say, the log value, a second as an exponential value, and the third as an arc sine value.

Such an all-encompassing, but basically simple, model has the advantage of making no assumptions about the nature of psychotherapy, the nature of personality, or the nature of personality change. It has the advantage of excluding no past or future explanations of the "dynamics" of therapeutic personality change. Indeed, future research will inevitably draw heavily upon current theory and clinical practice. Thus, the model is simply an empirical one that can be used equally well by psychoanalytic, client-centered, behavioristic, or eclectic researchers and practitioners who aim for more effective treatment.

The linear model also provides a convenient way of organizing the state of our present findings from psychotherapy research.

In attempting to review the research gains in knowledge of psychotherapy in the period from January 1960 to January 1964, we will also be tentatively specifying the known variables that give meaning and substance to the general linear model. To do so is to start with the goal itself: constructive personality or behavioral change.

CONSTRUCTIVE PERSONALITY CHANGE

Constructive personality change (CPC) has often seemed an illusive entity. Some have claimed that changes resulting from psychotherapy are so subtle that they defy measurement. This is utter nonsense!

Patients usually come to psychotherapy because they are so miserable that they are willing to pay hard money to alleviate their discomfort or because their lives are in such disorder that people around them have *demanded* that they change. Patients are asking for rather dramatic changes in themselves as a result of psychotherapy. As clinicians, we would be the first to say that successful psychotherapy does involve visible and significant changes; if it did not, we would not call it successful psychotherapy. Most often, constructive personality or behavioral change has seemed illusive because researchers have sought a single measure. Recent research from Wisconsin and Kentucky, as reported by Truax (82), as well as from the Camarillo Project, as reported by May and Tuma (52), shows again that personality change is far from a unitary phenomenon. Most patients show a mixture of positive and negative changes rather than a totally uniform positive or negative change.

What is needed is an attempt by researchers to obtain multiple measures of behavioral and personality change. A criterion index may be obtained by some simple and straightforward means, such as converting the multiple measures to standard scores and summing them. As psychologists, we long ago learned that even in the simple situation of conditioning experiments, measures of frequency, amplitude, and latency yielded different findings. Why should we be so naive as to expect one behavioral or personality measure alone to capture the intricacies and complexities of significant behavioral or personality change?

The point to be made is simply this: while strong arguments could be leveled against the infallibility of any one measure, if significant improvement occurred on a majority of varied indices, then we would be hard put to argue that the patient was not improved. Thus, research results would be less likely to become simply artifacts of the particular criterion measure used. A considerable body of important advances in personality measurement and indeed in the measurement of personality change has become available over recent years and is now more readily available to researchers.

An outcome criterion should include a number of different measures tapping significant areas of human functioning: self-report questionnaires, such as the MMPI and Q-sort; measures of gross functioning, such as discharge rates in institutions, productivity and earning power, academic standing, and other measures of educational and vocational adjustment; measures of relationship satisfaction, such as reported by a spouse, a close friend, a business associate, or a neighbor; gross behavioral measures, such as the Wittenborn Psychiatric Rating Scale; therapist judgment ratings; and a host of other measures of "face value" that almost any ingenious researcher could create.

Thus Graham (37) used a measure of sexual satisfaction and sexual activity level as an outcome measure, while Brown and Rickard (14) used coherence of speech taken from tape recordings as a separate measure. Endler (24) used the semantic differential to show an increase in self-evaluation post-therapy.

Indeed, a variety of meaures have been shown to reflect changes associated with psychotherapy. In a careful examination of perceptual changes, Seeman (65) found that most perceptual tasks did not reflect changes associated with therapy. One finding was positive: post-therapy patients were able to do better on the flicker-fusion test. As a result of the investigation, Seeman suggests a modification in the theorem of client-centered theory which implies that clients in general have perceptual distortion that will be modified by therapy. In general, they do not!

Spielberger, Weitz, and Denny (69) used improvement in academic performance as their criterion of adjustment and found that college freshmen with high anxiety scores who regularly attended group counseling sessions showed significantly greater improvement in grades than students who were not counseled or who did not regularly attend counseling. Employing scales from the Kelley Role Construct Repertory Test, Cartwright and Lerner (19) found improvement in psychotherapy related to the patient's need to change and the therapist's final level of understanding. In addition, Drasgow and Carkhuff (22) have given new meaning to an old instrument in tapping in on the ability of interest differences on the "Kuder-Neuropsychiatric keys" pre- and post- therapy to successfully differentiate from negative outcome. McGinnis (53) found the Barron Ego Strength Scale effective in differentiating alcoholic patients receiving group therapy as an adjunct to the regular A.A. program from patients receiving no group therapy.

The Camarillo study and the Wisconsin-Kentucky studies suggested that patients do not show uniform changes across all indices. Further evidence is given by Forsyth and Fairweather (29) who analyzed some 66 clinical variables, including those from a follow up study, to measure effects of psychotherapy. Their evidence clearly indicated that the criteria were nonunitary in nature. Ward adjustment, length of psychotherapy, and discharge measures tended to cluster together; but as a group they did not relate well to later follow-up adjustment. Community adjustment and social adjustment in group therapy (Finney Palo Alto Group Psychotherapy Scale) tended to cluster together, forming a second major criterion. The Wright study (96), done on an exit unit using essentially a "total push" type program vs. a control program, showed significant gains for the exit unit on discharge rate and employment rate, but not on inventory type measures.

Taken together, such studies indicate that only when we have variety of indices can we begin to make meaningful statements about constructive personality change. Thus, in the case of Wright's study, we might possibly suspect that the hospital administration had a hand in discharge rate and in immediate employment situations, and that perhaps this was the case of environmental manipulation rather than a case of any real significant change in the patients. In any event, such studies clearly indicate the need for a variety of indices of outcome measures.

THERAPIST VARIABLES

Research has begun to focus heavily upon therapist characteristics that appear related to significant outcome measures in studying the phenomena of psychotherapy. Impetus for such recent interest in the therapist has grown out of the work of Whitehorn and Betz (90), which suggested that the successful and unsuccessful (or A and B type) therapists differed in their attitudinal approach to psychotherapy. The successful therapist was warm and attempted to understand the patient in a personal, immediate, and idiosyncratic way whereas the less successful therapist tended to relate in a more impersonal manner, focusing upon psychopathology and a more external kind of "understanding." Betz (10, 11) has continued to find support for the hypothesis that the personality and interests of the therapist play a significant role in determining the effectiveness of the psychotherapeutic process, especially with process schizophrenics. McNair, Callahan, and Lorr (54) suggest that some modification in our enthusiasm is in order. They found that the type B therapist had significantly better therapy results than the type A therapist under one set of circumstances. They conclude that the relationship between therapist type and therapist results was dependent on the similarity of background and interest of patient and therapist.

Psychoanalytic (2, 40, 28, 64), client-centered (23, 47, 60, 61, 79, 80), and eclectic theorist (30, 59, 67, 75, 76) have in the past emphasized the importance of three therapist characteristics. They have stressed the importance of nonpossessive warmth, the therapist's maturity, integration or genuineness, and the therapist's sensitivity and accuracy in understanding the patient's inner experiences. Halkides (39) and Barrett-Lenard (6) investigated the importance of these three therapist behaviors (or conditions) from a client-centered point of view. Their evidence strongly suggests the relevance of the three therapist conditions for success with counseling cases, although a replication of the Halkides (39) study by Hart (41) failed at confirmation, even though Hart used the same data and essentially the same procedure.

A recent report (growing out of the Wisconsin program) reviewing a number of studies by Truax (81) focused essentially upon the three therapist characteristics. There were some differences in conception and measurement of the therapist conditions. It should be pointed out that the development of the concept of accurate empathy, as distinct from the earlier client-centered conception of empathy, grew out of the group psychotherapy research (79), where accurate empathy which stressed diagnostic accuracy or sensitivity to feeling or experiences from a slightly analytic point of view (2, 28), proved much more highly related to the criterion indices than did the better known empathy variable which grew out of the client-centered tradition. This series of studies was based upon a five-year research program in which a number of patients in intensive individual psychotherapy (lasting from six months to more than three and a half years) were compared with a carefully matched control group. Findings indicated that, (a) patients receiving psychotherapy and those receiving control conditions showed little difference in the average constructive personality change, but that, (b) patients whose therapist offered a high level of unconditional positive warmth, self-congruence or genuineness, and accurate empathic understanding, showed significant positive personality and behavioral change on a wide variety of indices, and (c) patients whose therapists offered relatively low levels of these conditions during therapy exhibited significant deterioration in personality and behavioral functioning. The evidence was clear-cut in showing that the three measurable therapist characteristics were clearly predictive of outcome, and that, in the samples studied, the number of therapists offering relatively high levels of these conditions approximated the number offering relatively low levels of these conditions, so that the average therapy patient outcome was not markedly different from that seen in the control group.

Bergin and Soloman (9), using the same accurate empathy scale in following up the empathy research of the earlier studies reported by Truax, presented evidence that accurate empathy was also significantly related to the therapist's ability to produce outcome in out-patients seen by fourth-year post-graduate clinical psychologists who had been trained in essentially psychoanalytic theory. Bergin and Soloman went further and related accurate empathic ability to personality characteristics of the therapist. One of their more intriguing findings was that accurate empathic ability was, within limits, positively related to the age of the therapist, thus suggesting that a maturational process of life experiencing provides a substrate for empathic ability.

Lesser (50) focused his research on patient-therapist similarity. His findings suggest that high actual similarity between patient and therapist led to below-average progress for patients (is that perhaps contaminated with the thought that for the therapist to be similar he must be sick?), but that the therapist's ability to accurately predict the degree of similarity between himself and his patient's Q-sort was significantly and positively related to the patients' progress. This seems to suggest again that the sensitive, empathic therapist who is able to accurately assess the patient and himself (high congruence?) is perhaps most effective.

Grigg (38), using a questionnaire technique, asked 249 clients to assess their own benefits from the counseling relationships. He found to his great surprise that there was no relationship between the client assessment of progress and the level of experience of the therapist involved. In his particular setting, the therapists seem not to have benefited from training. The data did indicate that clients felt that the inexperienced therapist or counselor was more likely to give advice, be active, and be interpretative. Perhaps these superficial aspects of degree of interpretativeness and degree of advice-giving are simply not very crucial in success.

As clinicians we often find that we feel we can work best with some patients rather than with others. In an "Uh huh" analogue study, Sapolsky (63) found that under the condition of experimenter-subject incompatibility there is virtually no response acquisition. Thus, the reinforcing value of the "Uh huh" is clearly contingent upon the "relationship" between experimenter and subject; if the relationship is compatible, then the "Uh huh" is reinforcing and there is response acquisition; if the relationship is incompatible, there is virtually no response acquisition, and hence we may assume little reinforcement value in the "Uh huh"! These findings seem to highlight the critical nature of the relationship, and perhaps point to the underlying role of therapist warmth.

In other studies by Truax, reported by Rogers (62), the findings indicated that the three therapist characteristics of accurate empathy, unconditional positive regard, and therapist genuineness were also related in individual psychotherapy to depth of patient self-exploration, which in turn was related to the outcome indices.

In a study by Spotts growing out of the Wisconsin program, reported by Rogers (62), findings suggest that positive regard or warmth, regardless of conditionality, was significantly associated with constructive personality change and patient engagement in the process of psychotherapy.

Many of us, as clinicians, have accepted as a basic part of our dogma, the idea that a good therapist shows a high degree of acceptance of others. Weiss, Krasner, and Ullmann (89) in a quasi-therapeutic analogue study were able to show that a hostile (nonempathic and nonwarm) experimenter decreased the number of verbal responses and, perhaps most significantly, that an experimenter who showered attention and assent or agreement (the warm supportive therapist) produced an increase in the subjects' frequency of self-reference statements. One very intriguing aspect of the study was the findings of greater emotional disturbance in the subjects during extinction with the experimenter who had previously showered attention and agreement upon them. One cannot help wondering whether perhaps the extinction period under those conditions seems something like a betrayal or incongruence in the therapist who had previously been attentive and agreeable and then had become aloof? In a related study, Streitfeld (73) used a scale of acceptance of self and others which he then compared to supervisor ratings of therapist ability and supervisor ratings of patient outcome. He found no relationships. In view of other evidence, his lack of findings seems likely to be due to the inadequacy of his homemade scale or in the supervisors' ratings.

A number of studies make us look again at traditional variables which we have considered in traditional ways. In the Cartwright and Lerner (19) study, only the therapist's final—not his initial—level of understanding of the patient was related to improvement in therapy. The Wisconsin finding (82) that too much accurate empathy, too early in therapy has a deleterious effect appears related. Thus, the initial level of therapist empathic understanding is perhaps not so crucial, and indeed may have a negative impact if too high, as the over-all, and especially the final, level of understanding. Interestingly enough, Waskow (88) found that "the more judgmental that a counselor was, the more the client tended to discuss and express his feelings," although it is difficult indeed to determine from this study the extent to which counselor judgmentalness may have been a function of client expression of feeling. However, the study serves to point up the need to further re-explore the efficacy of judgmentalness with certain "counseling-type" populations and to refine the different meanings of "judgmentalness." In addition, it leaves us without the critical knowledge of whether or not the client's expression of feeling is "good," that is, whether it is related to positive outcome with this particular population.

In studies (79, 84) designed to look at a number of therapist characteristics in group psychotherapy, comparative evaluations of conditions drawn from differing theoretical and clinical models were made upon hospitalized groups led by experienced therapists of widely differing approaches. In statistical analyses of 16 different therapist-influenced variables (including accurate empathy and warmth), concreteness or specificity of expression, a condition relatively under the direct control of the therapist, emerged as the major therapeutic contributor. Pope and Siegman (58), working with another related measure, offer the interpretation that therapist specificity may be anxiety reducing when the content area is neutral, but arousing when it is emotional.

In the study of group psychotherapy involving 16 dimensions or characteristics of group psychotherapy, the findings indicated that 14 therapeutic conditions were indeed associated with the criterion of intrapersonal or self-exploration, which other research has repeatedly shown to be significantly associated with various indices of constructive personality and behavioral change. (See next section on patient variables.) Using analysis of variance of multiple regression in the implementation of the model of the general linear equation, investigators discovered that seven of the conditions accounted for significant amounts of independent sources of variation in self-exploration: (1) therapist leadership; (2) therapist self-congruence or genuineness; (3) group concreteness or specificity of content discussion; (4) group empathy; (5) genuineness or self-congruence of group members; (6) group ego involvement; and (7) group cohesion. Each of the seven conditions accounted for *separate and independent* components of the amount and depth of self-exploration. Another important finding was that, while therapist accurate empathy, unconditional positive regard, and therapist self-congruence or genuineness were each individually related significantly to the criterion, the measurement of accurate empathy included the effective variance in unconditional positive regard. Thus, the therapist brought to the therapy situation two separate and independent personal or attitudinal characteristics: an accurate and warm understanding of the patient, and an honest openness to experiencing. A third important finding which should be mentioned was that the self-congruence had an essentially nonlinear relationship to the criterion, whereas a lack of genuineness or self-congruence on the part of the therapist indeed seemed to clearly inhibit self-exploration; beyond a minimal critical level, additional degrees of genuineness or self-congruence of the therapist were not related to increases in patient functioning. That datum suggests a change in the client-centered hypothesis to the effect that a lack of genuineness inhibits intrapersonal exploration and thus the concern should be with the presence of a conscious or unconscious facade or with "playing the therapist role."

A study using data obtained from individual psychotherapy with hospitalized schizophrenics (82) offered findings confirming much from the group therapy research. Again the degree of accurate empathy sufficiently accounted for the effective variance of unconditional positive warmth in predicting depth of patient self-exploration. The surprising finding, however, was that in predicting final case outcome, nonpossessive warmth or unconditional positive regard had a significant effect independent of the effect of therapist accurate empathy. That finding suggests that the client-centered hypothesis was to some degree in error and that the analytic hypothesis of an emotional, re-educative experience, as proposed by Alexander (2), was more correct.

In another study aimed at the role of therapist warmth, Strupp, Wallach, and Jenkins (77) found substantial correlations between the therapist's ratings of outcome of therapy and the patient's ratings of emotional-attitudinal variables relating to the quality of the therapeutic relationship, particularly the therapist's feelings of warmth and liking for the patient.

Cartwright and Vogel (20), using a Q-sort measure of outcome, found that in their setting more experienced therapists tended to be more successful than inexperienced therapists. This at least reflects well on their local training program, even if it does not illuminate the dimensions to which the increased experience might be related. The central question, of course, is what kind of experiences lead to better therapists? This they did not question.

In further attempts to untangle the complexities of therapist characteristics, Knupfer, Jackson, and Krieger (48) related supervisors' ratings of therapists' competence for 40 psychiatric residents with the residents' own self-report on a Q-sort. The data suggested that therapists who were rated as highly competent were both more self-confident and more expressive as individuals, whereas persons whom the supervisors felt to be less therapeutically competent presented themselves as weaker and more passive individuals on their self-Q-sorts. In a study getting at the same question, Combs and Soper (20) found statistically significant correlations ranging from .40 to .65 between supervisors' rank-orders of "good" and "bad" counselors and 12 aspects of the counselor's attitudes. Thus, "good" counselors tended to assume the internal rather than external frame of reference with others, to be people rather than thing-oriented, and to see people as able, dependable, and friendly rather than unable, undependable, and unfriendly.

After reading theoretical and clinical writings of a number of fairly well known clinicians and then listening to a psychotherapy session with a live patient, one is most often struck by the vast inconsistencies between what we practice and what we preach. In the Wisconsin and in the Kentucky projects it was often observed that a given therapist who was known by his co-workers to be very warm, friendly, supportive, and understanding sometimes came out with surprisingly low ratings on scales of warmth and accurate empathy when an objective evaluation was made of his tape recorded sessions with patients. By contrast, a therapist who talked harshly and heartlessly, using a mechanistic learning theory language, sometimes came out quite high in objective ratings of interactions with patients on the same measures of warmth and accurate empathy. Thus, some therapists talk about warmth and understanding but seem to be aloof and detached, while others talk mechanically and coldly about patients but are very warm, personal, and understanding in their encounter with patients. A very significant study by Wrenn (95) attempted to get at this puzzling observation in a more quantitative way. He asked 54 counselors to write responses to standard therapy situations which were designed to maximize theoretical differences in the way they might be handled. He found virtually no relationship between their concrete situational responses and their professed theoretical orientation. Does this mean that the analytic therapist might be quite existential, the existential therapist quite analytic, and even the behavior therapist quite client-centered? Perhaps it is time to look at *what we do rather than what we say we do*. With this in mind, we cannot help feeling the tragedy of the Menninger Psychotherapy Research Project. It is perhaps one of the best studies of its kind in investigating analytic and analytically-oriented psychotherapy. This tragedy, in view of the observation of other programs and the study by Wrenn, lies in the lack of complete recording of what actually went on during the analytic and analytically-oriented sessions. With the present hindsight, complete tape recordings or even video tape recordings would seem obvious necessities. There is much that can be gained from the more fragmentary and even pre-digested data available from the Menninger project, but looking back with current knowledge, we can see how much has been lost.

PATIENT VARIABLES

Increasing attention, in recent literature, has been given to the characteristics of patients which lead to constructive change as an outcome of psychotherapy. Truax (82) studied therapy and control groups of hospitalized schizophrenic patients and found no relationship between the traditional characteristics of age, sex, socioeconomic class, and initial degree of disturbance (Health-Sickness Scale) or even premorbid adjustment (Phillips Scale), and outcome measures using various indices of behavior and personality change for either therapy or control patients. Cabeen and Coleman (16) report similar findings in working with male sex-offender patients receiving formal group and adjunctive therapies. They found that older patients, less intelligent patients, homosexual offenders, and repeated offenders demonstrated improvement as often as the other patients. Wood and his associates (93, 94) offered further corroboration. Such traditional indices as degree of illness, diagnostic category, or presence of outpatient follow-up treatment had no relationship to the long-term degree of final improvement of hospitalized patients who had been in therapy. Only married patients were found to have benefited more than unmarried patients.

Stone, Frank, Nash, and Imber (72) took exception to the Truax, Wood et al. and Cabeen and Coleman findings concerning degree of disturbance. In a five year follow-up of 30 out-patients, Stone et al. found that patients who exhibited the greatest positive change were the sickest to start with (and had perhaps more room to change or their resultant data simply constituted the statistical phenomena of regression toward the mean). In further exploring other dimensions, Stone et al. found that patients changing most were younger (in contrast to the Cabeen and Coleman and the Truax findings) and for obscure reasons held religious preferences for Catholicism and Lutheranism.

When we consider patient prognostic indicators in the context of the research evidence indicating that certain specified therapeutic conditions offered by the therapist lead to constructive personality change, then we may strongly suggest that many patient prognostic indicators reflect simply the prejudices and biases of the therapists. Thus most therapists, and indeed other hospital and clinic personnel because of their prejudices, are usually unable or unwilling to provide high levels of therapeutic conditions to less desirable patients and therefore such patients show less constructive change. The suggestion is that therapists and others show, for example, less warmth and accurate empathic understanding to the patient who is less likable to the therapist because of his age, his religious preference, or even his type of emotional disturbance: how many psychopathic deviates, for example, receive high levels of warmth and accurate empathy from therapists?

In a study of more psychological characteristics, Stoler (71) found that more successful clients were liked to a significantly greater degree than less successful clients, and that client likability correlated significantly with Gendlin's Experiencing Strand of Walker's Process Scale. As mentioned earlier, Cartwright and Lerner (19) found the client's need to change in client-centered counseling directly related to improvement in counseling.

Heilbrun (44) tested the relationship between counseling readiness (a self-report measure) and four self-report personality variables, self-acceptance, tendency to make a good social impression, responsibility, and psychological-mindedness. He found strong and significant negative correlations for a large number of males and females on all measures except one: there was no relationship between self-acceptance and counseling readiness for the girls.

A number of studies have explored what it is that successful patients do in therapy. There is a great deal of convergence upon the patient's intrapersonal or self-exploratory experiences. Using a variety of indices of constructive behavioral and personality change, Truax (80) found significantly more depth of self-exploration and depth of experiencing in successful than in unsuccessful cases of hospitalized schizophrenics. Truax and Carkhuff (82) reviewed results indicating relatively clear-cut findings that the greater the degree of patient engagement in the deep intrapersonal or self-exploratory process, the greater the degree of constructive personality changes in the patient. Further analysis indicated that even during initial stages of psychotherapy (the second interview), the level of patient self-exploration was significantly predictive of final outcome (from 6 months to $3\frac{1}{2}$ years later). Wagstaff, Rice, and Butler (87) report similar findings in a study of client-centered counseling. Their data indicated that patients with successful outcome tended to explore themselves more in the course of psychotherapy, whereas patients who could be classified as therapeutic failures showed little self-exploration and emotional involvement. In a more specific study of client-centered counseling, Braaten (12) found that measures of self-reference and "private self" differentiated successful from unsuccessful cases. Tomlinson and Hart (78), employing the Walker process scale to measure depth of patient experiencing, self-exploration and rigidity of concepts, found

that the scale was able to differentiate successful from unsuccessful counseling cases.

CONTEXTUAL OR SITUATIONAL VARIABLES

Recent research has accorded very little attention to the potentially
critical contextual or situational variables that are generally controlled,
whether directly or indirectly, by the therapist, often without an awareness of their effect. We, as clinical researchers, have apparently abdicated
in this area in favor of the verbal conditioning people who have satu-
rated the literature with studies, few of which are in any way related to
outcome criteria or, indeed, in their analogue forms to the process of
therapy itself.

At the University of Kentucky studies exploring two situational
variables that are not tied to past theoretical models have begun to yield
results. These studies focus on (a) vicarious therapy pre-training for psychotherapy and (b) the use of "alternate sessions" in group psychotherapy where the therapist is himself absent from the therapy sessions
(79). The former, vicarious therapy pre-training (VTP), may be employed
in either group or individual psychotherapy. It simply involves presentation to prospective patients of a 30-minute tape recording of excerpts
of "good" patient therapy behavior. The tape itself illustrates in a very
concrete manner how clients often explore themselves and their feelings:
it thus provides cognitive and experiential structuring of "how to be
a good patient." In short, it allows for a vicarious experiencing of deep
psychotherapy prior to the initiation of the psychotherapeutic or counseling relationship. Recent research (83) completed using VTP in group
psychotherapy with both mental hospital and juvenile delinquent patients provides both clinical and research confirmation of its facilitative
effect. It was found that early psychotherapy sessions from groups receiving VTP showed significantly higher levels of self-exploration than
non-VTP groups having the same number of sessions. Further, VTP
resulted in significantly more successful outcomes in time-limited therapy
as judged by a variety of objective outcome criteria.

Wolf (91), Wolf and Schwartz (92), and Truax (79) have suggested,
especially in regard to group psychotherapy, that sessions in which the
therapist is absent, if alternated with regular group meetings, would
prove therapeutic and thus almost double the number of therapy hours
that a given therapist could offer. In initial studies (83) of alternate
sessions in group therapy, it was found that both hospitalized mental
patients and juvenile delinquents showed the same general depth of
intrapersonal exploration or process movement during the alternate sessions as they did during the regular therapy sessions. In fact, with the

juvenile delinquents, there was a tendency for the deepest level of therapeutic process to occur in the alternate sessions when the therapist was
absent! But—and this is a very big BUT—tentative findings indicate
that the alternate session groups are *not* significantly more improved in
relation to a variety of objective outcome criteria than nonalternate
session groups, which met only with the therapist. The suggestion is that
a depth of self-exploration is of little lasting value in and of itself without
the therapist present.[1] Perhaps the therapist facilitates an emergent
directionality out of an essentially directionless process of intrapersonal
exploration.

Studying the question of the frequency of therapeutic contact, Lorr,
McNair, Michaux, and Raskin (51) presented evidence to suggest that
some slight benefit accrues from more frequent therapy sessions when
compared to infrequent sessions.

Other than these studies, there is little research being reported in
the area of situational variables. In general, the recent literature on
situational variables is typified by findings such as those showing that
music played at a fast tempo increased the rate of speech of patients in
group therapy significantly more than the slow tempo (42). The potential relevance to outcome is obscure, to say the least.

PROCESS OF PROJECTION?

A great majority of the so-called process studies of psychotherapy
cannot actually be called studies of psychotherapy. More properly they
should be referred to as studies of two-person interactions. They may
or may not have anything at all to do with psychotherapy. The cheapness
with which they can be carried out has apparently recommended them
to a variety of investigators. Unfortunately, they usually simply relate
two unknown variables both of which may or may not be related to positive or negative outcome. To be sure, they are all quite interesting and
make excellent reading.

Perhaps one of the more popular of the so-called process studies of
psychotherapy was that reported by Speisman (68) who attempted to
deal with a potentially important variable, that of depth of interpretation. Unfortunately his depth of interpretation scale had not been related
to outcome and could have been very easily labeled a scale of "genetic
interpretation" or "historicality," or even a scale of plausibility of therapist response. In any event, he reports a superficial and moderate depth
of interpretation. Such studies make very interesting reading and are

[1] Theoretical objections to the use of alternate sessions have been made by Haim
Ginott in personal communications. S. S. Slavson, in his recent book, *Textbook in
Analytic Group Psychotherapy,* 1963, International Univer. Press, has also made theoretic
objections to the use of alternate sessions which correctly predict these findings of
greater patient process without greater outcome.

very intriguing, although they actually provide very little in the way of information and instead seem to provide a convenient projective device for theoretician and clinician alike. We are free to speculate. If we are devout believers in deep interpretations, then we are free to assume that greater resistance on the part of the patient is in fact a good thing since it shows we are dealing with significant material which helps the patient to come to grips with the core of his "being" or the central focus of his life problems. On the other hand, if we are devout believers in superficial interpretations (and if we are, we certainly would not call them superficial but instead might refer to them as responses dealing with the immediate "being" of the patient or the "here and now," etc.), then we are quite free to cite the Speisman study as evidence for our beliefs; we might interpret (or project) the lowered resistance on the part of the patient as an extremely positive happening since it facilitates self-exploration and allows him to come to terms with his "being" and to work through his relationship, problems, and life turmoils.

Clearly the plethora of studies of this type, labeled as "process" studies, have had a great attraction to researchers in recent years. The literature is filled with them. Many eminent researchers and theorists call for more of such studies, perhaps because they give the illusion of being simple and straightforward. Unfortunately, such encouragement has led many of our most gifted researchers into producing more such "projective" evidence.

In this area a very excellent study by Bandura, Lipsher, and Miller (5) discovered that the therapist's approach to hostile patient responses led to more patient expression of hostile content. Again such findings present a convenient projective device to the theoretician and even to future researchers, since we don't know whether this makes the patient more or less adjusted, or in fact in any way changes his personality or usual behavioral adjustment. We are free to speculate about the possible meaning of both therapist and patient variables in such studies. In the rarefied atmosphere of intricate theory building and description of dynamics we could go even further. The work of Gottschalk, Gleser, and their associates (32-35) shows able attempts to isolate and measure three different types of hostility in verbal samples and their studies could be co-joined with the Bandura et al. study. We could then theorize about which kind of hostility approach by the therapist would lead to increases and decreases in which kind of hostility emission rates in patients, and then make more interesting projections by guessing how it relates to outcomes.

The point being made is not that such studies are worthless and of no value to the growing science of human behavior and psychotherapy, since it seems likely that at least some of the hundreds of studies of this type being produced would be related to meaningful outcomes in psychotherapy. The point is that such studies have little value to psychotherapy per se. To have meaning they must build upon prior research which shows that at least one variable studied is relevant to outcome in psychotherapy. Thus if we knew that patients who showed positive behavioral and personality change were those who showed increasing expressions of certain kinds of hostility throughout psychotherapy, it would then become appropriate to determine therapist behaviors that produced changes in patient expressions of hostility. Without such prior information, it seems very likely that such studies are a waste of much needed creative skills and energy by the research investigator, and constitute an unfortunate stimulus for "projective" theories. We might expect the sum total of such studies, then, to tend to lead to confusion rather than clarity in the research literature even if they are both interesting and intriguing. In sum, they have!

Fortunately, some researchers have attempted to do research related to significant therapy outcomes, even though it is more difficult and more costly.

One fairly exciting finding dealing with both process and outcome of psychotherapy was that obtained by Butler (15) in an investigation of changes in Q-sorts using the self-sort. He found clear evidence that there were nonrandom positive and negative changes in patient self-sorts as early as the eighth interview of treatment in a counseling situation. Since other research has indicated nonrandom positive and negative change, or increased variance in outcome measures, as a result of psychotherapy and still further studies have attempted to isolate particular therapist, patient, and interaction processes that differentiate between the positive and negative nonrandom changes, findings such as Butler's become of great significance. It means that detectable changes can and do occur in even the early stages of the counseling relationship (which most clinicians for perhaps quite invalid reasons believe to be watered-down psychotherapy relationships).

This finding by Butler, combined with the positive findings of the Shlien, Mosak, and Dreikurs study (66) on time-limited client-centered and Adlerian psychotherapy, and the research dealing with long-term and short-term psychotherapy indicating that long-term psychotherapy might be the result of the dependency nurturing of the therapist, together suggest the need for further exploration of time-limited psychotherapy as well as a search of the effects of different lengths of predetermined time-limited therapy.

Cartwright (18) in a replication of her 1957 study (17), confirmed the earlier findings that there is an increase in self-consistency of patients in therapy. In light of the data reported by Truax indicating that, at least with schizophrenics, psychotherapy can clearly be for better or for worse, another almost overlooked aspect of her study assumes major significance. She found in analyzing her failure cases that they showed significant deterioration in adequacy of interpersonal relations! They did not simply not get better; they got worse. This extends the findings with schizophrenics to indicate that even with mildly disturbed populations some patients show clear negative deterioration in behavioral or personality functioning as a consequence of counseling or psychotherapy. It should be noted that the Truax studies also indicated that the therapeutic conditions of accurate empathy, unconditional positive regard, and therapist self-congruence tended to hold for counseling center clients as well as for schizophrenic patients. If we were to put these studies together, they would suggest that with the very mildly disturbed counseling cases as well as with the more severely hospitalized schizophrenic, therapists who offer low levels of conditions have patients who show deterioration in personality and in behavioral functioning.

Related to the research dealing with the process of psychotherapy are the studies of therapist and patient expectancies, preferences, and assessments of therapy. Among the plethora of studies concluding, in effect, that therapists prefer "better" patients, that is, those less sick and more sensitive, intelligent, and willing to talk about themselves and their problems, were a few studies showing the discrepant expectations of therapist and patient, particularly with regard to the length of treatment (31): the therapist thinks in longer terms and the patient in shorter terms of treatment. Feifel and Eells (27), using an open-ended questionnaire to get at differential assessments of therapy, found that therapists tended to stress changes in symptomatic relief and improvement in social relationships, whereas patients stressed self-understanding and self-confidence. In addition, the patients focused on the opportunity to talk over problems and emphasized the "human" characteristics of the therapist, while the therapist focused upon therapeutic technique. Gonyea (36) interpreted his findings to suggest that therapeutic relationship variables are correlated with therapist experience, but not with each other. The variety of scales which he employs are of a validity and reliability dubious enough to raise questions about both the findings and the interpretations.

The dimension of social class influences upon therapy again rears its ugly head. Moore, Benedek, and Wallace (57) found that psychiatrists were likely to rely upon drugs for lower-class and psychotherapy for upper-class women. Also, patients with a psychological view of their illness were significantly more likely to be treated by psychotherapy and more likely to improve. Thus, the significance of social class to the clinician seems to be primarily as it influences the patient's view of her illness, that is, patients from the same social class as the psychiatrist see illness as does the clinician and are consequently more effectively treated by him.

THERAPY LENGTH, CONTINUANCE, AND TERMINATION

Studies of the length of stay in psychotherapy seem to deserve separate consideration.

Continuance in psychotherapy has become legitimately a major problem, since in the no-cost or low-cost clinic or hospital situation the patient who comes into therapy may not be highly motivated to begin with, and abrupt termination initiated by the patient is frequent. Continuance reflects to some degree upon outcome, since if the patient doesn't participate in psychotherapy, he is not likely to show therapeutic change.

Bailey, Warshaw, and Eichler (4) checked various demographic factors relating to length of stay and amount of progress in therapy. Two factors proved significant: (a) the higher the patient's educational level and (b) the greater the experience in psychotherapy, the more likely the patient is to stay and improve in therapy. Strickland and Crowne (74) found that patients with high need for approval terminated therapy significantly earlier than patients with lower need for approval. It may be that need for approval is really a "sick" belief in which case the finding fits the mass of other data. Hiler (45) approached the continuance in therapy problem by analysis of sentence-completion test material. His evidence suggests that the patient who tends to continue in psychotherapy also tends to be more willing to reveal personal feelings, has a higher need achievement (as contrasted with Strickland and Crowne's low need for approval group), and has more psychological sophistication and perhaps hence more willingness to make frank admissions of inferiority. In a parallel study (46), Hiler obtained evidence to show that terminators tended to show more evidence of acting out and more paranoid and schizoid ideation whereas remainers tended towards more neurotic complaints of obsessive, phobic, depressed, and anxiety symptoms. In short, the sicker people terminate and the healthier people get treatment. The evidence currently available on continuation tends to point the same way. In another study dealing with the length of stay in therapy and the personality of the patient, Zolik and Hollon (97) obtained findings suggesting that healthier and more integrated but less independent patients tended to remain in therapy longest. Employing the Rorschach, Affleck and Mednick (1) report that the patient who is likely to continue is the more verbal individual who has a richer fantasy life and is better equipped to relate to his fellow human beings. Again, better patients stay longer!

Thanks to Stieper and Wiener (70) there is some evidence suggesting that the therapist plays a prominent role in so-called interminable therapy. He found no difference in the outcome measure of MMPI change between short-term cases and long-range cases lasting from 2.8 to 10 years when evaluated. Similarly Truax (82) found a slight negative relationship between length of treatment and outcome with hospitalized schizophrenics. Stieper and Wiener went further, and, using pooled judgments, arrived at a predictable dimension of "dependency nurturing" which was more characteristic of the therapist in the long-term rather than the short-term therapy cases.

Another study (82) in which psychotherapy was available in a fairly unstructured fashion in a ward of 24 chronic patients tried to relate patient and therapist activities during the initial interview of psychotherapy to termination or continuance. The only really surprising finding was that when the therapist was deeply empathic during the first interview, patients tended to discontinue treatment. This suggests that a relationship needs to be formed, perhaps particularly with the chronic schizophrenic, before deeply empathic responses frighten off the prospective patient. The data clearly confirm the correctness of the stress on "timing" of responses traditionally made by psychoanalytic writers.

In a follow-up of their earlier work, McNair, Lorr, and Callahan (54) found that therapists who were markedly interested in the patient's problems held significantly more patients in therapy. Employing self-report questionnaires, Mendelsohn and Geller (56) found that the greater the over-all similarity between therapist and patients, the greater the length of counseling (more friendship or dependency?).

THE QUESTION OF CAUSATION

One study (80), employing a balanced incomplete block design, was aimed at clarifying this relationship for accurate empathy. Analysis of the accurate empathy data indicated that different therapists indeed produced different levels of accurate empathy when interacting with the same set of patients.

The data, then, suggest that it is the therapist who determines the level of conditions, and in this case, specifically, of accurate empathy.

Similar findings have been obtained with other conditions. Using the same recorded interviews from the same patients and the same balanced incomplete block design, researchers made evaluations of the degree to which the patient engaged in the process of therapy. It was found that both the therapist and the patient made significant contributions to the patient's engagement in the process of therapy.

Another study by Truax and Carkhuff (86) has attacked experimentally the question of whether the patient's depth of self-exploration is controlled or determined by the level of conditions (accurate empathy and unconditional positive regard) offered by the therapist in initial interviews. First, relatively high conditions of accurate empathy and unconditional positive regard were presented; then the experimental variable of *lowered conditions* was purposefully introduced by the therapist and maintained for the next third of the interview, after which the experimental variable was deliberately withdrawn and high conditions were re-established. The data indicated that with hospitalized schizophrenic patients the attempted experimental operations were successful; that is, that the conditions of accurate empathy and unconditional positive regard were successfully lowered during the middle periods of the therapeutic interviews (and interestingly enough the level of congruence of the therapist was maintained, if not raised, during lowered condition). There was the predicted significant drop in depth of self-exploration while lowered conditions were present and a return to high self-exploration when conditions were raised. This held for each individual patient. The results clearly suggest a causal relationship between the level of conditions offered by the therapist and the patient's consequent level of self-exploration.

Another study by Heckel, Wiggins, and Salzberg (43) tried three strategies in attempting to extinguish patient delusional systems: (a) joining in with the patient, (b) encouragement, and (c) interviewing. Unfortunately none were effective.

Beyond these studies, few attempts have been made to experimentally manipulate meaningful variables in therapy: again we have abdicated in favor of the verbal conditioning analogues.

THE USE OF LAY THERAPISTS

Considerable interest has already focused upon the relevant variables for teaching both professional and lay therapists. A program for applying research knowledge, and even research instruments, to the training of professional and lay therapists has already been implemented at the University of Kentucky (85). Initial results of this program indicate that, after a training period of only four months involving four hours a week plus practicum time, lay therapists are able to provide moderately high levels of therapeutic conditions to hospitalized patients. In fact, the measured level of accurate empathy, unconditional positive regard, and therapist genuineness for the trained lay therapists meet or exceed those obtained on the average from a group of more experienced therapists in the Wisconsin program. Studies are now underway evaluating the effectiveness of lay therapists in terms of patient personality change, and thus will provide evidence of causality by directly relating specific training of therapists with patient outcome.

Although the characteristics of the lay therapists were not measured by Appleby (3), he found significant improvement in experimental groups of chronic schizophrenic patients who were treated by hospital aides functioning as lay therapists. Perhaps even more striking, Mendel and Rapport (55) presented data indicating that 70 percent of a group of 166 chronically disturbed female patients were maintained outside of the hospital at a minimally adequate level of functioning during a 51-month period of observation by being provided with half-hour monthly interactions with nonprofessional persons functioning as lay therapists.

SUMMARY AND IMPLICATIONS OF CURRENT RESEARCH

The findings reported during the four-year period just reviewed, while they constitute in reality only beginning steps, have considerable significance in their implications for the practice of psychotherapy, for the training of psychotherapists, and even for the general problems of prevention of psychological disturbances or emotional upset.

The history of psychotherapy research and the reports of the research efforts reviewed here have been those of primarily isolated and fragmentary reports. With more solid data it could be expected that more over-all analysis integrating divergent findings and assessing their relative contribution to effective psychotherapy would be in order.

The major finding growing from all research is that psychotherapy as currently practiced can be both helpful and harmful. That is perhaps a profoundly distressing finding.

The second major finding, that the field is now moving successfully toward identifying specific dimensions of psychotherapy, such as warmth —which if present to a high degree leads to constructive personality change, and if present to a low degree leads to negative or deteriorative personality change—is perhaps the most exciting and significant new development in the field.

Such findings have direct relevance to the field of preventive mental health. The evidence suggests that such identifiable therapeutic variables can be used in a model for psychotherapy, and that this model is a reversible model: the model can be used to predict positive psychotherapeutic personality change, and to predict damaging environmental factors which facilitate emotional disturbance or mental illness. Thus, for example, the evidence suggests that a lack of warmth or the presence of hostility indeed facilitates deteriorative personality change. It thus becomes conceivable that school counselors, teachers, and others can become skilled at identifying such environmental conditions and then take steps to change such an environment in an effort to prevent the predictable ensuing emotional upset or mental illness. Certainly, it seems likely, that if we can identify and quantify the effective elements in the psychotherapeutic relationship, then the same approach and tools can be used to identify the same elements in the parent-child relationship, the husband-wife relationship, or indeed in any other human encounter.

In essence, the implication is that the more we learn about how to help people, the more we also know about how not to hurt people. Thus, psychotherapy research is of potentially enormous significance to society in its contribution to facilitation of constructive development of the human individual.

Perhaps even more clearly, research findings identifying elements of effective psychotherapy are directly applicable to the training of psychotherapists.

The evidence that therapists do not always practice what they preach implies that the therapist in training could perhaps profit from less theoretical and intellectual training and more specific training of how to make operational the effective ingredients in psychotherapy. Specifically, measuring instruments used in current research could be directly applied to training programs. Thus tape recordings of psychotherapy rated very high in the known elements of effective psychotherapy could be selected to provide concrete examples for beginning therapists, and such scales could also be used to evaluate the trainee's own early therapy behavior to give him immediate and concrete informational feedback telling him how well he is learning to operate with his concepts.

Since the personality of the therapist and his personal characteristics loom as most central in the research evidence currently available, the training of the therapist in at least some areas involve personality change in the trainee. It might therefore be sensible to apply the known therapeutic elements to the training of the therapist himself. This implies that the teacher or supervisor should provide minimally high levels of therapeutic conditions and thus contribute to the trainee's personality growth, and also provide the trainee with a living, observable model of a therapist to be imitated.

Our current knowledge of effective ingredients in psychotherapy offers very direct implications for the current practices of psychotherapy. Since we have in the past, perhaps naively, believed that psychotherapy by its nature could rarely prove harmful, we have all too often allowed the beginning therapist to proceed directly from theory to an "on-the-job" training. It now seems certain that therapeutic encounters which provide low levels of therapist-offered conditions lead to significant harmful effects in the lives of our all too human patients. We may now need to rely more heavily and more universally on intermediate steps between theory and practice, such as role playing, in the training of therapists. It may mean that as supervisors and administrators we will be more concerned that prospective therapists be not only theoretically capable, but be personally able to offer at least minimal levels of therapeutic conditions.

The cluster of research evidence indicating that the degree of patient self-exploration is predictive of outcome in a wide variety of patient populations offers a promising lead towards enhancing the effectiveness of existing psychotherapies. The evidence suggests that psychotherapy relationships can be evaluated very early in the process of therapy to give some practical indication of the likelihood that the particular relationship will succeed in helping the patient. In cases that seem unlikely to succeed, the therapist, the hospital, or the clinic can first try to offer the patient a different therapist, and if this does not prove likely to succeed, they may offer other nonpsychotherapeutic helps.

Evidence describing the kinds of patients who are most likely to be helped in psychotherapy suggests that the traditional variables that most of us have accepted on faith are, in fact, irrelevant. Research shows the importance of marital status in successful outcomes and points to the importance of the patient's own need to change as well as his own emotional involvement. There is controversial evidence with respect to age and degree of disturbance and even at best the evidence is that if they are important at all they are not very important. The perhaps sobering evidence related to therapy continuance or termination is that healthy patients who seem to need it less actually are the ones who get more psychotherapy, while the sicker ones tend to terminate treatment prematurely. Putting together the evidence on patient and therapist similarly, we may say that it looks as though patients who are similar to their therapists are the ones who tend to continue in therapy but also show the least progress. Such findings suggest the potential usefulness of arranging the offering of psychotherapy under conditions that are not entirely under the control of the patient.

The relatively unexplored area of contextual or situational variables in psychotherapy has yielded some fruit. There seems to be some slight positive benefit from more frequent, when compared to less frequent, therapeutic contacts. Vicarious therapy pretraining seems to facilitate both the depth and extent of therapeutic process engaged in by the patient, and also contributes substantially to more favorable outcome.

The evidence from a variety of research studies concerning the characteristics and behavior of therapists has important personal meaning to us as therapists. It may mean that as therapists we can aim toward a more clear and sensitive awareness of the patient's inner-being, toward a greater ability to understand deeply the patient's moment-to-moment feelings and experiencings, and thus to make more accurate meanings out of the shifts in posture, slight inflections in tone, and the empty silences. It can mean that as therapists we can concentrate less upon our skills at intellectualized diagnostic formulations and more upon developing our skills at the moment-to-moment diagnosis of the patient's "being." These findings may mean that as therapists we can allow ourselves to express more openly our deep warmth and caring for the *person* who comes to us for help. The findings may mean that we can become more effective as we are more able personally to enter into a direct encounter with the person of the patient. We may thus risk confronting the patient as a person rather than as an institution; that our open or nondefensive intactness, our human authenticity or genuineness may also encourage the patient to deeply "be himself" within the relationship.

The available evidence may mean that as therapists we can be more helpful to the extent that we personally hold an optimistic view of man and can see within our patient his potential for being able, adequate, and likeable.

The evidence may also mean, that as we become more self-confident, more concrete and specific in our statements, and thus more expressive and less passive, we can become better able to blunt the harmful edge and sharpen the helpful edge of the two-edged sword which is the psychotherapeutic encounter itself. Finally, these research findings may mean that when we personally are unable to offer such personal conditions to a particular patient, then both our knowledge and our integrity can direct us to helping him find another therapist or another type of help.

TOWARDS BETTER PSYCHOTHERAPY RESEARCH

The research findings reviewed here represent major advances, if not breakthroughs, in our knowledge of effective psychotherapy. The studies themselves, however, are really only pilot studies and are thus suggestive rather than conclusive.

What can be done to make for more extensive and more certain knowledge of the ingredients of successful psychotherapy? This is not an obscure or academic question. It is a vital one. The evidence is that psychotherapy can be a significant force for human betterment, for facilitating human happiness, individual productivity, and perhaps even creativity, but that as it is currently practiced *it can be for better or for worse*. Without such vitally needed knowledge some patients are damaged by what passes as psychotherapy today; the evidence suggests that both the hospitalized schizophrenic and the college counseling client show marked and significant deterioration as effects of poor psychotherapy. Thus we must know with some immediacy the elements of psychotherapy leading to constructive (or deteriorative) change in the all too human patient we are seeking to help.

The evidence that high levels of identifiable therapist-offered "conditions" are strikingly related to constructive changes while low levels are related to deteriorative changes in the patient is at once sobering and exciting. While it raises a host of very serious practical and ethical questions for the fields of psychotherapy and counseling, it also points the way for research toward pinpointing the significant ingredients in effective psychotherapy and thus largely eliminating destructive "helping" relationships.

How, then, can we produce better research? Psychotherapy research does not basically lack sufficient methodology nor does it lack creative or even brilliant investigators so much as it lacks data. To do better research we need better data.

A perhaps formidable obstacle to better data and hence better research lies in the therapist himself. All too often we as therapists are willing to talk, speculate, and even theorize about what we do in the therapeutic encounter, but are unwilling to let the researcher see what we actually do—or even tolerate the silent and noncommittal tape recorder to hear us.

To make firm and rapid advances, a large mass of solid data is necessary. In large part, this means a very large number of psychotherapy cases from a wide variety of experienced therapists must be completely recorded along with varied indices of patient personality or behavioral change. This is a major but necessary task if we are to have solid knowledge.

We as clinicians and therapists must be willing to expose ourselves in the very personal encounter that is the fabric of psychotherapy to the risk of recording ourselves as we are—both our moments of deep understanding of the patient and our moments of awkward misunderstanding and perhaps even our rare moments of defensive cruelty.

Such a body of data, once collected, would be duplicated and made centrally available to investigators so that comparative findings would be available for evaluating the relative contribution of different patient, therapist, interaction, and contextual variables. It would almost inevitably lead to actualizing the significant variables in the multiple linear equation model, and thus add greatly to our knowledge of how effectively to produce constructive change in the patient.

Such data would also be invaluable for use in training counselors and therapists; the best examples could provide models for imitation and learning.

References

1. Affleck, D. C., and Mednick, S. A. The use of the Rorschach Test in the prediction of the abrupt terminator in individual psychotherapy. *J. consult. Psychol.*, 1959, *23*, 125-128.

2. Alexander, F. *Fundamentals of psychoanalysis.* New York: Norton, 1948.

3. Appleby, L. Evaluation of treatment methods for chronic schizophrenia. *Arch. gen. Psychiat.,* 1963, *8,* 8-21.

4. Bailey, M. A., Warshaw, L., and Eichler, R. M. A study of factors related to length of stay in psychotherapy. *J. clin. Psychol.,* 1959, *15,* 442-444.

5. Bandura, A., Lipsher, D. H., and Miller, P. E. Psychotherapists' approach-avoidance reactions to patients' expressions of hostility. *J. consult. Psychol.,* 1960, *24,* 1-8.

6. Barrett-Lennard, G. T. Dimensions of therapist response as causal factors in therapeutic change. *Genet. Psychol. Monogr.,* 1962, *76,* No. 43 (Whole No. 562).

7. Barron, F., and Leary, T. Changes in psychoneurotic patients with and without psychotherapy. *J. consult. Psychol.,* 1955, *19,* 239-245.

8. Bergin, A. E. The effects of psychotherapy: Negative results revisited. *J. counsel. Psychol.,* 1963, *10,* 244-250.

9. Bergin, A. E., and Soloman, Sandra. Personality and performance correlates of empathic understanding in psychotherapy. Paper read at *Amer. Psychol. Assoc.,* Philadelphia, Sept., 1963.

10. Betz, Barbara J. Bases of therapeutic leadership in psychotherapy with the schizophrenic patient. *Amer. J. Psychother.,* 1963, *17,* 196-212.

11. Betz, Barbara J. Differential success rates of psychotherapists with "process" and "nonprocess" schizophrenic patients. *Amer. J. Psychiat.,* 1963, *11,* 1090-1091.

12. Braaten, L. J. The movement from nonself to self in client-centered psychotherapy. *J. counsel. Psychol.,* 1961, *8,* 20-24.

13. Brayfield, A. H. Counseling psychology. *Ann. Rev. Psychol.,* 1963, *14,* 319-350.

14. Brown, E. C., and Rickard, H. C. Evaluation of a psychotherapy case in terms of change in a relevant behavior. *J. clin. Psychol.,* 1960, *16,* 93.

15. Butler, J. M. Self-concept change in psychotherapy. *Counseling Center Discussion Papers,* Univer. of Chicago, 1960, *6* (13), 1-27.

16. Cabeen, C. W., and Coleman, J. C. The selection of sex offender patients for group psychotherapy. *Int. J. group Psychother.,* 1962, *12,* 326-334.

17. Cartwright, Rosalind D. The effects of psychotherapy. *J. counsel. Psychol.,* 1957, *4,* 15-22.

18. Cartwright, Rosalind D. The effects of psychotherapy: A replication and extension. *J. consult. Psychol.,* 1961, *25,* 376-382.

19. Cartwright, Rosalind D., and Lerner, Barbara. Empathy, need to change, and improvement with psychotherapy. *J. consult. Psychol.,* 1963, *27,* 138-144.

20. Cartwright, Rosalind D., and Vogel, J. L. A comparison of changes in psychoneurotic patients during matched periods of therapy and no therapy. *J. consult. Psychol.,* 1960, *24,* 121-127.

21. Combs, A. W., and Soper, D. W. The perceptual organization of effective counselors. *J. counsel. Psychol.,* 1963, *10,* 222-226.

22. Drasgow, J., and Carkhuff, R. R. Kuder neuropsychiatric keys before and after therapy. *J. counsel. Psychol.,* 1964, *11,* 67-71.

23. Dymond, Rosalind. A scale for the measurement of empathic ability. *J. consult. Psychol.,* 1949, *13,* 127-133.

24. Endler, N. S. Changes in meaning during psychotherapy as measured by the semantic differential. *J. counsel. Psychol.,* 1961, *8,* 105-111.

25. Eysenck, H. J. The effects of psychotherapy: An evaluation. *J. consult. Psychol.,* 1952, *16,* 319-324.

26. Eysenck, H. J. The effects of psychotherapy. In H. J. Eysenck (Ed.), *Handbook of abnormal psychology.* New York: Basic Books, 1960, 697-725.

27. Feifel, H., and Eells, Janet. Patient and therapists assess the same psychotherapy. *J. counsel. Psychol.,* 1963, *27,* 310-318.

28. Ferenczi, S. The principle of relaxation and neo-catharsis. *Int. J. Psychoanal.,* 1930, *11,* 428-443.

29. Forsyth, R. P., and Fairweather, G. W. Psychotherapeutic and other hospital treatment criteria: The dilemma. *J. abnorm. soc. Psychol.,* 1961, *62,* 598-605.

30. Fox, R. E., and Goldin, P. C. The empathic process in psychotherapy: A survey of theory and research. Unpublished manuscript, 1963.

31. Garfield, S. L., and Wolpin, M. Expectations regarding psychotherapy. *J. nerv. ment. Dis.,* 1963, *137,* 353-362.

32. Gleser, G. C., Gottschalk, L. A., and Springer, K. J. An anxiety scale applicable to verbal samples. *Arch. gen. Psychiat.,* 1961, *5,* 593-605.

33. Gottschalk, L. A., Gleser, G. C., Daniels, R. S., and Block, S. L. The speech patterns of schizophrenic patients: A method of assessing relative degree of personal disorganization and social alienation. *J. nerv. ment. Dis.,* 1958, *127,* 153-166.

34. Gottschalk, L. A., Gleser, G. C., Magliocco, E. B. and D'Zmura, T. L. Further studies on the speech patterns of schizophrenic patients. *J. nerv. ment. Dis.,* 1961, *132,* 101-113.

35. Gottschalk, L. A., Springer, K. J., and Gleser, G. C. Experiments with a method of assessing the variations in intensity of certain psychological states occurring during two psychotherapeutic interviews. In L. A. Gottschalk (Ed.), *Comparative psycholinguistic analysis of two psychotherapeutic interviews.* New York: Int. Univer. Press, Inc., 1961, pp. 115-138.

36. Gonyea, G. G. The "ideal therapeutic relationship" and counseling outcome. *J. clin. Psychol.,* 1963, *19,* 481-487.

37. Graham, S. R. The effects of psychoanalytically oriented psychotherapy on levels of frequency and satisfaction in sexual activity. *J. clin. Psychol.,* 1960, *16,* 94-95.

38. Grigg, A. E. Client response to counselors at different levels of experience. *J. counsel. Psychol.,* 1961, *8,* 217-223.

39. Halkides, Galatia. An investigation of therapeutic success as a function of four variables. Unpublished doctoral dissertation, Univer. of Chicago, 1958.

40. Halpern, H., and Lesser, Leone. Empathy in infants, adults, and psycho-therapists. *Psychoanal. Rev.,* 1960, *47,* 32-42.

41. Hart, J. T. A replication of the Halkides study. Unpublished manuscript. Univer. of Wisconsin, 1960.

42. Heckel, R. V., Wiggins, S. L., and Salzberg, H. C. Conditioning against silences in group therapy. *J. clin. Psychol.,* 1962, *18,* 216-217.

43. Heckel, R. V., Wiggins, S. L., and Salzberg, H. C. Joining, encouraging, and intervening as means of extinguishing a delusional system. *J. clin. Psychol.,* 1963, *137,* 344-345.

44. Heilbrun, A. B., Jr. Male and female personality correlates of early ter-mination in counseling. *J. counsel. Psychol.,* 1961, *8,* 31-36.

45. Hiler, E. W. The sentence completion test as a predictor of continuation in psychotherapy. *J. consult. Psychol.,* 1959, *23,* 544-549.

46. Hiler, E. W. Initial complaints as predictors of continuation in psycho-therapy. *J. clin. Psychol.,* 1959, *15,* 244-245.

47. Jourard, S. I-Thou relationship versus manipulation in counseling and psychotherapy. *J. indiv. Psychol.,* 1959, 174-179.

48. Knupfer, G., Jackson, D. D., and Kreiger, G. Personality differences between more and less competent psychotherapists as a function of criteria of com-petence. *J. nerv. ment. Dis.,* 1959, *129.*

49. Krasner, L. The therapist as a social reinforcement machine. In H. H. Strupp and L. Luborsky (Eds.), *Research in psychotherapy.* Washington, D. C.: Amer. Psychol. Assoc., 1962. Vol. 2, 61-74.

50. Lesser, W. M. The relationship between counseling progress and empathic understanding. *J. counsel. Psychol.,* 1961, *8,* 330-336.

51. Lorr, M., McNair, D. M., Michaux, W. W., and Raskin, A. Frequency of treatment and change in psychotherapy. *J. abnorm. soc. Psychol.,* 1962, *64,* 281-292.

52. May, P. R. A., and Tuma, A. H. Choice of criteria for the assessment of treatment outcome. Paper read at West. Psychol. Assoc., Santa Monica, April 18, 1963.

53. McGinnis, C. A. The effect of group therapy on the ego-strength scale scores of alcoholic patients. *J. clin. Psychol.,* 1963, *19,* 346-347.

54. McNair, D. M., Callahan, D. M., and Lorr, M. Therapist "type" and patient responses to psychotherapy. *J. consult. Psychol.,* 1962, *26,* 425-442.

55. Mendel, W. M., and Rapport, S. Out-patient treatment for chronic schizo-phrenic patients; therapeutic consequences of an existential view. *Arch. gen. Psychiat.,* 1963, *8,* 190-196.

56. Mendelsohn, G. A., and Geller, M. H. Effects of counselor-client similarity on the outcome of counseling. *J. counsel. Psychol.,* 1963, *10,* 71-77.

57. Moore, R. A., Benedek, Elissa P., and Wallace, J. G. Social class, schizo-phrenia, and the psychiatrist. *Amer. J. Psychiat.,* 1963, *120,* 149-154.

58. Pope, B., and Seigman, A. W. Effect of therapist verbal activity level and

specificity on patient productivity and speech disturbance in the initial interview. *J. consult. Psychol.,* 1962, *26,* 489.

59. Raush, H. L., and Bordin, E. S. Warmth in personality development and in psychotherapy. *Psychiatry,* 1957, *20,* 351-363.

60. Rogers, C. R. *Client-centered therapy.* Cambridge, Mass.: Riverside Press, 1951.

61. Rogers, C. R. The necessary and sufficient conditions of therapeutic personality change. *J. consult. Psychol.,* 1957, *21,* 95-103.

62. Rogers, C. R. The interpersonal relationship: The core of guidance. *Harvard Educ. Rev.,* 1962, *32,* 416-429. (Following studies reported by C. R. Rogers)

   (Truax, C. B.). Comparison between high conditions therapy, low conditions therapy, and control conditions in the outcome measure of change in anxiety levels.

   (Truax, C. B.). Constructive personality change in schizophrenic patients receiving high conditions therapy, low conditions therapy, and no therapy.

   (Truax, C. B.). Effects of therapists and effects of patients upon the amount of accurate empathy occurring in the psychotherapeutic interaction.

   (Truax, C. B.). Effects of therapists and effects of patients upon the level of problem expression and experiencing occurring in the therapeutic interaction.

   (Truax, C. B.). The relationship between the patient's perception of the level of therapeutic conditions offered in psychotherapy and constructive personality change.

   (Truax, C. B., Liccione, J., and Rosenberg, M.). Psychological test evaluations of personality change in high conditions therapy, low conditions therapy, and control patients.

   (Spotts, J. E.). The perception of positive regard by relatively successful clients.

63. Sapolsky, A. Effect of interpersonal relationships upon verbal conditioning. *J. abnorm. soc. Psychol.,* 1960, *60,* 241-246.

64. Schafer, R. Generative empathy in the treatment situation. *Psychoanal. Quart.,* 1959, *28,* 342-373.

65. Seeman, J. Psychotherapy and perceptual behavior. *J. clin. Psychol.,* 1962, *18,* 34-37.

66. Shlien, J. M., Mosak, H. H., and Dreikurs, R. Effect of time limits: A comparison of client-centered and Adlerian psychotherapy. *Amer. Psychologist,* 1960, *15,* 415 (Abstract).

67. Shoben, E. J., Jr. Psychotherapy as a problem in learning theory. *Psychol. Bull.,* 1949, *46,* 366-392.

68. Speisman, J. C. Depth of interpretation and verbal resistance in psychotherapy. *J. consult. Psychol.,* 1959, *23,* 93-99.

69. Spielberger, C. D., Wietz, H., and Denny, J. P. Group counseling and the academic performance of anxious college freshmen. *J. counsel. Psychol.,* 1962, *9,* 195-204.

70. Stieper, D. R., and Wiener, D. N. The problem of interminability in outpatient psychotherapy. *J. consult. Psychol.,* 1959, *23,* 237-242.

71. Stoler, N. Client likeability: A variable in the study of psychotherapy. *J. consult. Psychol.,* 1963, *27,* 138-144.

72. Stone, A. R., Frank, J. D., Nash, E. H., and Imber, S. D. An intensive five-year follow-up study of treated psychiatric patients. *J. nerv. ment. Dis.,* 1961, *133,* 410-421.

73. Streitfeld, J. W. Expressed acceptance of self and others by psychotherapists. *J. consult. Psychol.,* 1959, *23,* 435-441.

74. Strickland, Bonnie R., and Crowne, D. P. Need for approval and the premature termination of psychotherapy. *J. consult. Psychol.,* 1963, *27,* 95-101.

75. Strunk, O., Jr. Empathy: A review of theory and research. *Psychol. Newsltr.,* 1957, *9,* 47-57.

76. Strupp, H. H. Nature of psychotherapists' contribution to the treatment process. *Arch. gen. Psychiat.,* 1960, *3,* 219-231.

77. Strupp, H. H., Wallach, M. S., Wogan, M., and Jenkins, Joan W. Psychotherapists' assessments of former patients. *J. nerv. ment. Dis.,* 1963, *137,* 222-230.

78. Tomlinson, T. M., and Hart, J. T., Jr. A validation study of the process scale. *J. consult. Psychol.,* 1962, *26,* 74-78.

79. Truax, C. B. The process of group psychotherapy. *Psychol. Monogr.,* 1961, *75,* No. 14 (Whole No. 511).

80. Truax, C. B. Therapeutic conditions. *Discussion papers, Wisconsin Psychiatric Institute,* Univer. of Wisconsin, 1961, *13.*

81. Truax, C. B. Effective ingredients in psychotherapy: An approach to unraveling the patient-therapist interaction. *J. counsel. Psychol.,* 1963, *10,* 256-263.

82. Truax, C. B., and Carkhuff, R. R. For better or for worse: The process of psychotherapeutic personality change. Invited address; Recent advances in the study of behavior change, Academic Assembly on Clinical Psychology, McGill Univer., Montreal, Canada, June 4, 1963.

83. Truax, C. B., and Carkhuff, R. R. The old and the new: The changing scene in theory and research in counseling and psychotherapy. *Personnel Guid. J.,* 1964, *42,* 860-866.

84. Truax, C. B., and Carkhuff, R. R. Concreteness: A neglected variable in research in psychotherapy. *J. clin. Psychol.,* 1964, *20,* 264-267.

85. Truax, C. B., Carkhuff, R. R., and Douds, J. Toward an integration of the didactic and experiential approaches to training in counseling and psychotherapy. *J. counsel. Psychol.,* 1964, *11,* No. 3.

86. Truax, C. B., and Carkhuff, R. R. The experimental manipulations of therapeutic conditions: Toward a resolution of the tough- and tender-

minded viewpoints in counseling and psychotherapy. *J. consult. Psychol.* (in press).

87. Wagstaff, A. K., Rice, L. N., and Butler, J. M. Factors of client verbal participation in therapy. *Counseling Center Discussion Papers,* Univer. of Chicago, 1960, *6* (9), 1-14.

88. Waskow, Irene E. Counselor attitudes and client behavior. *J. consult. Psychol.,* 1963, *27,* 405-412.

89. Weiss, R. L., Krasner, L., and Ullmann, L. P. Responsitivity to verbal conditioning as a function of emotional atmosphere and patterning of reinforcement. *Psychol. Rev.,* 1960, *6,* 415-426.

90. Whitehorn, J. C., and Betz, Barbara J. A study of psychotherapeutic relationships between physicians and schizophrenic patients. *Amer. J. Psychiat.,* 1954, *3,* 321-331.

91. Wolf, A. Group psychotherapy with adults: The alternate meeting. Paper read at Amer. Personnel Guid. Assoc., New York, Jan. 27, 1961.

92. Wolf, A., and Schwartz, E. K. *Psychoanalysis in groups.* New York: Grune & Stratton, 1962.

93. Wood, E. C., Rakusin, J. M., and Morse, E. Interpersonal aspects of psychiatric hospitalization: II. Some correlations between admission circumstances and the treatment experience. *Arch. gen. Psychiat.,* 1962, *6,* 39-45.

94. Wood, E. C., Rakusin, J. M., Morse, E., and Singer, R. Interpersonal aspects of psychiatric hospitalization: III. The follow-up survey. *Arch. gen. Psychiat.,* 1962, *6,* 46-55.

95. Wrenn, R. L. Counselor orientation: Theoretical or situational? *J. counsel. Psychol.,* 1960, *7,* 40-45.

96. Wright, F. H. The exit unit program for psychiatric patients. *J. counsel. Psychol.,* 1959, *6,* 116-120.

97. Zolik, E. S., and Hollon, T. N. Factors characteristic of patients responsive to brief psychotherapy. *Amer. Psychologist,* 1960, *15,* 387 (abstract).

Hope and Confidence

This reading reminds us not to become bogged down in process variables but to look for significant sources of variance and outcome in a wide range of measures. Perhaps those characteristics which partly describe the effective therapist also partly describe the effective, creative researcher and integrater of the literature: hope and confidence.

The reading also develops the basic perspective necessary for making an eclectic view not only meaningful but potent. Nevertheless, the general linear model it presents will aid us in efforts to develop preferred modes of treatment only if we continually redefine constructive personality change for each of the special treatment populations.

In spite of the assertion that the "basically simple model has the advantage of making no assumptions about the nature of psychotherapy, the nature of personality, or the nature of personality change," the model itself, and its choice of sets of variables, is replete with assumptions.

We doubt that the stance "I make no assumptions, I am only interested in what works" is related to good therapeutic outcome. Effective therapists know what works; we have begun to sense what we feel constitute the "effective ingredients." No apology is needed for making assumptions. Apologies are needed when the assumptions are not stated or not clear.

INTEGRATIONS AND IMPLICATIONS
FOR FACILITATIVE PROCESSES
AND CONSTRUCTIVE OUTCOMES

We have considered the challenges to the helping profession, dwelt on a variety of different attempts to account for the effective ingredients of truly therapeutic processes, and examined the evidence. We would like now to turn to some meaningful attempts to integrate the research with theory, practice, and training in counseling and psychotherapy.

The writers in this section run the gamut from a full treatment of the experimental approaches to the application of research in practice and training. Murray examines the raging vogue of behavioristic conditioning and concludes that learning theory does not necessarily dictate a therapist who is in effect an impersonal, programmed reinforcement machine. Bergin considers both the clinical and experimental approaches that have demonstrated their efficacy and those that promise improved therapeutic consequences in the future. Carkhuff makes generalizations from research findings to training and practice and draws the implications for training and "practice in preferred modes of treatment" built around a central core of primary facilitative conditions.

THE SOCIOTROPIC STANCE*

Edward J. Murray

Learning theory is an attempt to account for the acquisition, performance, and extinction of behavioral responses of all kinds. As such, it would seem to offer some help in explaining and improving the complex processes of psychotherapy. This writer has taken this position for some time and has made some small efforts to contribute to such an enterprise (Murray, 1963), following the learning analysis made by Dollard and Miller (1950).

In recent years, however, a new movement has emerged which also employs learning concepts and goes by various names such as behavior therapy (Eysenck, 1960; Shaw, 1961), conditioned reflex therapy (Salter, 1961), or reciprocal inhibition therapy (Wolpe, 1958). This group has claimed to have powerful new psychotherapeutic techniques specifically derived from learning theory. While applauding the general use of learning concepts, we have been more than a little disturbed at the direction this movement has taken. The therapy tends to be symptomatic, manipulative and impersonal. Furthermore, this sort of therapy has come to be equated with the learning approach in the mind of the public.

Nevertheless, this position can be profitably contrasted with that of Dollard and Miller (1950), Shoben (1949), Mowrer (1953), and this author (Murray, 1963). In order to highlight the differences between these groups, both of which use learning concepts, we will call them, in Boring's terms, "biotropic" and "sociotropic." Some of the chief differences in these approaches are listed in Table 1. Obviously this is a continuum and very few people would fit either extreme. The question as to which approach has more to offer the future development of psychotherapy can not be answered at the present time. A choice can not be made on the grounds of therapeutic effectiveness because, as Eysenck (1960) has pointed out, adequately controlled studies have been done on neither. At this stage of the game, all approaches should be encouraged.

The purpose of this paper is to question the assumption that the particular methods and techniques offered by the biotropes are new and more specifically derived from learning theory than other approaches. Actually, learning theory is an abstract, quasi-mathematical system with

* Learning theory and psychotherapy: Biotropic versus sociotropic approaches. *Journal of Counseling Psychology*, 1963, *10*, 250-255. Reprinted by permission of author and publisher.

TABLE 1

Biotropic Versus Sociotropic Approaches in the Application
of Learning Theory to Psychotherapy

Biotropic (for example, Eysenck, Salter, Wolpe, Shaw)	Sociotropic (for example, Dollard and Miller, Mowrer, Shoben, Murray)
1. Relatively greater reliance on classical Pavlovian conditioning.	1. More emphasis is placed on operant, or instrumental, learning.
2. Direct transposition of laboratory hardware into clinic, for example, PGR conditioning, bar pressing apparatus.	2. Translation of laboratory findings into verbal and expressive techniques.
3. More use of reinforcement based on physiological drives, for example, electric shock, candy bars, erotic pictures.	3. Social reinforcement and acquired drives more important, for example, approval, empathy, interest, understanding, respect, life goals of individual.
4. Primary stimulus generalization and discrimination central to psychopathology and therapy, for example, trains, buses, cars in phobias.	4. Secondary, or mediated, generalization and discrimination of most importance, for example, verbal symbols, feelings.
5. Restriction of interest to overt muscular responses and peripheral autonomic reactions in naive behaviorist tradition.	5. Recognition of important, although difficult to measure, cognitive processes such as thinking, fantasy, and dreams (which on the physiological level would be central brain mechanisms).
6. Transference is not part of treatment —"Personal relations are not essential."	6. The therapeutic relationship is seen as the key learning experience in all forms of therapy.
7. Causal factors in neurosis are seen as primarily genetic, physiological, and medical.	7. Cultural variables play a great role in determining disturbance, for example, social class, family relations, and social learning.
8. Affinity for the directive-organic school of psychiatry.	8. Affinity for the analytic-psychological school of psychiatry.
9. Techniques deemed of most importance include hypnosis, suggestion, progressive relaxation, drugs, and overt manipulation.	9. Point to techniques such as insight, labeling, permissiveness, and other subtle means of influencing behavior.
10. Learning theory presented as an alternative to traditional psychotherapy.	10. Adopt a strategy of first reinterpreting and then extending and modifying traditional therapy.

no intrinsic content. To use it in any empirical area, such as psycho-therapy, one must make many ancillary assumptions having to do with the nature of personality and psychopathology. The point which we wish to make is that a great many therapeutic methods can be derived from learning theory, depending on the way one approaches the problem.

IS BIOTROPIC BEHAVIOR THERAPY NEW?

Behavior therapy is often presented as a new approach to serve as an alternative to psychoanalytic or nondirective techniques. Certainly, the concepts of reciprocal inhibition, conditioned reflex, and avoidance conditioning sound like new techniques. But on close examination they turn out to be the rather old methods of hypnotic suggestion, moral persuasion, and punishment.

Reciprocal inhibition turns out to be the replacement of anxiety with the incompatible responses of eating, relaxation, or assertion by means of hypnotic, direct, or auto-suggestion (Wolpe, 1958; Salter, 1961). Thus, Salter will teach a patient auto-hypnosis and have him say, over and over, something like "I am grown up, my childish fears no longer bother me."

Is this a new therapy? How reminiscent it is of the kindly naive apothecary of Nancy who, as early as 1910, had people say "Every day, in every respect, I am getting better and better" (Coué and Brooks, 1961). In the last century, the Swiss psychiatrist DuBois developed a method which closely resembles reciprocal inhibition. He called it "moral orthopedics" (Bromberg, 1959). Relaxation goes back at least to 1891, when the nurse, Annie Payson Call, used muscular relaxation and "mind training" to relieve tension (Wolberg, 1954).

Avoidance conditioning consists of associating a noxious stimulus with bedwetting, over-eating, and other symptoms. In one case, vomiting was associated with pictures of a fetish (Raymond, 1960). The vomiting was induced twice an hour, 24 hours a day, for seven days, with no food or sleep permitted. The analogy with brainwashing is inescapable.

Nevertheless, punitive techniques antedate the biotropes. Beating, purging, and surprise baths were popular treatments in the 18th and 19th centuries. Symptomatic therapy included firing off a shot, or administering a douche, whenever a patient uttered a delusional statement. Benjamin Rush—the Revolutionary War patriot and psychiatrist—described a drug addict who was cured by having an artificial snake pop out of her opium box on to her shoulder (Bromberg, 1959).

Thus, it does not appear that the biotropes have new techniques specifically derived from learning theory, although a number of ingenious refinements have been added. A more important question is whether these biotropic techniques are more consistent with learning principles than the permissive approaches.

IS LEARNING THEORY LIMITED
TO SYMPTOMATIC TREATMENT?

One characteristic of biotropic therapy is the concentration on overt, isolated symptoms—tics, bedwetting, stuttering, phobias, writer's cramps, impotence, etc. (Eysenck, 1960). Rather than making this an understandable strategy of concentrating on the simpler, more observable problems first, they make a point of saying that the symptom *is* the neurosis. Eliminate the symptom and the neurosis is gone.

The various hypnotic, persuasive, and punitive techniques do seem to eliminate symptoms. However, they work best with isolated and weakly motivated responses after anxiety has been reduced—what Lehner (1954) calls a "habit residual." This is hardly a picture of the difficult problems faced by the mental health field today. Coercive treatment of strongly motivated symptoms may create further conflict. Beech (1960) found that highly anxious sufferers of writer's cramp often worsened with avoidance conditioning. Highly anxious patients may also show the substitution of a new symptom when the old one is removed (for example, Sandler, 1945). The biotropes claim this does not happen, but their evidence may be based on the low anxiety, habit residual type of symptom. In commenting on the punitive treatment of a boy with strongly motivated antisocial behavior, Bandura (1962) describes how each coercive therapeutic maneuver was followed by further symptomatic and antisocial escape responses.

Does modern learning theory really suggest a symptomatic treatment? Sophisticated learning theorists have been trying to include the inferred variables of motivation and symbolic behavior for years (for example, Hull, 1943). Dollard and Miller (1950) found it impossible to discuss neurosis or psychotherapy without referring to higher mental processes, cue-producing responses, and internal emotional reactions. Changes in these central processes may be necessary for therapy. Mowrer (1956) has emphasized the importance of an understanding of language and other symbolic behavior for the effective application of learning theory to problems like psychotherapy. Even Eysenck (1960) has modified the strictly symptomatic approach to include the visceral components of anxiety. If anxiety, why not other motives? Why not symbolic processes?

An example of how a learning-oriented therapist might concentrate on motives rather than habits is given by Kimble (1956) in discussing a case of juvenile delinquency. He points out that if one were interested in eliminating a bar-pressing response in a rat, one could either extinguish the habit by withholding food reinforcement or reduce hunger by feeding. The delinquent boy had socially-acceptable responses high in the habit hierarchy, he notes, with the antisocial ones appearing only with frustration. The frustration was primarily that of his need for companionship and affection from his father. The appropriate therapy, Kimble concludes, is to satisfy the boy's motives, not to try to alter his habits.

DOES LEARNING THEORY DEMAND A HIGHLY MANIPULATIVE THERAPY?

Biotropic therapists frequently take the position that learning theory suggests active, manipulative behavior on the part of the therapist. In addition to the hypnosis and punishment mentioned above, manipulation would include directive methods of changing the patient's extra-interview behavior. The practical issue here—whether direct manipulation is therapeutically effective—has never been adequately tested. The theoretical issue, with which we are concerned, is whether direct manipulation is derived from learning theory while other methods are not. Actually, many interview techniques can be derived from learning theory depending on the assumptions one wishes to make.

As an illustration, let us examine a case presented by Shaw (1961). He says that, on the basis of behavioral principles, he might suggest to a shy, lonely young lad, that he try greeting people occasionally. However, it is possible to deduce, in a casual way, two conflicting techniques for this case depending on certain assumptions. First, suppose we assume that one of the reasons for Shaw's young man being so shy was a distant and cold father who had never been interested in guiding his son. Suppose further that this conflict had generalized to the therapist. Then, one might predict, on the basis of learning principles, that it would be therapeutically useful for the therapist to make a suggestion about greeting people.

Suppose, instead, that the young man's shyness could be attributed to a domineering father—one of those constantly giving orders, suggestions, and generally trying to manipulate his son. We submit that, from a learning point of view, the patient's long range social learning would be jeopardized by suggesting that he greet people, since it would reinforce fear of the therapist. In other words, with these assumptions and with this case, learning theory suggests a nondirective therapy!

The discovery of the importance of selective verbal reinforcement in psychotherapy was a major scientific advance. However, an inference from this discovery—which we believe is erroneous—is that a behavioral therapy should be devised in which the therapist decides what is best for the patient and selectively reinforces that behavior.

The problem is that reinforcement has little meaning without the companion concept of motivation. Actually, the evidence now suggests (see Murray, 1963) that the effectiveness of approval and disapproval is based on anxiety related to an innate need for social contact, affection, love, or call it what you will. Selective reinforcement in psychotherapy has meaning only in relation to this motive. The evidence further suggests that the effectiveness of verbal reinforcement depends on the personalities of the patient and therapist, and their relationship. For this verbal reinforcement to be effective, the therapist must have a basic respect for the individual needs and integrity of the patient.

A related issue which becomes unnecessarily involved in discussions of behavior therapy concerns personal freedom. We have no doubt that, on philosophical grounds, personal freedom must be ultimately viewed as illusory. But, illusory or not, the *sense* of personal freedom is as real a psychological goal as the sense of being loved. What personal freedom may mean is that the individual can interact with his environment in such a way as to fulfill has own individual pattern of motives rather than someone else's. His motives are, of course, determined by his unique life experiences. A therapist imposing his own value hierarchy on a patient may be artificially altering the motivational priorities of the person and, thus, his sense of personal freedom. Behavior therapy can just as easily be designed to enhance the sense of personal freedom.

MUST THERAPY BASED
ON LEARNING PRINCIPLES BE IMPERSONAL?

The biotropic approach is nowhere at greater variance with dynamic forms of psychotherapy, than in de-emphasizing the therapeutic relationship (Eysenck, 1960). Yet, many of their therapeutic achievements may be explained in terms of the therapeutic relationship. It is generally understood, for example, that hypnosis is an intensified form of a dependency relationship. Wolpe (1958) seems to build up a relationship with his patients—in one case a woman was seen for 65 interviews over a 27-month period and it is clear from the summary that he had a good deal of empathy for her. In a recent study, Lazarus (1961) found that establishing a therapeutic relationship facilitated systematic desensitization treatment.

Similarly, there is little justification for Bandura's (1961) conclusion that methods derived from learning theory do not rely heavily on the development of affectionate responses on the part of the patient toward the therapist. In our sociotropic analysis of therapy (Murray, 1963), we have presented evidence suggesting that the extinction of anxiety about affectionate, sexual, hostile, and other feelings in the therapeutic relationship constitutes the core of therapy. Bandura, himself, has very nicely shown that the anxiety of the therapist can lead to avoidance behavior and thus prevent this extinction. Therapeutic progress depends on a positive relationship so that the learning process can take place. The evidence can thus be construed as demanding that the theory take into account the importance of a highly personal, warm therapeutic relationship.

Part of the antipathy to examining the relationship aspects of therapy, on the part of some learning oriented individuals, is a conception of the therapist as *E*—the detached, unimpassioned objective experimenter (Pascal, 1959). But this is an unnecessary confusion of the therapist and scientist roles. Actually, psychologists probably should not do research on their own personal therapy; it is better to study the other fellow's psychotherapy. Thus, there are three symbols involved: *P, T,* and *E.*

CONCLUSIONS

In this paper we have distinguished between two general approaches to applying learning principles to psychotherapy—the biotropic and sociotropic. We have tried to show that the symptomatic, manipulative, and impersonal kind of therapy espoused by the biotropes is not more specifically derived from learning theory than the permissive, interpersonal, and dynamic approaches of the sociotropes. Furthermore, the apparently new techniques of the biotropes are really the persuasive and coercive procedures of the past few centuries. While the sociotropes may be accused of simply reinterpreting dynamic psychotherapy, the biotropes have simply reinterpreted the directive and manipulative methods.

No attempt has been made to evaluate the effectiveness or promise of the two approaches. The major point is that quite different, sometimes diametrically opposed, therapeutic procedures can be derived from learning principles. The flesh one puts on the skeleton of learning principles depends on one's biological or social orientation, one's general views on the basic nature of man, and other ancillary assumptions. We hope that we have laid the ghost that learning oriented psychotherapy must be symptomatic, manipulative, and impersonal.

REFERENCES

Bandura, A. Psychotherapy as a learning process. *Psychol. Bull.,* 1961, *58,* 143-159.

Bandura, A. Punishment revisited. *J. consult. Psychol.,* 1962, *26,* 298-301.

Beech, H. R. The symptomatic treatment of writer's cramp. In H. J. Eysenck (Ed.), *Behavior therapy and the neuroses.* New York: Pergamon, 1960.

Bromberg, W. *The mind of man: A history of psychotherapy and psychoanalysis.* New York: Harper & Row, 1959.

Coué, E., and Brooks, C. H. *Better and better every day.* New York: Barnes & Noble, 1961.

Dollard, J., and Miller, N. E. *Personality and psychotherapy.* New York: McGraw-Hill, 1950.

Eysenck, J. H. (Ed.), *Behavior therapy and the neuroses.* New York: Pergamon, 1960.

Hull, C. L. *Principles of behavior.* New York: Appleton-Century-Crofts, 1943.

Kimble, G. A. Behavior theories and a counseling case: A symposium—reinforcement theory. *J. counsel. Psychol.,* 1956, *3,* 112-115.

Lazarus, A. A. Group therapy of phobic disorders by systematic desensitization. *J. abnorm. soc. Psychol.,* 1961, *63,* 504-510.

Lehner, G. F. J. Negative practice as a psychotherapeutic technique. *J. gen. Psychol.,* 1954, *51,* 69-82.

Mowrer, O. H. Neurosis, psychotherapy, and two-factor learning theory. In O. H. Mowrer (Ed.) *Psychotherapy: Theory and research.* New York: Ronald, 1953.

Mowrer, O. H. Behavior theories and a counseling case: A symposium—neoanalytic theory. *J. counsel. Psychol.,* 1956, *3,* 108-111.

Murray, E. J. Sociotropic-learning approach to psychotherapy. In P. Worchel and D. Byrne (Eds.), *Personality change.* New York: Wiley, 1963.

Pascal, G. R. *Behavioral change in the clinic: A systematic approach.* New York: Grune & Stratton, 1959.

Raymond, M. J. Case of fetishism treated by aversion therapy. In H. J. Eysenck (Ed.), *Behavior therapy and the neuroses.* New York: Pergamon, 1960.

Salter, A. *Conditioned reflex therapy.* New York: Capricorn, 1961.

Sandler, S. Somnambulism in the armed forces. *Ment. Hyg.,* April, 1945, 236-247.

Shaw, F. J. (Ed.). Behavioristic approaches to counseling and psychotherapy. *Univer. of Alabama Studies,* 1961, No. 13.

Shoben, E. J. Psychotherapy as a problem in learning theory. *Psychol. Bull.,* 1949, *46,* 366-392.

Wolberg, L. R. *The technique of psychotherapy.* New York: Grune & Stratton, 1954.

Wolpe, J. *Psychotherapy by reciprocal inhibition.* London: Oxford Univer. Press, 1958.

A Rehabilitation Learning Theory

Murray is correct. Learning theory does *not* dictate an impersonal programmed reinforcement machine, the efficacy of which is accounted for by the fact that it is dealing with "isolated and weakly motivated responses," or low anxiety "habit residuals." His points are especially relevant for behavior therapists who are interested in client relief and improved functioning in the many significant areas of life other than isolated symptomatology.

Murray shows that a variety of approaches might be incorporated within learning theory (and here he makes overtures in the direction of Alexander's integrative attempt). When we are guided by the principle of effectiveness, given a particular interaction of relevant variables, some of the techniques of the biotropic approaches, whatever their origin, may serve a complementary or supplementary function to the more sociotropic approaches. Indeed, the relationship conditions of the sociotropic approaches may facilitate the efficacy of the biotropic techniques.

We are puzzled by the developing and ironic rehabilitation of learning theory treatment. We find the behaviorists saying over and over: "What works, works." With this we most wholeheartedly agree. However, we are not impressed by the mechanisms which are posited after the fact to account for the phenomenon but which do not offer adequate explanation for the evolution of the phenomenon. We often ask our more behavioristic colleagues: "Why don't you raise your children in a calculated, manipulative, and impersonal way?" Fortunately for their children, the behaviorists, answer is usually that their theory only involves the treatment of already-developed symptoms.

In the following reading, Bergin takes the best evidence that researchers have developed and meaningfully translates it into therapeutic practice.

SOME IMPLICATIONS OF
PSYCHOTHERAPY RESEARCH
FOR THERAPEUTIC PRACTICE*
Allen E. Bergin

The material to follow is a digest of research findings which have implications for practice and research in psychotherapy. It has been formulated in terms of six conclusions and implications which

* Some implications of psychotherapy research for therapeutic practice. *Journal of Abnormal Psychology*, 1966, *71*, 235-246. Based in part on a paper presented at the Pre-Convention Institute of the Ontario Psychological Association, London, Ontario, February, 1964. Presented at a symposium: "Implications of empirical research for innovations in therapeutic practice and research." American Psychological Convention, Los Angeles, September, 1964.

appear justifiable and defensible. This catalogue of conclusions is based upon a comparative handful of research reports which have been carefully selected from the present empirical chaos for their relative adequacy of conceptualization, design, and outcome. Conclusions have been drawn only in those areas where the results appear to have substance and where they have been replicated; consequently, many areas of study are excluded.

THE DETERIORATION EFFECT

CONCLUSION 1. *Psychotherapy may cause people to become better-or worse-adjusted than comparable people who do not receive such treatment.*

Recently, a curious and provocative finding occurred in the preliminary results of the Wisconsin schizophrenia project conducted by Rogers, Gendlin, and Truax (Rogers, 1961; Truax, 1963; Truax and Carkhuff, 1964). It was that the patients in psychotherapy tended to become either better or worse in adjustment than their matched control-group counterparts.

At that time two earlier studies were analyzed (Barron and Leary, 1955; Cartwright and Vogel, 1960; Cartwright, 1956) in which similar findings had occurred; but being incidental to other results, they had not been emphasized in proportion to their true import (Bergin, 1963). Since then, four additional studies with similar findings have been discovered (Fairweather *et al.*, 1960; Mink, 1959; Powers and Witmer, 1951; Rogers and Dymond, 1954). In all seven studies, although there tends to be no difference in the average amount of change between experimentals and controls, there does tend to be a significant difference in *variability* of change. The criterion, or change, scores for treatment groups attain a much wider dispersion than do those of control groups, even though the mean change in both groups is quite similar. Typically, control Ss improve somewhat, with the varying amounts of change clustering about the mean. On the other hand, experimental Ss are typically dispersed all the way from marked improvement to marked deterioration. Now frequently documented, this information is alarming to say the least. Psychotherapy can and does make people worse than their control counterparts! Because of the controversial nature of this conclusion, the following material is presented as detailed substantiating evidence in its support.

Table 1 is reproduced from Cartwright's re-analysis (1956) of the well-known Barron and Leary study (1955). He comments on the data as follows:

> For many scales the variance results suggest that mean differences between the groups are absent because differences of two kinds, op-

posed in sign, are present. It seems that some therapy patients *deterio-rated* to a greater extent than did the waiting-list controls, while some therapy patients *did improve* significantly more than the controls.

TABLE 1

Variances of Discrepancy Scores on MMPI Scales for Individual Psychotherapy and Nontreatment Groups

MMPI Scale	Individual psychotherapy (N = 42) V^a	Nontreatment group (N = 23) V	F	p
1. Lie	19.89	23.43	1.18	
2. F	215.21	22.94	9.38	.01
3. K	55.95	31.70	1.76	
4. Hs	127.46	64.16	1.99	.05
5. D	244.30	93.32	2.62	.01
6. Hy	113.21	87.80	1.29	
7. Pd	155.00	89.68	1.73	
8. Pa	111.94	68.06	1.64	
9. Pt	208.51	73.27	2.85	.01
10. Sc	272.91	74.13	3.68	.01
11. Ma	126.79	75.34	1.68	
12. Es	43.56	14.82	2.94	.01

[a] Variances computed from SD data reported by Barron and Leary (1955, p. 243).

It should be noted that this occurred only for individual and not for group therapy.

It is a fascinating fact that Cartwright's observation has lain un-attended in the literature for years, while implicit in his statement is a clear means of resolving much of the controversy over negative re-sults in therapy outcome studies. It is even more fascinating that Cart-wright himself participated in a study (Rogers and Dymond, 1954) in which a similar phenomenon occurred, but just as the data in the Barron and Leary study, it was never emphasized in proportion to its true import. The classic features in this study apparently overshadowed the passing references to a *client-deterioration phenomenon*. While the study is properly famous for other reasons, it provides supporting bits of evidence for the thesis that negative change in therapy is not an isolated or chance occurrence. A careful reading of the report in-dicates that of 25 therapy *S*s, six or 24 percent, declined in self-ideal correlation between pre-therapy and follow-up testing. A quick computation of the mean change in self-ideal correlation indicates that those who increased averaged an increment of .49 in their correlations, whereas those who declined a decrement of —.40, a difference that is striking considering the fact that the mean pre-therapy correlations were not different for these two subgroups. While some chance fluctuations in scores are to be expected, these changes in both directions can hardly be attributed to the effects of imperfect test reliability. While the authors do not examine these possibilities in the data, they do allude to them in passing: "It is of interest, though it does not bear directly upon the hypothesis, that there has also been a marked increase in the degree of variation of correlations [self-ideal] over this period" (Butler and Haigh, 1954, p. 63).

It may be argued, of course, that decline in self-ideal correlation can be an indication of improved adjustment, particularly when the correlation is extremely high as in the case of some paranoid subjects. However, the pretest correlations of all six subjects who declined in this study were low, ranging from .28 to —.12. The question of whether self-ideal correlations actually measure adjustment at all is still a subject of some debate, so we would not want to draw conclusions about psychotherapy in general from data based on this measure alone. In another section of the same volume, an analysis of behavior observations made of the clients independently of therapist progress ratings (p. 228) yielded results similar to those found with the self-ideal measure: "During the whole period from pre-therapy to follow-up, observers saw a definite increase in the maturity of behavior of those clients whose therapy was rated as successful and a sharp decrease in the maturity of behavior of those clients rated as unsuccessful. The relationship was statistically significant."

While there are additional fragmentary evidences of deterioration phenomena in the book, these suffice to illustrate the point.

In a controlled study of counseling with high-school students, Mink (1959, p. 14) observes the same phenomenon: "Counseling affected the expression of social adjustments on the California Test of Personality. The forms of expression indicate both improvement and recession."

The excellent multi-factor design executed by Fairweather et al. (1960) yielded similar results:

Generally, significantly different variances occurred on most instruments between treatments and diagnosis. The control group usually had the smallest variance and the three psychotherapy groups the largest (p. 24). . . . In these three interactions, one or all of the three long-term psychotic groups in psychotherapy demonstrated changes in the maladaptive scale direction [MMPI] while the controls remain relatively the same or change in the adaptive direction (p. 9).

Cartwright and Vogel (1960) discovered the same type of differential effect in a neurotic sample using different criterion measures:

> Thus, as measured by the Q score, adjustment changes, regardless of direction, were significantly greater during a therapy period than during a no-therapy period (p. 122). . . . The post-therapy tests showed those in therapy with experienced therapists to have improved significantly on both tests, whereas those in therapy with inexperienced therapists not to have improved . . . ; in fact, they bordered on a significant decrease in health on the TAT (p. 127).

Turning back several decades to the Cambridge-Somerville youth study (Powers and Witmer, 1951) which was initiated in 1937, we find the same phenomenon with a group of pre-delinquent boys:

> . . . when the Study Services were effectual most of the boys did function better than their C-twins. This conclusion can be accepted, however, only if its opposite is also accepted: that some of the boys who were not benefited may have been handicapped in social adjustment by the organization's efforts. If this is true, we can conclude that the apparent chance distribution of terminal adjustment ratings . . . was due to the fact that the good effects of the Study were counterbalanced by the poor (p. 455).

Elsewhere the authors indicate that in a significant proportion of cases where the counselor's efforts were judged as poor, the boys "were more socially maladjusted than their control twin" (p. 509). It is unfortunate that this excellently designed and executed study is one leaned upon most heavily by Eysenck (1960, 1965) in his bold denial of the usefulness of psychotherapy, for while the study shows no difference between experimentals and controls, it demonstrates the efficacy of treatment as well as its deteriorative effect.

Finally, we cite the recent Wisconsin project on therapy of schizophrenia which has been published thus far only in tempting bits and pieces:

> . . . high levels of therapist-offered conditions during therapy are related to patient improvement, but . . . low levels . . . are related to patient deterioration, so that if all therapy combined is indiscriminately compared to control conditions there is little average change. Thus psychotherapy can be for better or for worse. . . . (Truax, 1963, p. 256).

Since the length of therapy varied in these seven studies from a few months to several years, it seems doubtful that the observed deterioration can be accounted for by the temporary regression that sometimes occurs during treatment. The views of most writers would indicate that the average deterioration due to this effect for a treatment group would be small after brief and lengthy periods of therapy but large in between; whereas the findings reported here suggest a consistent, rectangularly distributed, amount of regression regardless of the length of time transpired prior to obtaining outcome estimates. Unfortunately, so little controlled empirical work has been done with analytic therapies, which are presumably the richest sources of such data, that it is difficult to compare the findings reported here with what might be found if research were done on them.

Fortunately, these various data indicate that psychotherapy can make people considerably better off than control Ss. Therefore, contrary to the notions of some critics, psychotherapy can produce improvement beyond that which may occur due to spontaneous remission alone. Consistently replicated, this is a direct and unambiguous refutation of the oft-cited Eysenckian position (Eysenck, 1960, 1965).

A general paradigm is suggested by the double-edged effect observed in the studies cited which may be schematized as shown in Figure 1. Such a startling phenomenon certainly deserves a name, and *The Deterioration Effect* is suggested here.

It is interesting to note that a phenomenon similar to the great variability in the quality of therapeutic effects noted here has also been observed in relation to the accuracy of diagnostic evaluations (Garfield, 1963). Apparently, even well-known diagnosticians vary greatly in the accuracy of their judgments. When all of these judgments are pooled, average predictions or discriminations often are not different from chance estimates; but some individuals appear to far exceed chance predictions while others actually do worse than chance.

Implication No. 1. (a) We should not give up the practice of psychotherapy as some have advocated. (b) We should be more cautious and critical of our own practices, carefully eliminating any ineffective or harmful therapeutic techniques. We should find out whom we are making worse or better, and how, with all due speed. (c) We should find out if some therapists make people better and if some make them worse, or if individual therapists do both. After that, we have the ticklish business of making changes in technique, personality, or personnel as may be necessary to eliminate negative influences and accentuate positive ones.

NATURAL THERAPEUTIC CONDITIONS

CONCLUSION 2. (a) *It has been frequently replicated, and is now a well-established fact, that control Ss who do not receive psychotherapy change positively as a group with the passage of time. This is the so-*

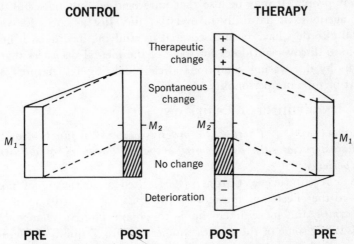

Fig. 1. The deterioration effect. Schematic representation of pre- and post-test distributions of criterion scores in psychotherapy outcome studies.

called "spontaneous remission" effect (Eysenck, 1952, 1960, 1965). (b) Three studies (Frank, 1961; Gurin, Veroff and Feld, 1960; Powers and Witmer, 1951) indicate that many of these disturbed persons who receive no formal psychotherapy seek and obtain help from various professional and nonprofessional sources such as friends, clergymen, physicians, teachers, and occasionally even psychotherapists (Bergin, 1963).

All this has typically been unknown to the researchers who were depending upon these so-called controls to be a base line for comparison with their treatment cases. It seems clear that this aid has an ameliorative effect since the people improve, although it would be impossible to substantiate this fully without further study of the influences upon control Ss in their "natural" habitat. To the extent that this position is correct, it further undermines the Eysenck-type position, because it shows that control Ss often change due to the influence of therapy or therapy-like procedures. Thus, "spontaneous remission" is just another name for the effects of informal therapy.

Implication No. 2. (a) Researchers who utilize control groups should carefully ascertain that these groups are indeed controls, or, if necessary, should directly measure the effects of non-experimental influences which they cannot control. (b) The fact that some of these previously uncontrolled influences are much like therapy, but frequently occur outside of a professional setting, implies that nonprofessional help can stimulate positive personality change. This may consist partly of individuals with "therapeutic personalities" who are sought out for counsel and catharsis by many people. It may be also that unrecognized, but powerful, therapeutic agents exist naturally in everyday life. Just as cures for various physical disorders have been discovered by studying health, so it may be possible to discover antidotes for some of the mental disorders that confront us by discovering conditions already existing in "nature" which support or promote personality integration.

INGREDIENTS OF THERAPY

CONCLUSION 3. *Therapeutic progress varies as a function of therapist characteristics such as warmth, empathy, adequacy of adjustment, and experience.*

In a recent review, Gardner (1964) cited a smattering of positive results to the effect that the more a therapist has an attitude of *liking and warmth,* the more likely he is to obtain positive change in his clients. While some of the studies enumerated are of questionable design or generalizability, they are relatively consistent when compared with many other areas of research.

A recent questionnaire study of patients' retrospective reports regarding their therapeutic experience (Strupp, Wallach, and Wogan, 1964), which was not reported by Gardner, further confirms this general finding. While the study is uncontrolled and appears to be contaminated by artifactually inflated correlations, it is of interest that it strongly emphasizes the importance of therapist warmth and genuineness in relation to patient-perceived outcome ($r. = .53$).

Additional data on this point come from the client-centered group in a series of studies with neurotics and psychotics. It should be noted that some of the therapists studied were *not* client-centered. These studies are consistent in discovering a significant relationship between operational measures of Rogers' concept of positive regard and independent indices of therapeutic progress or outcome (Truax and Carkhuff, 1964, 1965a; Barrett-Lennard, 1962). Measures of the therapist's attitudes have included ratings by both the therapist himself and the patient. Three types of analysis have resulted in similar results and in different studies with different samples of clients and therapists. It has thus become increasingly clear, within the limits of these studies, that a therapist's ability to be warm and positively inclined toward his patients is an effective therapeutic ingredient. The effects of intentional authoritarian demands or other forms of planned therapist aggression which are sometimes advocated have not been studied and thus cannot be compared with these findings.

Acknowledging the past confusion and contradiction involved in studies of *empathy,* we suggest that the recent data summarized at Chicago (Barrett-Lennard, 1962), Wisconsin (Truax, 1961a; Truax and

Carkhuff, 1964), and Kentucky (Truax and Carkhuff, 1965a; Carkhuff, Kodman and Truax, 1965; Dickenson and Truax, 1965; Truax and Wargo, 1965) offer promising leads. Analyses of recorded therapist behavior and ratings by clients of their therapists during the process of treatment have yielded consistently positive relationships between empathic understanding and outcome.

The strength of these findings lies in careful design (Rogers, 1961) and in the analysis of therapist behavior *in vivo,* which is unusual in empathy research. A new empathy measure has been operationalized by Truax (1961b) and is defined as accurate ". . . sensitivity to current feelings *and* the verbal facility to communicate this understanding in a language attuned to the patient's current being" (Truax and Carkhuff, 1964). While the scale is still crude and might not be accepted by analysts as measuring their "kind" of empathy, its usefulness has been relatively substantial in these studies.

The third characteristic, *adequacy of adjustment,* has not been studied as thoroughly as the others, but thus far the data are relatively consistent. Those therapists who are more anxious, conflicted, defensive, or "unhealthy" are least likely to promote change in their cases.

Several studies have indicated that supervisor and client ratings of the therapists' competence are negatively related to his degree of anxiety or maladjustment (Arbuckle, 1956; Bandura, 1956; Bergin and Solomon, 1963). Other studies have yielded similar findings when the therapist's actual in-therapy behavior and the patient's response to it was evaluated and used as a criterion of competence. For example, Bandura, Lipsher, and Miller (1960) found that therapists' hostility anxiety was directly associated with avoidance responses to patients' expressions of hostility toward them. The more hostility conflict a therapist had, the more likely he was to avoid his patients' hostility and consequently the patients' self-exploration in this area diminished and his conflicts remained unresolved. A practically identical result was found by Winder, Ahmad, Bandura and Rau (1962) with regard to dependency anxiety.

In another study (Bergin and Solomon, 1963) it was found that measures of the therapists' degree of personal disturbance correlate negatively with his level of empathy as measured by ratings of tape-recorded psychotherapy interviews. Independent measures of personality strength, on the other hand, correlated positively with degree of "live" empathy. In addition, ratings of therapist anxiety level correlated negatively with independent ratings of therapeutic competence.

Additional data came from the client-centered studies already cited with regard to warmth and empathy, in their examination of therapist congruence. Congruence (Rogers, 1957; 1959) means essentially the healthiness of the therapist in his relationship with his client—his spontaneity, nondefensiveness, openness, or genuineness. Like positive regard and empathy, this variable has also been related to therapeutic progress, and further confirms the general finding of a direct connection between level of therapist adjustment and therapeutic effectiveness.

The three elements of warmth, empathy, and congruence have been found, in the Wisconsin studies, to vary directly with outcome in both negative and positive directions. That is, when these therapist characteristics were at a low level, the patients were getting worse; when they were high, the patients improved (Truax and Carkhuff, 1964). These studies thus provide a partial answer to the question raised earlier as to how negative change occurred in the outcome studies reviewed, although they are limited in that the observed differences were not large, and there is also some question as to whether the division into high and low conditions was done before or after the fact. The other studies cited here in the same realm further clarify the point, although none of the data are precise enough to make practical selection decisions possible.

With regard to the much debated variable of therapist experience, it may be asserted that, in general, more experienced therapists are more effective and successful. This is based on four studies (Barrett-Lennard, 1962; Cartwright and Vogel, 1960; Chance, 1959; Fiedler, 1950a, 1950b, 1951), one of which suggests that highly inexperienced therapists may actually cause patient deterioration (Cartwright and Vogel, 1960).

Implication No. 3. (a) Since psychotherapists are effective partly as a function of personal adjustment, they should be selected for this quality and not solely on the basis of academic and intellectual abilities. Future practice of therapy should therefore be modified by new selection procedures which will bring healthier personalities to bear upon problems of pathology, and by closer self-scrutiny and exposure of one's work among present practitioners.

There is presently no evidence that personal therapy for a disturbed therapist can qualify him for practice and should not be depended upon until such evidence is provided. This does not, of course, prove that the experience of being treated cannot be useful to a student therapist whose functioning is within a relatively normal range. There are no studies in which treated neurotics have improved to a level of functioning which is similar to that of control normals even though they do change in level of adjustment; therefore, treatment should not be counted upon to take care of errors in selection. The behavior ratings and personality inventories used in the studies reviewed could provide a beginning in research geared specifically toward the selection problem.

(b) Given the necessary personal attributes, therapists should develop their abilities in the realm of warmth and empathic communication, particularly in the case of empathy which is known to be subject to training and experience influences. Further study should be conducted so that clear, measurable standards of performance can be required of aspirants to professional status before they are permitted to practice. As an example, the Truax Empathy Scale (Truax, 1961b) could be used as a beginning to assess one's level of functioning via analysis of recorded interviews.

(c) Inexperienced potential therapists should be very carefully introduced to practice with clients, perhaps with much more stringent care than is now commonly exercised. Since all beginners make many mistakes, it may be more useful and ethical to have them see more resilient, normal people until they reach a criterion level of interview performance, measured perhaps on dimensions such as warmth and empathy which appear to be accepted by most schools of therapy as vital though not necessarily sufficient for successful treatment.

CONCLUSION 4. *To date, the only school of interview-oriented psychotherapy which has consistently yielded positive outcomes in research studies is the client-centered approach (Rogers and Dymond, 1954; Shlien, Mosak, and Dreikurs, 1962; Truax and Carkhuff, 1964).*

The fact that other schools have not subjected their methods to systematic study of this sort is important but it should not deter us from accepting the fact that client-centered treatment has some positive value when properly conducted according to Rogers' paradigm (1957). The implications for practice seem quite clear, particularly in light of the consistently dismal reports on percentages of improvement in psychoanalytic therapy (Eysenck, 1965; Wolpe, 1964b).

It appears from these reports that the poorest results were obtained with more classical, long-term psychoanalysis, namely a lower percentage of improved cases than the 67 percent "spontaneous" remission rate. Briefer, analytically-oriented eclectic psychotherapy was more promising in that the percentage improvement equalled the spontaneous remission figure. This type of therapy was also used in some of the studies cited in this paper on the deterioration effect; therefore, despite the generally negative evidence, some analytically-oriented therapists must be having a positive effect beyond that occurring in control groups.

It should also be noted that the technique of "moderate interpretation" (Speisman, 1959), which derives from the analytic tradition, has potential therapeutic significance. Its definition is very similar to that given for "good" interpretation by various analysts (Fenichel, 1941) and it is related to productive patient self-exploration. It consists of responding to client affect just below the surface and labeling, identifying or emphasizing it. This does not involve making connections between past and present, being diagnostic or theoretical, nor telling the patient about feelings he "really has" when he is not experiencing them. It is, rather, an instance of good empathy. If one looks carefully at the definitions and operations for identifying accurate empathy and moderate or good interpretation, it is very difficult to distinguish between them. Truax and Carkhuff (1964) refer to this notion in an interesting comment:

> . . . "accurate empathy" has much in common with the "good psychoanalytic interpretation," in that it makes use of both verbal and nonverbal cues presented by the patient. It differs from some good psychoanalytic interpretations in its insistence that the therapist's empathic response focuses upon feelings and experiences of the patient from the patient's own unique viewpoint.

The importance of these observations should not be underestimated, for if they are accurate it appears that effective variables cut across schools of treatment and thus provide the basis for applying techniques on the basis of known effects rather than on doctrines promulgated by warring factions. This also indicates that titles, degrees, or years of training should not define the psychotherapist, but rather what the individual can do. Thus one might call himself "client-centered" and espouse the teachings of that school while at the same time presenting the low level of therapist empathy found to result in client deterioration. On the other hand, a psychoanalyst might be functioning at a high level according to the client-centered empathy scale.

CONCLUSION 5. *In spite of all so far stated about the possibilities for substantially improving consulting-room effectiveness, some stubborn facts still require confrontation. One is that even when the various sources of slippage and inadequacy are accounted for, interviews still do not generally produce very dramatic changes in people. Another is the now well-known fact that many types of people simply are not helped at all by this procedure.*

Studies of the relationship between client qualities and therapeutic outcome indicate consistently and clearly that positive outcome is limited or nil with many personality types. It is common for private practitioners and even clinics to either refuse to treat, or reluctantly accept for treatment, cases that do not fit their conception of psychotherapy. To a great extent this is realistic because traditional methods do not work with these cases. These "rejects" tend to be less intelligent, less anxious, less educated, less verbal and insightful, more concrete and action-oriented, more severely disturbed, more impulsive in the sociopathic sense, and often find the typical consulting room procedure rather meaningless (Barron, 1953; Cartwright, 1955; Fulkerson and Barry, 1961; Garfield and Affleck, 1961; Hollingshead and Redlich, 1958; Kirtner and Cartwright, 1958a, 1958b). This general observation has been made fairly frequently by various clinicians and is currently rather well-substantiated by the research literature.

Implication No. 5. The implication of these data, which only confirm an already widely believed idea, is that novel or modified techniques must be developed for dealing with a vast population whose problems are not amenable to standard methods. The importance of novel approaches is further emphasized by the fact that standard methods are not dramatically effective even in those cases where they are applicable, except in rare instances. The latter unusual cases would be a proper subject of study in themselves and may actually suggest innovations even though they arise in "traditional" therapy.

There are three primary sources of possible innovation that might alleviate this predicament. One is creative work in the clinical setting; another is naturally existing conditions in society; and another is that general area of research which is concerned with personality and behavior change such as studies of learning, attitude change, and personality development.

THE PROMISE OF BEHAVIOR THERAPY

CONCLUSION 6. *Studies of learning have thus far been very fruitful in generating principles and methods for promoting personality change. The work by Wolpe (1958), Lazarus (1963), Lang and Lazovik (1933), Lindsley (1963) and others has been both provocative and fruitful. The cases presented and research studies reported provide more positive evidence of the usefulness of these methods than is the case in any form of traditional interview or dynamic psychotherapy, including client-centered therapy.*

They involve clinical adaptation of learning principles, such as counterconditioning or extinction of anxiety symptoms, positive reinforcement in shaping adaptive responses and developing appropriate discriminations, aversive conditioning of maladaptive approach responses, and modeling. It is the effects of these methods which are important here. Wolpe (1964a) cites over 200 cases of neurosis in 89 percent of which he has obtained substantial recovery. Lazarus (1963), in England, reports 408 cases with a similar improvement rate. The striking aspect of these results is that they have been achieved with difficult symptom pictures in brief periods of time. Unfortunately, these are clinical reports by individual therapists who rate their own case outcomes. Independent criteria and control subjects are completely lacking, and it is difficult to discern how comparable their cases are with those reported in other studies. Still, it is rare to find such high rates of claimed cure even in the clinical literature.

A number of well-designed studies appear to substantiate the clinical reports of Wolpe and Lazarus. Lang and Lazovik (1963) were able to significantly alter snake phobias with brief desensitization procedures. Effects of testing and training in relaxation were controlled, and no symptom substitution occurred during six-months of follow-up. Lazarus (1961) demonstrated substantial and rapid change of phobic symptoms and impotence by group desensitization methods. A comparison group being treated by traditional interpretive group therapy showed considerably less improvement, only two of 17 cases becoming symptom-free after 22 sessions. These same cases were subsequently treated by group desensitization and after a mean of 10 sessions each, two-thirds were symptom-free. Paul (1964) found that desensitization procedures were far more effective in eliminating speech anxieties than brief insight therapy, an attention-placebo condition, and a no-therapy control condition.

In a study of operant conditioning methods, which are different from Wolpe's techniques, King, Armitage, and Tilton (1960) found that substantial changes could be effected even in schizophrenic cases. They were able to produce clinically observable improvement in cases so treated which was greater than the changes occurring in conventional interview therapy, recreational therapy, or no therapy. Allyon and Michael (1959) effected substantial positive changes in ward behavior of psychotics by programming the reinforcements of their hospital environment according to operant principles. Lovaas, Schaeffer, and Simmons (1966) appear to have induced important changes in the social behavior of difficult cases of childhood autism by systematic use of negative reinforcement. In a review, Lindsley (1963) argues for the general promise of operant techniques. The evidence thus far pertains primarily to simple motor and verbal behaviors. Conceivably, this approach will prove to be more useful with the more primitive behaviors of psychotics and small children than with the more complex, symbolically involved adult neuroses.

A most interesting development in behavior therapy involves the systematic application of principles of imitative or observational learning. Bandura (1965c) argues persuasively from the vantage point of extensive experimental work (Bandura, 1965a, 1965b) that modeling procedures provide powerful conditions for the acquisition of new responses and the modification of old ones. Though controlled clinical applications have just begun, they already lend considerable substance to Bandura's view (Berberich and Schaeffer, 1965; Frank, 1965; Hoehn-Saric et al., 1965; Krumboltz and Thoreson, 1964; Krumboltz and Schroeder, 1965; Krumboltz, Varenhorst, and Thoreson, 1965; Nelson and Bijan, 1965; Thoreson and Krumboltz, 1965; Truax and Carkhuff, 1965b).

Several extensive reviews further substantiate the generality of conclusion six (Bandura, 1965c; Bandura and Walters, 1963; Eysenck and

Rachman, 1965; Franks, 1964; Grossberg, 1964; Krasner and Ullmann, 1965; Ullmann and Krasner, 1965; Wolpe, 1964b).

In spite of the fact that the evidence is favorable, these techniques have been criticized by clinicians as removing symptoms without changing basic pathology and as being limited to very simple neuroses. Neither criticism, however, fits the evidence. Wolpe (1964a) cites data on 88 cases which indicate that a high proportion of complex neuroses can be successfully treated (89 percent) and in a much briefer time than is typical of traditional methods (Table 2).

TABLE 2

Comparison of Numbers of Sessions in Complex
and Simple Neuroses.[a]

	Number	Median number of sessions	Mean number of sessions
Complex neuroses	65	29	54.8
Simple neuroses	21	11.5	14.9
Whole group	86	23	45.4

[a] The total is only 86 because 2 cases that turned out to be schizophrenic are excluded.

The more telling critique of this work is Breger and McGaugh's point (1965) regarding the uncontrolled case reports, which are the basis for the high cure rates, and the rater bias in estimating outcomes encountered in many of the experimental studies. Faulty as a proportion of these reports are, the over-all record still represents the best there is in the field of psychotherapy.

In addition to the fact that difficult cases show improvement in a short time, these reports indicate that significant relapses are rare. This is perhaps the most persuasive evidence that behavior therapists are right when they assert that "symptoms" are not symptoms of psychoanalytic-style pathology, but that they are learned behaviors subject to modification via re-learning.

Some learning theorists have criticized Wolpe in particular, claiming that his techniques do not derive directly and logically from learning principles and thus do not have the scientific base he claims (Breger and McGaugh, 1965; Mowrer, 1963). While this may be true to some extent, it is irrelevant to the question of the technique's effectiveness and ignores the possibility that these clinical phenomena may eventually become the basis for reformulating learning theories in terms of complex, socially significant human behavior. In this case, one would not expect principles of behavior therapy to conform rigorously to conceptions derived largely from animal research.

Implication No. 6. The implications of this work seem quite clear. Since these techniques are effective with many types of symptomatology, they should be used. With regard to some of the more complex and difficult problems, behavior therapists argue that it would be better to spend time developing more complex social learning paradigms for treatment than to expand equal energy modifying less promising traditional interview methods. It appears that special effort should be devoted to integrating these methods with others and in some cases substituting them for the other methods. It would seem important to avoid a current tendency to isolate behavior therapies from the mainstream of treatment and thus create another rigid "school" which will gradually become as impervious to new ideas as the traditional schools already are.

CONCLUSION

In conclusion, it is only regrettable that consent upon so many topics of research has had to be excluded. Suffice it to say that the results in many of those not mentioned are not as yet amenable to synthesis. A good example is the material on the patient-therapist relationship. Nearly all of this research actually pertains to therapist qualities and has nothing to do with an analysis of interactional factors. An unusual exception is the work of Barrett-Lennard which was cited briefly in the discussion of therapist qualities. The few other useful facts in this domain were also included in that section. Another promising line of investigation is that on patient-therapist similarity; but the meaning of the data is still quite ambiguous (Sussman, 1964).

In spite of the fact that much of what is called psychotherapy research is appalling in its inadequacy, to have found a handful of reliable conclusions is gratifying. The groundwork seems well laid by these studies for initial steps at productive innovation in therapeutic treatment.

REFERENCES

Ayllon, T., and Michael, J. The psychiatric nurse as a behavioral engineer. *J. exp. anal. Behav.*, 1959, *2*, 323-334.

Arbuckle, D. S. Client perception of counselor personality. *J. counsel. Psychol.*, 1956, *3*, 93-96.

Bandura, A. Psychotherapist's anxiety level, self-insight, and psychotherapeutic competence. *J. abnorm. soc. Psychol.*, 1956, *52*, 333-337.

Bandura, A. Vicarious processes: a case of no-trial learning. In L. Berkowitz (Ed.), *Advances in experimental social psychology*, Vol. II. New York: Academic Press, 1965. (a) Pp. 3-48.

Bandura, A. Behavioral modification through modeling procedures. In L. Krasner and L. Ullmann (Eds.), *Research in behavior modification*. New York: Holt, Rinehart and Winston, 1965. (b). Pp. 310-340.

Bandura, A. Psychotherapy conceptualized as a social-learning process. Paper presented at the Kentucky Centennial Symposium on Psychotherapy, University of Kentucky, April, 1965. (c)

Bandura, A., Lipsher, D. H., and Miller, Paula E. Psychotherapists' approach-avoidance reactions to patients' expressions of hostility. *J. consult. Psychol.*, 1960, *24*, 1-8.

Bandura, A., and Walters, R. H. *Social learning and personality development*. New York: Holt, Rinehart and Winston, 1963. (Ch. 5)

Barrett-Lennard, G. T. Dimensions of therapist response as causal factors in therapeutic change. *Psychol. Monographs: General and Applied*, 1962, *76*, No. 43 (While No. 562).

Barron, F. Some test correlates of response to psychotherapy. *J. consult. Psychol.*, 1953, *17*, 235-241.

Barron, F., and Leary, T. Changes in psychoneurotic patients with and without psychotherapy. *J. consult. Psychol.*, 1955, *19*, 239-245.

Berberich, J., and Schaeffer, B. Establishment of verbal behavior through imitation. Paper read at Amer. Psychol. Assoc. Convention, Chicago, 1965.

Bergin, A. E. The effects of psychotherapy: Negative results revisited. *J. counsel. Psychol.*, 1963, *10*, 244-250.

Bergin, A. E., and Solomon, Sandra. Personality and performance correlates of empathic understanding in psychotherapy. *Amer. Psychologist*, 1963, *18*, 393. (Abstract)

Breger, L., and McGaugh, J. L. Critique and reformulation of "learning-theory" approaches to psychotherapy and neurosis. *Psychol. Bull.*, 1965, *63*, 338-358.

Butler, J. M., and Haigh, G. Changes in the relation between self-concepts and ideal concepts consequent upon client-centered counseling. In C. R. Rogers and R. F. Dymond (Eds.). *Psychotherapy and personality change*. Chicago: Univer. of Chicago Press, 1954. Pp. 55-75.

Cartwright, D. S. Success in psychotherapy as a function of certain actuarial variables. *J. consult. Psychol.*, 1955, *19*, 357-363.

Cartwright, D. S. Note on "changes" in psychoneurotic patients with and without psychotherapy. *J. consult. Psychol.*, 1956, *20*, 403-404.

Cartwright, Rosalind D., and Vogel, J. L. A comparison of changes in psychoneurotic patients during matched periods of therapy and no-therapy. *J. consult. Psychol.*, 1960, *24*, 121-127.

Chance, Erika. *Families in treatment*. New York: Basic Books, 1959.

Dickenson, W. A., and Truax, C. B. Group counseling with college underachievers: Comparisons with a control group and relationship to empathy, warmth, and genuineness. Unpublished manuscript, Univer. of Kentucky, 1965.

Eysenck, H. J. The effects of psychotherapy: An evaluation. *J. consult. Psychol.,* 1952, *16,* 319-324.

Eysenck, H. J. The effects of psychotherapy. In H. J. Eysenck (Ed.), *Handbook of abnormal psychology.* New York: Basic Books, 1960. Pp. 697-725.

Eysenck, H. J. The effects of psychotherapy. *Int. J. Psychiat.,* 1965, *1,* 97-178.

Eysenck, H. J., and Rachman, S. *The causes and cures of neurosis.* San Diego: Knapp, 1965.

Fairweather, G., Simon, R., Gebhard, M. E., Weingarten, E., Holland, J. L., Sanders, R., Stone, G. B., and Reahl, J. E. Relative effectiveness of psychotherapeutic programs: A multicriteria comparison of four programs for three different patient groups. *Psychol. Monographs: General and Applied,* 1960, *74,* No. 5 (Whole No. 492).

Fenichel, O. *Problems of psychoanalytic techniques.* Albany, N. Y.: *Psychoanal. Quarterly,* 1941.

Fiedler, F. E. The concept of the ideal therapeutic relationship. *J. consult. Psychol.,* 1950, *14,* 239-245. (a)

Fiedler, F. E. A comparison of therapeutic relationships in psychoanalytic nondirective, and Adlerian therapy. *J. consult. Psychol.,* 1950, *14,* 436-445. (b)

Fiedler, F. E. Factor analyses of psychoanalytic, nondirective, and Adlerian therapeutic relationships. *J. consult. Psychol.,* 1951, *15,* 32-38.

Frank, J. D. *Persuasion and healing.* Baltimore: Johns Hopkins Press, 1961.

Frank, J. D. The role of hope in psychotherapy. Paper presented at the Univer. of Kentucky Centennial Psychotherapy Symposium, April, 1965.

Franks, C. (Ed.) *Conditioning techniques in clinical practice and research.* New York: Springer, 1964.

Fulkerson, S. D., and Barry, J. R. Methodology and research on the prognostic use of psychological tests. *Psychol. Bull.,* 1961, *58,* 177-204.

Gardner, G. Gail. The psychotherapeutic relationship. *Psychol. Bull.,* 1964, *61,* 426-437.

Garfield, S. L. The clinical method in personality assessment. In J. Wepman and R. Heine (Eds.), *Concepts of personality.* Chicago: Aldine, 1963. Pp. 474-502.

Garfield, S. L., and Affleck, D. C. Therapists' judgments concerning patients considered for psychotherapy. *J. consult. Psychol.,* 1961, *25,* 505-509.

Grossberg, J. M. Behavior therapy: A review. *Psychol. Bull.,* 1964, *62,* 73-88.

Gurin, G., Veroff, J., and Feld, Sheila. *Americans view their mental health.* New York: Basic Books, 1960.

Hoehn-Saric, R., Frank, J. D., Imber, S. D., Nash, E. H., Stone, A. R., and Battle, C. C. Systematic preparation of patients for psychotherapy—I. Effects on therapy behavior and outcome. *J. Psychiat. Res.,* 1965, *2,* 267-281.

Hollingshead, A. B., and Redlich, F. C. *Social class and mental illness.* New York: Wiley, 1958.

King, G. F., Armitage, S. G., and Tilton, J. R. A therapeutic approach to schizophrenics of extreme pathology. *J. abnorm. soc. Psychol.,* 1960, *61,* 276-286.

Kirtner, W. L., and Cartwright, D. S. Success and failure in client-centered therapy as a function of client personality variables. *J. consult. Psychol.,* 1958, *22,* 259-264. (a)

Kirtner, W. L., and Cartwright, D. S. Success and failure in client-centered therapy as a function of initial in-therapy behavior. *J. consult. Psychol.,* 1958, *22,* 329-333. (b)

Krasner, L., and Ullmann, L. (Eds.) *Research in behavior modification: New developments and implications.* New York: Holt, Rinehart and Winston, 1965.

Krumboltz, J. D., and Thoreson, C. E. The effect of behavioral counseling in group and individual settings on information-seeking behavior. *J. counsel. Psychol.,* 1964, *9,* 324-333.

Krumboltz, J. D., and Schroeder, W. W. The effect of reinforcement counseling and model-reinforcement counseling on information-seeking behavior of high school students. *Personnel guid. J.,* 1966, in press.

Krumboltz, J. D., Varenhorst, Barbara, and Thoreson, C. E. Nonverbal factors in the effectiveness of models in counseling. Paper read at Amer. Personnel and Guidance Assoc. Convention, 1965, Minneapolis.

Lang, P. J., and Lazovik, A. D. Experimental desensitization of a phobia. *J. abnorm. soc. Psychol.,* 1963, *6,* 519-525.

Lazarus, A. A. Group therapy of phobic disorders by systematic desensitization. *J. abnorm. soc. Psychol.,* 1961, *63,* 504-510.

Lazarus, A. A. An evaluation of behavior therapy. *Behav. Res. Ther.,* 1963, *1,* 69-79.

Lindsley, O. R. Free-operant conditioning and psychotherapy. In J. H. Masserman (Ed.), *Current psychiatric therapies,* Vol. III. New York: Grune & Stratton, 1963. Pp. 47-56.

Lovaas, O. I., Schaeffer, B., and Simmons, J. Q. Building social behavior in autistic children by use of electric shock. In J. O. Palmer and M. J. Goldstein (Eds.), *Perspectives in psychopathology: Readings in abnormal psychology.* New York: Oxford Univer. Press, 1966. Pp. 222-236.

Mink, O. G. A comparison of effectiveness of nondirective therapy and clinical counseling in the junior high school. *School Counselor,* 1959, *6,* 12-14.

Mowrer, O. H. Freudianism, behavior therapy, and "self-disclosure." *Behav. Res. Ther.,* 1936, *1.*

Nelson, Karen, and Bijan, Guilani. Teaching social behaviors to schizophrenic children through imitation. Paper read at Amer. Psychol. Assoc. Convention, Chicago, 1965.

Paul, G. L. Effects of insight, desensitization, and attention placebo treatment of anxiety. Stanford, Calif.: Stanford Univer. Press, 1966.

Powers, E., and Witmer, Helen. *An experiment in the prevention of delinquency*. New York: Columbia Univer. Press, 1951.

Rogers, C. R., and Dymond, Rosalind F. *Psychotherapy and personality change*. Univer. of Chicago Press, 1954.

Rogers, C. R. The necessary and sufficient conditions of therapeutic personality change. *J. consult. Psychol.*, 1957, *21*, 95-103.

Rogers, C. R. A theory of therapy, personality, and interpersonal relationships, as developed in the client-centered framework. In S. Koch (Ed.), *Psychology; a study of a science*, Vol. III. New York: McGraw-Hill, 1959. Pp. 184-256.

Rogers, C. R. A theory of psychotherapy with schizophrenics and a proposal for its empirical investigation. In J. G. Dawson and N. P. Dellis (Eds.), *Psychotherapy with schizophrenics*. Baton Rouge: Louisiana State Univer. Press, 1961. Pp. 3-19.

Shlien, J. M., Mosak, H. H., and Dreikurs, R. Effect of time limits: a comparison of two psychotherapies. *J. counsel. Psychol.*, 1962, *9*, 31-34.

Speisman, J. C. Depth of interpretation and verbal resistance in psychotherapy. *J. consult. Psychol.*, 1959, *23*, 93-99.

Strupp, H. H., Wallach, M. S., and Wogan, M. Psychotherapy experience in retrospect: questionnaire survey of former patients and their therapists. *Psychol. Monographs: General and Applied*, 1964, *78*, No. 11 (Whole No. 588).

Sussman, Alice. Patient-therapist similarity as a factor in psychotherapy. Unpublished manuscript, Teachers College, Columbia Univer., 1964.

Thoreson, C. E., and Krumboltz, J. D. Relationship of counselor reinforcement of selected responses to external behavior. *J. counsel. Psychol.*, 1966, in press.

Truax, C. B. The process of group psychotherapy. *Psychol. Monographs: General and Applied*, 1961, *75*, No. 14 (Whole No. 511). (a)

Truax, C. B. A scale for the measurement of accurate empathy. *Psychiat. Inst. Bull.*, Wisconsin Psychiatric Institute, Univer. of Wisconsin, 1961, *1*, No. 10. (b)

Truax, C. B. Effective ingredients in psychotherapy. *J. counsel. Psychol.*, 1963, *10*, 256-263.

Truax, C. B., and Carkhuff, R. R. For better or for worse: The process of psychotherapeutic change. In *Recent advances in behavioral change*. Montreal: McGill Univer. Press, 1964.

Truax, C. B., and Carkhuff, R. R. The experimental manipulation of therapeutic conditions. *J. consult. Psychol.* 1965, *29*, 119-121 (a)

Truax, C. B., and Carkhuff, R. R. Personality change in hospitalized mental patients during group psychotherapy as a function of the use of alternate sessions and vicarious therapy pretraining. *J. clin. Psychol.*, 1965, *21*, 225-228. (b)

Truax, C. B., and Wargo, D. G. Human encounters that change behavior: For better or for worse. Unpublished manuscript, Univer. of Kentucky, 1965.

Ullmann, L., and Krasner, L. (Eds.) *Case studies in behavior modification.* New York: Holt, Rinehart and Winston, 1965.

Winder, C. L., Ahmad, Farrukh Z., Bandura, A., and Rau, Lucy. Dependency of patients, psychotherapists' responses, and aspects of psychotherapy. *J. consult. Psychol.,* 1962, *26,* 129-134.

Wolpe, J. *Psychotherapy by reciprocal inhibition.* Stanford, Calif.: Stanford Univer. Press, 1958.

Wolpe, J. Behavior therapy in complex neurotic states. *Brit. J. Psychiat.,* 1964, *110,* 28-34. (a)

Wolpe, J. The comparative clinical status of conditioning therapies and psychoanalysis. In J. Wolpe, A. Salter, and L. J. Reyna (Eds.), *The conditioning therapies.* New York: Holt, Rinehart and Winston, 1964. Pp. 5-20. (b)

In Reverse Order

Bergin's first two conclusions are discussed well in his earlier article. We would, however, like to make some increasingly extensive comments on Bergin's remaining conclusions in the reverse order.

Conclusion 6. We cannot agree more with the need to develop novel or modified techniques. A meaningful, social learning theory does appear a fruitful source for "generating principles and methods for promoting personality change."

Conclusion 5. We feel that the changes in client behavior will be as dramatic as the therapist is effective. The client will be limited by the therapist's resourcefulness. If the therapist does not move beyond the traditional interview, more than likely he will not effect dramatic changes. But if he relates the therapy to "real life" and even dares to move into the social environment with *and* without the client, we believe changes as dramatic as the therapist's life is effective will occur.

Conclusion 4. Perhaps Rogers' major *coup d'état* involved his labeling his school "client-centered." *All effective therapies are client-centered.* The conditions that the techniques of the nondirective school attempt to communicate most directly are not mysteriously incorporated in their techniques. They are the conditions of effective living. That is not to say that in the heightened experience of therapy, training in communicative skills is not necessary. Therapy is, after all, a communication process.

In an earlier work, Bergin suggested: ". . . it seems likely that some analysts are effective but when they are, they are probably doing client-centered therapy!" We might add that some nondirectivists are effective, but when they are, they are probably doing client-centered therapy. The results of the Wisconsin project demonstrated that the patients of non-directive therapists who were high on facilitative conditions improved in functioning while those of nondirective therapists who were low deteriorated.

Conclusion 3. Bergin suggests adding adequacy of adjustment, and experience to the list of critical therapist dimensions. In our society, persons who are empathic, congruent, respectful, and warm are considered psychologically healthy and adequately adjusted. As has been made clear by Truax and Carkhuff, the controversial construct of experience is primarily a function of the individual therapist. We know only too well those persons who have been practicing 30 years but who, in reality, have had one year's experience 30 times. (Gardner's point on "personal commitment" may be related when we consider the possibility that the principal effect of graduate training in the helping professions is to raise the intellectual defenses of the individual and remove him from any basic commitment with which he might have entered training, or from the possibility of acquiring that commitment.)

Bergin emphasizes the selection of future therapists on the basis of all of those dimensions that characterize the effective therapist. We must agree with the basic irrelevance of the current intellective indices for therapeutic practice. The lack of relationship of intellective indices with any criteria of productivity indicates that the problems of our present selection procedures go far beyond those of the professions of counseling and psychotherapy. Graduate schools in the helping professions would do well to provide the facilitative experiences that elicit the constructive behavior change necessary for effective therapeutic functioning. Ideally, training programs should provide a model for facilitative interpersonal functioning. Beyond certain limits, we find ourselves concerned with the model that the screening emphasis provides. The following article attempts a meaningful integration on the research in training and practice.

AN INTEGRATION OF PRACTICE
AND TRAINING*
Robert R. Carkhuff

THE CHALLENGE

If we were to do properly controlled research on the practice of medicine and found that, all other things being equal, patients who were treated by minimally trained, nonprofessional "friends" were more likely or even as likely to recover or be "cured" than the patients of physicians, we would be horrified and would call for extensive reform in professional medical practice. A careful review (Carkhuff, 1965a) of carefully controlled studies of the outcomes of our traditional training programs indicates that state of affairs in our counseling and therapeutic practices.

It is clear that our current training programs of all kinds have simply not established their efficacy in terms of a translation to client benefits. Instead we have trained individuals who, if we can borrow from quasi-outcome research, present a distressing composite picture in terms of their ability to judge the personality characteristics of others (Arnhoff, 1954; Kelly and Fiske, 1950; Luft, 1950; Taft, 1955; Weiss, 1963). While these indices remain of questionable relationship to client outcomes, they remain important goals of our traditional training programs.

Perhaps most importantly, the helping professions have not yet responded adequately to the critical challenges to the efficacy of our various guidance, counseling, and therapeutic activities with both adults (Eysenck, 1952; 1960) and children (Levitt, 1957) which established that clients and patients who are not counseled improve as often and to the same degree (and in some cases, such as in the case of psychoanalytic treatment, more often and to a greater degree) of improvement as those who are not. If these findings appear to be an indictment of our traditional modes of training and practice, then so be it. The picture is indeed a distressing one.

IN RESPONSE

In response to these challenges and in the hope of "sharpening up" our treatment and training practices, I should like to propose several

---

* Toward failure or fulfillment: Training and practice in counseling and psychotherapy. In *The counselor's contribution to facilitative processes*. Urbana, Illinois: R. W. Parkinson, 1966, pp. 1-18. Reprinted by permission.

avenues of approach. Several propositions flow from a basic assumption concerning the instances of counseling and psychotherapy in relation to all interpersonal processes. We will examine the evidence concerning the corollaries of each of these propositions.

Assumption: *Counseling and psychotherapy and their training processes are simply additional instances of all interpersonal processes.* We would be inclined to add, "no more, no less," but in all likelihood, "a little more and a little less" would be more appropriate. There is no evidence to suggest that these helping processes are any more or less critical than parent-child, teacher-student, and other significant human relationships between those designated as "more knowing" and "less knowing" by society. The direct implication of this proposition is that the same dimensions which are effective in the other instances of human encounters are effective in the counseling and therapeutic processes. To be sure, while the primary variables may be the same, the weights may vary with the given instances of the interpersonal processes involved (Carkhuff, 1963). It may be, for example, that the teachers' empathic understanding of their students will not be as significant a source of effect as that dimension will be in child-rearing or counseling. Nevertheless, our assumption, for which we will examine the evidence in a number of propositions and their corollaries, dictates the critical significance of a condition such as empathic understanding to all learning processes. In addition, secondary variables peculiar to a particular interaction of first person, second person(s), and situational variables may operate to facilitate or even retard the outcomes of the processes (Carkhuff, 1963). Here a most notable example would involve the varying effects of the application of nondirective techniques or the implementation of the traditional "shadowy" figure of the orthodox analyst with (1) functioning out-patient neurotic type populations, and (2) chronic and regressed hospitalized schizophrenic populations. It is clear to us from practice and research that the outcomes would be very different.

Further, there are suggestions that the effectiveness of the therapeutic processes may be accounted for in large part by the presentation of the inverse of those conditions which led to the development of the difficulty or the psychopathology in the first place. Thus, to follow the example of empathy, the absence of any real comprehensive depth of understanding by the significant figures in the developing child's environment may have led to his present difficulty. The institution of accurate empathic understanding in the counseling process may once again free the person for the self-exploration and experimentation critical to his constructive development.

In the hope that we may comprehend these interpersonal processes, we must attend more fully to first person, second person(s), and situational variables, alone and in their various interactions. The age, sex, race, socioeconomic status, etc. of the parent, teacher, or counselor are relevant. The specialized techniques employed as well as other specific influences upon the role concept of therapist must be investigated. These first person variables, in turn, may be meaningful only insofar as they interact with second person variables, especially including population types, if these can be reliably ascertained, in addition to other personal characteristics. Situational variables such as the environmental setting and the "atmosphere" in which therapy takes place as well as the "set" which the client has or has been given might also become extremely potent considerations.

There appear to be a number of general propositions which flow from this general assumption and which deserve special attention because of their critical significance. We will examine the research evidence concerning each of their corollaries.

PROPOSITION I. *All interpersonal processes may have constructive or deteriorative consequences.* It makes good logical sense that if we can effect positive gain in persons we can also effect negative consequences. It makes good logical sense that the deteriorated schizophrenic did not begin that way but rather is at least in large part a product of a succession of retarding relationships just as the psychologically healthy person is the end result of a number of facilitating relationships. Let us examine the evidence.

Corollary I. Counseling and psychotherapy may be "for better or for worse." Here the evidence offers a startling consistency. At all levels of development on the psychological health-psychopathology continuum, there is extensive data to indicate that the counseling and therapeutic processes may have constructive or deteriorative consequences. There is substantial evidence to indicate a significantly greater variability on the post-treatment change indices of the treatment groups over the control groups. A significant increase of both constructive and deteriorative consequences in treatment groups when compared to their controls has been found in programs of intensive research with hospitalized schizophrenics (Rogers, 1962; Truax, 1963; Truax and Carkhuff, 1964),[1] out-patient neurotics (Barron and Leary, 1955; Bergin, 1963; Cartwright and Vogel, 1960) and relatively nonpathological guidance populations (Mink and Isaksen, 1959).

In general, then, the relevant findings seem to offer an explanation for the puzzling mass of data already existing concerning the over-all

---

[1] According to a personal communication from Eysenck, Barendregt in Holland has found a significant increase in constructive and deteriorative consequences in the treatment of hospitalized patients.

lack of efficacy of the "helping" relationships. That is, the constructive gains from counseling by some clients are balanced out by the deteriorative changes from counseling by other clients. Consequently, when we average the increased number of positive and negative changes in the treatment group, we find "no average differences" on the change indices between the treatment and control groups. Together, these studies suggest one very consoling and one very distressing message to those of us who have dedicated our lives to "helping" others. Firstly, and in direct response to Eysenck's challenge, *we have an impact!* However, and secondly, the findings force us to take a long hard look at this impact which we have. *Counseling and therapy may be "for better or for worse!"*

Corollary II. Parent-child, teacher, teacher-student and other significant relationships may be "for better or for worse." Here there is a growing body of literature to suggest that child-rearing and teaching relationships may have constructive or deteriorative consequences. There is evidence in child-rearing to indicate the deteriorative results of early retarding parental relationships in terms of social maladjustment (Cass, 1953; Montalto, 1952), the manifestation of hostility (Chovest, 1962), and the emergence of schizophrenia (Bateson, 1956; Baxter, Becker, and Hooks, 1963; Bowen, 1960; Lidz, Cornelison, Fleck, and Terry, 1957; Lidz and Lidz, 1949; Weakland, 1960; Wynne, Ryckoff, Day, and Hirsch, 1958.) In the teaching area there is limited yet very promising support for the facilitating or retarding effects of teachers upon both the child's social adjustment (Truax, 1960) and learning achievement (Christensen, 1960).

Thus, collapsing the outcome indices explored, there is substantial support for the proposition that all interpersonal processes may be "for better or for worse." An oft-forgotten instance of interpersonal learning processes is that of graduate training in the helping professions. It deserves special attention simply because it is often forgotten.

Corollary III. Training in the helping professions may be "for better or for worse." First, let us point out here that there is a dearth of evidence concerning our traditional training programs. Our training programs have simply not been assessed in terms of their translation to the personal benefits of the trainees or, more importantly, client benefits. While we cannot cite the hundreds of programs which should have been researched, we can make the following statement loudly and clearly: *No traditional training programs have demonstrated their constructive consequences.* In the few instances where the outcomes of traditional training programs have been researched, there are strong indications that they contribute to a deterioration in interpersonal functioning. We need not mention again the work of Eysenck, Levitt, Kelly and Fiske, Taft, and Weiss. We should mention, though, the distressing finding of

Bergin and Solomon (1963) who discovered that *the clients of those trainees who have received the highest academic and practicum grades tend to deteriorate in functioning.* We know, on the other hand, from our lay counselor training programs (Appleby, 1963; Carkhuff and Truax, 1965a, 1965b; Harvey, 1964; Mendel and Rapport, 1963; Rioch, *et al.*, 1963) and, with some reservations, possibly some of the short-term guidance institutes (Demos, 1964; Demos and Zuwaylif, 1963; Hansen and Barker, 1964; Jones, 1963; Munger and Johnson, 1960; Munger, Myers, and Brown, 1963; Webb and Harris, 1963) that training may have constructive consequences in terms of facilitating the positive outcomes of schizophrenic patients, both in- and out-patient, out-patient neurotics, marital counseling cases and student-clients. The lay counselor training programs have been the only programs to consistently demonstrate their efficacy in terms of translation to the client benefits. Their results clearly suggest that lay counselors, trained and supervised, can do anything that professionals can do and sometimes more. Thus, at a variety of different developmental stages we find that "helping" relationships may be facilitative or deteriorative in terms of their intrapersonal and interpersonal results. The problem then becomes one of looking at outcome and then tracing back through the process (and this makes out a case for some form of the all-too-often neglected recording of the process) in an attempt to explicate those process variables which facilitate positive movement and those which inhibit this goal or even contribute to individual deterioration (Carkhuff and Truax, 1965). In spite of the bewildering array of theories and practices, there have been many recurring themes, concentrating, for example, on conditions envolving empathic understanding, warmth and respect, genuineness, concreteness, and other dimensions.

PROPOSITION II. *All effective interpersonal processes share a common core of conditions conducive to facilitative human experiences.* Again, it makes good logical sense to assume that many of those interpersonal conditions which would be facilitative in the parent-child relationship would also be facilitative in the teacher-student and counselor-counselee relationships and vice versa. What is the evidence?

Corollary I. Clients of counselors who offer high levels of facilitative conditions improve while those of counselors who offer low levels of these conditions deteriorate. Psychoanalytic, client-centered, and various eclectic theorists alike have emphasized: (a) the importance of the counselor's ability to sensitively and accurately understand the patient in such a manner as to communicate this deep understanding; (b) the importance of counselor respect and warmth and acceptance of the client; (c) the necessity for the counselor to be integrated, mature, and genuine within the counseling encounter. Other sources of more limited theory and research have variously supported dimensions such as concreteness or specificity of expression of both counselor and counselee, counselor self-disclosure, flexibility, and more dynamic personality characteristics. Many of these dimensions, especially those involving warmth and respect, empathy, genuineness, and concreteness have been related to constructive gain or deterioration in hospitalized schizophrenics, including both individual (Rogers, 1962; Truax, 1963; Truax and Carkhuff, 1964) and group psychotherapy (Truax, 1961; Truax, Carkhuff, and Kodman, 1965) as well as in out-patient neurotics or situationally-distressed populations (Barrett-Lennard, 1962; Bergin and Soloman, 1963; Halkides, 1958; Truax, 1963). The accumulation of studies offers substantial support for the relationship of a core of facilitative conditions to client and patient outcomes. These findings also constitute a second possible response to the challenges of Eysenck, Leavitt *et al.*, the first being the more treated clients get both "better" and "worse" than the controls. *The effective ingredients of psychotherapy may not be what we have traditionally considered to be the dimensions of counseling and psychotherapy.* Since a great part of the effectiveness of a given counselor may be accounted for by how effective and facilitative a human being he is, these conditions may be available to the control group clients and patients from other than the professional "helper." That is, *control groups may not be control groups.* In all probability, the likelihood of a given client seeking the help of a nonprofessional "helper" is minimal for those in the treatment group who have already been assigned counselors and minimal for those clients under control conditions. Thus, the clients under control conditions may find the facilitative relationship of counseling and psychotherapy (Bergin, 1963; Frank, 1961; Gurin, Veroff, and Feld, 1960; Powers and Witmer, 1951). The relationship of facilitative conditions to outcomes of their "learners" should also hold in other instances of interpersonal processes.

Corollary II. Children and students of parents, teachers, and other significant persons who offer high levels of facilitative conditions improve while those of persons who offer low levels of these conditions deteriorate. Here there is a growing body of evidence in support of the potency of related facilitative conditions in the teaching situation (Christensen, 1960; Davitz, 1964; Isaacson, McKeachie, and Milholland, 1963; Pace and Stern, 1958; Thistlethwaite, 1959; Truax, 1960; Willis, 1961;) and the child-rearing situation (Bateson, 1956; Baxter, Becker, and Hooks, 1963; Bowen, 1960; Cass, 1953; Chorost, 1963; Lidz, Cornelison, Fleck, and Terry, 1951; Lidz and Lidz, 1949; Montalto, 1952; Weakland, 1960; Wynne, Ryckoff, Day, and Hirsch, 1958). Again, there is limited evidence to indicate that the benefits accrued from the high-level conditions relationship are not restricted to social adjustment gains but are also evident in more traditional educational indices (Christensen, 1960).

It makes good sense that the effective teacher or parent is not simply the knowledgeable one who imparts his accumulated wisdom to a vulnerable learner. Rather, he would appear to be one whose more didactic offerings are made in the context of a relationship which finds the teacher tuned in on the student's wavelength of feeling and understanding, concerned for the student's comprehension and general welfare, genuine in the encounter and concrete in the cognitive and affective specifics, all of which bring us to our third corollary.

Corollary III. Trainees of mental health programs which offer high levels of facilitative conditions improve while those of programs which offer low levels of conditions deteriorate. Here we have no clearcut evidence other than that of our own extensive personal experiences. Graduate training centers are loath to ask the essential questions. However, there is inferential evidence to indicate both constructive and deteriorative consequences. Bergin and Solomon's (1963) research investigation of a traditional analytic program with no emphasis upon the experiential base of facilitative conditions found the post-internship trainees functioning at or near the very lowest level of empathy (a dimension which again correlated with client change indices) where the clinician is oblivious to the feelings of the client or essentially *immune to human encounters.* We can only conjecture concerning the level of conditions provided by their teachers and supervisors. In contrast, there are the lay counselor and other training programs of Carkhuff and Truax (1965a, 1965b), the specific intent of which was to provide an experiential base of facilitative conditions and concurrently a role model of a facilitative person for imitation or identification while didactically teaching the necessary discrimination and operationalization of facilitative conditions in human encounters. At the cessation of training the trainees were functioning at levels of empathy, positive regard, and genuineness and eliciting client process involvement (which also is a highly significant correlate of client change) essentially commensurate to those of a number of our most prominent and experienced therapists. In addition, *the clients of these trainees improved in functioning.*

Other such inferential evidence is available. Of necessity the support must be inferential because well-designed studies of the process and outcome of training are simply not available.

DISCUSSION AND IMPLICATIONS

There are a number of issues to which we might address ourselves in the context of these proposals. For example, we might ask, "How is it that a few good therapists get through some fairly 'retarding' programs?" The model would dictate that the high ego strength, psychologically healthy products of a number of facilitative relationships would be less severely affected by a retarding experience, although whether or not they reacted covertly or overtly against the experience would indicate whether or not they would remain or get thrown out of their training programs. I might add anecdotally here, that three of the most facilitative counselors and therapists of the ten or so whom I have come to know in my personal experience from the hundreds of therapists and therapies which we have studied in our major research programs, were thrown out of their programs, primarily for "clinical" reasons concerning their effective clinical work. The remainder of effective therapists by and large led a tenuous graduate and clinical existence, often scraping through with one principal facilitative supporter. I must grind a final axe here: psychological health always poses an affront to the disturbed unless the latter are seeking help; unfortunately, the retarding promulgators of retarding programs must often choose between reexamining their last 20 years of ineffective practice or destroying their more effective underlings.

There are a number of other implications of these propositions which we can systematize in order to study their significance.

IMPLICATION I. *All treatment and training "cults" or orientations and their techniques are the consequence of a particular interaction pattern of counselor, client, and contextual variables.*

The very evolution of the variety of cults of counseling and psychotherapy is attributable for the most part to a more or less unique interaction of variables. A particular group of therapists who, having many interests and beliefs in common, converge and linger in a given setting with all its implications and interact with a client population which is screened by themselves, the therapists or the setting to have many characteristics in common. Certain methods of approach soon come to connote more efficacious outcomes. A set of beliefs takes hold of the therapists and, shaped by what they believe to be effective practices, these therapists promulgate a theory of therapeutic practice. Unfortunately, it all too often ends there. The beliefs based upon generalizations from their own experience are passed on as doctrine and applied by their students in contexts involving a very different interaction of variables. If the trainee has not learned to trust his own experience or feedback and has not learned himself to be shaped by what is effective for him in terms of client outcome, he may even indoctrinate his students in his own externally-imposed theory and practice and the group will have succeeded in establishing a more-or-less dominant "cult" or school of counseling or psychotherapy. Rogers' (1965) growing emphasis upon the dimension of therapist congruence, and if he is pushed perhaps of therapist self-disclosure, has been a function of his willingness to attempt to apply nondirective techniques derived from college counseling center experiences with sophisticated, psychologically attained, intelligent, out-patient, neurotic-type populations to a hospitalized schizophrenic population (Carkhuff and Truax, 1965c). Needless to say, for a variety of reasons, the technique of reflection simply has its limitations with a catatonic schizophrenic patient. Other "cults" of counseling or psychotherapy have as severe or greater limitations when venturing out of their bailiwick. They simply have not exposed themselves as openly or responded as directly to their failures.

IMPLICATION II. *We can account for the greatest part of the counselor's or the trainer's effectiveness independent of his orientation and technique by assessing the level of facilitative conditions offered by the counselor.*

At this point in time we can account for the greatest part of the efficacy of a practitioner, whatever his orientation, by an assessment of the level of facilitative conditions and the consequent level of process involvement engaged in by his clients (Truax and Carkhuff, 1963, 1964, 1965.) Thus, the clients of psychoanalytic therapists who are high on empathy, respect, genuineness, and concreteness improve in functioning on a variety of change indices with little regard to the therapist's congnitive map of what is taking place and where it is going. The case is similar for the nondirectivists or the existentialists or the trait-and-factor-testing people or the vocational information-getting-and-giving group, all of which orientations have in all likelihood (although this has yet to be substantiated by research) an additional contribution to make to the efficacy of the process *given a particular interaction of variables.* A significant exception to the lack of evidence concerning the effect of a particular orientation is the work of the behavioristic conditioning school. Given experimentally-oriented counselors and therapists in experimental-type settings with neurotic anxiety reaction cases involving more or less isolated fears such as phobic reactions the evidence is undeniable. Even here, however, the learning theory model which dictates the mechanisms employed, does not necessarily dictate that the therapist be an impersonal programmed reinforcement machine. Indeed, everything that we know about the contingencies of reinforcement effect upon social variables dictates a very personal interaction. In this regard, Wolpe (1958), himself, concedes that as much as 60 percent of the effectiveness of the counterconditioning process may be due to "nonspecific relationship factors."

IMPLICATION III. *We have built our treatment and training programs around secondary factors which are a function of the particular interaction of variables.*

These secondary factors may account for a minimal albeit important amount of the efficacy of the process. However, if employed in the absence of the particular interaction of variables which gave them their

origin, these secondary factors may actually have deteriorative consequences. Built around this central core of primary, facilitative conditions
are the set of secondary factors predicated upon a particular interaction
of counselor, client, and contextual variables. We have already discussed
a possible interaction of variables in the case of the nondirective and
conditioning schools. Vocational counseling involving vocational information-getting-and-giving and testing which may facilitate the critical
decision-making processes of situationally distressed normals in educational and vocational settings is another possibility. The psychoanalytic
approach calculated to foster personality change or to reconstruction of
sophisticated out-patient neurotics with hysterical or obsessive compulsive
symptoms in psychiatric clinics is still another well known combination.
These modes of approach may well constitute possible "preferred modes
of treatment" given that particular interaction of variables and, *in the
context of high levels of facilitative conditions,* may contribute an additional amount of the effectiveness in effective processes. We have built
our training programs in psychiatry, clinical and counseling psychology,
social work and counselor education around these secondary factors which
may account for an additional amount of the variance in the change
indices given a particular interaction of variables. In the context of a
different combination of variables, these secondary factors may contribute nothing or may actually depress the efficacy at the client's expense—
the tragedy in inappropriate applications of doctrinaire modes of practice.

IMPLICATION IV. *Both professional and nonprofessional persons
can be brought to function at levels of facilitative conditions which effect
positive gains in others.*

In developing the different lay counselor training programs we have
simply attempted to sharpen up the communicative and sensitivity skills
of the trainees in an attempt to help them to become their most "facilitative selves." It is interesting that the different lay therapist programs
concentrate upon the central core of facilitative conditions almost to the
exclusion of theory and technique while the traditional programs have
concentrated upon theory and technique almost to the exclusion of the
facilitative conditions. It is also interesting to note that we have been
willing to pass off this "low-level" interpersonal training to the nonprofessionals and have eagerly sought to assess the outcomes of these
programs. The outcomes have, to be sure, been exciting. It is clear that
lay persons without professional qualifications can become facilitative
agents. Professional training, in appropriate perspective and properly
accomplished, ought to be able to effect similar results and indeed has
already done so (Carkhuff and Truax, 1965a). This can be most effectively accomplished in a program with a didactic focus upon the inter-

personal core of facilitative conditions in the context of the facilitative conditions which provide both an experiential base for the behavioral change implicitly sought in all training as well as a role model for identification and imitation (Truax, Carkhuff, and Douds, 1964). For doctoral level persons, in particular, there is a very real place for a full comprehension of the variety of other possible "preferred modes of treatment" in a particular combination of variables in order that the doctoral level person may provide the lay counselor with the supervision and consultation essential to the appropriate circumstances. In addition, the doctoral level person must possess the necessary skills to enable him to make enlightened and systematic inquiries into what we are professing to do, and to design and carry out and assess the efficacy of lay counselor training programs so critical to our meeting our mental health needs.

SUMMARY

In response to the many challenges to the helping professions we have posited, and examined a substantial body of evidence for, several fundamental propositions: counseling and psychotherapy are additional instances of all interpersonal processes which may have constructive or deteriorative consequences and which in their constructive instances largely are a function of a core of facilitative interpersonal dimensions. We have explored the many implications for training and practice. The ultimate appeal is not to the experience of the reader. We are witnessing the closing of the door on the golden age of psychoanalytic theory, practice, and research. It is apparent that we are on the threshold of a new golden age of impersonal behavior conditioning. This, too, must pass! The further removed that any mode of practice comes to be from the "truth" concerning the dimensions of effective human encounters, which each of us who has had a facilitative relationship knows deep inside of us, the greater is its likelihood of ultimate extinction.

REFERENCES

Appleby, L. Evaluation of treatment methods for chronic schizophrenia. *Arch. gen. Psychiat.*, 1963, *8*, 8-21.

Aspy, D. The effects of the level of facilitative conditions offered by teachers upon achievement indices. Unpublished doctoral dissertation, Univer. of Kentucky, 1965.

Barrett-Lennard, G. T. Dimensions of therapist response as causal factors in therapeutic change. *Psychol. Monogr.*, 1962, *76*, No. 43 (Whole No. 562).

Barron, F., and Leary, T. Changes in psychoneurotic patients with and without psychotherapy. *J. consult. Psychol.*, 1955, *19*, 239-245.

Bateson, G., Jackson, D., Haley, J., and Weakland, J. H. Toward a theory of schizophrenia. *Behav. Sci.*, 1956, *1*, 251-264.

Baxter, J. C., Becker, J., and Hooks, W. Defensive style in the families of schizophrenics and controls. *J. abnorm. soc. Psychol.*, 1963, *66*, 512-518.

Bergin, A. E. The effects of psychotherapy: Negative results revisited. *J. counsel. Psychol.*, 1963, *10*, 244-250.

Bergin, A. E., and Solomon, Sandra. Personality and performance correlates of empathic understanding in psychotherapy. Paper read at Amer. Psychol. Assoc., Philadelphia, September, 1963.

Bowen, M. A family concept of schizophrenia. In D. Jackson (Ed.), *The etiology of schizophrenia*. New York: Basic Books, 1960. Pp. 346-372.

Carkhuff, R. R. On the necessary conditions of therapeutic personality change. *Discuss. papers Wisconsin Psychiat. Instit.*, 1963, No. 47, 1-7.

Carkhuff, R. R. The search for an identity: A statement of some propositions underlying a new graduate training program in counseling psychology. *Counselor Educ. and Super.*, in press, 1966.

Carkhuff, R. R. Training in the counseling and therapeutic processes: Requiem or reveille? *J. Counsel. Psychol.*, 1966, *13*, 360-367.

Carkhuff, R. R., and Truax, C. B. Training in counseling and psychotherapy: An evaluation of an integrated didactic and experiential approach. *J. consult. Psychol.*, in press, 1965.

Carkhuff, R. R., and Truax, C. B. Lay mental health counseling: The effects of lay group counseling. *J. consult. Psychol.*, in press, 1965 (a)

Carkhuff, R. R., and Truax, C. B. Toward explaining success and failure in interpersonal learning processes. *Personnel guid. J.*, 1966, *44*, 723-728. (b)

Carkhuff, R. R., and Truax, C. B. The client-centered process as viewed by other therapists. In *The therapeutic relationship and its impact*. (C. R. Rogers, E. T. Gendlin and C. B. Truax, Eds.) Book in preparation, 1965. (c)

Cass, Loretta K. Parent-child relationships and delinquency. *J. abnorm. soc. Psychol.*, 1953, *47*, 101-104.

Chorost, S. B. Parent-child-rearing attitudes and their correlates in adolescent hostility. *Genet. Psychol. Monogr.*, 1962, *66*, (1), 49-90.

Christensen, C. M. Relationships between pupil achievement, pupil affect-need, teacher warmth, and teacher permissiveness. *J. educ. Psychol.*, 1960, *51*, 169-174.

Davitz, J. R. *The communication of emotional meaning*. New York: McGraw-Hill, 1964.

Demos, G. D. The application of certain principles of client-centered therapy to short-term vocational counseling. *J. counsel. Psychol.*, 1964, *11* 280-284.

Demos, G. D., and Zuwaylif, F. H. Counselor movement as a result of an intensive six-week training program in counseling. *Personnel. guid. J.*, 1963, *42*, 125-128.

Eysenck, H. J. The effects of psychotherapy: An evaluation. *J. consult. Psychol.*, 1952, *16*, 319-324.

Eysenck, H. J. The effects of psychotherapy: In *Handbook of abnormal psychology*. (H. J. Eysenck, Ed.). New York: Basic Books, 1960.

Fairweather, G. W., and Simon, R. A further follow-up comparison of psychotherapeutic programs. *J. consult. Psychol.*, 1963, *27*, 186.

Frank, J. D. *Persuasion and healing*. Baltimore, Md.: Johns Hopkins Press, 1961.

Gurin, G., Veroff, J., and Feld, Sheila. *Americans view their mental health*. New York: Basic Books, 1960.

Halkides, Galatia. An investigation of therapeutic success as a function of four variables. Unpublished doctoral dissertation, Univer. of Chicago, 1958.

Harvey, L. V. The use of nonprofessional auxiliary counselors in staffing a counseling service. *J. counsel. Psychol.*, 1964, *11*, 348-357.

Heilbrun, G. Results with psychoanalytic therapy. *Amer. J. Psychother.*, 1963, *17*, 427-435.

Isaacson, R. L., McKeachie, W. J. and Milholland, J. E. A correlation of teacher personality variables and student ratings. *J. educ. Psychol.*, 1963, *44*, 110-117.

Levitt, E. E. The results of psychotherapy with children. *J. consult. Psychol.*, 1957, *21*, 189-196.

Lidz, T., Cornelison, Alice, Fleck, S., and Terry, Dorothy. The intrafamilial environment of schizophrenic patients: II. Marital schism and marital skew. *Amer. J. Psychiat.*, 1957, *114*, 214-248.

Lidz, Ruth W., and Lidz, T. The family environment of schizophrenic patients. *Amer. J. Psychiat.*, 1949, *106*, 332-345.

Mendel, W. M., and Rapport, S. Out-patient treatment for chronic schizophrenic patients: Therapeutic consequences of an existential view. *Arch. gen. Psychiat.*, 1963, *8*, 190-196.

Mink, O. G., and Isaksen, H. L. A comparison of effectiveness of nondirective therapy and clinical counseling in the junior high school. *School Counselor*, 1959, *6*, 12-14.

Montalto, F. D. Maternal behavior and child personality. *J. Proj. Tech.*, 1952, *16*, 151-178.

Munger, P. F., Myers, R. A., and Brown, D. F. Guidance institutes and the persistence of attitudes. *Personnel guid. J.*, 1963, *41*, 415-419.

Pace, C. R., and Stern, G. G. An approach to the measurement of physiological characteristics of college environment. *J. educ. Psychol.*, 1958, *49*, 269-277.

Powers, E., and Witmer, Helen. *An experiment in the prevention of delinquency*. New York: Columbia Univer. Press, 1957.

Rioch, Margaret J., Elkes, C., Flint, A. A., Udansky, B. S., Newman, R. G., and Silber, E. NIMH pilot study in training mental health counselors. *Amer. J. Orthopsychiat.*, 1963, *33*, 678-689.

Rogers, C. R. The interpersonal relationship: The core of guidance. *Harv. educ. rev.*, 1962, *32*, 416-429.

Taft, R. The ability to judge people. *Psychol. Bull.*, 1955, *52*, 1-23.

Thistlethwaite, D. L. College press and student achievement. *J. educ. Psychol.,* 1959, *50,* 183-191.

Truax, C. B. Conditions relevant to constructive personality change in preschool children. Unpublished manuscript, Univer. of Iowa, 1960.

Truax, C. B. The process of group psychotherapy: Relationships between hypothesized therapeutic conditions and intrapersonal exploration. *Psychol. Monogr.,* 1961, *75,* No. 7 (Whole No. 511).

Truax, C. B. Effective ingredients in psychotherapy: An approach to unraveling the patient-therapist interaction. *J. counsel. Psychol.,* 1963, *10,* 256-263.

Truax, C. B., and Carkhuff, R. R. For better or for worse: The process of psychotherapeutic personality change. In *Recent advances in the study of behavior change.* Montreal, Canada: McGill Univer. Press 1964.

Truax, C. B., and Carkhuff, R. R. Significant developments in psychotherapy research. In *Progress in clinical psychology* (L. E. Abt and B. F. Reiss, Eds.). New York: Grune & Stratton, 1964, 124-155.

Truax, C. B., and Carkhuff, R. R. The experimental manipulation of therapeutic conditions. *J. consult. Psychol.,* 1965, *29,* 119-124.

Truax, C. B., Carkhuff, R. R., and Douds, J. Toward an integration of the didactic and experimental approaches to training in counseling and psychotherapy. *J. counsel. Psychol.,* 1964, *11,* 240-247.

Truax, C. B., Carkhuff, R. R., and Kodman, F. The relationships between therapist-offered conditions and patient change in group psychotherapy. *J. clin. Psychol.,* 1966.

Weakland, J. H. The "double-bind" hypothesis of such schizophrenia and three-party interaction. In D. Jackson (Ed.). *The etiology of schizophrenia.* New York: Basic Books, 1960.

Webb, A. P. and Harris, J. T. A semantic differential study of counselors in an NDEA institute. *Personnel guid. J.,* 1963, *42,* 260-263.

Weiss, J. H. The effect of professional training and amount and accuracy of information on behavioral prediction. *J. consult. Psychol.,* 1963, 27, 257-262.

Willis, Margaret. *The guinea pig after 20 years.* Columbus, Ohio: Ohio State Univer. Press, 1961.

Wolpe, J. *Psychotherapy by reciprocal inhibition.* London: Oxford Univer. Press, 1958.

Wynne, L. C., Rykoff, J. M., Day, Juliana, and Hirsch, S. J. Pseudomutuality in the family relations of schizophrenics. *Psychiat.,* 1958, *21,* 205-220.

All Anger Is Not Destructive

The previous article is the most systematic statement of our present thinking and sentiments. We believe that it highlights training as an additional instance of all learning experiences, the principal constructive or deteriorative effects of which may be accounted for by the central core of facilitative conditions.

Perhaps the most important message expressed involves the need for both our professional and our nonprofessional training programs to build around those conditions that have demonstrated their therapeutic efficacy. We call for greater investigation of potentially useful techniques and relevant and appropriate application of these techniques in the context of facilitative relationships. We stand in basic disagreement with the extremists on all sides. We disagree with the behaviorists who would do away with all aspects of interview-oriented therapy and who seek the answer in an increased armamentarium of techniques. We disagree with the traditional psychoanalysts who continue to practice their strange, mystical, and ritualistic cults to the exclusion of those conditions and techniques that can be therapeutically useful to clients and patients. We disagree with nondirectivists who actually believe that the only mode of effectively communicating the conditions of facilitative human encounters involves a pained and depressed voice beginning with, "You feel that you are. . . ," so that the client can become more fully his depressed self. Perhaps we are saying that we stand in basic disagreement to all doctrines of authoritarian extremism, which pervert and distort the dimensions of effective human interactions.

It is our hope that the reader, at this point, experiences mixed feelings of anger, guilt about time wasted, and some excitement. Our own anger comes from the fact that, for so long, we have compulsively and ritualistically perpetuated training practices that have made it more difficult for our students to become effective therapists. Moreover, we find that lay therapy training programs have proven to be extremely effective. We feel healthy anger toward our colleagues who continue to help their graduate students become increasingly neurotic during the course of their training, so that each new group of therapist-supervisors perpetuates "the initiation system": *If graduate training of therapists is not a fulfilling and facilitative experience, we have no business teaching or seeing patients.* Others, less fully trained, can do the job of therapy, and perhaps do it better.

We experience a sense of excitement when we consider it to be possible to identify a "core of primary facilitative factors." Yet it is important to stress once more that any given approach or special technique does not occupy enough of an area to warrant serving as the basis for entire training programs. Within the context and meaning of these readings, we face the problem that the great majority of training and clinical practice is carried on as if it were a sophisticated game: our failures are written off with the consoling thought that "we cannot win them all."

It is time we faced the lie we have lived and weigh the relative import of the contributions to our effectiveness made by our mentors and our clients. We need to ask how many of our supervisors had clients who improved? Did they, our teachers, really have something we wanted? Did we flourish in our experience with them? If not, why? Did they provide live, exciting models of people living fully and effectively?

There are other sobering memories and questions, and we will ask one more. Why, in contrast to his therapist, does the patient often sound more complete and human? *We are asking the reader to re-examine the investments he has made during his professional career.* Hopefully, such a spirit of inquiry will accompany him on his venture into the summary of this work with the feeling that *something must be done now and must be done confidently.*

SUMMARY

*"There is within man
a terrible
and profound hope."*

Andŕe Malraux

Emerging Directions: A Synthesis

In the introduction to this text we made ten points on which we differentiated our position from the more traditional orientations. (We could have listed many more points.) We will not return to these particular points except insofar as they are incorporated into our summary statements. In the following section, we will spell out as succinctly and as lucidly as possible the major propositions of our work. Together they constitute the beginnings of a personalized eclectic stance—perhaps a potent one.

In the first section we briefly review propositions accounting for the potential efficacy of counseling and therapy.

THE EFFICACY OF COUNSELING
AND THERAPY PRACTICES

1. *There is substantial basis for believing that some counselors and therapists can be effective.* By effective we mean that improvement can be registered on one or any number of potentially meaningful outcome or change indices. The question is: "In terms of the particular desired gains or changes involved, does the therapist leave the client better off than he found him?" In order to leave the client "better off," we have to find what practices lead to which of the desired gains or changes. The desired gains or changes, in turn, may be related to the early developmental level, deficits, or disfunctioning of the clients. For example, it

439

appears intuitively satisfactory in a hospital setting to relate outcome to income and employ those indices for outcome that accounted for the patient's incoming in the first place. We should emphasize again that while there is substantial basis for believing that counselors and therapists can be effective, *there is also substantial basis for believing that they can have deleterious effects.*

2. *There is substantial basis for believing that counseling and therapeutic efficacy is largely independent of therapeutic cults, schools, or disciplines of therapy.* The evolution of these cults is a peculiar function of a particular interaction of therapist, client, and situational variables. The prescribed behaviors of these cults is often superstitious in origin. The effectiveness of the processes are a consequence of dimensions that all schools (and indeed all human relations) hold in common. Here, again, we must allow for the complementary or supplementary effects of possible "preferred modes of treatment."

3. *There is substantial basis for believing that to be effective, counselors and therapists must be shaped by what is effective for the client.* Facilitative agents do not operate in vacuo. While in process they must be able to trust their motives; ultimately they must be able to trust the feedback that they get from their clients, and this feedback must indicate that on the relevant indices the client has improved. The process leading to improvement may involve a variety of modes of communication that are shaped by the unique interaction of therapist and client. If we treat all of our clients similarly we do not need them in the same room with us. *Whether or not we remain practitioners must be governed by whether or not our patients improve, and this must be decided by other clinical judgments than our own.*

4. *There is substantial basis for believing that the efficacy or inefficacy of counseling and psychotherapy is primarily a function of a central core of facilitative conditions.* The primary conditions of constructive gain or change involve deep sensitivities and genuine attitudinal conditions. These conditions cut across the wide variety of counseling and psychotherapy cults and elicit the therapeutic process movement. When in an open relationship they are made articulate, the conditions are communicated to the client via three principal sources of learning: (a) the experiential; (b) the didactic; and (c) the role model for identification that the facilitator provides.

5. *There is substantial basis for believing that in the context of the core facilitative dimensions, there are a variety of techniques that can account for an additional degree of effectiveness.* A variety of potential techniques will open doors to more effective living or diminish the significance of the handicaps that prevent the client from opening doors. Dimensions that cut across techniques often account for the efficacy of a

variety of techniques. We are continually impressed, for example, by the striking similarity between the relaxation conditioning of the behaviorists and hypnosis, between the repeated trials to extinction of the desensitization process and free association, and between the role rehearsal of behaviorists and psychodrama, all of which together provide an excellent transition back to real life. Perhaps most significant is the systematic approach that each involves. (Systematic approaches in general communicate the therapist's confidence, elicit client hope for improvement, and bring about additional improvement.) However, we must again reiterate our point that the efficacy or inefficacy of the potential secondary dimensions of possible preferred modes of treatment will in large part be contingent upon the communication of a central core of facilitative conditions. For an extreme example, we borrow from another area of endeavor: The noted biologist, von Bertalanffy (1960), indicates that even the effects of drugs are dependent upon the psychological atmosphere in which they are administered.

At this point, we will again briefly and generally discuss facilitative conditions and complementary techniques in an attempt to define what they are and what they are not.

CONDITIONS AND TECHNIQUES REVISITED

6. *There is substantial basis for believing that facilitative conditions are not entities in themselves to be communicated by prescribed techniques but rather that they are the dimensions of effective human encounters.* Empathic understanding, positive regard, genuineness, concreteness, self-disclosure, confidence, spontaneity, flexibility, and openness are artificial dissections of effective interpersonal processes. They are the conditions of facilitative human encounters and facilitative living, and neither entities in themselves nor techniques. Although some modes of communicating some of these conditions may be more effective than others, these modes must be incorporated into an effective way of living or they are not effective at all.

7. *There is substantial basis for believing that the variety of techniques available are rehabilitative in the sense that they are calculated to free the individual to engage more fully in the kinds of life activities in which he would have become involved if the facilitative conditions had been present originally.* We are essentially a rehabilitative rather than a preventive culture; the techniques we are discussing are not the means employed to achieve psychological health or prevent disfunctioning in child-rearing. Even when we are talking about counterconditioning of characteristics that were inappropriately learned in the first place, we are talking about the absence or inverse of conditions that led to the initial disabilities. We again point out that the variety of techniques

available provide levers to effective living but do not in themselves constitute effective living.

We will now briefly discuss propositions for a meaningful developmental theory.

TOWARD UNDERSTANDING DEVELOPMENTAL PROCESSES

8. *There is substantial basis for believing that interpersonal encounters, at all levels, may have constructive or deteriorative consequences.* Extensive evidence indicates the facilitative or retarding effects that intervention at any developmental level can have. Thus, a series of facilitative relationships will produce a more or less psychologically healthy person, partially dependent upon some of the original characteristics of that person. Similarly, the severely and chronically mentally ill patient may be viewed as the deteriorated consequence of a progression of severely retarding relationships. As can be seen in Figure 1, after the initial direction has been dictated, intervention at any point along the line by teachers, guidance counselors, and social workers (as well as coaches, ministers, and the like), may serve to intensify or significantly modify the original direction.

9. *There is substantial basis for believing that when therapeutic processes are effective they are effective primarily because they present the client with the inverse of those conditions that gave rise to the difficulties in the first place.* When the lack of a deep and comprehensive understanding, a lack of positive regard, and distant, ingenuine, and stereotyped (in essence, the conditions that many of the behavioristic conditioners advocate) relationships give rise to difficulties, including psychopathology and other manifestations of malfunctioning, the effective form of intervention involves the institution of facilitative conditions, the inverse of those conditions that gave rise to the difficulty in the first place. These conditions fill the gaps left in the psychological development of the individual.

10. *There is substantial basis for believing that the necessity for directness and explicitness of communication of facilitative conditions will vary with the degree of psychological development of the individuals involved.* Direct and explicit communication of facilitative conditions is necessary where the individual is least developed psychologically, that is, with psychotic and severely neurotic patients. With situationally distressed, but otherwise psychologically healthy individuals, however, the communication of conditions is often implicit. The communication between two psychologically healthy persons may be taken for granted. The question at the point of therapeutic intervention is: "What is the past learning history of the person before me?" The answer may dictate other

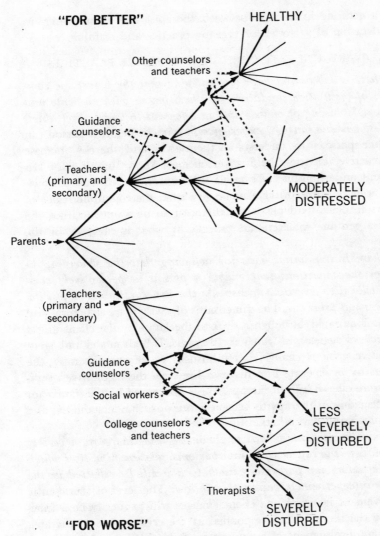

"FOR BETTER"

HEALTHY

Other counselors and teachers

Guidance counselors

Teachers (primary and secondary)

Parents

Teachers (primary and secondary)

Guidance counselors

Social workers

College counselors and teachers

Therapists

MODERATELY DISTRESSED

LESS SEVERELY DISTURBED

SEVERELY DISTURBED

"FOR WORSE"

FIG. 1. Systematic representation of the consequences of a series of "for better or worse" relationships.

variations of the theme, including, for example, the therapist's discovery in his interactional process with many delinquents of the need to demonstrate strength overtly and make himself a person with whom the delinquent can identify. Even here we present the delinquent with the dilemma: "I can make it in your world but choose a more fulfilling way of living."

The consideration of issues concerning client dimensions and whether or not the form of treatment is calculated or evolves in the course of a genuine interaction between therapist and client brings us to a consideration of a model for therapy practice and training.

TOWARD UNDERSTANDING FACILITATIVE PRACTICES

11. *There is substantial basis for believing that the perceptive communication of facilitative conditions to others begins with an acute and sensitive understanding of oneself and an openness to and respectfulness of the widest possible range of experience in oneself.* Before a person can enable other persons to understand themselves and thereby increase their constructive activities, the first person must know himself fully. His openness and understanding of himself will enable him to trust his own motives as well as the feedback that he gets from the communications of others. The feedback will allow the therapist to be shaped, within the context of a genuine interactional process, by what is effective for the client.

12. *There is substantial basis for believing that the structural dimensions of the conditions that enable a person to perceptively communicate facilitative conditions constitute the structural goals of facilitative interpersonal processes.* The dimensions of therapy are structural and not content-dominated, although a shift to the latter by the client might occur. A cycle of agentry, in which the therapist is both model and agent of constructive gain or change, is established. In effective therapy, the client comes to incorporate into his own life style the facilitative conditions that were offered him in therapy. He is influenced by the significant sources of learning in therapy to become more open, understanding, and respectful of himself and others.

13. *There is substantial basis for believing that there are a variety of crises points in the course of all interpersonal relationships after which the effectiveness of one party's approach to life will be reflected in the level of the interpersonal processes that follow.* The level of therapeutic process movement in which the client engages will primarily be a function of how the therapist has responded at the crisis points of therapy. Similarly, the development of a student or child will be in large part a function of how the teacher or parent has responded at the crisis points in the relationship. These points need not be major crises. In therapy, they may, for example, involve the client's telling the therapist that the therapist has not been listening or that the therapist does not understand him. How the therapist responds at these points will be reflected in the client's subsequent degree of self-exploration. If the therapist responds defensively, the client may come to ask himself whether this therapist has anything that the client wants or needs. If the therapist is open in his response, the client may come to trust the therapist's motives and value his effective living.

14. *There is substantial basis for believing that all of the conditions of interpersonal processes that hold in general hold specifically in training in the helping professions.* Again, we cannot emphasize too strongly the too-often neglected instance of training in the helping professions. The same conditions that hold in other instances where constructive gain and positive change are sought hold in graduate training. The goals for trainees should be similar to those for clients. Let us integrate training, as well as therapy, with life. Suffice it to say that *graduate students are actually people.*

TOWARD MEANINGFUL RESEARCH

15. *There is substantial basis for believing that replications of negative results do not demonstrate the impossibility of effective and facilitating human encounters.* The finding that human encounters, particularly therapist-patient interactions, can be "for better or for worse" supports the belief that therapy *can* work but too often does not. Those factors contributing to positive change must be identified, more fully understood, and tested with a wide variety of populations. If we determine that the combination of factors and their interactions vary from one group to another, a practical result should be the development of "preferred modes of treatment." Research should emphasize the following sets of variables which appear to be the most comprehensive: outcome, therapist, client, environmental (including cultural), contextual, and interactional. There is a need to identify more meaningful client dimensions such as amenability to given forms of treatment, for example, hypnosis and behavior therapy. In addition, we may need to research a *large* number of outcome indices in order to determine which of the following modes of treatment are to be preferred for specific outcomes: self-reports, expert reports, reports of significant others, and objective and possibly projective measures.

16. *There is substantial basis for believing that research testing the efficacy of these facilitating conditions in life situations other than counseling and therapy will contribute to a deeper and more meaningful understanding of all human encounters.* There is a need to study the more personal and relatively durable human relationships in life in order to learn more about effective treatment and training. Psychotherapy will remain only partially effective as long as we insist that it is unique and apart from the main stream of life. Ways and means of living effectively contribute to ways and means of effective counseling and psychotherapy. The very efficacy of various techniques may be dependent upon the quality and level of the conditions of effective living on which they are based or which they produce.

17. *There is substantial basis for believing that research identifying*

developmental factors and processes that contribute to the individual's ability to offer high levels of facilitating conditions will have implications for all human relationships. It is time to take a preventative stance instead of devoting all of our energies to ameliorative techniques. This area of study has implications for relationships such as parent-child and student-teacher, in which one person is assumed "more knowing" and one "less knowing." Perhaps we can identify optimum periods of a person's life for intervention with the maximum outcome benefits. More specifically, there is a need to research the conditions that lead to the early development of competence, confidence, openness, congruence, flexibility, and empathic understanding, as well as sensitivity to processes, factors, individuals, and groups that may prove destructive; in other words, to consider the implications for human relations in general.

TOWARD EFFECTIVE HUMAN RELATIONS

18. *There is substantial basis for believing that effective human relations in general incorporates the instance of counseling and psychotherapy.* If we view psychotherapy and counseling as reflecting and demonstrating the best aspects of human encounters, we are challenged to apply our skills, understanding, and insights to the cause of bettering all human relationships. It may be that we are fast approaching the juncture going beyond psychology, education, psychiatry, and social work and need to envisage a new, potent, and interdisciplinary science/art.

19. *There is substantial basis for believing that effective human relations are not the province of any one orientation or discipline such as psychology, but rather that they are the province of a much needed, new orientation.* Many in the helping professions look to psychology for advances and many model themselves after the lead of the behavioral science. Yet it appears that psychology has no room left for "people problems," the very concern which gave birth to the professional emphasis in the field. The symptom-reducing efforts of the behaviorists notwithstanding, in psychology and other behavioral sciences, the criteria of rigor has displaced the criteria of meaning. It is common for the student in an introductory psychology course to hear the professor say: "If you want to *learn* about people, major in psychology; if you want to help them, go into some other area of study." The very admission that he, the psychologist, cannot, or does not wish to translate his findings into people benefits, raises questions about the validity of his "learnings about people." Furthermore, the "scientists" who study animals rather than people cannot even generalize from the rat in the maze to the rat in the city dump. We are not interested only in statistical significance. *We are interested in human relevance.*

20. *There is substantial basis for believing that trained nonprofes-*

sionals can assume much of the burden for prophylactic and rehabilitative efforts for more effective living. Experimental lay-therapy training programs appear to demonstrate a level of efficacy as great or greater than the traditional programs designed to train professionals. Large-scale training facilities geared to significantly increasing the trainees level of interpersonal functioning will be translated into people benefits. Fully trained professionals as a group have failed to have a real or important impact, and those who are effective are too few in number. We have no alternative but to apply and test our knowledge to increasing the skills of individuals not admissible to the current training establishment.

SOME COMMENTS AND EXTENSIONS

Throughout modern history, Western man has pursued the constructive use of his material world. He has sought and succeeded in developing a massively complex physical environment that he has, in part, the power to control. We will not discuss here the misuse of the scientific, industrial, economic, and political manifestations of man's interrupted strides toward progress. We wish to emphasize instead an anti-materialistic characteristic of the modern age—the social forces and movements vigorously crying out for placement of human values at the forefront of man's consciousness. The constructive use of human life is no longer seen as a virtuous goal but as *the basic necessity.*

In the past, the most pressing and most basic problem of man, that of human relations, was often not given the attention it deserved. The religions of the world and even a few forms of government attempted to fill the gap, but were either diverted by the pull of different tides of interest or lacked the means to communicate at a utilitarian level. If we are not to fail for the same general reasons, we must translate our research and clinical findings into people benefits. Our professional lives must be devoted to the determination of what is, at this moment in history, most important. The creative and constructive outcomes of human relationship problems rest at the base of questions about the use and abuse of our physical and human resources.

It is our contention that the foregoing personalized and eclectic approach to these problems and their hoped-for solutions is consistent with our empirical and pragmatic culture. Psychotherapy (even its behavioristic manifestation) has been an import from Europe to the United States: allegiance to tradition or a school is more consistent with the continental image of a therapist than with the American image. The ability to break with the past and tear away from ritualistic tradition for its own sake is both an American characteristic and a strength. It is time, and hopefully not too late, to work within the context of our own cultural experience. In all other areas of our culture we have been sensitive to what works. We need now to apply this same perspective to therapy, so that the study of human relations becomes the vehicle by which human values come to life. When this step is taken, we stand on the threshhold of learning why the facilitating conditions facilitate and what makes helpful people helpful.

At present, each traditional approach or school would posit its own explanation to justify its stance and assumptions. Those of us not adhering to a school would then be left with the task of sifting through the abstractions in order to find common themes. *We can no longer afford such luxury.* Only an eclectic stance frees us to seek out the answers to human problems directly and economically. We must not settle for the lesser solution presented to us at a level far beyond the day-to-day stress of living.

From an eclectic stance we are free to research the basic core of facilitative conditions, and the selective use of techniques. (The point has been made earlier that these conditions provide the necessary context within which special techniques prove effective.) There is now no need for the artificial dichotomy separating rigor and meaningfulness. To choose one, we need not forego the other. Meaningful questions can and must be explored rigorously.

We have attempted throughout our work to integrate the basic core of facilitative conditions with learning in a social context, and preferred modes of treatment and techniques. We have emphasized that our goals for clients are to some extent culture-bound in that we want our clients to move forward to higher, more fulfilling lives. In other cultures these goals may not be either possible or valued. Beyond cultural or subcultural differences we must possess the courage to live fully and communicate this courage concretely to others. Without courage, learning and re-learning anything of real value to the human encounter is not possible. (This kind of openness and courage allows, even demands, that we be as aware of our anger as we are of our more tender feelings.)

To ignore, or to put off the establishment of an interdisciplinary approach to human relations, forfeits the leadership to those who will impose some one neurotic truth, stagnant and deteriorative. Implicit, if not explicit in our stance is the awareness that there may be a need to fight destructive and retarding forces when it is found that they are not amenable to facilitation. Without the recognition of this other side (the need to fight), there is little hope for finding more meaningful criteria, a way of implementing human values, or love and respect side by side in a better world.

We have presented what we believe to be a confident and hopeful stance. Without hope and confidence therapists would be forced to live a lie, and a world without hope and confidence is an all-encompassing casket.

AUTHORS' BIBLIOGRAPHY

Carkhuff, R. R. On the necessary conditions of therapeutic personality change. *Discussion papers, Wisconsin Psychiatric Institute,* Univer. of Wisconsin, 1963, *7,* 1-7.

Carkhuff, R. R., and Truax, C. B. The client-centered process as viewed by others. In *The therapeutic relationship and its impact: A study of psychotherapy with schizophrenics.* C. R. Rogers, E. T. Gendlin, and C. B. Truax, Eds. Madison, Wisconsin: Univer. of Wisconsin Press, in press, 1966.

De Charms, R., Levy, J., and Wertheimer, M. A note on attempted evaluation of psychotherapy. *J. clin. Psychol.,* 1954, *10,* 233-235.

Eysenck, H. J. The effects of psychotherapy: A reply. *J. abnorm. soc. Psychol.,* 1955, *50,* 147-148.

Eysenck, H. J. The effects of psychotherapy. In H. J. Eysenck (Ed.), *Handbook of abnormal psychology.* New York: Basic Books, 1960.

Goodstein, L. Behavior theoretical views of counseling. In *Theories of Counseling.* B. Steffire (Ed.). New York: McGraw-Hill, 1965.

Knight, R. P. Evaluation of the results of psychoanalytic therapy. *Amer. J. Psychiat.,* 1941, *98,* 434-446.

Luborsky, L. A note on Eysenck's article, 'The effects of psychotherapy: An evaluation.' *Brit. J. Psychol.,* 1954, *45,* 129-131.

Meehl, P. Psychotherapy. In *Annual review of psychology,* 1955, *6,* 357-378.

Raimy, V. (Ed.). *Training in clinical psychology,* Englewood Cliffs, N. J.: Prentice-Hall, 1950.

Renneker, R. E. Innovations in psychoanalytic practice. Address, Workshop in Psychotherapy, Centennial Celebration, Univer. of Kentucky, April, 1965.

Sanford, N. Clinical methods: Psychotherapy. In *Annual review of psychology,* 1953, *5,* 317-342.

Shoben, E. J. Counseling. In *Annual review of psychology,* 1956, *7,* 147-172.

Teuber, H. L., and Powers, E. Evaluating therapy in a delinquency prevention program. *Proc. Assoc. Res. Nerv. Ment. Dis.,* 1953, *31,* 138-147.

von Bertalanffy, L. Some biological considerations of the problem of mental illness. In *Chronic schizophrenia: Explorations in theory and treatment.* L. Appleby, J. M. Scher, and J. Cummings (Eds.). New York: Free Press of Glencoe, 1960.